Lecture Notes in Computer Science 6377

Commenced Publication in 1973
Founding and Former Series Editors:
Gerhard Goos, Juris Hartmanis, and Jan van Leeuwen

Rongbo Zhu   Yanchun Zhang   Baoxiang Liu
Chunfeng Liu (Eds.)

Information Computing and Applications

First International Conference, ICICA 2010
Tangshan, China, October 15-18, 2010
Proceedings

 Springer

Volume Editors

Rongbo Zhu
South-Central University for Nationalities
College of Computer Science
Wuhan 430073, China
E-mail: rongbozhu@gmail.com

Yanchun Zhang
Victoria University
School of Engineering and Science
Melbourne, VIC 8001, Australia
E-mail: yanchun.zhang@vu.edu.au

Baoxiang Liu
He'Bei Polytechnic University
College of Science
Tangshan 063000, Hebei, China
E-mail: liubx5888@126.com

Chunfeng Liu
He'Bei Polytechnic University
College of Science
Tangshan 063000, Hebei, China
E-mail: liucf403@163.com

Library of Congress Control Number: 2010935194

CR Subject Classification (1998): C.2, D.2, C.2.4, I.2.11, C.1.4, D.2.7

LNCS Sublibrary: SL 3 – Information Systems and Application, incl. Internet/Web and HCI

ISSN   0302-9743
ISBN-10   3-642-16166-9 Springer Berlin Heidelberg New York
ISBN-13   978-3-642-16166-7 Springer Berlin Heidelberg New York

springer.com

© Springer-Verlag Berlin Heidelberg 2010
Printed in Germany

Typesetting: Camera-ready by author, data conversion by Scientific Publishing Services, Chennai, India
Printed on acid-free paper   06/3180

Preface

Welcome to the proceedings of the International Conference on Information Computing and Applications (ICICA 2010), which was held in Tangshan, China, October 15–18, 2010.

As future-generation information technology, information computing and applications become specialized, information computing and applications including hardware, software, communications and networks are growing with ever-increasing scale and heterogeneity and becoming overly complex. The complexity is getting more critical along with the growing applications. To cope with the growing and computing complexity, information computing and applications focus on intelligent, selfmanageable, scalable computing systems and applications to the maximum extent possible without human intervention or guidance.

With the rapid development of information science and technology, information computing has become the third approach of science research. Information computing and applications is the field of study concerned with constructing intelligent computing, mathematical models, numerical solution techniques and using computers to analyze and solve natural scientific, social scientific and engineering problems. In practical use, it is typically the application of computer simulation, intelligent computing, internet computing, pervasive computing, scalable computing, trusted computing, autonomy-oriented computing, evolutionary computing, mobile computing, applications and other forms of computation addressing problems in various scientific disciplines and engineering. Information computing and applications is an important underpinning for techniques used in information and computational science and there are many unresolved problems worth studying.

The ICICA 2010 conference provided a forum for engineers and scientists in academia, industry, and government to address the most innovative research and development including technical challenges and social, legal, political, and economic issues, and to present and discuss their ideas, results, work in progress and experience on all aspects of information computing and applications.

There was a very large number of paper submissions (782), representing 21 countries and regions, not only from Asia and the Pacific, but also from Europe, and North and South America. All submissions were reviewed by at least three Program or Technical Committee members or external reviewers. It was extremely difficult to select the presentations for the conference because there were so many excellent and interesting submissions. In order to allocate as many papers as possible and keep the high quality of the conference, we finally decided to accept 214 papers for presentations, reflecting a 27.4% acceptance rate. And 76 papers are included in this volume. We believe that all of these papers and topics not only provided novel ideas, new results, work in progress and state-of-the-art techniques in this field, but also will stimulate future research activities in the area of information computing and applications.

The exciting program for this conference was the result of the hard and excellent work of many others, such as Program and Technical Committee members, external reviewers and Publication Chairs under a very tight schedule. We are also grateful to the members of the Local Organizing Committee for supporting us in handling so many organizational tasks, and to the keynote speakers for accepting to come to the conference with enthusiasm. Last but not least, we hope participants enjoyed the conference program, and the beautiful attractions of Tangshan, China.

September 2010

Rongbo Zhu
Yanchun Zhang
Baoxiang Liu
Chunfeng Liu

Organization

ICICA 2010 was organized by Hebei Polytechnic University, Hebei Scene Statistical Society, and sponsored by the National Science Foundation of China, Hunan Institute of Engineering. It was held in cooperation with *Lecture Notes in Computer Science* (LNCS) and *Communications in Computer and Information Science* (CCIS) of Springer.

Executive Committee

Honorary Chair	Jun Li, Hebei Polytechnic University, China
General Chairs	Yanchun Zhang, University of Victoria, Australia
	Baoxiang Liu, Hebei Polytechnic University, China
	Rongbo Zhu, South-Central University for Nationalities, China
Program Chairs	Chunfeng Liu, Hebei Polytechnic University, China
	Shaobo Zhong, Chongqing Normal University, China
Local Arrangement Chairs	Jincai Chang, Hebei Polytechnic University, China
	Aimin Yang, Hebei Polytechnic University, China
Steering Committee	Qun Lin, Chinese Academy of Sciences, China
	MaodeMa, Nanyang Technological University, Singapore
	Nadia Nedjah, State University of Rio de Janeiro, Brazil
	Lorna Uden, Staffordshire University, UK
	Yiming Chen, Yanshan University, China
	Changcun Li, Hebei Polytechnic University, China
	Zhijiang Wang, Hebei Polytechnic University, China
	Guohuan Lou, Hebei Polytechnic University, China
	Jixian Xiao, Hebei Polytechnic University, China
	Xinghuo Wan, Hebei Polytechnic University, China

	Chunying Zhang, Hebei Polytechnic University, China
	Dianchuan Jin, Hebei Polytechnic University, China
Publicity Chairs	Aimin Yang, Hebei Polytechnic University, China
	Xilong Qu, Hunan Institute of Engineering, China
Publication Chairs	Yuhang Yang, Shanghai Jiao Tong University, China
Financial Chair	Jincai Chang, Hebei Polytechnic University, China
Local Arrangement Committee	Lihong Li, Hebei Polytechnic University, China
	Shaohong Yan, Hebei Polytechnic University, China
	Yamian Peng, Hebei Polytechnic University, China
	Lichao Feng, Hebei Polytechnic University, China
	Yuhuan Cui, Hebei Polytechnic University, China
Secretaries	Kaili Wang, Hebei Polytechnic University, China
	Jingguo Qu, Hebei Polytechnic University, China
	Yafeng Yang, Hebei Polytechnic University, China

Program/Technical Committee

Yuan Lin	Norwegian University of Science and Technology, Norwegian
Yajun Li	Shanghai Jiao Tong University, China
Yanliang Jin	Shanghai University, China
Mingyi Gao	National Institute of AIST, Japan
Yajun Guo	Huazhong Normal University, China
Haibing Yin	Peking University, China
Jianxin Chen	University of Vigo, Spain
Miche Rossi	University of Padova, Italy
Ven Prasad	Delft University of Technology, The Netherlands
Mina Gui	Texas State University, USA
Nils Asc	University of Bonn, Germany
Ragip Kur	Nokia Research, USA
On Altintas	Toyota InfoTechnology Center, Japan

Suresh Subra	George Washington University, USA
Xiyin Wang	Hebei Polytechnic University, China
Dianxuan Gong	Hebei Polytechnic University, China
Chunxiao Yu	Yanshan University, China
Yanbin Sun	Beijing University of Posts and Telecommunications, China
Guofu Gui	CMC Corporation, China
Haiyong Bao	NTT Co., Ltd., Japan
Xiwen Hu	Wuhan University of Technology, China
Mengze Liao	Cisco China R&D Center, China
Yangwen Zou	Apple China Co., Ltd., China
Liang Zhou	ENSTA-ParisTech, France
Zhanguo Wei	Beijing Forestry University, China
Hao Chen	Hu'nan University, China
Lilei Wang	Beijing University of Posts and Telecommunications, China
Xilong Qu	Hunan Institute of Engineering, China
Duolin Liu	ShenYang Ligong University, China
Xiaozhu Liu	Wuhan University, China
Yanbing Sun	Beijing University of Posts and Telecommunications, China
Yiming Chen	Yanshan University, China
Hui Wang	University of Evry in France, France
Shuang Cong	University of Science and Technology of China, China
Haining Wang	College of William and Mary, USA
Zengqiang Chen	Nankai University, China
Dumisa Wellington Ngwenya	Illinois State University, USA
Hu Changhua	Xi'an Research Institute of Hi-Tech, China
Juntao Fei	Hohai University, China
Zhao-Hui Jiang	Hiroshima Institute of Technology, Japan
Michael Watts	Lincoln University, New Zealand
Tai-hon Kim	Defense Security Command, Korea
Muhammad Khan	Southwest Jiaotong University, China
Seong Kong	The University of Tennessee, USA
Worap Kreesuradej	King Mongkut Institute of Technology Ladkrabang, Thailand
Uwe Kuger	Queen's University Belfast, UK
Xiao Li	Cinvestav-IPN, Mexico
Stefa Lindstaedt	Division Manager Knowledge Management, Austria
Paolo Li	Polytechnic of Bari, Italy
Tashi Kuremoto	Yamaguchi University, Japan
Chun Lee	Howon University, Korea

Zheng Liu	Nagasaki Institute of Applied Science, Japan
Michiharu Kurume	National College of Technology, Japan
Sean McLoo	National University of Ireland, Ireland
R. McMenemy	Queen's University Belfast, UK
Xiang Mei	The University of Leeds, UK
Cheol Moon	Gwangju University, Korea
Veli Mumcu	Technical University of Yildiz, Turkey
Nin Pang	Auckland University of Technology, New Zealand
Jian-Xin Peng	Queen's University Belfast, UK
Lui Piroddi	Technical University of Milan, Italy
Girij Prasad	University of Ulster, UK
Cent Leung	Victoria University of Technology, Australia
Jams Li	University of Birmingham, UK
Liang Li	University of Sheffield, UK
Hai Qi	University of Tennessee, USA
Wi Richert	University of Paderborn, Germany
Meh shafiei	Dalhousie University, Canada
Sa Sharma	University of Plymouth, UK
Dong Yue	Huazhong University of Science and Technology, China
YongSheng Ding	Donghua University, China
Yuezhi Zhou	Tsinghua University, China
Yongning Tang	Illinois State University, USA
Jun Cai	University of Manitoba, Canada
Sunil Maharaj Sentech	University of Pretoria, South Africa
Mei Yu	Simula Research Laboratory, Norway
Gui-Rong Xue	Shanghai Jiao Tong University, China
Zhichun Li	Northwestern University, China
Lisong Xu	University of Nebraska-Lincoln, USA
Wang Bin	Chinese Academy of Sciences, China
Yan Zhang	Simula Research Laboratory and University of Oslo, Norway
Ruichun Tang	Ocean University of China, China
Wenbin Jiang	Huazhong University of Science and Technology, China
Xingang Zhang	Nanyang Normal University, China
Qishi Wu	University of Memphis, USA
Jalel Ben-Othman	University of Versailles, France

Table of Contents

Parallel and Distributed Computing

Trusted and Pervasive Computing

Internet and Web Computing

Multimedia Networking and Computing

Evolutionary Computing and Applications

Scientific and Engineering Computing

Intelligent Computing and Applications

A Non-strategic Microeconomic Model for Single-Service Multi-rate Application Layer Multicast

Morteza Analoui and Mohammad Hossein Rezvani

Department of Computer Engineering, Iran University of Science and Technology (IUST)
16846-13114, Hengam Street, Resalat Square, Narmak, Tehran, Iran
{analoui,rezvani}@iust.ac.ir

Abstract. This paper presents a non-strategic behavior model for the application layer multicast networks in which the natural selfishness of the peers is exploited in order to maximize the overall utility of the network. In the non-strategic solution concept, the decisions that a peer might make does not affect the actions of the other peers at all. In other words, it incorporates the non-strategic decisions in order to design the mechanism for the overlay network. We have modeled the application layer multicast network as a non-strategic competitive economy based on the theory of consumer-firm of microeconomics by leveraging the concept of Walrasian general equilibrium.

Keywords: Multicasting, Application Layer, Non-strategic Modeling, Microeconomics, Walrasian Equilibrium.

1 Introduction

To address the selfish behavior of the overlay peers in application layer multicasting networks, some works have used game theoretic approaches [1, 2, 3]. The game theoretic approaches, fall into the category of *"strategic behavior modeling"* in which the players seek to maximize their utility regard to the decisions that the other players might make. Also, another category of proposals exist in which the selfishness of the peers is controlled by means of distributed pricing [4, 5]. We believe that this problem could be investigated by microeconomics theories in which the goal is to maximize the aggregated utility of the consumers in conjunction with the maximizing the profit of the firms as the selfish agents of the system. In our mapping, the service provided by the overlay network can be viewed as the commodity and the behavior of the overlay peers can be mapped to that of the consumers in the economy. Also, the origin server and the peers who forward the content to their downstream peers can be thought as the firms of the economy.

A major contribution of this work is that unlike the game theoretic approaches, here the decision that a given peer might make, does not depend on the decisions taken by the other peers. Roughly speaking, our work falls into the category of *"non-strategic behavior modeling"* for which we have adopted the theory of *consumer-firm* developed in microeconomics. We have developed a mechanism which tries to find the equilibrium price in such a way that the total demanded bandwidth of the system equates its total supplied bandwidth. In microeconomics terminology, this method of finding

R. Zhu et al. (Eds.): ICICA 2010, LNCS 6377, pp. 1–8, 2010.
© Springer-Verlag Berlin Heidelberg 2010

equilibrium point is known as *"Walrasian general equilibrium."* The remainder of the paper is organized as follows: We discuss the related researches in Section 2. Section 3 introduces the model of the overlay network. Section 4 proposes the non-strategic behavior model developed for the application layer multicast networks. Section 5 presents the experimental analysis of the system. Finally, we conclude in Section 6.

2 Related Work

There already exists a significant body of research work toward self-organization in the application layer multicast networks. Some of the projects which have been carried out in the area of the application layer multicast include Narada [6], OMNI [7], SCRIBE [8], ZIGZAG [9] and NICE [10].

In the literature, utility-based approaches have been investigated for constructing bandwidth-efficient overlay trees. In such solutions, each peer is associated with a utility which is a function of its downloading rate. It has been shown in [11, 12] that finding among all possible trees, the one with optimal maximum utility or maximum bandwidth is a NP problem.

To address the selfishness of the users in the overlay network, some works have applied game theory [1, 2, 3]. In Wu *et al.* [1], an auction-based game theoretic approach is proposed in which the downstream peers submit their bids for the bandwidth at the upstream peers. They show that the outcome of this game is an optimal topology for the overlay network. Also, the authors of [2] have proposed an auction-based model to improve the performance of BitTorrent network.

A few other works have also been proposed to adjust the selfish behavior of the users within distributed pricing. Cui *et al.* [5] are the first to apply the priced-based resource sharing method to the overlay networks. Another priced-based work in the area of the overlay networks has been presented in [4]. They propose an intelligent model based on optimal control theory and also advise mathematical models that mimic the selfishness of the overlay users, represented by some forms of the utility functions. They show that, even when the selfish users all seek to maximize their own utilities, the aggregate network performance still becomes near-optimal.

3 The Model of the Overlay Network

We consider an overlay network consisting of an origin server and V peers denoted as $\mathcal{V} = \{1, 2, ..., V\}$. The multicast tree consists of the origin server as the root, a set of peers, and a set of physical links. The physical links are in fact the physical connections either the router-router connections, or the router-peer connections. Let us suppose that the overlay network consists of L physical links, denoted as $\mathcal{L} = \{1, 2, ..., L\}$. The capacity of each link $l \in \mathcal{L}$ is denoted by c_l. We represent the directed graph of the multicast session by a $(V+1) \times (V+1)$ adjacency matrix, denoted as $\mathbf{A}$. The $\mathbf{A}_{i,j}$ element of the matrix $\mathbf{A}$ denotes the flow that is originated from node i and is terminated in node j, namely $f_{i,j}$. Also, $x_{i,j}$ denotes the rate of the flow $f_{i,j}$. We put $\mathbf{A}_{i,j} = 1$ whenever there is a flow and zero otherwise. The multicast session consists of some unicast end-to-end flows, denoted as set $\mathcal{F}$:

$$\mathcal{F} = \{f_{i,j} \mid \exists\, i, j \in \mathcal{V} \; : \; \mathbf{A}_{i,j} = 1\} \tag{1}$$

Each flow $f_{i,j}$ of the multicast tree passes a subset of the physical links, denoted as

$$\mathcal{L}(f_{i,j}) \subseteq \mathcal{L} \tag{2}$$

Also, the set of the flows that pass through link l is denoted as follows

$$\mathcal{F}(l) = \{f_{i,j} \in \mathcal{F} \mid l \in \mathcal{L}(f_{i,j})\} \tag{3}$$

The set of all downstream nodes of each node i (children of node i) is denoted by $Chd(i)$ as follows

$$Chd(i) = \{v \in \mathcal{V} \mid \mathbf{A}_{i,v} = 1\} \tag{4}$$

We also define the parent of node i, namely $Par(i)$, as follows

$$Par(i) = \{v \in \mathcal{V} \mid \mathbf{A}_{v,i} = 1\} \tag{5}$$

4 Non-strategic Behavior Model for Application Layer Multicast

We consider the bandwidth of the service as the commodity in the overlay economy. We will further suppose that the preference of each consumer on the consumption domain $\mathfrak{R}_+$ can be represented by a utility function u_i that is continuous, strongly increasing, and strictly quasi-concave on $\mathfrak{R}_+$ [13]. The utility of each consumer i (peer i), namely u_i, is made up of an economic part and an empirical part in time slot t as follows

$$u_i(t) = \alpha\, u_i^{eco}(t) + (1 - \alpha)\, u_i^{emp}(t) \tag{6}$$

The time slot t starts when a new peer joins to the overlay economy or when an existing peer leaves the economy and lasts until the next occurrence of these events. The economic part of the utility, namely u_i^{eco}, is represented in Eq. (7) which is the benefit earned by consumer i from the allocated bandwidth.

$$u_i^{eco}(t) = \ln\left(1 + \frac{x_{Par(i),i}(t)}{B}\right) \tag{7}$$

Where, B denotes the maximum allowed bandwidth of the service. The empirical utility of consumer i in time slot t can be represented as follows

$$u_i^{emp}(t) = -\ln\left(1 + \frac{d_{Par(i),i}(t)}{D_i}\right) - \ln\left(1 + \frac{l_{Par(i),i}(t)}{L_i}\right) \qquad (8)$$

Each consumer i on joining the overlay economy is endowed with an income e_i. One can imagine that consumer i is provided with the income in terms of the amount of the service. We denote p as the price of each unit of the bandwidth in the overlay economy. Thus, the quantity $p.e_i$ can be thought as the "initial monetary income" of consumer i. The utility maximization problem of each consumer i in time slot t is as follows

$$\max_{x_{Par(i),i}(t,.)} u_i(t,.) \qquad (9)$$

$$\text{s.t.} \quad p(t).x_{Par(i),i}(t,.) + \sum_{l \in \mathcal{L}(f_{Par(i),i})} q_l(t-1) \le p(t).e_i + \sum_{\tau=0}^{t-1} \Pi_i(p(\tau)) \qquad (10)$$

$$x_{Par(i),i}(t,.) \le CD_i \qquad (11)$$

$$b \le x_{Par(i),i}(t,.) \le B \qquad (12)$$

Condition (10) states the "budget constraint" of peer i. The sum on the left-hand side of Eq. (10) is just the expenditure of consumer node i in which the first term represents the price of the demanded service and the other term (the sigma) is the sum of the prices of the all physical links that flow $f_{Par(i),i}$ has passed through in the previous time slot. Constraint (11) implies that the rate of the service that is demanded by consumer i should not be greater than its downlink capacity. Constraint (12) states that the rate at which the service is received should be in the interval between its minimum and its maximum allowed bandwidth. Let us define the income of consumer i, namely $m_i(p(t))$, as following:

$$m_i(p(t)) = p(t).e_i + \sum_{\tau=0}^{t-1} \Pi_i(p(\tau)) \qquad (13)$$

We denote the solution of consumer i's problem in time slot t as follows [14]:

$$x^*_{Par(i),i}(t, p(t), m_i(p(t)), \sum_{l \in \mathcal{L}(f_{Par(i),i})} q_l(t-1), CD_i, b, B) \tag{14}$$

The bundle x^* is in fact the *"Walrasian equilibrium allocation" (WEA)* of consumer i which forms his or her demanded bundle and mainly depends on the price and the income [13].

Clearly, each non-leaf peer acts as both consumer and firm in the overlay economy. When such a non-leaf peer acts as the firm, its optimization problem can be formalized as follows

$$\max_{y_j(t,.)} p(t).y_j(t,.) \tag{15}$$

$$\textbf{s.t.} \quad y_j(t,.) \le CU_j \tag{16}$$

$$y_j(t,.) \le K_j . x^*_{Par(i),i}(t,.) \tag{17}$$

$$y_j(t,.) = \sum_{k \in Chd(j)} x^*_{j,k}(t,.) \tag{18}$$

Where K_j denotes the number of children of node j and CU_j denotes its uploading capacity. Constraint (16) states that the amount of the bandwidth that is sold by peer j should not exceed its uploading capacity. Constraint (17), referred to as *"data constraint"*, implies that the amount of the bandwidth that is sold by peer j can not exceed the rate at which it has been bought by peer j. In other words, the intermediate peer j currently uploads to its downstream peers the service that it has downloaded from its upstream peer. Since peer j sells the service to its downstream peers, one can imagine that the production plan of firm j equates the sum of those rates. Constraint (18) just states this fact. The solution to Eq. (15) is in fact the production plan of firm j as follows

$$y^*_j(t, p(t), CU_j, x^*_{Par(j),j}(t,.), \{x^*_{j,k}(t,.) \mid k \in Chd(j)\}) \tag{19}$$

As is the case in microeconomics literature, the aggregate excess demand of the overlay economy in time slot t is defined as follows

$$z(p(t)) \equiv \sum_{i \in I} x^*_{Par(i),i}(t, p(t), m_i(p(t),.)) - \sum_{j \in J} y^*_j(p(t),.) - \sum_{i \in I} e_i \tag{20}$$

Where, I and J denote the set of consumers and the set of firms, respectively. If $z(p(t)) > 0$, the aggregate demand for the service will exceed the aggregate endowment of the users; indicating an excess demand for the service in the network. On the other hand, if $z(p(t)) < 0$, there will exist excess supply for the service. If $z(p^*(t)) = 0$, the Walrasian equilibrium is reached in which the price p^* is known as *Walrasian equilibrium price (WEP)*. With respect to the conditions that have been considered for the utility function and the production function, the existence of the WEP will be guaranteed by the *"Existence Theorem"*. Interested readers can refer to pages 210-211 of [13] to see the proof of this theory.

5 Experimental Analysis

Fig. 1 shows the price of the service versus the number of the overlay peers for different maximum number of allowed children, namely K_{max}. The figure shows that the price of the final rounds increases much slower than that of the early rounds for the all values of K_{max}. The reason lies in the fact that the overlay economy is a perfectly competitive market system. In such an economic system, when the number of consumers and the firms becomes sufficiently large, no single one of them, alone, has the power to significantly affect the market price. Clearly, the non-leaf peer adds the profit of each round of the service to its initial income. This enables such a peer to buy the service in higher quantity from the corresponding parent and in turn, to sell the service in higher quantity to its children. As the time passes, the non-leaf peer will reach to a state in which it will not has the budget limitation in order to buy the service from the corresponding parent (see Eq. (10)). At this time, the peer is merely restricted to its downlink capacity constraint and the service constraint itself, as stated in Eqs. (11) and (12). Thus, the peer can exploit the full potential of its downlink capacity to buy the service; leading to an increase in the quantity of the production. As the time passes, the number of such fully utilized peers increases in the system, especially in the upper levels of the multicast tree where the older peers are located. With respect to the above explanations, the gap between the demand and the supply decreases in the ultimate rounds. This, in turn, results in increasing $z(p(t))$ in Eq. (20) with much slower slope than before and causes the price not to rise rapidly in the ultimate rounds.

There is another interesting conclusion to be drawn from Fig. 1: As the value of K_{max} increases, the price of the service increases too. Our proposed algorithms at first look for the upper levels of the multicast tree in order to assign the appropriate parents to the new peers. Thus, the resultant multicast tree will typically have a near-balanced shape. Clearly, as the value of K_{max} increases, the relative number of the leaf nodes, i.e. the ratio between the number of the leaf nodes and the total number of the nodes, increases too. On the other hand, the leaf nodes are merely the consumers of the service and do not forward the service to the other nodes of the tree. Since the approximate percent of the leaf nodes is higher than 50%, it can be concluded that the number of the consumers is larger than the number of the firms. Therefore, the total demand of the market exceeds the total supply; resulting in ever increasing of the price during the time.

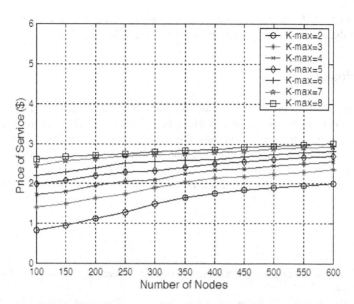

Fig. 1. The effect of node's degree on price for various populations

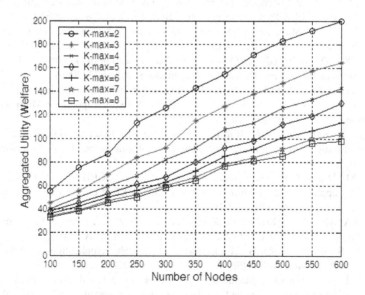

Fig. 2. The effect of node's degree on welfare for various populations

In microeconomics terminology, the aggregated utility of the economy is referred to as *"welfare"*. As it is evident from Fig. 2, the larger is the value of K_{max}, the lower will be the welfare of the system. From the above discussion, it is clear that the amount of increase in the price is proportional to the value of K_{max}. According to constraint (10), if the price increases, the consumers will afford less quantities of the bandwidth than before. This, in turn results in lower utility for them.

6 Conclusions

In this paper we have presented a model for the multi-rate application layer multicast networks based on the theory of consumer-firm. By considering the users as selfish utility maximizers, and by considering the service provided by the origin server as commodity, the model exploits the inherent selfishness of all the network users, so that the activities of the individual users could lead to the optimization of the utility for the whole network. The experimental analysis has proved the optimality of the system.

References

1. Wu, C., Li, B.: Strategies of Conflict in Coexisting Streaming Overlays. In: INFOCOM, pp. 481–489 (2007)
2. Levin, D., LaCurts, K., Spring, N., Bhattacharjee, B.: Bittorrent is an auction: analyzing and improving bittorrent's incentives. In: SIGCOMM, pp. 243–254 (2008)
3. Wu, C., Li, B., Li, Z.: Dynamic Bandwidth Auctions in Multioverlay P2P Streaming with Network Coding. IEEE Trans. Parallel Distrib. Syst. 19(6), 806–820 (2008)
4. Wang, W., Li, B.: Market-Based Self-Optimization for Autonomic Service Overlay Networks. IEEE J. on Selected Areas in Communications 23(12), 2320–2332 (2005)
5. Cui, Y., Xue, Y., Nahrstedt, K.: Optimal Resource Allocation in Overlay Multicast. IEEE Transactions on Parallel and Distributed Systems 17(8), 808–823 (2006)
6. Chu, Y., Rao, S.G., Seshan, S., Zhang, H.: A Case for End System Multicast. IEEE J. on Selected Areas in Communications special issue on Network Support for Multicast Communications 20(8), 1456–1471 (2002)
7. Banerjee, S., Kommareddy, C., Kar, K., Bhattacharjee, B., Khulle, S.: OMNI: An Efficient Overlay Multicast Infrastructure for Real-Time Applications. J. of Computer Networks 50(6) (2006)
8. Castro, M., Druschel, P., Kermarrec, A.-M., Rowstron, A.: SCRIBE: a large-scale and decentralized application-level multicast infrastructure. IEEE J. on Selected Areas in Communications 20(8), 1489–1499 (2002)
9. Tran, D.A., Hua, K.A., Do, T.: ZIGZAG: An Efficient Peer-To-Peer Scheme for Media Streaming. In: Proc. of IEEE INFOCOM, San Franciso, CA, USA (2003)
10. Banerjee, S., Bhattacharjee, B., Kommareddy, C.: Scalable Application Layer Multicast. In: Proc. of ACM SIGCOMM, Pittsburgh, PA, USA (2002)
11. Zhu, Y., Li, B., Pu, K.Q.: Dynamic Multicast in Overlay Networks with Linear Capacity Constraints. IEEE Transactions on Parallel and Distributed Systems 20(7), 925–939 (2009)
12. Zhu, Y., Li, B.: Overlay Networks with Linear Capacity Constraints. IEEE Transactions on Parallel and Distributed Systems 19(2), 159–173 (2008)
13. Jehle, G.A., Reny, P.J.: Advanced Microeconomic Theory. Addison-Wesley, Reading (2001)
14. Bertsekas, D.: Nonlinear Programming, 2nd edn. Athena Scientific, Belmont (1999)

Importance Measure Method for Dynamic Fault Tree Based on Isomorphic Node

Hong-Lin Zhang[1,*], Chun-Yuan Zhang[1], Dong Liu[2], and Gui-Wu Xie[3]

[1] School of Computer, National University of Defense Technology, Changsha, China
honglin518@gmail.com, cyzhang@nudt.edu.cn
[2] Key Lab of National Defense Technology, Academy of Equipment Command and
Technology, Beijing, China
ld5m@163.com
[3] 63880 Army, Luoyang, China
gw.xie@hotmail.com

Abstract. In order to enhance the measure efficiency in the research
field of importance measure for dynamic fault tree which contains some
structural information, a new method using this information is presented.
By means of creating an object for every node, identifying the isomorphic
nodes and computing only once for the same kind of isomorphic nodes,
this method reduces the number of states and the computation time.
This method also introduces the idea of perturbation and extends the
BI importance factor, then gives a concept of relative importance factor
which is obtained according to the type of independent module and has
no relation with the dependency within the independent module. The
importance factor can be computed by the combination of the relative
importance factors. Finally this method is applied on a real high reliability computer system. The analysis shows that this method can provide a
credible importance measure and greatly reduce the time expense if the
system structure has some replicate components or backups.

Keywords: isomorphic node; importance measure; modular analysis;
dynamic fault tree; reliability analysis

1 Introduction

The importance measure in the research of reliability analysis can show that
which component contribute at most to the system performance and disclose
the performance bottleneck of the system design. The reliability analyzer can use
the information about importance measure to enhance the system performance
at the least cost, and the information about importance measure also plays a
major role in the above critical systems.

Importance measure for static systems has been exhaustedly investigated, and
some importance factors have also been presented. Borgonovo [1] indicates the

---

* This research is partially supported by the National Natural Science Foundation of
China (60904082) and National Defence Pre-Research of China (51320010201).

R. Zhu et al. (Eds.): ICICA 2010, LNCS 6377, pp. 9–16, 2010.

relations among several importance factors. Choi [2] uses the imperfect minimal cut set to compute the importance measure, and Zio [3] applies the differential importance factor to measure the inter-importance among the components, but they can not applied to the dynamic fault tree. Liu [4] indicates that the uncertainty in input parameters is propagated through the model and leads to the uncertainty in the model out, and it gives a new computational method of delta. Duflot [5] proposes an MCS-wise truncation criterion involving two thresholds: an absolute threshold and a new relative threshold. Though the truncation method is required in some large and complex systems, it neglects some very useful structural information of these systems.

The model of Markov chain is a computation model which is based on the transition of states. In order to solve the problem of state explosion, the commonly efficient method is the modularization. Based on the idea of modularization, Amari [6] brings forward the method of digital numerical analysis (DNA). With respect to the systems which contain many redundancies and backups with the same reliability characters, Bobbio [7] provides a compact(parametric) way to model replicated components or subsystems, however the transformation from FT model to parametric BDD is a tedious process. Marquez [8] proposes a framework of hybrid Bayesian network to analyze DFT. Yuge [9] proposes a method to quantitatively analyze the priority AND gate of DFT. With respect to the gate of functional dependency (ab. FDEP), Xing [10] proposes an efficient analytical approach to handle functional dependence loops in the reliability analysis.

According to the structural characteristic of high reliable complex system, incorporated with the idea of object oriented, this paper proposes a method of importance measure based on isomorphic node (ab. IMIN). Firstly through the construction of object for each node in DFT, explores the reliability characteristic, and finds out the isomorphic node, so that IMIN uses the structural characteristic to simplify the state space and reduces the cost of solving. Secondly using the results from the first step, decomposes the fault tree into independent modules from top to the basic components. According to the type of each module, computes the relative importance, and then synthesizes to acquire the importance of basic events or parameters. The second step reduces the complexity from exponential level to polynomial level.

2   Modulation Based on Isomorphic Node

Modular analysis is always used to reduce the size of state space and the cost of solving when applying Markov model to the dynamic fault tree. One of the key questions is how to identify the independent modules and minimum independent modules. This section provides a novel method based on the isomorphic node, which identify not only the independent module, but also the isomorphic module.

Fault tree contains various nodes, such as basic event, top event and gate event. Each node can be considered as an object which characterizes the property of the event and sustains the later analysis.

Definition 1. *Each node in fault tree is considered as an object, which consists of the following properties: name, type, parent, children_num, children[], prob, prob_type, prob_fun, isomorphic_flag.*

name is the name and the identifier of the node. *type* is the type of the node. The property of *type* can has different definition and extension in the actual implementation. *parent* is the parent node of the node, and can be defined as the pointer of the parent node. *children_num* is the number of the children of the node. *prob* is the failure probability of the node. *prob_type* is the failure distribution type of the node. *prob_fun* is the function of the node, whose inputs are the failure probability of each children node and output is the failure probability of the node. *isomorphic_flag* is the property involved in the judgment of isomorphic, and it will play an important role in this paper, so that this property will be elaborated at the Definition 3. After the representation of each node, the fault tree can be represented as the set of objects $O = \{O_i | i \in [1, N]\}$, where N is the number of nodes in fault tree, and all the later analysis are based on the set.

Definition 2. *Node a and b is the event of fault tree, their corresponding objects are respectively O_a and O_b, a is independent with b, and the failure distribution function of a is equivalent with b, then call O_a is isomorphic with O_b.*

Theorem 1. *O_a and O_b are two objects of the object set of fault tree, if $O_a \cdot type = O_b \cdot type$, $O_a \cdot children\_num = O_b \cdot children\_num = m$, and all the elements of $O_a \cdot children[]$ are mutually independent with all the elements of $O_b \cdot children[]$, and there exists an order which makes $O_a \cdot children[i]$ is isomorphic with $O_b \cdot children[i](i \in [1, m])$, then O_a is isomorphic with O_b.*

This theorem is so obvious that we omit the proof.

Suppose all the basic events of fault tree are independent with each other, and are classified as m groups according their failure distributions. Each group has n_i basic events whose distribution functions are identical. Each node can be expressed as the function of basic events, and the form of the function is normalized. The normalization means a unique formal expression of the function. We can acquire the normalization of a function through the following process: firstly condense the expression; then transform the form according the order: *'node number'*, *'+'*, *'×'*. finally replace the basic events with their corresponding group. The final expression called $NORM$ string of the node is unique to the form of the expression of the node.

Definition 3. *The isomorphic property isomorphic_flag of object O_a contains two parts: θ and ID. Where θ is the set of all basic events involved in the object O_a, and ID is the identifier value of $NORM$ string. Each $NORM$ string correspond to an unique ID.*

In the implementation, under the condition that there is no conflict of the $HASH$ value, we can use the $HASH$ value of $NORM$ string as the identifier value of $NORM$ string.

Theorem 2. *O_a and O_b are two elements of the object set O in fault tree, if $O_a \cdot isomorphic\_flag \cdot \theta \cap O_b \cdot isomorphic\_flag \cdot \theta = \varnothing$, and $O_a \cdot isomorphic\_flag \cdot ID = O_b \cdot isomorphic\_flag \cdot ID$, then O_a is isomorphic with O_b.*

Proof. since $O_a \cdot isomorphic\_flag \cdot \theta = O_b \cdot isomorphic\_flag \cdot \theta = \varnothing$, so node a is independent with node b. since $O_a \cdot isomorphic\_flag \cdot ID = O_b \cdot isomorphic\_flag \cdot ID$, so $NORM_a = NORM_b$, and so the distribution function of O_a is equivalent with the distribution function of O_b. Based on the Definition 2, this theorem is proved.

3   Importance Measure with Relative Importance

Importance measure provides a quantitative guidance about the safety/risk significance of structure and system components. The results from the quantitative analysis can not be the unique basis for the decision, but they should be integrated into the whole decision support system.

The BI importance factor of basic event j, BI_j, is defined as the partial derivative of the risk metric with respect to basic event j

$$BI_j = \frac{\partial Y}{\partial x_j} \tag{1}$$

where Y is the system performance (such as reliability, safety, etc), x_j is the basic event j (or basic components, parameter, etc).

Suppose the function of system performance is $Y = \eta(A)$, where A is the factor vector which could affect the performance function Y. Q is the perturbation direction. Then after the perturbation, the performance function is changed to be $Y' = \eta(A_\delta)$. Therefore the importance factor BI can be extended as

$$BIE_Q = \frac{\partial Y}{\partial Q} = \lim_{\delta \to 0} \frac{Y' - Y}{\delta} \tag{2}$$

Suppose the independent module M_i consists of n_i submodules: $M_{i1}, M_{i2}, \ldots, M_{in_i}$, then the performance of module M_i can be expressed as $P_i = Y_i(P_{i1}, P_{i2}, \ldots, P_{in_i})$. The relative importance indicates the importance of submodule in its parent module. The definition of relative importance is defined as following:

Definition 4. *The relative importance of module M_{ik} (where $k \in \{1, 2, \ldots, n_i\}$) with respect to module M_i is*

$$RBI_{ik}^i = \frac{\partial P_i}{\partial P_{ik}} \tag{3}$$

We decompose the system S into n_0 independent modules $\{M_{01}, M_{02}, \ldots, M_{0n_0}\}$, each module M_{0i} is decomposed further into n_{0i} submodule $\{M_{0i1}, M_{0i2}, \ldots, M_{0in_{0i}}\}$. We have the following formulations: $P_S = P_0 = Y_0(P_{01}, P_{02}, \ldots, P_{0n_0})$, $P_{0i} = Y_{0i}(P_{0i1}, P_{0i2}, \ldots, P_{0in_{0i}})$.

During the process of decomposition, we guarantee that all the submodules of the same parent module are independent with each other. The importance of module M_{0ij}, i.e. the relative importance of M_{0ij} to system, can be computed as:

$$BI_{0ij} = RBI_{0ij}^0 = \frac{\partial P_0}{\partial P_{0ij}} = RBI_{0i}^0 \times RBI_{0ij}^{0i} \tag{4}$$

4 Case Example

Fig.1 is the structure of a prototype of on-board computer (OBC). OBC consists of three circuit boards: two CPU board and a power board.

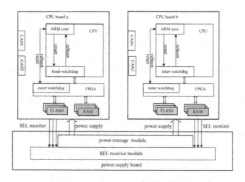

Fig. 1. The system structure of OBC

Power board supply power to two CPU boards. There is also a single-event latchup (SEL) monitor in power board. If SEL takes place in a CPU board, SEL monitor will cut off the power supply to the CPU board so as to protect the whole system.

Two CPU boards have the same architecture. Each CPU board has one CPU, one FPGA, three FLASH, three RAM and two redundant CAN interfaces. In order to detect single-event upset (SEU) effect, inner watchdog in CPU and outer

Table 1. Identifier for components of OBC

Identifier	Component	Identifier	Component
CAN	interface of CAN bus	FPGA	IC of FPGA
CPU	IC of CPU	NKRAM	TMR of RAM
IC	other IC in the CPU board	NKFLA	TMR of FLA
POW	power management module	IWD	inner watchdog
POD	SEL monitor module	OWD	outer watchdog
SEU	SEU effect in the IC of CPU	SEL	SEL effect in CPU board
OBC	OBC system	CB	CPU board

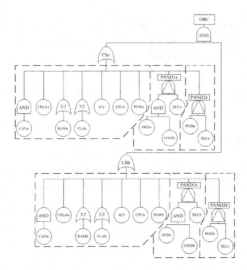

Fig. 2. The dynamic fault tree of the OBC system

watchdog in FPGA are used to monitor CPU work state. The storage system is composed of FLASH and RAM, both of which use TMR (Triple Modular Redundancy) technique to detect and correct errors happened in storage chips.

We use the symbols of Table 1 to identify the corresponding components of OBC. Table 1 also lists the other factors which affect the reliability of OBC, and consider the factor as a component, such as SEU, SEL. A_a represents the component A of CPU board a and A_b represents the component A of CPU board b for any symbol A.

We suppose that all components of OBC accord with the life of exponential distribution whose failure rate $\lambda = 3.0 \times 10^{-6} h^{-1}$.

Through the modulation of DFT in Fig. 2, we can get two independent static subtrees and four dynamic subtrees (depicted as dashed line). During the modulation, considering that the failure of FPGA can result in the failure of RAM and FLASH, and further the failure of system, we make FPGA as the input of OR gate to CB_a and CB_b, so that remove the FDEP gate. The subtree containing FDEP gate is seemed as a static subtree.

Since this fault tree has strong structural character, we can intuitively (or through the algorithm of identification of isomorphic node) find out the isomorphic nodes. The isomorphic nodes are listed as the following according the level from top to down: (CB_a, CB_b), $(FPGA_a, FPGA_b)$, (CAN_a, CAN_b), (RAM_a, RAM_b), (FLA_a, FLA_b), (IC_a, IC_b), (CPU_a, CPU_b), (POW_a, POW_b), $(PAND1_a, PAND1_b)$, $(PAND2_a, PAND2_b)$.

We compute the probability and relative importance at the time $t = 8760h$ (one year later) for all the components. we can obtain the importance of SEL_a to the system:

$$BI_{\lambda_{SEL_a}}^S = BI_{CB_a}^S \times BI_{PAND1_a}^{CB_a} \times BI_{SEL}^{PAND1_a} \times BI_{\lambda_{SEL}}^{SEL} = 10.29$$

Table 2. The BI importance of the parameter in OBC

param	BI	param	BI	param	BI
λ_{FPGA}	818.4	λ_{CAN}	41.4	λ_{RAM}	121.0
λ_{FLA}	121.0	λ_{IWD}	0.179	λ_{OWD}	0.179
λ_{SEU}	0.177	λ_{POD}	10.38	λ_{SEL}	10.29

The failure probability of OBC system after one year is 1.087%, the importance of other failure rate can be computed as the same way, depicted as table 2.

The importance of the failure rate of CPU, IC, POW are not listed in the table, which are the same as FPGA. Just as the shown of the table 2, because of the technology of triple model redundancy, the importance of RAM and FLA are decreased from the 818.4 to 121.0. The importance of the SEL and SEU are also decreased greatly, which is accordant with our design goal of tolerating the errors of sing-event effect (SEE).

IMIN, DNA (Discrete Numerical Analysis) [6] and MFT (Modular Fault Tree) [6] are all available to the system with high reliability and structural character. This case can also be modeled as a parametric fault tree, so that PBDD (parametric binary decision diagram) [7] is another available method. PBDD provides a compact(parametric) way to model replicated components or subsystems, so that it has approximate efficiency as IMIN. We implement the IMIN method, DNA method , MFT method and PBDD method on the same MATLAB platform to solve this case. IMIN method reduces the time expense 73.3% and 40.3% respectively compared to DNA method and MFA method. If we neglect the cost of tedious transformation from FT model to PBDD for the method of PBDD, the time expense of IMIN is 8.2% higher than that of PBDD.

5   Conclusion

Importance measure has many challenges in the filed of dynamic fault tree. It is one of the most key problems how to reduce the cost of solving and efficiently measure the importance of the system structure and the components. Based on the fact that the actual high reliable system has strong structural character, we propose a method of importance measure based on the conception of isomorphic node. We will further our research on this field from various factors and system performance.

References

1. Borgonovo, E.: Differential, criticality and Birnbaum importance measures: An application to basic event, groups and SSCs in event trees and binary decision diagrams. Reliability Engineering & System Safety 92, 1458–1467 (2007)
2. Choi, J.S., Cho, N.Z.: A practical method for accurate quantification of large fault trees. Reliability Engineering & System Safety 92, 971–982 (2007)

3. Zio, E., Podofillini, L.: Accounting for components interactions in the differential importance measure. Reliability Engineering & System Safety 91, 1163–1174 (2006)
4. Liu, Q., Homma, T.: A new computational method of a moment-independent uncertainty importance measure. Reliability Engineering & System Safety 94, 1205–1211 (2009)
5. Duflot, N., Berenguer, C., Dieulle, L., Vasseur, D.: A min cut-set-wise truncation procedure for importance measures computation in probabilistic safety assessment. Reliability Engineering & System Safety 94, 1827–1837 (2009)
6. Amari, S., Dill, G., Howald, E.: A new approach to solve dynamic fault trees. In: Annual Reliability and Maintainability Symposium 2003 Proceedings, pp. 374–379. IEEE Press, New York (2003)
7. Bobbio, A., Daniele, C.R., Massimiliano, D.P., Giuliana, F.: Efficient analysis algorithms for parametric fault trees. In: 2005 Workshop on Techniques, Methodologies and Tools for Performance Evaluation of Complex Systems, pp. 91–105. IEEE Press, New York (2005)
8. Marquez, D., Neil, M., Fenton, N.: Solving Dynamic Fault Trees using a New Hybrid Bayesian Network Inference Algorithm. In: 16th Mediterranean Conference on Control and Automation, pp. 1526–1531. IEEE Press, New York (2008)
9. Yuge, T., Yanagi, S.: Quantitative analysis of a fault tree with priority AND gates. Reliability Engineering & System Safety 93, 1577–1583 (2008)
10. Xing, L.D., Dugan, J.B., Morrissette, B.A.: Efficient Reliability Analysis of Systems with Functional Dependence Loops. Eksploatacja I Niezawodnosc-Maintenance and Reliability 3, 65–69 (2009)

Shortages of the Traditional Calculation of Interference Intensity of the Control Rules

Zhigang Li[1,2], Zhihai Wang[1], and Weijia Guo[2]

[1] School of Computer and Information Technology, Beijing Jiaotong University,
100044 Beijing China
[2] College of Computer and Automatic Control, Hebei Polytechnic University,
063009 Tangshan China
heutlzg@yahoo.com.cn, zhhwang@bjtu.edu.cn,
gowqjd2010qwoj@gmail.com

Abstract. Interference between the control rules is an important index of the static features of a fuzzy controller. The book named Principle and Application of Fuzzy Control gives the method to calculate it. A test was carried to check whether the method was coincident with the law of the interference intensity or not. In the test both the kind of the subset and the parameters of each subset were changed according to the law of the interference intensity. The test shows that it is not easy to put the method into use because of its intricacy, and the result couldn't be coincident with the law of the interference intensity in some case. So the method needs to be bettered.

Keywords: Regular fuzzy set; Interference intensity; Law of the interference intensity.

1 Introduction

Human's experience plays an important part in the traditional design of fuzzy control rules, which does work well in some fields. But in other fields where people knows little, the technology of data mining(DM) can abstract the latent modes and rules by the accumulated historical data and current data, which breaks the restraint of getting fuzzy control rules and refreshes the database dynamically by self-learning. So it is significant to carry out the work of data mining in the complicated industrial control.

The controlled object of the previous study of the subject is the collecting main pressure control system of the fifth coke-oven from Tangshan iron and steel company. After the integration and purification on the original data from the company, the main factors which affect the collecting main pressure were abstracted by the attribute reduction in rough set theory, and then the mechanical mode of the collecting main pressure control system was formed [1]. The center of every fuzzy subset in each variable was abstracted by all kinds of data mining, such as improved K-means algorithm [2] or related rules [3] or the dynamic clustering based on the batch and increment [4], and the related knowledge in statistics. The center of every fuzzy subset is dynamically adjusted by the new data until all the centers are stable, then the fuzzy control rules are abstracted by the relation between the subsets [5].

R. Zhu et al. (Eds.): ICICA 2010, LNCS 6377, pp. 17–24, 2010.
© Springer-Verlag Berlin Heidelberg 2010

Because the fuzzy control rules are produced automatically, in order to meet the requirements of control, the dynamic and static features must be analyzed. Interference between the rules is an important index of the static features of a fuzzy controller. So it becomes unavoidable to discuss the interference and its intensity between the rules. The book named Principle and Application of Fuzzy Control discusses the question and gives the method of calculating the interference intensity. But it is not easy to put the method into use because of its intricacy, and the test shows that the result couldn't be coincident with the law of the interference intensity.

2 Interference Intensity

2.1 The Definition of the Interference Intensity

If the rules interfere with each other, there must be a relation expression [6] as follows:

$$\underset{1 \le i \le n}{\exists} \ X_i \circ R \ne U_i \tag{1}$$

The definition shows that if the rules interfere with each other, there will be such a relationship following: $X_i \circ R \ne U_i$, so it is unavoidable to think about the calculation of the interference intensity

2.2 The Calculation of the Interference Intensity

Theorem 1: if the fuzzy relation ship (R) of the controller is the union of Cartesian product of X_i and U_i , and suppose that every fuzzy subset of the input is regular, then the subset U_i will meet the relation ship below

$$\underset{1 \le i \le n}{\forall} \ U_i \subseteq X_i \circ R \tag{2}$$

Regular fuzzy subset means that there is at least one x which belongs to X will meet the relation ship: $X_i(x) = 1$ for each X_i .

The calculation of the interference intensity [6]:

Suppose that the fuzzy relation of the controller is $R^{(0)}$, for an arbitrary input X_i , the control will be :

$$U_i^{(1)} = X_i \circ R^{(0)} \quad (i = 1,2,3 \cdots n) \tag{3}$$

Suppose that every X_i is regular fuzzy relation. Then there will be $U_i \subseteq U_i^{(1)}$ according to the theorem one. Construct the fuzzy relation: $R^{(1)}$

$$R^{(1)} = R^{(0)} \cup \bigcup_{i=1}^{n} [X_i \times (U_i \cup U_i^{(1)})] \tag{4}$$

Similarly:

$$U_i^{(2)} = X_i \circ R^{(1)} \tag{5}$$

$$R^{(2)} = R^{(1)} \cup \bigcup_{i=1}^{n} [X_i \times (U_i \cup U_i^{(2)})] \tag{6}$$

Continuously construct the fuzzy relation: $R^{(3)}$, $R^{(4)}$

R will be the union of $R^{(0)} , R^{(1)} , R^{(2)}$

$$R = \bigcup_{k=1}^{\infty} R^{(k)} = \bigcup_{k=1}^{\infty} \bigcup_{i=1}^{n} [X_i \times (U_i \cup U_i^{(k)})] \tag{7}$$

It is supposed that $U_i^{(0)} = U_i$, its degree of membership is:

$$\mu_R(x,u) = \sup_{\substack{0 \le k \le \infty \\ 1 \le i \le n}} [\mu_{X_i}(x) \wedge \mu_{U_i}^{(k)}(u)] \tag{8}$$

Thus

$$\mu_R(x,u) \le \max_{1 \le i \le n} \mu_{X_i}(u) = c(x) \tag{9}$$

$$\delta(x,u) = C(x) - R(x,u) \tag{10}$$

$\delta(x,u)$ is taken as the interference intensity. The average or the maximum will be taken as the interference intensity of the whole control rule list.

The quotation above shows that the method of calculating the interference intensity in the book is very intricate and it is not easy to put it into use. The test following will show the shortages of the method.

To make sure that every membership function corresponding to its subset is regular, every subset will be sampled from its center to its sides when the membership function is gotten. Every subset will be described with seven points.

3 The Test

The data, Table 1 and the control list1 in Table 2, are from the previous work of Data Mining [4]. The data in Table 1 have been normalized.

To expose the shortages of the method further, we shall produce the second and the third control rule list by revising some rules in control (list1). The name of the fuzzy subset of the control will be in the lower case if it is revised.

Table 1. Subset name and center of every variable

	Error	Error change	control
NB	-0.75095	-0.7175	-0.68875
NM	-0.43475	-0.38225	-0.49725
NS	-0.25318	-0.14321	-0.3695
ZO	-0.02162	-0.00304	0.01775
PS	0.199915	0.170563	0.35525
PM	0.431297	0.514609	0.528
PB	0.826642	0.7467	0.79775

Table 2. Rule list

Error	Error change	Control (list1)	Control (list2)	Control (list3)
NB	NB	PB	PB	PB
NB	NM	PB	PB	PB
NB	NS	PB	PB	PB
NB	ZO	PB	PB	PB
NB	PS	PB	pm	PB
NB	PM	PB	pm	PB
NB	PB	PB	ps	PB
NM	NB	PB	PB	PB
NM	NM	PB	PB	PB
NM	NS	PB	PB	ps
NM	ZO	PM	PM	ps
NM	PS	NS	NS	NS
NM	PM	NS	NS	NS
NM	PB	PM	PM	PM
NS	NB	PB	PB	pm
NS	NM	PB	PB	pm
NS	NS	PM	PM	PM
NS	ZO	NS	NS	NS
NS	PS	PB	ps	PB
NS	PM	NS	NS	ps
NS	PB	PM	ns	PM
ZO	NB	PB	PB	PB
ZO	NM	PM	PM	PM

Table 2. (*continued*)

ZO	NS	PS	PS	PS
ZO	ZO	PS	PS	PS
ZO	PS	PS	PS	PS
ZO	PM	PM	ns	PM
ZO	PB	NM	NM	NM
PS	NB	PM	PM	PM
PS	NM	PS	PS	PS
PS	NS	ZO	ZO	ZO
PS	ZO	NS	NS	NS
PS	PS	NS	NS	ps
PS	PM	NM	NM	NM
PS	PB	NB	NB	NB
PM	NB	PS	PS	ns
PM	NM	ZO	ZO	ZO
PM	NS	NS	NS	NS
PM	ZO	NM	NM	NM
PM	PS	NB	NB	NB
PM	PM	NB	NB	NB
PM	PB	NB	NB	NB
PB	NB	NB	zo	NB
PB	NM	NB	ns	NB
PB	NS	NB	NB	NB
PB	ZO	NB	NB	NB
PB	PS	NB	NB	NB
PB	PM	NB	NB	NB
PB	PB	NB	NB	NB

The method is an iterative course. The condition to put the recycle to an end is: the difference between each a pair of elements in the same position of the new produced R matrix and the previous one is less than 0.001. The average of $\delta(x,u)$ is taken as the interference intensity. We shall calculate the interference intensity in two cases

The first case: the configuration of the parameters of the error and error change and control is as follows:

The subset on the left bound adopts Z function ($f(a,b)$), a is its center, b is the center of the subset on the right. The subset on the right bound adopts S function ($f(a,b)$), a is the second center on the right, b is the first center on the right. For the other subsets there are four choices for them: gaussmf, trimf, gbellmf, trapmf.. The parameters are as follows:

Gauss function ($f(x,a,c)$), a =0.32, c is the center of the subset.

Triangle function ($f(x,a,b,c)$): b is the center of the subset, a is the center of the subset on the left, c is the center of the subset on the right.

Bell function ($f(x,a,b,c)$): a = 0.35, b = 1.25, c is the center of the subset.

Trap function ($f(x,a,b,c,d)$): the center of the trap is the center of the subset. a is the center of the subset on the left. b is the average value of the center of the trap and the center of the subset on the left. c is the average value of the center of the trap and the center of the subset on the right, d is the center of the subset on the right.

The reference book [6,7] gives the method to decrease the interference intensity: on the one hand, the subsets of the input shouldn't be overlapped too much, that is to say, the fuzzy subset of the input shouldn't be too dim, on the other hand, the subsets of the output shouldn't be too precise. This is the basis by which we set the parameters of each subset in the second case.

The second case: the configuration of the parameters of each subset is as follows:

The subset on the left bound adopts Z function. The subset on the right bound adopts S function, for the other subsets there are four choices for them: gaussmf, trimf, gbellmf, trapmf. The configuration of every subset follows such principle: the center of every subset won't be changed; the width of every subset of error and error change will become a half of its width before being revised. The subset of the control will cover the whole domain.

The result is shown in Table 3 to Table 6:

Table 3. Comparation of the interference intensity(guassy)

	Rule list 1	Rule list 2	Rule list 3	trend
Average of R(x,u) before revised	0.6458	0.6446	0.6505	
Average of C(x) before revised	0.8886	0.8886	0.8886	
intensity before revised	0.2428	0.2441	0.2382	Increase then decrease
Average of R(x,u) after revised	0.4972	0.4882	0.51	
Average of C(x) after revised	0.7807	0.7807	0.7807	
intensity after revised	0.2835	0.2925	0.2707	Increase then decrease

Table 4. Comparation of the interference intensity(triangle)

	Rule list 1	Rule list 2	Rule list 3	trend
Average of R(x,u) before revised	0.2494	0.2317	0.2597	
Average of C(x) before revised	0.8886	0.8886	0.8886	
intensity before revised	0.6393	0.6570	0.6289	Increase then decrease
Average of R(x,u) after revised	0.4646	0.4586	0.4707	
Average of C(x) after revised	0.7773	0.7773	0.7773	
intensity after revised	0.3127	0.3187	0.3066	Increase then decrease

Table 5. Comparation of the interference intensity(bell)

	Rule list 1	Rule list 2	Rule list 3	trend
Average of R(x,u) before revised	0.6069	0.605	0.6123	
Average of C(x) before revised	0.8886	0.8886	0.8886	
intensity before revised	0.2818	0.2836	0.2764	Increase then decrease
Average of R(x,u) after revised	0.4905	0.4768	0.5019	
Average of C(x) after revised	0.7812	0.7812	0.7812	
intensity after revised	0.2907	0.3044	0.2793	Increase then decrease

Table 6. Comparation of the interference intensity(trap)

	Rule list 1	Rule list 2	Rule list 3	trend
Average of R(x,u) before revised	0.2689	0.2519	0.2809	
Average of C(x) before revised	0.8886	0.8886	0.8886	
intensity before revised	0.6198	0.6368	0.6078	Increase then decrease
Average of R(x,u) after revised	0.4756	0.4765	0.4821	
Average of C(x) after revised	0.7773	0.7773	0.7773	
intensity after revised	0.3017	0.3008	0.2952	decrease

When we think over the results from table 3 to table 6, we shall find the shortages of the traditional calculation of the interference intensity. At first, the interference intensities of the same rule list will vary obviously when the types of the subset are different. When the parameters of the subset are revised according to the method to decrease the interference intensity which is from the references, we shall find that on the one hand, the trend changes in some case (trap subset), on the other hand, the interference intensities increase for some kinds of subset, decrease for others. The reason is that there will be more zeroes in the membership function when the overlap degree of the subsets of error and error change is decreased, so will the membership function of X_i, which means the downtrend of the input is strengthened. The downtrend may be masked in some cases because of the superposition of the calculation of $R(x,u)$, but will be exposed in other cases. In the calculation of $c(x)$, there is almost some rule which can make $c(x)$ get a big number for each x, then the downtrend of $c(x)$ is weakened. So the outcome may increase according to the method of the interference intensity.

4 The Conclusion

The test above indicates the result couldn't be coincident with the law of the interference intensity. The definition of the calculation method of the interference intensity shows that it is not easy to put it into use because of its intricacy. So the calculation method offered in the book named Principle and Application of Fuzzy Control still has shortages, could be improved.

References

1. Li, Z.G., Sun, Z.K.: Produce the Mechanism Model of Gas-Collecting Pipe Based on Rough Set. In: Dynamics of Continuous Discrete and Impulsive Systems, pp. 1356–1360. WATAM Press, Canada (2006)
2. Li, Z.G., Zhao, B.: An Incremental Partition-based Clustering Algorithm in a Batch Mode. In: Impulsive & Hybrid Dynamical Systems, pp. 2041–2044. WATAM Press, Canada (2007)
3. Li, Z.G., Li, F., Zhang, S.S., Wang, R.L.: The incremental updating algorithm about association rules based on the support rating of the item set. J. Engineering and Design of Computer 28, 4072–4074 (2007)
4. Li, Z.G., Wang, Z.L.: A New Clustering Analysis Used for Generating Fuzzy Control Rules. In: 5th International Conference on Fuzzy Systems and Knowledge Discovery, China, pp. 26–32 (2008)
5. Li, Z.G., Wang, Z.L., Sun, Z.K., Lv, Y.: A Stability Determining Algorithm on Fuzzy Rules Based on the Theory of Phase Track. In: International Symposium on Intelligent Information Technology Application, China, pp. 37–41 (2008)
6. Zhu, J.: Principle and Application of Fuzzy Control. China Machine Press, Beijing (2005)
7. Zhang, Z.K.: Fuzzy Mathematics' Application in Automation. Tsing University Press, Beijing (1997)
8. Li, H.J.: The Basis and Practical Algorithm of Fuzzy Mathematics. Science Press, Beijing (2005)
9. Yang, L.B., Gao, Y.Y.: Principle and Application of Fuzzy Mathematics. Huanan Polytechnic University Press, Guangzhou (2008)
10. Sun, Z.Q.: Theory and Technology of Intelligent Control. Tsing University Press, Beijing (1997)

Dynamic Data Replication Strategy Based on Federation Data Grid Systems

M. Zarina[1], M. Mat Deris[2], A.N.M.M. Rose[1], and A.M. Isa[1]

[1] Faculty of Informatics
University Darul Iman Malaysia
Gong Badak, Kuala Terengganu, Malaysia.
Zarina@udm.edu.my, anm@udm.edu.my, isa@udm.edu.my
[2] Faculty of Information Technology and Multimedia,
University Tun Hussein Onn Malaysia
Batu Pahat, Johor, Malaysia
mmustafa@uthm.edu.my

Abstract. Data access latency is one of the important factors of system performance in federated data grid. However, different replication strategies resulted in different access latency. This paper proposes a model of replication strategy in federated data grid that is known as dynamic replication for federation (DRF). DRF uses the concept of a defined 'network core area' (NCA) as the designated search area of which a search will be focussed. However, the area known as NCA is not static and it is bound to change if data requested cannot be found. This paper will also highlight how NCA is defined and reallocated if a search fails. Results from the analysis show that the DRF proposed in this paper is superior to Optimal Downloading Replication Strategy (ODRS) in terms of wide area network bandwidth requirement and in the average access latency data where the results was 48% higher than for $\rho_j = 0.3, 0.4, 0.$

Keywords: data grid, replication strategy, access latency, high performance.

1 Introduction

A data grid connects a collection of hundreds of geographically distributed parts of the world to facilitate sharing of data and resources [1]. Data grids enable scientists from universities and research laboratories to collaborate with one another to solve large-scale computational problems. The size of the data that needs to be accessed on data grid is on the order of terabytes or petabytes [3].

Data grid systems are classified into four categories: hierarchical, federation, monadic and hybrid [2]. Most current research works focus on hierarchical model. However there are still researches that deal with federation model that intends to provide scientific communities better availability and efficient access to massive data. The main factor that distinguishes federation from the hierarchical model is that the number of data source in federation model is more than one. As for the hybrid model, it is a complicated approach and lots of undergoing studies are looking into this

R. Zhu et al. (Eds.): ICICA 2010, LNCS 6377, pp. 25–32, 2010.

model. All of the models mentioned pay particular attention the aspect of data availability and access time.

In ensuring that data availability and access latency is at the optimum level, replication is one of processes that need to be further enhanced or studied. There are two methods of replication which are known as static and dynamic. As for static replication, after a replica has been created, it will stay exist in the same place unless it is deleted manually by users or its duration of existence has expired. On the contrary, dynamic replication takes into consideration the changes of the grid environments and automatically creates new replicas for popular data and move the replica to other sites when necessary in order to improve the performance of access time [4]. Jiang jianjin [5], has proposed an Optimal Downloading Replication Strategy (ODRS) to reduce access latency in federated data grid. However it encounters the problem of high probability of accessing data when the initial search failed. An area that needs to be looked at here is whether specifying scope of search can help alleviate the problem of high probability of accessing data.

In this research, dynamic replication for federated (DRF) data grid is proposed. The objective of this research is to minimize access latency by accessing data from the nearest node in the federation model within the cluster of the defined perimeter. The search of data will always focus to the area known as 'Network Core Area' (NCA). Initially, the inner most   core of the sub grid will be defined as the NCA, therefore the initial search will only focus within the defined NCA. If the search for data fails to materialize, the scope of search will now be extended to the chosen cluster in the outer core area of the same sub grid. The outer core area will now be known as the core area since it contains nodes that will be servicing the requested data. And then the outer core area will now be defined as the new NCA. For ρ_j,0.5,0.6,0.7 preliminary results show that the average access latency in DRF was 48% higher than ODRS. In addition; the usage of wide area network in ODRS was 66% whereas in DRF; the usage of wide area bandwidth within region and among was 53% and 13%, respectively. These results are significant since DRF uses a more effective range of bandwidth than ODRS.

2   Model and Problem Formulation

2.1   Federation Data Grids

In the following diagram (Fig. 1), Cluster 1 will be defined as the NCA, whereby the initial search will focus to. If the search failed to yield any desired results, the search will then be expanded into the area outside the Cluster 1, Sub Grid 1. The Sub Grid 1 will then be next area of search and therefore will be next known as the new NCA. The header in Cluster 1 will then relinquish its role as the main arbitrator for data request as Cluster 1 is no longer the NCA.

Fig. 1 gives an instance of grouping in federated data grid. There are two sub data grids and four clusters in this data grid, which is a logical independent system and any two clusters/sub grids peer to each other. For each sub grid, it consists of two or more clusters which each of cluster consist of several nodes. In each cluster there is one header node and the others are normal node normal node has finite local storage space

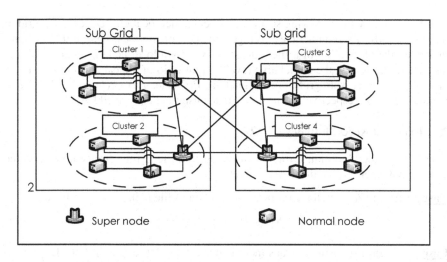

Fig. 1. An instance of grouping in federated data grid

to store data replica. A header node is in charge of storing index information of those nodes that belong to this cluster. A header node answers the request messages from normal nodes that belong to the same cluster with it and the request messages from other cluster or other sub grid.

2.2 Terms and Definitions

The same assumptions and approaches have deployed based on ODRS, but in ODRS, cases involved clusters only, whereas DRF involved clusters and sub grids.

Assuming that there are M nodes in the system, and a node n_k belongs to a cluster o_l only, with $k = 1,2,..., M$ and $l = 1,2, ..., S$ which S is all clusters in the system. A cluster o_l can only belong to a sub grid only. We assume that all data clusters and sub data grids have the same size m,s and $m,s \geq 2$. In this paper, we deal with homogeneous cases that cluster and sub grid can take the same size. We assume that the nodes belong to cluster o_l are $n_{(l-1)m+1}$, $n_{(l-1)m+2}$,..., $n_{1\times m}$, then a node n_k belongs to cluster $o_{[k/m]}$. Cluster $o_{[k/m]}$ belong to sub grid g_i are $o_{(i-1)s+1}$, $o_{(i-1)s+2}$,...., o_{ixs}, then a sub cluster o_l belongs to sub grid $g_{[l/s]}$.

There are N unique files f_j in the data grid, where $j =1, 2, ..., N$. For every node, the storage space is of the same size and it can store K file replicas, so the system can store MK file replicas. The data set stored in node n_k is D_k. Each file is associated with a normalized request rate of λ_j for file f_j per node, which is a fraction of all requests that are issued for the jth file.

For file f_j, there are r_j replicas uniformly distributed in the system, and we assume $r_j \geq 1$. For a node n_k, there is at most one replica of f_j in its storage space. For file f_j, the probability of having a replica in node n_k is p_j. In ODRS three elements of hit ratio that have been considered are as follows: $P(local\text{-}hit)$, $P(Intra\text{-}Grid\text{-}hit)$, $P(Inter\text{-}Grid\text{-}hit)$. We enhances the model by adding sub grids so that the hit ratio that are going to be taken into account are: $P(local\text{-}hit)$, $P(Cluster\text{-}hit)$, $P(Intra\text{-}Grid\text{-}hit)$ and $P(Inter\text{-}Grid\text{-}hit)$. As a consequence, when there is a request for a file; the request may be served by the following sequence : local node, local cluster, local sub grid or other sub grids. The cumulative (average) hit ratio of the local node is $P(local\text{-}hit)$, indicating the probability of a file requests served by a local node from any nodes in the system. Similarly, the cumulative (average) hit ratio of a local cluster, a local sub grid and of other sub grids are defined as $P(Cluster\text{-}hit)$, $P(Intra\text{-}Grid\text{-}hit)$ and $P(Inter\text{-}Grid\text{-}hit)$ respectively. The nodes in a cluster are connected LAN.

2.3 Expected Access Latency of DRF

According to the algorithm for a node n_k requesting file f_j, four events are considered and compute their probabilities respectively.

Case 1 : Event El_{kj}, which means there is a replica of file f_j in n_k, and we have

$$P(El_{kj}) = P(f_j \in D_k) = \gamma_j / M = \rho_j . \tag{1}$$

Case 2: Event Eo_{kj}, which means there is no replica of file f_j in n_k, but file f_j hits in the other nodes of cluster $o_{[k/m]}$.

Case 3: Event Eg_{lj}, which means there is no replica of file f_j in local cluster $o_{[k/m]}$ but file f_j hit in other clusters o_{-kj} of the same sub grid $g_{[l/s]}$.

Case 4: Event Eg_{-lj}, which means there is no replica of file f_j in sub grid $g_{[l/s]}$, therefore, file f_j must be hit in other sub grids. Then we have:

$$P(Eg_{-kj}) = (-\gamma_j / M)^{lm} = (-\rho_j)^{lm} . \tag{2}$$

From [5] we can get a replica of file f_j in other clusters/sub grids. So to solve the problem in **case 3** is:

$$P(Eg_{lj}) = P(Eo_{-kj}) - P(Eg_{-lj}) = (1 - \rho_j)^m - (1 - \rho_j)^{lm} . \tag{3}$$

Since there is at least one replica of f_j in data grid, the problem in **case 2** we have:

$$P(Ec_{lj}) = 1 - \rho_j - (1 - \rho_j)^m . \tag{4}$$

Having the probabilities above, we can compute the cumulative expected hit ratios now.

$$P(local - hit) = \sum_{j=1}^{N} \frac{\lambda_j}{\lambda} P(El_{kj}) . \tag{5}$$

$$P(cluster - hit) = \sum_{j=1}^{N} \frac{\lambda_j}{\lambda} P(Eo_{lj}) . \tag{6}$$

$$P(IntraGrid - hit) = \sum_{j=1}^{N} \frac{\lambda_j}{\lambda} P(Eg_{lj}) . \tag{7}$$

$$P(Intra-Grid-hit) = \sum_{j=1}^{N} \frac{\lambda_j}{\lambda} P(Eg_{-lj}) \ . \tag{8}$$

In our model, t_l is used as costs when accessing a file replica from a node's local storage space, from a remote node of the same cluster that this node belongs costs t_o, from a remote node of other cluster but same sub grid that this node belongs costs t_g and from a node of other sub grids costs t_G, with $t_l \leq t_o \leq t_g \leq t_G$. Fig. 2 shows the relationship between t_o, t_g and t_G. (t_l is not depicted here), in which   is the normalized request rate for file f_j at this node.

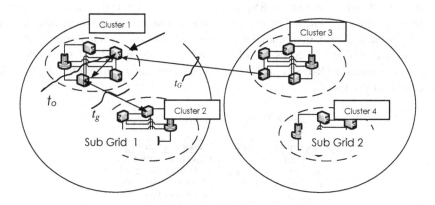

Fig. 2. Data access for DRF

$t(n_k, f_j)$ denotes the access latency of node n_k requesting file f_j. Applying Eq. (1) to Eq. (4), we can obtain the expected access latency for a file request. The expected access latency of node n_k requesting file f_j is $E(t(n_k, f_j))$. By considering the request rate of every file, we can compute the expected access latency for node n_k requesting any file in data grid:

$$t_k = \sum_{j=1}^{N} \frac{\lambda_j}{\lambda} \times E(t(n_k, f_j)). \tag{9}$$

Access latency for a node to request any is uniform across the system, because the system is symmetric.The objective of this paper is to minimize t, with the following constraints:

1) The number of all replicas in system is less than the total storage space of data grid.
2) The number of the replica of a file is at least one, and at most the system size, i.e. $1 \leq r_j \leq M$.

Then, the constrained optimization problem of this paper is:

$$\min\{t = \sum_{j=1}^{N} \lambda_j [t_o + t_{lo}\rho_j + t_{go}(1-\rho_j)^m + t_{Gg}(1-\rho_j)^{lm}]\}$$

$$s.t \quad \sum_{j=1}^{N} \rho_j \leq K, 1/M \leq \rho_j \leq 1, j = 1, 2, 3, \cdots, N.$$

(10)

3 Analytical Results

In [5] the performance of ODRS compared with several popular replication strategies through theoretical analysis. The replication strategies that were compared include Uniform Replication Strategy (URS), Square Root Strategy (SRS) and Proportional Replication Strategy (PRS). For each replication strategy, the comparisons include replication ratio distribution, cumulative expected hit and expected access latency. Zipf-like distribution is used as the file request distribution. Table 1 shows that the result of comparison, ORDS is the best on expected cumulative inter grid hit ratio and expected access latency.

Table 1. Comparison on replica strategy

Comparison Method	Ranking* of strategies
Cum. local hit ratio	**PRS,ODRS,SRS,URS**
Cum. intra grid hit ratio	SRS,ODRS,URS,PRS
Cum. inter grid hit ratio	ODRS,SRS,PRS,URS
Access latency	ODRS,SRS,PRS,URS

* Arranged from most to least significant

Table 2. System Parameters

Parameter	Value
Size of file (M Bytes)	1000
Intra-cluster connectivity bandwidth (Mbps)	1000
Inter-cluster connectivity bandwidth (Mbps)	100
Inter-grid connectivity bandwidth (Mbps)	10
System size M	1000
Nodes in cluster m	10
Clusters in sub grid	10
Storage space at each node (GB) K	10
Number of file N	100

3.1 System Parameters

The parameters used in analysis are shown in Table 1. The time for transferring a file between two nodes in the intra cluster, inter cluster 800 sec and inter sub grid is 1600 sec. The local hit does not need network bandwidth.

To demonstrate the advantages of the dynamic replica strategy, DRF will be compared with optimized downloading replication strategy (ODRS).

3.2 Cumulative Hit Ratio

From Equation (5) – (8), we can plot the graph for hit ratio according to the parameters in Table 2. The horizontal axis is a number of replica r_j per M or   and the vertical axis is the cumulative of hit ratio. From Equation (5) and Equation (6), we can see that cumulative local hit ratio and cumulative intra cluster is same with ORDS.

From Eq. (7) and (8) we can calculate the cumulative inter cluster hit ratio and inter grid hit ratios. From Table 1, we can see that the cumulative inter grid hit ratio of ODRS is the best (lowest) among four replication, so it requiresleast wide area network. In DRF, the inter grid hit ratio (from ODRS) can divided into inter cluster hit ratio (IC DRF) and inter sub grid hit ratio (ISG DRF). From Fig. 3, we can see that the cumulative inter sub grid hit ratio is the lowest and approaching zero, so it requires very least wide area network over region and the cumulative inter cluster hit ratio approaching ODRS. In summary; from the graph, the usage of wide area bandwidth in ODRS was 66% whereas in DRF; the usage of wide area bandwidth within region and among was 53% and 13%, respectively.

3.3 Access Latency

Table 1 shows that the access latency of ODRS is the lowest among four replication strategies. From Eq. (9) we can calculate the expected access latency for DRF. Fig. 4 shows that the values for access latency of DRF are lower than ODRS. From the graph, the average access latency in DRF is 48% higher than ODRS for $\rho_j = 0.3, 0.4, 0$.

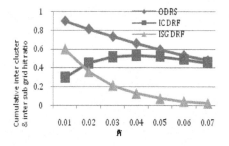
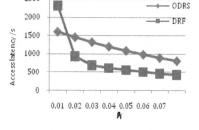

Fig. 3. Cumulative local hit ratio   **Fig. 4.** Access latency in analysis

4 Conclusion and Future Works

In this paper, the model for dynamic data replication strategy for federation data grid is proposed. The aim of this model is to access data from the nearest node as possible by using the concept of 'Network Core Area'. The NCA is mainly used to define, control and restrict the area of search. Accessing data will start with the local node as the designated NCA, if not found then from within the local cluster. If there is no file within the local cluster, then the search will be expanded to within local sub grid and will be further searched in other sub grids. If the requested data is not found at the nearest node, then after a certain threshold; the data will be replicated by the local node. By focussing the search to the nearest node, DRF has been proven successful in reducing the need of a greater bandwidth and at the same time minimizing expected data access latency of file. In addition, the algorithm on how to calculate hit file (threshold) will be investigated in so as to optimize the efficiency of the proposed model.

References

1. Chang, R.-S., Wang, C.-M., Chen, P.-H.: Complete and fragmented replica selection and retrieval in Data Grids. Future Generation Computer System, 536–546 (2007)
2. Venugopal, S., Buyya, R., Ramamohanarao, K.: A taxonomy of data grids for distributed data sharing, management and processing. ACM Computing
3. Lamehamedi, H., Shentu, Z., Szymanski, B., et al.: Simulation of dynamic data replication in data grids. In: Proceeding of the International Parallel and Distributed Processing Symposium. IEEE Computer Society, Washington (2003)
4. Tang, M., Lee, B.-S., Yeo, C.-K., Tang, X.: Dynamic replication algorithms for the multitier data grid. Future Generation Computer System 21, 775–790 (2005)
5. Jianjin, J., Guangwen, Y.: An Optimal Replication Strategy for data grid system. Front Computer. Sci. China 1(3), 338–348 (2007)

A Novel Approach for QoS Guided Metascheduler for P2P Grid System

D. Doreen Hephzibah Miriam and K.S. Easwarakumar

Department of Computer Science and Engineering,
Anna University, Chennai - 600025, India
doreenhm@gmail.com, easwara@cs.annauniv.edu

Abstract. Task scheduling is an integrated component of computing. One of the goals of P2P Grid task scheduling is to achieve high system throughput while matching application needs with the available computing resources. This matching of resources in a non-deterministically shared heterogeneous environment leads to concerns over Quality of Service (QoS). In this paper, we integrate Grid with P2P to propose, a novel approach for QoS guided task scheduling algorithm called QoS guided P2P Grid Metascheduler(QPGM) using Min Mean Computation algorithm, which gives improved performance on load balancing and generates an optimal schedule so as to complete the tasks in a minimum time and to utilize the resources efficiently. Simulation results demonstrate that QPGM task scheduling algorithm can get better effect for a large scale optimization problem.

Keywords: Peer-to-Peer, Grid, Quality of Service (QoS), Metascheduler, Task Scheduling.

1 Introduction

Several aspects of today's Grids are based on centralized or hierarchical services. However, as Grid sizes increase from tens to thousands of hosts, fault tolerance have been a key issue. To address this problem, functionalities should be decentralized to avoid bottlenecks and guarantees scalability. A way to ensure Grid scalability is to adopt P2P models and techniques to implement non-hierarchical decentralized Grid services and systems [10]. With the emergence of Grid and P2P computing, new challenges appear in task scheduling based on properties such as security, quality of service, and lack of central control within distributed administrative domains.

Grid scheduling is defined as the process of making scheduling decisions involving resources over multiple administrative domains. This process can include searching multiple administrative domains to use a single machine or scheduling a single job to use multiple resources at a single site or multiple sites. One of the primary differences between a Grid scheduler and a local resource scheduler is that the Grid scheduler does not "own" the resources at a site (unlike the local resource scheduler) and therefore does not have control over them. Furthermore,

R. Zhu et al. (Eds.): ICICA 2010, LNCS 6377, pp. 33–40, 2010.

often the Grid scheduler does not have control over the full set of jobs submitted to it. This lack of ownership and control is the source of many of the problems. Hence, we integrate P2P with Grid to perform metascheduling.

The main aim of this paper is to create an efficient and optimized QoS based Metascheduler algorithm for P2P Grid Systems taking into account of QoS parameters that can improve the performance and revolutionize the existing scheduling algorithms by achieving load balancing and optimum resource utilization.

The rest of this paper is organized as follows: Section 2 presents the related work. Section 3 describes the design of the scheduling system. Section 4 describes the QoS guided Metascheduler Algorithm. Section 5 mentions the simulation model. Section 6 describes the experimental evaluation. Finally, Section 7 gives the conclusion and future work.

2   Related Works

Intensive research has been conducted in grid task scheduling problem which is a NP complete problem [16]. A meta task is defined as a collecting of independent tasks with no data dependences. A meta task is mapped onto machine statically; each machine executes a single task at a time. In general, we take into account a set of meta tasks in the Grid environment. Some of the mapping heuristics algorithm are discussed below.

OLB (Opportunistic Load Balancing) [6] assigns each job in arbitrary order to the processor with the shortest schedule, irrespective of the Expected Time to compute(ETC) on that processor. **MET** (Minimum Execution Time) [7] assigns each job in arbitrary order to the processor on which it is expected to be executed fastest, regardless of the current load on that processor. **MCT** (Minimum Completion Time) [7] assigns each job in arbitrary order to the processor with the minimum expected completion time for the job. **Min-min** [13] establishes the minimum completion time for every unscheduled job, and then assigns the job with the minimum minimum completion time (hence Min-min) to the processor which offers it this time. **Max-min** [13] is very similar to Min-min. Again the minimum completion time for each job is established, but the job with the maximum minimum completion time is assigned to the corresponding processor. Longest Job to Fastest Resource- Shortest Job to Fastest Resource **(LJFR-SJFR)** [1] heuristic begins with the set U of all unmapped tasks. Next, the task with the overall minimum completion time from M is considered as the shortest job in the fastest resource (SJFR). Also the task with the overall maximum completion time from M is considered as the longest job in the fastest resource (LJFR).

In **Sufferage**, [13] for each task, the minimum and second minimum completion time are found in the first step. The difference between these two values is defined as the sufferage value. In the second step, the task with the maximum sufferage value is assigned to the corresponding machine with minimum completion time. In **XSufferage**, [3] Casanova et al gave an improvement to fix the problem, in Sufferage heuristic, when there is input and output data for the tasks, and resources are clustered. Sufferage problems are described in [3]. In **Qsufferage**, [14] Weng et al, presented to schedule the bag-of-tasks application in the grid environment. The algorithm considers the location of each tasks input data, while makespan and response ratio are chosen as metrics for performance evaluation. Li et al proposed a **multidimensional QoS** Constrained Resource Scheduling in [5]. Each of grid task agents diverse requirements is modeled as a quality of service (QoS) dimension, associated with each QoS dimension is a utility function. In **Segmented Min-Min** heuristic described in [15] tasks are first ordered by their expected completion times. Then the ordered sequence is segmented and finally it applies Min-Min to these segments. This heuristic works better than Min-Min. K. C. Nainwal et al proposes **QoS adaptive** Grid Meta scheduling algorithm in [9]. AGMetS uses availability to adapt to the underlying resource failures, thereby ensuring QoS even in the face of failures. Our proposal is to perform scheduling by integrating Grid and P2P techniques to perform Metascheduling taking into account of QoS parameters.

3   System Model for P2P Grid Metascheduler

Resource scheduling plays an important role among the whole task scheduling, a good resource scheduling algorithm can increase load balancing and reduce the implementation time of task scheduling. In P2P Grid model, Super- Peer schedules resources among a local range, so it will avoid search resources from whole Grid range and make resource scheduling time to reduce, as a result, the scheduling time of all tasks will be reduced. Secondly, because P2P technology has advantage of load balancing, it will increase resources utilization of Grid system.

The mapping heuristics discussed in Section 2 can be classified into two modes: online mode and batch mode. In **online mode**, the task is mapped to a resource as soon as it arrives to the scheduler. Task is considered only once for mapping and the mapping does not change once it is done. This mode of mapping is useful when arrival rate of tasks is low. In **batch mode**, First tasks are collected into a set and called metatask. Mapping of meta-task is performed at pre-scheduled times called mapping events. Mapping of each task is performed at every mapping event until it begins its execution. Both online and batch mode assume that estimates of expected execution times on each machine of every task is known in advance.

The system model of QoS guided P2P Grid Metascheduler(QPGM) is depicted in Figure 1. The system accepts total number of user jobs, processing requirements or average Million Instructions(MI) of those jobs, allowed deviation percentage of the MI, processing overhead time of each user job on the grid, granularity size of the job grouping activity and the available grid resources in the grid environment. From the inputs given by the user, Gridlets are generated according to the parameters defined in gridsim [2]. After gathering the details of user jobs and the available resources, the system randomly creates jobs with

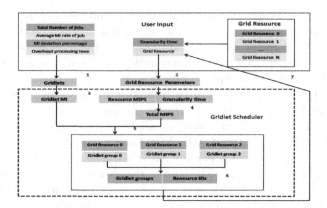

Fig. 1. P2P Grid Metascheduler Model

priority assigned to it according to the given average MI and MI deviation percentage. The scheduler will then select a resource and multiplies the resource Million Instructions per second(MIPS) with the given granularity size. The jobs are then gathered or grouped according to the resulting total MI of the resource, and each created group is stored in a list with its associated resource ID. Eventually, after grouping all jobs, the scheduler submits the job groups to their corresponding resources for job computation.

4   Task Scheduling Algorithm

4.1   QoS Guided P2P Grid Metascheduler(QPGM) Algorithm Description

Every task waiting to be scheduled using QPGM algorithm has the following two attributes: the Super-Peer that task belongs to; the type of QoS that task belongs to. In QPGM algorithm, the tasks that are waiting to be scheduled uses the principle of Min Min with Mean computation(MMC). The idea is to apply Min min first, then take the mean value of the completion time (CT) and again apply Min min to the task reselected having CT higher than mean CT computed. As a result, it ensures that expectation execution time of task ET is the shortest. It can be divided into three scenarios when Super-Peer schedules its own task, listed as follows:

1. If there are no other tasks that being executed or waiting for scheduling in the task queue memorizer of the Task Manager(TM), when TM receives the first high QoS task that user submits, it can search satisfaction demand resources in Resource available list(RAL) present in Resource Manager(RM). Then it searches whether existing valid resource queue in the respond resource group according to receiving resource. If resource queue is empty, search sub-tree of directory tree of resource group or leaf node, return collected information

---

Algorithm 1. QoS guided P2P Grid Metascheduler(QPGM) Algorithm

---

1. Divide all submitted tasks into two sets according to tasks QoS Request/supply and they belong to Super-Peer, place different set QoS_H and QoS_L;

2. For each task T_i in QoS_H set, it is submitted the Super-Peer that it belongs to, Super-Peer deals with this task according to the 3 situations that mentioned below;

   for $i = 1$ to m **do**
   // where m is a number of tasks in QoS_H set;
   if *(task_queue= =null AND resource_queue= =null)* **then**
      Super-Peer searches resources that the task request;
      Return the new state of resources;
      Scheduling this task using MMC approach;
   end
   if *(task_queue!=null AND resource_queue=!=null)* **then**
      Super-Peer makes this task to join in the waiting queue;
      Assign the resources to this task and waiting for scheduling;
      Return the new state of resources;
   end
   if *(task_queue!=null AND resource_queue= =null)* **then**
      Super-Peer makes this task to join in the waiting queue or transfer it to other Super-Peer according to the urgent situation of task;
   end
   end

3. For each task T_j in QoS L set, the Super-Peer still works according to the above procedure.

---

to TM and RM. RM can search the best new state of these resources in the RAL and return it to TM. It makes resource scheduling last disposing based on receiving RAL. At last, TM selects a group of the best quality resources to assign this task based on compounding and optimizing principle.

2. If there is other task or high QoS task to being executed in the task queue memorizer that user submitted, when task queue is empty in the TM and resource queue of resource group is not empty in the RM, because it has saved a set of better QoS resources that has been completed this task when it receives this kind of task first, there is resource queue that has been scheduled and is waiting for being assigned, thus, it is not necessary to submit searching resource request to RM. The RM can select a group of resource assign this task based on a certain compounding and optimizing principle after it analyzes the received information.

3. If there are other tasks to be waiting for resources and all high QoS resources have been occupied in the task queue memorizer that user submitted, but this task must be completed in a certain time, thus RM can make this task to join waiting queue, or submits it to the other Super-Peer, in which the Super-Peer deals with it according to (1) or (2) that mentioned above after it receives this task, finally, return the result to user. When user submits task

to Super-Peer, they may be meet such things that Super-Peer is not satisfied with *QoS* request/supply enough of user because local system loading is too much. The Super-Peer needs to transfer some tasks to other Super-Peer at once.

5   Simulation Environment

To evaluate QoS guided P2P Grid Metascheduler(*QPGM*) Algorithm, a simulation environments known as GridSim toolkit [2] had been used.GridSim has some good features for scheduling algorithms which are listed as follows. It allows modeling of heterogeneous types of resources. Resource capability can be defined (in the form of MIPS(Million Instructions Per Second) as per SPEC (Standard Performance Evaluation Corporation) benchmark). There is no limit on the number of application jobs that can be submitted to a resource. It supports simulation of both static and dynamic schedulers. GridSim had been used in many researches to evaluate the results such as [4], [8], [11], [12].

6   Experimental Results and Evaluation

To simulate QoS guided P2P Grid Metascheduler(QPGM) Algorithm, Gridsim toolkit is used. In the user interface of QPGM, the input data are to be given as discussed in the System Model explained in Section 3.

The request to initiate schedule will be triggered by the existing user or by a new user after registration. The gridlet to be scheduled could be selected from the available gridlets or it could be updated. The parameters for gridlet are its ID, Length, Input size, Output size as defined in gridsim toolkit [2]. On selecting the gridlet, the QPGM algorithm starts to execute the task either in batch mode or online mode as specified by the user. After execution of scheduling by *QPGM* , the output windows shows the result in the format shown in Figure 2 where it gives details of the gridlet ID, the status of execution,the total load, cost, the start and end time to execute the task along with total gridlet processing time.

Figure 3 shows the resource utilization graph for the gridlet scheduled using QoS guided P2P Grid Meta Scheduler(QPGM) algorithm. The Graph is plotted taking Resources along the horizontal axis and Resource characteristics ie. MIPS and Cost along the vertical axis. It shows how the MIPS and Cost are mapped to

Total Time: 23.92 seconds						
========================= SIMULATION RESULTS===						
Gridlet ID	STATUS	Resource Name/ID		Tctal Load	Cost	Start Time	Finish Time
6	SUCCESS	R1/5		2C.00	200.00	12.28	14.28
===						
Total Gridlet processing cost 200.00						
All the Gridlets are processed within the given granularity time						

Fig. 2. Output of QPGM

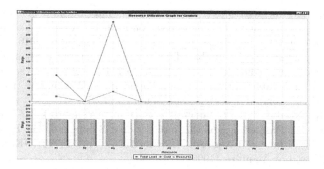

Fig. 3. Resource Utilization graph

the resources depending on the QoS of the task specified during input and Min min with mean computation methodology which is used for task scheduling. As a result, QPGM algorithm satisfies both user requirements in addition it provides better load balancing of the system.

7 Conclusion and Future Work

In this paper we have surveyed several conventional task scheduling algorithms in heterogeneous computing system, and analyzed the fault of conventional algorithms deeply. We present a novel approach for task scheduling using QoS guided P2P Grid Meta Scheduler(QPGM) algorithm, we embed P2P technology into Grid for the first time, composing of local Grid system and take advantage of Super-Peer to complete local task scheduling. The experimental results shows the proposed model gives better improvement in the quality of loading balancing and system resource utilization in comparison with the conventional methodologies. Many issues remain open, like deadline of task, execution cost on each resource, communication cost,structured topology etc. Some of the above mentioned issues are under consideration as a part of further work.

References

1. Abraham, A., Buyya, R., Nath, B.: Nature's heuristics for scheduling jobs on computational grids. In: Proceedings of 8th IEEE International Conference on Advanced Computing and Communications (ADCOM 2000), pp. 45–52 (2000)
2. Buyya, R., Murshed, M.: Gridsim: A toolkit for the modeling and simulation of distributed resource management and scheduling for grid computing. Concurrency and Computation: Practice and Experience (CCPE) 14(13), 1175–1220 (2002)
3. Casanova, H., Zagorodnov, D., Berman, F., Legrand, A.: Heuristics for scheduling parameter sweep applications in grid environments. In: HCW 2000: Proceedings of the 9th Heterogeneous Computing Workshop, Washington, DC, USA, p. 349. IEEE Computer Society, Los Alamitos (2000)

4. Chauhan, S.S., Joshi, R.C.: A weighted mean time min-min max-min selective scheduling strategy for independent tasks on grid. In: Advance Computing Conference (IACC), 2010 IEEE 2nd International, pp. 4–9 (19-20, 2010)
5. Chunlin, L., Layuan, L.: Utility based multiple QoS guaranteed resource scheduling optimization in grid computing. In: ICCTA 2007: Proceedings of the International Conference on Computing: Theory and Applications, Washington, DC, USA, pp. 165–169. IEEE Computer Society, Los Alamitos (2007)
6. Freund, R., Nccosc, T.K.: Smartnet: A scheduling framework for heterogeneous computing. In: Proceedings of the International Symposium on Parallel Architectures, Algorithms and Networks (ISPAN 1996), pp. 514–521. IEEE Computer Society Press, Los Alamitos (1996)
7. Freund, R.F., Gherrity, M., Ambrosius, S., Campbell, M., Halderman, M., Hensgen, D., Keith, E., Kidd, T., Kussow, M., Lima, J.D., Mirabile, F., Moore, L., Rust, B., Siegel, H.J.: Scheduling resources in multi-user, heterogeneous, computing environments with smartnet. In: 7th IEEE Heterogeneous Computing Workshop (HCW 1998), pp. 184–199 (1998)
8. Naghibzadeh, M., Etminani, K.: A min-min max-min selective algorithm for grid task scheduling. In: Proceedings of the 3rd IEEE/IFIP International Conference in Central Asia (2007)
9. Nainwal, K.C., Lakshmi, J., Nandy, S.K., Narayan, R., Varadarajan, K.: A framework for QoS adaptive grid meta scheduling. In: International Workshop on Database and Expert Systems Applications, pp. 292–296 (2005)
10. Talia, D., Trunfio, P.: Toward a synergy between P2P and Grids. IEEE Internet Computing 7(4), 94–96 (2003)
11. Sherwani, J., Ali, N., Lotia, N., Hayat, Z., Buyya, R.: Libra: a computational economy-based job scheduling system for clusters. Journal of Software: Practice and Experience 34(6), 573–590 (2004)
12. Yeo, C.S., Buyya, R.: Pricing for utility-driven resource management and allocation in clusters. International Journal of High Performance Computing Applications 21(4), 405–418 (2007)
13. Shoukat, M.M., Maheswaran, M., Ali, S., Siegel, H.J., Hensgen, D., Freund, R.F.: Dynamic mapping of a class of independent tasks onto heterogeneous computing systems. Journal of Parallel and Distributed Computing 59, 107–131 (1999)
14. Weng, C., Lu, X.: Heuristic scheduling for bag-of-tasks applications in combination with QoS in the computational grid. Future Generation Computer Systems 21(2), 271–280 (2005)
15. Wu, M.-Y., Shu, W., Zhang, H.: Segmented min-min: A static mapping algorithm for meta-tasks on heterogeneous computing systems. In: HCW 2000: Proceedings of the 9th Heterogeneous Computing Workshop, Washington, DC, USA, p. 375. IEEE Computer Society, Los Alamitos (2000)
16. Zhu, Y.: A survey on grid scheduling systems. In: Dong, G., Lin, X., Wang, W., Yang, Y., Yu, J.X. (eds.) APWeb/WAIM 2007. LNCS, vol. 4505, pp. 419–427. Springer, Heidelberg (2007)

Failure Recovery Mechanism in Neighbor Replica Distribution Architecture

Ahmad Shukri Mohd Noor[1] and Mustafa Mat Deris[2]

[1] Department of Computer Science, Faculty of Science and Technology,
Universiti Malaysia Terengganu, 21030 Kuala Terengganu, Malaysia
ashukri@umt.edu.my
[2] Faculty of Multimedia and Information Technology Universiti Tun Hussein Onn Malaysia
86400 Parit Raja, Batu Pahat, Johor Darul Takzim, Malaysia
mmustafa@uthm.edu.my

Abstract. Replication provide an effective way to enhance performance, high availability and fault tolerance in distributed systems. There are numbers of fault tolerant and failure recovery techniques based on replication. These recovery techniques such as Netarkivet's data grid and fast disaster recovery mechanism for volume replication systems were implemented in two-replica distribution technique(TRDT) or primary-backup architecture. However, these techniques have its weaknesses as they inherit irrecoverable scenarios from TRDT such as double faults, both copies of a file are damaged or lost, missing of the content index in index server table and index server has generated checksum error in content index. In this paper we propose the failure recovery based on the Neighbor Replication Distribution technique (NRDT) to recover the irrecoverable scenarios and to improve the recovery performance. This technique considered neighbors have the replicated data, and thus, maximize the fault tolerant as well as reliability in failure recovery. Also, the technique outperform the TRDT in failure recovery by reducing the irrecoverable cases in TRDT. It also tolerates failures such as server failures, site failure or even network partitioning due to it has more the one back up or replica.

Keywords: Fault Tolerant, Detection, Fault Failure Recovery, Distributed Computing, RepblicationTechnique.

1 Introduction

Early research on data grids predicted the benefits from data replication for performance, data availability, and fault tolerance [1],[2],[3],[4]. Zhang and colleagues [5] propose an algorithm for dynamically locating data replica servers within a grid in order to optimize performance, and improve fault tolerance of grid data replication services. Replication of data or processes is an effective way to enhance performance, provide high availability and fault tolerance in distributed systems [6]. One of the most popular replication technique for fault tolerant and failure recovery is two-replica distribution technique (TRDT) or primary–backup technique. TRDT has been

R. Zhu et al. (Eds.): ICICA 2010, LNCS 6377, pp. 41–48, 2010.

proposed by Shen et al [7]. There are numbers of fault tolerant and failure recovery techniques based on TRDT namely Netarkivet's data grid and fast disaster recovery mechanism for volume replication systems. Netarkivet's data grid developed for the national Danish web archive, and is used for storing large amounts of crawled web pages [8].While to optimize the disaster recovery mechanisms. Yanlong et al. [9] presented a fast disaster recovery mechanism. It tracks the incremental changes as they happen. However these research projects inherit the TRDT weaknesses of irre-coverable failure scenarios.

This paper focus on improving fault tolerant and the recovery performance in dis-tributed or grid environment by reducing irrecoverable scenarios. We utilized the Neighbor Replication Distribution Technique (NRDT) technique to optimize the fail-ure recovery. Furthermore we introduced an index server (IS) and a heartbeat moni-toring server (HBM) to this technique.

The rest of the paper is organized as follows: Section 2 presents the background of the research with two-replica distribution technique(TRDT). The failure recovery problems faced by this technique were also mentioned here. The Neighbor Replica-tion Distribution technique (NRDT) architecture details with the proposed failure recovery mechanism and dealing with node failure illustrated in section 3. Section 4 discusses the recovery performance of proposed mechanism. The research findings and conclusion is given in Section 5 and section 6 respectively.

2 Two-Replica Distribution Technique

Most of replication techniques for fault tolerant and failure recovery are using pri-mary backup or two replica distribution technique [6].TRDT has been proposed by Shen et al. [7]. In this technique, each node has an equal capacity of storage and all data have two replicas on different nodes and all nodes have two data replicas [7].The TRDT fault tolerant and recovery mechanism composed of Primary and Backup (or Secondary), and its architecture is shown in Fig. 1.

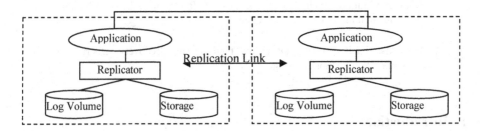

Fig. 1. A Architecture of typical two-replica distribution technique [9]

2.1 TRDT Irrecoverable Scenarios

In this section, we will discuss TRDT irrecoverable scenarios. For simplicity, let con-sider in this TRDT model there are three nodes, two for data replica and one for index server . We name the data replica nodes as j-1 and j and the index server as idx. Each operation acts on a single file f in the replicas. Before carrying out any other action, the system checks the current status of the file on both nodes   and in the index server (idx).

Let :

$D_{idx}(f)$ *is the checksum of the file f found in the content index(registered with server)*

$D_{j-1}(f)$ *is The checksum of f in replica Dj-1*

$D_j(f)$ *is The checksum of f in replica Dj*

Here are some irrecoverable scenarios that suffered by TRDT:-

i. Some failure scenarios in particular double faults. where both copies of a file are damaged or lost.

Case 1: idx and any one of data replica nodes failed.

$$Didx(f_n) \cup D_j(f_n) = 0 \tag{1}$$

$$Didx(f_n) \cup D_{j-1}(f_n) = 0 \tag{2}$$

Case 2: Both nodes of data replica fail, no backup file can be recovered.

$$D_j(f_n) \cup D_{j-1}(f_n) = 0 \tag{3}$$

ii. Another scenario where the content index has registered a wrong checksum for a file or Deletion of the content index. This will result in many files having $Didx(f) = 0$. If the server mistakenly deleted content index files or the content index corrupted ,thus there is no index to be referred for recovery purposes.

3 Neighbor Replication Distribution Technique (NRDT)

In NRDT, all nodes are logically organised in the form of two-dimensional n x n grid structure [16]. If there are nodes in environment where N = n2, then it will logically organise in the form of n x n grid.For example, if a grid consists of nine nodes, it will logically be organise in the form of 3 x 3 grids as shown in Fig. 2. Each node has it own master data file.

3.1 The NRDT Failure Recovery Mechanism

HBM will monitor and detect the failure occurrence for the application that has been registered with AR. This fault detection component will continuously monitor the system and update the current status of each application in the IS and provide a space for recovery actions to be taken in a variety of ways such as kill and restart, fail-over, virtual IP and others. While the for the purpose of improving the reliability, fault tolerance and failure recovery of the model. We have made installed IS and HBM in two different nodes as depict in figure 2.

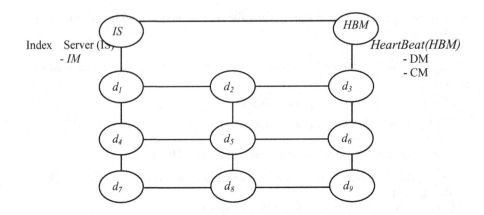

Fig. 2. NRDT Architecture with IS and HBM

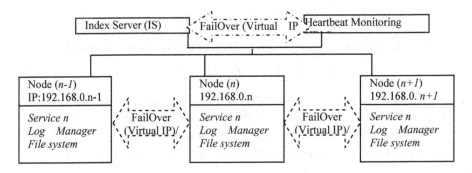

Fig. 3. NRDT recovery mechanism

They back each other where IS has replica of HBM and vice versa. HBM server will detect the failure occurrence and all the transactions status needs to be indexed by HBM for references and further action to be taken during recovery process. There two main component in HBM. 1- Detection Manager(DM). Detect any failures in participating nodes. 2-Coordinator manager(CM). If there is a failed node, CM will decide the candidate node that can virtually backup the service of failed node by using Virtual IP.The main component in IS is Index Manager (IM). IM stores all indexed content of checksum data file in participating node.

Once a new replica is elected, this replica takes over the role of a primary. Transferring the primary services from a faulty primary to a working one and constitutes the recovery step. A closer picture of recovery mechanism is shown in figure 3.

4   Performance of NRDT Failure Recovery Mechanism

IS keep a set of checksum datafile value, S = { s1,s2...sn) in table format. This datafile that reside in every replicas is considered register to IS if and only if the datafile checksum is stored in the IS table as shown in table1.

Table 1. Index Server (IS) register checksum datafile in table format

S	F_1	f_2	f_3	f_4	f_5	f_6	f_7	f_8	f_9
c_1	S_1	S_2		S_4					
c_2	S_1	S_2	S_3		S_5				
c_3		S_2	S_3			S_6			
c_4	S_1			S_4	S_5		S_7		
c_5		S_2		S_4	S_5	S_6		S_8	
c_6			S_3		S_5	S_6			S_9
c_7				S_4			S_7	S_8	
c_8					S_5		S_7	S_8	S_9
c_9						S_6		S_8	S_9

let $D_{i,j}(f_n)$ is the checksum function for file f_n in replica $c_{i,j}$.

Definition: if a data file f_n in replica $c_{i,j}$ node is registered with IS and it is a valid data .we can define that

$$D_{i,j}(f_n) = \{x \mid x \in S \text{ and } x \neq \emptyset \} \tag{4}$$

A number of scenarios will be discussed in this section. In each scenario, the recovery operation as depict in function in table 2 will be to discuss well as the possibilities to recover the failures.

Table 2. Function of recovery operation

$fr_{idx}(f_{ci}^n)$	Corrects a wrong entry for datafile n within replica node C_i in the cental content
$fd_i(f_n)$	Delete corrupted file n
$fc_i(f_n)$	recover file n from effected node to the operating one.
$D_i(f_n)$	Generate checksum for the file n in node i

Case 1: For example, Let If there is master file (f_n) damaged in $C_{i,j}$ HBM then detected the failure, it will then notify the status to .Then IS will check the file registration with content index. If the file is registered, then IS refer to Index table for the damaged file and check the neighbor for the effected node. IS choose one of it neighbor then file recovery take place. This election is done by comparing the checksum of the file in fail node.

In our technique, IS use following condition to recover the file it neighbor.

$$D_{i,j-1}(f_n) \cap D_{i,j+1}(f_n) \cap D_{i-1,j}(f_n) \cap D_{i+1,j}(f_n) = \{x \mid x \in S \text{ and } x \neq \emptyset \} \tag{5}$$

Case 2: In the scenario where double faults happened, where both copies of a file are damaged or lost in two neighboring node, failure recovery with NRGT still can recover the damaged file as in this technique, there are at least $\geq 2 + 1$ node alive (at least 2 replica + 1 the master file). So if both copies damaged still there at least one replica can operate the service and that the same time refer to IS and recover the damage file in infected node.

Let master file (f_n) store in $C_{i,j}$ and have replica in $C_{i+1,j}$ and $C_{i,j-1}$. Assume that the file (f_n) is damaged in two node $C_{i,j}$ and $C_{i+1,j}$. The file recovery process can still take place as there is a undamaged file in node $C_{i,j-1}$. The IS will refer to $C_{i,j-1}(f_n)$ to recover (f_n) in node $C_{i+1,j}$ and $C_{i,j-1}$.
Thus,

$$D_{i,j-1}(f_n) \cap D_{idx}(f_n) = \{ \; x \mid x \neq \varnothing \; \} \tag{6}$$

Thus it solve the problem of double faults where both copies of file in two nodes are damaged or lost that cannot be in TRDT.

Case 3: The content index has registered a wrong checksum or deletion of the content index. This will result in many files having $Didx(f_n) = \varnothing$ or $Didx(f_n) = \{d'\}$

If the server mistakenly deleted content index files or the content index files corrupted, thus there is no index to be referred for recovery purposes. In this case the IS server become unreliable. Thus HBM will take over the service of the IS.
Confirmation on the IS stability can be check by follow definition:-

$$D_{i,j-1}(f_n) \cap D_{i,j+1}(f_n) \cap D_{i-1,j}(f_n) \cap D_{i+1,j}(f_n) = \{x \mid x \notin S \text{ and } x \neq \varnothing\} \tag{7}$$

Then compare the checksum the file (f_n) in each neighboring node with index content for confirmation that index content table having problem(s).

$$D_{i,j+1}(f_n) \cap D_{idx}(f_n) = D_{i-1,j}(f_n) \cap D_{idx}(f_n) = D_{i+1,j}(f_n) \cap D_{idx}(f_n) = D_{i,j-1}(f_n) \cap D_{idx}(f_n) = \{ \; \} \tag{8}$$

then it compare with HBM index content

$$D_{i,j-1}(f_n) \cap D_{i,j+1}(f_n) \cap D_{i-1,j}(f_n) \cap D_{i+1,j}(f_n) \cap D_{hbm}(f_n) = \{x \mid x \in S \text{ and } x \neq \varnothing\} \tag{9}$$

Then it is confirmed that IS content index had problem.

Solution: Recover IS content index with the HBM content index and restore checksum table for the f_n in IS.

$$fc_{idx}(f_n) = . \; fc_{hbm}(f_n) \tag{10}$$

(Note: As we mentioned previously IS store replica (log, service, volume, data) of HBM and vice versa. Thus, when one server malfunction the other one will back the service.)

In such case, if the system not sure whether a data file does not register with IS or IS is unreliable, NRDT recovery mechanism will check the service with HBM since HBM has the replica service of IS (incase of IS malfunction or failed.).

5 Research Findings

Replication of data or processes is an effective way to provide high availability, enhance performance and fault tolerance in distributed systems Replication is a key technique to achieve fault tolerance in distributed and dynamic environments. The proposed failure recovery mechanism has been simulate in mathematical model and is proven that this model can reduce   the unsolved scenarios faced TRDT. While by installing IS and HBM in two different node it can improve the reliability, fault tolerance and failure recovery in the model mechanism. The overall finding as follow:

i.   The indexing of the applications that register to the service allows the construction of reliable recovery mechanism as HBM and IS will provide the necessary information needed to run the specific recovery service.

ii. Running IS and HBM in two different node can overcome the problem where the content index has registered a wrong checksum, deletion of the content index or malfunction service n in TRDT.These scenario happen usually when the server not stable(malfunction). So in our model mechanism, if the current server (IS) malfunction, it can be supported by the other one(HBM).However this is not like primary-buck mechanism. In our model initially IS and HBM have their service run concurrently. So when one server failed and at the same time while the failed server being recovered the other server have to run two services on one site.

iii. In the scenario where double faults happened, where both copies of a file are damaged or lost in two node which this kind failure cannot be recovered in TRDT. The NRDT recovery mechanism still can recover the damaged file as in this technique, due to in NRDT, there at least ≥ 2 + 1 node alive (at least 2 replica + 1 the master file).

6 Conclusion

Replication is a rising fault tolerant technique, and disaster recovery mechanisms play an important role in replication systems. The right replication technique can be an effective way in providing enhanced performance, high availability and fault tolerance in distributed systems. NRDT fault tolerant and failure recovery mechanism is presented to recover the data and service   at the primary node and to improve the recovery efficiency by retaining availability of data or service with maintaining a sufficient number of replicas, so that at least one is always available to continue a process. The model has proved that it can eliminate the irrecoverable from two-replica distribution technique such as double faults where both copies of a file are damaged or lost, missing of the content index. Thus it optimize the fault tolerant and failure recovery as well as improve data and service scalability, reliability, availability.

References

1. Chervenak, A., et al.: The Data Grid: Towards an Architecture for the Distributed Management and Analysis of Large Scientific Data Sets. Journal of Network and Computer Applications, 187–200 (2001)
2. Hoschek, W., et al.: Data management in an international data grid project. In: Proceedings of GRID Workshop, pp. 77–90 (2000)
3. Stockinger, H., et al.: File and object replication in data grids. In: Tenth IEEE Symposium on High Performance and Distributed Computing, pp. 305–314 (2001)
4. Dabrowski, C.: Reliability in grid computing systems Concurrency Computatation. Practice and Experience. Wiley InterScience, Hoboken (2009), http://www.interscience.wiley.com
5. Zhang, Q., et al.: Dynamic Replica Location Service Supporting Data Grid Systems. In: Sixth IEEE International Conference on Computer and Information Technology (CIT 2006), p. 61 (2006)
6. Erciyes, K.: A Replication-Based Fault Tolerance Protocol Using Group Communication for the Grid. In: Guo, M., Yang, L.T., Di Martino, B., Zima, H.P., Dongarra, J., Tang, F. (eds.) ISPA 2006. LNCS, vol. 4330, pp. 672–681. Springer, Heidelberg (2006)
7. Shen, H.H., Chen, S.M., Zheng, W.M., Shi, S.M.: A Communication Model for Data Availability on Server Clusters. In: Proc. Int'l. Symposium on Distributed Computing and Application, Wuhan, pp. 169–171 (2001)
8. Niels, H.: A formal analysis of recovery in a preservational data grid. In: Christensen the 14th NASA Goddard - 23rd IEEE Conference on Mass Storage Systems and Technologies, College Park, Maryland, USA, May 15-18 (2006)
9. Wang, Y., Li, Z.-h., Lin, W.: A Fast Disaster Recovery Mechanism for Volume Replication Systems. In: Perrott, R., Chapman, B.M., Subhlok, J., de Mello, R.F., Yang, L.T. (eds.) HPCC 2007. LNCS, vol. 4782, pp. 732–743. Springer, Heidelberg (2007)

Autonomous Discovery of Subgoals Using Acyclic State Trajectories

Zhao Jin[1], Jian Jin[2], and WeiYi Liu[1]

[1] School of Information Science and Engineering, Yunnan University,
Kunming, 650091, P.R. China
jzletter@sina.com
[2] Hongta Group Tobacco Limited Corporation
Hongta Road 118, Yuxi, 653100, P.R. China
jinjianem@sina.com

Abstract. Divide and rule is an effective strategy to solve large and complex problems. We propose an approach to make agent can discover autonomously subgoals for task decomposition to accelerate reinforcement learning. We remove the state loops in the state trajectories to get the shortest distance of every state from the goal state, then these states in acyclic state trajectories are arranged in different layers according to the shortest distance of them from the goal state. So, to reach these state layers with different distance to the goal state can be used as the subgoals for agent reaching the goal state eventually. Compared with others, autonomy and robustness are the major advantages of our approach. The experiments on Grid-World problem show the applicability, effectiveness and robustness of our approach.

Keywords: Reinforcement Learning, Acyclic State Trajectory, Subgoals, State Layers, Grid-World.

1 Introduction

Reinforcement Learning(RL) has attracted many researchers because of the notion of agent can learn on itself to select optimal actions mapping its states to maximize reward, without the aid of an intelligent teacher(e.g., human)[1][2]. But the iterative learning process of RL make it only works well on problems with small state space[3].

For scaling up the application of RL, Divide and rule as an effective strategy to solve large and complex problem is introduced to accelerate RL[4][5][6]. By task decomposition, the overall task is decomposed into some sub-tasks, then these sub-tasks will be accomplished in an easier and quicker manner, so learning is accelerated.

Task decomposition can accelerate learning significantly, but how discover subgoals for task decomposition remains an open problem[7][8]. In most existing RL approaches with task decomposition, subgoals are usually given by sophisticated human according to the prior knowledge of problem domain, which makes the task decomposition is problem-specific, and also weaken agent's autonomy, which is the major advantage of RL, furthermore, these approaches would lose acceleration capability when prior knowledge of problem domain is not available, or the sub-goals can not be given by human because the problem is too large and complex.

R. Zhu et al. (Eds.): ICICA 2010, LNCS 6377, pp. 49–56, 2010.

Some researchers have tried to find ways to make agent can discover autonomously sub-goals. Takahashi[9] presented a method of self task decomposition for modular learning system, but agent still needs instructions given by a coach (human). McGovern[10] and menache[11] proposed similar methods to discover the "bottleneck" regions in the state space to be the subgoals. The visiting frequencies of each state in accumulated state trajectories are counted to draw histogram for detecting the bottlenecks to be subgoals. Chen[12] and Kazemitabar[13] presented similar methods to find the states which are not only visited frequently in the whole space but also have a relative high visiting frequency in their neighboring regions performing a critical role in connecting the neighbor states to be the subgoals. Their works make agent can discover autonomously subgoals, but large amount of state loops existed in the state trajectories makes the visiting frequencies of the bottleneck states do not stand out, so the efficiency to discover bottlenecks or connected components is low, moreover, they method are limited to state space which exists bottleneck regions.

In this paper, we proposed an approach to make agent can discover autonomously subgoals using acyclic state trajectories. During the learning process, we record every state trajectory agent experienced in every training episode, and remove all state loops existed in the state trajectory to acquire acyclic state trajectory. By removing these repeated states that formed state loops, each state in an acyclic state trajectory will get the shortest distance from the goal state, and this distance is measured by the number of steps that agent move form this state to the goal state. Next, each state is arranged into different layers according to the shortest distance of it from the goal state. All states in the same layers has the same distance from the goal state, so no matter agent reaches which state in the same layer, the distance (steps) of agent from the goal state is same. These state layers with different distance from the goal state are just like the first ring road, the second ring road, and so on, to surround the center of city. Therefore, the whole state layer could be a subgoal. By this way, even there are no bottleneck regions in the state space, the whole state layer also could be a subgoal for agent reaching the goal state eventually.

By organizing the states in layers according to the distance of them from the goal state in the acyclic state trajectories, agent can discover autonomously subgoals from the state layers, and the subgoal combined from a whole layer states makes our approach is robust and general. The experiments on Grid-World show the applicability, effectiveness and robustness of our approach.

The rest of this paper is organized as follows. Section 2 gives the algorithm to eliminate the state loops existed in state trajectory. Section 3 presents the approach to discover subgoals from acyclic state trajectories. Section 4 is the experiments to illustrate the applicability, effectiveness and robustness of our approach. Sections 5 is conclusions.

2   Remove State Loops in the State Trajectory

In RL, for agent can explore the overall state space to find the optimal policy, the randomness of select action is necessary[2]. So, even in a very small state space, the state trajectory may be very long, because large amount of state loops are included in the state trajectory.

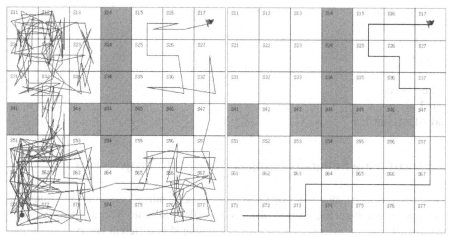

(a) State trajectory with state loops   (b) Acyclic state trajectory

Fig. 1. Removing state loops in state trajectory

We use the classical Grid-World problem shown in Fig.1(a) to give an example. In Fig.1(a), the square with flag is the goal state, and the square with a green circle is the start state. The squares colored dark grey is obstacle. The agent can move up, right, down and left by one square in its one step. The problem faced by agent is to find the optimal policy, here is the shortest route from the start state to the goal state. The red lines from the start state to the goal state show a real state trajectory with many state loops. In order to get the shortest distance of each state from the goal state, these state loops in state trajectory should be removed. Algorithm 1 gives the way to remove state loops in state trajectory.

The black lines in Fig.1(b) shows the acyclic state trajectory computed from the state trajectory shown in Fig.1(a). By removing the state loops, the shortest distance of each state from the goal state is acquired.

Algorithm 1. Removing state loops in state trajectory
Input
    e: an state trajectory, defined as a list of states
Output
    e': an acyclic state trajectory, defined as a list of states
Step 1. Initialization:
    Create a null list: e'
    Let $i \leftarrow 0$
    Let s is a state, and $s \leftarrow e[i]$
Step 2. While $i < e.length$ do
    If s does not exist in e'
        Add s into e'
    Else if s has existed in e'
        Let $index_s \leftarrow$ the index of s in e'

Delete the elements of e' form $index_s$ to the end of e'
        Add s into e'
    End if
    Let $i \leftarrow i + 1$
    Let $s \leftarrow e[i]$
    End While
Step 3. Return e'
End Algorithm 1

3   Discovering Subgoals Using Acyclic State Trajectories

After these repeated states that form the state loops are removed, each state in the acyclic state trajectory will get the shortest distance from the goal state. These states surrounding the goal state in different distance can be arranged in different layers according to the distance of them from the goal states. These state layers can naturally be subgoals for agent reaching the goal state, just like the third ring road, the second ring road and the first ring road can naturally be subgoals for reaching the center of city.

By this way, we enlarge the scope to discover subgoal, not only the bottleneck region can be the subgoal, but also the collection of states can be subgoal, which makes our approach is more robust and general. The way to arrange states in different layers is shown in Algorithm 2.

Algorithm 2. Creating layered state space
Input
    s_g: the goal state
    $total\_ast$: the accumulated acyclic state trajectories
Output
    L_sp: the layered state space
Step 1. Initialization:
    Create a null list set: L_sp
    Create a null list l_1 , and add s_g into l_1
    Add l_1 into L_sp
    $k \leftarrow 1$
Step 2. While $k <$ the length of $total\_ast$ Do
    Create the kth state layer l_k, and add l_k into L_sp
    For each acyclic state trajectory t in $total\_ast$ Do
        Find the index i of s_g in t
        If $t[i - k]$ is not null
            If $t[i - k]$ not exist in any layer between
            $L\_sp[2]$ and $L\_sp[k - 1]$
                Add $t[i - k]$ into l_k
            End if
            For each state layer l_m between $L\_sp[k + 1]$
            and $L\_sp[k + m]$ Do
                If $t[i - k]$ exist in l_m

Remove $t[i-k]$ from l_m
    End if
   End for
  End If
 End For
End While

Step 3. Return L_sp

End Algorithm 2

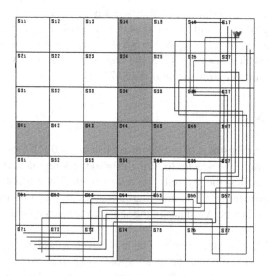

Fig. 2. The sketch map of accumulated acyclic state trajectories

S71 -> S61 -> S82 -> S83 -> S84 -> S65 -> S55 -> S56 -> S57 -> S47 -> S37 -> S36 -> S26 -> S16 -> S17

S71 -> S72 -> S73 -> S63 -> S64 -> S65 -> S66 -> S76 -> S77 -> S67 -> S57 -> S47 -> S37 -> S36 -> S26 -> S27 -> S17

S71 -> S72 -> S82 -> S83 -> S84 -> S65 -> S55 -> S56 -> S66 -> S67 -> S57 -> S47 -> S37 -> S27 -> S17

S71 -> S72 -> S73 -> S63 -> S64 -> S65 -> S66 -> S56 -> S57 -> S47 -> S37 -> S27 -> S17

S71 -> S72 -> S73 -> S63 -> S64 -> S65 -> S66 -> S56 -> S57 -> S47 -> S37 -> S27 -> S26 -> S16 -> S17

S71 -> S72 -> S73 -> S63 -> S64 -> S65 -> S55 -> S56 -> S57 -> S47 -> S37 -> S36 -> S35 -> S25 -> S15 -> S16 -> S17

S71 -> S61 -> S82 -> S83 -> S64 -> S65 -> S66 -> S76 -> S77 -> S67 -> S57 -> S47 -> S37 -> S36 -> S35 -> S25 -> S26 -> S27 -> S17

S71 -> S72 -> S73 -> S83 -> S64 -> S65 -> S66 -> S56 -> S57 -> S47 -> S37 -> S27 -> S17

Fig. 3. Accumulated acyclic state trajectories

Fig.2 and Fig.3 show the accumulated acyclic trajectories after agent finished 8 time training episodes. Fig.4 shows the layered state space created by Algorithm 2 according to the accumulated acyclic trajectories shown in Fig.2 and Fig.3.

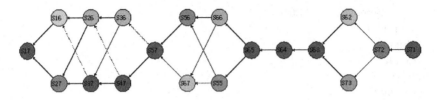

Fig. 4. Layered state space

When we get the layered state space shown in Fig.4, these state layers with different distance from the goal state could be used as the sub-goals for agent reaching the goal state eventually. For example, in Fig.4, the 5th state layer which has only state $s57$ and the 9th state layer which has only state $s64$ can be used as two sub-goals for agent reaching the goal state $s17$ from the start state $s71$.

4 Experiments

We first illustrate the robustness of our approach in a clean 6×6 Grid-World, shown in Fig.5(a), which has no any obstacles to form the bottleneck regions. After agent finished 36 time training episodes, the layered state space created by Algorithm 2 is shown in Fig.5(b). The experiment result is amazing, all states in the original state space are arranged perfectly in layers. All states in the same layer has the same distance from the goal state.

If agent selects the 6th state layer which includes states $\{s55, s44, s33, s22, s11, s66\}$ to be a sub-goal, then the overall learning task is decomposed equally into two smaller sub-tasks, and the whole state space is also

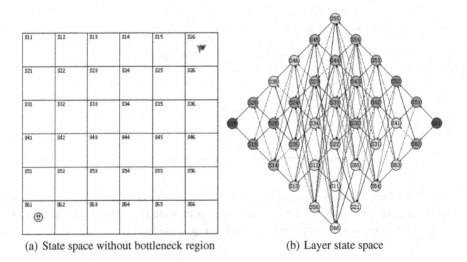

(a) State space without bottleneck region   (b) Layer state space

Fig. 5. Creating layered state space from State space without bottleneck region

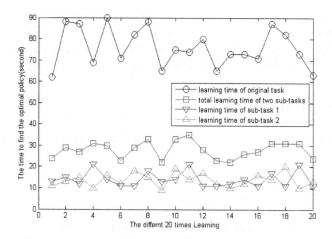

Fig. 6. The learning time comparison

divides equally into two smaller state spaces, then these two sub-tasks can be accomplished easily and quickly in smaller state space, so learning is accelerated. From this experiment, it is obvious that our approach is robust and general, even in such a clean state space the sub-goals for task decomposition also can be discovered clearly and easily.

Next, we compare the time to find the optimal policy in two situations. One situation is the overall learning task is not decomposed, agent learns the task in the original state space; another situation is the layered state space is created from the original state space, and one of state layer is used to be sub-goal to decompose the overall learning task into two smaller sub-tasks. We perform 20 times different learning in a 6×6 Grid-World. The comparison results are shown in Fig.6. The line marked as "learning time of original task" is the time to find the optimal policy without task decomposition, marked as "total learning time of two sub-tasks" is the total time of two sub-tasks to find their optimal policies, marked as "learning time of sub-task 1" is the time to find the optimal policy in sub-task 1, and the line marked as "learning time of sub-task 2" is the time to find the optimal policy in sub-task 2.

From Fig.6, it is obvious that task decomposition can significantly reduce the learning time, even the overall task is only decomposed into two sub-tasks using only a subgoal. This experiment shows our approach is very effective.

5   Conclusion

The strategy of divide and rule applies RL is very successful, but how discover subgoals for task decomposition is not tackled in depth. These existing approaches either need the assistance of human, or are limited to specific state space.

We proposed an approach to make agent can discover autonomously subgoals for task decomposition. Compared with others, our approach has two advantages:1) the discovery of subgoals is performed by agent itself without human's aid; 2) the approach is robust, which is not limited to specific problem state space, but is applicable widely.

Acknowledgment

This work was supported by the National Natural Science Foundation of China (No. 60763007).

References

1. Mitchell, T.M.: Machine Learning. McGraw-Hill, New York (1997)
2. Sutton, R.S., Barto, A.G.: Reinforcement Learning:An Introduction. MIT Press, Cambridge (1998)
3. Kaelbling, L.P.: Reinforcement Learning: A Survey. Journal of Artificial Intelligence Research 4, 237–285 (1996)
4. Dietterich, T.G.: Hierarchical Reinforcement Learning with the MAXQ Value Fuction decomposition. Journal of Artificial Intelligence Research 13, 227–303 (2000)
5. Barto, A.G., Mahadevan, S.: Recent Advance in Hierarchical Reinforcement Learning. Discrete Event Dynamic System: Theory and applications 13(4), 41–77 (2003)
6. Girgin, S., Polat, F., Alhajj, R.: Improving reinforcement learning by using sequence trees. Machine Learning, vol. 4. Springer, Netherlands (2010)
7. Shi, C., Huang, R., Shi, Z.: Automatic Discovery of Subgoals in Reinforcement Learning Using Unique-Direction Value. In: Proceeding the 6th IEEE International Conference on Cognitive Informatics, pp. 480–486. IEEE Computer Society, Los Alamitos (2007)
8. Chiu, C., Soo, V.: Cascading Decomposition and State Abstractions for Reinforcement Learning. In: 2008 Seventh Mexican International Conference on Artificial Intelligence, pp. 82–87. IEEE Computer Society, Washington (2008)
9. Takahashi, Y., Nishi, T., Asada, M.: Self Task Decomposition for Modular Learning System through Interpretation of Instruction by Coach. In: Bredenfeld, A., Jacoff, A., Noda, I., Takahashi, Y. (eds.) RoboCup 2005. LNCS (LNAI), vol. 4020, pp. 640–647. Springer, Heidelberg (2006)
10. McGovern, A., Barto, A.G.: Automatic Discovery of Subgoals in Reinforcement Learning using Diverse Density. In: Proceedings of the Eighteenth International Conference on Machine Learning, pp. 361–368. Morgan Kaufmann, San Francisco (2001)
11. Menache, I., Mannor, S., Shimkin, N.: Q-Cut - Dynamic Discovery of Sub-goals in Reinforcement Learning. In: Elomaa, T., Mannila, H., Toivonen, H. (eds.) ECML 2002. LNCS (LNAI), vol. 2430, pp. 187–195. Springer, Heidelberg (2002)
12. Chen, F., Gao, Y., Chen, S., Ma, Z.: Connect-based subgoal discovery for options in hierarchical reinforcement learning. In: Proceedings of the Third International Conference on Natural Computation, pp. 698–702. IEEE Computer Society, Los Alamitos (2007)
13. Kazemitabar, S.J., Beigy, H.: Automatic Discovery of Subgoals in Reinforcement Learning Using Strongly Connected Components. In: Köppen, M., Kasabov, N., Coghill, G. (eds.) ICONIP 2008. LNCS, vol. 5506, pp. 829–834. Springer, Heidelberg (2009)

Numerical Computing and Forecasting to Land Subsidence in Coastal Regions of Tangshan

Jing Tan[1,2], Zhigang Tao[1,3], and Changcun Li[1]

[1] College of Resources and Environment, Hebei Polytechnic University
Tangshan Hebei 063009, China
[2] College of Qinggong, Hebei Polytechnic University
Tangshan Hebei 063009, China
[3] State Key Laboratory for Geomechanics & Deep Underground Engineering
Beijing 100083, China
hblgdxtj@126.com

Abstract. Coastal areas are an important part of Tangshan, which groundwater has been over exploited for a long time. The hazard of land subsidence has appeared and kept aggravating continuously. By studying the hydrogeology and engineering geology condition, a new understanding of deformation mechanism of land subsidence in Tangshan coastal areas has been found. According to the distribution of groundwater funnel(GF) and monitor data of groundwater, firstly, the mathematical model of developing tendency of GF is established and it is verified the results are similar with the real results. Then the conception of groundwater dynamics coefficient has been introduced and the development tendency model is established according to the depth value of GF center water above. Finally, combine the mathematical model and the rate of land subsidence, establish the numerical analysis model about land subsidence. The results conform to the truth of subsidence of coastal areas.

Keywords: Land Subsidence, Hazard of Environment, Scientific Computing, Tangshan Coastal Regions.

1 Introduction

Land Subsidence has become a major part of geological disaster research[1]. Currently, the land subsidence is main to study its causes[2-3], mechanisms[4-6], monitoring[7-8], predictions[9-11], and measures preventing [12-13]. Because of the narrow range of engineering computing and computer applications in the past, the research of land subsidence is slow. While the rapid development of science and technology provides land subsidence research with a good foundation.

Tangshan coastal areas will be the busy part of economics in the future, with the development of society, the groundwater has been over exploited for a long time and the hazard of land subsidence has appeared and kept aggravating continuously. Tangshan is an important coastal city in Bohai economic circle, which will develop to the southern coastal areas as the next major aim, and speed up the pace of migration to

R. Zhu et al. (Eds.): ICICA 2010, LNCS 6377, pp. 57–64, 2010.
© Springer-Verlag Berlin Heidelberg 2010

the coastal areas gradually, advanced in "the Eleventh Five-Year Plan". However, the southern coastal areas are characteristic of the fragile geological environment, the lack of freshwater resources and the threat of land subsidence already. For example, two subsidence exploitation funnels have appeared in Jiantuozi and Tanghai in 1985, where the mean value of land subsidence is 400mm-1800mm, and the ground is below the sea level modern 1753 km^2, which is a major environmental problem to have impact on economics directly.

The authors use modern scientific technology, calculate and predict the development trend of land subsidence in coastal areas of Tangshan, and provide scientific basis of prevention and control of land subsidence in coastal areas.

2   Evolution Feature of Groundwater Depression Funnel

Tangshan has a total of four large scale groundwater depression funnels in the end of 2000, that is, Ninghe-Tanghai funnel in Pingyuan area, Qianying funnel, multi-level drop funnel and Guye funnel[14].

2.1   Status of Groundwater Depression Funnel

(1) Ninghe - Tanghai groundwater depression funnel. It is from Laoting in the east to Tianjin Ninghe in the west ,from Bohai Bay in the south to the basic direction along the brackish-fresh water in the northern boundary, in some areas such as the Xigezhuang in Fengnan has been extended to the northern boundary of brackish-fresh water. The type is groundwater subsidence funnel.

The funnel is located in the Binhai Plain hydro geologic zone, the exploitation layer is the deep confined fresh water, with salt water floor above 40-120m depth. Exploitation depth is about 120-360m, individual areas are over 400m. In 2000 the funnel area in low water level is 3145.8 km^2, reducing 29.4 km^2 compared to the year 1995. The centre of funnel is located in Hanggu, the center depth of water is 82.54 m, water level is -82.06 m, decreasing 9.39 m compared to the year 1995 . According to statistics, the total of motor-pumped wells are 5688 in the funnel region in 2000, reducing by 79 compared to the year 1995, motor-pump well density is 1.81 / km^2; the total of groundwater exploitation is 168.21 million m^3, increasing 9.2 million m^3 compared to the year 1995, the number of mining modules is 53500 m^3/km^2a.

(2) Qianying deep water depression funnel

Qianying funnel distributes in the mining camps and external, which is affected by dewatering of the Kailuan Mine. Closures water level is 2.00m, funnel area is 196km2 in 2000, expanding 15.5km^2 compared to 1995. Center depth of water is 55.01m in 2000, increasing 3.81m compared to 1995. The total of dewatering is 6.58 million m^3 in 2000, increasing 260,000 m^3 compared to 1996.

2.2   Trend Prediction of Groundwater Depression Funnel

Based on 1986-2000 funnel center depth and affecting area, in the condition of taking full account of government departments curbing over exploited groundwater, use gray theory GM (1,1) model series to predict factors such as area of groundwater

Table 1. Forcast table of transformational trend on two groundwater funnel from 2000 to 2015

Factors year	Ninghe - Tanghai groundwater subsidence funnel			Qianying depth-level subsidence funnel		
	Affected area (km²)	Center water depth (m)	Center water level height (m)	Affected area (km²)	Center water depth (m)	Center water level height (m)
2001	3190.4	77.6175	-77.1383	196.8293	55.3713	-37.2355
2002	3228.5	78.3426	-77.8638	198.3600	56.1488	-38.0349
2003	3267.1	79.0744	-78.5961	199.9027	56.9372	-38.8515
2004	3306.1	79.8131	-79.3352	201.4574	57.7368	-39.6857
2005	3345.6	80.5587	-80.0814	203.0241	58.5475	-40.5377
2006	3385.6	81.3113	-80.8345	204.6031	59.3696	-41.4081
2007	3426.0	82.0709	-81.5947	206.1943	60.2033	-42.2971
2008	3466.9	82.8376	-82.3621	207.7979	61.0487	-43.2052
2009	3508.4	83.6114	-83.1367	209.4139	61.9059	-44.1328
2010	3550.3	84.3925	-83.9186	211.0426	62.7752	-45.0803
2011	3592.7	85.1808	-84.7078	212.6839	63.6567	-46.0482
2012	3635.6	85.9766	-85.5044	214.3379	64.5506	-47.0368
2013	3679.0	86.7797	-86.3086	216.0049	65.4570	-48.0467
2014	3723.0	87.5904	-87.1203	217.6848	66.3762	-49.0782
2015	3767.5	88.4087	-87.9396	219.3777	67.3082	-50.1319

depression, the center water depth and the center water level height in 2010, 2015 (Table 1). To simplify the calculations, the paper uses MATLAB 6.5 software to program, which can output results and trend graphs at the same time, and make the results more intuitive.

After scientific computing, Ninghe-Tanghai groundwater depression funnel has a regularly increasing trend of affected area, the center water depth and the center water level height space. Affected area is from 3190.4km² in 2001 to 3767.5km² in 2015, changing largely; the center water depth is from 77.62m in 2001 to 88.41m in 2015 , dropping about 10m.

Qianying depth-level depression funnel also has a regularly increasing trend of affected area, the center water depth and the center water level height space. Affected area is from196.83km² in 2001 to 219.38km² in 2015, changing small; the center water depth is from 55.37m in 2001 to 67.31m in 2015 , dropping about 11m. the center water level height is -37.24m in 2001 to -50.13m in 2015, changing largely.

3 Mathematical Model of Groundwater Depth

3.1 The Meaning of "Coefficient of Storage"

At present, coefficient of storage parameter is obtained by pumping test and its calculation in land subsidence, however, pumping test is short-term, which is still in the elastic deformation stage confined to the aquifer, and land subsidence can be the result of long-term excessive exploitation of groundwater, which makes the permanent drawdown of groundwater. And even if the measures would be taken to cease mining, the water level can not be recovered yet, and this loss results in the additional load of water layer, which makes deformation because of the pressure of overburden soil originally changing aquifer in turn.

"Coefficient of storage" means that when the head of groundwater fall down a unit, the total of released water is from a unit area, thickness of the aquifer is equal to the thickness of the soil column [15]. Based on the theory, the authors will introduce the concept of coefficient of storage in dynamics, combine with the center water depth values above, and predict the trend of coastal areas of Tangshan together in the next 10 years.

3.2 Model

In order to establish the mathematical model of the aquifer compression caused by the exploitation of confined aquifer, assume that: (1) Soil particles and water can not be compressed; (2) generalize the aquifer and get the mean parameters; (3) there is no supply in portrait; (4) underground water moves according to Darcy's law; (5) the direction of underground water moving points to funnel center; (6) groundwater is near the former level before exploitation; (7) only consider the vertical compression when the lateral compression of aquifer is constrained[13]. Through mathematical derivation, we can get:

$$H(r,t) = \sum_{m=0}^{\infty} \frac{4H_0}{(4m+1)\pi} \sin\left[\frac{(4m+1)\pi}{2r_0} r\right] e^{-\frac{(4m+1)^2 \pi^2}{4r_0^2 \lambda} t} \tag{1}$$

H_0 is the maximum drawdown of depression funnel. If t and r_0 are determined, the above formula would be used to determine the contour of the time depression funnel, which can predict the trend of the deep groundwater level around funnel.

3.3 Model Application in Coastal Areas of Tangshan

(1) Aquifer and exploitation of the coastal areas of Tangshan

According to status of groundwater exploitation and the characteristics of regional hydrogeology, the fresh level in shallow coastal areas of Tangshan is stable many years, has very little extraction, the basic balance of supply and drainage, also; little salt mining. From the well depth of view, well depth is in the 220m ~ 450m, no more than 450 m in the exploitation. It shows that the deep freshwater aquifer is the third aquifer, so the land subsidence is due to the compression of the third aquifer.

(2) Parameters Selection

On the long-term observe dates of groundwater dynamics, combine with previous groundwater subsidence funnel each district and predictions of the center water depth, it can be get the parameters each district the next 2015 (Table 2).

Table 2. Main parameters of every subsidence funnel in Tangshan coastal areas　(2015)

Funnels	Maximum Drawdown (H_0/m)	Permeability Coefficient (K/m)	Thickness of Hydrous Layer (M/m)	Mining time (t/d)	Affected Radius (r_0/km)
Ninghe	89	1.0	230	50*365	30
Tanghai	52	1.1	230	35*365	26
Jiantuozi	80	1.1	230	35*365	26
Caozhuangzi	26	1.2	230	28*365	15

3.4　Results

To simplify the calculation and improve the efficiency of the model, this paper takes VB 6.0 as the second development platform, programs the preparation of the water table depth. The program is characteristic of simple interface, easy operation, inputting set parameters, showing results and graphics and other functions.

In the interface of calculating results, it will show a distribution diagram of groundwater level depth with a circle of groundwater depression funnel and the number of equivalent lines impacted within the groundwater depression funnel. The space of each groundwater equivalent line is 2.5km in graphics, the value of each equivalent line is in accordance with the dates in "results zone".

We can find that groundwater depression funnel in Tangshan coastal areas have a rapid development, even have the state of aggregation. If the groundwater exploited by human can not be checked effectively in Tangshan coastal areas, it would form a large funnel region that Ninghe, Jiantuozi and Tanghai link together. If so, it would cause great difficulties for controlling land subsidence, and make groundwater dry of Tangshan coastal areas.

4　Prediction of Tangshan Coastal Land Subsidence

4.1　Calculation Model

According to equation (1), the groundwater depth value can be calculated in predicted areas, then the water level declining value can be derived from the base year to the forecast year according to the following formula.

Assume affected radius of each funnel areas is the fixed value from the base year to the forecast one, that is, $r=cons$. Then the formula of groundwater declining value within impacting of groundwater funnels follows equation (2).

$$\Delta H(r, \Delta t) = \sum_{m=0}^{\infty} \frac{4H_0}{(4m+1)\pi} \sin\left[\frac{(4m+1)\pi}{2r_0}r\right] e^{-\frac{(4m+1)^2\pi^2}{4r_0^2\lambda}t_0} - \sum_{m=0}^{\infty} \frac{4H_0}{(4m+1)\pi} \sin\left[\frac{(4m+1)\pi}{2r_0}r\right] e^{-\frac{(4m+1)^2\pi^2}{4r_0^2\lambda}t_1} \qquad (2)$$

There t_0 - the time difference of funnel from the forming year to the base year;
　　　t_1 - the time difference of funnel from the forming year to the forecast year.

Then according to formula (2), the total of land subsidence is got with a different radius of each funnel in the study areas:

$$S = \overline{A} \bullet \Delta H(r, \Delta t) \qquad (3)$$

There $\overline{A}$ - annual sedimentation rate, mm/a·m;
      S -ground sedimentation rate, mm.

Table 3. Groundwater depth of on every subsidence funnel in Tangshan coastal areas

funnels	Ninghe		Tanghai		Jiantuozi		Caozhuangzi	
	Computing Value	Conversion Value	Computing Value	Computing Value	Computing Value	Conversion Value	Computing Value	Conversion Value
2.5	3.6	85.4	2.3	49.7	3.6	76.4	0.2	25.8
5	7.1	81.9	4.6	47.4	7.1	72.9	0.4	25.6
7.5	10.5	78.5	6.8	45.2	10.4	69.6	0.5	25.5
10	13.7	75.3	8.8	43.2	13.5	66.5	0.6	25.4
12.5	16.7	72.3	10.6	41.4	16.3	63.7	0.7	25.3
15	19.4	69.6	12.2	39.8	18.7	61.3	0.7	25.3
17.5	21.7	67.3	13.5	38.5	20.7	59.3	—	—
20	23.7	65.3	14.5	37.5	22.2	57.8	—	—
22.5	25.3	63.7	15.1	36.9	23.3	56.7	—	—
25	26.5	62.5	15.4	36.6	23.7	56.3	—	—
27.5	27.2	61.8	—	—	—	—	—	—
30	27.4	61.6	—	—	—	—	—	—

4.2 Calculation Recognition

The period of model identification ranges from 2001 to 2005, the forecast period ranges from 2006 to 2015. The purpose is to reflect the original physical model actually with the mathematic model after generalization. In the recognition process, the people must have the large amount of reliable information on the basis of hydro geological and analyses thoroughly, and perfect scientific information according to the feedback dates, step by step, until the simulated results are consistent with historical observations. Compare the real values to predicted values, it can be found that a the model has a high precision in coastal areas of Tangshan from 2001 to 2005, and the relative error is less than 5%.

4.3 Results

Macro-analyze the field dates in 1983-1996 and 2005, the sedimentation mean rate is20.13mm/a·m in 1983 -1989, 39.29mm / a • m in 1992-1996, that is annual sedimentation rate of 1992-1996 is 1.9 times 1983-1989 . And 20mm / a • m ~ 65mm / a • m in 2000, the average sedimentation rate is 43mm / a • m. Obviously it reflects fully the lag effect of releasing water in clay layer, with the increasing exploitation of groundwater, water levels continuing to decline, and land subsidence significantly accelerated. The development stage of land subsidence begins in 1992, according to the evolution of Tianjin and Hangu, if the ground water extraction keeps the status quo, the rapid subsidence will continue for decades. So it is more reasonable to use the status quo than the average annual sedimentation rate to forecast. In status quo conditions, Tanghai region will increase by 352.59 mm in 2015; Jiantuozi will increase by 393.40 mm in 2015; Caozhuangzi will increase by 47.62 mm in 2015.

Water demand will continue to increase with the economic development of the coasts in Tangshan. With the continuous declining of groundwater levels and land subsidence, keep the status of mining conditions, the total settlement in funnel districts as Tanghai, Nanpu Development, Caozhuangzi, Ninghe are: 1905.43 mm, 1917.50 mm, 839.35 mm and 2385.97 mm in 2015.

5 Conclusion

According to the historical observation dates of distribution and factors of main groundwater depression funnel current in Tangshan coastal areas, establish the mathematic model of groundwater depression funnel trend, and the model has been identified.

According to the concept of storage water coefficient in groundwater dynamics, establish the mathematical model of groundwater level depth. Make use of the model to calculate and obtain groundwater level depth value about four sub-coastal areas of Tangshan.

Make use of the ground sedimentation rate, combine the mathematical model of groundwater level depth, link the above two, and establish the numerical land subsidence model of coastal areas in Tangshan. Use the validated model to predict the situation of the coastal areas of Tangshan in next 10 years.

The development trend of land subsidence in coastal areas will be intensified in the next 10 years. In order to develop the regions' economy better, the government must take strong and effective measures to curb the excesses of the exploitation of groundwater eliminate the development of ground subsidence fundamentally.

References

1. Papers Choices of Foreign Land Subsidence Technical Methods. Shanghai Geology Department. Geological Publishing, Beijing (1981)
2. Yuan, M., Yan, Y.: Status quo anslysis of ground subsidence in Suzhou City. Journal of Natural Disasters 1, 129–133 (2010)
3. Yang, L.-z., Zhang, G.-h., Liu, Z.-y., et al.: Relationship between deep groundwater resources composition and land subsidence under the condition of exploitation in Dezhou, Shangdong, China. Geological Bulletin of China 4, 111–119 (2010)
4. Li, J., Helm, D.C.: A nonlinear viscous model for aquifer compression associated with ASR applications. In: Carbognin, L., Cambolat, G., Ivan Johnson, A. (eds.) LAND SUBSIDENACE, Proceedings of the Sixth Internation Symposium on Land Subsidence, vol. II, Padova, La Garangola, Via Montona, pp. 319–330 (2000)
5. Ling, Y.: Computation Model and Prediction for Surface subsidence Caused by Pumping from Double-Layer Aquifer. Building Science 5, 65–68 (2010)

6. Xu, M., Wang, W., Yu, Q.: Ground Water and Land Subsidence Optimum Controlling Numerical Simulation in Tianjin Binhai New Are. Urban Geology 1, 13–18 (2010)
7. Zhu, Y., Chen, H., Zhang, D., et al.: Subsidence of Suzhou Area from 1995-2000 Detected by Persistent Scatterers for SAR Interferometry Technique. Advances in Earth Science 10, 90–96 (2010)
8. Bo, H., Hansheng, W.: Monitoring Ground Subsidence with Permanent Scatterers Interferometry. Journal of Geodesy and Geodynamics 30(2), 34–39 (2010)
9. Cai, D., Cheng, W., Fang, L., et al.: Research on Monitoring Statistical Model of Urban Land Subsidence. Bulletin of Surveying and Mapping 1, 19–22 (2010)
10. Zhang, K.-j., Xi, G.-y., Zhang, L.-b.: Application of Fuzzy Comprehen- sive Evaluation Based on Variable-weight Method in the Hazard Evaluation for Land Subsidence. Bulletin of Surveying and Mapping 1, 49–51 (2010)
11. Yang, M., Lu, J.: Characteristics and Prediction of Ground Settlement Around Deep Excavation in Shanghai. Journal of Tongji University (Natural Science) 2, 48–53 (2010)
12. Zhao, W.-t., Li, L.: The mechanism of land subsidence and its prevention measures in Suzhou-Wuxi-Changzhou area. The Chinese Journal of Geological Hazard and Control 1, 92–97 (2009)
13. Li, T.-x., Wu, L.-j., Wu, X.-h., et al.: Current Situation and Countermeasures to Land Subsidence in Hebei Plain. Journal of Changjiang Engineering Vocational College 2, 32–35 (2009)
14. Geological Environment Monitoring Stations in Hebei Province. Geological Environment Monitoring Report of Tangshan City, Hebei Province, pp. 61–70 (2001)
15. Liu, J., Jin, X., Zhang, J.: A mathematical model about subsidence due to groundwater aquifer. Modern Geology 12(3), 419–423 (1998)

Stochastic Newsboy Inventory Control Model and Its Solving on Multivariate Products Order and Pricing

Jixian Xiao[1], Fangling Lu[1], and Xin Xiao[2]

[1] College of Science, Hebei Polytechnic University, Tangshan 063009, China
[2] Hebei Normal University of Science & Technology, Qinhuangdao 066004, China
xiaojix@yahoo.com.cn, yayatou-1986@163.com

Abstract. In this paper based on the traditional stochastic inventory control problem, namely, the Newsboy problem, considered the factor of inventory item which has an impact on the decision-making model, a new model is built up. While assuming the form of demand to meet the adding form, and considering the impact of the price on the demand rate and the impact of the demand rate on inventory item, we discuss a new subscription model, and give corresponding calculation methods to determine the optimal order quantity and optimal sales price. Model in this paper is an extension of existing models, while the known model is a special case of this model. At last an simple example is given.

Keywords: Newsboy stochastic inventory control model, Adding form, Inventory item.

1 Introduction

1.1 Theory of Inventory

In the human production, economy, trade and other social activities, inventory of materials is essential. Stock inventory control theory is to study the inventory control system, to use the quantitative method to study the actual inventory of various complex issues, to explore the optimal inventory policy for the inventory system. Inventory control is to reduce the amount of funds used and inventory costs of materials as much as possible under the premise of ensuring normal production or the need of the goods for sale. The main problem is how much inventory should be maintained is the most reasonable, when adds purchase is the most appropriate time, and how many stock to add symbols the most economic principles.

1.2 Theory of Stochastic

Stochastic inventory control problem is divided into two categories, which are multi-period stochastic inventory control model and single-cycle stochastic inventory control model. Single-cycle random-type inventory problem is the so-called Newsboy

R. Zhu et al. (Eds.): ICICA 2010, LNCS 6377, pp. 65–72, 2010.

problem. The most basic Newsboy question is that there is a certain period of time with continuous probability distribution of demand is known items, known in advance of its purchase price and sale price, and per unit of unsold residual value (or disposal price) . If the penalty cost per unit is also known, then how to choose the order so that the system expected profit maximum. Newsboy problem reflects our real life, many of the reality, as some popular products, such as perishable foods. In the past few decades, to the problem for the Newsboy in stock, in order to better solve the practical problems, such as airline tickets, hotel room reservations etc, the models extended and improved based on Newsboy model are emerging.

In this paper based on the Newsboy problem, considered the factor of inventory item which has an impact on the decision-making model, a new idea appeared. While assuming the form of demand to meet the adding form, and considering the impact of the price on the demand rate and the impact of the demand rate on inventory item, we build up the new subscription model.

2 Model Assumption and Notation Setting

In order to simplify the inventory system, we make the following assumptions at first. Suppliers make the first order and instantaneous supply at the beginning of the cycle. Retailers order at the beginning of the sales period, and the order volume is Q. Fixed order cost per order is K. Unit cost of purchased products is c. Retailer's selling price is p. Sales cycle is T. Product inventory storage fee per time per unit is h. If there is products not sold at the end of sales, manufacturers recover full recovery as price v or all of the processing cut at a discount price v. If there are shortages in the sales generated during the period, each unit costs arising out of loss is s. The profit retailers have in the sales is $\Pi(p,Q)$.

Demand rate retailers face is $d(p,t,\varepsilon)$. $D(p,\varepsilon)$ is the demand during the sales cycle. We can know that

$$D(p.\varepsilon) = \int_0^T d(p,t,\varepsilon)dt .$$ (1)

Here, ε is a random variable defined on the interval $[A,B]$, whose distribution function and probability density function are $F(\cdot)$ and $f(\cdot)$. Let μ and σ be mean and standard deviation of ε.

3 Analysis

3.1 Situation 1

If order quantity is less than demand during the period of sales, that is:

$$\int_0^T d(p,t,\varepsilon)dt \le Q .$$

System costs include ordering costs, inventory storage fees, the normal sales charge, and recycling (processing) fee income.

Ordering costs is $K + Qc$.

Inventory storage fees is $h \cdot \int_0^T (Q - \int_0^t d(p,t,\varepsilon)dt)dx$, $0 \leq x \leq T$.

The normal sales charge is $p \int_0^T d(p,t,\varepsilon)dt$.

Recycling (processing) fee income is $v \cdot [Q - \int_0^T d(p,t,\varepsilon)dt]$.

At this point, the retailer's profit in the sales period is:

$$\Pi_1(p,Q) = p \int_0^T d(p,t,\varepsilon)dt + v \cdot [Q - \int_0^T d(p,t,\varepsilon)dt]$$
$$- [h \cdot \int_0^T (Q - \int_0^t d(p,t,\varepsilon)dt)dx + K + Qc] \tag{2}$$

3.2 Situation 2

If order quantity is more than demand during the period of sales, that is $\int_0^T d(p,t,\varepsilon)dt > Q$.

System costs include ordering costs, inventory storage fees, the normal sales charge, out of stock fee.

Ordering cost is $K + Qc$.

Inventory storage fees:

$$h \cdot \int_0^{t_0} (Q - \int_0^t d(p,t,\varepsilon)dt)dx, \qquad 0 \leq x \leq t_0.$$

Here,

$$Q = \int_0^{t_0} d(p,t,\varepsilon)dt. \tag{3}$$

From the formula, we can get the value of t_0, and the normal sales charge is pQ.

Out of stock fee is $s[\int_0^T d(p,t,\varepsilon)dt - Q]$.

Then in this situation, the retailer's profit in the sales period is:

$$\Pi_2(p,Q) = pQ - s \cdot [\int_0^T d(p,t,\varepsilon)dt - Q]$$
$$- h \cdot [\int_0^{t_0} (Q - \int_0^t d(p,t,\varepsilon)dt)dx] - (K + Qc) \tag{4}$$

4 the Building and Solving of Model

4.1 Normal Model of The Problem

From the above formulas (3) and (4), we can get the expected profit of the retailer:

$$E[\Pi(p,Q)] = \int_A^c \Pi_1(p,Q)f(\varepsilon)d\varepsilon + \int_c^B \Pi_2(p,Q)f(\varepsilon)d\varepsilon \tag{5}$$

The problem is to find the best $p*, Q*$ to make the retailer's profit expectations to be maximized, which means that to solve the following question:

$$\max_{p,Q} E[\Pi(p,Q)] \qquad (6)$$

Solving the problem is more complicated, usually we establish the corresponding model based on the actual problem, and then use genetic algorithms or neural network algorithm to solve.

4.2 Demand of Adding Form

Here we discuss a simplified case. Random demand form of price elasticity has two forms, one adding form, the other product form. Now we choose the adding form. Let:

$$D(p,\varepsilon) = y(p) + \varepsilon. \qquad (7)$$

Let linear relationship exists between demand and price. It means:

$$y(p) = a - bp.$$

From (1) and (7), we can know that:

$$d(p,t,\varepsilon) = \frac{y(p) + \varepsilon}{T}. \qquad (8)$$

We can know from (8) that demand rate is dependent on price changes, and that the demand rate is constant for variable time.

Let $z = Q - y(p)$, and put (4) and (5) into (2) and (3):

$$\Pi_1(z, p) = p(a - bp + \varepsilon) - K - c(a - bp + z)$$
$$+ v(z - \varepsilon) - \frac{hT}{2}(2z + a - bp - \varepsilon) \qquad , \varepsilon \le z. \qquad (9)$$

$$\Pi_2(z, p) = p(a - bp + z) + s(z - \varepsilon) - K - c(a - bp + z)$$
$$- \frac{hT(z + a - bp)^2 - hT^2(z + a - bp)^2}{2(a - bp + \varepsilon)} \qquad , \varepsilon > z. \qquad (10)$$

Directly to solve the optimization problem is clearly more complicated. We can transform the variables. Put (9) and (10) into (5):

$$E[\Pi(p,z)] = \int_A \Pi_1(p,z) f(\varepsilon) d\varepsilon + \int^B \Pi_2(p,z) f(\varepsilon) d\varepsilon.$$

Seek first-order partial derivatives of $E[\Pi(p,z)]$ to z and p :

$$\frac{\partial E[\Pi(p,z)]}{\partial z} = v + (p + s - v)[1 - F(z)] - \frac{hT^2(z + a - bp) f(z)}{2}$$
$$- c - 1 + \int_z^B \left[hT(1 + \frac{a - bp + z}{a - bp + \varepsilon}) + \frac{hT^2(a - bp + z)}{a - bp + \varepsilon} \right] f(\varepsilon) d\varepsilon.$$

$$\frac{\partial E[\Pi(p,z)]}{\partial p} = a + bc + \mu - 2bp + \int_A \frac{hTb}{2} f(\varepsilon) d\varepsilon$$

$$+ \int_z^B \frac{hT[bp(2z + 2a - bp)(a - bp + \varepsilon) - b(z + a - bp)^2]}{2(a - bp + \varepsilon)^2} f(\varepsilon) d\varepsilon.$$

$$- \int_z^B (\varepsilon - z) f(\varepsilon) d\varepsilon$$

At the same we can get the second-order partial derivatives of $E[\Pi(p,z)]$ to z and p. For the fomla are too long to show. Let $p > c > v$ as normal, if second-order partial derivatives are more than zero, we can not get the solution directly for the problem is very complex. If not, we can know that for a certain z, $E[\Pi(p,z)]$ is a concave function of p. From the Lemma9.4.1 of the reference [1], for the certain z, the optimal sailing price p^* can worked out from $\dfrac{\partial E(\Pi(z,p))}{\partial p} = 0$ directly.

Transform (6) into a one-dimensional optimization problem of z:

$$\max_z E[\Pi(z, p(z))].$$

Then, from the first order optimality conditions, we can get that:

$$\frac{dE[\Pi(z, p(z))]}{dz} = 0 \qquad (21)$$

Form (11) we can get the value z^*, and obtain the corresponding optimal selling price p^* and the corresponding optimal order quantity Q^*.

Here, we can also use the basic genetic algorithm to solve this problem, as following steps.

Step 1. Initialization. Enter various parameters: population size M, termination T, the crossover probability p_c (generally take 0.4 to 0.99), and mutation probability p_m (usually taken 0.0001 ~ 0.1). Set counter evolution termination $t \leftarrow 0$.

Step 2. Individual evaluations. Calculate each individual' fitness in the group $P(t)$.

Step 3. Selection operators. Choose the selection operator of roulette.

Step 4. Crossover operations. Single-point crossover can be chosen in this problem. First do random matching on the group, and then set the crossover point randomly, and each cross-point position is selected by the probability of uniform distribution.

Step 5 Mutation operations. With a smaller probability it is an occurrence of mutation operation.

After operations of selection, crossover and mutation we can get the next generation of the group, that is $P(t+1)$.

Step 6 Termination of conditions. If $t \leq T$, then $t \leftarrow t+1$, turn to Step 2. If $t > T$, then the individual with the greatest fitness gotten from the evolutionary process will be get out as the optimal solution. Terminate calculations.

5 Example

A certain retailer distributes a kind of wall calendar. Fixed order cost per order is 10 yuan. Retailer's selling price is p . Sales cycle is 10 days. Product inventory storage fee per time per day is 0.01yuan.The wholesale price of the calendar is 6 yuan each. After the season of selling calendar, the calendars which are not sold are deal 3 yuan each. If shortages occur within the selling season, then shortage cost due to each calendar is 5 yuan each. Based on previous data accumulated, demand of retailers face is $D(p,\varepsilon) = a - bp + \varepsilon = 200 - 10p + \varepsilon$, where ε is a random variable defined on the interval $[10,20]$, which obeys uniform distribution.

The problem is to find the best $p*, Q*$ to make the retailer's profit expectations to be maximized.

5.1 Solution

If order quantity is less than demand during the period of sales, that is:

$$\int_0^{10} d(p,t,\varepsilon)dt \leq Q.$$

System costs include ordering costs, inventory storage fees, the normal sales charge, and recycling (processing) fee income.

Ordering costs is $10 + 6Q$.

Inventory storage fees:

$$0.01 \cdot \int_0^{10} (Q - \int_0^x d(p,t,\varepsilon)dt)dx, \qquad 0 \leq x \leq 10.$$

The normal sales charge is $p \int_0^{10} d(p,t,\varepsilon)dt$.

Recycling (processing) fee income is $3 \cdot [Q - \int_0^{10} d(p,t,\varepsilon)dt]$.

At this point, the retailer's profit in the sales period is:

$$\Pi_1(p,Q) = p \int_0^{10} d(p,t,\varepsilon)dt + 3 \cdot [Q - \int_0^{10} d(p,t,\varepsilon)dt]$$
$$- [0.01 \cdot \int_0^{10} (Q - \int_0^x d(p,t,\varepsilon)dt)dx + 10 + 6Q]$$

If order quantity is more than demand during the period of sales, that is $\int_0^{10} d(p,t,\varepsilon)dt > Q$.

System costs include ordering costs, inventory storage fees, the normal sales charge, out of stock fee.

Ordering costs is $10 + 6Q$.

Inventory storage fees:

$$0.01 \cdot \int_0^{t_0} (Q - \int_0^x d(p,t,\varepsilon)dt)dx, \qquad 0 \le x \le t_0 .$$

Here $Q = \int_0^{t_0} d(p,t,\varepsilon)dt$.

From the formula, we can get the value of t_0, and the normal sales charge is pQ .

Out of stock fee is $6[\int_0^{40} d(p,t,\varepsilon)dt - Q]$.

Then in this situation, the retailer's profit in the sales period is:

$$\Pi_2(p,Q) = pQ - 6 \cdot [\int_0^{40} d(p,t,\varepsilon)dt - Q]$$
$$- 0.01 \cdot [\int_0^{t_0} (Q - \int_0^x d(p,t,\varepsilon)dt)dx] - (10 + 6Q)$$

For ε is a random variable defined on the interval $[10,20]$, which obeys uniform distribution. The mean of ε is $\mu = 15$.

From the Lemma9.4.1 of the reference [1], we can get the approximate optimal solution $z^* \approx 18$, $p^* \approx 13.8$, $Q^* \approx 80$, $E[\Pi(p,Q)] \approx 538.3$.

5.2 Comparison

When $h = 0$ and $K = 0$, the problem has worked out. The result is $z^* \approx 18$, $p^* \approx 13.8$, $Q^* \approx 81$, $E[\Pi(p,Q)] \approx 588.3$.

Compared with the above answer, when the system costs includes inventory storage fees. We should appropriately increase in price, and reduce the order so that expected revenue optimization. The result is also consistent with the actual situation.

6 Conclusion

As the expression of objective function is more complex, and it has the probability function and integration, we can make use of nonlinear programming knowledge to set up search method, or the genetic algorithm optimization to solve. From the above model and solution process, we can know that Newsboy demand products rely on the price of the Joint Decision Model on Ordering and Pricing can be get from letting $h = 0$. Model in this paper is an extension of existing models, while the known model is a special case of this model.

References

1. Zhou, Y., Wang, S.: Inventory Control Theory And Methods. Science Press, Beijing (2009)
2. Liu, B., Zhao, R., Wang, G.: Uncertain Programming and Its Application. Tsinghua University Press, Beijing (2003)
3. Xia, S.: Operations Research. Tsinghua University Press, Beijing (2003)

4. Yu, W., Li, J., Lv, X.: Research of Inventory Strategies Based on Markov Chain. Enterprise Management and Information Technology (13), 5–8 (2009)
5. Cao, L., Han, R., Chen, D.: Optional PResearch of Inventory Control on Stochastic Demand And Recovery. Wuhan University of Technology (1), 169–172 (2009)
6. Axsater, S., Marklund, J., Silver, E.A.: Heuristic methods for centralized control of one-warehouse n-retailer inventory systems. Manefacturing and Service Operations Management 4(1), 75–97 (2002)
7. Goyal, S.K.: On Improving The Single-vendor Single-buyer Integrated Production Inventory Model With a Generalized Policy. European Journal of Operational Research 125(2), 429–430 (2000)
8. Goyal, S.K., Szendrovits, A.Z.: A Constant Lot Size Model with Equal and Unequal Sized Batch Shipments Between Production Stages. Engineering Costs and Production Economics 10(1), 203–210 (1986)
9. Wang, D.: Single-supplier Multi-vendor Integrated Production Inventory Models. Systems Engineering Technology 21(1), 92–96
10. Lu, L.: A One-vendor Multi-buyer Integrated Inventory Model. European Journal of Operationl Research 81(2), 312–323 (1995)
11. Qian, L.: Application of Simulated Annealing Algorithm in Localization of Distribution Center. Communication Satandardization (8) (2008)
12. Niaoer, Y.: The Thinking of Inventory Control. China Academic Journal Electronic Publishing House, 88–89 (2009)

Grey Correlation Analysis on the Influential Factors the Hospital Medical Expenditure

Su-feng Yin[1], Xiao-jing Wang[2], Jian-hui Wu[1], and Guo-li Wang[1]

[1] Hebei Province Key Laboratory of Occupational Health and Safety for Coal Industry,
Division of Epidemiology and Health Statistics North China Coal Medical College,
Tangshan 063000, China
[2] Kailuan Hospital Affiliated North China Coal Medical University
TangShan 063000, China
ysfdzy@yahoo.com.cn

Abstract. To investigate the implementation of Grey Correlation Analysis in the research of the hospitalization fee, to analyze the influential factors of the hospitalization expenses, and to provide proof for medical expenses containing measurements. To analyzed the in patient hospital fee of the top ten diseases of internal medicine inpatient in a hospital by Grey correlation analysis The grey correlation analysis shows the correlative degree between each kind of expense and their rankings are as follows: pharmaceutical fee 0.938, bed fee 0.8411, laboratory test fee 0.8331, radiation diagnosis fee 0.7655, and examination fee 0.6108. It indicates that for the internal medical disease, the dominating factor in hospital expenditure is the pharmaceutical fee. It is the medicine expenses which should be cut mostly in order to control the excessive increase of hospital medical expenditure. In the study of hospital medical expenditure, the grey correlation analysis fully utilized information and data, and led to more reasonable conclusions.

Keywords: Medical expenses; Grey correlation analysis, factors.

1 Introduction

The analysis on in-patient hospital fee is the core content of benefit evaluation of hospital economic management and it is also an important aspect of hospital comprehensive assessment. Although the studies on this field were increasing, analysis methods such as conventional liner model was showed with some disadvantage because the data distribution about in-patient hospital fee of different types disease are not normal[1] and some potential confounding factors were difficult to control [2]. The increase of in-patient hospital fee was influenced by objective and subjective factors, of which its connotation and extension are difficult to define and information was showed with grayed characteristics [3]. In order to reflect the nature of this data, the current study was aimed to apply the gray relational analysis to evaluate the in-patient hospital fee so that all information was overall comprehensive used as well as the relationship of cofounding factors were dynamic showed. Furthermore the present study will provide

R. Zhu et al. (Eds.): ICICA 2010, LNCS 6377, pp. 73–78, 2010.
© Springer-Verlag Berlin Heidelberg 2010

the evidence for taking effect measures, using reasonable of medical resources, controlling the increase of medical costs and improving cost models of different type diseases.

2 Theory and Procedure of Grey Correlation Analysis

Grey relational analysis is the main elements of deng's theory of gray system and it is a system analysis technique [4]. Grey correlation analysis is to analyze the close relation between the main behavioral factors and relative behavioral factors in gray system and then the major factors or secondary factors are determined, which attributes the system development. Its main idea is to determine the degree of close relationship on the base of geometric similarity between main behavioral sequence and related sequence. In addition its basic tool is to calculate the relevancy, which services as the marker to weight the close relation and mutual comparison. If the tendency changes in the curve is the same as or similar to, then the corresponding sequences were thought to be a close relation. Otherwise the relation was thought to be minor [5]. The analysis steps are as follows:

(1) Determine the analysis sequence: According to the study goals, reference and comparison sequences were determined. Reference sequence was expressed with $X_0(k)$, $X_0(k) = \{x_0(1), x_0(2), ..., x_0(n), ...\}$.

(2) Variables transformation: the methods such as the average values method, the initial value method, and interval-based method were applied to transform the raw data to dimensionless ones. Then we can get reference sequence $Y_0(k)$ and comparison sequence $Y_i(k)$ (i=1, 2, ..., m ; k=1, 2······, n).

(3) Calculate the absolute difference between sequence and get the difference: calculate absolute difference at each point between reference sequence and comparison, which consist of absolute difference $\Delta_{0i}(k)$, $\Delta_{0i}(k) = |y_o(k) - y_i(k)|$.

(4) Identify the absolute maximum and minimum difference among the absolute difference sequence. They are expressed as Δ_{max} or Δ_{min} .

(5) Calculate correlation coefficient

$$\gamma_{oi(k)} = \frac{\Delta_{min} + \zeta \times \Delta_{max}}{\Delta_{0i}(k) + \zeta \times \Delta_{max}} .$$

Note: ζ is identify factor, $\zeta \in [0,1]$, the value is 0.5.

(6) Calculate correlation degree and sort

$$R_{oi} = \frac{1}{n} \sum_{k=1}^{n} \gamma_{oi(k)} .$$

Sort the correlation degree between several comparison sequences and reference sequence from the biggest to smallest number. The biggest value of correlation degree means the closet correlation, indicating the largest contribution of the studied factors.

3 Factors Impacted on In-Patient Hospital Fee Analysis by Gray Correlation Analysis

3.1 The Raw Data about In-Patient Hospital Fee

All data came from the database of cases record of a hospital in Tangshan City. The retrospective method was selected to choose the top 10 diseases of the internal medicine in 2008 and the total cases were 1026. The data related to in-patient hospital fee were selected for analysis. According to the analysis demand, the charge items were summary and set the variable name: X_0 presented for the total fee, X_1 presented for bed charge, X_2 for pharmacy charge, X_3 laboratory fee, X_4 for other diagnosis and therapy fee, X_5 for radiation diagnosis fee. All variables were numerical. The data were showed in table 1.

Table 1. The detail fee of top ten diseases of internal medicine (unit: yuan)

Type	X_0	X_1	X_2	X_3	X_4	X_5
1	151513.92	15300.36	112499.06	12366.40	10098.60	1249.50
2	672557.03	36634.00	538841.82	21126.90	74972.31	982.00
3	316339.83	32016.40	198281.08	25534.30	58394.55	2113.50
4	258799.07	18790.60	182765.65	16084.70	40137.62	1020.50
5	160968.68	17353.60	118919.48	11593.30	11680.30	1422.00
6	191790.94	14363.40	126681.44	11716.70	37289.40	1740.00
7	208435.91	12388.60	138949.22	12521.90	44093.19	483.00
8	182618.28	132199.56	132199.56	13842.90	20647.82	1119.00
9	327470.87	20217.00	264563.46	8734.30	33749.11	207.00
10	92221.51	9487.00	65438.94	7999.10	8693.47	603.00

3.2 Factors Impacted on In-Patient Hospital Fee Analysis by Grey Correlation Analysis

The total in-patient hospital fee was served as the reference sequence and other item fee as the comparison sequences. Because the reference sequence and comparison sequences were all economic series and showed the same polarity, the initial value method was applied to transform the original data. The absolute differences $\Delta_{0i}(k)$ between comparison and reference sequences were calculated and identify the maximum and minimum values. $\triangle$ max equaled to 3.6945 and $\triangle$ min was 0.0000. As motioned before, $\zeta = 0.5$ [3].

Correlation coefficient is calculated and showed in Table 2 and Table 3.

Table 2. Message sequence differences

Type	$\triangle_{01}$	$\triangle_{02}$	$\triangle_{03}$	$\triangle_{04}$	$\triangle_{05}$
1	0.0000	0.0000	0.0000	0.0000	0.0000
2	2.0446	0.3508	2.7305	2.9581	3.6530
3	0.0046	0.3254	0.0231	3.6945	0.3964
4	0.4800	0.0835	0.4074	2.2665	0.8914
5	0.0718	0.0053	0.1249	0.0942	0.0757
6	0.3270	0.1397	0.3183	2.4267	0.1268
7	0.5660	0.1406	0.3631	2.9906	0.9891
8	0.2374	0.0302	0.0859	0.8393	0.3097
9	0.8400	0.1904	1.4550	1.1807	1.9956
10	0.0114	0.0270	0.0381	0.2522	0.1261

Table 3. Correlation coefficient of all item fee and total fee by gray correlation analysis

Type	γ_{01}	γ_{02}	γ_{03}	γ_{04}	γ_{05}
1	1.0000	1.0000	0.0000	1.0000	1.0000
2	0.4746	0.8404	0.4035	0.3823	0.3358
3	0.9975	0.8502	0.9876	0.3333	0.8233
4	0.7937	0.9568	0.8193	0.4490	0.6745
5	0.9626	0.9971	0.9367	0.9515	0.9606
6	0.8496	0.9297	0.8530	0.4322	0.9358
7	0.7655	0.9293	0.8357	0.3818	0.6513
8	0.8861	0.9839	0.9556	0.6876	0.8564
9	0.6874	0.9066	0.5594	0.6101	0.4807
10	0.9939	0.9856	0.9798	0.8799	0.9361

we sort all correlation coefficient of all item fee and total fee, which showed in Table 4. Table 4 data showed that the rank of impact of various item fee on total fee are as followed, pharmacy charge (R_{02}), bed charge (R_{01}), laboratory fee (R_{03}), radiation diagnosis fee (R_{05}) and diagnosis fee (R_{04}).

Table 4. The correlative degree and rank of all item fee and total fee

	R_{01}	R_{02}	R_{03}	R_{04}	R_{05}
Correlative degree	0.8411	0.9380	0.8331	0.6108	0.7655
Rank	2	1	3	5	4

4 Conclusion

Grey relational analysis is a quantitative comparison or description method on factors change of systems as time change in the development process. This analysis doesn't require a large sample size or a special data distribution. It is more reasonable to analysis in-patient hospital fee compared with conventional analysis. [6] [7] [8]

Traditional Chinese medicine charge showed to be a top factor regarding of effect on total in patient hospital fee and it is also the main cause which resulted in in-patient hospital fee increase in division of internal medicine. The follow are bed charge, laboratory fee, radiation diagnosis fee and other diagnosis fee. For disease of the internal medicine, the control of pharmacy charge is the key to decrease the in-patient hospital fee. Bed charge reflected the days stayed in hospital, which is related to disease severity, therapy methods and quality. Therefore improving the diagnosis and service will help in deducing hospital days and then controling in-patient hospital fee. The charger of internal medicine should focus on reducing overhead income, putting an end to unreasonable describing or other inappropriate medical care. In addition work should be done on diagnosis and treatment technology and effort in order to improve the operational efficiency of hospitals. If so, the goals of high-quality, high efficiency, low consumption will be achieved and then promote rational use of health resources [9, 10].

References

1. Wu, J.J.: Hospitalization constitutes the top ten diseases in the distribution of medical expenses. China Health Resources 5, 19–21 (1999)
2. Mo, C.M., Ni, Z.Z.: Medical cost factors in multiple linear regression analysis of the problems and improvement. Modern Preventive Medicine, 33–34 (2002)
3. Deng, J.L.: Grey theory. Huazhong University Press, Shanghai (2002)
4. Liu, X.M., Xu, R.: Deng's application of gray correlation analysis model. Statistics and Decision, 23–25 (2008)

5. Guo, C.W.: Influence factor analysis of the new gray correlation analysis method to hospitalization costs. Researches in Medical Education 8, 886–888 (2009)
6. Chen, J.H., Sun, L., Wu, J.J.: Gray Correlation Analysis of the In-Patient Costs Chinese Patients with Viral Hepatitis. Medicine and Philosophy (Clinical Decision Making Forum Edition) 7, 66–67 (2009)
7. Zhou, X., Wang, P.: Application of the gray correlation analysis in medicine. Liaoning Journal of Traditional Chinese Medicine, 938–939 (2006)
8. Yu, Y.P., Li, D.Z.: Medical quality of the Grey Relational Analysis. Chinese Journal of Health Statistics, 195–196 (2007)
9. Yu, Q., Wang, Y.T., Bao, J.: Analysis of medical expense and influencing factors of inpatients with medical insurance. Chinese Hospital Management 3, 21–23 (2008)
10. Lu, J.: Growth factors in hospitalization costs of acute appendicitis Grey relational analysis. Chongqing Medicin 11, 2483–2484 (2008)

Discrete Construction of order-k Voronoi Diagram

Ye Zhao[1], Shu-juan Liu[2], and Yi-li Tan[3]

[1] Department of Mathematics and Physics, Shijiazhuang Tiedao University,
Hebei Shijiazhuang 050043, China
[2] Mathematics and Information Science College, Hebei Normal University,
Hebei Shijiazhuang 050031, China
[3] College of Science, Hebei Polytechnic University, Hebei Tangshan 063009, China
ye_box@163.com

Abstract. The order-k Voronoi diagrams are difficult to construct because of their complicated structures. In traditional algorithm, production process was extremely complex. While discrete algorithm is only concerned with positions of generators, so it is effective for constructing Voronoi diagrams with complicated shapes of Voronoi polygons. It can be applied to order-k Voronoi diagram with any generators, and can get over most shortcomings of traditional algorithm. So it is more useful and effective. Model is constructed with discrete algorithm. And the application example shows that the algorithm is both simple and useful, and it is of high potential value in practice.

Keywords: Voronoi diagram, discrete, order-k.

1 Introduction

As a branch of Computational Geometry, Voronoi diagram has been quickly developed on account of the development of theory and the need of application. We have already noted that the concept of the Voronoi diagram is used extensively in a variety of disciplines and has independent roots in many of them. Voronoi diagram was appeared in meteorology, biology discipline and so on [1, 2, 3]. Order-k Voronoi diagram is an important concept of it. And it can be used for spatial interpolation, which is applied in statistical estimation as well as in cartography. The multiplicatively weighted order-k Voronoi diagram has been used for retail trade area analysis. More and more people pay attention to the algorithm that can construct order-k Voronoi diagram fast and effectively [4, 5, 6]. We investigate a discrete method for constructing, and it proved to be satisfactory by experiment.

2 Definitions

2.1 Definition 1 (A Planar Ordinary Voronoi Diagram) [7]

Given a finite number of distinct points in the Euclidean plane
$P = \{p_1, p_2, \cdots, p_n\} \subset R^2$, where $2 < n < +\infty$, $x_i \neq x_j$, for $i \neq j$, $i, j \in I_n$.

R. Zhu et al. (Eds.): ICICA 2010, LNCS 6377, pp. 79–85, 2010.
© Springer-Verlag Berlin Heidelberg 2010

We call the region given by

$$V(p_i) = \left\{ x \middle| \|x - x_i\| \le \|x - x_j\| \; for \; j \ne i, j \in I_n \right\}, \tag{1}$$

the planar ordinary Voronoi polygon associated with p_i, and the set given by:

$$V = \{V(p_1), V(p_2), \cdots, V(p_n)\}, \tag{2}$$

the planar ordinary generated by P (or the Voronoi diagram of P). [8] We call p_i of $V(p_i)$ the generator point or generator of the ith Voronoi, and the set $P = \{p_1, p_2, \cdots, p_n\}$ the generator set of the Voronoi diagram (in the literature, a generator point is sometimes referred to as a site), as shown in Fig. 1.

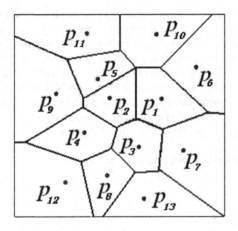

Fig. 1. A planar ordinary Voronoi diagram, and there are 13 points in the plane

2.2 Definition 2 (Order-k Voronoi Diagram)

In the ordinary Voronoi diagram [9], a generator is a point p_i, or a generator set $P = \{p_1, p_2, \cdots, p_n\}$ of points, we consider the family of generalized Voronoi diagrams generated by a set of all possible subsets consisting of k points out of P, i.e.

$$A^{(k)}(P) = \{\{p_{11}, \ldots, p_{1k}\}, \ldots, \{p_{l1}, \ldots, p_{lk}\}\}. \tag{3}$$

Here $p_{ij} \in P$, $l = \frac{n!}{k!(n-k)!}$. We call this family the higher-order Voronoi diagram.

Here the 'order' means the number of points constituting a generator and 'higher' means more than one point. Note that 'higher' does not refer to the dimension of a space [10].

Let $A^{(k)}(P)$ be the set of all possible subsets consisting of k points out of P, i.e. We call the set given by:

$$V\!\left(P_i^{(k)}\right)=\left\{p\left|\max_{p_h}\!\left\{d\!\left(p,p_h\right)\!\middle|p_h\in P_i^{(k)}\right\}\right\}\le\min_{p_h}\!\left\{d\!\left(p,p_j\right)\!\middle|p_j\in P\setminus P_i^{(k)}\right\}\right.\!\cdot \tag{4}$$

The order-k Voronoi polygon associated with $P_i^{(k)}$, and the set of order-k Voronoi polygons, $\mathrm{V}\!\left(A^{(k)}(P),d,R^m\right)=\mathrm{V}^{(k)}=\left\{V(P_1^{(k)}),\dots,V(P_n^{(k)})\right\}$, the order-$k$ Voronoi diagram generated by P, as shown in Fig. 2.

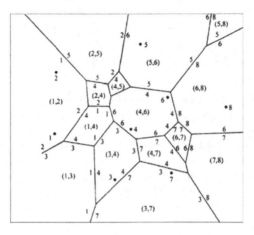

Fig. 2. An order-2 Voronoi diagram in which the region with the symbol $\{i,j\}$ indicates the order-2 Voronoi polygon of $\{p_i,p_j\}$.

3 Discrete Construction of Order-k Voronoi Diagram

3.1 Outline of Discrete Algorithm

Suppose that there are n generator points in the Euclidean plane, and we will construct order-k $(2\le k\le n-1)$ voronoi diagram. First, we divide colors range of computer into k parts, and assign different colors within first part for different generator points. Then use discrete algorithm constructing Voronoi diagram. In the process of spreading out, every time before assign a color value to a pixel, we should make a judgment: assign a pixel the color of the generator point if it is background color; assign it the color of the $(i+1)$th $(1\le i\le k-1)$ part if it is the color of the ith part; and stop spreading out if it is the color of the kth part. The procedure end when all points on screen are marked color. This time, we get the Voronoi diagram.

3.2 Algorithm

Input: $p_1,p_2,\cdots,p_n,k$. p_i is generator, k is the order.
Output: order-k Voronoi diagrams generated by those generators.

Step 1: suppose the colors range of possibilities is from
         1 to N , an divide it into K parts:
         $1 \sim N_1$, $N_1 + 1 \sim N_2$, ..., $N_{k-1} + 1 \sim N_k$.
         Here, $N_K \leq N$, $N_1 - N_0 = N_2 - N_1 = \cdots = N_K - N_{K-1}$, $n \leq N_1 - 1$.
         Assign generator points p_i with color i, $i = 1, 2, ..., n$;
Step 2: Built linked lists, that holds generators' data
         including: abscissa 'x', ordinate 'y', color 'i';
Step 3: Initialize screen as white color. define a
         pointer p to linked lists, $j = 1$;
Step 4: Generate data sheet of Δx, Δy, and r2
Step 5: When p is not empty, do loop:
   {
     (1) Read data of row k :Δx, Δy, and r2;
     (2) read p->x, p->y, p->color;
   if   p->color=0
         then {SetPixel (p->x ± Δx, p->y ± Δy, p->color= $N_1 + p$ -
>color);
     else if p->color=the color of the ith part
             then { SetPixel (p->x ± Δx, p->y ± Δy, $N_1 + p$ -
>color); }
     else {
           record the point;
           if points form a closed circumference
             then delete the node which 'p' pointed to from
               list;
           if 'p' point to the end of
             then k++, let 'p' point to the first node of list;
           else p++;}
   }
Step 6: Do landscape and portrait scanning for screen
         separately. When color of one pixel point is
         different with the next one, assign black color to
         it;
Step 7: Do landscape and portrait scanning for screen
         separately. Let pixel point white color if it is
         not black;
End.

3.3 Judgment of Region of Order-k Voronoi Diagram

In the generation of process, we need always judge how many times a pixel be deal
with. The method is as the following:

We suppose that there are n generator points. First, Assign color value c_i
($i = 1, 2, ..., n$, $c_i \in [a, b]$) to every generator point, and the color of other pixel is white
(value is 0). Given: $s > \sum c_i$. If a pixel was assigned a color, the color of the pixel is

the sum of value in present and s. And it is denoted as ss. Now if a pixel was deal with d times, $\lfloor ss/s \rfloor = d$.

When the color value of a pixel is k, it belongs to a region of order-k Voronoi diagram generated by that generator point that extend to it. This time, we can do deal with next pixel. Otherwise, let the color value of the pixel is the sum of value in present, value of generator point and s.

4 Practical Application

Now we take 3 generator points as the example, and construct order-k Voronoi diagram using discrete algorithm. Fig. 3 show us the generation of process.

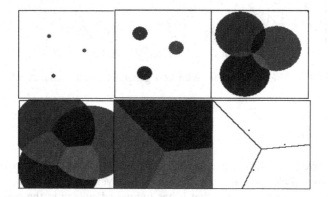

Fig. 3. Discrete production process of an order-2 Voronoi diagram with 3 generator points

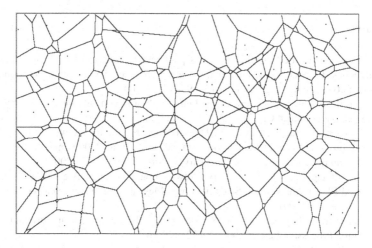

Fig. 4. The order-2 Voronoi diagram with 100 generator points constructed with discrete algorithms

We construct the order-k Voronoi diagram with 100 generator points and 200 generator points respectively by VC++6.0. As shown in Fig. 4 and Fig. 5.

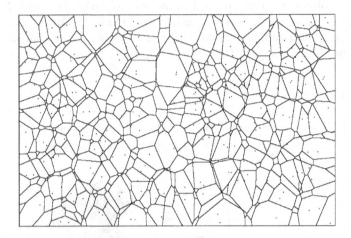

Fig. 5. The order-2 Voronoi diagram with 200 generator points constructed with discrete algorithms

5 Conclusions

In this paper, we give a discrete algorithm of constructing order-k Voronoi diagram. The method is simple, practical and has strong universality and remarkable effect. The experimental results indicate that it has unique advantage in the construction of order-k Voronoi diagrams, and it is of high potential value in practice.

References

1. Voronoi, G., Nouvelles: Applications des parameters continues a la theories des forms quadratiques. Premier Mémoire: Sur quelques Proprieteés des formes quadratiques positives parfaits. J. Reine Angew, Math. 133, 97–178 (1907)
2. Clarkson, K.L.: New applications of random sampling in computational geometry. J. Discrete and Computational Geometry 2, 195–222 (1987)
3. Sud, A., Govindaraju, N., Gayle, R., Dinesh Manocha, Z.: Interactive 3D distance field computation using linear factorization. In: Proceedings of the 2006 Symposium on Interactive 3D Graphics and Games, Redwood City, California, pp. 14–17 (2006)
4. Qian, B., Zhang, L., Shi, Y., Liu, B.: New Voronoi Diagram Algorithm of Multiply-Connected Planar Areas in the Selective Laser Melting. J. Tsinghua Science & Technology 14, 137–143 (2009)
5. Aurenhammer, F., Drysdale, R.L.S., Krasser, H.: Farthest line segment Voronoi diagrams. Information Processing Letters 100, 220–225 (2006)
6. Chen, J., Zhao, R., Li, Z.: Voronoi-based k-order neighbour relations for spatial analysis. J. ISPRS Journal of Photogrammetry and Remote Sensing 59, 60–72 (2004)

7. Lee, I., Lee, K.: A generic triangle-based data structure of the complete set of higher order Voronoi diagrams for emergency management. Computers, Environment and Urban Systems 33, 90–99 (2009)
8. Cabello, S., Fort, M., Sellarès, J.A.: Higher-order Voronoi diagrams on triangulated surfaces. J. Information Processing Letters 109, 440–445 (2009)
9. Wu, Y., Zhou, W., Wang, B., Yang, F.: Modeling and characterization of two-phase composites by Voronoi diagram in the Laguerre geometry based on random close packing of spheres. Computational Materials Science 47, 951–996 (2010)
10. Ferenc, J.-S., Néda, Z.: On the size distribution of Poisson Voronoi cells. Physica A: Statistical Mechanics and its Applications 385, 518–526 (2007)

Double Verifiably Encrypted Signature-Based Contract Signing Protocol

Chaoping Wang[1], Aimin Yang[2], and Yan Sun[3]

[1] School of Mathematics Physics and Information Science,
Zhejiang Ocean University, Zhoushan 316000, China
jianmowww@yahoo.com.cn
[2] College of Science, Hebei Ploytechnic University, Tangshan 063009, China
aimin_heut@163.com
[3] Operations Research Center, Shijiazhuang Army Command Academy,
Shijiazhuang 050084, China
wlyuan2010@foxmail.com

Abstract. Wang et al. proposed a double verifiably encrypted signature (DVES) scheme which can be used to design the contract signing protocol systems. In this paper, we propose an efficient contract signing protocol based on the DVES scheme. A semi-trusted third party is involved in our protocol to ensure firness. Moreover, the new contract signing protocol satisfies the desirable properties: unforgeability, opacity, extractability, timeliness, effectiveness and fairness.

Keywords: double verifiably encrypted signature; aggregate signature; contract signing; timeliness; fairness.

1 Introduction

A fair exchange protocol ensures that either the two exchanging parties get the exchanged messages or none of them obtain anything. The contract signing protocol is a kind of fair exchange protocol where two parties aim to exchange their digital signature on an agreed contract. Contract signing protocols can be partitioned into two categories: protocols that use trusted third party either on-line or off-line (optimistic protocols) [1] and protocols without trusted third party [2].

The second category protocols without trusted third party are based on gradual and verifiable release of information. Hence, if one participant stops the protocol prematurely, both participants have roughly the same computational task in order to find the other participant's signature. A security problem can arise in a setting where the participant A has much more hardware power than the participant B. Then the actual time needed for finishing the computation would be unbalanced favorably for A. These protocols are impractical, and only realize weak fairness. To realize strong fairness, Pagnia et al.[3] proved that a trusted third party (TTP) must be included into the fair exchange protocol. So, we are interested in protocols from the first category.

R. Zhu et al. (Eds.): ICICA 2010, LNCS 6377, pp. 86–93, 2010.

Optimistic contract protocols depend on a trusted third party (TTP), but in such a way that the TTP is not actively involved in case all signers are honest; only for recovery purposed the TTP might become active [4]. Optimistic contract signing protocols have been first described for synchronous networks [4,5]. The first optimistic fair contract signing protocol [4] is based on verifiably encrypted signature (VES), and then generalized by [6]. In these schemes, one party encrypts his signature with the TTP's public key, and proves to the other party that he indeed encrypted his valid signature. After receiving his expected contract signature from the other party, he proceeds to open the encryption. If the other party refuses to do so after getting his signature, the TTP can decrypt the encrypted signature, and then sends the result to him. However, all these schemes involved expensive and highly interactive zero-knowledge proofs (ZKP) in the exchange phase which greatly reduces the efficiency. To improve efficiency, Park et al. [7] proposed a non-interactive optimistic fair exchange protocol based on regular RSA signatures. The ZKP is only used in the setup phase in [7]-this is a one-time cost. Recently, the notion of non-interactive contract signing protocol has attracted a great extension [8,9,10,11,12,13,16].

In [15], Boneh et al. have proposed a verifiable encrypted signature scheme using aggregate signature. Wang et al. followed this concept to create a double verifiable encrypted signature (DVES) [16]. Based on the DVES scheme, they presented an efficient contract signing protocol. In order to avoid the possible misuse of signature on the contract by the TTP, they adopted the concept of semi-trusted third party (STTP) to conceal the signers' privacy, introduced by Franklin et al.[14].

Our results. In this paper, we propose a new efficient contract signing protocol based on the double verifiable encrypted signature scheme [16]. The new scheme also employs the off-line STTP to conceal the signers' privacy. The new proposed protocol consists of three sub-protocols: *Main contract signing protocol, Abort* and *Dispute-solving*. Since both the signers u_A and u_B can contact the STTP to settle the disputes before the deadline, so the new protocol is more flexible and practical. Moreover, the new contract signing protocol satisfies the security properties: unforgeability, opacity, extractability, timeliness, effectiveness, semi-trusted and fairness.

Organization of the paper. The rest of the paper is organized as follows. Section 2 describes the concepts of the bilinear pairings and DVES. The new contract signing protocol is presented in Section 3. We analyze the security of the proposed protocol in Section 4. Finally, Section 5 concludes the paper.

2   Preliminary

2.1   Bilinear Pairings

Let G_1, G_2 and G_e be three (multiplicative) groups of the same prime order q. Let P be an arbitrary generator of G_1, meaning that $qP = \mathcal{O}$, where $\mathcal{O}$ denotes the zero element of G_1, and Q be an arbitrary generator of G_2. Assume that solving the discrete logarithm problem (DLP) is difficult in all G_1, G_2 and G_e. A mapping function $e : G_1 \times G_2 \to G_e$ which satisfies the following conditions is called a bilinear pairing:

1. Bilinearity: Let $P \in G_1$, $Q \in G_2$, and $a, b \in Z_q^*$. Then the equation $e(aP, bQ) = e(P, Q)^{ab}$ holds.
2. Non-degeneracy: There exists $P \in G_1$ and $Q \in G_2$ such that $e(P, G) \neq 1$.
3. Computability: For $P \in G_1$ and $Q \in G_2$, there exists an efficient algorithm to compute $e(P, Q)$.

2.2   Double Verifiable Encrypted Signature (DVES)

Assume there exists a computable φ form G_2 to G_1, with $\varphi(Q) = P$, and a hash function $H : \{0, 1\}^* \to G_1$.

1. DVES generation: Assume the signer u_A has a secret key $x_A \in Z_q$ and a public key $y_A = Q^{x_A} \in G_2$. The signer creates a signature encrypted with the public keys of the two users, namely u_B and STTP, as follows.
   (a) u_A computes $\sigma_A = h^{x_A}$, where $h = H(M) \in G_1$.
   (b) u_A picks two random numbers r_B and r_T from Z_q.
   (c) u_A computes $\mu_B = \varphi(Q)^{r_B}, \mu_T = \varphi(Q)^{r_T}, \rho_B = \varphi(y_B)^{r_B}, \rho_T = \varphi(y_T)^{r_T}$.
   (d) u_A creates an aggregate signature $\omega_A = \sigma_A \rho_B \rho_T$.
2. Publicly verify: For a signature ω_A, a message M and the public keys y_B and y_T, one can make a verification by computing $h = H(M)$ and checking whether the equation $e(\omega_A, Q) = e(h, y_A)e(\mu_B, y_B)e(\mu_T, y_T)$ holds.
3. The decryption needs two users' efforts. The signer u_A's signature can be recovered by the equation $\sigma_A = (\omega_A / \mu_B^{x_B}) / \mu_T^{x_T} = (\omega_A / \mu_T^{x_T}) / \mu_B^{x_B}$.

3   New Contract Signing Protocol

Before describing the new protocol, we introduce some notations. Mes_{RI}, Mes_{EA}, Mes_{DS} and Mes_{AP} represent "Request is invalid.", "Exchange aborted.", "Dispute-solving." and "Abort the protocol.", respectively. Label ℓ is used to identify a specific protocol instance, and links all messages generated in this instance. T is a deadline which chosen by the initiator signer. $A \to B : Mes$ denotes that A sends the message Mes to B. "$||$" denotes the concatenation. We also assume the communication channel between the signers is unreliable, while the communication channel between the signers and the STTP is resilient. In the following, we describe the new contract signing protocol as a sequence of rounds, each round consists of multiple messages.

Setup. According to the security parameter k, the STTP publishes the public parameters G_1, G_2, G_e, P, Q, $\mathcal{O}$, q e, where G_1, G_2, G_e be three (multiplicative) groups of the same prime order q, P be an arbitrary generator of G_1, meaning that $qP = \mathcal{O}$, where $\mathcal{O}$ denotes the zero element of G_1, and Q be an arbitrary generator of G_2, e be a bilinear pairing. There exists a computable φ from G_2 to G_1, with $\varphi(Q) = P$, and a hash function $H : \{0,1\}^* \to G_1$.

Key Generation. With the public parameters G_1, G_2, G_e, P, Q, $\mathcal{O}$, q, e provided by the STTP, u_A picks a random number $x_A \in Z_q$ as her secret key and computes $y_A = Q^{x_A} \in G_2$ as the public key. Similarly, u_B and the STTP have their secret/public key pairs (x_B, y_B) and (x_T, y_T), respectively.

Main Contract Signing Protocol. Let M be the contract to be signed. u_A wants to exchange his contract signature σ_A on M for u_B's contract signature σ_B on M. The main process is shown as follows:

As a initiator, the signer u_A computes $h = H(M\|\ell\|T)$ and his contract signature $\sigma_A = h^{x_A}$. Then, u_A picks two random numbers $r_{AB}, r_{AT} \in Z_q$, and computes $\mu_{AB} = \varphi(Q)^{r_{AB}}$, $\mu_{AT} = \varphi(Q)^{r_{AT}}$, $\rho_{AB} = \varphi(y_B)^{r_{AB}}$, $\rho_{AT} = \varphi(y_T)^{r_{BT}}$, $\omega_A = \sigma_{AB}\rho_{AB}\rho_{AT}$. Then, u_A sends $\{\ell, T, \mu_{AB}, \mu_{AT}, \omega_A\}$ to the signer u_B. Denotes

Step 1. $u_A \to u_B : \{\ell, T, \omega_A, \mu_{AB}, \mu_{AT}\}$.

Upon receiving $\{\ell, T, \omega_A, \mu_{AB}, \mu_{AT}\}$, if u_B does not agree the deadline T, he stops the protocol. Otherwise, he computes $h = H(M\|\ell\|T)$, and uses u_A's public key y_A and the STTP's public key y_T to check whether the equation $e(\omega_A, Q) = e(h, y_A)e(\mu_{AB}, y_B)e(\mu_{AT}, y_T)$ holds. If the equation holds, u_B computes his contract signature $\sigma_B = h^{x_B}$, and picks two random numbers $r_{BA}, r_{BT} \in Z_q$, and computes $\mu_{BA} = \varphi(Q)^{r_{BA}}$, $\mu_{BT} = \varphi(Q)^{r_{BT}}$, $\rho_{BA} = \varphi(y_A)^{r_{BA}}$, $\rho_{BT} = \varphi(y_T)^{r_{BT}}$, $\omega_B = \sigma_{BA}\rho_{BA}\rho_{BT}$. Then, u_B sends $\{\ell, \mu_{BA}, \mu_{BT}, \omega_B\}$ to the signer u_A. Denotes

Step 2. $u_B \to u_A : \{\ell, \omega_B, \mu_{BA}, \mu_{BT}\}$.

Otherwise, u_B stops the protocol.

If u_B is timeout, the contract signing protocol ends without dispute. Upon receiving $\{\ell, \omega_B, \mu_{BA}, \mu_{BT}\}$, u_A uses u_B's public key y_B and the STTP's public key y_T to check whether the equation $e(\omega_B, Q) = e(h, y_B)e(\mu_{BA}, y_A)e(\mu_{BT}, y_T)$ holds. If the equation holds, u_A sends his signature σ_A to u_B. Denotes

Step 3. $u_A \to u_B : \sigma_A$

Otherwise, u_A asks the STTP to execute the *Abort* algorithm to abort the protocol.

Upon receiving σ_A from u_A, u_B uses u_A's public key y_A to check whether the equation $e(\sigma_A, Q) = e(h, y_A)$. If the equation holds, u_B sends his signature σ_B to u_A. Denotes

Step 4. $u_B \to u_A : \sigma_B$.

If u_B does not receive σ_A or only receives an invalid σ_A from u_A, he asks the STTP to execute the *Dispute-solving* algorithm to settle the dispute before the deadline.

Upon receiving σ_B from u_B, u_A uses u_B's public key y_B to check whether the equation $e(\sigma_B, Q) = e(h, y_B)$. If the equation holds, the contract signing protocol ends without dispute. If u_A does not receive σ_B or only receives an invalid σ_B from u_B, he asks the TTP to execute the *Dispute-solving* algorithm to settle the dispute before the deadline.

Abort. If the signer u_A claimed that he does not receive ω_B or only receives an invalid ω_B, he can ask the STTP to execute the *Abort* algorithm to abort the protocol before the deadline. The main process describes as follows:

1. $u_A \rightarrow STTP : \{\ell, T, u_A, u_B, \sigma_{AP}, Mes_{AP}\}$
2. STTP has three possible cases:

   (a) If (Invalid) $STTP \rightarrow u_A : \{\ell, \sigma_{RI}, Mes_{RI}\}$
   (b) Else if (STTP's State = *Dispute-solving*) $STTP \rightarrow u_A/u_B : \alpha_B/\alpha_A$
   (c) Else $STTP \rightarrow u_A/u_B : \{\ell, \sigma_{EA}, Mes_{EA}\}$

In detail, if the signer u_A wants to abort the protocol, he has to send the message $\{\ell, T, u_A, u_B, \sigma_{AP}, Mes_{AP}\}$ to the STTP, where $\sigma_{AP} = h(Mes_{AP}||\ell)^{x_T}$. The STTP checks its validity, if any validation fails, the STTP sends the messages σ_{RI} and Mes_{RI} to the signer u_A, where $\sigma_{RI} = h(Mes_{RI}||\ell)^{x_T}$. If the STTP is at the state of *Dispute-solving*, and sends $\alpha_B = \omega_B/\mu_{BT}^{x_T}$ and $\alpha_A = \omega_A/\mu_{AT}^{x_T}$ to the signer u_A and u_B, respectively. Otherwise, the STTP computes his signature $\sigma_{EA} = h(Mes_{EA}||\ell)^{x_T}$ about the label ℓ and the message Mes_{EA}, then, sends them to the signer u_A and u_B, respectively. After that, the STTP will no longer respond to any requests for the two signers except for a new contract signing.

Dispute-solving. If the signer u_A or u_B claims that she/he does not receive the contract signature or only receives an invalid contract signature from the other party, u_A or u_B can ask the STTP to execute the *Dispute-solving* algorithm. We classify this algorithm into two cases : (1) the signer u_A executes the *Dispute-solving* algorithm; (2) the signer u_B executes the *Dispute-solving* algorithm. The main process is shown as follows:

The signer u_A or u_B executes the *Dispute-solving* algorithm.

1. $u_A/u_B \rightarrow STTP : \{\ell, T, u_A, u_B, \{\mu_{AB}, \mu_{AT}, \omega_A\}, \{\mu_{BA}, \mu_{BT}, \omega_B\}, \sigma_{DS}, Mes_{DS}\}$
2. The STTP has three possible cases:

   (a) If (Invalid) $STTP \rightarrow u_A/u_B : \{\ell, \sigma_{RI}, Mes_{RI}\}$
   (b) Else if (STTP's State = *Abort*) $STTP \rightarrow u_A/u_B : \{\ell, \sigma_{EA}, Mes_{EA}\}$
   (c) Else $STTP \rightarrow u_A/u_B : \alpha_B/\alpha_A$

In detail, if the signer u_A or u_B executes the *Dispute-solving* algorithm, he has to send $\{\ell, T, u_A, u_B, \{\mu_{AB}, \mu_{AT}, \omega_A\}, \{\mu_{BA}, \mu_{BT}, \omega_B\}, \sigma_{DS}, Mes_{DS}\}$ to the STTP, where $\sigma_{DS} = h(Mes_{DS}||l)^{x_A}$. The STTP checks whether the equations $e(\omega_A, Q) = e(h, y_A)e(\mu_{AB}, y_B)e(\mu_{AT}, y_T), e(\omega_B, Q) = e(h, y_B)e(\mu_{BA}, y_A)e(\mu_{BT}, y_T)$ and $e(\sigma_{DS}, Q) = e(h(Mes_{DS}||\ell), y_A)$ hold. If not, the STTP sends $\{\sigma_{RI}, Mes_{RI}\}$ to u_A or u_B. If the STTP is at the state of *Abort*, then, sends $\{\sigma_{EA}, Mes_{EA}\}$ to the signer u_A and u_B, respectively. Otherwise, the STTP computes $\alpha_A = \omega_A/\mu_{AT}^{x_T}$ and $\alpha_B = \omega_B/\mu_{BT}^{x_T}$, then, sends α_B and α_A to u_A and u_B, respectively. After that, the STTP will no longer respond to any requests for the two parties except for a new contract signing.

4   Security Analysis

Based on the description of the new contract signing protocol in Section 3, it is easy to see that the components of aggregate signatures are existential unforgeable against adaptive chosen message attacks [17], because they are the short signature proposed by Boneh et al. [18]. Besides the above requirement, the new contract signing protocol satisfies the following desirable properties : unforgeability, opacity, extractability, timeliness, effectiveness, semi-trusted and fairness.

Theorem 1. The new contract signing protocol is unforgeability and opacity.

Proof. Due to the space limitation, we omit the detail of the proof. Then, we refer the reader to the Theorem 4.4 and Theorem 4.5 of [19] for more details.

Theorem 2. The new contract signing protocol satisfies the extractability.

Proof. The mapping function φ has the following property that has been described in [15]: $e(\varphi(U), V) = e(\varphi(V), U), \forall U, V \in G_2$. Consequently, the extractability is correct since

$$e((\omega_A/\mu_{AB}^{x_B})/\mu_{AT}^{x_T}, Q) = e(\omega_A, Q) \cdot e(\mu_{AB}, y_B)^{-1} \cdot e(\mu_{AT}, y_T)^{-1}.$$

And (ω_A, Q) can be derived as follows.

$$\begin{aligned}
e(\omega_A, Q) &= e(\sigma_A \varphi(y_B)^{r_{AB}} \varphi(y_T)^{r_{AT}}, Q) \\
&= e(\sigma_A, Q) \cdot e(\varphi(y_B)^{r_{AB}}, Q) \cdot e(\varphi(y_T)^{r_{AT}}, Q) \\
&= e(h, y_A) \cdot e(\varphi(y_B), Q)^{r_{AB}} \cdot e(\varphi(y_T), Q)^{r_{AT}} \\
&= e(h, y_A) \cdot e(\varphi(Q)^{r_{AB}}, y_B) \cdot e(\varphi(Q)^{r_{AT}}, y_T) \\
&= e(h, y_A) \cdot e(\mu_{AB}, y_B) \cdot e(\mu_{AT}, y_T).
\end{aligned}$$

The result is that $e((\omega_A/\mu_{AB}^{x_B})/\mu_{AT}^{x_T}, Q) = e(h, y_A) \cdot e(\mu_{AB}, y_B) \cdot e(\mu_{AT}, y_T) \cdot e(\mu_{AB}, y_B)^{-1} \cdot e(\mu_{AT}, y_T)^{-1} = e(h, y_A)$. Based on the analysis, the STTP only computes $\alpha_A = \omega_A/\mu_{AT}^{x_T}$, and sends it to the signer u_B. Finally, the signer u_B computes $\alpha_A/\mu_{AB}^{x_B} = \sigma_A$. So, the extractability needs two users' efforts. The new contract signing protocol satisfies the extractability.

Theorem 3. The new contract signing protocol is effectiveness.

Proof. If both signers of the new contract signing protocol (CSP) perform properly, they can obtain each other's contract signature without any involvement of the STTP when the protocol ends. So, the CSP is effectiveness.

Theorem 4. The new contract signing protocol satisfies the timeliness.

Proof. In order to realize timeliness, we choose a deadline T for the execution of the CSP. According to the new CSP, before the deadline T, both signers can ask the STTP to execute the *Dispute-solving* algorithm to settle disputes, or the initial signer asks the STTP to execute the *Abort* algorithm to abort the protocol. So, the new CSP can finish in a limited time, and does not undermine the fairness.

Theorem 5. The employed third party of the new contract signing protocol is a semi-trusted third party.

Proof. Normal Case : The STTP need not take part in the protocol. Thus, he can not obtain the exchange signatures.

Dispute Case : We can see that the STTP can obtain the messages $\{\mu_{AB}, \mu_{AT}, \omega_A\}$ and $\{\mu_{BA}, \mu_{BT}, \omega_B\}$ in the *Dispute-solving* phase from the signer u_A or u_B. The STTP can decrypt them by computing α_A and α_B, but only obtains two ciphers: one is the signer u_A's contract signature encrypted with u_B's public key, and the other is the signer u_B's contract signature encrypted with u_A's public key. Instead, the signer u_A and u_B can compute $\sigma_B = \alpha_B/\mu_{BA}^{x_A}$ and $\sigma_A = \alpha_A/\mu_{AB}^{x_B}$, respectively, when they received the $\mu_{BT}^{x_T}$ and $\mu_{AT}^{x_T}$ from the STTP. However, the STTP can verify this message but cannot decrypt it.

So, the third party employed in the new efficient contract signing protocol is semi-trusted third party, and he cannot obtain the signers' signatures.

Theorem 6. The new contract signing protocol satisfies the fairness.

Proof. Due to the space limitation, we will give the proof in the full version.

5   Conclusion

In this paper, we presented a new contract signing protocol based on the double verifiable encrypted signature [16]. Both signers can contact the STTP and solve the possible cases whenever they want before the deadline. Moreover, the new contract signing protocol satisfies unforgeability, opacity, extractability, timeliness, effectiveness, semi-trusted and fairness.

References

1. Asokan, N., Shoup, V., Waidner, M.: Optimistic fair exchange of digital signatures. In: Nyberg, K. (ed.) EUROCRYPT 1998. LNCS, vol. 1403, pp. 591–606. Springer, Heidelberg (1998)
2. Garay, J.A., Pomerance, C.: Timed Fair Exchange of Standard Signatures. In: Wright, R.N. (ed.) FC 2003. LNCS, vol. 2742, pp. 190–207. Springer, Heidelberg (2003)
3. Pagnia, H., Gartner, F.C.: On the impossibility of fair exchange without a trusted third party. Tech. Rep. TUD-BS-1999-02, Darmstadt University of Technology (March 1999)
4. Asokan, N., Schunter, M., Waidner, M.: Optimisitic Protocols for Fair Exchange. In: The 4th ACM Conf. on Computer and Communications Security, pp. 7–17. ACM, New York (1997)
5. Pfitzmann, B., Schunter, M., Waidner, M.: Optimal Efficiency of Optimisitic Contract Signing. In: ACM PODC 1998, pp. 113–122. ACM, New York (1998)

6. Camenisch, J., Damgárd, I.B.: Verifiable encrytion, group encrytion, and their applications to group signatures and signature sharing schemes. In: Okamoto, T. (ed.) ASIACRYPT 2000. LNCS, vol. 1976, pp. 331–345. Springer, Heidelberg (2000)
7. Park, J.M., Chong, E.K.P., Siegel, P.J.: Constructing fair exchange protocols for e-commerce via distributed computation. In: ACM PODC 2003, pp. 172–181. ACM, New York (2003)
8. Zhang, Q., Wen, Q.Y., Chen, G.L.: Efficient fair contract signing protocol from bilinear pairings. In: Proc. of 2008 International Symposium on Electronic Commerce and Security, pp. 333–337 (2008)
9. Shao, Z.H.: Fair exchange protocol of signatures based on aggregate signatures. Computer Communications 31(10), 1961–1969 (2008)
10. Minh, N.H., Moldovyan, N.A.: Protocols for Simultaneous Signing Contracts. In: Proc. of The 2009 International Conference on Advanced Technologies for Communications, pp. 31–34 (2009)
11. Shao, Z.H.: Fair exchange protocol of Schnorr signatures with semi-trusted adjudicator. Computers and Electrical Engineering (2010), doi:10.1016/j.compeleceng.2010.03.005
12. Wang, G.L.: An Abuse-Free Fair Contract Signing Protocol Based on the RSA Signature. IEEE Transactions on Information Forensics and Security 5(1), 158–168 (2010)
13. Sun, Y.B., Gu, L.Z., Qing, S.H., Zheng, S.H., Sun, B., Yang, Y.X., Sun, Y.: Timeliness Optimistic Fair Exchange Protocol Based on Key-Exposure-Free Chameleon Hashing Scheme. In: Proc. of ICACT 2010, pp. 1560–1564 (2010)
14. Franklin, M.K., Reiter, M.K.: Fair exchange with a semi-trusted third party. In: Proc. of the 4th ACM Conference on Computer and Communications Security, pp. 1–5. ACM, New York (1997)
15. Boneh, D., Gentry, B.L., Shacham, H.: Aggregate and verifiabley encrypted signatures from bilinear maps. In: Biham, E. (ed.) EUROCRYPT 2003. LNCS, vol. 2656, pp. 416–432. Springer, Heidelberg (2003)
16. Wang, C.H., Kuo, Y.S.: An Efficient Contract Signing Protocol Using the Aggregate Signature Scheme to Protect Signers' Privacy and Promote Reliability. ACM SIGOPS Operating Systems Review 39(4), 66–79 (2005)
17. Goldwasser, S., Micali, S., Rivest, R.: A digital signature scheme secure against adaptive chosen-message attacks. SIAM Journal on Computing 17(2), 281–308 (1988)
18. Boneh, D., Lynn, B., Shacham, H.: Short signatures from the Weil pairing. In: Boyd, C. (ed.) ASIACRYPT 2001. LNCS, vol. 2248, pp. 514–532. Springer, Heidelberg (2001)
19. Boneh, D., Gentry, C., Lynn, B., Shacham, H.: Aggregate and verifiably encrypted signatures from bilinear maps. Cryptology ePrint Archive, Report 2002/175 (2002), http://eprint.iacr.org/2002/175

Semantic Memory for Pervasive Architecture

Sébastien Dourlens and Amar Ramdane-Cherif

Laboratoire d'Ingénierie des systèmes de Versailles (LISV),
Université de Versailles Saint Quentin
Centre Universitaire de Technologie
10-12, Avenue de l'Europe 78140 Vélizy
{sdourlens,rca}@lisv.uvsq.fr

Abstract. Pervasive environments become a reality and involve a large variety of networking smart devices. This ambient intelligence tends to complex interactions. Lots of researches have been done on intelligent and reactive architectures able to manage multiple events and act in the environment. In the Robotics domain, a decision process must be implemented in the robot brain or a collective intelligence to accomplish the multimodal interaction with humans in human environment. We present a semantic agents architecture giving the robot and other entities the ability to well understand what is happening and thus provide more robust processing. We will describe our agent memory. Intelligence and knowledge about objects in the environment is stored in two ontologies linked to a reasoner an inference engine. To share and exchange information, an event knowledge representation language is used by semantic agents. This pervasive architecture brings other advantages: cooperation, redundancy, adaptability, interoperability and platforms independent.

Keywords: cognitive memory, pervasive architecture, semantic agents, ontology, knowledge representation language, web service.

1 Related Work

The study of intelligent systems have been done using multiple technologies in different scientific domains: Multi Agent systems (MAS), Ambient Intelligence (AmI), Architecture modeling (AM), Artificial intelligence (AI), Formal logic (FL), Knowledge representation languages (KRL) from Description Logic (DL), knowledge management (KM), Information Retrieval (IR), Multi Agent Systems (MAS), Multimodal Interaction (MI), Human Robot Interaction (HRI). Intelligence will come from mixed technologies managing environment data fully or partially observable, deterministic or stochastic, episodic or sequential, dynamic or static, symbolic, possibilistic or probabilistic, in space and time. Our approach mixes all perceived events in a structured semantic memory integrated in agents. Our multimodal architecture is based on multi agent systems. Lots of architectures have been designed in the aim to be embodied in a robot, in a house, in the city or to simply bring an intelligent software component into a system. We focus on intelligent architecture integrating semantic agents, semantic services as structural components, ontology as knowledge

R. Zhu et al. (Eds.): ICICA 2010, LNCS 6377, pp. 94–102, 2010.

base [1], inference systems and KRL as communication protocol. We agree with the fact that ontologies offer rich representations of machine-interpretable semantics ensuring interoperability and integration [2] because of the non explicit information processed by existing complex architectures. The genericity of the architecture components is a key of success of designing non dedicated applications open to several domains and mixing different technology. MAS are a useful paradigm for ambient intelligence. This architectural choice permits to model widely open, distributed and ubiquitous architecture [3] and [4]. Agents are autonomous programming objects able to communicate. Intelligent robots often need awareness model and user fusion model, using KRL in a software agents' organization permit to these robots to reason [5]. We will adapt this work to Human Robot Interaction. Agents may act socially around a common goal in groups of agents called agencies. Web services were designed by the W3C in the goal to standardize software services in an interoperable way. Our agents will interact as web services. They are connected with other agents and environment using the Simple Object Access Protocol (SOAP [18]) for Service Oriented Architecture (SOA) in the XML format. To obtain semantic agents and services, we need to add a KRL into our agents to give the ability to query, store or produce knowledge. In our work, semantic agents will be used to compose or adapt the architecture, to query the knowledge base and communicate with software and hardware services. Our objective is to represent and store the semantic events and extract the meaning of a situation. Ontology Web language v2 (OWL [19]) permits to describe relationships using classes, individuals, properties in a hierarchical structure called a domain ontology in the formal XML. It appears to be a useful storage base and may be coupled with a reasoner. Reasoners are inference systems based on description logic like KAON2 [20], Pellet [21], JESS [22], Fact++ [23] to realize the matching operation. Recent languages appears to try to solve this issue, new Extensible Multimodal Annotation (EMMA) [6, 24], a standard language proposal from the W3C consortium is able to represent multimodal fusion and fission in a very procedural way. [15] also presents an example of multimodal applications on mobile as a proof of concepts. MurML [7], MMIL [8], MutliML [9] are pure XML and are based on a natural language processing (NLP) parser made by a combinatory categorical grammar (CCG) [10] at an intermediate level of recognition of gestures and speech utterances. It is an interesting approach well suited for speech recognition. Our solution is grammar independent. [11] proposes a robot mark-up language approach based on standard XML technology. Other languages more suitable, powerful and simple as KRL like Knowledge Interchange Format (KIF [25]) or Narrative KRL (NKRL) exist [12]. NKRL is a language very close to the frames and slots idea proposed by Minsky [13] and refined by Quillian [14]. The language we use in this article is very close to frames and NKRL but our ontologies and the inference system are different, the result will be more adapted to robot architecture. To respect background behind OWL (completeness calculus and consistency checking), we introduced in the memory of our agent similar meta-concepts like properties, relationships and individuals types. One difference is the n-ary relationships implied by the use of frames and slots. This gives us the ability to import or export any OWL knowledge bases into the agent memory. In addition, the transition from frame to XML is very easy. Our ontologies use concepts and models fully compliant with FIPA [26] standards from IEEE Computer Society. Meaning of the situation must be quickly extracted to take a reactive decision. This meaning is very important to obtain a correct interpretation. Meaning of the situation and situation refinement require developing a description of the current relationships among entities and events in the environment context. The extraction of the meaning to understand what is happening as well as ontological storage of the events is very important for the interpretation. Multimodal Interaction refers to two important processes of interaction are well presented in [16] Information fusion refers to particular mathematical functions and algorithms for data combination. Multimodal fission, in the opposite way, is the process to physically act or show any reactions to the inputs or the current situation. According to decision rules taking following the fusion process, the fission will split semantic results of the decision into single actions to be sent to the actuators. Multimodal fusion is a central question to solve and provide effective and advanced human-computer interaction by using complementary or redundant modalities. Multimodal fusion helps to provide more informative, exact, complete, reliable interpretation. Dependency between modalities allows reciprocal disambiguation and improves recognition in the interpretation of the scene. Essential requirements for multimodal fusion and fission engines are the management of modalities with events, cognitive algorithms, formal logic and context representation of robotics systems or simulation environment. In this document, we bring functional and exchangeable components to fulfill these requirements. Our architecture realizes fusion and fission processes using all environment knowledge stored in the semantic agent memory.

2 Pervasive Architecture

Proposed architecture is composed of intelligent agents able to manage several multimodal services (figure 1). Services are directly connected to the environment controlling sensors or actuators, or are simple software services. They are in charge of internal of the robot or external inputs and outputs in a ubiquitous network. In our pervasive architecture, semantic agents and services can be embedded into the robot, the house, the city or anywhere on Internet. Human makes part of the environment and can interact with the robot by input modalities like gestures, body movements, voice or touch of a screen. It appears obvious that our intelligent robot has to manage multimodal inputs and outputs related to different contexts facing uncertain, noise and complex tasks to realize. This implies to process and to exchange a large amount of events. Architecture must be well-conceived to reduce this complexity, events combination and knowledge must be well organized. On the figure 2, Semantic Services are able to create and communicate with KRL with events. Semantic services role is to send any information from hardware sensors, execute a software function or execute orders to control actuators. Services can be seen as reactive agents with no cognitive part but enough exchangeable knowledge and code to realize the process they are designed to. Semantic agents are more complex because they are cognitive or functional. They possess their own abilities and program to achieve their tasks and goals. Agents contain an embedded inference system able to process the matching operation and then answer queries. Scenarios or execution schemes are stored in their knowledge base. Agents and Services interact to the environment in two manners: - the network between them and - the web services sensors and actuators. Semantic Agent contains its knowledge base, its inference engine and its communication module. Semantic service has code and standard memory (properties and methods in generic programming object model), the communication module and the hardware controller module. The hardware controller enables the service to receive information from a sensor or to drive an actuator. The communication module contains the network card and its semantic functionalities to send and receive events.

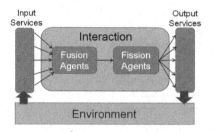

Fig. 1. Multimodal architecture

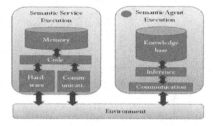

Fig. 2. Architecture components

3 Semantic Memory Design

Semantic agents and semantic services communicate with events. These events are written in knowledge representation language using concepts (formal T-BOX of concepts) and instances of concepts (formal A-BOX of concepts). They are directly included in the agent memory. This memory contains a domain ontology called *Concepts Ontology* and a second ontology called *Models Ontology*. The second one embeds templates of events (formal T-BOX of models) under the form of predicates and instances of events called *facts* (formal A-BOX). Concepts, Events models, Query models and instances are stored in ontologies. Instances are facts, happened scenario and context knowledge. In addition, concept ontology is fully compatible OWL2. Models are filled with concepts and instances of concepts to give the facts. All inserted facts coming from the network fully link concepts, models and instances storing hierarchically the knowledge and intelligence of facts (figure 3). Agent memory is composed of a Meta ontology, a Concepts ontology and a Models ontology (Fig. 4). The Meta ontology contains the different types of relationships, models and roles used in the two other ontologies. These ontologies are stored in a SQL database within

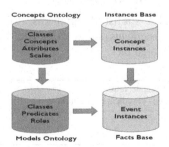

Fig. 3. Knowledge base content

about 8 tables. One frame query is equivalent to one SQL query sent to the database and the matching is directly done in a very fast way because of the complexity due to the storage of the ontology in database tables at the time of creation of concepts and models. To build the concept ontology, standardized OWL editors used can be Protégé, Swoop or any others OWL v2 compliant. Then OWL files can be imported into the agent knowledge base with the editor we developed.

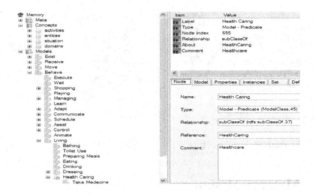

Fig. 4. Ontologies in the agent memory

4 Events Communication and Storage

KRL is a semantic formal language L that can describe events in a narrative way. It is fully used to build event messages and store facts directly the models classes of the models ontology of the agent memory. The formal system is composed of the formal language based on variable arity relations in logic of predicates (event frames). It permits to realize semantic inference in order to extract the meaning of the situation. Ontologies are useful and powerful structures to store the events and extract this meaning. Inference system may use models to match the instances of the ontologies. In NKRL, frames are predicates with slots that represent pieces of information. A slot is represented by a role associated to an argument. A predicate P is a semantic *n-ary* relationship between Roles and Arguments and represents a simple event or a composed event; it is denoted by the following formula.

$$P((R_1\ A_1)\ldots (R_n\ A_n)),\tag{1}$$

where R is a list of roles and A is a list of arguments. Roles R_n are the possible roles (dedicated variables storing arguments) in the event and A_n are the possible values or instances of concepts in the stored fact.

Name: <RootPredicate>:<PredicateName>
Natural language description: '<Predicate Description>'
<RootPredicate>
   <Role1> <Arguments1>
   <Role2> <Arguments2>

Fig. 5. Event model description

The figure 5 shows a sample model written with the NKRL syntax. The list of all roles is part of the Meta ontology of the agent memory. Role can be OBJECTIVE, SOURCE, BENEFICIARY, MODALITY, TOPIC, CONTEXT, MODULATOR, DATE. Models of events are models of predicates and instances of predicates specific to a situation. For example, "Move" is an informative term called root predicate (an event model of the Models Ontology) expressing a movement of anything.

5 Semantic Memory in Agents

A fusion agent (FA) is a semantic agent which has the role to extract a specific meaning. The matching operation of the inference engine will extract the required meaning in the dialog context. Once information are extracted from the knowledge base, the fusion agent will be able to create a composed event that will be also stored in the knowledge base and eventually shared with others agents by sending it to others agents in the network. Each fusion agent is specialized to a task or a domain to compose new events or to act in the environment using linked semantic services. This specialization is done by a composition agent. All fusion agents have a program that consists to execute a loop of these five following steps:

1. Take a model of event (rules and scenarios are stored in memory)
2. Fill roles with known or wanted arguments
3. Query the knowledge base (its own memory)
4. Get list of matching events
5. Compose a new (composed) event.

A fission agent is a semantic agent which has the role to manage actuators services. Fission agent acts exactly like the fusion agent except that in addition they will produce order events for all future jobs to be executed directly by services at a specific time. For the fission agent model, only the meaning will be of different types because events will be orders or plans called "execution events" and sent to actuators.

```
Behave: PutThatHere      MODEL
    SUBJECT: COORD(ArmShowsObject, ArmShowsPosition, SpeechOrder)
    SENDER: COORD(GestureSensors, VocalSensors)
      DATE: date time
        LOCATION: location

Behave: PutThatHere      FACT
    SUBJECT: COORD(ArmShowsObject, ArmShowsPosition, SpeechOrder)
    SENDER: COORD(GestureDetectionVideo1, GestureDetectionVideo1, VocalRecognition1)
      DATE: 09/04/2010 10:04
      LOCATION: room 5
```

Fig. 6. "Behave: PutThatHere" model and fact

Famous example of "Put That Here" [17] is represented by a model and one of its instances on figure 6. It's a composed event that represents "a human giving an order and pointing an object and a location". In this example, one instance of our fusion agents is in charge to merge events that happen in a same period of time. It uses an event model waiting for the three events "ArmShowsObject", "ArmShowsPosition" and "SpeechOrder". Event instance or fact appears at 10:04 sent by the two services "GestureDectectionVideo1" and "VocalRecognition1". The first service is in charge of the detection of gestures produced by human. The second service uses one or several mikes to recognize a speech sentence. These services have the ability to send their basic event in parallel to any agents and are embedded in the robot or are parts of the house, thus they are connected to the robot agents. At a scheduled interval of time and after new events took place in its memory, our agent composes an instance of the *Behave:PutThatHere* model. The interpretation of events happening in environment is very simple and fast. The matching operation will give a true description of the event.

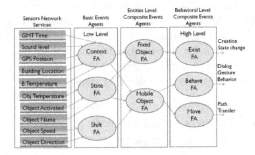

Fig. 7. Agency of fusion agents

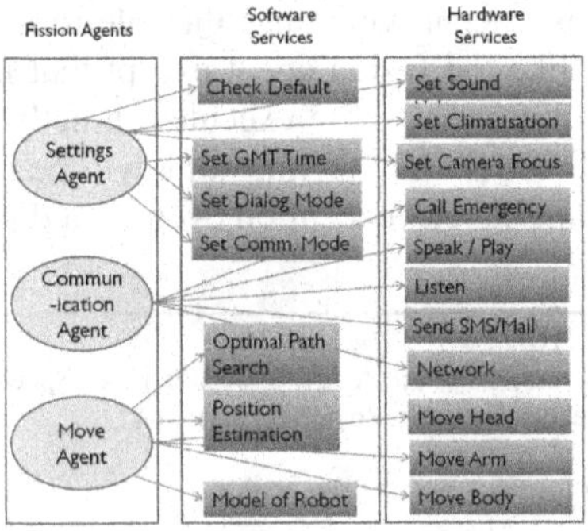

Fig. 8. Agency of fission agents

A more complex pervasive architecture is a composition of several fusion agents (figure 7) to build composed events that will be sent on the network and stored by the other agents memory (past facts on the figure 3) to think, to act or to adapt the architecture itself. The figure 8 presents an example of agency of fission agents and actuators services realized by three fission agents. Agents are represented as disks, services as boxes and arrows represent the composition. The choice of software services and hardware services depends on the conceived robotics application.

6   Conclusion and Future Work

We presented in this paper semantic components for pervasive architectures with the ability to solve robotic interaction. Agents have been extended with a semantic memory using a KRL and composed of two Concepts and Event Models ontologies. Semantic memory permits to store and access the meaning of facts happening to the entities and objects in the environment. Integration mechanisms are based on deductive rules and derivation of new information from existing information at different levels of abstraction. Adaption of the architecture can be realized by reconfiguring agencies. For future work, we will present different robotic applications to assist users in their daily tasks already in progress.

References

1. Guarino, N.: Formal ontology, conceptual analysis and knowledge representation. Human-Computer Studies 43(5/6), 625–640 (1995)
2. Leo, O.: Ontologies for semantically Interoperable Systems. In: Proceedings of the Twelfth International Conference on Information and Knowledge Management, New Orleans, LA, USA, pp. 366–369. ACM Press, New York (2003)
3. Macal Charles, M., North Michael, J.: Tutorial on agent-based modeling and simulation part 2: How to model with agents. In: Perrone, L.F., Wieland, F.P., Liu, J., Lawson, B.G., Nicol, D.M., Fujimoto, R.M. (eds.) Proceedings of the 2006 Winter Simulation Conference (2006)
4. Allan, R.: Survey of Agent Based Modeling and Simulation Tools. Technical Report (2009), http://epubs.cclrc.ac.uk/work-details?w=50398
5. Erik, B., Ivan, K., John, S., Kokar, M.M., Subrata, D., Powell, G.M., Orkill, D.D., Ruspini, E.H.: Issues and Challenges in Situation Assessment (Level 2 Fusion). Journal of Advances in Information Fusion 1(2) (December 2006)
6. Michael, J., Paolo, B., Burnett Daniel, C., Jerry, C., Dahl Deborah, A.: MacCobb Gerry and Ragget Dave: EMMA: Extensible MultiModal Annotation markup language. W3C Recommendation (February 2009)
7. Kranstedt, A., Kopp, S., Wachsmuth, I.: Murml: A multimodal utterance representation markup language for conversational agents. In: Proc. of the AAMAS, Workshop on Embodied conversational agents - Let's specify and evaluate them (2002)
8. Frédéric, L., Denis, A., Ricci, A., Romary, L.: Multimodal meaning representation for generic dialogue systems architectures. In: Proc. on Language Resources and Evaluation (LREC 2004), pp. 521–524 (2004)
9. Manuel, G., Alois, K.: MultiML - A General Purpose Representation Language for Multimodal Human Utterances. In: ICMI 2008, Chania, Crete, Greece (2008)
10. Mark, S., Jason, B.: Combinatory Categorial Grammar to appear. In: Borsley, R., Borjars, K. (eds.) Non-Transformational Syntax. Blackwell, Malden (2005)
11. Jun-young, K., Ji Young, Y., Shinn Richard H.: An Intelligent Robot Architecture based on Robot Mark-up Languages. In: Proceedings of IEEE International Conference on Engineering of Intelligent Systems (ICEIS), pp. 1–6 (2006)
12. Piero, Z.G.: Representation and Processing of Complex Events. In: Association for the Advancement of Artificial Intelligence AAAI Spring Symposium (2009)

13. Marvin, M.: Matter, Mind and Models. In: Proceedings of IFIP Congress, Spartan Books, Wash. D.C, pp. 45–49 (1965); Reprinted in Semantic Information Processing. A short paper proposing a theory of self-knowledge and the illusion of free will (1965)
14. Quillian Ross Semantic memory.: Ph.D. thesis, Carnegie Intstitute of Technology (1966); Minsky, M. (ed.) Semantic Information Processing, p. 262. MIT Press, Cambridge (1968)
15. Michael, J.: Building Multimodal Applications with EMMA. In: ICMI-MLMI 2009, November 2-4. ACM, Cambridge (2009), 978-1-60558-772-1/09/11
16. Frédéric, L.: Physical, semantic and pragmatics levels for multimodal fusion and fission. In: Seventh International Workshop on Computational Semantics (IWCS-7), Tilburg, The Netherlands, pp. 346–350 (2007)
17. Bolt, R.: "Put That Here": Voice and gesture at the graphics interface. In: Proceedings of the 7th Annual Conference on Computer Graphics and Interactive Techniques (1980)
18. SOAP website, http://www.w3.org/TR/soap12-part0
19. OWL website, http://www.w3.org/TR/owl-features/
20. KAON website, http://kaon2.semanticweb.org
21. Pellet website, http://clarkparsia.com/pellet
22. JESS website, http://www.jessrules.com
23. FACT++ website, http://owl.man.ac.uk/factplusplus/
24. EMMA website, http://www.w3.org/TR/emma
25. FIPA website, http://www.fipa.org

Fair E-Payment Protocol Based on Certificateless Signature and Authenticated Key Exchange

Ming Chen[1], Kaigui Wu[1], and Jie Xu[1,2]

[1] College of Computer, Chongqing University,
400044 Chongqing, China
[2] School of Computing, University of Leeds, UK
chenming9824@yahoo.com.cn,
kaiguiwu@cqu.edu.cn, jxu@comp.leeds.ac.uk

Abstract. E-payment protocol allows two or more users to securely exchange e-cash and digital product among them over an open network. There are some problems in the E-payment applications of cross-domain and cross-organization scenarios because of certificate-based authentication and digital signature, like inconsistent public key certificates and a heavy certificate management burden. ID-based cryptography is adopted to solve those problems, but it suffers the key escrow issue. Certificateless cryptography has been introduced to mitigate those limitations. A certificateless signature and authenticated key exchange scheme (CL-SAKE for short) is proposed, and its security is proved in the extended random oracle model. As an application, an E-payment protocol based on the new CL-SAKE is then proposed, which achieves unforgeability and un-reusability of e-cash, customer anonymity and fair exchange.

Keywords: certificateless signature, certificateless authenticated key exchange, electronic payment, fairness.

1 Introduction

E-Payment Protocol is an important means of payment to realize E-commerce. With the staggering development of E-commerce, E-payment protocol has aroused the attention of many scholars all over the world. The first E-payment protocol was proposed by Chaum [1] in 1982. Over the next 30 years, E-payment has been well studied and many E-payment protocols have been put forward. However, most E-payment systems [2] adopt certificate-based public key cryptography (CA-PKC). A critical weakness of CA-PKC, existing in cross-domain and cross-organization E-commerce applications, is a heavy burden of certificate management. Some scholars recently have adopted identity-based cryptography (ID-PKC) [3] to E-cash systems [4,5] in order to deal with the weakness of CA-PKC-based systems. In ID-PKC, the user's public key is derived from his identifier, and the corresponding private key is generated by a trusted third party named as private key generator (PKG). ID-PKC has a main advantage over CA-PKC, which avoids the difficulties and application limitations from users' certificate. Nevertheless, it has a fatal flaw, so-called the key escrow issue [6]. A malicious PKG who has the users' long-term private keys can

R. Zhu et al. (Eds.): ICICA 2010, LNCS 6377, pp. 103–110, 2010.

impersonate anyone, which gives rise to major risks in the system. In addition, Yang and Chang [7] proposed a non-signature authenticated encryption scheme on Elliptic curve and based on this scheme they constructed a fair electronic payment system. Lin and Liu [8] proposed a new electronic payment scheme for digital content transactions that fulfilled fair exchange and customer anonymity. A main contribution of Lin's work is that their scheme encourages venders' motivation to create high-quality digital contents because it immediately apportions sales revenue to payees. And other scholars focused on the mobile payments scenario [9].

Different from the works mentioned above, an E-payment protocol, based on certificateless signature and authenticated key exchange (CL-SAKE), is proposed in this paper. Certificateless cryptography (CLC) [6] has been introduced to circumvent the key escrow issue inherent to ID-PKC. In CLC, a partially trusted authority called Key Generation Center (KGC) helps to generate the private key for each user but cannot access the full private key of any user. The public key of users is computed from public parameters and a secret value chosen by the user. Hence, CLC does not need an additional certificate to bind the user to her public key, and avoids the key escrow issue. Then, Liu et al [10] presented a certificateless signcryption scheme, Zhang et al [11] pointed out a certificateless authenticated key agreement protocol, and Wang et al [12] put forward a certificateless E-cash scheme. Inspired by these works, we propose an E-payment protocol that adopts a CL-SAKE mechanism to establish a secured transaction and to generate e-cash and repudiable evidence. Our signature algorithm achieves the existentially unforgeable against chosen message attacks (EUF-CMA) under the CDH intractability assumption. Moreover, we show our key exchange scheme, extended from SCK-1 scheme in [13], realizes provably secure implicit authentication, and we prove that the new E-payment protocol achieves e-cash's unreusability, users' anonymity and payment's fairness.

The rest of this paper is organized as follows: the proposed CL-SAKE and E-payment protocol are detailed in Section 2. We analyze the proposed schemes in Section 3. Finally, some concluding remarks are given in Section 4.

2   Certificateless E-Payment Protocol

We introduce firstly some preliminaries that form the basis of our schemes.

Let k be a security parameter and q be a k-bit prime number. Let G_1 and G_2 be two cyclic groups of the same large prime order q. We assume that G_1 is additive group and G_2 is multiplicative group, respectively. Let $e\colon G_1 \times G_1 \to G_2$ be an admissible pairing which satisfies the following properties:

Bilinearity: For $\forall (P,Q) \in G_1$ and $\forall (a,b) \in Z_q^*$, there exist $e(aP,bQ)=e(P,Q)^{ab}$.

Non-degeneracy: there exist $(P,Q) \in G_1$, such that $e(P,Q) \neq 1$.

Computability: For $\forall (P,Q) \in G_1$, one can compute $e(P,Q) \in G_2$ in polynomial time.

Typically, the used pairing is a modified Weil pairing or Tate pairing on a super singular elliptic curve or abelian variety [3]. Next, we describe two assumptions, the Computational Diffie-Hellman (CDH) and the Bilinear Diffie–Hellman (BDH).

Definition 1 (CDH): For $a,b \in_R Z_q^*$, given $(P,aP,bP) \in G_1$, computing $abP \in G_1$ is hard.

Definition 2 (BDH): For unknown $a,b,c \in_R Z_q^*$, given $(P,aP,bP,cP) \in G_1$, computing $e(P,P)^{abc} \in G_2$ is hard.

2.1 Certificateless Signature and Authenticated Key Exchange

The CL-SAKE consists of seven algorithms, including Setup, Partial-Key-Generation, Set-Private-Key, Set-Public-Key, Sign, Signature-verify and Key-Exchange.

Setup: This algorithm takes as input $l \in Z^*$, and outputs $params = (G_1,G_2,e,P,P_0, H_1,H_2,l)$. Where, (G_1,G_2,e) is as above, P is a generator of G_1, $s \in Z_q^*$ and $P_0 = sP$ are *master-key* and public key of KGC, respectively. $H_1 : \{0,1\}^* \to G_1$ and $H_2 : \{0,1\}^{*2} \times G_1^5 \times G_2 \to \{0,1\}^l$ are secure one-way hash functions.

Partial-Key-Generation: This algorithm takes as input $(params,s,ID_i)$, and outputs $D_i = sQ_i$ as the partial key for the entity i. Here, $Q_i = H_1(ID_i)$, $ID_i \in \{0,1\}^*$ is the identifier of i.

Set-Private-Key: This algorithm takes as input $(params,ID_i,D_i)$, and outputs $S_i = (x_i,D_i)$ as the private key of i. Here, $x_i \in_R Z_q^*$ is selected randomly.

Set-Public-Key: This algorithm takes as input $(params,ID_i,D_i,x_i)$, and outputs $P_i = x_iP$ as the public key of i.

Sign: This algorithm takes as input $(params,M,D_i,x_i)$, picks randomly $r \in Z_q^*$, and outputs (σ,R). Where, $\sigma = (r+x_i)Q+D_i$, $Q = H_1(M)$, and $R = rP$.

Signature-verify: This algorithm takes as input $(params,M,ID_i,P_i,\sigma,R)$, and outputs *accept* or *reject*. The verifying equation is as follows.

$$e(\sigma,P) = e(Q,(r+x_i)P)e(Q_i,sP) = e(Q,R+P_i)e(Q_i,P_0). \tag{1}$$

Key-Exchange: Assume that entities A and B have key pairs (S_A,P_A) and (S_B,P_B) respectively. They run the key exchange as follows.

A selects $r_A \in Z_q^*$ at random, computes $R_A = r_AP$, and sends (ID_A,P_A,R_A) to B.

When B receives (ID_A,P_A,R_A) from A, he chooses $r_B \in Z_q^*$, calculates $R_B = r_BP$, and sends (ID_B,P_B,R_B) to A. Then, he computes $K_B = e(R_A,D_B)e(r_BP_0,Q_A)$ and the session key $SK_{BA} = H_2(ID_A,ID_B,R_A,R_B,r_BR_A,r_BP_A,x_BR_A,K_B)$.

When A receives (ID_B,P_B,R_B) from B, she computes $K_A = e(R_B,D_A)e(r_AP_0,Q_B)$ and the session key $SK_{AB} = H_2(ID_A,ID_B,R_A,R_B,r_AR_B,x_AR_B,r_AP_B,K_A)$.

In every run, the session ID is (ID_A,ID_B,R_A,R_B). Obviously, $r_AR_B = r_Ar_BP = r_BR_A$, $K_A = e(R_B, D_A)e(r_AP_0, Q_B) = e(sR_B, Q_A)e(r_AP, sQ_B) = e(r_BP_0, Q_A)e(R_A, D_B) = K_B$, $r_BP_A = r_Bx_AP$

$= x_A R_B$, $r_A P_B= r_A x_B P= x_B R_A$, and $SK_{AB}=SK_{BA}$. So, in order to calculate a same session key as B, entity A must embed her private key S_A and a temporary secret value r_A, which achieves the implicit authentication from B to A, and vice versa.

2.2 E-Payment Protocol

The new E-payment protocol involves four entities, that is, consumer C, vender V, bank B and a trusted third party T. The identifier and key pairs of the four entities are (ID_C, S_C, P_C), (ID_V, S_V, P_V), (ID_B, S_B, P_B) and (ID_T, S_T, P_T), respectively. We assume that C and V have opened an account I_i ($i \in \{C, V\}$) at B.

E-cash Generation. When C needs the e-cash, he establishes secure communication link with B by CL-AKE. C sends related information to B (We assume C and V have reached a consensus on *money*-the price of product). If the account balance of C is greater than or equal to *money*, an e-cash, *payment*, is generated and sent to C, and the corresponding moneys are frozen. If not, *false* would be sent back.

$$C \rightarrow B : E_{SK_{CB}}(ID_C, ID_V, ID_T, ID_{pro}, I_C, money, t_1)$$
$$B \rightarrow C : E_{SK_{BC}}(payment) / false$$

Here, *payment*=$(ID_C,ID_V,ID_T,ID_{pro},money,t_2,t_3,Cert_B)$, and $Cert_B=Sig_B(ID_C, ID_V, ID_T, ID_{pro},money,t_2,t_3)$. $Sig_X(M)$ means the X's signature on message M by using our signature algorithm, and $E_{SK}(N)$ denotes encrypted message by session key SK. ID_{pro} is an index of product. t_1 and t_2 are timestamps, and t_3 is an deadline of *payment*.

Payment. Firstly, C and V run the CL-AKE, and then they exchange e-cash and digital product as follows.

$$C \rightarrow V : E_{SK_{CV}}(payment)$$
$$V \rightarrow C : E_{SK_{VC}}(product)$$
$$C \rightarrow V : E_{SK_{CV}}(Sig_C(payment, t_4))$$

In the process, V checks whether *payment* is valid or not. That is, V verifies $Cert_B$ and checks time of validity. If the *payment* is valid, *product* will be sent to C. If C verifies that *product* is valid, C sends a payment confirmation $Sig_C(payment, t_4)$ to V.

Compensation. We introduce compensation sub-protocol to deal with the possible misbehaviors of participants in payment sub-protocol. If dishonest C does not confirm payment after received *product*, V can apply for compensation. V and T run the CL-AKE, and do as follows.

$$V \rightarrow T : E_{SK_{VT}}(payment, product)$$
$$T \rightarrow V : E_{SK_{TV}}(Sig_T(payment, t_5)) / false$$

In the process, T should check the validity of *payment* and *product* (here, assume that T can verify the validity of products. Relevant technology may refer to [14]). If *payment* and *product* are both verified, *payment* is signed with a timestamp t_5 and sent to V by T. Then, T sends *product* to C.

$$T \rightarrow C : E_{SK_{TC}} (product)$$

Settlement. V establishes secure link with B by CL-AKE, and does as follows.

$$V \rightarrow B : E_{SK_{VB}} (payment_1, Sig_{C_1}(payment_1, t), \cdots)$$

B checks e-cash and payment confirmation. If they are both valid, moneys will be deposited into V's account. Note that settlement operations should be finished in the validity of the e-cash, and the payment confirmation signed by C or T is valid. In addition, V can do one-time settlement for multiple e-cashes.

3 Analysis and Discussion

3.1 Proof of Security

Before analyzing CL-SAKE, we review the adversaries in CLC [6]. A CL-SAKE should resist the attacks from two types of adversaries denoted as "AdvI" and "AdvII". An AdvI models an outsider adversary who does not know the *master-key*, but has the ability to replace the public key of any entity with a value of her choice. AdvII models a malicious KGC who knows *master-key*, but cannot replace the user's public key.

We will use the random oracle model extended by Chen [13] and Zhang [11] to model our CL-SAKE. The model is defined by two games between a challenger CH and an adversary $Adv \in \{Adv$I, AdvII$\}$. Adv is modeled by a probabilistic polynomial-time Turing machine. All messages go through the Adv. Participants only respond to the queries by Adv and do not directly communicate among themselves. As the article space limitations, the following brief description is our proof ideas but not details.

Theorem 1. The proposed CL-Sign scheme is existentially unforgeable against chosen message attacks under the CDH intractability assumption.

Proof: If AdvI intends to forge signature of entity i, it needs to have the partial key D_i. If AdvI wants to obtain the D_i, it needs to resolve CDH problem. Suppose that the CDH assumption holds, AdvI cannot forge i's signatures. Meanwhile, in the case of unknown x_i, AdvII also has to resolve CDH problem in order to get x_iQ_i. Thus, suppose that the CDH assumption holds the proposed CL-Sign meets unforgeability.

Theorem 2. The proposed AKE scheme is a secure certificateless AKE protocol.
   The proof of Theorem 2 follows Lemmas 1 - 4.

Lemma 1. In the presence of a benign adversary [13], both participants always agree on the same session key, and this key is distributed uniformly at random.

Proof: Suppose that two parties i and j follow CL-AKE and Adv is benign. They will agree on the same key according to analysis in 2.1. Since r_i and r_j are randomly selected by i and j, the session key can be considered as the output of the cryptographic hash function H_2 on a random input, and is uniformly distributed over $\{0, 1\}^l$. □

Lemma 2. Under the assumptions that the BDH problem is intractable, the advantage of an *Adv*I against our CL-AKE is negligible in the extended random oracle model.

Proof: Note that the *Adv*I is the same as the adversary defined in [13]. Chen had proved that the SCK-1 is secure in the random oracle model. So, CL-AKE extended from SCK-1 is also secure in the *Adv*I model. In order to compute K_i for *Adv*I who impersonates party i, he must request *CH*-query to solve the BDH problem. □

Lemma 3. Under the assumptions that the CDH problem is intractable, the advantage of an *Adv*II against our CL-AKE is negligible in the extended random oracle model.

Proof: Suppose that there exists an *Adv*II who can win the games [11] with a non-negligible advantage $\varepsilon(k)$ in polynomial-time t. Then we can show that there is an algorithm *CH* solved the CDH problem in G_1 with non-negligible probability. That is, given an input (P, aP, bP) (specifically, let $x_iP=aP$ and $r_jP=bP$ for an *Adv*II who impersonates initiator i, or let $x_jP=aP$ and $r_iP=bP$ for an *Adv*II who impersonates responder j), we show how *CH* can solve the CDH problem in G_1, i.e. to compute abP (specifically, x_ir_jP for an un-regular initiator or x_jr_iP for an un-regular responder). □

Lemma 4. Our CL-AKE has the forward secrecy if the CDH problem is hard.

Proof: Suppose that two parties i and j agreed on session key SK_{ij} using our CL-AKE, and later, their private keys were compromised. Let r_i and r_j be the ephemeral secret values used to establish SK_{ij}, and they are not exposed. Clearly, to compute the r_ir_jP without the knowledge of r_i and r_j, the adversary must solve the CDH problem. By the CDH assumption, this is impossible. Hence, our CL-AKE has the forward secrecy. □

Theorem 3. The proposed E-payment protocol achieves the unforgeability and unreusability of e-cash.

Proof: Before generating the e-cash, the identity of C must be verified by B. Hence, the e-cash signed by B is unforgeable. Since the CL-SAKE is secure. In addition, each e-cash is bound up with a specific sale transaction by bank's signature and cannot be used to pay for other products, which realizes the unreusability of e-cash. □

Theorem 4. The proposed E-payment protocol meets the anonymity of users.

Proof: It is easy to see that both C and V do not know any true Identity but ID number and public key of their counterparty in the transaction process. ID number, defined as a random bit string, and public key of user are unrelated with user's Identity. Hence, our E-payment protocol achieves the anonymity of users. □

Theorem 5. The proposed E-payment protocol is a fair exchange protocol.

Proof: Suppose that B and T are honest participants that do not conspire with C or V who would engage in misbehaviors. We identify three misbehaviors of destroying fairness defined in [15]. The details are given as follows.

Case 1. *C* sends an incorrect e-cash to *V* in Payment sub-protocol. *V* will detect an error when he verifies the *Cert$_B$* or timestamp, and would not send product to *C*.

Case 2. *V* receives a valid e-cash but does not deliver correct product to *C*, he would not attain the payment confirmation from *C*. If he wants to obtain the payment confirmation from *T* in compensation sub-protocol, he must send valid product to *T*.

Case 3. *C* receives valid product, but does not send *Sig$_C$(payment,t$_4$)* to *V*. Then, *V* sends compensation request to *T* and receives *Sig$_T$(payment,t$_5$)* from *T*.

Based on above analyses, our E-payment protocol shows good quality of fairness. □

3.2 Comparisons

E-payment protocols have seldom been considered in the certificateless setting. Table 1 compares our scheme with two protocols, a certificateless E-cash scheme proposed by Wang et al [12] and an ID-based E-cash scheme proposed by Wang et al [4].

Table 1. Comparisons among different schemes

schemes	signature	unforgeability	un-reusability	anonymity	fair exchange
[4]	blind	yes	no	user's	traceability
[12]	blind	yes	no	bank's	traceability
our scheme	short	yes	yes	user's	fairness

Different from our scheme, References [4,12] achieve anonymity by employing blind signature, but do not take the un-reusability of E-cash into account. In addition, References [4,12] realize the traceability of behaviors, and we contribute compensation sub-protocol to achieving fairness at the period of exchange. The traceability cannot fully ensure that the protocol is finally fair, for external arbitration is uneasy.

4 Conclusions

Digital product transactions will grow tremendously in the coming years. Well-designed E-payment protocol is a critical successful factor on such transactions, and must ensure unforgeability and un-reusability of e-cash, customer anonymity, and fair exchange. This paper proposes an E-payment protocol based on CL-SAKE that aims at circumventing the key escrow issue inherited in ID-based schemes and the certificate management burden in CA-based cryptosystems. The security of proposed CL-SAKE is proved in the extended random oracle model, and the E-payment scheme ensures all properties listed ahead. Next, the performance evaluating will be implemented to measure whether the protocol performance is acceptable or not.

Acknowledgments. We would like to thank anonymous referees for their useful comments. This work is supported in part by the Major Research plan of the National Natural Science Foundation of China under Grant No.90818028.

References

1. Chaum, D.: Blind signatures for untraceable payments. In: Proceedings of Crypto 1982, pp. 199–203. Springer, Heidelberg (1982)
2. Huang, Y.L., Shieh, S.P., Ho, F.S.: A generic electronic payment model supporting multiple merchant transactions. Compute Security 19(5), 452–465 (2000)
3. Boneh, D., Franklin, M.K.: Identity-based Encryption from the Weil Pairing. In: Kilian, J. (ed.) CRYPTO 2001. LNCS, vol. 2139, pp. 213–229. Springer, Heidelberg (2001)
4. Wang, C.J., Tang, Y., Li, Q.: ID-Based Fair Off-Line Electronic Cash System with Multiple Banks. Journal of Computer Science and Technology 22(3), 487–493 (2007)
5. Chen, X., Zhang, F., Liu, S.: ID-based restrictive partially blind signatures and applications. Journal of Systems and Software 80(2), 164–171 (2007)
6. Al-Riyami, S.S., Paterson, K.G.: Certificateless public key cryptography. In: Laih, C.-S. (ed.) ASIACRYPT 2003. LNCS, vol. 2894, pp. 452–473. Springer, Heidelberg (2003)
7. Lin, S.J., Liu, D.C.: An incentive-based electronic payment scheme for digital content transactions over the Internet. Journal of Network and Computer Applications 32, 589–598 (2009)
8. Yang, J.H., Cheng, C.C.: An Efficient Fair Electronic Payment System Based Upon Non-Signature Authenticated Encryption Scheme. International Journal of Innovative Computing, Information and Control 5(11A), 3861–3873 (2009)
9. Dahlberg, T., Mallat, N., Ondrus, J., Zmijewska, A.: Past, present and future of mobilepayments researcha literature review. Electron Comm. Res. Appl. 7(2), 165–181 (2008)
10. Liu, Z., Hu, Y., Zhang, X., et al.: Certificateless signcryption scheme in the standard model. Information Sciences 180(1), 452–464 (2010)
11. Zhang, L., Zhang, F., Wu, Q., Domingo-Ferrer, J.: Simulatable certificateless two-party authenticated key agreement protocol. Information Sciences 180(2), 1020–1030 (2010)
12. Wang, S., Chen, Z., Wang, X.: A New Certificateless Electronic Cash Scheme with Multiple Banks Based on Group Signatures. In: Proceedings of IEEE International Symposium on Electronic Commerce and Security 2008, pp. 362–366. IEEE Computer Society, Los Alamitos (2008)
13. Chen, L., Cheng, Z., Smart, N.P.: Identity-based key agreement protocols from pairings. Int. J. Inf. Secur. 6(4), 213–241 (2007)
14. Ray, I., Ray, I., Natarajan, N.: An anonymous and failure resilient fair-exchange e-commerce protocol. Decision Support Systems 39(3), 267–292 (2005)
15. Pagnia, H., Vogt, H., Gärtner, F.C.: Fair Exchange. The Computer Journal 46(1), 55–76 (2003)

Short Signature from the Bilinear Pairing

Leyou Zhang[1], Yupu Hu[2], and Qing Wu[3]

[1] Department of Applied Mathematics, Xidian University, Xi'an,
Shaanxi 710071, China
[2] Key Laboratory of Computer Networks and Information Security, Xidian University
[3] School of Automation, Xi'an Institute of Posts and Telecommunications, Xi'an,
710061, China
leyouzhang77@yahoo.com.cn

Abstract. Short digital signatures are essential to ensure the authenticity of messages in low-bandwidth communication channels and are used to reduce the communication complexity of any transmission. A new short signature scheme based on the bilinear pairing in the standard model is introduced. The proposed scheme has short public parameters and the size of the signature achieves 160 bits. In addition, under the n-Exponent Computational Diffie-Hellman Problem(n-CDH), the new scheme is provable security. To the best of authors knowledge, this is the first scheme whose signature size achieves 160 bits based on the bilinear pairing.

Keywords: Short signature, bilinear pairing, standard model, provable security.

1   Introduction

Short signature schemes are needed in environments with space and bandwidth constraints.There are several important practical reasons mentioned in [1] for the desirableness of short signatures. For example, on wireless devices such as PDAs, cell phones, RFID chips and sensors, battery life is the main limitation. Communicating even one bit of data uses significantly more power than executing one 32-bit instruction [2]. Reducing the number of bits to communicate saves power and is important to increase battery life. Also, in many settings, communication is not reliable, and thus the number of bits one has to communicate should be kept as few as possible.

1.1   Related Works

Short signature is an active research area. As mentioned in [3,4], there are two paradigms of shortening signatures at present.

- Shorten the total length of a signature and the corresponding message. In such schemes[5,6], one encodes a part of the message into the signature thus shortening the total length of the message-signature pair. For long messages, one can then achieve a DSA signature overhead of length of 160 bits.

R. Zhu et al. (Eds.): ICICA 2010, LNCS 6377, pp. 111–118, 2010.

- Shorten the signature directly. This technique is to shorten the signature directly while preserving the same level of security. Boneh, Lynn and Shacham [7] used a totally new approach to design such short digital signatures in 2001. Their scheme is based on the Computational Diffie-Hellman (CDH) assumption on elliptic curves with low embedding degree. A number of desirable schemes were proposed at present.

Currently, provable security is the basic requirement for the public key cryptosystem. The provably secure short signature schemes are based on two security model. One is the random oracles model. The other is standard model. Most of practical efficient schemes are provable secure in the random oracles model. Random oracle model is a formal model at present, where a hash function is considered as a black-box that contains a random function. However, many results have shown that security in the random oracle model does not imply the security in the real world. Security in the standard model usually provides a higher security level than security in the random oracle model. Gennaro, Halevi and Rabin [8] firstly proposed practical secure signature schemes under the strong RSA assumption in the standard model. In 2004, Boneh and Boyen [9] proposed a short signature scheme from bilinear groups which is secure under the Strong Diffie- Hellman assumption without using random oracles. Later, Zhang F. *et al*[4], Wei and Yuen [10] also proposed some short signature schemes in the standard model. However, it is also true that schemes providing security in the random oracle model are usually more efficient than schemes secure in the standard model. Table 1 gives a summary of signature size of the different schemes.

Table 1. Signature size of the different schemes

Scheme	[3]	[6]	[7]	[11]	[13]	[14]	[4]	[9]	[10]	[15]
Model	RO	RO	RO	RO	RO	RO	SM	SM	SM	SM
Size(bits)	160	160	160	160	160	320	320	320	320	320

In Table 1, RO and SM denote the random oracle model and standard model respectively. Size is the signature size.

1.2   Our Contribution

We construct a new short signature in the standard model from the bilinear pairing. The size of new signature achieves 160 bits, which is shorter than the available at present. The security of our scheme depends on the n-CDH assumption.

2   Preliminaries

2.1   Bilinear Pairing

Let G and G_1 be two (multiplicative) cyclic groups of prime order p and g be a generator of G. A bilinear map e is a map $e : G \times G \longrightarrow G_1$ with the following properties:

   (i) bilinearity: for all $u, v \in G, a, b \in \mathbb{Z}_p$, we have $e(u^a, v^b) = e(u, v)^{ab}$;
   (ii) non-degeneracy: $e(g, g) \neq 1$;
   (iii) computability: there is an efficient algorithm to compute $e(u, v)$ for all $u, v \in G$.

2.2   Hardness Assumption

Security of our scheme will be reduced to the hardness of the n-CDH problem in the group. We briefly recall the definition of the n-CDH problem:

Definition 1. (n-Exponent Computational Diffie-Hellman Problem) Given a group G of prime order p with generator g and elements $g^a, g^{a^2}, \cdots, g^{a^n} \in G$ where a is selected uniformly at random from $\mathbb{Z}_p$ and $n \geq 1$, the n-CDH problem in G is to compute $g^{a^{n+1}}$.

Note that it was shown in [11] that n-CDH problem is equivalent to CDH problem for $n = 1$.

Definition 2. We say that the (t, ε) n-CDH assumption holds in a group G, if no adversary running in time at most t can solve the n-CDH problem in G with probability at least ε.

2.3   Security Definition

A signature scheme is made up of three algorithms, KeyGen, Sign, and Verify, for generating keys, signing, and verifying signatures, respectively.

The standard notion of security for a signature scheme is called existential unforgeability under a chosen message attack [12-18], which is defined using the following game between a challenger and an adversary A:

Setup: The challenger runs algorithm KeyGen to obtain a public key PK and a private key SK. The adversary A is given PK.

Queries: Proceeding adaptively, A requests signatures on at most q_s messages of his choice $M_1, \cdots, M_{q_s} \in \{0, 1\}$, under PK. The challenger responds to each query with a signature $\sigma_i = Sign(SK, M_i)$.

Forgery: A outputs a pair (M, σ) and wins the game if
   (1) M is not any of $(M_1, \cdots, M_{q_s})$;
   (2) Verify(PK,M, σ)= *Valid*.

We will use a weaker notion of security which we call existential unforgeability under a weak chosen message attack. Here we require that the adversary submit all signature queries before seeing the public key. This notion is defined using the following game between a challenger and an adversary A:

Query: A sends the challenger a list of q_s messages $M_1, \cdots, M_{q_s} \in \{0, 1\}$, where q_i is one of the following:

Response: The challenger runs algorithm KeyGen to generate a public key PK and private key SK. Next, the challenger generates signatures $\sigma_i = Sign(SK, M_i)$. The challenger then gives A the public key PK and signatures σ_i.

Forgery: Algorithm A outputs a pair (M, σ) and wins the game if
(1) M is not any of $(M_1, \cdots, M_{q_s})$;
(2) Verify$(PK, M, \sigma) = Valid$.

Definition 3. A signature scheme is (t, ε) existentially unforgeable under a weak adaptive chosen message attack if no probabilistic polynomial time(running in time at most t) adversary has a non-negligible advantage ε in the above game.

3   New Short Signature from the Bilinear Pairing

In this section, we describe our schemes as follows:

3.1   An Initial Scheme

KeyGen. Let G be a group of prime order p and g be a random generator of G. Pick $\alpha, \alpha_1, \cdots, \alpha_n, \beta_1, \cdots, \beta_n$ in $\mathbb{Z}_p$ at random. Set $g_1 = g^\alpha$. Then choose g_2 randomly in G. The public key is

$$PK = (g, g_1, g_2).$$

The private key is

$$SK = (\alpha, \alpha_1, \cdots, \alpha_n, \beta_1, \cdots, \beta_n).$$

Note: We omit the public keys corresponding to $(\alpha_1, \cdots, \alpha_n, \beta_1, \cdots, \beta_n)$ since they are not used at the phase of *Verify*.

Sign. Message is represented as bit-strings of length n. Let $M = (m_1, \cdots, m_n)$ be a n-bit message to be signed, where $m_i \in \{0, 1\}$. Signer first generates the auxiliary information parameters as follows: Let $h_0 = g$, then for $i = 1, \cdots, n$, compute

$$h_i = (h_{i-1})^{\alpha_i^{m_i} \beta_i^{1-m_i}}.$$

The auxiliary information parameter h_n is published as public key. Then the signature is computed as

$$\sigma = (\sigma_1, \sigma_2) = ((g_2 h_n)^\alpha, h_n).$$

Verify. Given the signature σ, message M and the public keys, verifier accepts the signature if and only if the following holds.

$$e(\sigma_1, g) = e(g_1, g_2\sigma_2).$$

Correctness: If σ is valid, one can obtain

$$e(\sigma_1, g) = e((g_2 h_n)^\alpha, g) = e(g_2 h_n, g^\alpha) = e(g_1, g_2\sigma_2).$$

3.2   New Short Signature Scheme

KeyGen. Let G be a group of prime order p and g be a random generator of G. Pick $\alpha, \alpha_1, \cdots, \alpha_n, \beta_1, \cdots, \beta_n$ in $\mathbb{Z}_p$ at random. Set $g_1 = g^\alpha$. Then choose g_2 randomly in G. Compute $t_{0i} = e(g_1, g^{\alpha_i})$ and $t_{1i} = e(g_1, g^{\beta_i})$ for $1 \le i \le n$. The public key is

$$PK = (g, g_1, g_2, \{t_{0i}\}, \{t_{1i}\}, v),$$

where $v = e(g_1, g_2)$. The private key is

$$SK = (\alpha, \alpha_1, \cdots, \alpha_n, \beta_1, \cdots, \beta_n).$$

Sign. Message is represented as bit-strings of length n. Let $M = (m_1, \cdots, m_n)$ be a n-bit message to be signed, where $m_i \in \{0, 1\}$. Signer first generates the auxiliary information parameters as follows: Let $h_0 = g$, then for $i = 1, \cdots, n$, compute

$$h_i = (h_{i-1})^{\alpha_i^{m_i} \beta_i^{1-m_i}}.$$

The auxiliary information parameter h_n is published as public key. Then the signature is computed as

$$\sigma = (g_2 h_n)^\alpha.$$

Verify. Given the signature σ, message M and the public keys, verifier accepts the signature if and only if the following holds.

$$e(\sigma, g) = v \prod_{i=1}^{n} p_i,$$

where

$$p_i = \begin{cases} t_{0i} \ if \ m_i = 1 \\ t_{1i} \ if \ m_i = 0 \end{cases}.$$

Correctness: If σ is valid, one can obtain

$$e(\sigma, g) = e((g_2 h_n)^\alpha, g) = e(g_2 h_n, g^\alpha) = e(g_1, g_2) e(g_1, h_n)$$

$$= v e(g_1, g^{\sum_{i=1}^{n} \alpha_i^{m_i} \beta_i^{1-m_i}}) = v \prod_{i=1}^{n} e(g_1, g^{\alpha_i^{m_i} \beta_i^{1-m_i}}) = v \prod_{i=1}^{n} p_i.$$

3.3   Efficiency

The size of our initial scheme achieves $2|G_1|$ which is similar with the previous schemes in the standard model. But our new scheme has a signature of 160 bits. It is the shortest signature in the standard model at present. Table 2 gives the comprehensive comparison among our signature scheme and other schemes. We

Table 2. Comparison of Efficiency

Scheme	Hardness	Security Model	Signature Size	Verify
[4]	k+1-SRP	Standard	320	$2e$
[9]	q-SDH	Standard	320	$2e$
Ours	n-CDH	Standard	160	$1e$

assume that all these short signature schemes are using the GDH group derived from the curve $E/F_{3^{163}}$ defined by the equation $y^2 = x^3 - x + 1$. This group provides 1551-bit discrete log security.

Note: In Table 2, we denote by e a computation of the pairing.

4   Security Proof

We only give the security proof of our second scheme since the proof of the first one is similar with it.

Theorem. If n-CDH assumption holds, then our scheme is secure.

Proof: Assume that there is an an adversary A that breaks the proposed scheme with advantage ε, we show how to build an adversary B that solves the decisional n-CDH problem with advantage $\frac{\varepsilon}{2n}$. For a generator $g \in G$ and $\alpha, c \in Z_p$, set $y_i = g^{\alpha^i} \in G$. Algorithm B is given as input a random tuple $(g, y_1, \cdots, y_n)$. B works by interacting with A as follows:

Init. A first outputs a message $M^* = (m_1^*, \cdots, m_n^*)$ that it wants to attack.

Setup. To generate the system parameters, B sets $g_1 = y_1$. Then it selects randomly a $\gamma \in Z_p^*$ and sets $g_2 = y_n g^\gamma = g^{\alpha^n + \gamma}$. It chooses $a, \alpha_i, \beta_i \in Z_p^*$ for $1 \le i \le n$ and computes

$$g_{0i} = \begin{cases} g^{\alpha_i} & if \ m_i^* = 0 \\ y_1^{\alpha_i} & if \ m_i^* = 1 \end{cases},$$

$$g_{1i} = \begin{cases} y_1^{\beta_i} & if \ m_i^* = 0 \\ g^{\beta_i} & if \ m_i^* = 1 \end{cases},$$

where $1 \le i \le n$. It implicitly sets to private key
$$(a\alpha, \alpha_i \alpha^{m_i^*}, \beta_i \alpha^{1-m_i^*}), 1 \le i \le n,$$
and the public key
$$PK = (g, g_1, g_2, \{t_{0i}\}, \{t_{1i}\}, v)$$
where $t_{0i} = e(g_1, g_{0i})$, $t_{1i} = e(g_1, g_{1i})$ for $1 \le i \le n$ and $v = e(g_1, g_2)$.

Signature Queries. A issues up to q private signature queries. Each query q_i works as follows: Suppose A asks for the signature corresponding to an message $M_i = (m_{i1}, \cdots, m_{in})$. The only restriction is that $M_i \ne M^*$. It means that there exists at least an j such that $m_{ij} \ne m_j^*$. To respond the query, B first derives the auxiliary information parameters as follows:

$$h_1' = \begin{cases} g^{\alpha_1^{m_{i1}} \beta_1^{1-m_{i1}}} & if \ m_{i1} \ne m_1^* \\ y_1^{\alpha_1^{m_{i1}} \beta_1^{1-m_{i1}}} & if \ m_{i1} = m_1^* \end{cases},$$

$$h_2' = \begin{cases} h_1^{\alpha_2^{m_{i2}} \beta_2^{1-m_{i2}}} & if \ m_{i2} \ne m_2^* \\ y_1^{\alpha_2^{m_{i2}} \beta_2^{1-m_{i2}}} & if \ m_{i2} = m_2^* \wedge m_{i1} \ne m_1^* \\ y_2^{\alpha_2^{m_{i2}} \beta_2^{1-m_{i2}}} & if \ m_{i2} = m_2^* \wedge m_{i1} = m_1^* \end{cases}$$

$\vdots$

Finally, $H' = (h_0(= g), h'_1, \cdots, h'_n)$ is obtained. For simplify, we suppose that k denotes the number of positions such that $v_i = v_i^*$. Then one can obtain $h'_n = y_k^{\tau(M_i)}$, where $\tau(M_i) = \prod_{j=1}^{n} \alpha_i^{m_{ij}} \beta_i^{1-m_{ij}}$ and $k < n$. Finally, B sets $h_i = h'_i/(y_n g^\gamma)$ and constructs the signature as follows:

$$\sigma = (h'_n)^{a\alpha}.$$

In fact, one can obtain

$$\sigma = (h'_n)^{a\alpha}$$
$$= (y_n g^\gamma h'_n/(y_n g^\gamma))^{a\alpha}$$
$$= (g_2 h_n)^{a\alpha}$$

Thus, B can derive a valid signature for M_i.

Notice that, from the received inputs, A gets no information at all about the M^* chosen by B, thus such a choice will be identical to the challenge message with probability $1/2^n$.

Forgery. Finally, A outputs a forged signature σ^* for M^*. Using this signature, B can give the solution to the given the n-CDH problem. In fact,

$$\sigma^* = (g_2 h_n)^{a\alpha} = g_2^{a\alpha}(h_n)^{a\alpha} = y_{n+1}^a g_1^{a\gamma}(h_n)^{a\alpha}.$$

If σ^* is valid, then $h_n = y_k^{\tau(M^*)}$ and $(h_n)^{a\alpha} = y_{k+1}^{\tau(aM^*)}$. Hence

$$(\sigma^*/(y_{k+1}^{a\tau(M^*)} g_1^{a\gamma}))^{a^{-1}} = y_{n+1}.$$

Probability. Following the above, if A has an advantage ε against our scheme, B will solve the decisional n-CDH problem with advantage $\frac{\varepsilon}{2^n}$.

5   Conclusion

In this paper, we propose a short signature scheme which is more efficient than other short signature schemes proposed so far. Based on the n-CDH problem, we provide a rigorous proof of security for our scheme in the standard model.

Acknowledgements

This work is supported in part by the Nature Science Foundation of China under grant 60970119,60803149 and the National Basic Research Program of China(973) under grant 2007CB311201.

References

1. Bellare, M., Neven, G.: Multi-signatures in the plain public-key model and a general forking lemma. In: Proceedings of the 13th ACM Conference on Computer and Communication Security, pp. 390–398 (2006)
2. Barr, K., Asanovic, K.: Energy aware lossless data compression. In: Proceedings of the ACM Conference on Mobile Systems, Applications and Services (2003)
3. Tso, R., Okamoto, T.: Efficient Short Signatures from Pairing. In: 2009 Sixth International Conference on Information Technology: New Generations, pp. 417–422. IEEE Press, New York (2009)
4. Zhang, F., Chen, X., Susilo, W., Mu, Y.: A new short signature scheme without random oracles from bilinear pairings, Cryptology ePrint Archive, Report 2005/386 (2005), http://eprint.iacr.org/2005/386.pdf
5. Tso, R., Gu, C., Okamoto, T., Okamoto, E.: Efficient ID-based digital signatures with message recovery. In: Bao, F., Ling, S., Okamoto, T., Wang, H., Xing, C. (eds.) CANS 2007. LNCS, vol. 4856, pp. 47–59. Springer, Heidelberg (2007)
6. Zhang, F., Susilo, W., Mu, Y.: Identity-based partial message recovery signatures (or How to shorten IDbased signatures). In: S. Patrick, A., Yung, M. (eds.) FC 2005. LNCS, vol. 3570, pp. 45–56. Springer, Heidelberg (2005)
7. Boneh, D., Lynn, B., Shacham, H.: Short signatures from the Weil pairing. In: Boyd, C. (ed.) ASIACRYPT 2001. LNCS, vol. 2248, pp. 514–532. Springer, Heidelberg (2001)
8. Gennaro, R., Halevi, S., Rabin, T.: Secure hash-and-sign signature without the random oracle. In: Stern, J. (ed.) EUROCRYPT 1999. LNCS, vol. 1592, pp. 123–139. Springer, Heidelberg (1999)
9. Boneh, D., Boyen, X.: Short signatures without random oracles. In: Cachin, C., Camenisch, J.L. (eds.) EUROCRYPT 2004. LNCS, vol. 3027, pp. 56–73. Springer, Heidelberg (2004)
10. Wei, V.K., Yuen, T.H.: More Short Signatures without Random Oracles.Cryptology ePrint Archive: Report 2005/463
11. Zhang, F., Safavi-Naini, R., Susilo, W.: An efficient signature scheme form bilinear pairing and its application. In: Bao, F., Deng, R., Zhou, J. (eds.) PKC 2004. LNCS, vol. 2947, pp. 277–290. Springer, Heidelberg (2004)
12. Goldwasser, S., Micali, S., Rivest, R.: A digital signature scheme secure against adaptive chosenmessage attacks. SIAM J. Comput. 17(2), 281–308 (1988)
13. Du, H., Wen, Q.: Efficient and provably-secure certificateless short signature scheme from bilinear pairings. Computer Standards and Interfaces 31, 390–394 (2009)
14. Shao, Z.: A provably secure short signature scheme based on discrete logarithms. Information Sciences 177, 5432–5440 (2007)
15. Kang, L., Tang, X., Lu, X.: A Short Signature Scheme in the Standard Model. Cryptology ePrint Archive, Report 2007/398 (2007), http://eprint.iacr.org/2007/398.pdf
16. Zhang, F., Chen, X., Mu, Y.: A new and efficient signature on commitment values. International Journal of Network Security 7(1), 100–105 (2008)
17. Zhang, M., Yang, B., Zhong, Y.: Cryptanalysis and Fixed of Short Signature Scheme without Random Oracle from Bilinear Parings. International Journal of Network Security 12(2), 159–165 (2011) (Will appear)
18. Guo, F., Mu, Y., Chen, Z.: Efficient batch verification of short signatures for a single-signer setting without random oracles. In: Matsuura, K., Fujisaki, E. (eds.) IWSEC 2008. LNCS, vol. 5312, pp. 49–63. Springer, Heidelberg (2008)

The Construction of an Individual Credit Risk Assessment Method: Based on the Combination Algorithms

Jiajun Li, Liping Qin, and Jia Zhao

Economics Research center, Northwestern Polytechnical University
Xi'an, Shaanxi, P.R. China, 710129
aiqinliping@sina.com

Abstract. As the rapid growth of personal credit business, we have always been seeking to establish an effective risk assessment model to achieve low costs and better accuracy of decision-making. Over the past few years, the so-called combined algorithms have appeared in many fields, but they are always useless in the field of individual credit risk assessment. So we constructed a practical method based on combined algorithms, and we tested it empirically. The result shows that the application of the method can achieve better accuracy than the BP neural network.

Keywords: risk assessments, combined algorithms, accuracy.

1 Introduction

Credit risk assessment is a method to predict the corresponding credit risk, and financial institutions can use the models based on this method to assess the risk of a loan. With the extension of personal financial services, there is the risk loss of loan default. More and more Chinese scholars are doing research on the individual credit risk, but it is still difficult to get rid of the main subjective inference[1] . The application of combined algorithms has always been one of the popular individual credit risk assessment areas. Some combined classification algorithms has been used to identify risks. In fact, it is a key issue of the application to improve the accuracy of credit risk assessment, because the improvement of the accuracy will save enormous assessment costs. In fact, the work in both the machine learning and statistical pattern recognition shows that combined classification algorithms are the effective technique to improve the classification accuracy[2] , because the credit risk assessment methods based on combined algorithms can effectively overcome the single credit risk assessment techniques in the assessment. Based on this, we constructed a method based on principal component analysis, decision trees, cluster analysis, discriminant analysis technique, and applied it to individual credit risk assessment.

R. Zhu et al. (Eds.): ICICA 2010, LNCS 6377, pp. 119–126, 2010.

2   The Way and Structure Used to Construct the Method

The combination of algorithms is to train more than one classification algorithm with the same task, and then combine the results of all the algorithms. To construct a combination, we need to choose the proper method and structure.

According to Bhekisipho Twala (2010), the common methods to construct a combination include bagging[3][4], boosting[5][6][7], stacking[8]. Both of the first two use the classification algorithms generated by the same dataset. The last one can get a combination based on different learning algorithms. Therefore, we use the last one to construct a method (that is, a combination) to assess individual credit risks.

Multiple classifier systems can be classified into three architectural types[9]: static parallel (SP), multi-stage (MS) and dynamic classifier selection (DCS). Because the DCS is more flexible and adaptable, we use it to construct the method.

3   To Design the Method

Common theories of credit risk assessment include[1] : the standard theory of mathematical statistics and the data mining theory. Some of the standard theory of mathematical statistics can be used for individual credit risk assessment, which are linear probability models, Logit models, Probit models, and discriminant analysis. And the individual credit risk assessment methods of data mining theory include classification (the models are the ones such as decision trees models, neural networks etc.), clustering, association rules analysis, forecasting, surveillance and other isolated spots.

According to Xu Xiangyang's research[1] we constructed the method as follows: First, use the Principal Component Analysis (PCA) to identify the main factors from a number of individual credit risk factors; Second, classify the sample dataset based on Decision Trees (DTs) , and get m subsets of samples; Third, do the Cluster Analysis (CA) for each subset, and obtain the sub-cluster sample sets on behalf of the local distributions; fourth, do the Discriminant Analysis(DA) for the testing dataset to which the results of the classification is well known, and get the accuracy of the method (Fig. 1 shows an example).

3.1   The Principal Component Analysis

The Principal Component Analysis[10] (PCA) is a method of data dimensionality, and its basic idea is to recombine a certain number of relevant indicators into a new group of comprehensive indicators unrelated to each other to replace the original indicators. The number of the new indicators is smaller, which keep the principal information of the original ones, so the advantages of the PCA are obvious. First, it reduces the number of indicators; second, it maintains the original information; third, it eliminates the correlation between indicators.

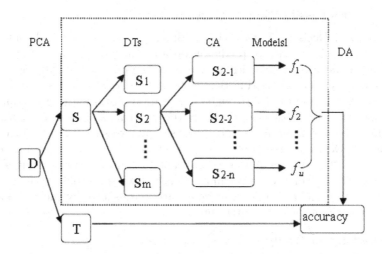

Fig. 1. This is the general view of the method. D presents the whole dataset. S presents the training dataset. S_i ($i=1,2,\cdots,m$) presents the i-th subset of S. S_{i-j}($i=1,2,\cdots,m$) ($j=1,2,\cdots,n$) presents the j-th sub-cluster sample set of the i-th subset of S. T presents the testing dataset.

Because, in general, the contributions of the given indicators in personal credit datasets are different, we have to get rid of the ones with lower contributions. So we do the Principal Component Analysis to get the key indicators. Steps to apply the Principal Component Analysis to the individual credit risk data processing are as follows:

First, construct the original data matrix according to the indicators:

$$X = \begin{bmatrix} x_{11} & x_{12} & \cdots & x_{1p} \\ x_{21} & x_{22} & \cdots & x_{2p} \\ \vdots & \vdots & \ddots & \vdots \\ x_{n1} & x_{n2} & \cdots & x_{np} \end{bmatrix} = (X_1, X_2, \cdots, X_p) \tag{1}$$

Second, the dimensions of the selected indicators are different, and we need to eliminate the impact of the dimensions, so we standardize the original indicators. So we make the following change: $x_{ij}^* = (x_{ij}-\overline{x_j})/s_j$ (i=1,2,$\cdots$,n; j=1,2,$\cdots$,p). Here, set $x_{ij}-\overline{x_j}=\lambda$, then $\overline{x_j}=\sum\limits_{i=1}^{n} x_{ij}/n$, $s_j^2=\sum\limits_{i=1}^{n} \lambda^2/(n-1)$ (j=1,2,$\cdots$,p).

Then, calculate the correlation matrix and the Eigen values and eigenvectors of the correlation matrix.

At last, calculate the principal components, and range the obtained Eigen values by the principle of descending order, and we can determine the number of main factors by the standard of 85% [11] or more of the accumulated variance contribution rates. Finally, get the feature vector, and then we can determine the final principal components and related factors.

3.2   The Pre-classification of Decision Trees

The method of Decision Trees (DTs) is different from all other classification methods for the invariance of predictor variables in its monotone transformation, and this invariance provides immunity to the presence of extreme values. Here, we use the method[12] Hua Bei used and the Decision Trees algorithm to classify the training dataset for rough classifications. Decision trees can predict their respective credit classes according to the applicant's attributes. In order to determine the class of an unknown type of sample, we should firstly start from the root of a Decision Tree. Then decide whether to continue according to the classification attribute value, and if you want to continue, which node should you choose, the left or the right child node. And we shall continue it until we reach the end or the leaf node. The target attribute shown by the leaf node is the predict value of the target attribute.

3.3   The Cluster Analysis

The Cluster analysis is a mathematical statistics method to classify the data with similar characteristics[13] . Because its classification results are almost free from the influence of data errors or anomalies, cluster analysis performs better in individual credit risk assessments, compared with other data mining methods. We do the Cluster Analysis for the subset of each leaf node, and get the sub-cluster sample set on behalf of the local distribution.

The following six steps[14] shows the process to cluster the personal credit data: choose the variables; standardize the data; calculate the similarity (distance) matrix; choose the clustering technology; determine the number of classes; interpret the results of clustering. And they focus on the choice of clustering technology. We choose the CURE[15] (clustering algorithm representatives) in this paper. Set the sample sets as $S=\{S_i\}(i=1,2,\cdots,m)$, and the steps to use the CURE for individual credit risk assessments are as follows:

(1)Use the Hierarchical Cluster Procedures to cluster S_i, and get the initial guess of the classifications, then speed up the algorithm;

(2)Reject the outliers by using the following method:
If {a class growths slowly}
Then {reject the class}
And if {the number of the classes is lower than the threshold }
Then {delete the classes of only one or two data}

(3)Cluster the local classes. Use the representative points in step (1) to represent the various classes, and shrink or move to the center of the class according to the shrinkage factor α .

(4)Label the samples with the corresponding class labels, and we can get the sub-cluster sample sets $S_{i-j}(i=1,2,\cdots,m)$ $(j=1,2,\cdots,n)$.

From the description of the algorithm, we know that in the algorithm there are both hierarchical clustering method of composition and the division of the components. The advantage of it is its better ability to eliminate the noise and deal with isolated points, and it can form any shapes of the classes. For large databases, it has better scalability in the premise of the quality of clustering.

3.4   Fit the Models

We can fit the sub-cluster sample sets $S_{i-j}(i=1,2,\cdots,m)$ $(j=1,2,\cdots,n)$ to models one by one. For each sub-cluster sample set, the specific modeling method can be the method based on neural network, fuzzy C-means clustering algorithm, genetic algorithm, expert scoring method etc. Here, we recommend the BP artificial neural network model to fit the sub-cluster sample sets, and then we can get their respective distribution functions $f_v(v=1,2,\cdots,u)$.

As a non-parametric method, the BP artificial neural network model overcomes the traditional methods in the abilities of the comprehensive analysis and the overall generalization, and it can improve the evaluation results.

3.5   The Discriminant Analysis

Now we separately set the mean value and the covariance of $S_{i-j}(i=1,2,\cdots,m)$ $(j=1,2,\cdots,n)$ as μ_{i-j} and $\Sigma_{i-j}(i=1,2,\cdots,m)$ $(j=1,2,\cdots,n)$. In order to determine that a given sample s is from which sub-cluster data set, we classify s according to the standard of the smallest distance. Specific methods are as follows:

(1)Calculate the Mahalanobis distance $d_{i-j}^2(s)$ $(i=1,2,\cdots,m)$ $(j=1,2,\cdots,n)$ between the sample s and every sub-cluster sample set;

(2)Compare the size of each $d_{i-j}^2(s)$ $(i=1,2,\cdots,m)$ $(j=1,2,\cdots,n)$, and classify s as the sub-cluster sample set which has the smallest distance. And its implementation is as follows:

If $\{d_{k-l}^2(s) = \min\{d_{i-j}^2(s)|i=1,2,\cdots,m;j=1,2,\cdots,n\}\}$

Then$\{s \epsilon s_{i-j}\}$

3.6   The Calculation of the Accuracy

Through the Discriminant Analysis, we know which one within the testing dataset belongs to which sub-cluster sample set, and can use the corresponding distribution function $f_v(v=1,2,\cdots,u)$ to get the corresponding function value, that is, the credit score g . For the convenience of the calculation, it is assumed that the applicants are only divided into two kinds:G("good") and B("bad") (of course, in reality they will be divided into more levels[16]). Provide that if $g \geq g_0$ (g_0 is a given value, which can be determined according to the actual situation), then provide the loans, or else refuse the application. Then we can compare the results obtained from this method to the real situations, and calculate the accuracy of the method. The specific calculation method is $p = t/T$, and p presents the accuracy of the method, T presents the number of the applicants within the testing dataset, t presents the number of the samples which are classified wrongly.

Of course, we can also measure the method by the costs of the loans, and if we set the cost as C, then we can get the computational method as follows:

If{the predicted class is the same as the real one}, Then{c=0};

And if {reject G}, Then {c=C_1};

And if {provide loans to B}, Then {c=C_2}. ($C_1 > C_2 > 0$)

4   The Empirical Analysis

To test the practicality of the proposed method, we tested it empirically, and designed a contrast experiment. Because we focused on the accuracy of this individual credit risk assessment, we designed the contrast experiment without regarding to the run time.

4.1   The Introduce of the Dataset

This paper introduced the UCI German credit dataset which had been successfully used in many papers[17] . The dataset contains a total of 1,000 samples, and each sample has 20 attributes (including 7 numerical attributes and 13 categorical ones).

4.2   The Processes of the Analysis

First, we attempted to use the Principal Component Analysis or Factor Analysis to get a series of indicators which is the most explanatory from the given ones. However, because each indicator within this dataset is independent of others, we introduced all the 20 indicators to the Empirical Analysis. The whole dataset was divided into the training dataset and the testing dataset randomly according to the principle of 400 : 600.

Second, when using the decision tree for pre-classification, we took the discrete condition attribute (that is, the purpose of loan) as the nodes of the decision tree, and divided the training dataset roughly. Then we got 10 subsets, that is S_i (i=1,2,$\cdots$,10).

Third, to apply the CURE, we used the CLUSTER process of SAS to analysis S_i (i=1,2,$\cdots$,10) respectively. And then we used the BP artificial neural network model to model each sub-cluster sample set $S_{i-j}(i=1,2,\cdots,m)$ $(j=1,2,\cdots,n)$ one by one.

At last, by using the DISCRIM process of SAS, we do the Discriminant Analysis for the testing dataset. Referring to the experimental results which LI Jiajun (2008) got, we set: $g_0 = 60$. Comparing to the given results, we knew $p = t/T = 73.51\%$.

4.3   The Comparison of Experimental Results

Through the comparative study, Abdou, etc. gave the result that the average rate of the neural network model to classify is higher than that of other methods[18]. Khashman applied the BP neural network model to the same dataset as we used in this paper, and got the result that the highest accuracy of the testing dataset is 73.17% [19]. However the method we proposed here can achieve the accuracy of 73.51% when it's used to assess the testing dataset, which is better than that of the neural network model. So it proved that this method of the standard theory of mathematical statistics and the data mining theory could avoid the deficiencies of the single algorithm and get better predictions.

5 Conclusions

We propose a method based on combined algorithms which is different from the ones that just combine the machine learning approaches. It is the rational combination of the standard theory of mathematical statistics and the data mining theory and it can be used for personal credit classification. The Empirical Analysis proved that this method can be effectively applied in practice, and has a higher accuracy of prediction than that of the BP artificial neural network model.

Of course, this is just an ordinary method. In fact, because the results of the same dataset is limited, there is not any combined algorithm which is best for all the datasets. So the future research could focus on the design of specific combined algorithms for specific datasets and the simulation studies.

References

1. Xiangyang, X., Jike, G.: Research on Personal Credit Scoring Model based on Clustering. Financial Electronics 9, 229–231 (2006)
2. Kittler, J., Hatef, M., Duin, R.P.W., Matas, J.: On combining classifiers. IEEE Transaction on Pattern Analysis and Machine Intelligence 20, 226–239 (1998)
3. Breiman, L.: Bagging predictors. Machine Learning 26, 123–140 (1996)
4. Bauer, E., Kohavi, R.: An empirical comparison of voting classification algorithms: Bagging, boosting and variants. Machine Learning 36, 105–139 (1999)
5. Schapire, R.: The strength of weak learns ability. Machine Learning 5, 197–227 (1990)
6. Drucker, H., Cortes, C., Jackel, L.D., Lecun, Y., Vapkin, V.: Boosting and other ensemble methods. Neural Computation 6, 1289–1301 (1994)
7. Freund, Y., Schapire, R.: A decision theoretic generalization of on-line learning and an application to boosting. Journal of Computing and Systems 55, 119–139 (1996)
8. Wolpert, D.: Stacked generalization. Neural Networks 5, 241–259 (1992)
9. Twala, B.: Multiple classifier application to credit risk assessment. Expert Systems with Applications 37, 3326–3336 (2010)
10. Jiuqing, H.: System Engineering. China Statistical Publishing House, Beijing (1999)
11. Yuanzheng, W., Yajing, X.: Cause of SAS software applications and statistics. Mechanical Industry Publishing House, Beijing (2007)
12. Bei, H.: Research on credit card approval models based on data mining technology. Computer Engineering and Design 6, 2989–2991 (2008)
13. Everitt, B.: Cluster analysis. Halsted-Wiley, New York (1974)
14. Hegazy, Y.A., Mayne, P.W.: Objective site characterization using clustering of piezocone data. Geotechnical Engineering Division 128, 986–996 (2002)
15. Guha, S., Rastogi, R., Shim, K.: Cure: an efficient clustering method for large databases. In: Proc. 1998 ACM-SIGMOD Int. Conf. Management of Data (DIGMOD 1998), Seattle, WA, pp. 73–84 (June 1998)
16. Jiajun, L., Yaya, L.: The improvement of the customer credit rating Based on subjective default. Financial forum 3, 26–30 (2008)

17. Asuncion, A., Newman, D.J.: UCI Machine Learning Repository. University of California School of Information and Computer Science, Irvine (2007)
18. Abdou, H., Pointon, J., Elmasry, A.: Neural nets versus conventional techniques in credit scoring in Egyptian banking. Expert Systems and Applications 35, 1275–1292 (2008)
19. Khashman, A.: Neural networks for credit risk evaluation: Investigation of different neural models and learning schemes. Expert Systems with Applications (2010)

Method for Evaluating QoS Trustworthiness in the Service Composition

Lei Yang, Yu Dai, and Bin Zhang

College of Information Science and Engineering, Northeastern University
yanglei@ise.neu.edu.cn

Abstract. QoS driven service selection as an important way to satisfy user's constraint on quality and maintain the runtime performance of services, has received much attention. This paper proposes a method for evaluating the QoS trustworthiness which reflects the possibility that the service can perform as its estimated QoS. Besides this, trustworthiness QoS driven service selection is also proposed. The experiments shows the proposed approach can reflect the dependent relation between estimated QoS and the environmental context effectively, and can insure the accuracy of trustworthiness evaluation. Meantime, the proposed service selection approach can improve the actual runtime performance of the selected service.

Keywords: Service; service selection; QoS; trustworthiness.

1 Introduction

With the development of web service, composing available services to satisfy user's requirement has become an important way to constructing the application [1]. Since services run in a highly variable environment, their quality may change which will affect the performance of the composite service. For this problem, researchers have done a lot of works in the field of QoS driven service selection [2, 3, 4].

Currently, most of these works assume that the estimated QoS is absolutely effective and unchangeable. However, in the reality, the assumption cannot always be held on. One of the important reasons is that the difference between the historical reflected data about the quality is always neglected. For example, the response time of a service in the daytime may be a big difference from the response time at night due to the change of the network traffic. Similarly, the response time of a service will be changed when the environment to access the service is changed due to the user of the service moving to another place. Then, directly using an approach of computing the average (which is always used by several works) response time to give an estimated QoS may cause the estimated one far from the actual one. Another important reason is that at the beginning the reflected data of the QoS may be a small amount. Then the method by computing the average to estimate QoS cannot reflect the real situation. For example, service A is invoked 100 times, 90 of which are invoked successfully. If using the current method, the success rate is 0.9 by computing the average. Imaging there is another service B invoked 10 times, 9 of which are successfully invoked. If using the current method, the success rate is also 0.9 by computing the average. In the

R. Zhu et al. (Eds.): ICICA 2010, LNCS 6377, pp. 127–134, 2010.

reality, service users would like to trust the QoS of A since it is invoked more times. However, the average method cannot distinguish these situations. Then, using such an estimated QoS to select services for the application cannot meet the user's require-ment. And then a re-selection or the punishment will be needed which may cause extra delay or the punishing cost [5].

In this paper, we propose a method for evaluating the probability (here, we name it QoS trustworthiness) that the service can perform as its estimated QoS. In the method, the estimated QoS is computed with the consideration of the environment factors, which can ensure the personalized QoS estimation. Besides this, the ways for evaluat-ing the QoS trustworthiness in the large and small number of reflected data respectively are given. Then, the paper presents how to put the proposed QoS and its trustworthiness into the problem of service selection and the experiments shows the better performance of the approach.

2   Method for Evaluating QoS Trustworthiness in the Context of Environment

2.1   Trustworthiness QoS Model

In this paper, for similarity of the description, we use a vector $e=<t, u, ct>$ to express the environment when and who to use the service. Here, t is the time to use the ser-vice, e.g. 8:00-9:00 AM May 1st 2009; u is the service requester; ct is the time interval to use the service, e.g. 8:00-9:00 AM.

As the service runs on the internet, its performance will be affected by the status of the internet, i.e. the network traffic will affect the response time as some service re-ceive the input parameter via the internet. Generally speaking, the network traffic will be different in different time duration, i.e., the daytime's network traffic will be very different from the nights'. Therefore, considering such dependent relation will be important when estimating the QoS. The service can be invoked by different users from different locations. Then, as the location and the preference of the users are different, then the reflected data obtained from them will be different, which will affect the effectiveness of the QoS estimation. For example, a user with good temper may give a good reputation to a service while a user with bad temper who is espe-cially intolerable with the long response time may give a bad evaluation to the same service. Therefore, such an environment may also affect the effectiveness of the QoS estimation. This paper respects these environment factors, aiming at give a QoS value which is closer to the actual one. Then, based on this idea, the formatted definition of the trustworthiness QoS model is given.

Definition 1. Trustworthiness QoS Model. For service s, in the context of environ-ment e, the quality of it can be defined as $QoS_e(s)=<q_e^1(s), q_e^2(s),..., q_e^n(s)>$. Here, $\forall k, 1 \leq k \leq n$, q_e^k is the QoS attribute k, i.e., the response time, $q_e^k(s)$ is the func-tion which gives the estimated value of q_e^k, and $q_e^k(s).v$ (here, for simplicity, we use $v_e^k(s)$ to signify it) is the trustworthiness of the QoS attribute k if the value of k is $q_e^k(s)$.

2.2 Evaluation for QoS Trustworthiness in the Case of Large Number of Reflected Data

In the following, we will discuss the method of QoS estimation in the context of environment. And then the method for evaluation of the QoS trustworthiness is introduced.

In this paper, for simplicity, we use the vector $V_{e,s}$ to signify the estimated QoS value, $V_{e,s}=<v^1_{e,s}, v^2_{e,s}, ..., v^n_{e,s}>$. Here, $\forall i, 1 \leq i \leq n$, $v^i_{e,s}$ is the estimated value of the QoS attribute i of service s in the context of environment e. we use the vector $RQ_{e,s}$ to signify the reflected data in the context of environment e, $RQ_{e,s}=<rq^1_{e,s}, rq^2_{e,s},...,$ $rq^n_{e,s}>$. Here, $\forall j, 1 \leq j \leq n$, $rq^j_{e,s}$ is the reflected value of the QoS attribute i of service s in the context of environment e. The set of the vectors of the reflected data can be signified as $SetRQ_s=\{RQ_{e1, s}, RQ_{e2, s}, ..., RQ_{em, s}\}$. During the different time interval, the reflected data may be different to a large extent. For the relation between the response time and the net speed as well as the computer utility, we will classify the elements in the set of $SetRQ_s$ into 3 classes $SetRQ_s^A$, $SetRQ_s^B$ and $SetRQ_s^C$, according to 3 time interval, that is, the time interval A from 8:01 to 18:00, the time interval B from 18:01 to 23:00 and the time interval C from 23:01 to 8:00. We use $member(RQ_{ek, s}, SetRQ_s^x)$ to signify the membership between $ek.ct$ and x (seen in equation 1). If for each element $RQ_{ek, s}$ in the set $SetRQ_s^T$, the membership between $ek.ct$ and T is the biggest, then the element $RQ_{ek, s}$ is in the set $SetRQ_s^T$ (Here, $T=\{A, B, C\}$).

$$Cover(ek.ct, x) = \begin{cases} 1, ek.ct.down \geq x.down \wedge ek.ct.up \leq x.up \\ \dfrac{x.up - ek.ct.down}{ek.ct.up - e.ct.down}, ek.ct.down \geq x.down \wedge ek.ct.up > x.up \\ \dfrac{ek.ct.up - x.down}{ek.ct.up - e.ct.down}, ek.ct.down < x.down \wedge ek.ct.up \leq x.up \\ 0, ek.ct.down < x.down \wedge ek.ct.up > x.up \end{cases} \tag{1}$$

Here, *down* and *up* are respectively the up and low boundaries of the time interval.

By classifying the elements in the set of $SetRQ_s$, the dependent relationship between the reflected QoS data and the time interval can be shown. Then, in the different time interval the QoS can be estimated personally, which will minimize the distance between the estimated QoS and the actual one. Besides, we also notice that the service requester can also affect the reflected QoS data due to their different locations, different preferences and other factors. That is to say, in the same time interval, different service requesters may report different reflected QoS data. For this reason, to insure the effectiveness of the estimated QoS, such dependent relation between the QoS and the service requester should be considered. This paper will compute the personal estimated QoS by determining which QoS reflected data will be used in the QoS estimation according to the similarity degree of the requester reflected QoS. Definition 2 gives the definition and the way to compute the similarity degree of the requester reflected QoS.

Definition 2. Similarity Degree of the User Reflected QoS. Such degree is used to evaluate the similarity of the reflected QoS data reported by two different service users in the same time interval.

In this paper, according to Reference [6], the services common used by the two service requesters can be seen as a multidimensional space and the reflected QoS vector reported by a service user can be seen as a point in the space. Then, the similarity degree can be computed according to the geometric distance between the points. If the distance is closer, the two requesters will be more similar. Formally, the services common used by the service users u_r and u_i can form a set of $Share^i = \{s_i^1, s_i^2, \ldots, s_i^n\}$. Equation (2) gives the way to compute the similarity degree.

$$SimU(u_r, u_i) = \begin{cases} 1 - \dfrac{1}{n}\sum_{x=1}^{n} SimRQ_x, n \geq 1 \\ 0, n = 0 \end{cases} \tag{2}$$

Here, $SimRQ_x$ is the similarity degree towards the service s_i^x between u_r and u_i (seen in Equation (3)).

$$SimRQ_x = \frac{1}{3} \times \sum_{f=1}^{3} \sqrt[3]{\sum_{y=1}^{k} \frac{\left(\overline{rq_{s_i^x, z_f}^{u_r, y}} - \overline{rq_{s_i^x, z_f}^{u_i, y}}\right)^2}{\left(\overline{rq_{s_i^x, z_f}^{u_r, y}}\right)^2}}{k} \tag{3}$$

Here, $\overline{rq_{s_i^x, z_f}^{u_r, y}}$ and $\overline{rq_{s_i^x, z_f}^{u_i, y}}$ are the average of the reflected data of QoS factor y reported by u_r and u_i in the time interval z_f respectively. Here, z_f can be A, B or C. k is the number of the QoS factors.

When $SimU$ is bigger than the threshold $Threshold_{user}$, the reflected QoS reported by the requester u_r and u_i has a high similarity degree. Then, for a service requester u_r (here, we use the term of service requester to signify the actor who will use the service at time t, and the term service user to signify the actor who has used the service in the past time.) in the time interval ct and at the time t (that is to say, in the context of environment $e = <t, u_r, ct>$), if u_r uses the service s, the estimated QoS of the service can be computed as follows. Imagine the set of the vectors of the reflected data is $SetRQ_s = \{RQ_{e1, s}, RQ_{e2, s}, \ldots, RQ_{em, s}\}$. Firstly, according to the time interval ct, determine which subset of $SetRQ_s$ will be used for estimation. Then, the set $SetRQ_s^A$, $SetRQ_s^B$ or $SetRQ_s^C$ will be chosen. For simplicity, here, we signify such set as $SetRQ_s^X$. Secondly, in the set of $SetRQ_s^X$, determine which reflected data will be used for estimation according to the similarity degree. Then, in the set of $SetRQ_s^X$, the reflected data reported by the user whose similarity degree with the service requester u_r is higher than $Threshold_{user}$ will be used for estimation. We will use $EstimQ_s = \{rq_{e1, s}, rq_{e2, s}, \ldots, rq_{em, s}\}$ to signify the set of reflected data which can be used for QoS estimation. Finally, we will compute the estimated QoS based on $EstimQ_s$ according to the current methods. For the QoS factor q^k, such as response time and reputation, in the context of environment e, the estimated value can be computed as (4).

$$v_E^k = \frac{\sum_i rq_{e_i, s}^k}{n} \tag{4}$$

Here, n is the number of elements in the set of $EstimQ_s$. $rq_{e_i,s}$ is an element in the set of $EstimQ_s$ and $rq^k_{e_i,s}$ is the reflected data of factor k.

As the dynamics of the environment the services operate, the QoS can be changed sometimes which may affect the users' satisfaction. In this sense, it should be measured whether the estimated QoS will be similar to the actual one especially in the dynamic environment. We call such a measurement the QoS trustworthiness. The QoS trustworthiness in this paper is a possibility that the service can perform with the QoS as pre-estimated one.

The changes of the QoS may be caused either by service providers, who can minimize the price for invoking the service, or by the network, whose higher network load may affect the data transmission time. Compared with changes caused by service providers, changes caused by the Network may occur more frequently. Changes caused by the Network may affect the data transmission speed and thus, affect the response time of the composite service. Therefore, we try to predict the response time. In this paper, we will use our former work [7] to compute the possibility that the service can perform with the QoS as expected one (that is, the trustworthiness degree of the response time). As the limitation of the paper, we will not discuss it in detail.

2.3 Evaluation for QoS Trustworthiness in the Case of Small Number of Reflected Data

When the reflected data is small, i.e., the service is newly published, the way for estimating the QoS based on the average computation will not reflect the actual performance of the service. In this situation, the QoS published by the service provider will be used to represent the estimated value. However, the service provider may publish the better QoS as a result of the business interest. In this situation, the trustworthiness QoS should be evaluated also.

Service is published by the service provider. The reputation of the provider is related to the quality of the published service. Thus, in the case of small number of reflected data, the reputation of the service provider can be used to reflect the trustworthiness of the QoS.

The business reputation (BR) is the reputation in the business which the provider belongs to. The business reputation is initially obtained according to the rank of the provider at the time when the service provider is registered. For the limitation of the paper, we will not discuss the problem of how to update the business reputation.

The service reputation (SR) is the trustworthiness of a kind of service provided by the provider. In the interval of e.ct, the SR (seen in Equation (5)) can be computed as the average different degree between the service s and the other services with the same kind as s.

$$SR_e(s.provider) = \begin{cases} \dfrac{\sum_j \sum_x cd_{e_x,s^j}}{n} \\ 0, n = 0 \end{cases} \tag{5}$$

Where, *s.provider* is the provider of service *s*, the services provided by *s.provider* and same kind as service *s* forms a set $PS=\{s^1, s^2, ..., s^n\}$. cd_{e_x,s^i} is the distance between the reflected data and the published QoS of s^i, which can be computed as (6).

$$cd_{e,s} = \sum_k w^k * cd_{e,s}^k \qquad (6)$$

Where, w^k is the user's preference. $cd_{e,s}^k$ is the distance of the QoS factor k between the reflected data and the published QoS of s^i, which can be computed as (7).

$$cd_{e,s}^k = \begin{cases} \dfrac{rq_{e,s}^k - pubQoS^k}{pubQoS^k}, rq_{e,s}^k > pubQoS^k \\ 0, rq_{e,s}^k \le pubQoS^k \end{cases} \qquad (7)$$

Based on the above analysis, in the case of small reflected data, the trustworthiness of QoS of service *s* can be computed as:

$$trust_e = w_{BR} * BR_e(s.provider) + w_{SR} * SR_e(s.provider) \qquad (8)$$

Where, w_{BR} and w_{SR} ($0 \le w_{BR}, w_{SR} \le 1$ and $w_{BR} + w_{SR} = 1$) are the weight of the business and service reputations respectively.

3   Trustworthiness QoS Driven Service Selection

The aim of the trustworthiness QoS driven service selection is to find the service which can satisfy the constraint of the service requester and has the highest utility in the context of the environment *e*. The problem can be formally described as:

$$\max_{s_i \in cand} \{F(s_i, e)\}$$
$$s.t. q^{ik} \le c^k, k \in [1, n] \qquad (9)$$

Where, *cand* is the set of the candidate services which can satisfy the functional requirement of the service requester; c^k is the constraint towards the QoS factor k; $F(s_i, e)$ is the utility of the service and Equation (10) gives its computation.

$$F(s_i, e) = \sum_k t_e^k(s_i) * f_{ik} * wu^k \qquad (10)$$

Where, $t_e^k(s_i)$ is the QoS trustworthiness of QoS factor k of service s_i; f_{ik} is the score of the estimated value of QoS factor k of the service s_i and wu^k is the weight of the QoS factor.

$$f_{ik} = \begin{cases} \dfrac{q_e^k(s_i) - q_{min}^k}{q_{max}^k - q_{min}^k}, q_{max}^k > q_{min}^k \\ \dfrac{q_{min}^k - q_e^k(s_i)}{q_{min}^k - q_{max}^k}, q_{max}^k < q_{min}^k \end{cases} \qquad (11)$$

Where, $q_e^k(s_i)$ is the estimated value of the factor k of the service s_i in the context of e. q^k_{max} and q^k_{min} are the best and worst values of the factor k in the candidate set *cand*. Here, the range of f_{ik} is 0 to 1.

Such a problem is a multi-object optimization, the solution to which is simple. Then, this paper will not discuss how to solve the selection problem in detail.

4 Related Works and Experimentation

In order to satisfy the users' requirements, QoS driven service selection has become a hot issue. Ref.[9] gives a method for QoS prediction based on collaborative filtering. The method considers the dependent relations between the users and the QoS estimation. Similarly, Ref.[10] focuses on the relations between the users and the QoS estimation also and uses a method of computing the reflect similarity to measure the trust-ability of the reflected data. Ref. [8] gives a method for evaluating QoS trustworthiness based on the reflected data. However, this method can be only used in the case of the large number of reflected data. In this section, we will verify the effectiveness of our approach by the experimentation.

Publish 10 new web services and select 10 different users in the testing system. In the same time interval, let the users invoke the services. For each service, after the number of invocation is above 10, 50, 150, 500, 1000 and 2000, use the proposed method to evaluate the QoS trustworthiness. Takes the average trustworthiness of the 10 services and compares the relation between the number of the invocation and the average trustworthiness (seen in Fig. 1).

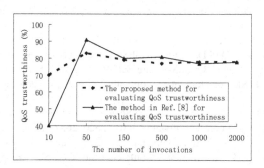

Fig. 1. Relation between the number of the invocation and the QoS trustworthiness

Fig.1 shows that, the QoS trustworthiness computed using the proposed method can ensure the accuracy when the number of invocations is above 500. However, the QoS trustworthiness computed using the method in Ref.[8] can ensure the accuracy when the number of the invocations is above 1000. Meantime, when the number of invocations is small, the QoS trustworthiness computed using the proposed method is closer than the one when the number of invocations is large.

5 Conclusions

This paper proposes a method for evaluating the QoS trustworthiness to reflect the distance between the estimated QoS and the actual one. The contributions of the paper includes: (1) The way for estimating QoS in the context of the environment is presented; (2) The ways for evaluating the QoS trustworthiness in the large and small number of reflected data respectively are given; (3) The proposed QoS and its trustworthiness are put into the problem of service selection. The experimentation shows the better performance of the approach. The work is supported by the national natural science foundations (No. 60903008, 60773218), the Fundamental Research Funds for the Central Universities (No. 90404011) and Dr. start-up foundation of Liaoning Province (No.20091022).

References

1. Yu, Q., Liu, X., Bouguettaya, A., et al.: Deploying and Managing Web Services: Issues, Solutions and Directions. VLDB Journal 17(3), 537–572 (2008)
2. Mohammad, A., Dimitrios, S., Thomas, R.: Selecting Skyline Services for QoS-based Web Service Composition. In: International World Wide Web Conference, pp. 11–20. ACM Press, Raleigh (2010)
3. Zeng, L., Benatallah, B., Ngu, A., et al.: QoS Aware Middleware for Web Services Composition. IEEE Transactions on Software Engineering 30(5), 311–327 (2004)
4. Danilo, A., Barbara, P.: Adaptive Service Composition in Flexible Processes. IEEE Transaction on Software Engineering 33(6), 369–384 (2007)
5. Canfora, G., Penta, M.D., Esposito, R., et al.: QoS-Aware Replanning of Composite Web Services. In: International Conference on Web Services, pp. 121–129. IEEE Press, Orlando (2005)
6. Li, Y., Zhou, M.H., Li, R.C., Cao, D.G., Mei, H.: Service Selection Approach Considering the Trustworthiness of QoS Data. Journal of Software 19(10), 2620–2627 (2008)
7. Dai, Y., Yang, L., Zhang, B.: QoS-Aware Self-Healing Web Service Composition Based on Performance Prediction. Journal of Computer Science and Technology 24(2), 250–261 (2009)
8. Li, Y., Zhou, M.H., Li, R.C., et al.: Service Selection Approach Considering the Trustworthiness of QoS Data. Journal of Software 19(10), 2620–2627 (2008)
9. Shao, L., Zhang, J., Wei, Y., et al.: Personalized QoS Prediction for Web Services via Collaborative Filtering. In: International Conference on Web Service, pp. 439–446. IEEE Press, Salt Lake City (2007)
10. Hu, J.Q., Zou, P., Wang, H.M., Zhou, B.: Research on web Service Description Language QWSDL and Service Matching Model. Chinese Journal of Computers 28(4), 505–513 (2005)

Three-Party Password-Based Authenticated Key Exchange Protocol Based on Bilinear Pairings

Fushan Wei*, Chuangui Ma, and Qingfeng Cheng

Department of Information Research,
Zhengzhou Information Science Technology Institute,
Zhengzhou, 450002, China
weifs831020@163.com

Abstract. Three-party password-based authenticated key exchange (3-party PAKE) protocols enable two communication parties, each shares a human-memorable password with a trusted server, to establish a common session key with the help of the trusted server. We propose a provably-secure 3-party PAKE protocol using bilinear pairings, and prove its security in the random oracle model. The proposed protocol requires four communication steps, which is more efficient than previous solutions in terms of communication complexity. In addition to the semantic security, we also present the authentication security to resist the undetectable on-line dictionary attacks.

Keywords: bilinear pairings, password, three-party, authenticated key exchange, random oracle model.

1 Introduction

Password-based authenticated key exchange (PAKE) protocols allow users to securely establish a common key over an insecure channel only using a low-entropy and human-memorable password. PAKE protocols are widely used for user authentication and secure communications in real applications, such as internet banking and remote user authentication. The problem of designing a secure PAKE protocol was proposed by Bellovin and Merritt [3] in 1992, and has since been studied extensively. A great deal of password authenticated key exchange protocols have been proposed in recent years [4,5,11,17]. Most of them considered different aspects of 2-party PAKE protocols.

Although 2-party PAKE protocols are quite useful for client-server architectures, they are not suitable for large-scale communication environment. In 2-party PAKE scenarios where a client wants to communicate with many other users, the number of passwords that the client needs to remember would be linear in the number of possible partners. It is very inconvenient in key management

---

* This work is supported by the National High Technology Research and Development Program of China (No.2009AA01Z417) and Key Scientific and Technological Project of Henan Province (No. 092101210502).

R. Zhu et al. (Eds.): ICICA 2010, LNCS 6377, pp. 135–142, 2010.
© Springer-Verlag Berlin Heidelberg 2010

for client-to-client communications in large-scale communication environment. To avoid this inconvenience, password-based authenticated key exchange in the 3-party model was proposed.

Due to the practical aspects, 3-party PAKE protocols have been become the subject of extensive work in recent years. The first work of 3-party PAKE protocol was proposed by Needham and Schroeder [9] in 1978, which inspired the Kerberos distributed system. In 1995, Steiner et al. [13] proposed a 3-party PAKE protocol, which was improved by Lin et al. [12] in 1996. In 2005, Abdalla, Fouque and Pointcheval [1] presented a generic construction of 3-party PAKE protocol from any secure two-party PAKE protocol, and this is the first provably-secure PAKE protocol in the 3-party setting. Wang et al. [14] found Abdalla et al.'s generic construction was vulnerable to undetectable on-line dictionary attacks. With enhancing it by adding the authentication security notion for the treatment of undetectable attacks, they presented another generic construction for 3-party PAKE protocols. Even though the generic construction is quite attractive, it is not particularly efficient, and more efficient solutions are preferable. In 2005, Abdalla and Pointcheval [2] also proposed an efficient 3-party PAKE protocol and put forth its security proof by using their security model. Since then, there have been some published works aimed to improve either the security or the communication performance [6,7,10,16].

We consider 3-party PAKE protocols in the asymmetric "PKI model" (where, in addition to a password, the client has the public key of the server), especially those based on bilinear pairings. Although the pairing operation takes high computation, it reduces the communication cost of the protocol significantly. In the wireless-Internet, wireless nodes are devices with particular mobility, computation and bandwidth requirements (cellular phone, pocket PC, palm pilot, laptop computer). The wireless medium places severe restrictions when designing cryptographic mechanisms, such as radio propagation effects, bandwidth, limited battery life, etc. Sometimes it is more important to reduce the communication cost in the wireless-Internet. So 3-party PAKE protocols using bilinear pairings are particularly suitable for implementation on wireless devices. Despite the practical importance, the research on pairing-based 3-party PAKE protocols is far from maturity. Until now, to the best of our knowledge, the only one 3-party PAKE protocol using bilinear pairing was proposed by Wen et.al [15] in 2005, they claimed that their protocol was provably-secure against active adversaries in the random oracle model. However, Nam et al. [8] showed that Wen et al.'s protocol can't resist a man-in-the-middle attack and the claim of provable security was seriously incorrect.

In this paper, we use bilinear pairings to propose a provably-secure 3-party password-based authenticated key exchange protocol, which is a two-round protocol with mutual authentication between the client and the server. We prove the novel protocol is secure in the random oracle model under the hardness of Gap Bilinear Diffie-Hellman (GBDH) problem and Gap Diffie-Hellman (GDH) problem. The protocol can also resist undetectable on-line dictionary attacks. Compared with other kindred protocols in terms of the security properties and efficiency, the proposed protocol has stronger security and higher efficiency in communication cost.

The remainder of this paper is organized as follows. In section 2, we recall the communication model and some security definitions of 3-party PAKE protocols. In section 3, we review some building blocks. Then we propose our scheme and prove its security in section 4. We conclude this paper in section 5.

2   The Formal Model

In this section, we recall the security model for 3-party password authenticated key exchange protocols introduced in [2].

2.1   Communication Model

Protocol participants. The participants in a 3-party PAKE setting consist of two sets: $\mathcal{U}$, the set of all clients and $\mathcal{S}$, the set of trusted servers. The set $\mathcal{S}$ is assumed to involve only a single trusted server for the simplicity of the proof, which can be easily extended to the case considering multiple servers. Here we further divide the set $\mathcal{U}$ into two disjoint subsets: $\mathcal{C}$, the set of honest clients and $\mathcal{E}$, the set of malicious clients. That is, the set of all users $\mathcal{U}$ is the union $\mathcal{U} = \mathcal{C} \cup \mathcal{E}$. The malicious set $\mathcal{E}$ corresponds to the set of inside attackers, who exist only in the 3-party setting.

Long-lived keys. Each client $U \in \mathcal{U}$ holds a password pw_U. Each server $S \in \mathcal{S}$ holds a vector $pw_S = \langle pw_U \rangle_{U \in \mathcal{U}}$ with an entry for each client. pw_U and pw_S are also called the long-lived keys of client U and server S. We consider 3-party PAKE protocols in the asymmetric "PKI model", so in this setting, the server S also has its own public and private key pair, the long-lived key of the server also includes the private key.

Protocol execution. The interaction between an adversary $\mathcal{A}$ and the protocol participants occurs only via oracle queries, which model the adversary's capabilities in a real attack. During the execution, the adversary may create several concurrent instances of a participant. These queries are as follows, where $U^i(S^j$, respectively) denotes the i-th (j-th, respectively) instance of a participant $U(S$, respectively).

- $Execute(U_1^{i_1}, S^j, U_2^{i_2})$: This query models passive attacks, where the attacker gets access to honest executions among the client instances $U_1^{i_1}$ and $U_2^{i_2}$ and trusted server instance S^j by eavesdropping. The output of this query consists of the messages that were exchanged during the honest execution of the protocol.
- $SendClient(U^i, m)$: This query models an active attack against clients, in which the adversary may intercept a message and then either modify it, create a new one, or simply forward it to the intended participant. The output of this query is the message that the participant instance U^i would generate upon receipt of message m.
- $SendServer(S^j, m)$: This query models an active attack against the server, in which the adversary sends a message to server instance S^j. It outputs the message that server instance S^j would generate upon receipt of message m.

- *Reveal*(U^i): This query models the misuse of the session key by instance U^i. The query is only available to $\mathcal{A}$ if the targeted instance actually holds a session key sk and it returns to the adversary the session key sk.
- *Test*(U^i): This query is allowed only once, at any time during the adversary's execution. This query is used to measure the semantic security of the session key of instance U^i, if the latter is defined. If the key is not defined, it returns $\perp$. Otherwise, it returns either the session key held by instance U^i if $b = 1$ or a random key of the same size if $b = 0$, where b is the hidden bit selected at random prior to the first call.

2.2   Security Notions

Partnering. We use the notion of partnering based on session identifications and partner identifications. More specifically, let the session identification of a client instance be a function of the partial transcript of the conversation between the clients and the server before the acceptance. Let the partner identification of a client instance be the instance with which a common secret key is to be established. We say U_1^i and U_2^j are partners if the following conditions are satisfied: (1) Both U_1^i and U_2^j accepted; (2) Both U_1^i and U_2^j share the same session identification; (3) The partner identification for U_1^i is U_2^j and vice-versa; (4) No instance other than U_1^i and U_2^j accepts with a partner identification equal to U_1^i or U_2^j.

Freshness. The freshness notion captures the intuitive fact that a session key is not "obviously" known to the adversary. An instance is said to be **fresh** in the current protocol execution if it has accepted and neither it nor its partner have been asked for a Reveal-query.

AKE semantic security. Consider an execution of the key exchange protocol $\mathcal{P}$ by the adversary $\mathcal{A}$ in which the latter is given access to all oracles. The goal of the adversary is to guess the value of the hidden bit b used by the Test oracle. Let *Succ* denote the event in which the adversary successfully guesses the hidden bit b used by Test oracle.

The advantage of $\mathcal{A}$ in violating the AKE semantic security of the protocol $\mathcal{P}$ and the advantage function of the protocol $\mathcal{P}$, when passwords are drawn from a dictionary $\mathcal{D}$, are defined as follows:

$$Adv_{\mathcal{P},\mathcal{D}}^{ake}(\mathcal{A}) = 2 \cdot Pr[Succ] - 1$$

$$Adv_{\mathcal{P},\mathcal{D}}^{ake}(t, R) = max\{Adv_{\mathcal{P},\mathcal{D}}^{ake}(\mathcal{A})\}$$

where maximum is over all $\mathcal{A}$ with time-complexity at most t and using resources at most R (such as the number of oracle queries).

A 3-party password-based key exchange protocol $\mathcal{P}$ is said to be semantically secure if the advantage $Adv_{\mathcal{P},\mathcal{D}}^{ake}$ is only negligible larger than $kn/|\mathcal{D}|$, where n is number of active sessions and k is a constant. Note that $k = 1$ is the best one can hope for since an adversary that simply guesses the password in each of the active sessions has an advantage of $n/|\mathcal{D}|$.

3 Building Blocks

In this section, we introduce some building blocks on which our protocol and proof of security will rely. We first give the definition of bilinear pairing, then introduce the GDH and the GBDH assumptions.

3.1 Bilinear Pairings

Let G_1 be a finite additive cyclic group of prime order q in an elliptic curve E, P be a generator of G_1, and G_2 be a cyclic multiplicative group of the same order. Let $\hat{e} : G_1 \times G_1 \longrightarrow G_2$ be a map which satisfies the following conditions:

(1) Bilinearity: For any P, Q and $R \in G_1$, we have $\hat{e}(P + Q, R) = \hat{e}(P, R) \cdot \hat{e}(Q, R)$ and $\hat{e}(P, Q + R) = \hat{e}(P, Q) \cdot \hat{e}(P, R)$. In particular, for any $a, b \in Z_q$, we have $\hat{e}(aP, bP) = \hat{e}(P, P)^{ab}$.

(2) Non-degeneracy: There exists $P, Q \in G_1$, such that $\hat{e}(P, Q) \neq 1$, in other words, the map does not send all pairs in $G_1 \times G_1$ to the identity in G_2.

(3) Computability: There is an efficient algorithm to compute $\hat{e}(P, Q)$ for all $P, Q \in G_1$.

In the setting of prime order groups, the Non-degeneracy is equivalent to $\hat{e}(P, Q) \neq 1$ for all $P, Q \in G_1$. So, when P is a generator of G_1, $\hat{e}(P, P)$ is a generator of G_2. Such a bilinear map is called a bilinear pairing.

3.2 Diffie-Hellman Assumptions

GDH assumption. Let G be a finite additive cyclic group of prime order q in an elliptic curve E, P is a generator of G. The GDH assumption can be defined by considering experiment Exp^{GDH}: we choose two random elements $u, v \in Z_q$, compute $U = uP$ and $V = vP$, and then give U and V to an adversary $\mathcal{A}$. Moreover $\mathcal{A}$ can send some Decisional Diffie-Hellman (DDH) oracle queries (which means given (U, V, K), the adversary can determine whether $K = CDH(U, V)$ by DDH oracle). Let K be the output of $\mathcal{A}$. $Exp^{GDH}(\mathcal{A})$ outputs 1 if $K = GDH(U, V) = uvP$ and 0 otherwise. We denote $Succ_G^{GDH}(t)$ be the maximal success probability that $Exp^{GDH}(\mathcal{A})$ outputs 1 over all PPT adversaries running within time t. We say that GDH assumption holds in G if $Succ_G^{GDH}(\mathcal{A})$ is negligible.

GBDH assumption. Let G_1, G_2, P and $\hat{e}$ be defined as above. Define $BDH(U, V, W) = Z$, where $U = uP, V = vP, W = wP$ and $Z = \hat{e}(P, P)^{uvw}$. We say GBDH assumption for $(G_1, G_2, \hat{e})$ holds, if for any PPT adversary $\mathcal{A}$, with the help of Decisional Bilinear Diffie-Hellman (DBDH) oracle (which means given (U, V, W, Z), the adversary can determine whether $BDH(U, V, W) = Z$ easily by using DBDH oracle):

$$Pr[\mathcal{A}(q, G_1, G_2, P, U = uP, V = vP, W = wP)] = BDH(U, V, W) \leq \epsilon(k),$$

where $u, v, w \in Z_q$, and where $\epsilon(k)$ is negligible. The probability is taken over the coin tosses of $\mathcal{A}$, the choice of q, P and the random choices of u, v, w in Z_q.

4 3-Party Password-Based Protocol Using Bilinear Pairings

In this section, we describe our 3-party PAKE protocol based on bilinear pairings, and prove its security in the random oracle model.

4.1 Description of the Scheme

Let G_1 be an additive cyclic group of a prime order q, and G_2 be a multiplicative cyclic group of the same order. Let P,Q be generators of G_1, and $\hat{e} : G_1 \times G_1 \rightarrow G_2$ be a bilinear pairing. Let $\mathcal{G}$ be a full domain hash function from $\{0,1\}^*$ to Z_q^*, $H_i : \{0,1\}^* \rightarrow \{0,1\}^{l_i} (i = 0, 1, 2)$ be hash functions which map a string of arbitrary length to a string of l_i bit. Let $H : \{0,1\}^* \rightarrow G_1$ be a hash function which maps a string of arbitrary length to an element in G_1. Let A, B be the identifications of the clients and S be the identification of the server, pw_A be the password shared between the client A and the server S, pw_B be the password shared between the client B and the server S, s be the secret key of the server and $P_S = sP$ be the corresponding public key. We assume that the private key of the server can never be compromised by the adversary.

As illustrated on Figure 1,the protocol runs among two clients A, B and a server S, and the session key space SK associated to this protocol is $\{0,1\}^{l_0}$

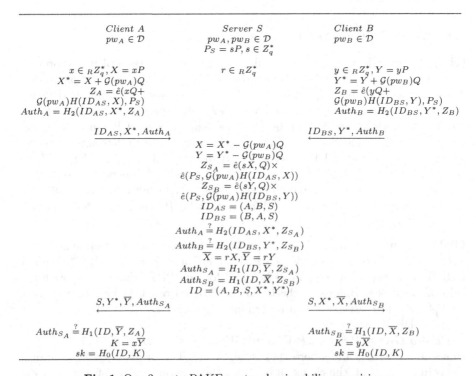

Fig. 1. Our 3-party PAKE protocol using bilinear pairings

equipped with a uniform distribution. The client A(B, respectively) and the server S initially share a lightweight string pw_A (pw_B, respectively), the password, uniformly drawn from the dictionary $\mathcal{D}$. The protocol consists of two rounds of messages.

4.2   Security

In this subsection, we deal with the AKE semantic security. For simplicity, we omit the discussion to key privacy with respect to the server and the mutual authentication goal. Due to lack of space, we also omit the proof of Theorem 1.

Theorem 1. (AKE semantic security) *Let G_1,G_2 and $\hat{e}$ be defined as above, such that GDH assumption holds in G_1, and GBDH assumptions holds for $(G_1, G_2, \hat{e})$. Let $\mathcal{D}$ be a uniformly distributed dictionary of size N. For any adversary $\mathcal{A}$ within a time bound t, with less than q_{send} (i.e. $q_{sendserver} + q_{sendclient}$) active interactions with the parties and q_{exe} passive eavesdroppings (Execute-queries), and asking q_g and q_h hash queries to $\mathcal{G}$ and any H_i oracles, respectively. Then*

$$Adv_{3PAKE,\mathcal{D}}^{AKE}(t, q_{exe}, q_{send}, q_g, q_h) \leq 2\frac{q_{send}}{N} + 2\frac{q_{sendclient}}{N} + \frac{q_h^2 + 4q_{sendclient}}{2^{l_1}} + \frac{q_h^2 + 2q_{sendserver}}{2^{l_2}} + \frac{(q_{exe} + q_{send} + q_g)^2}{(q-1)} + 8q_h Succ^{GBDH}(t') + 2q_h Succ_{G_1}^{GDH}(t')$$

5   Conclusion

This paper presents a three-party password authenticated key exchange protocol based on bilinear pairings in the asymmetric "PKI model", and prove its security under the GBDH and GDH assumptions in the random oracle model. Compared with previous solutions, the proposed protocol have the advantage of not only stronger security but also high efficiency in communication cost. For the reason that transmitting radio signals on resource-constrained wireless devices usually consumes much more power than computation does, thus the proposed protocol is particularly suitable for implementation on these devices due to its acceptable computation cost and low communication cost.

References

1. Abdalla, M., Fouque, P., Pointcheval, D.: Password-Based Authenticated Key Exchange in The Three-Party Setting. In: Vaudenay, S. (ed.) PKC 2005. LNCS, vol. 3386, pp. 65–84. Springer, Heidelberg (2005)
2. Abdalla, M., Pointcheval, D.: Interactive Diffie-Hellman Assumptions with Applications to Password-Based Authentication. In: Patrick, A., Yung, M. (eds.) FC 2005. LNCS, vol. 3570, pp. 341–356. Springer, Heidelberg (2005)
3. Bellovin, S., Merritt, M.: Encrypted Key Exchange: Password-Based Protocols Secure Against Dictionary Attacks. In: Proc. of IEEE Symposium on Research in Security and Privacy, pp. 72–84 (1992)

4. Bellare, M., Pointcheval, D., Rogaway, P.: Authenticated Key Exchange Secure Against Dictionary Attacks. In: Preneel, B. (ed.) EUROCRYPT 2000. LNCS, vol. 1807, pp. 139–155. Springer, Heidelberg (2000)
5. Canetti, R., Halevi, S., Katz, J.: Universally Composable Password-Based Key Exchange. In: Cramer, R. (ed.) EUROCRYPT 2005. LNCS, vol. 3494, pp. 404–421. Springer, Heidelberg (2005)
6. Chen, T., Lee, W., Chen, H.: A Round-And Computation-Efficient Three-Party Authenticated Key Exchange Protocol. Journal of System and Software 81(9), 1581–1590 (2008)
7. Kim, H., Choi, J.: Enhanced Password-Based Simple Three-Party Key Exchange Protocol. Computers and Electrical Engineering 35(1), 107–114 (2009)
8. Nam, J., Lee, Y., Kim, S., Won, D.: Security Weakness in a Three-Party Pairing-Based Protocol for Password Authenticated Key Exchange. Information Sciences 177(6), 1364–1375 (2007)
9. Needham, R.M., Schroeder, M.D.: Using Encryption for Authentication in Large Networks of Computers. Communications of the Association for Computing Machinery 21(12), 993–999 (1978)
10. Sun, H.M., Chen, B.C., Hwang, T.: Secure Key Agreement Protocols for Three-Party Against Guessing Attacks. The Journal of Systems and Software 75, 63–68 (2005)
11. Shin, S., Kobara, K., Imai, H.: Very-Efficient Anonymous Password-Authenticated Key Exchange And Its Extentions. In: Bras-Amorós, M., Høholdt, T. (eds.) AAECC 2009. LNCS, vol. 5527, pp. 149–158. Springer, Heidelberg (2009)
12. Sun, C.L., Sun, H.M., Hwang, T.: Three-Party Encrypted Key Exchange: Attacks And a Solution. ACM Operating System Review 34(4), 12–20 (2000)
13. Steiner, M., Tsudik, G., Waidner, M.: Refinement And Extension of Encrypted Key Exchange. ACM Operating Systems Review 29(3), 22–30 (1995)
14. Wang, W., Hu, L.: Efficient And Provably Secure Generic Construction of Three-Party Password-Based Authenticated Key Exchange Protocols. In: Barua, R., Lange, T. (eds.) INDOCRYPT 2006. LNCS, vol. 4329, pp. 118–132. Springer, Heidelberg (2006)
15. Wen, H.A., Lee, T.F., Hwang, T.: Provably Secure Three-Party Password-Based Authenticated Key Exchange Protocol Using Weil Pairing. IEEE Proceedings-Communications 152(2), 138–143 (2005)
16. Yoneyama, K.: Efficient And Strongly Secure Password-Based Server Aided Key Exchange. In: Chowdhury, D.R., Rijmen, V., Das, A. (eds.) INDOCRYPT 2008. LNCS, vol. 5365, pp. 172–184. Springer, Heidelberg (2008)
17. Yang, J., Zhang, J.F.: A New Anonymous Password-Based Authenticated Key Exchange Protocol. In: Chowdhury, D.R., Rijmen, V., Das, A. (eds.) INDOCRYPT 2008. LNCS, vol. 5365, pp. 200–212. Springer, Heidelberg (2008)

Bayesian Network Based on FTA for Safety Evaluation on Coalmine Haulage System

Wensheng Liu, Liwen Guo, and Ming Zhu

College of Resources and Environment, Hebei Polytechnic University,
Tangshan 063009, China
wincherlliu@163.com, guoliwen@heut.edu.cn, hbzhuming@163.com

Abstract. Safety evaluation is one of the most effective countermeasures to improve the safety in enterprises. Bayesian network based on FTA is a new safety evaluation method. On the basis of FTA, combining with the advantages of Bayesian network, the new method relax the harsh conditions of FTA which make it used in a wider area. This method is applied to the safety evaluation of underground haulage system in one mining area of Kailuan Coal Group Corporation Ltd. Through the result of the analysis we point out the most important factors influencing the safety state. The corresponding countermeasures are put forward too. The evaluation result indicates that this method is easy and can be popularized.

Keywords: Safety Assessment; Faulty Tree Analysis; Bayesian Networks; Coalmine Production System.

1 Introduction

The Coalmine Production System is a large-scale system which is made of man, machine and environment [1]. The working unit and spatial distribution are extremely complicated with the gas and coal dust explosion, water inrush, underground fire, roof accident, gas outburst, electromechanical accidents happening frequently. The coalmine production system has tridimensional distribution in spatial and dynamic development in time. The accident of coalmine has the characteristics of Dynamics, randomness, fuzziness. Different disasters are connected with each other in time and space which make the safety assessment necessary for the coalmine production in order to analyze the reason and reduce the accident rate.

However, literatures concerning safety assessment in coal mine are still very limited up to now. According to the characteristics of coalmine production system, safety assessment methods consisted of Process Safety Review methods, Safety Checklist Analysis, Fault Tree Analysis (FTA),etc [1].

Fault tree analysis method has the following characteristics: describing the cause and the logic relationship between the accident in detail; Finding potential risk factors and state easily; finding out accident-controlling elements and the unsafe state of the key link; Easy for mathematical logic operation and quantitative calculation and computerized analysis. This method is of high precision evaluation results which need

R. Zhu et al. (Eds.): ICICA 2010, LNCS 6377, pp. 143–149, 2010.

some certain mathematical foundation and data (For example, the probability of basic events). The default hypothesis of this method are: (1) Events are binary; (2) Events are independent of each other; (3) The relationship of event and the causes are expressed by logic gate. Fault tree analysis method can effectively handle the safety index of coal-mine production system. However, the following disadvantages limits its promotion application. (1) Its assumptions are harsh; (2) It can not handle the relationship problem between each node (basic events); (3) Calculation is complicated in practical.

2   Introduction of Bayesian Networks

Over the last decades, Bayesian networks (BNs) have become a popular tool for modeling many kinds of statistical problems [1]. We have also seen a growing interest for using BNs in many application areas such as the reliability analysis, forecasting, classifying, causal analysis, diagnostic analysis, etc [2, 3, 4, 5]. However, this method has not been widely applied to Safety Assessment from beginning, especially in the coal-mine production system. In this paper we will discuss the properties of the modeling framework that make BNs particularly well suited for safety assessment applications, and put forward the countermeasures to prevent accidents inclined haulage accident.

A BN consists of three main elements: (1) a set of variables $(X_1, X_2, ...)$ that represent the factors relevant to a particular system or problem; (2) the relationships between these variables that quantify the links between variables and (3) the set of conditional probability tables (CPTs) that quantify the links between variables and are used to calculate the state of nodes. The first two elements form the qualitative part and the third element form the quantitative part. An example of a BN over the variables $(X_1, X_2, ...)$ is shown in Fig. 1, only the qualitative part is given.

Fig. 1. An example of BN

As shown in figure 1, the nodes representing variables which interact with each other. These interactions are expressed as links between variables; the links, however, are not permitted to form a closed loop. A node representing variable X_3 is linked to two parent nodes, X_1, X_2 and two child nodes(X_4, X_5), on which it is dependent. The links or 'edges' are expressed as probabilistic dependencies, which are quantized through a set of conditional probability tables (CPTs). For each variable the tables express the probability of that variable being in a particular state, given the states of its parents. For variables without parents, an unconditional distribution is defined.

Each variable is described by the CPF of that variable given its parents in the graph, i.e., the collection of $CPF\{f(x_i|pa(x_i))\}_{i=1}^n$. The underlying assumptions of conditional independence encoded in the graph allow us to calculate the joint probability function as

$$f(x_1, x_2, ..., x_n) = \prod_{i=1}^{n} f\left(x_i | pa(x_i)\right) \tag{1}$$

The main task of Bayesian network is reasoning: Given a set of variables' observations which we name it evidence (E), Calculating another variable posterior probability distribution. Many researchers have proposed many algorithms for reasoning, including accurate reasoning and approximate algorithm [2].

3   Safety Evaluation Model Based on Bayesian Network(BN)

On the base of fault tree analysis, we used Bayesian network to model safety assessment. First, we illustrate how to convert Fault tree to BN. Then we take Haulage Vehicle Accident of coalmine for an example to illustrate how to relax fault   tree analysis hypothesis to establish a more appropriate assessment model.

The conversion algorithm proceeds along the following steps:

(1) for each leaf node of the FT, create a root node in the BN; however, if more leaves of the FT represent the same primary event, create just one root node in the BN; (2) assign to root nodes in the BN the prior probability of the corresponding leaf node in the FT; (3) for each gate of the FT, create a corresponding node in the BN. label the node corresponding to the gate whose output is the Top Event of the FT as the Fault node in the BN; (4) connect nodes in the BN as corresponding gates are connected in the FT; (5) for each gate in the FT assign the equivalent CPT to the corresponding node in the BN. (see Fig. 2).

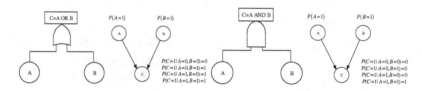

Fig. 2. FT transferred into BN

4   Example Analysis

Rail haulage system is a important part of the whole coalmine production system. Of the whole haulage accidents, the frequency caused by the Rail haulage is 50%, the death toll is 48%. So the safety of laneway rail haulage affects the whole coal haulage system. We use the method illustrated above to the safety evaluation of underground transportation system in one mine area of Kailuan Coal Group Corporation Ltd and analyzes the advantage of the new method compared with the traditional FTA.

4.1 Model Transformation

A FT of laneway rail haulage system of Kailuan Coal Group Corporation Ltd is as follow figure 3. The number, Type code, Name of events and probability value is as the table 1. The probability value of table 1 is from some history statistical data of Kailuan Coal Group Corporation Ltd.

From the FT, we can see that the two main factors resulting the laneway haulage accident are crash death (A) and crush injury (B).

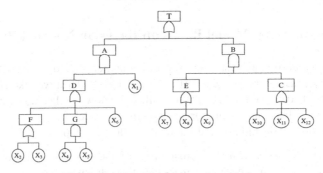

Fig. 3. The FT of the laneway in coalmine

Table 1. The number, type ID, event name and probability of the laneway haulage accident

type ID	Event name	probability	type ID	Event name	probability
A	crash death	-	X_4	vehicle lost in Laneway	0.005
B	crush injury	-	X_5	Illegal commanding	0.01
C	People in danger	-	X_6	parking in rail turnout	0.002
D	illegal parking in rail	-	X_7	Not belling when Tuning and passing turnout	0.007
E	illegal drive	-	X_8	Not slowing down when tuning and passing turnout	0.02
F	illegal fixing in rail	-	X_9	Not looking out when tuning and passing turnout	0.008
G	Illegal crashing	-	X_{10}	Pulling vehicle	0.003
X_1	driver inattention	0.003	X_{11}	sitting on head stock	0.006
X_2	Harvesters accident	0.02	X_{12}	Walking on the track	0.005
X_3	locomotive accident	0.004	T	haulage accident happened on laneway	-

Using the method illustrated above, we transferred the FT to BN and processed the simulation. The BN model is as the Fig. 4.

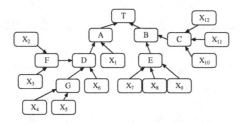

Fig. 4. FT transferred into BN of laneway haulage

The prior probabilities of the root node in BN are given by $X_1 \sim X_{12}$ listed in table 1. The probability of the non-root nodes is computed by the root nodes and the CPT. We list the top event CPT as example, Table2. The other CPTs is not listed one bye one in this paper in order to save space.

Table 2. The CPT of event T

	A	happened		Not happened	
	B	happened	Not happened	happened	Not happened
T	happened	1	1	1	0
	Not happened	0	0	0	1

4.2 Advantage of the New Method

Closer to accurate value. Through the prior probabilities of the root node in BN is given by $X_1 \sim X_{12}$, we got the prior probability of top event (T): $P(T)=0.000560557$. Using the minimal cut sets leading approximation progress of the traditional FTA method, we got the probability of top event (T): $P(T)=0.00056815$. Comparing the two result, we can see that the new method' result is according with the fact which the result of minimal cut sets leading approximation progress of the FTA is Slightly greater than the actual value [3, 4].

Backward reasoning. If the top event occurred at a time, we can use the BN's backward reasoning function to compute the posterior probability of every basic event, find some important factors which affect the top event significantly. The important factors make staff to pay special attention to in the production process. The backward reasoning is a special function that the FTA method doesn't have. For example, supposing there happened haulage accidents in the laneway. We use the backward reasoning function to compute the posterior probability of every basic event $X_1 \sim X_{12}$ which are listed in table 3

Table. 3. The prior probability and posteriori probability of basic events of laneway haulage safety assessment in the coalmine

event	prior prob- abilities	posteriori probability	event	prior probabilities	posteriori probability
X_1	0. 003	0.141236	X_7	0. 007	0.174992
X_2	0. 02	0.124208	X_8	0. 02	**0.499976**
X_3	0. 004	0.0248106	X_9	0. 008	0.199991
X_4	0. 005	0.00525923	X_{10}	0. 003	0.185809
X_5	0. 01	0.102579	X_{11}	0. 006	**0.371619**
X_6	0. 002	0.0124208	X_{12}	0. 005	**0.309682**

From the table 3 we can see that the posteriori probability can be used as the important degree which the basic event affect the top event. The posteriori probability of basic event X_8 (Not slowing down when tuning and passing turnout) is 0.499976 which is the largest of the whole numbers. So, we can conclude that the X_8 is the most sensitive factors affecting the top event. By reducing the incidence rate of X_8, we can reduce the incidence rate of top event. The other two larger probabilities are X_{11} and X_{12}. Reducing these two probabilities, we can also reduce the top event significantly.

5   Conclusion

Coalmine production system is a complicated system consisting of man, machine and environment which make its safety assessment always a hot topic all the time. Bayesian network based on FTA is a new method used in the safety assessment which combines the advantage of Bayesian networks and FT. The new method can get a accurate result compared to the FTA, and it can find the most important factors to the top event by the backward reasoning function. In one word, the new method this paper put forward can make us get more useful information in the safety assessment of the coalmine production system and its application prospects is wide.

References

1. Hou, Y.-b., Pan, R.-f., Wu, J.-y., Wang, B.-p.: Coal mine safety evaluation based on the reliability of expert decision. Procedia Earth and Planetary Science 1(1) (September 2009)
2. State Administration of Work Safety Supervision:Safety evaluation. China Coal Industry Publishing Pouse, Beijing (January 11, 2002)
3. Jesen, F.V.: Bayesian Networks and Decision Graphs. Springer, New York (2001)
4. Dorner, S., Shi, J., Swayne, D.: Multi-objective modeling and decision support using a Bayesian network approximation to a non-point source pollution model. Environmental Modeling & Software 22(2) (2007)
5. Jones, B., Jenkinson, I., Yang, Z., Wang, J.: The use of Bayesian network modelling for maintenance planning in a manufacturing industry. Reliability Engineering & System Safety 95(3) (March 2010)

6. Hassen, H.B., Masmoudi, A., Rebai, A.: Causal inference in biomolecular pathways using a Bayesian network approach and an Implicit method. Journal of Theoretical Biology 253(4) (August 21, 2008)
7. Hanea, D., Ale, B.: Risk of human fatality in building fires: A decision tool using Bayesian networks. Fire Safety Journal 44(5) (July 2009)
8. Ziegler, V.: Approximation. Information Processing Letters 108(2) (September 30, 2008)
9. Chao, W., Rang, M.T.: Mine safety system engineering. Central South University of Technology Press (1992)
10. Qiong, D.: Safety system engineering. North West University of Technology Press (2008)

Multi-factor Evaluation Approach for Quality of Web Service*

Qibo Sun, Shangguang Wang**, and Fangchun Yang

State Key Laboratory of Networking and Switching Technology,
Beijing University of Posts and Telecommunications, Beijing, China
qbsun@bupt.edu.cn, sguang.wang@gmail.com, fcyang@bupt.edu.cn

Abstract. Accurate evaluation of QoS (Quality of Services) is critical for web services in business applications. In this paper a multi-factor evaluation approach is propose to evaluate QoS of web service. This approach synthetically considers service providers, the context of customers, and historical statistics to evaluate the QoS. The experimental results demonstrate that our approach can effectively obtain accurate QoS evaluation for web services.

Keywords: Web service; QoS evaluation; fuzzy synthetic evaluation method; non-uniform mutation operator.

1 Introduction

With the increasing popularity of the development of service oriented applications, measuring the quality of services becomes an imperative concern for service consumers. The level of QoS has great influence on degree of the service usability and utility, both of which influence the popularity of web service (WS) [1]. Since a service has several quality attributes (e.g. availability, reliability and response time), whose values may be influenced by various factors, it is very difficult to accurately evaluate QoS [2]. In addition, published QoS from service providers are not always accurate and trustworthy in practice application. The reasons are as follows. First, service providers may publish malicious QoS (the QoS is higher than the actual service level). For example, in finance, online transaction or e-commerce applications, in order to attract a large number of customers in a short time and obtain lots of illegal profits, some service providers publish some false or exaggerated QoS to deceive service customers. As a result, some customers suffer economic losses. Second, many existing QoS evaluation approaches utilize the expectations of historical statistics to get close to the actual QoS values [3], which overlooks the context of service customers.

At present QoS evaluation has gained much attention in recent years due to the growth of online transactions and e-business activities in service-oriented environments.

* The work presented in this study is supported by the National Basic Research and Development Program (973program) of China (No.2009CB320406);the National High Technology Research and Development Program (863program) of China (No.2008AA01A317); the Foundation for Innovative Research Groups of the National Natural Science Foundation of China (No.60821001).
** Corresponding author.

R. Zhu et al. (Eds.): ICICA 2010, LNCS 6377, pp. 150–157, 2010.

The authors of [4] proposed an adaptive service selection approach. In this approach, a quality model is proposed. In this model five quality attributes (e.g. availability, execution time, data quality) considered are calculated by QoS aggregation functions. Although this approach is very effective to web service selection, the disadvantage is lacking in considering the trust of QoS attributes. The authors of [3] proposed an approach considering the trustworthiness of QoS data for service selection. In this approach, for the QoS data from service providers, the authors adopted an exponential function to revise the providers' QoS data while the statistics of past runtime data is insufficient, which is valid for obtaining trust QoS data. The authors of [5] identified a set of QoS metrics in the context of WS workflows, and proposed a unified probabilistic model for describing QoS values of a broader spectrum of atomic and composite Web service. The authors of [6] proposed an approach, namely bayesian network based Qos assessment model. The salient feature of this model is that it can predict the providers' capability in various combinations with users' QoS requirements, especially to the provider with different service levels.

In this paper based on our previous work on a framework for monitoring QoS [7-8] we present a multi-factor evaluation approach (MEA) to evaluate QoS of WS. The aim is that every service is assigned its actual QoS value and fairly competes with existing services for market share. In MEA, we adopt fuzzy synthetic evaluation method to obtain the evaluation of service providers and the context of customers respectively. Then slight non-uniform mutation operator is proposed and used to compute the weights of QoS from service providers, historical statistics and the context of customers. Finally, QoS can be calculated with weighted average method. Experimental results indicate that MEA can effectively evaluate QoS of WS.

The remainder of this paper is organized as follows. MEA are proposed in Section 2. We evaluate our approach experimentally in Section 3. Finally, Section 4 is our conclusions.

2 Multi-factor Evaluation Approach

In MEA, QoS evaluated (q_i, the i-th QoS attribute value of a web service) would be a synthetic calculation of multiple QoS sources, i.e. the three kinds of QoS data: QoS published ($\underline{q_i}$) from service providers, QoS monitored ($\overline{q_i}$) from history statistics and QoS inferred ($\tilde{q_i}$) from the context of customers. So we propose a multi-factor evaluation approach (MEA) to synthesize the three QoS sources above to evaluate QoS. MEA contains three steps as follows.

Step 1. Obtain the evaluation values of service providers and the context of customers by fuzzy synthetic evaluation method (FSEM). FSEM has various attributes concerning evaluation of objects and performs a comprehensive assessment and general appraisal on related factors to produce the overall assessment [9].

Suppose that domain $U_1 = \{u_{11}, u_{12}, u_{13}, u_{14}\}$ denotes a set of evaluated factors (they are logic location, reputation, use-count and brand of service providers' items in this study); $V = \{v_1, v_2, v_3, v_4, v_5\}$ denotes a set of evaluation grades, and $v_j (j = 1 \cdots 5)$

denotes a probable evaluation which is described as very poor, poor, normal, good and excellent. The appraisal object, i.e. the service provider has a fuzzy relation matrix R_1 from U_1 to V :

$$R_1 = (r_{ij})_{4 \times 5} = \begin{bmatrix} r_{11} & \cdots & r_{15} \\ \vdots & \vdots & \vdots \\ r_{41} & \cdots & r_{45} \end{bmatrix} \qquad (1)$$

where r_{ij} (i =1$\cdots$4) denotes the membership degree, the appraisal object is measured as v_j considering attribute u_{1i}.

Since the obtained appraisal matrix R_1 is not enough to appraise the operator yet, a fuzzy subset W_1 in U_1, called weight set, that is, $W_1 = \{w_{11}, w_{12}, w_{13}, w_{14}\}$,in which $\sum_{i=1}^{4} w_{1i} = 1$ and $0 \leq w_{1i} \leq 1$. The weight W_1 denotes the relative importance of the various evaluated factors expressed by decision makers (i.e. service customers in this study). Moreover, a fuzzy subset B_1 in V , called the decision making set, is also introduced, and denotes the overall fuzzy appraisal:

$$B_1 = W_1 \circ R_1 = \{b_{11}, b_{12}, b_{13}, b_{14}, b_{15}\} \qquad (2)$$

$$b_{1j} = \sum_{i=1}^{4} (w_{1i} \times r_{ij}), j = 1 \cdots 5 \qquad (3)$$

where " $\circ$ "denotes fuzzy mapping.

Similarly, we can obtain the evaluation value of the context of customers according to the $U_2 = \{u_{21}, u_{22}, u_{23}, u_{24}\}$ (they are transmission rate, throughput, network bandwidth and network delay of the context items in this study. Note that the specific factors described in different WS environment can vary, e.g. it may replace throughput with packet loss in wireless network environment.

Step 2. Based on Michalewicz's non-uniform mutation [10], a slight non-uniform mutation operator (SNMO) is proposed to calculate the weights of three QoS sources according to the evaluation values of Step 1.

For each individual X_i^t create an offspring X_i^{t+1} by a non-uniform mutation as follows. if $X_i^t = \{x_1, \cdots, x_k, \cdots, x_n\}$ is a chromosome and the muted element X_i^{t+1} is created as the following vector

$$X_i^{t+1} = \{x_1, \cdots, x_k', \cdots, x_n\}, x_k' = \begin{cases} x_k + \Delta(t, U - x_k) & \text{if } rand \leq 0.5 \\ x_k - \Delta(t, x_k - L) & \text{otherwise} \end{cases}$$

where t is the generation number, *rand* is a uniformly distributed random number between 0 and 1, L and U are the lower and upper bounds of the variable x_k respectively. The function $\Delta(t, y)$ returns a value in the range [0, y]. When t increases, $\Delta(i, y)$ approaches to zero as the following function:

$$\Delta(t, y) = y \cdot (1 - r^{(1 - t/T)^b}) \qquad (4)$$

where r is a uniform random number from [0,1], T is the maximal generation number, and b is a system parameter determining the strength of the mutation operator.

SNMO proposed is similar to Michalewicz's non-uniform mutation, but $\Delta(t, y)$ is different as follows:

$$\Delta(t, y) = y \cdot \left[\alpha \cdot (1 - r^{(1-t/T)^b}) + \beta \cdot \exp(-\frac{t}{B}) \right] \quad (5)$$

where t is the estimate number (EN), T is the maximal estimate number, α and β are the operator weights that are set according to practical WS environment, b and Then, three weights of QoS sources can be calculated as follows.

To the weight $\overline{w}_1$ of service providers, we assume that the evaluation result of a service provider is mb_1. Then the y of (5) is mapped as $\overline{y}$ as follows:

$$\overline{y} = \begin{cases} mb_1, if \ \ mb_1 < \delta \\ \delta, others \end{cases} \quad (6)$$

where $\delta(0 < \delta < 1)$ is the system parameter that is set according to practical WS environment. Then, the $\overline{w}_1$ is calculated by the following equation:

$$\overline{w}_1 = \overline{y} \cdot \left[\alpha \cdot (1 - r^{(1-t/T)^{b_1}}) + \beta \cdot \exp(-\frac{t}{B}) \right] \quad (7)$$

To the weight $\overline{w}_2$ of historical statistics, since historical statistics are from QoS monitoring [7], the QoS monitored ($\overline{q}_i$) is trustworthy. Then, $\overline{w}_2$ can be calculated as follows.

$$\overline{w}_2 = \begin{cases} 1 - \overline{w}_1 - \overline{w}_3, if \ (1 - \overline{w}_1 - \overline{w}_3) > \delta \\ \delta, \ \ \ \ others \end{cases} \quad (8)$$

where $\overline{w}_3$ is the weight of the context of customers.

To the weight $\overline{w}_3$ of the context of customers, $\overline{w}_3$ is calculated by the following equation:

$$\overline{w}_3 = \begin{cases} \delta - \overline{w}_1, \ \ if \ (\overline{w}_1 + \overline{w}'_3) > \delta \\ \delta, \ \ elseif \ \ \overline{w}'_3 > \delta \\ \overline{y} \cdot (rand^{(1-t/T)^{b_2}} - \exp(-t/B)), others \end{cases} \quad (9)$$

with
$$\overline{y} = \begin{cases} mb_2, mb_2 < \delta \\ \delta, others \end{cases}$$

Step 3. Evaluate QoS with three weights calculated in Step 2.

Having obtained $\{\overline{w}_1, \overline{w}_2, \overline{w}_3\}$, QoS evaluated ($q_i$) can be obtained by weighted average method as follows:

$$q_i = \overline{w}_1 \ddot{q}_i + \overline{w}_2 \overline{q}_i + \overline{w}_3 \tilde{q}_i \tag{10}$$

with $\sum_{i=1}^{3} \overline{w}_i = 1$ and $\overline{w}_i > 0$.

3 Experiments

In this experiment, three of some PC machines were used to act as an evaluate server (Q-Peer [7-8]), a customer client and a router. The router is a PC that runs Qualnet4.5 [11], which emulates numerous complex network scenarios and equipments, The two other PCs are connected through this router to emulate the dynamics of WS environment. To evaluate the performance of MEA, Some experiments have been performed on QoS evaluation. All experiments were taken on the evaluate server. The machine (Intel Core2 2.8GHz processor, 2.0GB of RAM) is running under Java 1.8, Windows XP SP3, MATLAB 7.6, lpsolve5.5. All parameters are set according the web service environment.

3.1 Experimental Results on Effectiveness

In this section, this experiment takes the response time (a QoS attribute) of web services as an example to validate MEA. Since service providers published some malicious QoS, MEA is used to adjust these malicious data to actual values. In this experiment, we simulate 5 service providers, 5 customers. The normal response time of 5 services are located in 15.3, 21.9, 28.3, 35.1, 39.5 (millisecond), but values published as 56.5, 60.8, 65.2, 70.7, 75.4. It is very clear that QoS published is much larger than their actual QoS. The experimental results of 5 web services (WSs) are shown in Fig. 1.

From Fig. 1, the response time evaluated (q_i) of each service is obtained by MEA. The effectiveness of MEA is verified as follows. MEA is able to amend $\underline{q}_i$ by once evaluation and the evaluated values are close to normal values. For example, in WS3 (web service 3) $\underline{q}_3 = 62.5$, but the normal value should be 28.3. At the first evaluation, the value is adjusted from 65.2 to 41.1. Although the value does not reach its normal value, compared with $\underline{q}_i$ the adjusted value is closer to normal value. With the increasing EN, MEA gradually revises these malicious values to near their actual values. For example, $\underline{q}_5 = 75.4$, but the normal value is 39.5. After 100 times evaluation, this value gradually reduces from 75.4 to the vicinity of 39.5. Although the value is not equal to 39.5, but this value is an actual QoS. The reason is that $\overline{w}_1$ gradually decreases, but $\overline{w}_2$ increases at the later stage, which make $\overline{w}_2$ have a greater influence on QoS evaluation. In addition, this value contains QoS inferred ($\tilde{q}_i$) to current customers. So they are actual QoS. Moreover, compared with q_i, although q_i gradually declines and closes to actual values, it occurs non-uniform mutations during decline. The mutations make the results keep more information and reduce the negative effect of extreme adjustment, which makes the evaluate values objective.

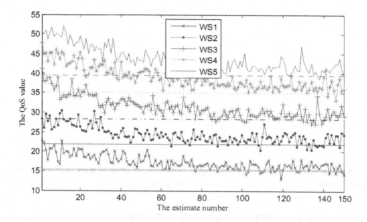

Fig. 1. QoS evaluation to malicious QoS

3.2 Experiment Comparisons

In this experiment to further valid MEA. we compared it on QoS deviation of composition service with the approach of [4]. For illustration purposes, the capital letters "TCS" represent the evaluated result of MEA. The capital letters "CS" represent the results of the approach in [4]. The capital letters "OPT1" represent the overall Utility [4] of composition service from the service Repository [7]. The capital letters "OPT2" represent its overall Utility from QoS monitoring [7]. The capital letters "ST" represent the deviation between the "OPT1"and "OPT2" (i.e., the overall Utility (QoS aggregation value) of composition service is not the same as the execution result), which is calculated by ST=|OPT1-OPT2/OPT2. The smaller the difference between ST and zero (zero is a ideal value) is, the better the capproach is, otherwise the worse.

We compare the deviation of TCS and CS with respect to the number of service candidates and service classes as shown in Fig. 2. In Fig. 2(a), the number of service candidates is 3-10, in which contain 5-30 malicious service. In Fig. 2(b), the number of service candidates is 20-50. When the number of service classes is 5 or 10, in which there is at least one malicious service candidate. While the number of service classes is 15- 50, there are at least 12 service classes and each service class contains at least one malicious service candidate.

From Fig. 2, regardless of the increasing number of service candidates or service classes, the deviation of TCS is far less than that of CS. The deviation of TCS in average is more close to 0. In Fig. 2 (a), the deviation of TCS in average is 0.169, but the deviation of CS is 0.378. In Fig. 2 (b), the deviation of TCS in average is 0.13, while that of CS is 0.37. The results indicate that the performance of TCS is better than that of CS. This means that more reliable composition service can be obtained by MEA ,which significantly improve web service selection process in composition system.

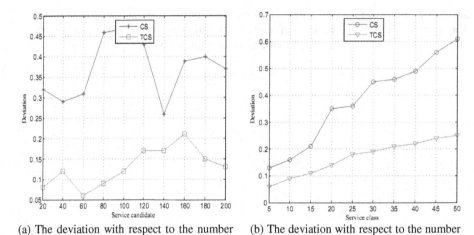

(a) The deviation with respect to the number of service candidates.

(b) The deviation with respect to the number of service classes.

Fig. 2. Comparisons on deviation of services composition

4 Conclusions

In this paper, we propose a multi-factor evaluation approach (MEA) to evaluate quality of web service. In MEA, we adopt fuzzy synthetic evaluation method to obtain the evaluation values from service providers and the context of customers. Then a slight non-uniform mutation operator is proposed to calculate the weight values of three QoS source (service providers, historical statistics and the context of customers). Finally, QoS evaluated can be effectively obtained by the weighted average method. Experimental results indicate that MEA is effective. Moreover, it significantly improves web service selection process.

References

1. Qi, Y., Bouguettaya, A.: Computing Service Skyline from Uncertain QoWS. IEEE Transactions on Services Computing 3, 16–29 (2010)
2. Le-Hung, V., Aberer, K.: Towards Probabilistic Estimation of Quality of Online Services. In: IEEE International Conference on Web Services, pp. 99–106. IEEE Press, New York (2009)
3. Li, Y., Zhou, M.-H., Li, R.-C., Cao, D.-G., Mei, H.: Service selection approach considering the trustworthiness of QoS data. Ruan Jian Xue Bao/Journal of Software 19, 2620–2627 (2008)
4. Ardagna, D., Pernici, B.: Adaptive service composition in flexible processes. IEEE Transactions on Software Engineering 33, 369–384 (2007)
5. Hwang, S.-Y., Wang, H., Tang, J., Srivastava, J.: A probabilistic approach to modeling and estimating the QoS of web-services-based workflows. Information Sciences 177, 5484–5503 (2007)

6. Guoquan, W., Jun, W., Xiaoqiang, Q., Lei, L.: A Bayesian network based Qos assessment model for web services. In: IEEE International Conference on Services Computing, pp. 498–505. IEEE Press, New York (2007)
7. Li, F., Yang, F., Shuang, K., Su, S.: A Policy-Driven Distributed Framework for Monitoring Quality of Web Services. In: IEEE International Conference on Web Services, pp. 708–715. IEEE Press, New York (2008)
8. Su, S., Li, F., Yang, F.C.: Iterative selection algorithm for service composition in distributed environments. Science in China Series F-Information Sciences 51, 1841–1856 (2008)
9. Kuo, Y.-F., Chen, P.-C.: Selection of mobile value-added services for system operators using fuzzy synthetic evaluation. Expert Systems with Applications 30, 612–620 (2006)
10. Deep, K., Thakur, M.: A new mutation operator for real coded genetic algorithms. Applied Mathematics and Computation 193, 211–230 (2007)
11. QualNet 4.5.1 User's Guide,
    http://www.scalable-networks.com/support/
    system-requirements/qualnet-4-5-1/

Execution-Aware Fault Localization Based on the Control Flow Analysis

Lei Zhao, Lina Wang, Zuoting Xiong, and Dongming Gao

Computer School of Wuhan University, 430072, Wuhan, Hubei, P.R. China
The Key Laboratory of Aerospace Information Security and Trust Computing.
Ministry of Education, China
zhaolei.whu@gmail.com, lnwang@whu.edu.cn, tinaxiong1218@gmail.com,
gaodm.whu@gmail.com

Abstract. Coverage-based fault localization techniques assess the suspiciousness of program entities individually. However, the individual coverage information cannot reveal the execution paths and to some extent it simplifies the executions. In this paper, the control flow analysis is adopted to analyze the executions first. Second, the edge suspiciousness is used to calculate the failed executions distribution to different control flows. By comparing different failed executions distributions of blocks covered by the same failed execution path, we propose the bug proneness to quantify how each block contributes to the failure. Similarly, the bug free confidence is also proposed to represent the possibility of bug free for blocks covered by a passed execution path. At last, the weighted coverage information statistic is proceeded and the weighted coverage based fault localization technique is brought out. We conduct several experiments to compare our technique with an existing representative technique by using standard benchmarks and the results are promising.

Keywords: Automated debugging, weighted coverage-based fault localization, bug proneness, bug free confidence.

1 Introduction

Software debugging is a tedious, challenging and error-prone process in software development. It is desirable to automate the debugging as much as possible. Fault[1] localization is a vital step of debugging[1]. Coverage based fault localization (CBFL) techniques have been proposed to support software debugging[2][3][4]. CBFL techniques filter statements of programs which are unrelated to bugs by comparing the execution statistics of passed executions and failed executions. Empirical studies have shown that CBFL techniques can be effective in guiding programmers to examine code and find faults.

---

[1] In this paper, we use *bugs* and *faults* interchangeably, that is *bug localization* and *fault localization* have the same meaning.

R. Zhu et al. (Eds.): ICICA 2010, LNCS 6377, pp. 158–165, 2010.
© Springer-Verlag Berlin Heidelberg 2010

The entities that executed during the failed executions more likely contain bugs than entities that executed during passed executions. If the number of failed executions that executed a certain entities is larger, the entities is much more likely containing bugs. However, the bug suspiciousness are computed individually among such CBFL techniques. In addition, with the impact of random test cases, the coverage of individual program entity cannot reflect the whole complex program executions[4]. Therefore, we claim that the individual coverage information to some extent simplifies the program executions, which may lead to the inaccurate results of CBFL techniques. Several researches [2][6] also points out that CBFL techniques are always able to locate the entities at which the program failed, while these entities do not contain bugs.

The control flow analysis is an appropriate way to solve above problems[5][6][7]. If a block b contains bug, all the executions that executed b may trigger the bug and perform failed. That is, different execution paths following different control flows are thought to be failed paths, and the ratios of failed executions among different control flow paths are similar. By contrast, if b is bug free, even if b is executed in failed executions, the possibility that all the executions are failed is rather low. To sum up, the distribution of failed executions among different control flows can indicate the bug proneness of blocks or other program entities. For all the entities in the program, the failed executions of different entities are different from one another, so for entities which lie in the same control flow, the bug proneness of each entity is different too. Capturing this character, we note the bug proneness as a weighted feature, and propose a novel fault localization approach based on the weighted coverage information. This is the main idea of our paper.

Our approach first use the program control flow graph to organize the executed traces, and then by contrasting the distribution of failed executions between the previous and successor blocks, we assess the bug proneness of the two blocks. Similarly by contrasting the distribution of passed executions between the previous and successor blocks, the bug free confidence of the two blocks is also assessed. For the next, the bug proneness and bug free confidences of all blocks which lie in a certain paths are normalized quantified. At last, some experiments are designed to confirm the efficiency of our approach.

The main contribution of this paper consists of three aspects: 1) By contrasting the distribution of executions between the previous and successor blocks, we propose a novel method to estimate the bug proneness and bug free confidence of blocks covered by the same execution path. 2) Weighted coverage based fault localization method is proposed in this paper, and to our knowledge until now, we are the first to propose the weighted coverage. 3) To some extent, our method is able to be universally used to update several previous methods. The experiments results show that our approach is promising.

The paper is organized as follows: Section 2 gives related work and a motivation example. Section 3 presents our analysis model and our technique, followed by some experimental evaluations and discussion in Section 4. Section 5 concludes this paper and presents our future work.

2 Methodology

2.1 Preliminaries

Definition 1. $EG = \{B, E, Path\}$ *is used to denote the execution graphs in this paper, where* $B = \{b_1, b_2, \cdots, b_m\}$ *is the set of basic blocks of the program,* $Path = \{path_1, path_2, \cdots, path_n\}$ *is the set of control flows, which is also noted as execution paths is the following section of this paper, and* $E = \{e_1, e_2, \cdots, e_k\}$ *is the control flow edges that start from one block to another.*

In the following sections of this paper, the notation $e(b_i, b_j)$ is usually used to represent the edge that goes from block b_i to block b_j. The notation $e(*, b_j)$ is used to represent all the edges that go to b_j. The notation $e(b_i, *)$ is used to represent all the edges that start from b_i.

2.2 Analysis Model

In this section we use the failed execution paths shown in Figure 1 to illustrate the calculation of bug proneness. We note $\{s, d\}$ as a failed execution path as shown in Figure 1. There must be a bug in either s or s. So the fault localization is to determine which node has more possibilities to lead to the failed execution and which node has higher bug proneness.

If the bug is located at s instead of d, then other execution paths which cover s are likely to trigger the bug in s and lead to failed executions. At the same time, the executions which cover d instead of s may be passed executions. On the contrary, if the bug is located at d instead of s, then the executions which cover s are likely to be passed executions while executions covering d may be failed executions. As a conclusion, the bug proneness of s can be measured through analyzing the distribution probability of failed executions to control flows which cover d. The comparison between distribution probabilities of failed executions to control flows covering s and d can be taken as the quantification of bug proneness.

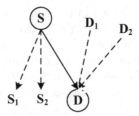

Fig. 1. An example of execution paths for approach illustration

2.3 Edge Suspiciousness Calculation

Existing researches point out that it is not appropriate to use the coverage frequency as the bug coverage rate in an edge and in this paper we choose the suspiciousness definition formula mentioned in [6]to solve this problem.

$$\theta^{\times}(e_i) = \frac{failed(e_i)}{failed(e_i) + passed(e_i)} \tag{1}$$

As shown above, $failed(e_i)$ represents the number of failed executions that cover e_i, and $passed(e_i)$ represents the number of passed executions that cover e_i.

2.4 Quantification of Bug Proneness

The equation of $prob_{in}^{\times}(e(s,d))$ is given as below,

$$prob_{in}^{\times}(e(s,d)) = \frac{\sum_{\forall e(*,d)} * \theta^{\times}(e(s,d))}{\sum_{\forall e(*,d)} [\theta^{\times}(e(*,d))]} \tag{2}$$

where $\theta^{\times}(e(s,d))$ represents the edge suspiciousness of $e(s,d)$, $\sum_{\forall e(*,d)}[\theta^{\times}(e(*,d))]$ represents the sum of suspiciousness of all the edges that go to d, and $\sum_{\forall e(*,d)}$ represents the number of edges that go to d. The reason for set $\sum_{\forall e(*,d)}$ in Equation2 is to distinguish the two cases that one is that sum of suspiciousness of edges going to d except $e(s,d)$ equals to 0, the other is that these is no other edges going to d except $e(s,d)$.

The equation of $prob_{out}^{\times}(e(s,d))$ is given as below.

$$prob_{out}^{\times}(e(s,d)) = \frac{\sum_{\forall e(s,*)} * \theta^{\times}(e(s,d))}{\sum_{\forall e(s,*)} [\theta^{\times}(e(s,*))]} \tag{3}$$

where $\theta^{\times}(e(s,d))$ represents the edge suspiciousness of $e(s,d)$, $\sum_{\forall e(s,*)}[\theta^{\times}(e(s,*))]$ represents the sum of suspiciousness of all the edges that go from s, and $\sum_{\forall e(s,*)}$ represents the number of edges that go from s.

Reexamining the executions in Figure1. If all the executions along $e(s,d_1)$ and $e(s,d_2)$ are passed executions while the executions along $e(s_1,d)$ and $e(s_2,d)$ are failed executions, then d has higher bug proneness. According to the Equation1, the value of both $\theta^{\times}(e(s,d_1))$ and $\theta^{\times}(e(s,d_2))$ are equal to 0, while the value of $\theta^{\times}(e(s_1,d))$ and $\theta^{\times}(e(s_2,d))$ are larger than 0. In such case, the value of $prob_{in}^{\times}(e(s,d))$ is less than $prob_{out}^{\times}(e(s,d))$. By contrast, if all the executions along $e(s,d_1)$ and $e(s,d_2)$ are failed executions while the executions along $e(s_1,d)$ and $e(s_2,d)$ are passed executions, then s has higher bug proneness. The value of $prob_{in}^{\times}(e(s,d))$ is larger than $prob_{out}^{\times}(e(s,d))$. Based on such analysis, the values of $prob_{in}^{\times}(e(s,d))$ and $prob_{out}^{\times}(e(s,d))$ can indicate the bug proneness of s and d oppositely. We will use $prob_{in}^{\times}(e(s,d))$ and $prob_{out}^{\times}(e(s,d))$ to qualify the value of bug proneness of s and d.

The ratio of bug proneness of s to bug proneness of d is designed as below

$$proneness(s) : proneness(d) = \frac{prob_{in}^{\times}(e(s,d))}{prob_{out}^{\times}(e(s,d))} \tag{4}$$

where $proneness(s)$ and $proneness$ denote the value of bug proneness of s and d respectively.

2.5   Normalization of Bug Proneness

By comparing the probability of edge suspiciousness, the ratio of bug proneness of two consecutive blocks can be quantified. However, there are many blocks covered by the same execution path and different execution paths cover different blocks. In order to calculate which block mostly contribute to a failed execution, the bug proneness must be normalization.

$path = \{b_1 \rightarrow b_2 \rightarrow \cdots \rightarrow b_n\}$ is employed here to represent a failed execution path, and $\{b_{i-1} \rightarrow b_i \rightarrow b_{i+1}\}$ is a part of the execution path. b_{i-1} is the pioneer block of b_i, and b_{i+1} is the successor block of b_i. The ratio of bug proneness of b_{i-1} to that of b_{i+1} can be calculate by the transfer of b_i. Therefore, for the execution path of $path = b_1 \rightarrow b_2 \rightarrow \cdots \rightarrow b_n$, the ratio of bug proneness of blocks from b_1 to b_n is

$$
\begin{aligned}
proneness(b_1) : proneness(b_2) : &\cdots : proneness(b_n) = \\
&prob_{in}^{\times}(e(b_1, b_2)) : \\
&prob_{out}^{\times}(e(b_1, b_2)) : \\
&\cdots : \\
&\frac{\prod_{i=1}^{i=n} prob_{out}^{\times}(e(b_{i-1}, b_i))}{\prod_{i=1}^{i=n} prob_{in}^{\times}(e(b_{i-1}, b_i))}.
\end{aligned}
\tag{5}
$$

The ratio may be not exact and normalization is further processed. We select the maximum value of Equation5, and then each value of Equation5 is divided by the maximum value, so that all the values are between $(0, 1]$.

2.6   Quantification of Bug Free Confidence

The coincidental correct brings passive impact to the effectiveness of fault localization techniques, and moreover it has been proved to be pervasive[8]. In order to weaken the impact, the bug free confidence is employed to qualify the possibility of bug free for blocks. $\theta^{\surd}(e_i) = \frac{failed(e_i)}{failed(e_i) + passed(e_i)}$ is used to represent the ratio of passed executions to the sum of passed and failed executions that cover e_i. $prob_{in}^{\surd}(e(s,d)) = \frac{\sum_{\forall e(*,d)} * \theta^{\surd}(e(s,d))}{\sum_{\forall e(*,d)} [\theta^{\surd}(e(*,d))]}$ and $prob_{out}^{\surd}(e(s,d)) = \frac{\sum_{\forall e(s,*)} * \theta^{\surd}(e(s,d))}{\sum_{\forall e(s,*)} [\theta^{\surd}(e(s,*))]}$ are designed which represent the ratio of $\theta^{\surd}(e_i)$ to the sum of $\sum_{\forall e(*,d)} [\theta^{\surd}(e(*,d))]$ and $\sum_{\forall e(s,*)} [\theta^{\surd}(e(s,*))]$ respectively. For a passed execution paths, after the ratio of bug free confidence of consecutive block have been calculated, the normalization will be proceeded as 5. The notation of bug free confidence is noted as $confidence(b)$.

2.7   Block Suspiciousness Calculation

The difference of the coverage information in this paper is that the coverage statistics is based on bug proneness and bug free confidence, which is named as weighted coverage. The weighted failed coverage calculation is as below

$$w\_failed(b) = \sum (failed(path_i | b \in path_i)) * proneness_i(b), \qquad (6)$$

where $failed(path_i | b \in path_i)$ represent the number of failed executions of $path_i$ that covers b and $proneness_i(b)$ represents the bug proneness of b related to $path_i$. Similarly, the weighted passed coverage calculation is as below

$$w\_passed(b) = \sum (passed(path_i | b \in path_i)) * confidence_i(b), \qquad (7)$$

where $passed(path_i | b \in path_i)$ represent the number of passed executions of $path_i$ that covers b and $confidence_i(b)$ represents the bug free confidence of b related to $path_i$.

When the bug free confidence and bug proneness values have been gotten, the weighted failed coverage and weighted passed coverage can be adopted into suspiciousness calculation equations, such as Tarantula, SBI and so on. Following the equation of SBI, the suspiciousness of blocks is designed as

$$suspiciousness(b) = \frac{w\_failed(b)}{w\_failed(b) + w\_passed(b)} \qquad (8)$$

3   Experiments and Analysis

In this section, the experiments will be conducted to evaluate the effectiveness of our technique. The linux program $flex$ from SIR[9] is used as the subject program. It is a real-lift program which has been adopted to evaluate other CBFL techniques. There are 19 bugs in the v1 version of $flex$ program. It must be mentioned that the 8th, 12th, 13th, 16th and 18th bugs cannot be located because there is no test cases that can trigger the bugs. For such bugs, the percentage of code examined is 100%. In the following results analysis, we just take the 18th bug as representation.

In our experiment, we select a typical CBFL technique to compare with our approach. Tarantual is often chosen as alternatives for comparison in other evaluations of fault-localization techniques. In previous researches, the ratio of the number of statements which are needed to be examined until the bug is fixed is commonly used to metric the effectiveness of techniques. In our experiments, we also use the ratio of the number of statements which are needed to be examined to metric our techniques. The comparisons of the percentage of code examined for every bug are given in order to further analyze the results. As shown is Figure2, the bars with plot lines represent the results of our method and the bars with solid lines refer to the results of Tarantula. The x-axis means the number of every bug and the y-axis refers to the percentage of code inspected

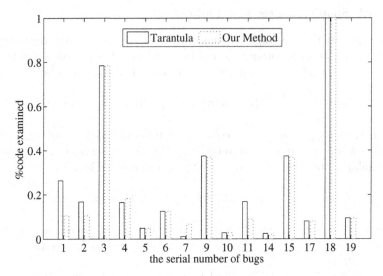

Fig. 2. The comparisons of percentage of code inspected for every bug

until the bug has been fixed. The length of the bar refers to the percentage of code needed to be inspected until the bug is fixed. So the shorter the length of the bar is, the less effort to fix the bug is needed. From the results we can see that our results are better than Tarantula when fixing the 1st, 2nd, 8th, 10th, 11th, 12th bugs and the benefit is obvious.

However, the percentage of code examined when fixing the 4th and 7th of Tarantula is less than that of our approach. We analyzed the possible reason for the shortage of our approach and found that multiple different control flows executed in the same execution were the causes. For example, the 7th bug of flex is a simple error of assignment in the function of *yyparse*, and the bug locates in the *case*31 branch of the *switch(yyn)* condition in the function of *yyparse*. However, we found that *yyparse* function were called several times in an failed execution and the execution paths are different. As a result, our approach regards the *switch(yyn)* condition statement may be the cause of several failed executions. For the next, we plan to solve the research issue by detailed control flow analysis.

4   Conclusion and Future Work

In this paper, we propose the execution aware fault localization technique. During this approach, we adopt the control flows analysis to analyze the program executions and then qualify the failed executions distribution to different control flows. By comparing the failed executions distribution of blocks covered by a failed execution path, we design the bug proneness to qualify how each block contributes to the failure and the bug free confidence to qualify how confident of bug free of every block. We conduct comparison experiments to compare the effectiveness of existing representative techniques with ours using standard benchmarks and the results are promising. For the future, We are planing to combine the test cases generation[10] with fault localization techniques so as to design the fault localization oriented approaches of test cases clustering.

Acknowledgment. This work was funded by the major project of Chinese National Natural Science Foundation (90718006),the National High Technology Research and Development Program of China (2009AA01Z442), and the Self-research program for Doctoral Candidates (including Mphil-PhD) of Wuhan University in 2008.

References

1. Agrawal, H., Horgan, J., Lodon, S., Wong, W.: Fault Localization using Execution Slices and Dataflow Tests. In: 6th IEEE International Symposium on Software Reliability and Engineering, pp. 143–151. IEEE Press, Toulouse (1995)
2. Jones, J.A., Harrold, M.J.: Empirical evaluation of the Tarantula Automatic Fault-Localization Technique. In: 20th IEEE/ACM International Conference on Automated Software Engineering, pp. 273–282. IEEE Computer Society Press, California (2005)
3. Santelices, R., Jones, J.A., Yu, Y., Harrold, M.J.: Lightweight Fault-Localization using Multiple Coverage Types. In: 31st Internation Conference on Software Engineering, pp. 56–66. IEEE Computer Society Press, Vancouver (2009)
4. Wong, E., Qi, Y.: Effective program debugging based on execution slices and inter-block data dependency. Journal of Systems and Software 79(2), 891–903 (2006)
5. Jiang, L., Su, Z.: Context-Aware Statistical Debugging: From Bug Predictors to Faulty Control Flow Paths. In: 22nd IEEE/ACM International Conference on Automated Software Engineering, pp. 184–193. IEEE Computer Society Press, Georgia (2007)
6. Zhang, Z., Chan, W.K., Tse, T.H.: Capturing Propagation of Infected Program States. In: The Joint 12th European Software Engineering Conference and 17th ACM SIGSOFT Symposium on the Foundations of Software Engineering, pp. 43–52. ACM Press, Amsterdam (2009)
7. Chilimbi, T., Liblit, B., Mehra, K., Nori, A., Vaswani, K.: HOLMES: Effective Statistical Debugging via Efficient Path Profiling. In: 31st Internation Conference on Software Engineering, pp. 34–44. IEEE Computer Society Press, Vancouver (2009)
8. Wang, X., Cheung, S.C., Chan, W.K., Zhang, Z.: Taming Coincidental Correctness: Refine Code Coverage with Context Pattern to Improve Fault Localization. In: 31st Internation Conference on Software Engineering, pp. 45–55. IEEE Computer Society Press, Vancouver (2009)
9. Do, H., Elbaum, S.G., Rothermel, G.: Supporting Controlled Experimentation with Testing Techniques: an Infrastructure and its Potential Impact. Empirical Software Engineering 10(4), 405–435 (2005)
10. Yu, Y., Jones, J.A., Harrold, M.J.: An Empirical Study of the Effects of Test-suite Reduction on Fault Localization. In: 30th Internation Conference on Software Engineering, pp. 201–210. IEEE Computer Society Press, Leipzig (2008)

Retraction: The Influence of Cacheable Models on E-Voting Technology

Chen-shin Chien[1] and Jason Chien[2]

[1] Department of Industrial Education,
National Taiwan Normal University, Taipei County, Taiwan
chiendoc@ntnu.edu.tw
[2] China Unversity of Science and Technology Computing Center
China Unversity of Science and Technology, Taipei County, Taiwan
jason034@cc.cust.edu.tw

Several conference proceedings have been infiltrated by fake submissions generated by the SCIgen computer program. Due to the fictional content the chapter "The Influence of Cacheable Models on E-Voting Technology" by "Chen-shin Chien and Jason Chien" has been retracted by the publisher. Measures are being taken to avoid similar breaches in the future.

R. Zhu et al. (Eds.): ICICA 2010, LNCS 6377, pp. 166–172, 2010.
© Springer-Verlag Berlin Heidelberg 2010

An Efficient HybridFlood Searching Algorithm for Unstructured Peer-to-Peer Networks

Hassan Barjini, Mohamed Othman*, and Hamidah Ibrahim

Department of Communication Technology and Network, Universiti Putra Malaysia,
43400 UPM, Serdang, Selangor D.E., Malaysia
hassan.barjini@gmail.com, mothman@fsktm.upm.edu.my

Abstract. Searching in peer-to-peer is started by flooding technique. This technique produces huge redundant messages in each hop. These Redundant messages limit system scalability and cause unnecessary traffic in a network. To improve this searching technique and reduce redundant messages, this paper proposes a novel algorithm called HybridFlood. In HybridFlood algorithm, flooding scheme divided into two phases. At the first phase the algorithm follows flooding by limited number of hops. In the second phase, it chooses nosey nodes in each searching horizon. The nosey nodes are nodes, which have the most links to others. These nodes maintain the data index of all clients. The proposed algorithm extends the search efficiency by reducing redundant messages in each hop. Simulation results show that the proposed algorithm decreases 60% of redundant messages and saves up to 70% of searching traffic.

Keywords: peer-to-peer; searching; redundant messages.

1 Introduction

There are many searching techniques, which have been proposed for peer-to-peer networks. They can be classified into two basic categories searching for the structured and the unstructured peer-to-peer networks [1].

The structured P2P system is established through connections between the peers and the central servers, such as Napster [2], SLP [3], which support all applications. The main fault of searching in the structured or centralized peer-to-peer is its vulnerability and single point failures.

Flooding search has some well known merits such as low latency, maximum scope or coverage, highly reliability and determinism to return results. However, despite all its merit, it produces too many redundant messages and a huge traffic overload, which in turn cause limitation of system scalability.

The current study attempts to develop and improve flooding search technique. The improved technique is reduces redundant messages and alleviates traffic and

---

* The author is also an associate researcher at the Lab of Computational Science and Informatics, Institute of Mathematical Research (INSPEM), University Putra Malaysia.

R. Zhu et al. (Eds.): ICICA 2010, LNCS 6377, pp. 173–180, 2010.

network overloads. This technique minimizes the searching cost and maximizes the efficiency in peer-to-peer networks. To achieve these approaches, we have developed HybridFlood algorithm. The algorithm is divided into two phases. In the first phase, it follows standard flooding by a limited number of hops. In the second phase, it chooses nosey nodes in each horizon. Nosey node is a node, which has the most links to its neighbors. The main responsibility of these nosey nodes is keeping an index of their entire neighbors' data. This is to trace each query to ensure that it is send to exact peer's address. Integrating these two phases, will decrease most redundant messages and will save high rate of searching traffic in the peer-to-peer network.

The reminder of this paper is organizing as follows: section two review, previous literature about searching in unstructured P2P system. Section three describes HybridFlood searching algorithm. Section four discusses the performance evaluations and the last section has the concluding remarks.

2   Related Work

The well known searching technique is flooding search. Flooding technique has significant merits such as: simple algorithm, large coverage, high reliability, moderate latency, and deterministic results. Most of the searching schemes exploit the flooding algorithm to gain these merits, but despite these merits it produces huge overshooting messages.

Many alternative schemes have been proposed to address this problem. Expanding Ring and Iterative Deepening are the pioneer choice of these endeavors. These techniques confined searching scope by limiting Time To Live (TTL) value. Although these schemes mitigate loads and traffic, but still produce many duplicate messages and no guarantee of successful query [4].

For decreasing more overshooting message the next version of flooding is random walk [4]. The main policy behind random walk is to choose randomly only one peer from immediate neighbors. In this scheme, no nodes are visited more than once, so it gains: minimum search cost, loads and traffic. Despite these merits, it is almost non deterministic, non reliable, and high variable performance.

For remedy random walk's faults, there is an extension version of random walker in literature, which is called Random Breadth-First-Search (RBFS) [5] or Teeming [6]. In this scheme at each step, the node propagates the query messages only to a random subset of its neighbors. Although in comparison to flooding the overshooting messages dramatically decrease, but the algorithm is probabilistic and query might not reach some large network segment [7].

There are many other activities to improve the flooding scheme by modifying the algorithm. They are implementing hierarchical structure and using super peers [8]. Gnuttela2 and KaZaa/FastTrack [1] are based on the hierarchical structure. These techniques divide peers into two groups; super peers and leaf peers. Super peer acts as a server receive queries from its clients or other super peer. First they check their clients. If the resource is found, then they reply to the requester peers. Otherwise they send queries to other super peers. However, a main drawback of this approach is vulnerability to single point failure and the limitation number of clients supported by each super peer.

3   Search Algorithm

The main idea behind this technique is to develop the flooding scheme. Hybrid-Flood combined flooding and super peer technique to both benefit from merits and to limit their faults. In HybridFlood algorithm, flooding is divided into two phases. In the first phase, it follows flooding with a limited number of hops. In the second phase, nosey nodes are selected in each searching horizon.

Thus, it is important to investigate the optimum number of hops in the first and second phase. To achieve these goals, we investigate the trend of new peer's coverage and the trend of redundant messages.

3.1   Trend of New Peers Coverage

Assume an overlay network is Random Graph. Each node presents as a peer. Peers are connected to neighbors by edges. Outdegree of each node represents the numbers of its neighbors. Assume we have N node with average outdegree d, hence by flooding technique the search progresses as a tree. So the total number of messages which propagating from each peer up to hop t ("TM_t") is equal to [9].

$$TM_t = \sum_{i=1}^{t} d(d-1)^i \tag{1}$$

If there is no loop node in the topology, then the total number of new peers visited so far ("TP_t") is equal to:

$$TP_t = \sum_{i=1}^{t} d(d-1)^i \tag{2}$$

Thus, the coverage growth of messages [10] in hop t ("CGR_t") can be represented as:

$$CGR_t = \frac{TP_t}{TP_{t-1}} \tag{3}$$

It is equal to:

$$CGR_t = \frac{\sum_{i=1}^{t} d(d-1)^i}{\sum_{i=1}^{(t-1)} d(d-1)^i} \tag{4}$$

So the coverage growth rate of messages is equal to:

$$CGR_t = 1 + \frac{(d-1)^{t-1}}{\sum_{i=0}^{(t-2)} (d-1)^i} \tag{5}$$

By simplifying equation (5):

$$CGR_t = 1 + \frac{(d-2)}{1 - \frac{1}{(d-1)^{t-1}}} \tag{6}$$

3.2 Trend of Redundant Messages

Redundant message ($"R_t"$) in each hop is equal to number of messages propagated ($"M_t"$) minus number of new peers ($"P_t"$) visited at the same hop.

$$R_t = M_t - P_t \tag{7}$$

Redundant messages in each topology generate by loop nodes. Assume we have just in second hop a loop, so the number of redundant messages in hop t becomes:

$$R_t = d(d-1)^t - [d(d-1)^t - (d-1)^{t-2}] \tag{8}$$

By simplifying equation (8)

$$R_t = (d-1)^{t-2} \tag{9}$$

Clearly, the total number of redundant messages ($"TR_t"$) generated up to hop t is equal to:

$$TR_t = \sum_{i=3}^{t}(d-1)^{i-2} \tag{10}$$

3.3 Description of HybridFlood Scheme

In this paper starting hops are low-hops and the rest as high-hops. HybridFlood designed in two phases. At first in low-hops it processes flooding, for benefiting high coverage growth rate of messages and low redundant messages. Then at second by high-hops, when there are too many redundant messages and low coverage growth rate of messages, HybridFlood is not following flood algorithm, instead it starts selecting nosey nodes. Nosey nodes construct with little cost by using local information. The nodes in each cluster just compare their outdegree and the node with most outdegree becomes the nosey node. The nosey nodes are selected in dynamic fashion *(DNN)*. The main responsibilities of the nosey nodes are first maintaining the cache indexes of its clients and second responding to query messages instead of its clients in the cluster.

3.4 Searching Algorithm in the Second Phase

The following algorithm explains searching algorithm in this phase.

```
Algorithm for searching in nosey nodes:
{
    Nosey_node_search(F:file);
            If ( F in C)    //C ( is cache of nosey node)
                {return Found};
            else
            for ( All DNN link to this Nosey node)
                {
```

```
      if (F in C (of other DNN))
      return(Found)
      else
      return( !Found)
    }
}
```

When the queries reach in nosey node, first it looks up its cache if found then it returns the address of client for getting file otherwise it checks other nosey nodes in its level.

4   Performance Evaluation

The main goal of this evaluation is to compare HybridFlood with flooding. HybridFlood implemented into two phases. In the first phase, it performs "M" hops in flooding and in the second phase it continues by choosing nosey nodes. So there is an interesting question,which must be investigated.

– What is the effect of increasing or decreasing "M" in the performance of HybridFlood?

4.1   Performance Metrics

For evaluating each method, we used three metrics:

1. Queries success rate.
2. Number of redundant messages.
3. Number of latency.

In [11], the queries success rate defines as the probability that a query is successful. Thus the fraction of the number of results finds per query to total packets broadcasted is queries success rate. This metric evaluates the efficiency and the quality of the search algorithm. As much as this metric improves the quality and the efficiency of search also improves. The second metric, presents the rate of system scalability. As much as the number of redundant messages increases the scalability of the system decreases. The last metric is the latency, as far as the latency increases the efficiency of the system decreases and vice versa.

4.2   Network Topology

To perform this evaluation, we have used Gnutella topology collected during the first six months of 2001, which has provided by Clip 2 Distributed Search Solution . The name of this topology is T1, it has 42882 nodes. The average degree of T1 is 3.4 and average 2-hop neighbors peer is 34.1.We set the replication ratio 0.01, since there are more than 40,000 nodes. The resources are copied uniformly in more than 400 nodes. Each search is for 50 results.

4.3   The Effect of Increasing or Decreasing of "M" in the First Phase of HybridFlood

For evaluation, we compare the HybridFlood with the flooding algorithm in T1 topology. Figures 1- 3 presented (by stack chart) the results for three metrics, in flooding with different M when the value of M is equal to 2, 3, and 4. Figure 1 shows the success rate of flooding and HybridFlood with different M. Here flooding has the lowest and HybridFlood ($M = 2$) has the most success rate. It shows HybridFlood ($M = 2$) has more than five time success rate than flooding. The trend of increasing success rate in various arrangements of HybridFlood is not uniform. By increasing M in HybridFlood this trend decreased. Table 1 presents the detail of this metric.

The results of the number of redundant messages for flooding and Hybrid-Flood with different M have shown in Figure 2. It shows redundant messages in HybridFlood ($M = 2$) decreased 60% more than flooding. The result shows

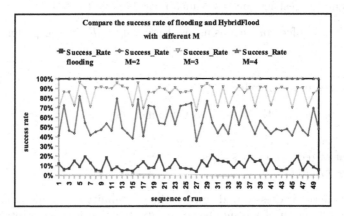

Fig. 1. Success rate in flooding and HybridFlood with different M

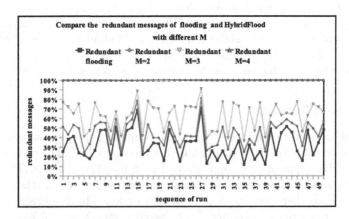

Fig. 2. Redundant messages in flooding and HybridFlood with different M

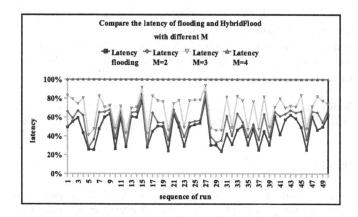

Fig. 3. Latency in flooding and HybridFlood with different M

Table 1. The comparison of metrics (%)

Metrics	Sum	Flooding	HybridFlood		
			$M = 2$	$M = 3$	$M = 4$
Average of Success Rate	100	9.1	45.5	30.5	14.9
Average of Redundant Messages	100	30.9	11.3	16.8	41.0
Average of Latency	100	44.5	7.9	12.6	35.0

HybridFlood ($M = 2$) produced minimum redundant messages. The trend of decreasing redundant messages is not uniform in HybridFlood with different M.

The results of evaluation for latency are in Figure 3. It shows the latency of HybridFlood ($M = 2$) decreased 80% more than flooding. The results show flooding has maximum and HybridFlood ($M = 2$) has minimum latency. According to above performance metrics, HybridFlood search, is more efficient than flooding, it can reduce too many redundant messages and traffic load while receiving the sufficient amount of the results by low latency. Our result proved the best arrangement for HybridFlood is M=2. The main reason is in the second hop, there are maximum coverage growth rate and almost minimum redundant messages. This has been proved by our analytical investigation in equations (6) and (10).

5   Conclusion

In this paper, we consider the main problem of flooding search. It generates huge redundant messages, which threaten scalability of the system. We proposed new searching technique, which combines flooding by super peer techniques. This HybridFlood technique benefiting both merits of flooding and super peer and limiting their drawbacks. In the first phase, we used flooding to gain more coverage growth rate and fewer redundant messages. In the second phase, we use super peers to gain low broadcast and redundant messages, and achieve the high searching speed. We have shown our algorithm is more efficient than flooding. The construction of our searching technique is scalable, simple and easy to implement in the real system. Our future research plans include consideration about the optimum size of cache memory, number of redundancy nosey nodes and period of updating its cache.

Acknowledgements. The research was supported by the Malaysian Ministry of Higher Education, Fundamental Research Grant (FRGS) 01-11-09-734FR.

References

1. Meshkova, E., Riihijärvi, J., Petrova, M., Mähönen, P.: A survey on resource discovery mechanisms, peer-to-peer and service discovery frameworks. Computer Networks 52(11), 2097–2128 (2008)
2. Alderman, J.: Sonic Boom: Napster, MP3 and the New Pioneers of Music. Basic Books (2000)
3. Guttman, E., Perkins, C., Veizades, J.: Service location protocol, version 2. Technical report, Sun Microsystems (1999)
4. Lv, Q., Cao, P., Cohen, E., Li, K., Shenker, S.: Search and replication in unstructured peer-to-peer networks. Performance Evaluation Review ACM USA 30, 258–259 (2002)
5. Zeinalipour-Yazti, D., Kalogeraki, V., Gunopulos, D.: pfusion: A p2p architecture for internet-scale content-based search and retrieval. IEEE Transactions on Parallel and Distributed Systems 18, 804–817 (2007)
6. Dimakopoulos, V.V., Pitoura, E.: On the performance of flooding-based resource discovery. IEEE Transactions on Parallel and Distributed Systems 17, 1242–1252 (2006)
7. Zeinalipour-Yazti, D., Kalogeraki, V., Gunopulos, D.: Information retrieval techniques for peer-to-peer networks. Computing in Science and Engineering 6, 20–26 (2004)
8. Yang, B., Garcia-Molina, H.: Designing a super-peer networks. In: 19 (ed.) Proceedings of the International Conference on Data Engineering, pp. 49–62. IEEE Computer Society Press, Los Alamitos (2003)
9. Aberer, M.H.: An overview on peer-to-peer information systems. In: WDAS- Proceedings, pp. 171–188. Carleton Scientific (2002)
10. Jiang, S., Guo, L., Zhang, X., Wang, H.: Lightflood: Minimizing redundant messages and maximizing scope of peer-to-peer search. IEEE Transactions on Parallel and Distributed Systems 19, 601–614 (2008)
11. Lin, T., Lin, P., Wang, H., Chen, C.: Dynamic search algorithm in unstructured peer-to-peer networks. IEEE Transactions on Parallel and Distributed Systems 20, 654–666 (2009)

Ontology Model for Semantic Web Service Matching

Jiaxuan Ji, Fenglin Bu, Hongming Cai, and Junye Wang

School of Software, Shanghai Jiao Tong University, Shanghai, P.R. China
jiaxuan.j@gmail.com, bu-fl@cs.sjtu.edu.cn,
cai-hm@cs.sjtu.edu.cn, cannon.sjtu@gmail.com

Abstract. Service and resource discovery has become an integral part of modern network systems, in which area all researches are aiming at RESTful Web services and SOAP Web services separately. Basically, a RESTful Web service is a simple Web service implemented by using HTTP protocol and the principles of REST, and does not address features such as security. On the other hand, the SOAP Web service is more feature rich, at the cost of increased complexity, yet still lacks a true resource-centric model. As there are apparent differences between RESTful Web services and traditional SOAP Web services, it's difficult to perform service comparison, matching and evaluation. Therefore, the gap between them needs to be eliminated, and we prefer to employ ontology, which is a formal representation of the knowledge by a set of concepts within a domain and the relationships between those concepts. In this paper, a service registry framework based on ontology model is proposed, which is called Concept Operation Ontology Model (COOM), to avoid the differences between RESTful Web services and traditional SOAP Web services, and illustrate the Web service matching mechanism based on this ontology model. The result shows that this service registry framework has unified the interface of RESTful Web services and SOAP Web services, and returned the best service alternatives with higher similarity when performing service matching.

Keywords: Service Registry; Ontology Modeling; Service Matching.

1   Introduction

A typical SOA (Service-oriented Architecture) has three main parts: a provider, a consumer and a registry. A registry provides the foundations for service discovery and selection. Up until now, the software industry has adopted SOA by using Web service technologies [1]. REST (Representational State Transfer) is a style of software architecture for distributed hypermedia systems such as the World Wide Web. It was proposed and defined in 2000 by Roy Fielding in his doctoral dissertation [2].

The RESTful Web service has its superiority, but it cannot entirely replace the traditional SOAP Web service. Many research groups do the researches of RESTful Web services and SOAP Web services separately, but there lack the researches of how to search services by merging these two kinds of services together. The way of bridging the gap between RESTful Web services and traditional SOAP Web services on searching becomes a new problem in Web service technology.

R. Zhu et al. (Eds.): ICICA 2010, LNCS 6377, pp. 181–188, 2010.
© Springer-Verlag Berlin Heidelberg 2010

The rest of this paper is organized as follows. Section 2 summarizes the researches worked in recent years related to our studies. In section 3, we introduce a new ontology model called Concept Operation Ontology Model (COOM), and present every part of COOM detailed. The service registry framework based on this ontology model is introduced in section 4. Section 5 describes an example based on our approach. Last section (Section 6) concludes this paper.

2   Related Work

Web service technologies bring a dynamic aspect to overall Web usage. However, the current understanding about Web services fails to capture enough semantic data. By presenting the semantics of service descriptions, the matchmaker enables the behavior of an intelligent agent to approach more closely that of a human user trying to locate suitable Web services. But the matching is only based on the input and output, which is not complete. Matthias Klusch [3] gives us an approach called OWLS-MX for matchmaking of service functionality. OWLS-MX allows service query concepts known in its local matchmaker ontology, but is not integrated with the UDDI registry standard for Web service discovery. Katia Sycara [4] describes the implementation of the DAML-S/UDDI Matchmaker that expands on UDDI by providing semantic capability matching, and presents the DAML-S Virtual Machine that uses the DAML-S Process Model to manage the interaction with Web service.

Now, RESTful Web Services are gaining more popularity. SA-REST [5] is similar to SAWSDL [6], as it semantically annotates RESTful Web services. Because there are no WSDL files for RESTful Web services, it adds the annotations to Web pages that describe the services. hRESTs and microWSMO [7] are similar approaches to SA-REST. Another approach called Semantic Bridge for Web Services (SBWS) is introduced in [8], and it annotates WADL documents linking them to ontology. Paper [9] presents a service indexing and matching method based on functionality and semantic domain ontology for RESTful Web Services. Paper [10] proposes a REST-based resource-oriented approach to integrate enterprise resources efficiently, in which RESTful resource meta-model is proposed.

All these researches concerned RESTful Web services and SOAP Web services separately. The argument is that SOAP, when used as an RPC-style interaction, can result in situations in which the HTTP protocol verb used (POST) is inconsistent with the semantic of the operation, which could be GET, PUT or DELETE. In this paper, we propose a service registry framework based on ontology model to avoid the differences between RESTful Web services and traditional SOAP Web services. Furthermore, we also illustrate the Web service matching mechanism based on this ontology model to enhance the flexible of service matching.

3   Concept Operation Ontology Model (COOM)

The COOM focuses on concepts and operations, and it consists of Concept Ontology Layer, Operation Ontology Layer and Association Ontology. As shown in figure 1.

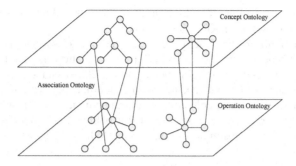

Fig. 1. The Structure of Concept Operation Ontology Model (COOM)

Concept Ontology Layer and Operation Ontology Layer connected by Association Ontology. Each of them is represented by a class. The association class inherits from the concept ontology, and also from the operation ontology. The instance of the associate class is a service which can either be a SOAP Web service or a RESTful Web service.

3.1 Concept Ontology Layer in COOM

The Concept Ontology is composed of a series of nouns, which mean resources in the real world. Each noun is represented by a class. It can be divided into two types of organization. One type contains the concepts involved in the same application field by the association property, and provides a concept template. We emphasize the relationship between the concepts and the cooperation relationship. It is like a type of things, but its definition is more extensive.

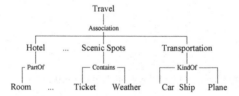

Fig. 2. Travel Template in Concept Ontology Layer collects all the things related on travel

As shown in figure 2, when you want to travel, you will undoubtedly concern the hotel, scenic spots and transportation. They are the related concepts with traveling. Room is a part of hotel and can be a subclass of the hotel class. When searching scenic spots, you will focus on the ticket price, local weather and so on. Scenic spots contain them. Transportation can be car, ship, and plane. The relationship between them is Kind-Of.

The concept ontology is not only tree-structured, but also net-structured. For example, the hotel which is near the scenic spot can have the relationship of nearby with the scenic spot, and also is a partner of transportation. These concepts comprise a concept template of traveling. It is different from the online shopping which related to the concepts of books, toys, EXPRESS and so on.

Another type tightly gathers the resources of the same classification into a set, and to provide a concept pattern. The relationship in this pattern is mainly expressed as same-as, kind-of, part-of, contain, associate, uncorrelated and so on. A concept of book can be extended to magazine, newspaper, journal, publication, reference, and encyclopedia. They all form a collection of the same concepts of resources, and provide a concept pattern. When a user asks for a publication and fails, the ontology system will recommend the similar books, in order to help the user to find the suitable book rapidly.

3.2 Operation Ontology Layer in COOM

The Operation Ontology is composed of a series of verbs, which mean the operation between the concepts. Each verb is also represented by a class. Corresponding to the concept ontology layer, operation ontology can also be divided into two types of organization. One type contains all the association operation in the same application field based on concept template. For example, the operation ontology involved in traveling contains verbs such as reserve, buy, search and pay. They collaborate with each other. Another type gathers the operation operate the same class of concepts, and provides an operation pattern. As shown in figure 3, ordering books can be represented by different words, such as buy, select, find, and get. These verbs take part in the cooperation between concepts in the concept template of the concept ontology.

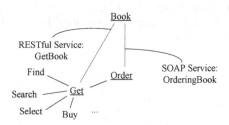

Fig. 3. Get Pattern in Operation Ontology and two kinds of Services linked in this model

This part is the key of merging RESTful Web services and SOAP Web services. The operation in REST architecture style, which is GET, PUT, POST, and DELETE, will establish close links with the verbs in the operation of SOAP services. Generally, whichever of these two kinds of services can be found easily and quickly through this ontology model.

3.3 Association Ontology

The association class inherits from a concept class and an operation class. Services, either the RESTful Web services or SOAP Web services are the instances of an association class. Each operation can operate all concepts in the concept pattern, and a concept in the same concept pattern can be operated by all the operation in the same operation pattern. Thus, the services of the similar function are gathered together tightly. The similarity between the services can be calculated by the matching algorithm which we will introduce to you in next section.

4 Overall Framework and Similarity Matching Algorithm

Figure 4 shows the overall service registry framework, and it consists of applications, semantization module, register module, matching module, ontology system, unified interface service pool and services DB.

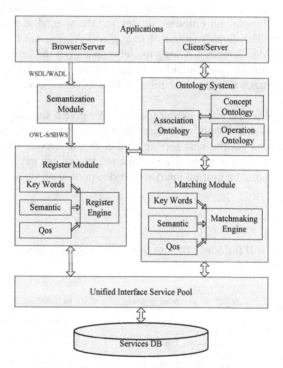

Fig. 4. The Service Register Framework

The providers provide WSDL and WADL documents, which we need to add semantic information. After the semantization, the register engine in the register module will save these useful information including key words, semantic information and QoS information to register module. When registering a new service, the service module will interact with the ontology, find the service location, and create a new service instance in association class to make the searching convenient for the service requester.

The requesters search the services through the key words. The ontology system will split combined words into verbs and nouns and locate them, confirm its adjacent concept ontology in the concept pattern and operation ontology in the operation pattern, find the services in the association ontology and calculate their similarity in the matching module. Here, we give a definition for the service matching score.

The service matching score between a web service S and a query service Q, $Sim_{sm}(S,Q)$, is a function of its concept pattern matching score and its operation pattern matching score is as follows.

$$Sim_{sm}(S,Q) = \alpha_{concept}Sim_{cpm}(S,Q) + \beta_{operation}Sim_{opm}(S,Q). \tag{1}$$

In the above formula, $Sim_{cpm}(S,Q)$ and $Sim_{opm}(S,Q)$ are similarity scores calculated by the concept pattern matching and the operation pattern matching method respectively. The concrete similarity matching algorithm refers to the paper [11]. In formula (1), $\alpha_{concept}$ and $\beta_{operation}$ must satisfy: $\alpha_{concept}+\beta_{operation}=1$, $0<\alpha_{concept}<1$, $0<\beta_{operation}<1$. The optimal values of $\alpha_{concept}$ and $\beta_{operation}$ in the algorithm are on the basis of the characteristics of the concrete domain ontology model and the special semantic relationships between concepts. The default values of $\alpha_{concept}$ and $\beta_{operation}$ are both 0.5. The basic principle is that if the domain ontology model emphasizes the semantic relationships between concepts, then $\alpha_{concept}$ should be larger; on the contrary, if the domain ontology model emphasizes the semantic relationships between operations, then $\beta_{operation}$ should be larger.

The larger score is, the more similar they are. We give a similarity threshold to get the appropriate services. When more than one service is returned, QoS is needed for further calculation to get the best service. Either SOAP service or RESTful service will find in this ontology system. The service requesters can get available Web service endpoints through the unified interface service pool in services DB.

5   Case Study

In this section, we will introduce the use of COOM and matching algorithm through a concrete example.

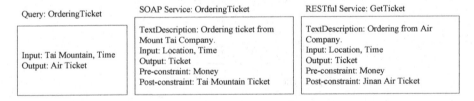

Fig. 5. SOAP Web Service and RESTful Web Service for Ordering Ticket

As shown in figure 5, the requester sends the request for the air ticket to the Tai Mountain. The target service is GetTicket. But there is just OrderingTicket in the service registry. How can system understand that the OrderingTicket service is the right service, and find it in more than one similar service?

5.1   An Example about Ordering Air Ticket Using COOM

In general, developers combine a verb and a noun for denoting the name of an operation, such as getPrice or get_price. Every distinct operation and message that follows each naming denomination would be treated as a different word. In order to bridge different naming conventions, we search the word GetTicket and split it into get and ticket that can use in the concept operation ontology model.

We establish the COOM based on the method proposed above, and use association ontology to build the connection. Each service is modeled under the association class as an instance. By building the concept operation ontology model, the system can merge the RESTful Web services and SOAP Web services well.

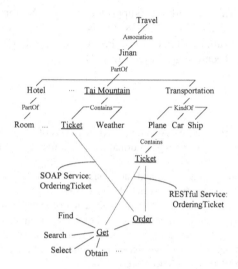

Fig. 6. Services in Concept Operation Ontology Model

As shown in figure 6 in the operation template, we can find Order, and through the association relations, it can be known that Get has the same meaning of Order. Furthermore, we notice that there is a SOAP service named as OrderingTicket, and a RESTful service named as GetTicket. Both of them are ticket reservation services. We need to calculate the similarity in the next step to find the most suitable service. After using the similarity matching algorithm, the similarity of RESTful Web Service: GetTicket is larger. So the GetTicket service is returned to the service requester.

5.2 Discussion

By splitting service name into verbs and nouns to establish the COOM, the system can merge the RESTful Web services and SOAP Web services well. When a service request comes, the most suitable service, either RESTful Web service or SOAP Web service will be returned to the service requester.

6 Conclusion

In this paper, we proposes a novel ontology model for unified web service interface. COOM and Web service matching mechanism is inspired by traditional information retrieval methods, signature matching methods. It is designed to calculate semantic and structural similarity between a desired service and a set of advertised services, so as to eliminate the gap between RESTful Web services and SOAP Web services.

In the future, further research work will be carried out in the management of ontology. Furthermore, the accuracy and efficiency of the matching algorithms will be re-evaluated and enhanced. In addition, validation of service consumers' discovery request to ensure the consistency between QoS requirements will be investigated.

Acknowledgments. This research is supported by the National Natural Science Foundation of China under No.70871078, the National High Technology Research and Development Program of China ("863" Program) under No.2008AA04Z126, and Shanghai Science and Technology Projects 09DZ1121500.

References

1. Grefen, P., Ludwig, H., Dan, A., Angelov, S.: An analysis of Web services support for dynamic business process outsourcing. Information and Software Technology 48(11), 1115–1134 (2006)
2. Fielding, R.T.: Architectural Styles and the Design of Network-based Software Architectures. PhD thesis, University of California, Irvine (2000)
3. Klusch, M., Fries, B., Sycara, K.: OWLS-MX: a hybrid Semantic Web service matchmaker for OWL-S services. International Journal of Web Semantics 7(2) (2009)
4. Sycara, K., Paolucci, M., Anolekar, A., Srinivasan, N.: Automated discovery, interaction and composition of Semantic Web services. Web Semantics: Science, Services and Agents on the World Wide Web 1(1), 27–46 (2003)
5. Sheth, A.P., Gomadam, K., Lathem, J.: SA-REST: Semantically Interoperable and Easier-to-Use Services and Mashups. IEEE Internet Computing 11, 91–94 (2007)
6. Farrel, J., Holger, L. (eds.): Semantic Annotations for WSDL and XML Schema. W3C Working Draft, April 10 (2007)
7. Kopecky, J., Gomadam, K., Vitvar, T.: hRESTS: An HTML Microformat for Describing RESTful Web Services. In: IEEE/WIC/ACM International Conference on Web Intelligence and Intelligent Agent Technology, pp. 619–625 (2008)
8. Battle, R., Benson, E.: Bridging the Semantic Web and Web 2.0 with Representational State Transfer (REST). Web Semantics 6, 61–69 (2008)
9. Nan, L., Hongming, C.: Functionality semantic indexing and matching method for RESTful Web Services based on resource state descriptions. In: 2nd International Workshop on Computer Science and Engineering (2009)
10. Junye, W., Lirui, M., Hongming, C.: A REST-based Approach to Integrate Enterprise Resources. In: International Forum on Computer Science-Technology and Applications, vol. 3 (2009)
11. Ganjisaffar, Y., Abolhassani, H., Neshati, M., Jamali, M.: A similarity measure for OWL-S annotated web services. In: IEEE/WIC/ACM International Conference on Web Intelligence, Hong Kong (2006)

Approaches to Improve the Resources Management in the Simulator CloudSim

Ghalem Belalem, Fatima Zohra Tayeb, and Wieme Zaoui

Dept. of Computer Science, Faculty of Sciences, University of Oran (Es Senia),
Algeria
BP 1524, El M'Naouer, Oran, Algeria
ghalem1dz@gmail.com, fatimazohra.tayeb@yahoo.fr,
zwieme@yahoo.com

Abstract. In Cloud Computing, service availability and performance are two significant aspects to be dealt with. These two aspects can deteriorate or even stopping the services of Cloud Computing, if they are not taken into account. Users see that cloud computing delivers elastic computing services to users on the basis of their needs. This paper aims at improving operation of service of the Cloud Computing environment. Cloud service must be available some is the situations and powerful being by a response time reduced at a user's request. To meet this aim, we propose, in this paper, two approaches which aim at returning a better availability of Datacenters without deteriorating the performances for the answers of the users. The first uses the principle of the messages of availability and the second uses the principle of reservation in advance.

Keywords: Cloud Computing, CloudSim, Broker, Message of availability, Reservation.

1 Introduction

With cloud computing, companies can scale up to massive capacities in an instant without having to invest in new infrastructure, train new personnel, or license new software. Cloud computing is of particular benefit to small and medium-sized businesses which wish to completely outsource their Datacenter infrastructure, or large companies which wish to get peak load capacity without incurring the higher cost of building larger Datacenters internally. The CloudSim simulator was proposed to simulate and evaluate the various approaches suggested with the platforms of Cloud Computing [4]. The execution of the simulator allows making announce a whole of the breakdowns in the treatment of the requests subjected by the users. This work aims to achieve two objectives:

a. The first objective is to reduce or eliminate various failures encountered during the submission of job (cloudlet) in the simulator CloudSim.
b. The second goal is to optimize resource management simulator. For these two objectives, we propose two approaches we will compare the end of the paper. The first approach is based on the message of availability and the second approach is based on the technique of reservation in advance.

R. Zhu et al. (Eds.): ICICA 2010, LNCS 6377, pp. 189–196, 2010.
© Springer-Verlag Berlin Heidelberg 2010

The rest of the paper is structured as follows: in Section 2, we define cloud computing environments as an important scientific trend; we give, in this section, the main objectives of these new environments. Section 3 is dedicated to the simulator CloudSim and problems encountered in version *B0.5*. We present, in Section 4, our two approaches to prevent and better manage resources in the simulator CloudSim. The different experiments are presented in Section 5. We end our paper with a summary and some extension work that we will consider doing so.

2   Cloud Computing

Many researchers try to define grids and clouds in different ways: From [1], a cluster is a type of parallel and distributed system, which consists of a collection of inter-connected stand-alone computers working together as a single integrated computing resource. From [8], a computational grid is a hardware and software infrastructure that provides dependable, consistent, pervasive, and inexpensive access to high-end computational capabilities. From [3], Cloud Computing is a type of parallel and distributed system that consists of a collection of computers interconnected, virtualized and presented as a single processing unit. This system based on a SLA (Service Level Agreement) with a negotiation mechanism between the service provider and the consumer of this service. Clouds appear to be a combination of clusters and Grids. However, this is not the case. Clouds are the next-generation of Datacenters with virtualized nodes through hypervisor technologies, dynamically provisioned on demand to meet a specific service-level agreement, which is established through a negotiation and accessible as a service via Web Service technologies such as SOAP and REST. But there are a set of characteristics that helps distinguish clouds from cluster and Grid, cloud computing platforms possess characteristics of both clusters and Grids, with its own special attributes and capabilities such as for virtualization, dynamic services with Web Service interfaces and Clouds are promising to provide services to users without reference to the infrastructure on which these are hosted. Recently, several academic and industrial organizations have started investigating and developing technologies and infrastructure for Cloud Computing such as Amazon Elastic Compute Cloud [11], Google App Engine, Microsoft Azure, Sun Grid [3] and Aneka [6, 12].

3   CloudSim Toolkit

Several Grid simulators, such as GridSim [2], SimGrid [10], and GangSim [7] have been developed, these toolkits are capable of modelling and simulating the Grid application (e.g. execution, scheduling, allocation, and monitoring) in a distributed environment which consists of multiple Grid organisations, but none of these are able to support the infrastructure and application-level requirements arising from Cloud computing paradigm like modelling of on-demand virtualization enabled resource [4]. Hence, Cloud infrastructure modelling and simulation toolkits must provide support for economic entities for enabling real-time trading of services between customers and providers. Among the currently available simulators developed, only GridSim offers support for economic-driven resource management and application scheduling simulation.

Figure 1 shows the conception of the CloudSim toolkit [5]. At the lowest layer, we find the SimJava that implements the core functionalities required for higher-level simulation [9], such as event queuing and processing, creation of system components (services, host, Datacenter, broker, virtual machines), communication between components, and management of the simulation clock.

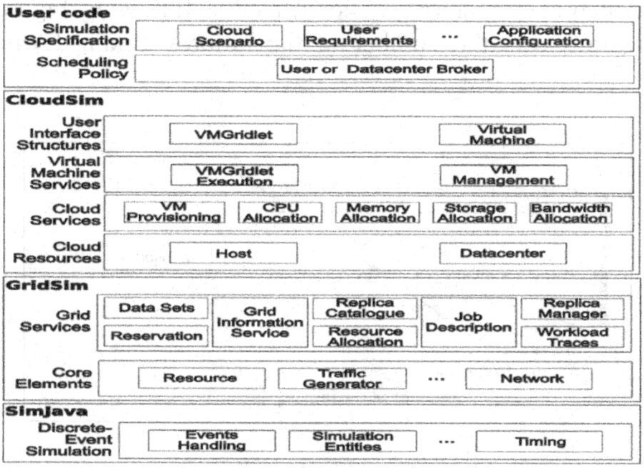

Fig. 1. CloudSim Architecture [5]

In the next layer follows the GridSim toolkit that support high level components for modelling multiple Grid components, such as networks, resources, and information services. The CloudSim is implemented as layer by extending the core functionality of the GridSim layer. CloudSim provides support for modelling and simulation of virtualized Datacenters environments such as management interfaces for VMs, memory, storage, and bandwidth. CloudSim layer manages the creation and execution of core entities (VMs, hosts, Datacenters, application) during the simulation period. This layer handle the provisioning of hosts to VMs on the basis of user requests, managing application execution, and dynamic monitoring. The final layer in the simulation stack is the User Code that exposes configuration functionality for hosts (number of machines, their specification and so on), applications (number of tasks and their requirements), VMs, number of users and their application types, and broker scheduling policies. A Cloud application developer can write an application configurations and Cloud scenarios at this layer to perform a cloud computing scenario simulations.

4   Extension of CloudSim Simulator

CloudSim is a toolkit of simulation; its behavior is primitive and does not satisfy all the users' requests. At the beginning of simulation, Datacenters are recorded in a directory called GIS. Broker, acting on behalf of a user, consults this directory and obtains the list of all Datacenters. It sends to the first element of this list a VM_create message (to create the virtual machine and to make there carry out Cloudlet), if this creation fails, it remakes the same thing with second Datacenter and so on.

If Broker traverses all the list and finds all Datacenters taken, CloudSim declares a "failed" and the request (the request) of the user is rejected.

To illustrate these situations of failures of certain requests, we launched a simulation with CloudSim, we fixed the number of Datacenters at 6, the number of processors elements to 2, the number of virtual machines with 2, the number of Cloudlet with 4 per user and we varied the number of the users from 5 to 50 per step of 5. The result of this simulation is shown by the following Figure (Fig. 2). The curve of this figure shows the number of the failures obtained while varying the number of users.

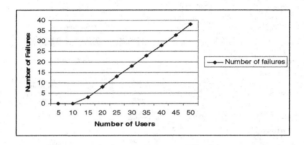

Fig. 2. Number of Failures in CloudSim

to cure the "failures" of the CloudSim simulator, we proposed two approaches into which no request of the users is rejected and consequently, all the users are satisfied. The first approach is based on the messages of availability and second is based on the reservation in advance.

4.1   Approach Based on the Messages of Availability

For this approach, we extended class GIS to obtain a new class CIS (Cloud Information Service). One of the principal characteristics of this new class is the use of a queue for the virtual machines (VMs) not create. The operation of this approach can be schematized by the activity chart of UML of Figure 3.

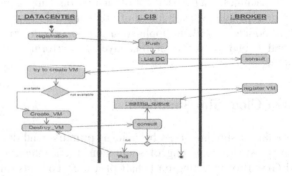

Fig. 3. Activity chart of UML of approach based on the messages of availability

When Broker receives the failures of creation on behalf of all Datacenters, it records the characteristics of these VMs in the queue on the level of CIS. This recording is in fact to send a message VM-Set of Broker towards the CIS. dice which Datacenter (DC) is released (with the destruction of VM of which Cloudlet at the end of execution), a message of the type DC_Available will be to send by DC to the CIS, the reception of this message causes to depilate the first element (if the queue is not empty), according to the policy of scheduling FIFO (First In First Out). This element of the VM_characteristics type will be sent in the VM_Create message intended for Datacenters free. Thus, no request is likely to be rejected.

4.2 Approach Based on the Reservation in Advance

Our second approach is based on the mechanism of reservation in advance. When the broker does not manage to allocate a virtual machine at all available DataCenters, it enters a process of reservation in advance by sending a message to all DataCenters, this message contains its identifier in the system and its requirements in terms for resources, and it will be put on standby of first DataCenter which will answer him.

When DataCenter finishes the treatment of a virtual machine, it checks its queue of the reservations, if it is full, it will take the first message and will answer its owner by a message by indicating to him that it will deal with its reservation, then it will be put on standby of a confirmation or cancellation. When the broker receives a message of first DataCenter which is able to deal with its reservation, it will answer this latter by a message of confirmation of reservation and send to the remainder of DataCenters a message of cancellation of reservation. If DC receives the Cancel message, it depilates the first element of the file of confirmation without creation. If DC receives the message VM-Ok, it depilates the first element of the file of confirmation, recovers the characteristics of VM and creates the virtual machine (see Figure 4).

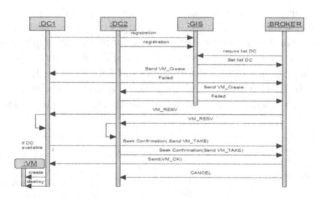

Fig. 4. Stages of approach based on Reservation in advance

4.3 Approach Based on the Reservation in Advance with Balancing of Load

The approach, based on the reservation in advance that we proposed, presents a problem of waste of time due to a lack of equity in the allocation of the functions. With the reception of a cancellation of the Broker, DC does not try any more to create

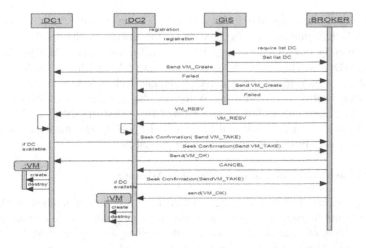

Fig. 5. Stages of approach based on reservation in advance with load balancing

other VMs of the queue (like already seen in Figure 5), which implies their creation in only DC which received a confirmation.

Including load balancing, we perform an optimization of this approach. DC receives a Cancel message of the Broker, it depilates the first element of the file of confirmation without creation; checks if the file is not empty and if it is the case, it asks the confirmation for second VM of the file (see Figure 5).

5 Study of Performances of the Approaches Proposed

In all simulations we have launched our two proposed approaches, we have minimized, even sometimes avoided, for discharges of user requests. In other words, both approaches provide almost total availability for processing applications.

For the purpose of studying the performances of the approaches suggested from a point of view of response time of the executions of Cloudlets, we launched two series of simulations. In the first series (see Figure 6), we fixed the number of Datacenters at 6, the number of PE with 2, the number of virtual machine with 2 and numbers of

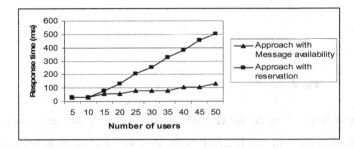

Fig. 6. Variation of Response Time for the Approaches Suggested

users with 20, then we have varied the number of Cloudlets from 5 to 50 per step of 5.The result of this simulation is shown by the following figure.

We notice that the curve of the approach containing message is below that of the curve of the approach containing reservation in advance. Therefore, we can conclude that the approach containing messages of availability gives a better performance than it second approach. In the second series of simulation (see Figure 7), we fixed the number of Datacenters at 6, the number of PE with 2, the number of virtual machine with 2 and numbers it of Cloudlet with 4 per user, then we have varied the number of users from 5 to 50 per step of 5.

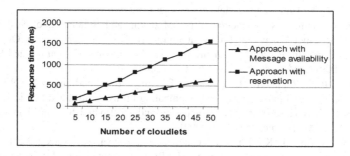

Fig. 7. Variation of response time for the approaches suggested

The result obtained by this simulation is schematized by this figure. The same conclusion is confirmed as previously, i.e., than the curve of the approach containing reservation in advance is above the curve of the approach containing messages of availability, which confirms the conclusion which the approach containing messages is better than the approach containing reservation.

6 Conclusions and Future Work

The recent efforts to design and develop Cloud technologies focus on defining novel methods, policies and mechanisms for efficiently managing Cloud infrastructures. The principal objective that we aimed at solving, it is the satisfaction of the users, while avoiding rejecting some requests subjected by the customers of Cloud Computing. We proposed in this paper two approaches, to deal with and to carry out all the requests subjected to Cloud Computing. In the first approach we proposed to use the messages of availability to collect information of availability of Datacenters, then to retransmit the requests on standby towards these Datacenters available. For the second approach, we proceeded by the reservation in advance within each Datacenter. We studied the performances of the two approaches propose from a point of view of response time. Several future tracks can be the subject of extension of this work. We can quote:

-    Equip the first approach by an agent which allows to select most suitable Datacenter for the assumption of responsibility of the requests;
-    Use a multi-agent system between data centers, where agents can negotiate among themselves to select the data center to the most appropriate Cloudlet.

References

1. Buyya, R.: High Performance Cluster Computing: Architectures and Systems, vol. 1. Prentice Hall, Upper Saddle River (1999)
2. Buyya, R., Murshed, M.: GridSim: A Toolkit for the Modeling and Simulation of Distributed Resource Management and Scheduling for Grid Computing. The Journal of Concurrency and Computation: Practice and Experience (CCPE) 14(13-15) (2002)
3. Buyya, R., Yeo, C.S., Venugopal, S., Broberg, J., Brandic, I.: Cloud Computing and Emerging IT Platforms: Vision, Hype, and Reality for Delivering Computing as the 5th Utility, Technical Report, GRIDS-TR-2008-14, Grid Computing and Distributed Systems Laboratory, The University of Melbourne, Australia (2008)
4. Buyya, R., Ranjan, R., Calheiros, R.N.: Modeling and Simulation of Scalable Cloud Computing Environments and the CloudSim Toolkit: Challenges and Opportunities, Keynote Paper. In: Proceedings of the 7th High Performance Computing and Simulation (HPCS 2009) Conference, Leipzig, Germany (2009)
5. Calheiros, R.N., Ranjan, R., De Rose, C.A.F., Buyya, R.: CloudSim: A Novel Framework for Modeling and Simulation of Cloud Computing Infrastructures and Services, Technical Report, GRIDS-TR-2009-1, Grid Computing and Distributed Systems Laboratory, The University of Melbourne, Australia (2009)
6. Chu, X., Nadiminti, K., Jin, C., Venugopal, S., Buyya, R.: Aneka: Next-Generation Enterprise Grid Platform for e-Science and e-Business Applications. In: Proceedings of the 3th IEEE International Conference on e-Science and Grid Computing (e-Science 2007), Bangalore, India (2007)
7. Dumitrescu, C.L., Foster, I.: GangSim: a simulator for grid scheduling studies. In: Proceedings of the IEEE International Symposium on Cluster Computing and the Grid (2005)
8. Foster, I., Kesselman, C., Tuecke, S.: The anatomy of the grid: Enabling Scable Virtuel Organizations. International Journal of Super Computer Applications 15(3), 1–10 (2001)
9. Howell, F., Mcnab, R.: SimJava: A discrete event simulation library for java. In: Proceedings of the first International Conference on Web-Based Modeling and Simulation (1998)
10. Legrand, A., Marchal, L., Casanova, H.: Scheduling distributed applications: the SimGrid simulation framework. In: Proceedings of the 3rd IEEE/ACM International Symposium on Cluster Computing and the Grid (2003)
11. Pandey, S., Dobson, J.E., Voorsluys, W., Vecchiola, C., Karunamoorthy, D., Chu, X., Buyya, R.: Workflow Engine: fMRI Brain Image Analysis on Amazon EC2 and S3 Clouds. In: The Second IEEE International Scalable Computing Challenge (SCALE 2009) in Conjunction with CCGrid 2009, Shanghai, China (2009)
12. Vecchiola, C., Chu, X., Buyya, R.: Aneka: A Software Platform for.NET-based Cloud Computing. In: Gentzsch, W., Grandinetti, L., Joubert, G. (eds.) High Performance & Large Scale Computing, Advances in Parallel Computing. IOS Press, Amsterdam (2009)

Introducing a New Predicate Network Model Constructed Based on Null Hypothesis Testing for Software Fault Localization

Saeed Parsa, Azam Peyvandi-Pour, and Mojtaba Vahidi-Asl

{parsa,m_vahidi_asl}@iust.ac.ir, az_peyvandypour@comp.iust.ac.ir

Abstract. The aim of this paper is to introduce a new statistical approach for software fault localization. To this end, a novel weighted predicate tree, *P-network*, has been introduced. The main contribution of the paper is to consider the behavior of branch statements, namely predicates, together, in failing and passing executions and detect those predicates having different behavior as fault relevant predicates. In order to assess the difference in behaviors of predicates together a null hypothesis testing has been used. The predicates with higher different ratios in failing and passing runs are selected as the nodes of the *P-network*. By using a BFS method on *P-network* all faulty predicates could be found. After that, by ranking the faulty predicates we are able to find the most relevant faulty ones, which might help the debugger easily locate the bug. The experiments on Siemens test suite reveal promising results.

Keywords: Statistical Software Debugging, Fault Localization, Faulty Predicates, Null Hypothesis, Breadth First Search.

1 Introduction

Having bug free software is the ideal of software companies. However, as more complex software becomes, the less probable it contains no latent fault [1][5]. Manual localization of the existing software faults could be really cumbersome and time-consuming. This has encouraged many researchers over past few years to develop new methods for automatic software debugging [2][3][6][7]. Among these methods, statistical software debugging techniques have achieved significant and promising development [1][4].

The aim of statistical software debugging is to collect program run-time data from both successful and failed executions and perform statistical analysis on the data to detect the causes for program failure [3]. To collect data some probes are inserted in the source code before branch statements. These branch statements, namely predicates, are those statements which determine the execution paths of the program [2]. The aim is to find those predicates in faulty paths, which mostly manifest the effect of the fault. Two outstanding statistical approaches for fault localization using conditional probabilities are *cooperative bug isolation* by Liblit [1] and *Sober* by Liu[2]. Liblit has introduced two conditional probabilities for each predicate *p* in the program:

R. Zhu et al. (Eds.): ICICA 2010, LNCS 6377, pp. 197–204, 2010.
© Springer-Verlag Berlin Heidelberg 2010

$$Context(p)=\text{Probability}(\text{program fails}|\ p \text{ is evaluated}) \tag{1}$$

$$Failure(p)=\text{Probability}(\text{program fails}|\ p \text{ is evaluated as True})$$

The first probability in (1) estimates whether a predicate has ever been evaluated as *True* or not in failing executions. It computes the ratio of failing executions to all executions where predicate p is ever observed. The second probability considers the same ratio where the predicate has evaluated only as *True*. Liblit, then computes the difference between *Context(p)* and *Failure(p)* as *Increase(p)*. A predicate with higher *Increase(p)* ranks as top fault relevant predicates. In other words, this approach calculates how much the execution of a predicate in failing runs in contrast to the passing ones may increase the probability that the predicate is relevant to the program failure. However, the Liblit's approach fails to work when a predicate has been evaluated as *True* in all executions. In these situations, The *Increase(p)* factor would be zero meaning that the predicate has no relevancy with the fault, which is not correct in all cases. To resolve the drawback, *Sober* [2] considers the execution of each predicate as a *Bernoulli* trial with head probability θ. It computes two distributions: f(θ|*passing executions*) and f(θ|*failing executions*). It uses these two distributions to present the evaluation bias of predicate p in each passing and failing executions. Evaluation bias for predicate p, depicted by n_t/n_t+n_f describes the number of times the predicate is evaluated as *True* to the number of times it has been observed (i.e. *True* or *False*) in a specific passing or failing execution. The technique in *Sober*, applies a null hypothesis based on the equality of variance and median for both failing and passing runs. In cases that there is a high difference between f(θ|*passing executions*) and f(θ|*failing executions*) it ranks the predicate as a high bug relevant one.

The problem with *Sober* is that it considers each predicate in isolation from other predicates and does not consider their mutual effects on each other. Therefore, it may lose its power for certain type of faults. The problem becomes worse when a fault is relevant to more than one predicate and if one of the predicates are eliminated the fault may disappear [4]. Furthermore, most of the existing debugging techniques may fail when there are multiple bugs in the program [10].

It is obvious that predicates have different interactions together in different executions. In each execution a sequence of predicates are executed. Because of this specific interaction in each individual run, the termination status might be successful or failure. However, studying the presence or absence of a predicate in different executions [6] or the number of times it has been evaluated as *True* to the number of times it has been observed [9] do not always lead to the location of bugs. Hence, in this paper we have developed an approach which analyzes the joint evaluation of predicates. In other words, we consider the number of times a specific predicate, p_i, has been evaluated as *True* together with a particular predicate, p_j, in an individual execution. This could be shown as a simple ratio, name it $p(i,j)$-ratio:

$$p(i,j)\text{-ratio}= \frac{The-number-of-times-predicate-i-is-evaluated-as-True}{The-number-of-times-predicate-j-is-evaluated-as-True} \tag{2}$$

For each two predicates in the program this ratio could be calculated. Considering the ratio as a random variable, we may have different values in different passing and failing executions. The average *p(i,j)-ratio* in passing executions could manifest the normal interaction of predicates p_i and p_j. Therefore, by contrasting the interaction of two predicates in failing and passing runs, the abnormal predicates could be detected. In order to contrast the behavior, in this paper, we have used a null hypothesis testing. Here, the question is: for which predicates the ratio should be computed? To solve the problem, we have constructed a weighted tree, called *P-network*. Since the program result is manifested directly in one (or more) predicate(s), these predicates are located in the root of the tree. Using the null hypothesis, we could decide whether a predicate should be selected as the child of a subject node in the network or not. After constructing the *P-network*, by considering the weights of the edges, the heavy-weighted paths are marked as suspicious ones. The predicates located in suspicious paths are ranked as faulty predicates and the top predicates are known as the most bug relevant predicates.

The remainder of this paper is organized as follows: in section 2, the description of the proposed statistical approach is presented with an example. The experimental results on Siemens test suite are manifested in section 3. Finally concluding remarks are expressed in section 4.

2 A Description of the Proposed Statistical Approach

The proposed statistical approach is performed in two main stages: 1)*p-network* construction 2) ranking faulty predicates. These stages are described in the following sub-sections.

In order to collect program runtime behavior, it should be properly instrumented. After the instrumentation process of the program, the execution is started with different failing and passing test cases. We would like to know the number of times that a predicate *X* has been evaluated with particular predicate, like *Y* in both failing and passing runs. Therefore, the collected data should contain the number of times each predicate has been evaluated as *True* in a specific execution. To this end, a counter has been inserted before each control instruction (i.e. *if-else*, *switch-case*, loops and return value instructions). The collected data is logged to be analyzed with statistical hypothesis testing.

2.1 Construction of *P-Network*

As mentioned earlier, a predicate network (or *P-network* for short) is a weighted tree which may contain repeated nodes. The aim of building such tree is to investigate which predicates may affect the result predicate in failing executions. To find the result predicates the locations in program code which mostly reveal the outcome (such as outputs, *print* & *print* to file and etc. instructions) are determined. Then, the closest predicate to that location is identified as the result predicate. A *P-network* could act as a cause-effect chain for the program failure. A part of *P-network* for the sixth version of *Printtokens2_2.0* is shown in Fig. 1 where the fault is located in line.

358 in function *"static int is_num_constant(str)"*.

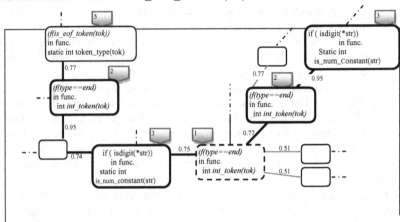

Fig. 1. The *P-network* for the sixth version of program Printtokens2_2.0; the result predicate is the dashed box and the paths with heavy weights are shown in bold. These paths contain the fault relevant predicates. The faulty predicates which are manifested in both paths are shown in bold boxes.

The root of the *P*-network is the result predicate, p_r, and the tree is constructed based on the null hypothesis testing in an iterative process. The iterative process is started from choosing the children of the root. Consider the average ratio of all predicates with the resultant predicate, p_r, in failing and passing runs is $\overline{p}(r, j) - ratio$ for all remaining predicates i in the program. After computing the ratios, the null hypothesis testing, is applied to select those predicates which are mostly observed with p_r in failing runs but not in passing ones. Such predicates, having the discriminated average ratio with the result predicate (i.e. p_r/p_i) between failing and passing runs are selected as the children of the root and the ratios form the weights of the edges. In the next step, the node with the highest ratio is regarded as the subject node and its children are selected in the same manner. After that the second child of root with the highest ratio satisfying the null hypothesis is selected as the subject node and the process is repeated until no node could be found satisfying the null hypothesis. The details of using null hypothesis testing are described in 2.2.

2.2   Using Null Hypothesis Testing for Filtering the Predicates

In statistics, hypothesis testing is to verify an assertion about a distribution of a random variable or other statistical properties [8][9]. The null hypothesis testing could be used when we want to verify whether a property in the statistical data is true or not. Therefore, we may have two symbols: H_0 for the null hypothesis that we want to test and H_1 for the alternative hypothesis. Based on the application, we have chosen null hypothesis test concerning means of the two populations: passing and failing. Here, we want to test the overall behavior of two individual predicates together, p_i/p_j, in both passing and failing runs. Therefore, the null hypothesis is regarded against the alternative as shown below:

$$H_0 : \mu_p = \mu_f$$
$$H_1 : \mu_p \neq \mu_f \tag{3}$$

Where μ_p are the median of p_i/p_j in passing and failing runs, respectively. In other words, we want to study, weather the behavior of predicates together (i.e. the ratio of p_i/p_j) is similar in both populations of runs (i.e. passing and failing). If not, based on the amount of difference, which is measured with the Z statistic, described later, the predicates are marked as suspicious ones. After some experiments on passing executions with 2000 runs in average, we found the population acting normal [8]. Since the number of failing executions is more than 30 with finite variance for many experimented programs, we applied central limit theorem to justify using the test of normal populations [11]. In order to accept or reject the assertion, the Z normalized static is used:

$$z = \frac{\overline{X} - \mu_p}{\sigma / \sqrt{n}} \tag{4}$$

Where X is a random variable representing the $p(i,j)$–ratio in failing runs and   is the mean of X. The parameter   is the standard deviation of X's in failing executions and n is the number of failing runs. The computed Z-value is compared with $z_{\alpha/2}$, the boundaries of the critical regions. If it is in the range of $[z_{\alpha/2}, z_\alpha]$, the H_0 assertion is satisfied and hence there is no considerable difference in interaction of two predicates in passing and failing runs. Otherwise, the interaction could be suspicious.

2.3 Ranking Faulty Predicates

The next step after building the network is marking the suspicious paths. The aim is to find nodes with highest weights. To this end, a breadth first search (BFS) method is applied to mark those paths. As shown in Fig. 1, the root labeled '1' has the highest ratio with '2' and '3'. Thus, these two predicates with their corresponding edges are marked as nodes in suspicious paths. Predicate '2' connected to the node '3' has a considerable weight; therefore, it is also marked as a suspicious node in the path: 1->2->3. Another marked path as highlighted in Fig. 1 is: 1->3->2->5.

The final step is the ranking of predicates based on their presence and their corresponding weights in suspicious network paths. To this end, for each individual predicate we compute the proportion of suspicious paths the predicate has been appeared. A predicate with high appearance and higher ratios with the result predicate is ranked top of the other. By selecting a proper threshold the top predicates are reported as the most effective faulty predicates to the user. To calculate the indirect ratio of a predicate i with the result predicate, it is required only to multiply the weights in the edges that connect the result predicate with the subject node (predicate i).

3 Experimental Results

In order to study the accuracy of the proposed approach, we have used Siemens test suite as the subject programs. Siemens contains seven programs in language C: print_tokens, print_tokens2, schedule, schedule2, tcas, replace and tot_info. Each program has some versions. In each version one fault has been seeded manually. Each program is provided with failing and passing test cases. The test suite has been provided from software infrastructure repository (sir)[12].

In order to experiment the proposed approach, we have considered two important criterions: the number of detected faults and the amount of code that should be inspected manually to locate the main causes of faults.

To implement the proposed approach, first, each faulty version has been instrumented manually. To collect the run-time data, the programs have been executed with different failing and passing test cases. After data collection, we have applied our proposed statistical approach. The result was an individual *P-network* for each faulty version. A part of *P-network* for version 6th of program Print_tokens2 has been shown in Fig. 1. After marking the paths in network based on the weights of edges, the faulty predicates for each version has been identified. The last step, as discussed earlier was the ranking of predicates in all marked paths to find the most effective faulty predicates. For each case, the top 5% of predicates with highest scores were selected as the most effective faulty ones. The average number of detected faults for each version is presented in Fig. 2.

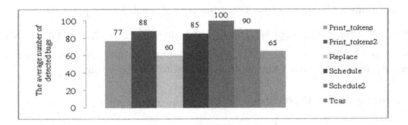

Fig. 2. The average number of detected bugs in Siemens test suite

As shown in Fig. 2, the proposed approach has detected a proper number of faults in comparison with the similar approaches. However, we have faced some problems. For some versions, the fault was located in the header file (e.g. some values have been changed). For those types of faults we could not detect the faulty predicates correctly. We also have difficulties to collect data from some versions of programs replace and tot_info due to segmentation faults in a number of runs. We believe that if we could fix the problem and complete our data set for those programs, the proposed approach is capable to detect their seeded faults appropriately. But, the main strong point of our approach was its capability to detect bugs when the failing population contains 6 or more failing test cases.

Obviously, the number of detected faults is not solely enough to assess the accuracy of a debugging technique. As mentioned before, in most of statistical techniques, only the control statements are instrumented and therefore to find the cause of bugs, user should scrutinize the code manually. This inspection is based on the control and data dependency between statements of the program. Therefore, another criterion for evaluating the efficiency of debugging methods is to compute the average amount of manually inspected code for finding the buggy statement. In Fig. 3 the results of this case study for all seven programs in Siemens are shown.

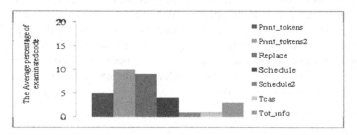

Fig. 3. The percentage of examined code in Siemens test suite

Since two well-known statistical debugging methods related to our work is done by Liblit [6] and Liu (i.e. Sober) [2] we compared our proposed technique with their works in Fig. 4.

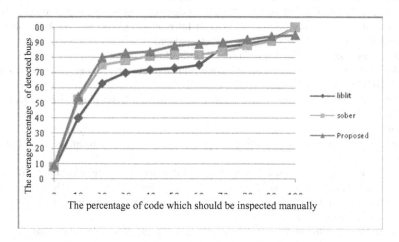

Fig. 4. The comparison of proposed approach with two other approaches

As shown in Fig. 4, in overall our proposed approach could detect the bugs with less amount of manually code inspection comparing with *Liblit* and *Sober*. But with more 80% scrutinize, the other two approaches were better, since we could not detect all the existing bugs as mentioned earlier.

4 Concluding Remarks

In this paper a new statistical approach for software debugging has been introduced. The approach in a backward manner, starts from the result predicates of the program and tries to find faulty predicates which have highly effect on the result predicate. To study the interactive behavior of predicates on program termination status, we have considered a ratio between particular predicates. this ratio, acts as a random variable, computes the number of times a predicate has been evaluated *True* in a specific run to *True* evaluations of another predicate in that execution. The average of the ratios in passing executions reveals the normal behavior of those predicates together. We applied a null hypothesis testing to detect abnormal ratios and use these predicates to construct our proposed tree, namely *P-network*. By marking heavy weighted paths in tree using BFS method, the faulty predicates have been found and by ranking those predicates, we found most effective ones. Our evaluation on Siemens suite, revealed the accuracy of the proposed approach.

References

1. Liblit, B.: Cooperative Bug Isolation. PhD thesis, University of California, Berkeley (2004)
2. Liu, C., Yan, X., Fei, L., Han, J., Midkiff, S.P.: Sober: Statistical model-based bug localization. In: 10th European Software Eng. Conf./13th ACM SIGSOFT Int'l Symposium Foundations of Software Engineering, Lisbon, pp. 286–295 (2005)
3. Jiang, L., Su, Z.: Context-aware statistical debugging: from bug predictors to faulty control flow paths. In: Twenty-Second IEEE/ACM International Conference on Automated Software Engineering, pp. 184–193. ACM Press, Atlanta (2007)
4. Arumuga Nainar, P., Chen, T., Rosin, J., Liblit, B.: Statistical debugging using compound Boolean predicates. In: International Symposium on Software Testing and Analysis, pp. 5–15. ACM Press, London (2007)
5. Zeller, A.: Why Programs Fail: A Guide to Systematic Debugging. Morgan Kaufmann, San Francisco (2006)
6. Liblit, B., Naik, M., Zheng, A., Aiken, A., Jordan, M.: Scalable Statistical Bug Isolation. In: Int'l Conference Programming Language Design and Implementation, Chicago, pp. 15–26 (2005)
7. Fei, L., Lee, K., Li, F., Midkiff, S.P.: Argus: Online statistical bug detection. In: Baresi, L., Heckel, R. (eds.) FASE 2006. LNCS, vol. 3922, pp. 308–323. Springer, Heidelberg (2006)
8. Freund, J.E., Miller, I., Miller, M.: Mathematical statistics with applications, 7th edn. Prentice Hall, Englewood Cliffs (2004)
9. Hastie, T.J., Tibshirani, R.J., Friedman, J.: The Elements of Statistical Learning: Data Mining Inference and Prediction. Springer, New York (2001)
10. Zheng, A.X., Jordan, M.I., Liblit, B., Naik, M., Aiken, A.: Statistical debugging: simultaneous identification of multiple bugs. In: ICML 2006: Proceedings of the 23rd International Conference on Machine Learning, pp. 1105–1112. ACM Press, New York (2006)
11. SAS Institute Inc.: SAS/STAT User Guide. Release 6.03 Edition, SAS Institute Inc., Cary, NC (1988)
12. Software-artifact infrastructure repository, http://sir.unl.edu/portal

Image Segmentation Based on FCM
with Mahalanobis Distance

Yong Zhang[1,*], Zhuoran Li[1], Jingying Cai[1], and Jianying Wang[2]

[1] College of Computer & Information Technology, Liaoning Normal University,
Dalian, China
[2] College of Mathematics, Liaoning Normal University,
Dalian, China
cony678@gmail.com

Abstract. For its simplicity and applicability, fuzzy c-means clustering algorithm is widely used in image segmentation. However, fuzzy c-means clustering algorithm has some problems in image segmentation, such as sensitivity to noise, local convergence, etc. In order to overcome the fuzzy c-means clustering shortcomings, this paper replaces Euclidean distance with Mahalanobis distance in the fuzzy c-means clustering algorithm. Experimental results show that the proposed algorithm has a significant improvement on the effect and efficiency of segmentation comparing with the standard FCM clustering algorithm.

Keywords: Fuzzy c-means clustering; Mahalanobis distance; image segmentation.

1   Introduction

Image segmentation is a major research topic for many image processing researchers. Image segmentation can be defined as the classification of all the picture elements or pixels in an image into different clusters that exhibit features. Most computer vision and image analysis problems require a segmentation stage in order to detect objects or divide the image into regions, which can be considered homogeneous according to a given criterion, such as color, motion, texture, etc. Using these criterions, image segmentation can be used in several applications including video surveillance, medical imaging analysis, image retrieval and object classification [1].

There are many different approaches to image segmentation. FCM clustering algorithm is widely used in image segmentation for its simplicity and applicability. Fuzzy c-means (FCM) method [2] is an unsupervised clustering algorithm that has been applied successfully to a number of problems involving feature analysis, clustering and classifier design. Furthermore, on the basis of FCM, much more optimized clustering methods have been proposed. For instance, Wu and Yang have proposed an alternative fuzzy c-means [3]. Xing and Hu have proposed the fuzzy c-means algorithm based mixtures of expert model to improve the unlabeled data classification [4].

---

* Corresponding author.

R. Zhu et al. (Eds.): ICICA 2010, LNCS 6377, pp. 205–212, 2010.
© Springer-Verlag Berlin Heidelberg 2010

Kang et al. have proposed the improved fuzzy c-means algorithm based on adaptive weighted average to solve noise samples [5].

Classical fuzzy c-means algorithm is based on Euclidean distance, which can only be used to detect spherical structural clusters. However, accuracy dealing with high dimensional data is not fine. To improve the problem, this paper replaces Euclidean distance with Mahalanobis distance in the FCM algorithm.

In order to overcome the fuzzy c-means clustering shortcomings, this paper replaces Euclidean distance with Mahalanobis distance in the fuzzy c-means algorithm. Experimental results in image segmentation show the proposed algorithm is effective and advantageous.

The remainder of this paper is organized as follows. Section 2 briefly introduces the related work. We propose image segmentation method based on FCM method with Mahalanobis distance in Section 3. The experimental results are reported in Section 4. Section 5 concludes this paper.

2   Related Work

2.1   Fuzzy c-Means Clustering

Clustering plays an important role in data analysis and interpretation, and also is an important branch of unsupervised clustering system in statistical pattern recognition. It is based on partitioning of a collection of data points into a set of different clusters where objects inside the same cluster show some considerable similarity. Fuzzy clustering technique based on fuzzy set theory, are widely used in pattern recognition and data mining and other fields.

The fuzzy c-means algorithm (FCM) is a well-known algorithm to cluster data in unsupervised learning and has been applied successfully in many areas [6]. It partitions a given data set $X = \{x_1, x_2, ..., x_l\}$ including l data points into c fuzzy subsets that are characterized by representatives $p = \{p_1, p_2, ..., p_c\}$. The process of subdividing a data set X into distinct subsets with homogeneous elements is called clustering. With fuzzy clustering each datum x_j belongs to all clusters p_i simultaneously, but to different degrees u_{ij} with $U = [u_{ij}] \in [0,1]^{c \times l}$. The FCM algorithm performs clustering by minimizing the objective function of weighted distances given in following

$$J_{FCM}(U, p; X) = \sum_{j=1}^{l} \sum_{i=1}^{c} u_{ij}^m d_{ij}^2 = \sum_{j=1}^{l} \sum_{i=1}^{c} u_{ij}^m \left\| x_j - p_i \right\|^2 \tag{1}$$

taking the constraints

$$\forall i \in \{1, ..., c\}, \ j \in \{1, ..., l\} : 1 \geq u_{ij} \geq 0 \tag{2}$$

$$\forall j \in \{1, ..., l\} : \sum_{i=1}^{c} u_{ij} = 1 \tag{3}$$

into account. u_{ij} represents the membership of the data point x_j from with respect to the ith cluster. The parameter m is the weighting exponent which determines the fuzziness of the clusters. $\|x_j - p_i\|$ is the norm and defines a measurement of similarity between a data point and the cluster center prototypes, respectively.

Minimization of the objective function is an iterative optimization algorithm which can be summarized as the following steps:

(1) Initialization

Fix the number of clusters c; fix the weighting exponent m, $1 < m < \infty$; fix the iteration limit T; and fix the termination threshold $\varepsilon > 0$. Initialize u_{ij} ($i \in \{1,...,c\}$ and $j \in \{1,...,l\}$) of datum x_j belonging to cluster p_i such that $1 \geq u_{ij} \geq 0$ and $\sum_{i=1}^{c} u_{ij} = 1$.

(2) $t=1$

(3) Compute the cluster centers by the following equation:

$$p_i^{(t)} = \frac{\sum_{j=1}^{l} (u_{ij}^{(t-1)})^m x_j}{\sum_{j=1}^{l} (u_{ij}^{(t-1)})^m}, 1 \leq i \leq c. \tag{4}$$

(4) Update the membership matrix U by the following equation:

$$u_{ij}^{(t)} = \frac{1}{\sum_{k=1}^{c} \left(\frac{\|x_j - p_i^{(t)}\|}{\|x_j - p_k^{(t)}\|} \right)^{\frac{2}{m-1}}}, 1 \leq i \leq c, 1 \leq j \leq l. \tag{5}$$

(5) If $\max_{1 \leq i \leq c} \|p_i^{(t)} - p_i^{(t-1)}\| < \varepsilon$ or $t > T$ then stop

else $t=t+1$ and go to step 3.

2.2 The Mahalanobis Distance in the Feature Space

Let X be a $l \times n$ input matrix containing l random observations $x_i \in R^n$, $i = 1,...,l$. The squared Mahalanobis distance d_M from a sample x_i to the population X is defined as follows:

$$d_M(x_i, X) = (x_i - p)^T \Sigma^{-1} (x_i - p) \tag{6}$$

where p is a mean vector of all samples, Σ is the covariance matrix calculated as:

$$\Sigma = \frac{1}{l}\sum_{j=1}^{l}(x_j - p)(x_j - p)^T \tag{7}$$

Originally, the Mahalanobis distance can be defined as a dissimilarity measure between two random vectors of the same distribution with covariance matrix Σ. If the covariance matrix is the identity matrix, the Mahalanobis distance reduces to the Euclidean distance.

3 Proposed Image Segmentation Method

3.1 FCM Algorithm Based on Mahalanobis Distance

Distance metric is a key issue in many machine learning algorithms, such as clustering problems [7-10]. These methods above are all based on Euclidean distance metric and only be used to detect the data classed with same super spherical shapes. The commonly used Euclidean distance metric assumes that each feature of data point is equally important and independent from others. This assumption may not be always satisfied in real applications, especially when dealing with high dimensional data where some features may not be tightly related to the topic of interest.

In this paper, we focus on learning a Mahalanobis distance metric in the FCM algorithm. The Mahalanobis distance is a measure between two data points in the space defined by relevant features. Since it accounts for unequal variances as well as correlations between features, it will adequately evaluate the distance by assigning different weights or importance factors to the features of data points. Only when the features are uncorrelated, the distance under a Mahalanobis distance metric is identical to that under the Euclidean distance metric. In addition, geometrically, a Mahalanobis distance metric can adjust the geometrical distribution of data so that the distance between similar data points is small [11].Thus it can enhance the performance of clustering or classification algorithms. When some training cluster size is smaller than its dimension, it induces the singular problem of the inverse covariance matrix.

This section presents a modified FCM algorithm based on Mahalanobis distance. To make use of the FCM algorithm for fuzzy clustering, we extend the original FCM algorithm into the modified algorithm by replacing Euclidean distance with Mahalanobis distance.

FCM algorithm based on Mahalanobis distance minimizes the following objective function

$$\min J(U,V,\Sigma) = \sum_{i=1}^{c}\sum_{k=1}^{l} u_{ik}^{m} D_{ik}^{2} \tag{8}$$

subject to

$$\sum_{i=1}^{c} u_{ik} = 1, \ 0 \le u_{ik} \le 1 \tag{9}$$

where $D_{ik}^2 = (x_k - p_i)^T \Sigma^{-1}(x_k - p_i)$ is a squared Mahalanobis distance. A data set $X = \{x_1, x_2, ..., x_l\}$ includes l data points dividing into c fuzzy subsets that are characterized by representatives $p = \{p_1, p_2, ..., p_c\}$. u_{ik} represents the membership of the data point x_k from with respect to the ith cluster. The parameter m is the weighting exponent which determines the fuzziness of the clusters.

The formulation of optimization using Lagrange multiplier method is as following:

$$L = \sum_{i=1}^{c} \sum_{k=1}^{l} u_{ik}^m (x_k - p_i)^T \Sigma^{-1}(x_k - p_i) + \sum_{k=1}^{l} \alpha_k (1 - \sum_{i=1}^{c} u_{ik}) \qquad (10)$$

The optimization problem is implemented by iteratively updating clustering centers, covariance matrices and membership degrees according to Eq.11-Eq.14 until the stopping criterion is satisfied [12].

$$p_i = \frac{\sum_{j=1}^{l}(u_{ij})^m x_j}{\sum_{j=1}^{l}(u_{ij})^m}, 1 \le i \le c. \qquad (11)$$

$$F_i = \frac{\sum_{j=1}^{l}(u_{ij})^m (x_j - p_i)(x_j - p_i)^T}{\sum_{j=1}^{l}(u_{ij})^m}, 1 \le i \le c. \qquad (12)$$

$$D_{ij}^2 = (x_j - p_i)^T [\rho_i \det(F_i)^{1/n} F_i^{-1}](x_j - p_i), \qquad (13)$$
$$1 \le i \le c, \ 1 \le j \le l.$$

$$u_{ij} = \frac{1}{\sum_{k=1}^{c}(D_{ij}/D_{kj})^{2/m-1}}, 1 \le i \le c, 1 \le j \le l. \qquad (14)$$

In Eq.12, F_i is the fuzzy covariance matrix of the ith cluster.

3.2 Algorithm Description

Image segmentation algorithm based on FCM algorithm with Mahalanobis distance is executed in the following steps.

Input: source image file before segmentation
Output: target image file after segmentation
Algorithm:
    Step 1: Initialization
        Read source image file, and transform it into a data set $X = \{x_1, x_2, ..., x_l\}$, where l is the number of pixels.

Fix the number of clusters c; fix the weighting exponent m, $1 < m < \infty$; Fix the iteration limit T and the termination threshold $\varepsilon > 0$; Initialize the membership matrix $U^{(0)}$; Initialize clustering centers $p^{(0)}$.

Step 2: $t=1$

Step 3: Calculate the cluster centers $p^{(t)}$ using Eq.11

Step 4: Calculate the covariance matrix $F^{(t)}$ using Eq.12

Step 5: Calculate the squared Mahalanobis distance $(D^2)^{(t)}$ using Eq.13

Step 6: Update the membership matrix $U^{(t)}$:

   For $1 \leq j \leq l$ do

       if $D_{ij} > 0$ for $1 \leq i \leq c$, update $u_{ij}^{(t)}$ using Eq.14

       otherwise $u_{ij}^{(t)} = 0$ if $D_{ij} > 0$, and $u_{ij}^{(t)} \in [0,1]$ with $\sum_{i=1}^{c} u_{ij}^{(t)} = 1$

   End for

Step 7: If $\max\limits_{1 \leq i \leq c} \left\| p_i^{(t)} - p_i^{(t-1)} \right\| < \varepsilon$ or $t > T$ then stop

   else $t=t+1$ and go to (3).

Step 8: Image segmentation using the obtained membership matrix U.

4 Experimental Results

This section provides three images to verify the efficiency of the proposed method. We evaluated our proposed method on three images, and compared it with FCM algorithm. Experiments were done in Matlab 7.0.

Suppose that the initial parameters in FCM algorithm with Mahanabois distance are weighting exponent $m=2$, iteration limit $T=100$, number of clusters $c=3$, and termination threshold $\varepsilon = 1e-5$.

Experimental results obtained from the standard FCM-based method and the proposed method are shown in Figures 1-3, respectively. It is obvious from these comparisons that the proposed segmentation method has better segmentation effect than that of the standard FCM method.

    (a)   (b)   (c)

Fig. 1. Experimental comparison: lena (a) original image; (b) segmentation image using standard FCM; (c) segmentation image using the proposed method

Fig. 2. Experimental comparison (a) original image; (b) segmentation image using standard FCM; (c) segmentation image using the proposed method

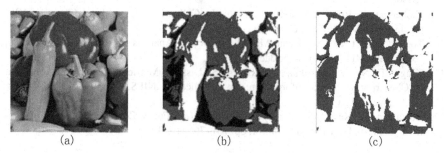

Fig. 3. Experimental comparison: penna (a) original image; (b) segmentation image using standard FCM; (c) segmentation image using the proposed method

5 Conclusion

This paper presents an image segmentation method based on FCM algorithm with Mahalanobis distance. The proposed method overcomes the fuzzy c-means clustering shortcomings in image segmentation. We first replace Euclidean distance with Mahalanobis distance in the fuzzy c-means algorithm, and then optimize the initial clustering centers using particle swarm optimization method. Experimental results in image segmentation show the proposed algorithm is effective and advantageous.

Acknowledgments. This work is partially supported by the National Natural Science Foundation of China under Grant No. 60873110. This work is also supported by the Doctor Start-up Foundation of Liaoning Province (No. 20081079), and Science Research Plan of Liaoning Education Bureau (No. 2008347).

References

1. Luis, G.U., Eli, S., Sreenath, R.V., et al.: Automatic Image Segmentation by Dynamic Region Growth and Multiresolution Merging. IEEE Trans. on Image Processing 10, 2275–2288 (2009)
2. Bezdek, J.C.: Pattern Recognition with Fuzzy Objective Function Algorithms. Plenum, New York (1981)

3. Wu, K.L., Yang, M.S.: An Alternative Fuzzy C-Means Clustering Algorithm. Pattern Recognition 35, 2267–2278 (2002)
4. Xing, H.J., Hu, B.G.: Adaptive Fuzzy C-Means Clustering-based Mixtures of Experts Model for Unlabeled Data Classification. Neuro computing 71, 1008–1021 (2008)
5. Kang, J.Y., Min, L.Q., Luan, Q.X., et al.: Novel Modified Fuzzy C-Means Algorithm with Applications. Digital Signal Process 2, 309–319 (2009)
6. Hoppner, F., Klawonn, F.: A Contribution to Convergence Theory of Fuzzy C-Means and Derivatives. IEEE Trans. on Fuzzy Systems 5, 682–694 (2003)
7. Yang, L., Lin, R.: Distance Metric Learning: a Comprehensive Survey. Technical Report, Michigan State University (2006)
8. Weinberger, K., Blitzer, J., Saul, L.: Distance Metric Learning for Large Margin Nearest Neighbor Classification. In: Advances in NIPS, pp. 1473–1480. MIT Press, Cambridge (2006)
9. Globerson, A., Roweis, S.: Metric Learning by Collapsing Classes. In: Advances in NIPS, pp. 451–458. MIT Press, Cambridge (2006)
10. Torresani, L., Lee, K.C.: Large Margin Component Analysis. In: Advances in NIPS, pp. 1385–1392. MIT Press, Cambridge (2007)
11. Xing, E.P., Ng, A.Y., Jordan, M.I., Russell, S.: Distance Metric Learning, with Application to Clustering with Side-information. In: Advances in NIPS, pp. 505–512. MIT Press, Cambridge (2002)
12. Gustafson, E., Kessel, W.: Fuzzy Clustering with a Fuzzy Covariance Matrix. In: Proc. IEEE Conf. on Decision and Control, pp. 761–766 (1979)

A Novel AHP and GRA Based Handover Decision Mechanism in Heterogeneous Wireless Networks

Jianqing Fu[1], Jiyi Wu[1,2], Jianlin Zhang[2], Lingdi Ping[1], and Zhuo Li[1]

[1] School of Computer Science and Technology, Zhejiang University,
310008 Hangzhou, P.R. China
[2] Key Lab of E-Business and Information Security, Hangzhou Normal University,
310036 Hangzhou, P.R. China
{Jianqing_fu,dr_pmp,zhangjohn,ldping,byte}@zju.edu.cn

Abstract. The next-generation of wireless systems represents a heterogeneous environment with different access networks technologies that differ in bandwidth, latency or cost. The most challenging problem is the seamless vertical mobility across heterogeneous networks. In order to improve the accuracy and efficiency of the vertical handover for such heterogeneous networks, this paper proposes a novel handover network decision mechanism with Q_OS provision based on analytic hierarchy process (AHP) and grey relational analysis (GRA) methods. We have successfully simulated and tested our approach using the OPNET simulation tool. The simulation results revealed that the proposed algorithm can not only work efficiently for 3G (TD-SCDMA), WLAN (IEEE 802.11),4G system but also reduce the complexity of implementation significantly.

Keywords: AHP, GRA, Handover, Decision mechanism.

1 Introduction

Present day wireless communications networks and devices are experiencing a paradigm shift. Rapid growth of mobile computing and emergence of new wireless technologies like Bluetooth, GPRS, UMTS, WiFi, WiMAX, DVB-H, etc would result in evolution of wireless networks towards heterogeneous all-IP mobile infrastructure [1][2].Conventional single interface mobile terminals are also evolving into multi-mode terminals. Currently, these multimode terminals do not possess true multimode functionality. They are limited to use only one radio interface at a time. But in the given heterogeneous scenario, these terminals should have true multimode functionality that would enable user applications to switch automatically between active interfaces that best suit them based on user preferences, application requirements and interface capabilities, and to use multiple radio interfaces simultaneously. Traditional horizontal handover decision mechanisms that mainly depend on signal strength for decision making are unable to realize the above requirements.

Three main types of network selection methods have been proposed for the heterogeneous systems. In the traditional methods such as [3], only the radio signal strength

R. Zhu et al. (Eds.): ICICA 2010, LNCS 6377, pp. 213–220, 2010.
© Springer-Verlag Berlin Heidelberg 2010

(RSS) threshold and hysteresis values are considered and processed in a fuzzy logic based algorithm. However, with a vision of multi-network environment and universal access, the traditional algorithm is not sufficient to make a handoff decision, as they do not take into account the current context or user's preference. When more handoff decision factors are considered, a number of two-dimension cost functions such as [4], are developed. In one dimension, the function reflects the types of services requested by the user, while in the second dimension, it represents the cost to the network according to specific parameters. In [5], a model is proposed based on a handover decision evaluated, from the user point of view, as the most convenient handover to his specific needs (cost and QoS). A comparison of three of these models was established in [6] with attributes (bandwidth, delay, jitter, and BER).It showed that SAW and TOPSIS provide similar performance to the traffic classes used. In [7][8], a NN based vertical handover algorithm is proposed to satisfy user bandwidth requirements. The context-aware handover concept is based on the knowledge of the context information of the mobile terminal and the networks in order to take intelligent and better decisions [9].

In this paper, keeping mobile users always best connected (ABC) is considered as design goal, and QoS characteristics in matter of user's preference, service application and network condition are adopted as decision factors. AHP is responsible to derive the weights of QoS parameters based on user's preference and service application. GRA takes charge of ranking the network alternatives through faster and simpler calculations. UMTS and WLAN are considered as network alternatives in this paper.

The rest of the paper is organized as follows. Section 2 highlights the related work. Section 3 illustrates the design of the decision model. Section 4 and 5, respectively, describe the implementation of the model and simulation results. Finally, section 6 concludes the paper and further research.

2 Proposed Handover Decision Mechanism

2.1 AHP Implementation

AHP is carried out using the following three principles: decomposition, pairwise comparison, and synthesis of weights[10].

(1)Decomposition
By using AHP, problems are decomposed into a hierarchy of criteria and alternatives as presented in Fig 1. The topmost level is the goal of the analysis, selecting the best handover network. The second level is composed of general criteria such as handover history, security[11], QoS, Cost and power consumption. Because QoS is very subjective, we divided it into several sub-criteria representing the level 3 of the AHP tree. These sub-criteria are availability, reliability, bandwidth and timing. The last level of criteria, level 4, contains the division of the sub-criteria. Availability is divided into Received Signal Strength (RSS), Signal Noise Ratio (SNR) and Coverage Area (CA), reliability into Bit Error Rate (BER) and Error-Correction (EC) and finally timing into delay, jitter and latency.

The information from the hierarchical tree is then synthesized to determine the relative ranking of alternatives. We decided not to include the cost of connection into the QoS AHP tree since, as in many complex decisions, costs should be set aside until the benefits of the alternatives are evaluated. So if the user profile strongly favours the cost of the network over other criteria, it will be evaluated by separating QoS from costs, mobile history and power consumption hierarchical trees and then outputs will be combined. Also, the power consumption is separated from other criteria simply because it only affects the decision if the battery level of the mobile receiver is critically low. Thus its weight is either very strong or very week.

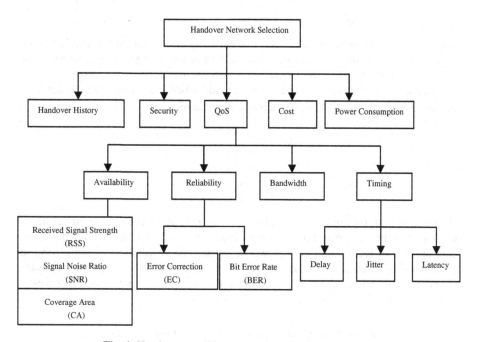

Fig. 1. Handover candidate network evaluation factor tree

(2)Pairwise Comparison

Once the hierarchy is constructed, elements at each level are compared each other in pairs with respect to their parents at the next higher level. The judgments are made based on user's intuition, experience and knowledge, and translated into numerical values on a scale of 1 to 9 according to the intensity of contribution to the objective, as shown in Table 1. The smaller one in a pair is chosen as a unit and the larger one is estimated as a multiple of that unit and assigned a number based on the perceived intensity of importance. Similarly, the reciprocals of these numbers are used to show how many times one is less important than another.

In formula (1),each entry a_{ij} could be straightforwardly represented as the ratio of the weights of the two elements, i.e. w_i/w_j, where w_i $(i=1,2,...,n)$ is the weights of the decision factors and n is the number of decision factors. If we construct all w_i into a weight matrix $(W)^T=[w_1,w_2,...,w_n]$, it is observed that AW=nW. Thus, the weight vector becomes the eigenvector of A and the number of elements becomes the eigenvalue.

For an example, we construct the next 4×4 matrix A_{QoS} as Table 2, the level 3 pairwise matrix of the AHP tree for QoS factor in Fig.1.

$$A = \begin{bmatrix} a_{11} & a_{12} & a_{13} & \cdots & a_{1n} \\ a_{21} & a_{22} & a_{23} & \cdots & a_{2n} \\ a_{31} & a_{32} & a_{33} & \cdots & a_{3n} \\ \cdots & \cdots & \cdots & \cdots & \cdots \\ a_{n1} & a_{n2} & a_{n3} & \cdots & a_{nn} \end{bmatrix} = \begin{bmatrix} w_1/w_1 & w_1/w_2 & w_1/w_3 & \cdots & w_1/w_n \\ w_2/w_1 & w_2/w_2 & w_2/w_3 & \cdots & w_2/w_n \\ w_3/w_1 & w_3/w_2 & w_3/w_3 & \cdots & w_3/w_n \\ \cdots & \cdots & \cdots & \cdots & \cdots \\ w_n/w_1 & w_n/w_2 & w_n/w_3 & \cdots & w_n/w_n \end{bmatrix} \qquad (1)$$

However, the AHP matrices are often not perfectly consistent due to user's random judgments. As a result, the eigenvector with the maximum eigenvalue (λmax) is chosen as the weight matrix. The closer λmax is to n, the higher the consistency of the assessments is. Comparisons have to be remade when the Consistency Index (CI), calculated by formula (2), fails to reach a required level.

$$CI = \frac{\lambda_{max} - n}{n - 1} \qquad (2)$$

$$CR = \frac{CI}{RI} \qquad (3)$$

CI should be non-negative, and the closer it is to zero, the more consistent the matrix is. This CI is then compared to a Random Index (RI), which is the average CI over a large number of reciprocal matrixes whose entries are randomly (and uniformly) selected from the interval [1/n,n],as shown in Table 2. The ratio of CI to RI for the same dimension matrix is referred as Consistency Ratio (CR). It is suggested that assessments are acceptable if CR 10%.

Table 1. Scale of relative importance for pairwise comparison

Intensity	Definition
1	equal importance
3	moderate importance
5	strong importance
7	demonstrated importance
9	extreme importance
2n	intermediate value
1/n	when $X_i/X_j = n$

Table 2. 4×4 matrix A_{QoS}

Factors	availability	bandwidth	reliability	timing
availability	1	2	1/3	1
bandwidth	1/2	1	1/4	1
reliability	3	4	1	3
timing	1	1	1/3	1

After calculated the maximum eigenvalue (λ_{max}=4.0459) for A_{QoS} on MATLAB,

$$CI_{Q_oS} = \frac{\lambda_{max} - n}{n-1} = \frac{4.0459 - 4}{4-1} = 0.0153 \text{, get } RI_{Q_oS} = 0.90 \text{ (n=4) form Table 3 and}$$

$$CR_{Q_oS} = \frac{CI_{Q_oS}}{RI_{Q_oS}} = \frac{0.0153}{0.90} = 0.017 \text{, were obtain. Our matrix } A_{QoS} \text{, has good consis-}$$

tency and is acceptable, as CR_{QoS} much less than 0.1.

Table 3. Random index

Dimension	1	2	3	4	5	6	7	8	9	10	11	...
RI	0	0	0.58	0.90	1.12	1.24	1.32	1.41	1.45	1.49	1.51	...

(3)Synthesis of weights

However, the weights achieved from every AHP matrix are only local weights with respect to the corresponding parent. The final weight of each element with respect to the goal can be achieved through multiplying the local weight by the weight of the corresponding parent.

$$A_{Q_oS} = \begin{bmatrix} 1 & 2 & 1/3 & 1 \\ 1/2 & 1 & 1/4 & 1 \\ 3 & 4 & 1 & 3 \\ 1 & 1 & 1/3 & 1 \end{bmatrix}, e_0 = \begin{bmatrix} 1/4 \\ 1/4 \\ 1/4 \\ 1/4 \end{bmatrix};$$

$$e_1' = A_{Q_oS}e_0 = \begin{bmatrix} 1.083 \\ 0.688 \\ 2.75 \\ 0.833 \end{bmatrix} => e_1 = \begin{bmatrix} 0.202 \\ 0.129 \\ 0.514 \\ 0.156 \end{bmatrix};$$

$$e_2' = A_{Q_oS}e_1 = \begin{bmatrix} 0.787 \\ 0.515 \\ 2.104 \\ 0.658 \end{bmatrix} => e_2 = \begin{bmatrix} 0.194 \\ 0.127 \\ 0.518 \\ 0.162 \end{bmatrix};$$

$$e_3' = A_{Q_oS}e_2 = \begin{bmatrix} 0.783 \\ 0.516 \\ 2.094 \\ 0.656 \end{bmatrix} => e_3 = \begin{bmatrix} 0.193 \\ 0.127 \\ 0.517 \\ 0.162 \end{bmatrix}.$$

The last step of AHP is synthesizing local priorities in each level into global priorities through multiplying local priorities by the corresponding parent's priority with respect to the objective. Here we give the example of 4×4 matrix A_{QoS} to show the process of weights.

When $e_2=e_3$, we finish the operating process. As a result, the eigenvector with the maximum eigenvalue (λ_{max}) is chosen as the weight matrix. Here $\lambda_{max}=0.783+0.516+2.094+0.656=4.049$, is much close to the figure we get from professional mathematical tool.

The eigenvector was the best way to get a ranking of priorities from a pairwise matrix, which has been demonstrated mathematically. The priority vector is obtained from normalized Eigen vector of the matrix. We can see that the most important criteria for a most reliable–profile are the reliability (51.70%) and the availability (19.31%).The other criteria, bandwidth (12.75%) and timing (16.18%) are less important.

2.2 GRA Implementation

(1)Bound Definition and Data Normalization

Before calculating the grey relational coefficients, the elements of each option need to be normalized based on three situations, larger-the-better, smaller-the-better, and nominal-the-best. Assuming n options $(E_1, E_2..., E_n)$ are compared, and each option has k elements. Then each option is presented as $E_i = \{e_i(1), e_i(2), \cdots e_i(n)\}$, where i=1,2,...,n. In the situation of larger-the-better, the element is normalized as.

$$e_i^*(j) = \frac{e_i(j) - L_j}{U_j - L_j} \tag{4}$$

In the situation of smaller-the-better, the element is normalized as

$$e_i^*(j) = \frac{U_j - e_i(j)}{U_j - L_j} \tag{5}$$

In the situation of nominal-the-best, the element is normalized as

$$e_i^*(j) = 1 - \frac{|e_i(j) - M_j|}{\max\{U_j - M_j, M_j - L_j\}} \tag{6}$$

where j=1,2,...k, $U_j = \max\{e_1(j), e_2(j), \cdots e_n(j)\}$, $L_j = \min\{e_1(j), e_2(j), \cdots e_n(j)\}$, and M_j is the moderate bound of element j.

(2)Grey Relational Coefficient Calculation

The upper bound in larger-the-better, the lower bound in smaller-the-better, and the moderate bound in nominal-the-best, are chosen to compose the ideal option, $E_0 = \{e_0(1), e_0(2), \cdots e_0(k)\}$.The grey relational coefficient can be achieved as following:

$$\Gamma_{0,i} = \frac{\Delta_{min} + \Delta_{max}}{\Delta_i + \Delta_{max}}$$

Where $\Delta_i = \sum_{j=1}^{k} w_j |e_0(j) - e_j^*(j)|$, w_j is the jth element's weight.

$\Delta_{max} = \max_{(i,j)} = (|e_0(j) - e_j^*(j)|)$ and $\Delta_{min} = \min_{(i,j)} = (|e_0(j) - e_j^*(j)|)$, where $\dfrac{\max_{(i,j)}()}{\min_{i,j}()}$ is

the function of computing the maximum/minimum value of a set of numbers varying with i and which are independent. The option with largest GRC is selected due to the highest similarity to the ideal situation.

3 Performance Evaluation

In this Section, we evaluate the performance of the proposed vertical handover network selection algorithm through simulation using the OPNET simulator. The algorithm is made by C program and inserted MN (mobile station) node model. The MN node model has 3 network interface cards, So it can communicate with 3G(TD-SCDMA), WLAN(IEEE 802.11) , 4G network respectively. Table 4 listed the testing network parameters.

Table 4. Evaluation network parameter

Attribute	TD-SCDMA	WLAN	4G
Cost per Byte(%)	100	10	30
Total Bandwidth(mbps)	2	54	100
Allowed Bandwidth(mbps)	0.2	2	5
Utilization(%)	10	20	20
Packet delay(ms)	400	100	100
Packet Jitter(ms)	50	15	20
Packet Loss(per 10^6)	100	15	15

4 Conclusions

In this paper, we developed a novel network selection algorithm for next generation networks. We integrated QoS factors, weighting factors, and network priority factors to select the best network for mobile user. AHP was adopted to achieve weighting factors and GRE was utilized to prioritize the networks. The simulation results revealed that the proposed mechanism can not only work efficiently for a 3G (TD-SCDMA), WLAN (IEEE 802.11), 4G system but also reduce the complexity of implementation significantly.

References

1. Kim, B., Yang, J., You, I.: A survey of NETLMM in all-IP-based wireless networks. In: Proc. of the International Conference on Mobile Technology, Applications and Systems, Article No. 60, September 10-12. ACM, Yilan (2008)

2. Park, Y., Park, T.: A Survey of Security Threats on 4G Networks. In: Workshop on Security and Privacy in 4G Networks Member, pp. 1–6 (2008)
3. Tripatlii, N.D., Reed, J.H., Vanlandinghum, H.F.: Adaptive handoff algorithm for cellular overlay systems using fiizzy logic. In: Pro. of the IEEE 49th Veliicnlar Technology Conference, vol. 2, pp. 1413–1418 (1999)
4. Park, H., Yoon, S., Kim, T., Park, J., Do, M.: Vertical handoff procedure and algorithm between IEEE802.11 WLAN and CDMA cellular network. In: Pro. of the Mobile Communications: 7th CDMA International Conference, Seoul, Korea, pp. 103–112 (2003)
5. Calvagna, A., Di Modica, G.: A user-centric analysis of vertical handovers. In: Pro. of the Second ACM International Workshop on Wireless Mobile Applications and Services on WLAN Hotspots, pp. 137–146 (2004)
6. Stevens-Navarro, E., Wong, V.: Comparison between vertical handoff decision algorithms for heterogeneous wireless networks. In: Pro. of the IEEE Vehicular Technology Conference (VTC-Spring), vol. 2, pp. 947–951 (2006)
7. Pahlavan, K., Krishnamurthy, P., Hatami, A., Ylianttila, M., Makela, J., Pichna, R.: Handoff in hybrid mobile data networks. IEEE Personal Communications 7(2), 34–47 (2010)
8. Guo, Q., Zhu, J., Xu, X.: An adaptive multi-criteria vertical handoff decision algorithm for radio heterogeneous network. In: Pro. of the IEEE International Conference on Communications, ICC 2005, vol. 4, pp. 2769–2773 (2005)
9. Wei, Q., Farkas, K., Prehofer, C., Mendes, P., Plattner, B.: Contextaware handover using active network technology. Computer Networks 50(15), 2855–2872 (2006)
10. Kassar, M., Kervella, B.: An overview of vertical handover decision strategies in heterogeneous wireless networks. Computer Communications 31, 2607–2620 (2008)
11. Yan, Z., Zhou, H., Zhang, H., Luo, H.: A dual threshold-based fast vertical handover scheme with authentication support. In: Pro. of the International Conference on Mobile Technology, Applications and Systems, Article No. 89, September 10-12. ACM, Yilan (2008)

Annotating Flickr Photos by Manifold-Ranking Based Tag Ranking and Tag Expanding

Zheng Liu, Hua Yan

School of Computer Science and Technology, Shandong Economic University, Ji'nan
Shandong 250014, China
Lzh_48@126.com

Abstract. This paper presents a novel automatic Flickr photos annotation method by ranking user-supplied tags and expanding the top ranked user-supplied tags. Firstly, user-supplied tags are filtered to obtain initial tags by noisy tags pruning. Secondly, the initial tags are ranked using manifold-ranking algorithm. In manifold-ranking process, the photo to be annotated is divided into several regions, and then these regions are acted as queries to launch the manifold-ranking algorithm which ranks the initial tags according to their relevance to the queries. Next, using Flickr API, top ranked initial annotations are expanded by a weighted voting policy. Finally, we combine top ranked initial tags with expanding tags to construct final annotations. Experiments conducted on Flickr photos demonstrate the effectiveness of the proposed approach.

Keywords: Flickr photo annotation, Manifold-ranking, Tag ranking, Tag expanding, Visual word model.

1 Introduction

In recent years, we have witnessed a rapid development of Web photo community site(e.g. Flickr, Photosig) which enables users to manage and share digital photos. Such social photo repositories allow users to upload personal photos and annotate content with descriptive keywords called tags. With the rich tags as metadata, users can more conveniently organize and access shared photos. Making full use of the tags provided by Flickr, a high efficient method can be proposed to annotate Flickr photos.

Several pioneering works related to Flickr tags have been proposed. Liu et al. proposed an approach to rank the tags for each image according to their relevance levels[1]. A novel Flickr distance was proposed to measure the visual similarity between concepts according to Flickr[4]. In paper [5], a learning based tag recommendation approach has been introduced to generate ranking features from multi-modality correlations, and learns an optimal combination of these ranking features by the Rankboost algorithm.

The source data for the annotating process is user-supplied tags. After tag ranking and tag expanding, the final annotations can be obtained. Our Flickr photo annotation method is made up of four stages, which is shown in Fig.1.

R. Zhu et al. (Eds.): ICICA 2010, LNCS 6377, pp. 221–228, 2010.

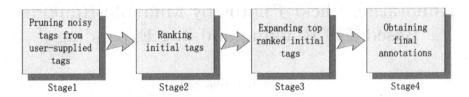

Stage1   Stage2   Stage3   Stage4

Fig. 1. Overview of our methods

The rest of the paper is organized as follows. Manifold-ranking based initial user-defined tag ranking and tag expanding are described in section 2 and 3 respectively. In section 4, the experimental results are present to demonstrate the performance of our method. Section 5 concludes the whole paper.

2   Initial Tags Ranking

To avoid noisy or uncorrelated tags, we submit each tag as a query to Wikipedia, and only the tags which have a coordinate in Wikipedia are reserved. After the un-related tags pruning, the rest of user-supplied is name initial tags(denoted as Γ).

2.1   Two-Level Tag Similarity Measuring Mechanism

We design a two-level policy considering both image content and tag semantic to measure tag similarity. At first, We define a method named NFD which is analogous to NGD[7] to compute the concurrence similarity between tags based on their co-occurrence. NFD between two tags can be estimated based on Flickr as follows.

$$NFD(t_i, t_j) = \frac{\max\{\log f(t_i), \log f(t_j)\} - \log f(t_i, t_j)}{\log G - \min\{\log f(t_i), \log f(t_j)\}} \tag{1}$$

where t_i and t_j represent the two tags in consideration. $f(t_i)$ and $f(t_j)$ are the numbers of images containing tag t_i and tag t_j respectively, which can be obtained by performing search by tag on Flickr website using the tags as keywords. $f(t_i, t_j)$ is the number of the images returned by Flickr when typing t_i and t_j as the search term. Moreover, G is the total number of photos in Flickr. The concurrence similarity between tag t_i and tag t_j is then defined as follows.

$$\gamma_s(t_i, t_j) = \exp[-NFD(t_i, t_j)] \tag{2}$$

Visual features are also considered in the tag similarity measuring mechanism. We use the visual word model and SIFT features[12] to measure image similarity. To construct codebook, we use corel5k dataset[10] as training data. All SIFT descriptors in the image of corel5k dataset are grouped into clusters which are named visual words by vector quantization with the Linde-Buzo-Gray

(LBG) algorithm[9]. After vector quantization, all images are represented as a D-dimensional vector, and the value of D is equal to the number of visual words. In our experiments, 2000 visual words are used for all photos.

Supposing that visual words vector h_u and h_v are D-dimensional vectors of visual word frequencies, which come from image I_u and image I_v respectively. We submit tag t_i to Flickr to obtain a photo collection $\delta(t_i)$. The visual similarity between t_i and t_j is calculated using cosine similarity as follows.

$$\gamma_v(t_i, t_j) = \frac{\sum\limits_{u \in \delta(t_i), v \in \delta(t_j)} \frac{h_u^t h_v}{\|h_u\| \|h_v\|}}{|\delta(t_i)| \cdot |\delta(t_j)|} \tag{3}$$

where u and v are the images belonged to $\delta(t_i)$ and $\delta(t_j)$ respectively, and h_k denotes visual feature vector extracting from image k. To explore the complementary nature of semantic similarity and visual similarity, we combine them as follows.

$$\gamma(t_i, t_j) = \lambda \cdot \gamma_s(t_i, t_j) + (1 - \lambda) \cdot \gamma_v(t_i, t_j) \tag{4}$$

2.2 Similarity between Tag and Image Region

After segmenting the image by Normalized cuts[11], the unlabeled image can be represented by region set Θ, the initial value of which is denoted as $\Theta^{(0)}$.

$$\Theta^{(0)} = \bigcup_{j=1}^{n} S_j, \ S_j \bigcap S_k = \emptyset \,, j \neq k \tag{5}$$

where S_i is the descriptor of i-th segment. To reduce computation cost and increase robustness against segmentation errors, we set a threshold β to combine visual similar segments into one region set. We combine the segment S_x and S_y into region set R_z, if the following condition is satisfied.

$$\exp(-\frac{\|F(S_x) - F(S_y)\|^2}{\sigma^2}) < \beta \tag{6}$$

where F_x and F_y are the visual feature vectors of region S_x and S_y. Visual features used in this subsection are as follows. Four descriptors are defined and used in the MPEG-7 standard which are Colour Layout (CLD), Colour Structure (CSD), Dominant Colour (DCD), and Edge Histogram (EHD). Texture feature based on Gabor Filters (GF) and Grey Level Co-occurrence Matrix(GLCM). Additionally, to emphasis invariance to saturation, Hue-Saturation-Value (HSV) color system is also considered.

Next, we compute the visual feature vectors of R_z by a weighting fusion approach based on the area percentage scheme.

$$F(R_z) = \frac{\alpha_x}{\alpha_x + \alpha_y} F(S_x) + \frac{\alpha_y}{\alpha_x + \alpha_y} F(S_y) \tag{7}$$

where α_i is the percentage of the image covered by segment S_i. Then, we update the current state of segment set $\Theta^{(t)}$ as follows.

$$\Theta^{(t+1)} = (\Theta^{(t)} - S_x - S_y) \cup R_z \tag{8}$$

When the updating process of Θ converges, if there are some isolated segments in Θ, we transform the isolated segment descriptor S_k to R_k. Then, the converged state of Θ is denoted as $\Theta^{(f)}$, and $\Theta^{(f)} = \{R_1, R_2, \ldots, R_q\}$.

We measure the similarity between tags and the regions in Flickr photo by image content analyzing. Firstly, the initial tag t_i is submitted to Flickr, and then top M photos(denoted as ψ_{t_i}) returned from Flickr are obtained. Secondly, the photos belonged to ψ_{t_i} are segmented by normalized cuts. Finally, K-means is applied to cluster the segments of ψ_{t_i} into k parts $C^{t_i} = \{C_1^{t_i}, C_2^{t_i}, \ldots \ldots, C_k^{t_i}\}$ according to feature vector, and the centroid set are $M^{t_i} = \{m_1^{t_i}, m_2^{t_i}, \ldots \ldots, m_k^{t_i}\}$ where $m_l^{t_i}$ is the centroid of the l-th cluster in C^{t_i}. Hence, the relevance between tag and image region is computed as follows.

$$\zeta(t_i, R_j) = \min\{\exp(-\frac{\left\| m_l^{t_i} - FR_j \right\|^2}{\sigma^2}), 1 \le l \le k\} \tag{9}$$

2.3   Manifold-Ranking Process

We use the manifold-ranking algorithm[8] to rank tags. The main idea of manifold-ranking lies in that given a set of points $\chi = \{x_1, \ldots, x_q, x_{q+1}, \ldots, x_n\} \subset \mathrm{R}^m$, the first q points are the queries which form the query set, and the remaining points are to be ranked according to their relevance to the queries. In this paper, the regions in $\Theta^{(f)}$ act as queries in the manifold-ranking process and the initial tags serve as the rest points in χ. The distance between data point x_i and x_j is computed as follows.

$$d(x_i, x_j) = \begin{cases} \gamma(x_i, x_j). & x_i, x_j \in \Gamma \\ \zeta(x_i, x_j). & x_i \in \Gamma, x_j \in \Theta^{(f)} \\ \exp(-\frac{\left\| F_{x_i} - F_{x_j} \right\|^2}{\sigma^2}). & x_i, x_j \in \Theta^{(f)} \end{cases} \tag{10}$$

After manifold-ranking process, top ranked tags set(denoted as Γ^T) are reserved.

3   Expanding the Top Ranked Initial Tags

We apply a Fickr API which is named flickr.tags.getRelated to obtain related tags, and then use a weighted voting policy to expand the top ranked tags. Supposing tag t_i is denoted as the i-th tag in the top ranked tag set Γ^T, the related tags of which returned by Flicir API are represented as $R(t_i)$. We merge all the related tags together and eliminate duplicated tags to build up the candidate expanding tag set Γ^E.

$$\Gamma^E = \bigcup_{t_i \in \Gamma^T} R(t_i) = \{e_1, e_2, \ldots, e_k\} \tag{11}$$

To make the expanding tags more relevant to the photo which is to be annotated, two factors are considered in our weighted voting policy. Firstly, the influence of higher ranked initial tags to voting results was boosted. Secondly, the semantic relevance between tags is taken into account as well. The weighted voting strategy computing a score for candidate tag e_j is designed as follows.

$$wv(e_j, t_i) = \begin{cases} \frac{|\Gamma^T| - i + 1}{|\Gamma^T|} & e_j \in R(t_i) \\ 0 & e_j \notin R(t_i) \end{cases} \qquad (12)$$

Based on voting score calculated from Eq.12, the final ranking score of each candidate expanding tag is computed as follows.

$$score(e_j) = \sum\nolimits_{t_i \in \Gamma^T} wv(e_j, t_i) \cdot \gamma(e_j, t_i) \qquad (13)$$

In the end, the final annotations are constructed by combining top ranked user-defined tags with expanding tags.

4   Experimental Results and Analysis

We collected 2000 Flickr photos as experimental dataset, with 20 categories and 100 photos in each category. Each photo category is built up by submitting a popular tag of Flickr and we download 100 photos which have at least 10 initial tags. We arrange 20 volunteers to judge the performance of our approach, and then integrate all volunteers' opinions to get the overall performance evaluation. We design three different experiment schemes to test the performance of our approach. There are four parameters left to be set in the algorithm:λ,α,σ and the number of iteration. In this experiment, the above four parameters are set as 0.4, 0.99, 1 and 50 respectively.

In experiment 1, we evaluate the performance of the proposed tag ranking method. Normalized Discounted Cumulative Gain (NDCG) is used as the metric to measure ranking performance[6]. In this experiment, each annotation of an image is labeled as one of the five levels: Strong Relevant (score 5), Relevant (score 4), Partially Relevant (score 3), Weakly Relevant (score 2), and Irrelevant (score 1). To compute NDCG, 20 volunteers are assigned to rate the relevancy of each annotation with the score from 1 to 5. After computing the NDCG value of each image's annotation list, we can average them to obtain an overall performance evaluation of the annotation ranking capability. The NDCG performance under different photo categories is shown in Fig.2. We select the top 10 tags in all cases, which include: 1) Initial tags, 2) Liu's method [1] and 3) our approach. As initial tags are not ranked, we use the user submitting order as the tag ranking results.

From Fig.2 we can see that the tag ranking performance of our approach is superior to initial tags. Compared with Liu's method, our approach performs better in some situations, such as wedding, bird, dog, cat, automobile etc. We find that in these cases there are some salient and visual similar objects in the

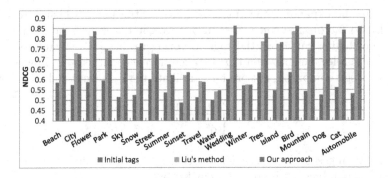

Fig. 2. NDCG performance under different photo categories

photos. The reason lies in two aspects. Firstly, using local features, our approach could effectively recognize salient objects. Secondly, our tag similarity measuring policy is more reasonable, as we use NFD to represent tag concurrence similarity and adopt SIFT feature based method to measure visual similarity.

Experiment 2 shows the tag expanding performance of our weighted voting scheme. We choose expanding tags from candidate expanding tags by a ranking score computing (shown in Eq.13). Hence, NDCG can also be used in tag expanding performance estimating. Fig.3 demonstrates tag expanding performance, which compares tag expanding policy without weighted voting. To abandon the weight voting, we should modify the first case of Eq.13. when $e_j \in R(t_i)$, we let $wv(e_j, t_i) = 1$. From Fig.3, some conclusions can be drawn. 1) Tag expanding performance highly depends on the ranking accuracy of initial tags. 2) Our weighted voting policy can boost tag expanding performance evidently.

Experiment 3 mainly test the effectiveness of the two-level tag similarity measuring mechanism. Two metrics are adopted in this experiment. The first metric is average precision of top N annotations($AP@N$), which evaluates how many annotations in top N position are relevant to the unlabeled image. To compute $AP@N$, a boolean function $ifTrue(\alpha_i)$ is defined in advance. The value of $ifTrue(\alpha_i)$ is set 1, when α_i is a correct annotation, otherwise, $ifTrue(\alpha_i)$ is set 0.

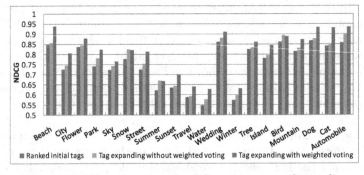

Fig. 3. NDCG performance for different tag expanding policy

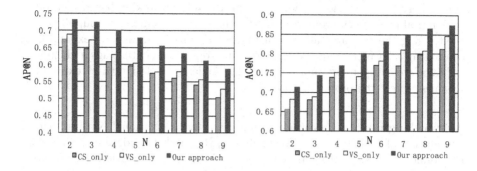

Fig. 4. Precision when the number of final annotations varying

Fig. 5. Coverage rate when the number of final annotations varying

Supposing we require volunteers to make the evaluations, and the number of volunteers is U. $AP@N$ is in Eq.14.

$$AP@N = \frac{1}{U} \sum_{j=1}^{U} \frac{\sum_{i=1}^{N} ifTrue(\alpha_i)}{N} \tag{14}$$

Another metric is average coverage rate of top N annotations($AC@N$), which estimates if top N annotations at least include one relevant annotation. A boolean function $ifCover(N)$ is defined in advance. The value of $ifCover(N)$ is set 1, only if at least one relevant annotation in Top N annotation, otherwise, $ifCover(N)$ is set 0. Averaging all users' opinions, $AC@N$ is solved as is shown in Eq.15.

$$AC@N = \frac{1}{U} \sum_{j=1}^{U} ifCover(N) \tag{15}$$

We compare our method with the following two cases: 1) only using concurrence similarity in tag similarity measuring (denoted as CS_only), 2) only using visual similarity in tag similarity measuring(denoted as VS_only). In this experiment, the final annotations include three top ranked initial tags which locate in the first three positions, and the other positions in final annotations are made up of expanding tags. From the experimental results shown in Fig.4 and Fig.5, several conclusions can be drawn: 1) Adopting two-level tag similarity measuring method in our approach could enhance the overall annotation performance in $AP@N$ and $AC@N$. 2) After tag ranking and expanding process, more relevant annotations are located in top positions.

5   Conclusions

Annotating photos through user-supplied tags mining is a popular way to index and organise photos. This paper proposes a Flickr photo-oriented automatic image annotation approach by manifold-ranking based tag ranking and weighted voting based tag expanding. We perform a manifold-ranking based method to rank initial tags which are obtained by pruning noisy tags in user-supplied tags. Next, using the relevant tags which Flickr API provides, tags are expanded by computing relevance score. Then, combining top ranked initial tags and expanding tags, we can get the final annotations. At last, we design three experiment schemes to test the proposed approach.

Acknowledgments. This work is supported by the National Natural Science Foundation of China (Grant No.60970048), Research Foundation of Shandong Economic University ("Research on Key Problems of Automatic Image Annotation", 2008).

References

1. Liu, D., Hua, X.S., Yang, L., Wang, M., Zhang, H.J.: Tag ranking. In: WWW 2009, pp. 351–360 (2009)
2. Sigurbjornsson, B., van Zwol, R.: Flickr tag recommendation based on collective knowledge. In: WWW 2008, pp. 327–336 (2008)
3. Xu, H., Zhou, X., Wang, M., Xiang, Y., Shi, B.: Exploring Flickr's related tags for semantic annotation of web images. In: CIVR 2009 (2009)
4. Wu, L., Hua, X.-S., Yu, N., Ma, W.-Y., Li, S.: Flickr distance. In: MM 2008, pp. 31–40 (2008)
5. Wu, L., Yang, L.J., Yu, N.H., Hua, X.S.: Learning to Tag. In: WWW 2009 (2009)
6. Jarvelin, K., Kekalainen, J.: IR evaluation methods for retrieving highly relevant documents. In: SIGIR 2000 (2000)
7. Cilibrasi, R.L., Vitnyi, P.M.B.: The Google Similarity Distance. IEEE Transactions on Knowledge and Data Engineering 19(3), 370–383 (2007)
8. Zhou, D., Weston, J., Gretton, A., Bousquet, O., Schölkopf, B.: Ranking on data manifolds. In: NIPS 2003 (2003)
9. Linde, Y., Buzo, A., Gray, R.: An Algorithm for Vector Quantizer Design. IEEE Transactions on Communications 28, 84–94 (1980)
10. Duygulu, P., Barnard, K., de Freitas, J., Forsyth, D.A.: Object recognition as machine translation: Learning a lexicon for a fixed image vocabulary. In: Heyden, A., Sparr, G., Nielsen, M., Johansen, P. (eds.) ECCV 2002. LNCS, vol. 2353, pp. 97–112. Springer, Heidelberg (2002)
11. Shi, J., Malik, J.: Normalized cuts and image segmentation. In: CVPR 1997, pp. 731–743 (1997)
12. Lowe, D.: Distinctive Image Features from Scale-Invariant Keypoints. IJCV 60(2), 91–110 (2004)

Application of Chaos in Network Video Security

Zhenxin Zhang[1], Jigang Tong[1], Zengqiang Chen[1], W.H. Ip[2], C.Y. Chan[2],
and K.L. Yung[2]

[1] Department of Automation, Nankai University,
Tianjin 300071, P.R. China
[2] Department of Industrial and Systems Engineering,
The Hong Kong Polytechnic University,
Hong Kong
nkzhangzx@163.com, chenzq@nankai.edu.cn, mfwhip@inet.polyu.edu.hk,
mfcychan@inet.polyu.edu.hk, mfklyung@polyu.edu.hk

Abstract. Network video makes communication much easier. But data
security becomes a troublesome issue. Fully using the characteristic of
chaotic systems, the embedded system gets designed to enhance the security of network video. The FPGA and uclinux are adopted as the
platform. The Qi hyper chaotic, Logistic mapping, Baker mapping and
Cat mapping algorithm is applied to video encryption. Combination of
on-line and off-line encryption, random encryption and double encryption methods make the security of data stronger. The system has been
tested to run a long time and proved to be stable with a high security. As a platform, the system implements the complex algorithms at a
very low cost: a 87MHz processor and 10M memory. But it still has the
potential to develop more complex algorithms and applications. So the
system has a broad prospect both in the area of application and research.

Keywords: chaos, FPGA, encryption, video in network.

1 Introduction

Today, the network is very popular. In the network environment, communication
and resource sharing make people's production and life more convenient and efficient. As a wonderful information carrier, video gets more and more attention,
but at the same time, network video security has also become a serious problem,
people want an efficient and convenient solution. For this situation, people began to get the chaotic system into the encryption area, using the many features
of chaotic systems to improve data security. In literature [2], chaotic systems
and network environment are analyzed, pointing out the basic requirements and
analysis methods of research, which lay the foundation for this area; literature
[3] confirmed the feasibility and high security of Baker mapping for image encryption; In literature [1] and [4], multiple chaotic encryption programs have
been demonstrated, and get a positive conclusion. However, in literature [2], the
object of study is just for images. In literature [1] and [4], the object is video,
but only one equation is adopted, and the platform is still the computer. In this

R. Zhu et al. (Eds.): ICICA 2010, LNCS 6377, pp. 229–236, 2010.

regard, this paper take full advantage of flexible and efficient characteristics of embedded system, and multiple equations are used for video encryption. At the same time, random encryption, on-line encryption, off-line encryption, double encryption and other methods are adopted to optimize the chaotic encryption system, which further improves the system's security. The project has passed the practical test.

2   Design Overview

Figure 1 shows a typical application of the system.

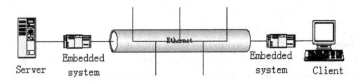

Fig. 1. Typical applications of the embedded System

The embedded system has an internal and an external network interface, as long as the network parameters were set on different network segments, it would work properly. General flow is as follow: the server compresses video data and passes it to the server-side embedded system which will encrypt and forward it. The client-side embedded system decrypts the data packets, and the client could play it in real time after decompressing. The embedded system needs to complete the data forwarding function, but also deal with large amounts of data of network video, while achieving the encryption and decryption functions.

3   Platform Construction

Xilinx Sparton3s500e FPGA is adopted as the platform, and the hardware system is constructed with several Xilinx IP cores: a 87M processor named Microblaze; a system bus named PLB; two ethernet controllers named ethernetlite and some other controllers.

With the hardware constructed, the uclinux could be transplanted. Linux has a good performance in network and multiple tasks controlling, which is the reason we adopt it.

4   Software Design on Target Board

The program flow chart is shown in Figure 2. First, initialize the network parameters of interface A and B and start to listen on them: if a handshake package is received from EthB, data routing function gets began; When a data package

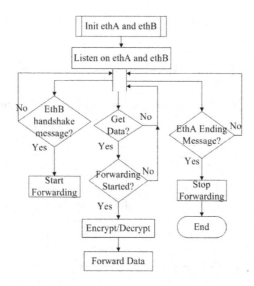

Fig. 2. The program flow chart on target board

comes, it gets encrypted or decrypted and forwarded out if the routing function
has been started, otherwise it would be discarded directly. If the end package
arrives from EthA , routing Function would be stopped. Program uses select()
way to simultaneously listen on various events rather than multiple threads to
optimize system. During the actual test, in multi-threaded mode, the load of the
CPU is close to 100%, but less than 10% in the select() mode.

5   Implementation of Encryption/Decryption Algorithms

5.1   Overview

Many characteristics of chaos such as the sensitivity to initial values, mixed nature, certainty and long-term unpredictability can be contacted with the feature
of confusion and proliferation in the traditional cryptography area. This design
adopt the Cat mapping, Baker mapping which are based on scrambling principle and logistic mapping, Qi hyper chaotic system which are based on confusing
principle. Scrambling principle means to change the position of data instead of
changing values. Take the two-dimensional discrete Baker mapping as an example. For a data rectangle of $N \times N$, n_i is the key and n_i is divisible by N. For
the key of $(n_1, n_2 \cdots n_i)$:

$$
\begin{aligned}
N_i &= n_1 + n_2 + \cdots + n_i \\
n_i | N, i &= 1, 2, \cdots k \\
n_1 + n_2 + &\cdots + n_k = N
\end{aligned}
\tag{1}
$$

$\forall (r, s)$, with the limit of

$$N_i \leq r < N_i + n_i \quad and \quad 0 \leq s < N$$

The following conclusion could be got:

$$B_{(n_1,n_2,\cdots n_k)}(r,s) = \left(\frac{N}{n_i}(r - N_i) + s \bmod \frac{N}{n_i}, \frac{n_i}{N}\left(s - s \bmod \frac{N}{n_i}\right) + N_i \right) \quad (2)$$

Figure 3 shows the block scrambling square generated by the discrete Baker mapping.

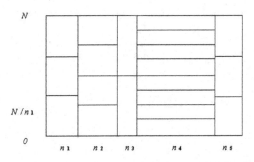

Fig. 3. Block scrambling square generated by the discrete Baker mapping

The confusing principle is to generate a chaotic sequence and XOR it with the data. So the confusing principle will just change the value of the data. For example, Logistic mapping is a one-dimensional discrete-time nonlinear dynamic system. Figure 4 points out the distribution of its iteration results. We use one embranchment to encrypt video.

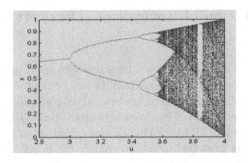

Fig. 4. Bifurcation diagram of logistic mapping

5.2   Implementation of Encryption and Decryption

In accordance with the various chaotic system equations, select a set of suitable initial values, and use linux C language to complete the encryption and decryption program.

Cat mapping and Baker mapping comply with the scrambling principle. Get the key into equation to generate a chaotic sequence and exchange the data using the sequence as index. In the decryption process, using the same key and do the anti-scrambling. The Logistic mapping and the Qi hyper chaotic comply with the confusing principle. First, put the key in the equation and iterate 1000 times to get into some bifurcation. Treat this place as a starting point and continue iterating to generate a chaotic sequence. At last, XOR with the sequence and the data to complete the confusion. In the decryption process, carry out the same operation to restore the data.

5.3   On-Line Encryption and Off-Line Encryption

On-line encryption means to generate a key for each fragment randomly. So both the client and server should generate a special chaos sequence for each fragment in real time. Obviously, the random key enhances the security of the data. However, the computation is so large that the embedded system couldn't sustain. A compromise scheme is to reduce the encrypted length. Experiments show if 500 bytes are encrypted inside a 1300 bytes fragment, we can get a very satisfied result. Table 1 shows the CPU resource occupancy of Cat mapping and Baker mapping in the compromised On-line mode.

Table 1. CPU occupancy of Cat mapping and Baker mapping

	Cat mapping	Baker mapping
On-line encryption	29.9%	45.3%

In the Off-line mode, the key is fixed. A chaotic sequence is generated during the program initialization stage and will be reused during all the following works. So it completely avoids the large computational problem. Table 2 shows the CPU occupancy of logistic mapping and Qi hyper chaotic in both the On-line and Off-line mode.

Table 2. Contrast between the On-line and Off-line mode

CPU occupancy	Logistic mapping	Qi hyper chaos
On-line	68.5%	95%
Off-line	1.3%	1.5%

5.4   Randomly Select Encryption Scheme and Double Encryption

Because the object of the encryption is fragment instead of the entire data stream, it is feasible to choose different algorithm for each fragment. As shown in Figure 5, the field "type" defines the encryption algorithm. In fact, we use the system time to generate a random number, and mapping it into the range of the field "type", which further enhance the data security.

If different algorithms were used on one fragment simultaneously, it would not result in incompatibility problems. Therefore, each fragment could be encrypted

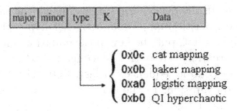

Fig. 5. The "type" field in a fragment

two times to enhance data security: First, randomly select between the Logistic mapping and Qi hyper chaotic to encrypt data and put the type code in the high four bit of the field "type". Second, randomly select between the Cat mapping and Baker mapping for the secondly encrypt, and put the type code in the low four bit of "type". Table 3 shows the CPU occupancy with different combinations of double encryption.

Table 3. CPU occupancy of double encryption

	Cat mapping Logistic mapping	Cat mapping Qi hyper chaos	Baker mapping Logistic mapping	Baker mapping Qi hyper chaos
CPU%	35.5%	37.9%	53.7%	58.6%

6   Performance Test

Take Baker mapping and Qi hyper chaotic equations working in double encryption mode as an example. Two sets of keys for the Baker mapping are:

$$KB_1 = (L, n_1, n_2, n_3, n_4) = (9, 4, 8, 16, 16)$$
$$KB_2 = (L, n_1, n_2, n_3, n_4) = (9, 4, 8, 16, 8)$$

Two sets of keys for the Qi hyper chaotic are:

$$KQ_1 = (x_0, x_1, x_2, x_3) = (-0.12345, -0.54321, 1.12345, 4.54321)$$
$$KQ_2 = (x_0, x_1, x_2, x_3) = (-0.12345, -0.54321, 1.12345, 4.54322)$$

In the program, KB_1 and KB_2 are used to encrypt the video. In figure 6, figure (a) is the original video, and the other figures are decrypted video with different

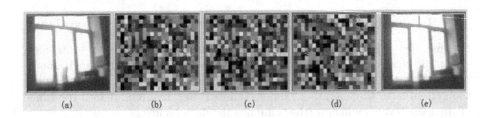

Fig. 6. key sensitivity test

combination of keys, which are listed as follow: Figure (b):KB_1 and KQ_2; Figure (c):KB_2 and KQ_1;Figure (d):KB_2 and KQ_2; Figure (e):KB_1 and KQ_1.

Figure 6 shows that only when both keys are entirely correct, it can properly decrypt the video. If any key had an extremely small difference, the video couldn't be restored. Figure 6 and Table 3 show that the various combinations of double encryption may achieve encryption and decryption with a high security and the resource-limited embedded platform could fulfill it. In actual test, the embedded system runs in the LAN environment for 48 hours continuously, and it remained stable and trouble-free.

7   Conclusions

Use chaotic systems in network video encryption area to enhance security. By constructing FPGA hardware platform and transplanting uclinux, a set of easy to use and efficient embedded encryption and decryption system is build. And numerous improvements are made: Present on-line encryption, off-line encryption, random encryption and double encryption methods to improve the security of the system. From the point of using view, configuring the system is the same as a traditional router, which eliminates the trouble of re-learning for ordinary users. This design took advantage of lower frequency processor (87Mhz) with less memory capacity (10M) to achieve a variety of complex chaotic algorithms, it has a high cost-effective and will has a broad prospect. The system has passed the test of continuously running for 48 hours.

Acknowledgments. This work is supported in part by the Natural Science Foundation of China (No. 60774088), the Specialized Research Fund for the Doctoral Program of Higher Education of China (No. 20090031110029), the Foundation of the Application Base and Frontier Technology Research Project of Tianjin (No. 08JCZDJC21900). And the research is partially supported under the Hong Kong Polytechnic University under Grant No. G-YG44.

References

1. Meng, Z., Zhongxin, L., Qinglin, S., Zengqiang, C., Zhuzhi, Y.: Chaos Based Video Compression and Encryption Algorithms. Control Engineering of China 12(5), 482–485 (2005)
2. Alvarez, G., Li, S.: Some Basic Cryptographic Requirements for Chaos-Based Cryptosystems. International Journal of Bifurcation and Chaos 16(8), 2129–2151 (2006)
3. Mao, Y., Chen, G., Lian, S.: A Novel Fast Image Encryption Scheme Based on 3D Chaotic Baker Maps. International Journal of Bifurcation and Chaos 14(10), 3613–3624 (2004)
4. Chiaraluce, F., Ciccarelli, L., Gambi, E., Pierleoni, P., Reginelli, M.: A New Chaotic Algorithm For Video Encryption. IEEE Transactions on Consumer Electronics 48(4) (2002)

5. Wang, Y.-h., Wang, l.-p.: A Blind Digital Watermarking Embedding Technology Based on Chaotic Sequences and DCT. Journal of Hengshui University 12(1), 33–35 (2010)
6. Lin, J.-q., Si, X.-c., Meng, W.-x., Zhao, J.-y.: Image encryption algorithm based on chaotic system. Application Research of Computers 2, 697–698, 703 (2010)
7. Liao, X.: New Efficient Algorithm of Image Encryption Based on Combined Chaotic Maps. Journal of Wenzhou University Natural Science 1, 33–40 (2010)
8. Ye, R.-s., Wu, S.-x.: A 4D Symmetric Chaotic System and Its Application on Image Hiding. Computer Technology and Development 1, 93–96 (2010)
9. Richard Stevens, W.: Advanced Programming in the UNIX Environment. Posts & Telecom Press, Beijing (2008)
10. Corbet, J., Rubini, A., Kroab-Hartman, G.: LINUX Device Driver. China Electric Power Press, Beijing (2006)
11. Yang, H.: Embedded system development of FPGA based on EDK tools. Machinery Industry Press, Beijing (2008)
12. Xue, X., Ge, Y.: Design Guide on Xilinx ISE9.X PFGA/CPLD. Posts & Telecom Press, Beijing (2007)
13. Getting Started with the MicroBlaze Development Kit - Spartan-3E 1600E Edition, http://china.xilinx.com/
14. Embedded Linux/Microcontroller Project, http://www.uclinux.org

Integration of Complementary Phone Recognizers for Phonotactic Language Recognition

Yan Deng, Weiqiang Zhang, Yanmin Qian, and Jia Liu

Tsinghua National Laboratory for Information Science and Technology,
Department of Electronic Engineering, Tsinghua University, Beijing 100084, China
y-deng05@mails.thu.edu.cn

Abstract. This paper takes an investigation into building and fusing multiple phone recognizers in the phonotactic system for language recognition. The phone recognizers are built using both phonetic and acoustic diversification. The phonetic diversification is achieved by training multiple phone recognizers on speech corpus of different languages. While the acoustic diversification is implemented in several ways, including using different acoustic features, different phone modeling techniques and training paradigms. As some phone recognizers are highly correlated with each other, we propose a performance optimization (PO) criterion to select a set of complementary phone recognizers for fusion. Experimental results on the NIST 2007 Language Recognition Evaluation (LRE) 30-s test set show the effectiveness of the proposed approach.

Keywords: Phonotactic language recognition, parallel phone recognition followed by vector space modeling (PPRVSM), fusion, fMPE.

1 Introduction

Language recognition is to identify the language spoken in a given utterance. Two categories of systems are widely used for language recognition: the acoustic systems and the phonotactic systems. The acoustic systems use Gaussian Mixture Models (GMM) [1] or support vector machines (SVM) [2] to model the long-term spectral characteristics. And the phonotactic systems adopt N-gram language model [3], binary tree [4] or SVM [5] to model the lexical constraints of different languages. Many state-of-the-art systems incorporate both to achieve the optimal performance [6] [7]. This paper will focus on the phonotactic approach.

A typical phonotactic system consists of a phone recognizer as the front-end and a language model as the back-end. The front-end phone recognizer is often used to convert speech into phone sequences or lattices [3] [8], from which the phonetic N-gram statistics are estimated. The back-end usually includes a set of language models, one per each target language. One prevailing phonotactic system is the phone recognizer followed by vector space modeling (PRVSM) [5], in which the phonetic N-gram statistics are concatenated into a super-vector and then modeled by SVM.

Generally, the phone recognizer is independent of the target languages. Then the phone set may not be large enough to cover all the sound units that will appear in

R. Zhu et al. (Eds.): ICICA 2010, LNCS 6377, pp. 237–244, 2010.
© Springer-Verlag Berlin Heidelberg 2010

target languages. So the phone recognizer is error prone. As a common solution, several phone recognizers are used in parallel to obtain better performance than the individual one. The parallel front-ends can be constructed in two ways. The first approach is to use multiple phone recognizers of different languages to improve the phone coverage, which is referred to as the phonetic diversification [3]. The other one is to employ phone recognizers using different features or acoustic models to emphasize on different acoustic aspects of the speech, which is called the acoustic diversification [9]. In this paper, we will combine the two approaches to train multiple front-ends. Actually, not all the front-ends are complementary. Then a criterion is proposed in this paper to select the most complementary phone recognizers to construct the best front-ends.

This paper is organized as follows. In section 2, we give a brief description of the phonotactic system. The construction and fusion of complementary phone recognizers will be discussed in detail in section 3. Section 4 presents the experimental results on the NIST 2007 LRE test set, followed by a conclusion in section 5.

2 Phonotactic Language Recognition

The phonotactic approach is one of the most effective techniques for language recognition. It is based on the assumption that the rules governing the allowable combination of phones can be different between languages. In phonotactic systems, the front-end is used to convert the input speech into phone sequences or lattices for following analysis and the back-end is used to perform language classification. The phonotacitc system employed in this paper is the prevailing parallel PRVSM (PPRVSM). In the PPRVSM system, phone lattice is adopted due to its superiority over 1-best phone sequence [8].

Given a speech segment O and the language models θ_i, the language recognition problem can be described as finding the language with the highest posterior probability $P(l \mid O, \theta_i)$. For the lattice based PPRVSM, it can be formulated as follows:

$$l^* \approx \arg\max_l \sum_S P(S \mid \theta_i) f(S \mid O, \theta_\Lambda) . \tag{1}$$

where θ_Λ is the model parameters of the phone recognizer, $f(S \mid O, \theta_\Lambda)$ is the probability of generating the phone sequence S and $P(S \mid \theta_i)$ is the language model probability of S. The computation of Eq. (1) is implemented in two stages:

(1) Phonotactic feature extraction. Several phone recognizers are used to convert the speech into phone lattices, from which the expected counts of phonetic N-grams $s_i...s_{i+N-1}$ are calculated [8]:

$$c(s_i...s_{i+N-1} \mid L) = \sum_{S \in \ell} p(S \mid L) c(s_i...s_{i+N-1} \mid S) .$$

where, $p(S \mid L)$ is the probability of the sequence S in the lattice L, $c(s_i...s_{i+N-1} \mid S)$ is the occurrence of $s_i...s_{i+N-1}$ in S. The probability of the N-gram $s_i...s_{i+N-1}$ in the lattice is computed as follows:

$$p(s_i...s_{i+N-1} \mid \mathcal{L}) = \frac{c(s_i...s_{i+N-1} \mid \mathcal{L})}{\sum_i c(s_i...s_{i+N-1} \mid \mathcal{L})} \ .$$

The probabilities are then concatenated to construct the phonotactic features.

(2) Vector space modeling (VSM). The VSM used in this paper is similar to [10]. The key point of VSM is the sequence kernel construction. In general, the kernel between two phonotactic feature vectors can be represented as follows:

$$K(X_1, X_2) = \sum_i p_n(s_i...s_{i+N-1} \mid \mathcal{L}_1) * p_n(s_i...s_{i+N-1} \mid \mathcal{L}_2) \ .$$

where $p_n(s_i...s_{i+N-1} \mid \mathcal{L}_1) = \dfrac{p(s_i...s_{i+N-1} \mid \mathcal{L}_1)}{\sqrt{p(s_i...s_{i+N-1} \mid all)}}$. The kernel matrix is then used for SVM training and scoring. The scores are fused to produce the final decision.

3 Integration of Complementary Phone Recognizers

3.1 Construction of Phonetic and Acoustic Diversification

In the PPRVSM system, the phonetic and acoustic diversification can be combined to generate multiple phone recognizers. Details are presented in the following.

The phonetic diversification is obtained by training phone recognizers of different languages. It will be good if the languages have complementary phone sets, which will make sure that the sound units appearing in all target languages can be covered by the phone sets. The approach is effective in building multiple phone recognizers. But the major difficulty is that phone or word transcription is required. Then it will be a great challenge in the following conditions: (1) there is only one language with labeled speech data; (2) the labeled training samples are not enough to train a good phone recognizer. An alternative is to train phone recognizers using different acoustic models. That is the acoustic diversification.

The realization of acoustic diversification can be implemented by using different acoustic features or acoustic models trained on the same speech data with the same phone set. Generally, the phone lattices obtained by acoustic diversification are homogeneous as the same phone set is used. So we'd better train different acoustic models that will generate phone lattices containing error patterns complementary to each other. Then simple methods such as simply changing the number of model parameters are infeasible. As they yield only slight changes in phone lattices. Therefore, different acoustic features, modeling techniques and training paradigms are favorable to construct complementary phone recognizers on the same speech corpora.

In this paper, we will take all of these diversifications into consideration. First of all, we build multiple phone recognizers to obtain phonetic diversification. Four language dependent phone recognizers are developed, including Czech, Hungarian, Mandarin and Russian. They come from different language families and comparable in performance. Then, different model architectures are adopted. For the Czech, Hungarian and Russian phone recognizers, artificial neural network (ANN)/hidden markov model (HMM) is used to model the acoustic variation within phones [11]. While for Mandarin, HMM is employed. Finally, we take different acoustic features and training techniques into consideration. The commonly used Mel-frequency cep-stral coefficients (MFCC) and perceptual linear prediction (PLP) features are both used. Meanwhile, the maximum likelihood (ML) and feature-domain minimum phone error (fMPE) training are adopted to train the HMM phone models. fMPE is a previ-ously introduced form of discriminative training using the same objective function as MPE. It is done by transforming the acoustic feature with a kernel-like method. The details can be found in [12].

3.2 Fusion of Complementary Phone Recognizers

Researchers have shown that simply combing the n-best systems is not a good choice for integration of multiple subsystems for speaker recognition [13]. It is also the truth for language recognition. This can be seen from Fig.1, in which the correlation coeffi-cients matrix of the scores as shown. We use the spearman's rank correlation coeffi-cient of scores produced by language recognition systems using different phone recognizers. High correlation can be observed between some phone recognizers, which hints that no benefits will arise from integrating these phone recognizers. Thus, it is important to decide which one(s) to choose and how to combine the results. The performance optimization (PO) approach is proposed in this paper.

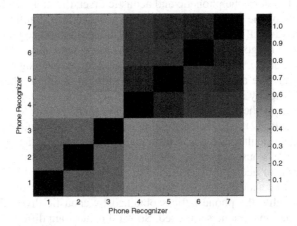

Fig. 1. Correlation coefficients matrix of different phone recognizers

The PO approach can be implemented as follows. First, selecting n complementary phone recognizers from M phone recognizers using a combinatorial optimization method, with a total number of combinations equal to C_N^n. As the phone recognizers developed in our experiment is less than 10, then C_N^n is small. So we can examine through all combinations to find the global optimum solution. Then, the combination is performed by adopting a score fusion method. Recent experiments have shown that the linear fusion method is simple to implement and yields good results in language recognition [14]. Then, we will adopt the linear fusion method.

For the trial x, the scores of N target languages produced by the i-th phone recognizer can be denoted as $s_i(x) = [s_{i1}(x),...,s_{iN}(x)]$. A transformation function is then defined as follows:

$$s(x) = \alpha_1 s_1(x) + \alpha_2 s_2(x) + ... + \alpha_M s_M(x) + \beta .$$

where α_i is a scalar, β is an N-dimensional vector. $\{\alpha_1, \alpha_2, ...\alpha_M, \beta\}$ constitutes a set of transformation parameters which are estimated by using a conjugate gradient descent algorithm to minimize a linear regression function [14].

4 Experiments

We perform experiments to study the integration of multiple complementary phone recognizers in the PPRVSM system. Both detection cost function (DCF, Cavg*100) and equal error rate (EER) are used to summarize the results.

4.1 Experimental Setup

The experiments are performed on the NIST 2007 LRE date set under the closed condition. The task is to recognize 14 languages: Arabic, Bengali, Chinese, English, Farsi, German, Hindustani, Japanese, Korean, Russian, Spanish, Tamil, Thai and Vietnamese. There are 7530 utterances in total. The training data we use comes from different sources including Callfriend, the evaluation and development data provided by NIST in the previous LRE. As the speech is relatively long, we use the voice activity detection to segment each speech utterance into 30 seconds.

In our experiments, four language dependent phone recognizers are used to construct a set of complementary front-ends. The Czech, Hungarian and Russian frontends are developed by the Faculty of Information Technology of the Brno University of Technology (BUT) [11]. Besides the three phone recognizers, we also developed a Mandarin phone recognizer using the Hidden Markov Models (HMM) architecture and trained on the conversational telephone data including about 30 hours of speech. There are 64 phone models for the phone recognizer. Each phone model is a tied-state left-to-right context-dependent (CD) HMM with 32 Gaussians per state. The CD models have the advantage of handling the context variability compared with context-independent ones [15].

For acoustic feature extraction, standard 12 MFCC coefficients with energy are extracted every 10 ms over a 25 ms hamming window. These features are augmented by their first and second order Deltas, resulting in a 39 dimension feature vector. To remove the channel variability, cepstral mean subtraction and variance normalization are both applied. Also the PLP feature is extracted to provide additional acoustic diversification. The parameters and configuration for PLP extraction are almost the same as the MFCC feature except that C0 is used instead of energy.

As with normal fMPE training in speech recognition, we need to generate lattices by decoding the training data with a weak language model [16], which are used to produce the MPE statistics. Also we need Gaussians to obtain Gaussian posteriors. In this study, 1000 Gaussians are used in calculating the offset features with context width 5. For experiments, we typically run 3-4 iterations of fMPE optimization.

4.2 Experimental Results

We build several phone recognizers to achieve both phonetic and acoustic diversification for integration. The performance of different phone recognizers is given in Table 1. Mandarin-MFCC means that the MFCC feature is used for the Mandarin phone recognizer, which is trained using the ML training paradigm. While Mandarin-MFCC-fMPE means that the MFCC feature and the fMPE training method are used. It is the same for Mandarin-PLP and Mandarin-PLP-fMPE. From Table 1, we can see that these phone recognizers are comparable in performance. For these phone recognizers, different language specific phone set, different acoustic features, different modeling techniques and training approaches are adopted to realize the phonetic and acoustic diversification for integration.

Table 1. Performance of Different Phone Recognizers

Phone Recognizer	EER (%)	DCF, Cavg*100
Czech	4.75	4.53
Hungarian	3.48	3.04
Russian	4.24	4.04
Mandarin-MFCC	2.93	2.68
Mandarin-MFCC-fMPE	2.65	2.35
Mandarin-PLP	2.97	2.74
Mandarin-PLP-fMPE	2.41	2.36

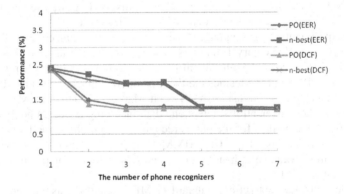

Fig. 2. Comparison of PO and n-best for integration

The second experiment is carried out to realize the integration of complementary phone recognizers. Comparisons of the PO and n-best approaches are given in Fig. 2. When we take a combination of the seven phone recognizers, the EER can decrease to 1.25% and the DCF reaches 1.20. There is a great improvement in performance in comparison with the best single phone recognizer, about a relative reduction of 50% both in EER and DCF. But this is achieved at the expense of increasing the complex and runtime of the system. However, when we use the PO approach, we can obtain almost the same performance using only three phone recognizers. The EER is 1.29%

and the DCF becomes 1.22, which are similar to those obtained by fusing seven phone recognizers. However, five phone recognizers are needed if we use the n-best approach. So the PO approach can be employed to select the most complementary phone recognizers when there are a lot of phone recognizers to fuse.

5 Conclusion

In this paper, we have built several complementary phone recognizers for integration using both phonetic and acoustic diversifications. For phonetic diversification, we train multiple phone recognizers on speech data and phone sets of different languages. While for acoustic diversification, different acoustic features, modeling techniques and training paradigm are all used. To select complementary phone recognizers for integration, we proposed the PO approach. Using this approach, only three phone recognizers are needed to achieve almost the same performance as using seven. The final performance on the NIST 2007 LRE 30-s test set reaches an EER of 1.29% and a DCF of 1.22, a relative reduction of about 50% in both EER and DCF when compared with the best single phone recognizer. It is almost the best result as reported so far.

Acknowledgments. This project is supported by National Natural Science Foundation of P. R. China and Microsoft Research Asia (60776800), National Natural Science Foundation of P. R. China and Research Grants Council (60931160443), National High Technology Research and Development Program of China (863 Program) (2006AA010101, 2007AA04Z223, 2008AA02Z414, 2008AA040201).

References

1. Torres-Carrasquillo, P.A., Singer, E., Kohler, M.A., Greene, R.J., Reynolds, D.A., Deller, J.R.: Approaches to Language Identification Using Gaussian Mixture Models and Shifted Delta Cepstral Features. In: Proceedings of ICSLP 2002, pp. 33–36 (2002)
2. Campbell, W.M., Campbell, J.P., Reynolds, D.A., Singer, E., Torres-Carrasquillo, P.A.: Support Vector Machines for Speaker and Language Recognition. Computer, Speech and Language 20(2-3), 210–229 (2006)
3. Zissman, M.A.: Comparison of Four Approaches to Automatic Language Identification of Telephone Speech. IEEE Transactions on Speech and Audio Processing 4(1), 31–44 (1996)
4. Navratil, J.: Recent Advances in Phonotactic Language Recognition Using Binary Decision Trees. In: Proceedings of ICSLP 2006, pp. 421–424 (2006)
5. Li, H., Ma, B., Lee, C.-H.: A Vector Space Modeeling Approach to Spoken Language Identification. IEEE Transactions on Audio, Speech and Language Processing 15(1), 271–284 (2007)
6. Torres-Carrasquillo, P.A., Singer, E., Campbell, W., Gleason, T., McCree, A., Reynolds, D.A., Richardson, F., Shen, W., Sturim, D.: The MITLL NIST LRE 2007 Language Recognition System. In: Proceedings of Interspeech 2008, pp. 719–722 (2008)
7. Matejka, P., Burget, L., et al.: BUT Language Recognition System for NIST 2007 Evaluations. In: Proceedings of Interspeech 2008, pp. 739–742 (2008)
8. Gauvain, J.L., Messaoudi, A., Schwenk, H.: Language Recognition Using Phone Lattices. In: Proceedings of ICSLP 2004, pp. 1283–1286 (2004)

9. Sim, K.C., Li, H.: On Acoustic Diversification Front-end for Spoken Language Identification. IEEE Transactions on Audio, Speech and Language Processing 16(5), 1029–1037 (2008)
10. Deng, Y., Zhang, W.-Q., Liu, J.: Language Recognition Based on Discriminative Vector Space Model. Journal of Nanjing University of Science and Technology 33(sup.1), 138–144 (2009)
11. Matejka, P., Schwarz, P., Cernocky, J., Chytil, P.: Phonotactic Language Identification Using High Quality Phoneme Recognition. In: Proceedings of Eurospeech 2005, pp. 2237–2240 (2005)
12. Povey, D., Kingsbury, B., Mangu, L., Saon, G., Soltau, H., Zweig, G.: fMPE: Discriminatively Trained Features for Speech Recognition. In: Proceedings of ICASSP 2005, pp. 961–964 (2005)
13. Hou, T., Liu, J.: Vector Angle Minimum Criteria for Classifier Selection in Speaker Verification Technology. Journal of Chinese Electronics 19(1), 81–85 (2010)
14. Brummer, N., Leeuwen, D.: On Calibration of Language Recognition Scores. In: Proceedings of IEEE Odyssey—Speaker Language Recognition Workshop, pp. 1–8 (2006)
15. BenZeghiba, M.F., Gauvain, J.L., Lamel, L.: Context-Dependent Phone Models and Models Adaptation for Phonotactic Language Recognition. In: Proceedings of Interspeech 2008, pp. 313–316 (2008)
16. Schluter, R., Muller, B., Wessel, F., Ney, H.: Interdependence of Language Model and Discriminative Training. In: Proceedings of IEEE ASRU Workshop, pp. 119–122 (1999)

Performance Analysis of IEEE 802.11a Based on Modified Markov Model in Non-saturation Conditions

Feng Gao[1], Zehua Gao[1,2], Liu Wen[1], Yazhou Wang[2], Jie Liu[2], and Dahsiung Hsu[1]

[1] Key Laboratory of IPOC, [2] Key Laboratory of UWC
University of Posts and Telecommunications, Beijing, China
gfbupt@sina.com

Abstract. The maximum nominal data rate specified in IEEE 802.11a is up to 54Mbps. However, in practice, we found that the data rate which users could get is much lower than that. In order to accurately estimate the ability of IEEE 802.11a to support data services, we improved the existing two-dimensional Markov chain models of the backoff window scheme, and analyzed the efficiency of the IEEE 802.11a standard for wireless LANs in non-saturation conditions from the perspective of framing efficiency and medium access control (MAC) layer transport efficiency in this paper. Specifically, we derived an analytical formula for the protocol actual throughput. The results showed that the throughput of non-saturation could exceed the saturated one. To a certain degree of non-saturation, the network throughput can be optimal. And under the condition of different frame length, the performance in RTS/CTS mode is different with that in basic access model which can be measured by a switching threshold we give in the last of the paper.

Keywords: IEEE 802.11a, protocol efficiency, MAC layer, Markov chain model, non-saturation conditions.

1 Introduction

In recent years, wireless local area network (WLAN) has become extremely popular. The IEEE 802.11 protocols are the dominating standards for WLAN. Particularly, IEEE 802.11a operating at 5.8 GHz band is not restricted by compatibility and has little interference with systems using the same frequency. The maximum nominal data rate specified in IEEE 802.11a is up to 54Mbps [1~2]. However, in actual situation, its actual user data rate is much lower than that.

The main restriction lies in Physical layer and MAC layer [3~5]. Thus the MAC protocol is the main element for determining the efficiency in sharing the limited bandwidth of the wireless channel. In order to accurately estimate the ability of IEEE 802.11a to support data services and direct network capacity planning, the non-saturation throughput of IEEE 802.11a is analyzed from the perspective of frame forming efficiency and MAC layer channel transport efficiency in this paper.

The analysis on IEEE 802.11 DCF performance has been a research focus since the standards has been proposed. In Ref. [6], Bianchi proposes a two-dimensional Markov chain model to analyze the DCF performance in the assumption of saturation

R. Zhu et al. (Eds.): ICICA 2010, LNCS 6377, pp. 245–252, 2010.

state and ideal channel conditions. Based on this work, many enhancements have been done focusing on different aspects. In Ref. [7], Haitao Wu improves Bianchi's model by considering the retry limits specified by the IEEE 802.11 MAC protocol. Ref. [8] derives a better Markov chain model for IEEE 802.11 standards; where consideration is given to the finite retry attempts and the freezing of bakeoff counter. However, most of the current research assumes the network in saturation conditions, i.e. the transmission queue of each station is assumed to be always nonempty. To actual WLAN, non-saturated state is more representative and the network performance is significantly affected by the non-saturation degree. Ref. [9] model the DCF using Parallel Space-Time Markov Chain (PSTMC), in which frame arrivals are tracked by monitoring the transmission queue during transitions between successive states of the space-time Markov chain. Ref. [10] provides a model which has ability to predict the optimal network throughput and the network capacity. Based on this feature, Ref. [10] introduces a new method to estimate the lower bound of network capacity. Ref. [11] extends Bianchi's model to include a waiting state that indicates non-saturation conditions of stations but not considering limited number of retries and backoff suspension. So as to accurately analyze DCF operation and calculate the non-saturation throughput of IEEE 802.11a, this paper further extends the aforementioned model of Ref. [11] and proposes a new Markov chain model with considerations of the retry limits and freezing of bakeoff counter.

2 Throughput Analysis

The MAC layer of IEEE 802.11a still employs MAC protocol defined in IEEE 802.11. This protocol incorporates two access schemes: DCF and point coordination function (PCF). Specifically, DCF is the fundamental mechanism to access the medium, including two transmission models – Basic access model and RTS/CTS model. In practical applications, DCF protocol is used more frequently [1~2].

In this paper, η is defined as the efficiency of the IEEE 802.11a for wireless LANs in non-saturation conditions. If we consider ideal channel condition without errors, η can be expressed as[4~5]

$$\eta = \eta_{\text{Frame}} \cdot \eta_{\text{DCF}} \qquad (1)$$

The calculation of framing efficiency have been introduced in detail in the Ref. [4 ~ 5].This paper has the same assumption as in Ref. [3]~[9]: the channel is error-free and no hidden terminals. Consider a fixed number n of contending stations. Moreover, at each transmission attempt, each packet collides with constant and independent probability P regardless of the number of retransmissions suffered. Furthermore, we introduce a waiting state and a probability P_I, where P_I represents for non-saturation degree of the network. When station successfully sends a data packet, this station will keep waiting state with probability of P_I, otherwise it will generate a new frame and trigger new bakeoff procedure in the probability of $(1- P_I)$.

Following the modelling and analysis proposed in Ref. [6], let $\{s(t), b(t)\}$ be a two-dimensional, discrete-time Markov chain, which is shown in Fig.1.

In this model, m is the retry limit, indicating that a packet will be discarded after an unsuccessful transmission at the m stage. The backoff CW will be exponentially increased until it reaches the maximum backoff window size $(CW_{max}+1)$.Hence, it can be expressed as [2]:

$$\begin{cases} W_i = 2^i W_0, i \leq m' \\ W_i = 2^{m'} W_0, i > m' \end{cases} \quad (2)$$

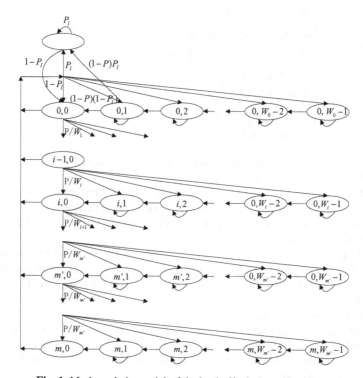

Fig. 1. Markov chain model of the backoff window scheme

In this Markov chain, the only non-null one-step transition probabilities are shown as (3):

These transition probabilities account, respectively, for :

1. The backoff counter decrements when the channel is idle;
2. The station enters into state (0,0) from state (0,1) when the station senses the channel busy and there are new packets to be transmitted;
3. The station returns to the WAIT state from state (0,1) When the station senses the channel busy and there is no packet to be transmitted;
4. The backoff stage increases and a new initial bakeoff value is chosen after an unsuccessful transmission;
5. When the station senses the channel busy, backoff process is interrupted and transfer into freezing state;

$$\begin{cases}
P\{i,k\,|\,i,k+1\}=1-P, k\in[0,W_i-2], i\in[0,m], k+i>0 \\
P\{0,0\,|\,0,1\}=(1-P)(1-P_I) \\
P\{WAIT\,|\,0,1\}=(1-P)P_I \\
P\{i,k\,|\,i-1,0\}=P/W_i, k\in[0,W_i-1], i\in[0,m] \\
P\{i,k\,|\,i,k\}=P, k\in[1,W_i-1], i\in[0,m] \\
P\{0,k\,|\,i,0\}=(1-P)/W_0, k\in[1,W_0-1], i\in[0,m-1] \\
P\{0,0\,|\,i,0\}=(1-P)(1-P_I)/W_0, i\in[0,m-1] \\
P\{WAIT\,|\,i,0\}=(1-P)P_I/W_0, i\in[0,m-1] \\
P\{0,k\,|\,m,0\}=1/W_0, k\in[1,W_0-1] \\
P\{0,0\,|\,m,0\}=(1-P_I)/W_0 \\
P\{WAIT\,|\,m,0\}=P_I/W_0 \\
P\{0,0\,|\,WAIT\}=1-P_I \\
P\{WAIT\,|\,WAIT\}=P_I
\end{cases} \tag{3}$$

6. The station enters backoff stage 0 and chooses a new value k (k≠0) for the backoff counter after a successful transmission;

7. The station enters backoff stage 0 and chooses 0 for the backoff counter k after a successful transmission when there are new packets to be transmitted;

8. The station returns to the WAIT state after a successful transmission when there is no packet to be transmitted;

9. At the last backoff stage, the station enters backoff stage 0 and chooses a new value k (k≠0) for the backoff counter after a successful or unsuccessful transmission;

10. At the last backoff stage, the station enters backoff stage 0 and chooses 0 for the backoff counter k after a successful or unsuccessful transmission when there are new packets to be transmitted;

11. At the last backoff stage, the station returns to the WAIT state after a successful or unsuccessful transmission when there is no packet to be transmitted;

12. The station enters into state(0,0) from the WAIT state when there are new packets to be transmitted;

13. The station stays in the WAIT state in the probability of PI.

Let $b_{i,k}=\lim_{t\to\infty}P\{s(t)=i,b(t)=k\}, i\in[0,m], k\in[0,W_i-1]$ and $b_0=\lim_{t\to\infty}P\{s(t),b(t)=WAIT\}$ be the stationary distribution of the Markov chain. According to the state diagram shown in Fig. 1, the steady state equations can be derived

$$b_{i,0}=b_{0,0}\cdot p^i, i\in[0,m] \tag{4}$$

The state probability is derived from the rate balance equations of the state transition diagram shown in Fig.1

$$b_{i,k}=\frac{W_i-k}{W_i(1-P)}\cdot b_{i,0}, \quad 0\le i\le m, 1\le k\le W_i-1 \tag{5}$$

In steady state, we also have

$$b_{0,1}(1-P)P_I + b_{0,0}P_I/W_0 = b_{WAIT}(1-P_I) \Leftrightarrow b_{WAIT} = \frac{b_{0,0}P_I}{(1-P_I)}$$

Therefore, by using the normalization condition $\sum_{i=0}^{m}\sum_{k=0}^{W_i-1} b_{i,k} + b_{WAIT} = 1$ for the stationary distribution, we have

$$b_{0,0} = \begin{cases} \dfrac{2(1-p)^2(1-2p)(1-P_I)}{W_0(1-p)(1-(2p)^{m+1})(1-P_I)+(1-2p)^2(1-p^{m+1})(1-P_I)+2P_I(1-p)^2(1-2p)}, & m \le m' \\ \dfrac{2(1-P)^2(1-2P)(1-P_I)}{P_1+P_2+P_3+P_4}, & m > m' \end{cases} \tag{6}$$

Where

$$P_1 = W_0(1-(2P)^{m'+1})(1-P)(1-P_I), \quad P_2 = W_0P(1-2P)(2P)^{m'}(1-P^{m-m'})(1-P_I)$$

$$P_3 = (1-2P)^2(1-P^{m+1})(1-P_I), \quad P_4 = 2P_I(1-P)^2(1-2P)$$

As any transmission occurs when the backoff counter is equal to zero, regardless of the backoff stage, it is

$$\tau = \sum_{i=0}^{m} b_{i,0} = \sum_{i=0}^{m} p^i b_{0,0} = \frac{1-p^{m+1}}{1-p} \cdot b_{0,0} \tag{7}$$

The conditional collision probability P that at least one of the n-1 remaining stations transmits in a time slot can be expressed as

$$p = 1-(1-\tau)^{n-1} \tag{8}$$

Using equations (6)~(8), P and τ can be solved by numerical techniques.

In this paper, DCF protocol efficiency factor is defined as:

$$\eta_{DCF} = \frac{P_s P_{tr} t_{Frame}}{(1-P_{tr})\sigma + p_s P_{tr}T_s + P_{tr}(1-p_s)T_c} \tag{9}$$

Where, tFrame is the average time of transmitting one frame and it can be solved by method indicated above. σ is the duration of an empty slot time. Tc and Ts are the average durations the medium is sensed busy due to a collision and a successful transmission respectively. The probability Ptr that there is at least one transmission in the considered slot time and the probability Ps that a transmission occurring on the channel is successful are respectively given by [6]

$$P_{tr} = 1-(1-\tau)^n \tag{10}$$

$$p_s = \frac{n\tau(1-\tau)^{n-1}}{P_{tr}} = \frac{n\tau(1-\tau)^{n-1}}{1-(1-\tau)^n} \tag{11}$$

The average length of a slot time in (9) is calculated considering that a system time slot: the time slot is empty with probability (1-Ptr); it includes a successful transmission with probability PsPtr; with probability Ptr (1-Ps) it contains a collision.

The values of Ts and Tc depend on the access mechanism, considering the ACK and CTS timeout effect in basic model and RTS/CTS model [6].

3 Model Validation

The specific parameters used in the experiment is showed in Table 1, the number of mobile devices in the network is set to 5,15,25,35 respectively.

Table 1. IEEE 802.11a MAC layer and PHY layer parameters (DSSS) [2]

The rate of physical layer	54Mbps
ACK/RTS/CTS rate	24Mbps
Propagation delay	1us
Slot time	9us
SIFS	16us
DIFS	34us

In the IEEE 802.11a basic access mode and RTS / CTS mode, $m = 6$, $m' = 6$. Under different conditions of the load, the probability of node transmitting packets in a slot can be obtained by equation (7), as shown in Figure 2:

As shown in figure 2, when the network is under very light load ($P_I > 0.999$), τ and n (the number of active nodes) is independent. And when the network load increases ($P_I < 0.999$), both in the basic access mode and the RTS/CTS mode, τ will increase significantly as n decreases.

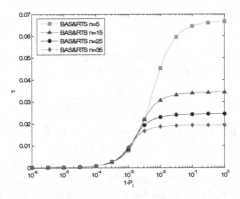

Fig. 2. the probability of a station transmitting data within a time slot

After we obtained p and τ, we substituted them into equation (9) to get η_{DCF}. Assume that length of MSDU is 1024 Byte in each station; the efficiency of the IEEE 802.11a standard in non-saturation conditions is shown in figure 3:

As shown in figure 3, when $1 - P_I \in (0, 10^{-3})$, the system throughput increases rapidly as the load increases and reached the maximum in both modes. When $1 - P_I \in (10^{-3}, 1)$ and in RTS/CTS modes the system throughput has been maintained at the maximum, which did not changes with the system load $1 - P_I$, showing a strong stability.

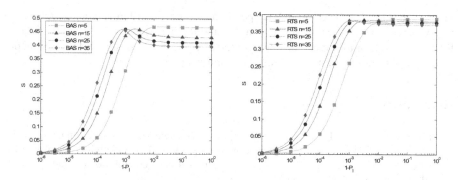

Fig. 3. the efficiency of IEEE 802.11a under basic and RTS/CTS mode

RTS/CTS mode solved the hidden terminal problem in wireless networks while brought additional cost. As shown in Figure 3 in the case of frame size of 1024 Bytes, RTS system's throughput is no higher than the basic access mode.

To ensure the optimum performance, the DCF protocol defines a RTS threshold to control the switching of the two access modes. When the data frame length is greater than the RTS threshold value, RTS/CTS access mode is used. Otherwise the basic access mode is adopted.

When $P_I = 0.9$, the switching thresholds between the basic mode and the RTS/CTS mode of various active nodes number are shown in Figure 4. After the estimation of the number of the active nodes, the result can be set according to Figure 4 so as to get the best performance.

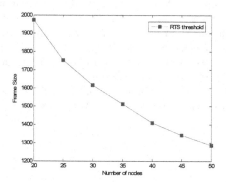

Fig. 4. RTS Threshold of various active nodes

4   Conclusions

In this paper, a new two-dimensional Markov chain model of the backoff procedure is proposed, and the efficiency of the IEEE 802.11a standard for wireless LANs in non-saturation conditions is analyzed on two fronts, which are framing efficiency and DCF transport efficiency. Specifically, we derive an analytical formula for the protocol throughput. The throughput performance under different non-saturation of the system is analyzed using the very model and the performances of basic mode and RTS/CTS mode are compared. We promoted a threshold to start RTS/CTS mode under various number of nodes to reach the optimal performance.

References

1. IEEE 802.11- 1997. IEEE standard for information technology —— telecommunications and information exchange between system——local and metropolitan area networks specific requirements, Part 11: Wireless medium access control (MAC) and physical (PHY) layer specifications (1997)
2. IEEE 802.11a——1999. IEEE standard for information technology —— telecommunications and information exchange between system——local and metropolitan area networks specific requirements, Part 11: Wireless medium access control (MAC) and physical (PHY) layer specifications for high-speed physical layer in the 5GHz (1999)
3. Jiang, L.S., Chen, W.P.: Analysis of wireless LAN MAC layer channel transport efficiency. Modern Electronics Technique 29(7), 4–6 (2006) (in Chinese)
4. Wen, L., Gao, Z.H., Gao, F.: Performance Analysis of IEEE 802.11a in Non-saturation Conditions. In: Proc. of IEEE IC-NIDC, pp. 837–841 (2009)
5. Wen, L., Gao, F., Gao, Z.H.: Performance Analysis of IEEE 802.11a. Data Communication 4, 19–21 (2009) (in Chinese)
6. Bianchi, G.: Performance analysis of the IEEE 802.11 distributed coordination function. IEEE Journal on Select Area in Commun. 18(3), 535–547 (2000)
7. Wu, H.T., Peng, Y., Long, K.P., et al.: Performance of reliable transport protocol over IEEE 802.11 wireless LAN: analysis and enhancement. In: IEEE INFOCOM, New York, America, June 23-27, pp. 599–607 (2002)
8. Vardakas, J.S., Sidiropoulos, M.K., Logothetis, M.D.: Performance behaviour of IEEE 802.11 distributed coordination function. IET Circuits Devices Syst. 2(1), 50–59 (2008)
9. Ghaboosi, K., Latva-aho, M., Yang, X.: A New Approach on Analysis of IEEE 802.11 DCF in non-Saturated Wireless Networks. In: Proc. of IEEE VTC, pp. 2345–2349 (2008)
10. Nghia, T.D., Robert, A.M.: A New Markov Model for Non-Saturated 802.11 Networks. In: Proc. of IEEE CCNC 2008, pp. 420–424 (2008)
11. Xu, Y.Y., Wang, S.Z., Xu, C.C.: Throughput analysis of IEEE 802. 11 WLANs in non-saturated conditions. Computer Science 33(6), 42–43 (2006) (in Chinese)

Soft Set Theory for Feature Selection of Traditional Malay Musical Instrument Sounds

Norhalina Senan[1], Rosziati Ibrahim[1], Nazri Mohd Nawi[1],
Iwan Tri Riyadi Yanto[2], and Tutut Herawan[3]

[1] Faculty of Information Technology and Multimedia
Universiti Tun Hussein Onn Malaysia, Johor, Malaysia
[2] Department of Mathematics
Universitas Ahmad Dahlan, Yogyakarta, Indonesia
[3] Department of Mathematics Education
Universitas Ahmad Dahlan, Yogyakarta, Indonesia
{halina,rosziati,nazri}@uthm.edu.my,
iwan015@gmail.com, tutut81@uad.ac.id

Abstract. Computational models of the artificial intelligence such as soft set theory have several applications. Soft data reduction can be considered as a machine learning technique for features selection. In this paper, we present the applicability of soft set theory for feature selection of Traditional Malay musical instrument sounds. The modeling processes consist of three stages: feature extraction, data discretization and finally using the multi-soft sets approach for feature selection through dimensionality reduction in multi-valued domain. The result shows that the obtained features of proposed model are 35 out of 37 attributes.

Keywords: Soft Set Theory; Feature selection; Traditional Malay musical instruments.

1 Introduction

In handling most of the data mining problems, feature selection is very crucial in finding the most significant set of features. The purpose of feature selection are to handle the "curse of dimensionality", enhancing generalization capability, and reducing learning and computational cost. The theory of soft set proposed by Molodtsov in 1999 [1] is a new mathematical tools for dealing with the uncertain data. One of the potential applications is to be used as the dimensionality reduction and decision making method which has been discussed in [2-5]. However, most of the current applications are deal with the Boolean information system. To date, less effort has been done in handling the non-Boolean dataset especially for the categorical dataset. In this paper, we propose feature selection method based on soft set theory for handling categorical dataset of Traditional Malay musical instruments sounds. To accomplish this study, the dataset consists of 1116 instances with 37 attributes from two categories of features schemes which are perception-based and MFCC is exploited. In order to utilize the soft set theory, it is essential to transform the original

R. Zhu et al. (Eds.): ICICA 2010, LNCS 6377, pp. 253–260, 2010.

dataset (continuous values with non-categorical form) into discretized values with categorical form. For that, equal width and equal frequency binning algorithm in [6] is employed as the discretization method. Afterwards, the multi-soft sets method proposed in [7] and the concept of soft dimensionality reduction in multi-valued information system in [8] are adopted to select the best feature set from the large number of features available. The rest of this paper is organized as follows: Section 2 discuss a related work on feature selection of musical instruments sounds. The theory of soft set will be explained in Section 3. Section 4 describes the modeling process of this study. A discussion of the result can be found in Section 5 followed by the conclusion in Section 6.

2 Related Work

The idea of soft set theory as dimensionality reduction methods have been proposed and discussed by [2-5]. Maji et al. [2] applied a soft set theory in the decision making problem with the help of Pawlak's rough reduct. The reduct soft set algorithm which defined from the rough set theory is employed as a reduction method. Then the weighted choice value is embedded in the algorithm to select the optimal decision. In [3-5], studies on parameterization reduction of soft sets and its applications are presented. Two major problems in [2] are highlighted in their study which are the result of computing reduction is incorrect and the algorithm to compute the reduction and then to select the optimal objects are not reasonable. To improve these problems, they presented a new definition of parameterization reduction of soft sets with the concepts of attributes reduction in rough set theory. However, all these methods are adopted for the dataset represented in the form of a Boolean-valued information system. In the real application, a given dataset may have varied form of values. For that, Herawan and Mustafa [7] proposed an alternative approach for handling multi-valued information system, so called multi-soft sets. In [8], Herawan et al. proposed the idea of attribute reduction in multi-valued information system under multi-soft sets approach. They found that the obtained reducts are equivalent to the Pawlak's rough reducts. To date, this approach is not yet being applied in handling a non-categorical dataset with continuous values. Thus, in our study, this approach will be applied as feature selection method for Traditional Malay musical instruments classification problem.

3 Soft Set Theory

Throughout this section U refers to an initial universe, E is a set of parameters, $P(U)$ is the power set of U and $A \subseteq E$.

3.1 Soft Set

Definition 1. (See [1].) *A pair* (F, A) *is called a soft set over U, where F is a mapping given by* $F : A \rightarrow P(U)$.

In other words, a soft set over U is a parameterized family of subsets of the universe U. For $\varepsilon \in A$, $F(\varepsilon)$ may be considered as a set of ε-elements of the soft set (F, A) or as the set of ε-approximate elements of the soft set. Clearly, a soft set is not a (crisp) set. Based on the definition of an information system and a soft set, in this section we show that a soft set is a special type of information systems, i.e., a binary-valued information system.

Proposition 1. (See [7].) *If (F, A) is a soft set over the universe U, then (F, A) is a binary-valued information system $S = (U, A, V_{\{0,1\}}, f)$.*

Definition 2. (See [2].) *The class of all value sets of a soft set (F, A) is called value-class of the soft set and is denoted by $C_{(F,A)}$.*

3.2 Multi-soft Sets

The "standard" soft set deals with a binary-valued information system. For a multi-valued information system $S = (U, A, V, f)$, where $V = \bigcup_{a \in A} V_a$, V_a is the domain (value set) of attribute a which has multi value, a decomposition can be made from S into $|A|$ number of binary-valued information systems $S = (U, A, V_{\{0,1\}}, f)$. From Proposition 1, we have

$$S = (U, A, V, f) = \begin{cases} S^1 = (U, a_1, V_{\{0,1\}}, f) & \Leftrightarrow (F, a_1) \\ S^2 = (U, a_2, V_{\{0,1\}}, f) & \Leftrightarrow (F, a_2) \\ \vdots & \vdots \quad \vdots \\ S^{|A|} = (U, a_{|A|}, V_{\{0,1\}}, f) & \Leftrightarrow (F, a_{|A|}) \end{cases}$$

$$= ((F, a_1), (F, a_2), \cdots, (F, a_{|A|}))$$

We define $(F, A) = ((F, a_1), (F, a_2), \cdots, (F, a_{|A|}))$ as a *multi-soft sets* over universe U representing a multi-valued information system $S = (U, A, V, f)$ [7].

3.3 AND and OR Operations in Multi-soft Sets

The notions of AND and OR operations in multi-soft sets are given below.

Definition 3. *Let $(F, E) = ((F, a_i) : i = 1, 2, \cdots, |A|)$ be a multi-soft sets over U representing a multi-valued information system $S = (U, A, V, f)$. The* AND *operation between (F, a_i) and (F, a_j) is defined as*

$$(F, a_i) \text{AND} (F, a_j) = (F, a_i \times a_j),$$

where

$$F(Va_i, Va_j) = F(Va_i) \cap F(Va_j), \forall (Va_i, Va_j) \in a_i \times a_j, \text{ for } 1 \leq i, j \leq |A|.$$

Definition 4. *Let* $(F,E) = \left((F,a_i) : i = 1,2,\cdots,|A| \right)$ *be a multi-soft sets over U representing a multi-valued information system* $S = (U,A,V,f)$. *The* OR *operation between* (F,a_i) *and* (F,a_j) *is defined as*

$$(F,a_i)\text{OR}(F,a_j) = (F,a_i \times a_j),$$

where

$$F(Va_i,Va_j) = F(Va_i)\bigcup F(Va_j), \forall(Va_i,Va_j) \in a_i \times a_j, \text{for } 1 \leq i,j \leq |A|.$$

Thus, both AND and OR operations in multi-soft sets over U define a soft set over $U \times U$.

4 The Modeling Process

The modeling process of this study comprises five main phases which are data acquisition, feature extraction, feature selection and data classification as shown in Fig. 1. Matlab functions were utilized in this study. The details for each phase as follows:

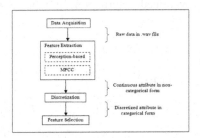

Fig. 1. The modeling process

4.1 Data Acquisition

The raw sounds samples of Traditional Malay musical instruments were downloaded from personal [9] and Warisan Budaya Malaysia web page [10]. The dataset comprises four different families which are membranophones, idiophones, aerophones and chordophones. In order to generate relevance dataset, the editing process explained in [11] is conducted.

4.2 Feature Extraction

In this phase, two categories of features schemes which are perception-based and MFCC features were extracted. All 37 extracted features from these two categories are shown in Table 1. The first 1-11 features represent the perception-based features and 12-37 are MFCC's features. The mean and standard deviation were then calculated for each of these features. These features are extracted using the formula in [11].

4.3 Discretization

The decision table used in this study is in the form of continuous value with non-categorical features (attributes). In order to employ the soft set approach proposed by [7,8], it is essential to transform the dataset into categorical ones. For that, the equal width binning in [6] is used. In this study, this unsupervised method is modified, to be suited in our problem. The algorithm first sort the continuous valued attribute, then the minimum xmin and the maximum xmax of that attribute is determined. The interval width, w, is then calculated by:

$$w = \frac{x_{max} - x_{min}}{k^*},$$

where k^* is a user-specified parameter for the number of intervals to discretize of each target class. The interval boundaries are specified as $x_{min} + w_i$, where $i = 1, 2, \cdots, k$. Afterwards, the equal frequency binning method is used to divide the sorted continuous values into k interval where each interval contains approximately n/k data instances with adjacent values of each class [6].

Note that, a data table may be redundant in two ways. The first form of redundancy is easy to notice: some objects may have the same features. A way of reducing data size is to store only one representative object for every set. The second form of redundancy is more difficult to locate, especially in large data tables. Some columns of a table may be erased without affecting the classification power of the system. This concept can be extended also to information systems, where we do not distinguish between conditional and class attributes. Using the entire attribute set for describing the property is time-consuming, and the constructed rules may be difficult to understand, to apply or to verify [12]. In order to deal with this problem, attribute reduction is required. The objective of reduction is to reduce the number of attributes, and at the same time, preserve the property of information.

In the following sub-section, we present an application of multi-soft sets for finding reduct. After transforming the dataset from non-categorical attributes into categorical form, this new decision table need to be converted into multi-soft sets.

4.4 Feature Selection (Reduction) Using Soft Set Theory

A reduct is a minimal set of attributes that preserve the classification. In order to express the idea more precisely, we need some preliminaries definitions as follow.

Definition 5. Let $(F, A) = ((F, a_i) : 1 \leq i \leq |A|)$ be multi-soft sets over U representing a multi-valued information system $S = (U, A, V, f)$, a set of attributes $B \subseteq A$ and b belongs to B. Attribute b is said dispensable (superfluous) in B if

$$C_{\left(F, b_1 \times \cdots \times b_{|B \setminus \{b\}|}\right)} \neq C_{\left(F, b_1 \times \cdots \times b_{|B|}\right)},$$

where $(F, a_i \times a_j) = (F, a_i) \text{AND} (F, a_j)$. Otherwise b is said indispensable in B.

To further simplification of a data table, we can eliminate some dispensable attributes from the table in such a way that we are still able to discern objects in the table as the original one.

Definition 6. Let $(F,A) = ((F,a_i):1 \le i \le |A|)$ be multi-soft sets over U representing a multi-valued information system $S = (U, A, V, f)$. A set of attributes $B \subseteq A$ is called independent (orthogonal) set if all its attributes are indispensable.

Definition 7. Let $(F,A) = ((F,a_i):1 \le i \le |A|)$ be multi-soft sets over U representing a multi-valued information system $S = (U, A, V, f)$ and a set of attributes $B \subseteq A$. A subset $B*$ of B is a reduct of B if $B*$ is independent and $C_{\left(F, b_1 \times \cdots \times b_{|B*|}\right)} \ne C_{\left(F, a_1 \times \cdots \times a_{|B|}\right)}$.

Thus a reduct is a set of attributes that preserves classes. It means that a reduct is the minimal subset of attributes that enables the same classification of elements of the universe as the whole set of attributes. In other words, attributes that do not belong to a reduct are superfluous with regard to classification of elements of the universe. While computing multi-soft sets is straightforward, but the problem of finding minimal reducts in information systems is NP-hard. It is shown in [13] that the proposed soft set-based reducts are equivalent with that Pawlak's rough set-based reduct [14].

5 Results and Discussion

5.1 Data Representation

The distribution of the dataset is summarized in Table 1. It can be represented in decision table form as $S = (U, A \cup \{d\}, V, f)$. There are 1116 instances in the universe U, with 37 attributes of A as the set of condition attributes and the family of the instruments as the decision attribute d. The distribution of all instances in each class is uniform with no missing values in the data.

Table 1. Summary of Data Distribution

Attribute	Description	#1	#2	#3
ZC	Zero Crossing	456	438	222
MEANZCR	Mean of Zero Crossings Rate	134	638	344
STDZCR	Standard Deviation of Zero Crossings Rate	1092	16	8
MEANRMS	Mean of Root-Mean-Square	724	386	6
STDRMS	Standard Deviation of Root-Mean-Square	350	498	268
MEANC	Mean of Spectral Centroid	198	528	390
STDC	Standard Deviation of Spectral Centroid	166	430	520
MEANB	Mean of Bandwidth	206	336	574
STDB	Standard Deviation of Bandwidth	480	474	162
MEANFLUX	Mean of Flux	484	494	138
STDFLUX	Standard Deviation of Flux	692	304	120
MMFCC1	Mean of the MFCCs #1	1116	0	0
MMFCC2	Mean of the MFCCs #2	984	96	36
MMFCC3	Mean of the MFCCs #3	302	516	298
MMFCC4	Mean of the MFCCs #4	692	352	72
MMFCC5	Mean of the MFCCs #5	596	392	128
MMFCC6	Mean of the MFCCs #6	822	246	48

Table 1. *(continued)*

MMFCC7	Mean of the MFCCs #7	840	222	54
MMFCC8	Mean of the MFCCs #8	924	142	50
MMFCC9	Mean of the MFCCs #9	730	380	6
MMFCC10	Mean of the MFCCs #10	938	136	42
MMFCC11	Mean of the MFCCs #11	950	122	44
MMFCC12	Mean of the MFCCs #12	950	144	22
MMFCC13	Mean of the MFCCs #13	1010	42	64
SMFCC1	Standard Deviation of the MFCCs #1	1116	0	0
SMFCC2	Standard Deviation of the MFCCs #2	856	218	42
SMFCC3	Standard Deviation of the MFCCs #3	772	196	148
SMFCC4	Standard Deviation of the MFCCs #4	778	256	82
SMFCC5	Standard Deviation of the MFCCs #5	724	264	128
SMFCC6	Standard Deviation of the MFCCs #6	786	176	154
SMFCC7	Standard Deviation of the MFCCs #7	846	172	98
SMFCC8	Standard Deviation of the MFCCs #8	864	162	90
SMFCC9	Standard Deviation of the MFCCs #9	808	220	88
SMFCC10	Standard Deviation of the MFCCs #10	752	292	72
SMFCC11	Standard Deviation of the MFCCs #11	898	156	62
SMFCC12	Standard Deviation of the MFCCs #12	986	98	32
MFCC13	Standard Deviation of the MFCCs #13	840	148	128

5.2 Feature Selection

To find the reducts (relevant features), the proposed model is implemented in MATLAB version 7.6.0.324 (R2008a). It is executed on a processor Intel Core 2 Duo CPUs. The total main memory is 1 gigabyte and the operating system is Windows XP Professional SP3. For that, the dataset is first discretized into 3 categorical values as shown in Table 2. The result shows that the proposed model successfully generates the best features set with 35 attributes from 37 of original full attributes. It is found that {MMFCC1, SMFCC1} is the dispensable set of attributes. Thus, the relevant features (reduct) is A–{MMFCC1, SMFCC1}.

6 Conclusion

In this paper, the soft set theory has been used as feature selection (attribute reduction) technique to identify the best features of Traditional Malay musical instrument sounds. To perform this task, two categories of features schemes which are perception-based and MFCC which consist of 37 attributes are extracted. The equal width and equal frequency binning discretization technique is then employed to transform this continuous-value with non-categorical features (attributes) into categorical form. Afterward, the multi-soft sets approach is adopted for feature selection through dimensionality reduction in multi-valued domain. It is found that 35 best features are successfully generated by the proposed model. For that, our future work will examine others feature selection technique and examine the effectiveness of the selected features towards the classification performance.

Acknowledgement

This work was supported by the Universiti Tun Hussein Onn Malaysia (UTHM).

References

1. Molodtsov, D.: Soft Set Theory-First Results. Computer and Mathematics with Applications 37, 19–31 (1999)
2. Maji, P.K., Roy, A.R., Biswas, R.: An Application of Soft Sets in a Decision Making Problem. Computer and Mathematics with Applications 44, 1077–1083 (2002)
3. Chen, D., Tsang, E.C.C., Yeung, D.S., Wang, X.: The Parameterization Reduction of Soft Sets and its Applications. Computer and Mathematics with Applications 49, 757–763 (2005)
4. Chen, D., Tsang, E.C.C., Yeung, D.S., Wang, X.: Some Notes on the Parameterization Reduction of Soft Sets. In: Proceeding of International Conference on Machine Learning and Cybernetics, vol. 3, pp. 1442–1445 (2003)
5. Kong, Z., Gao, L., Wang, L., Li, S.: The normal parameter reduction of soft sets and its algorithm. Computers and Mathematics with Applications 56, 3029–3037 (2008)
6. Palaniappan, S., Hong, T.K.: Discretization of Continuous Valued Dimensions in OLAP Data Cubes. IJCSNS, International Journal of Computer Science and Network Security 8, 116–126 (2008)
7. Herawan, T., Mustafa, M.D.: On multi-soft sets construction in information systems. In: Huang, D.S., et al. (eds.) ICIC 2009. LNCS, vol. 5755, pp. 101–110. Springer, Heidelberg (2009)
8. Herawan, T., Rose, A.N.M., Mustafa, M.D.: Soft set theoretic approach for dimensionality reduction. In: Ślęzak, D., et al. (eds.) DTA 2009. CCIS, vol. 64, pp. 180–187. Springer, Heidelberg (2009)
9. Shriver, R.: Webpage, http://www.rickshriver.net/hires.htm
10. Warisan Budaya Malaysia: Alat Muzik Tradisional, http://malaysiana.pnm.my/kesenian/Index.htm
11. Senan, N., Ibrahim, R., Nawi, N.M., Mokji, M.M.: Feature Extraction for Traditional Malay Musical Instruments Classification. In: Proceeding of International Conference of Soft Computing and Pattern Recognition, SOCPAR 2009, Malacca, pp. 454–459 (2009)
12. Zhao, Y., Luo, F., Wong, S.K.M., Yao, Y.Y.: A General Definition of an Attribute Reduct. In: Yao, J., Lingras, P., Wu, W.-Z., Szczuka, M.S., Cercone, N.J., Ślęzak, D. (eds.) RSKT 2007. LNCS (LNAI), vol. 4481, pp. 101–108. Springer, Heidelberg (2007)
13. Herawan, T., Mustafa, M.D., Abawajy, J.H.: Matrices representation of multi soft-sets and its application. In: Taniar, D., et al. (eds.) ICCSA 2010, Part III. LNCS, vol. 6018, pp. 201–214. Springer, Heidelberg (2010)
14. Pawlak, Z., Skowron, A.: Rudiments of rough sets. Information Sciences 177(1), 3–27 (2007)

ETSA: An Efficient Task Scheduling Algorithm in Wireless Sensor Networks

Liang Dai*, Yilin Chang, and Zhong Shen

State Key Laboratory of Integrated Service Networks
Xidian University
Xi'an 710071, China
ldai1981@gmail.com, {ylchang,zhshen}@xidian.edu.cn

Abstract. To minimize the execution time (makespan) of a given task, an efficient task scheduling algorithm (ETSA) in a clustered wireless sensor network is proposed based on divisible load theory. The algorithm consists of two phases: intra-cluster task scheduling and inter-cluster task scheduling. Intra-cluster task scheduling deals with allocating different fractions of sensing tasks among sensor nodes in each cluster; inter-cluster task scheduling involves the assignment of sensing tasks among all clusters in multiple rounds to improve overlap of communication with computation. ETSA builds from eliminating transmission collisions and idle gaps between two successive data transmissions. Simulation results are presented to demonstrate the impacts of different network parameters on the number of rounds, makespan and energy consumption.

Keywords: wireless sensor networks; divisible load theory; multi-round task scheduling.

1 Introduction and Motivation

Divisible load theory [1] provides an effective solution to wireless sensor networks for task scheduling [2-5]. Different from other heuristic solutions of task scheduling problem in wireless sensor networks [6, 7], this scheme can get not only the optimal solution, but also the analytic solution, thus ensuring the consistency of the results of scheduling.

Divisible load scheduling algorithm can be divided into single-round scheduling algorithms [2-5] and multi-round scheduling algorithms [8, 9]. Single-round scheduling algorithms were applied to wireless sensor networks in [2-5]. Although the authors derived closed-form solutions to obtain the optimal finish time, the network topology discussed in those papers is single-level tree structure. Multi-round scheduling algorithm has the characteristics of better computation and communication overlap, thus properly reducing the scheduling overhead.

Therefore, we present a multi-round task scheduling algorithm (ETSA) in clustered(multi-level tree) wireless sensor networks. The goal of this algorithm

* This work was supported by the National Natural Science Foundation of China (No.60972047), and the 111 project (No.B08038).

R. Zhu et al. (Eds.): ICICA 2010, LNCS 6377, pp. 261–268, 2010.

is to minimize the overall execution time (hereafter called makespan) and fully utilize network resources.

2   Efficient Scheduling Algorithm

2.1   Intra-cluster Task Scheduling

In order to ensure that tasks are processed orderly, SINK allocates tasks to each cluster according to the task-processing rate of each cluster, which guarantees that the task execution time of all clusters in each round remains the same.

Definition: The task-processing rate of a cluster is the average rate the cluster takes to complete the intra-cluster tasks, that is the number of tasks dealt (measurement and reporting data) per unit of time.

Assuming there are k nodes in a cluster, according to divisible load theory, the cluster's task-processing rate is as follows:

$$S = (1 + \sum_{i=2}^{k} \prod_{j=2}^{i} h_j)/(1/s_1 + 1/b_1) \tag{1}$$

where $h_i = (1/s_{i-1})/(1/s_i + 1/b_i)$, $i = 2, \cdots, k$. s_i is node i's measuring rate, and b_i states node i's transmitting rate to cluster head.

Proof: α_i is defined as the fraction of sensing task assigned to node n_i by the cluster head. By definition we can see:

$$\sum_{i=1}^{k} \alpha_i = 1 \tag{2}$$

So, the time for node n_i measuring its tasks and reporting results to cluster head are α_i/s_i and α_i/b_i, respectively.

Fig.1 illustrates the timing diagram for a set of sensor nodes, indexed from n_1 to n_k, in one cluster. All sensor nodes start to measure data at the same time. Once the previous node finishes transmitting data, the other one completes its measuring task and starts to report its data.

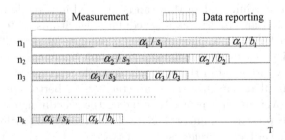

Fig. 1. Timing diagram for intra-cluster task-processing

In Fig.1, one can set up the following corresponding recursive load distribution equations:

$$\alpha_{i-1}/s_{i-1} = \alpha_i/s_i + \alpha_i/b_i, i = 2, 3, ...k \tag{3}$$

Rewriting the above set of equations as:

$$\alpha_i = h_i \alpha_{i-1} \tag{4}$$

where $h_i = (1/s_{i-1})/(1/s_i + 1/b_i)$, $i = 2, 3, ...k$.

Using Eq. (2) and (4), the largest workload for the node can be solved as:

$$\alpha_1 = 1/(1 + \sum_{i=2}^{k} \prod_{j=2}^{i} h_j) \tag{5}$$

Similarly, the workloads of other nodes given by Eq.(4) can be obtained:

$$\alpha_i = \prod_{j=2}^{i} (h_j)/(1 + \sum_{i=2}^{k} \prod_{j=2}^{i} h_j) \tag{6}$$

From Fig.1, finish time of measuring and reporting data for the cluster is:

$$T = (1/s_1 + 1/b_1)/(1 + \sum_{i=2}^{k} \prod_{j=2}^{i} h_j) \tag{7}$$

We can get the task-processing rate of the cluster:

$$S = (1 + \sum_{i=2}^{k} \prod_{j=2}^{i} h_j)/(1/s_1 + 1/b_1) \tag{8}$$

It's not difficult to see that in the homogeneous network environment, every cluster have the same parameters, and their task-processing rate is:

$$S = (1 - h^k)/(1/s + 1/b)(1 - h) \tag{9}$$

where $h = (1/s)/(1/s + 1/b)$

2.2 Inter-cluster Task Scheduling

The following notations will be used throughout this paper:

W_{total}: total amount of workload that resides at SINK; W_{ji} :number of tasks assigned to cluster i in round j; S_i: rate of cluster i's task-processing; B_i: down-link communication speed SINK to cluster head i; B_i': uplink transmission rate cluster head i to SINK; t_j: processing time of round j; W_j: size of the total load dispatched during round j; φ_i: information utility constant[5] of cluster head i(Information utilization constant is based on a technique of information accuracy estimation. Through estimating accuracy of information, cluster head can know the approximate percentage of data fusion.).

Thus, the entire load for cluster i in round j can be sensed (measured, transmitted) is W_{ji}/S_i. In round j, the time for SINK sending tasks to cluster i and for cluster head i sending the fused data are W_{ji}/B_i and $\varphi_i W_{ji}/B_i'$, respectively.

In practical wireless sensor network environment, communication and computing latency caused by pre-initialization are inevitable.

Suppose affine cost parameters are as follows:

α_i: computing latency of cluster i; β_i(resp. β_i'): communication latency incurred by SINK to initiate a data transferring to cluster head i. (resp. start-up time for communication from the cluster head i to SINK).

Fig. 2 describes the procedure of SINK dispatching the tasks to each cluster, each cluster measuring and reporting data, as well as cluster heads reporting the fused data to SINK. In this paper, we assume that there are total n clusters in a stable stage, where C_i, $i = 1, \cdots, n$ represents each cluster.

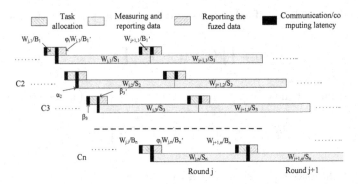

Fig. 2. Process of multi-round scheduling algorithm

As the computational cost of each cluster remains the same, so there are:

$$\alpha_i + W_{ji}/S_i = t_j, j = 1, \cdots, M - 1 \tag{10}$$

where t_j is only related to the number of rounds j, and M is the optimal scheduling round. The sum of tasks allocated to every cluster in round j is equal to the tasks in round j:

$$W_j = \sum_{i=1}^{n} W_{ji} \tag{11}$$

From the Eq. (10) and Eq. (11) we can compute:

$$W_{ji} = a_i W_j + b_i \tag{12}$$

where $a_i = S_i / \sum_{k=1}^{n} S_k$, $b_i = (S_i / \sum_{k=1}^{n} S_k) \sum_{k=1}^{n} (S_k \alpha_k) - S_i \alpha_i$.

As shown in Fig. 2, when the time for intra-cluster nodes processing the tasks in round j is exactly equal to the sum of the time for SINK sending sub-tasks to all cluster heads in round $j + 1$ and receiving the fused data from all the cluster heads in round j, the best bandwidth utilization is achieved, that is:

$$\sum_{i=1}^{n} [(W_{j+1,i}/B_i) + \beta_i + (\varphi_i W_{j,i}/B'_i) + \beta_i'] = t_j \tag{13}$$

Utilizing Eq. (10), Eq. (12) and Eq. (13), we have:

$$W_{j+1} = W_j * \frac{1 - \varphi_i \sum_{i=1}^{n} (S_i/B'_i)}{\sum_{i=1}^{n} (S_i/B_i)} + \frac{\sum_{i=1}^{n} (S_i\alpha_i)}{\sum_{i=1}^{n} S_i \sum_{i=1}^{n} (a_i/B_i)} - \frac{\sum_{i=1}^{n} (\beta_i + b_i/B_i + \beta_i' + \varphi_i b_i/B'_i)}{\sum_{i=1}^{n} (a_i/B_i)} \tag{14}$$

Simplify the Eq. (14) as follows:

$$W_j = \theta^j (W_0 - \eta) + \eta \tag{15}$$

where $\theta = [1 - \varphi_i \sum_{i=1}^{n} (S_i/B'_i)]/ \sum_{i=1}^{n} (S_i/B_i)$,

$$\eta = \frac{\sum_{i=1}^{n} (S_i\alpha_i)}{[\sum_{i=1}^{n} (S_i/B_i) + \varphi_i \sum_{i=1}^{n} (S_i/B'_i)] - 1} - \frac{\sum_{i=1}^{n} S_i \sum_{i=1}^{n} (\beta_i + b_i/B_i + \beta_i' + \varphi_i b_i/B'_i)}{[\sum_{i=1}^{n} (S_i/B_i) + \varphi_i \sum_{i=1}^{n} (S_i/B'_i)] - 1}$$

Also the total load is equal to the sum of the tasks allocated in all rounds:

$$\sum_{j=0}^{M-1} W_j = W_{total} \tag{16}$$

The following constraint relations can be obtained:

$$G(M, W_0) = (W_0 - \eta)(1 - \theta^M)/(1 - \theta) + M\eta - W_{total} = 0 \tag{17}$$

The problem of minimizing the total task finish time in scheduling algorithm[8] is described below:

$$EX(M, W_0) = \sum_{j=0}^{M-1} t_j + \frac{1}{2} \sum_{i=1}^{n} [(W_{0,i}/B_i) + \beta_i + (\varphi_i W_{M-1,i}/B'_i) + \beta_i'] \tag{18}$$

The minimization problem can be solved through Lagrange multiplication.

$$W_0 = (1 - \theta)/(1 - \theta^M)(W_{total} - M\eta) + \eta \tag{19}$$

After solving W_0 and M, the sizes of all the chunks $W_{j,i}$ can be obtained.

3   Wireless Energy Use

In this section, the energy model of the ETSA algorithm is presented in detail and the equations of energy consumption of individual sensor nodes are derived. The model is based on first-order radio model [10]. The energy to sense and transmit a unit sensory data are denoted by e_s, and e_{tx}, respectively. The distance between the sender and the receiver is d.

The energy use for individual sensor nodes j in cluster i is outlined as follows:

$$E_{i,j} = \alpha_{i,j}(e_s + e_{tx}d^2), i = 1, \cdots, k, j = 1, \cdots, n_i \tag{20}$$

4   Performance Evaluation

In this section, we investigate the effects of three network parameters, such as the number of clusters, computation/communication latency, and measurement/communication speed, on the number of rounds, makespan and energy consumption in homogeneous network. In the simulation, the following energy parameters are adopted: transmitting a unit of sensor reading over a unit distance takes $e_{tx}=200nJ$, measuring one unit of sensor reading needs $e_s=100nJ$, and the distance between the sender and the receiver is $d=100m$. There are 20 nodes in each cluster. The simulation results are shown in Fig. 3 to Fig. 6.

Firstly, Fig. 3 plots the M values computed by ETSA versus computation/communication latency when they vary among 0 and 1.0. As can be seen from Fig. 3, M decreases with either the communication or computation latency increasing, owing to the reason that fewer rounds may result in less overhead.

Next, the makesapn against the number of clusters are plotted in Fig. 4. In Fig. 4(a), the value of s is chosen from 4 to 10, while b is fixed to 1.0. Fig. 4(b) shows that when the communication speed of sensor nodes increases, the makespan of

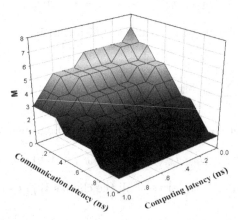

Fig. 3. Impact of communications and computing latency on the number of rounds

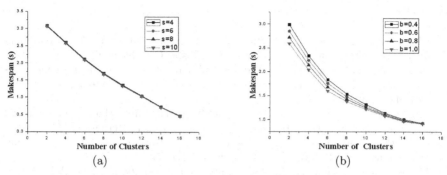

Fig. 4. Impact of measuring speed and bandwidth on the makespan

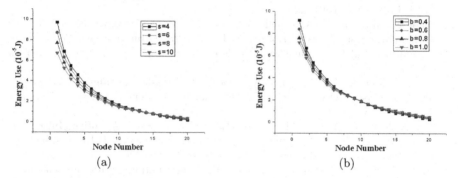

Fig. 5. The impact of measuring speed and bandwidth on the energy consumption

a given task is reduced. It can be found that the four lines in Fig. 4(b) converge when the number of clusters becomes large.

Then, the third simulation is about the energy consumption of intra-cluster nodes. SINK and cluster heads are not taken into account because generally, SINK has no energy constraint and the chosen cluster heads have the possibly enough energy. The network is configured with 20 clusters. Without loss of generality, the intra-cluster sensor nodes in the first cluster are chosen to study the energy consumption. Fig. 5(a) shows the higher the intra-cluster node's measuring speed, the more evenly the tasks allocated to each node, hence the smaller the energy consumption of the node. Fig. 5(b) presents the larger communication speed between nodes, the smaller the energy consumption of the node.

5   Conclusions

As the wireless sensor network node with limited energy, so the tasks should be completed as quickly as possible, and the network resources should be fully utilized. In this paper, we present a multi-round task scheduling algorithm (ETSA) in clustered wireless sensor networks. The algorithm enables to reasonably distribute tasks to each sensor, then effectively reduces the time-consuming and energy-consuming of task completion.

References

1. Bharadwaj, V., Ghose, D., Robertazzi, T.G.: Divisible load theory: A new paradigm for load scheduling in distributed systems. Cluster Computing 6(1), 7–18 (2003)
2. Moges, M.,, Robertazzi, T.G.: Wireless sensor networks: scheduling for measurement and data reporting. IEEE Transactions on Aerospace and Electronic Systems 42(1), 327–340 (2006)
3. Liu, H., Yuan, X., Moges, M.: An Efficient Task Scheduling Method for Improved Network Delay in Distributed Sensor Networks. In: 3rd International Conference on Testbeds and Research Infrastructures for the Development of Networks and Communities, pp. 1–8. IEEE Press, New York (2007)
4. Liu, H., Shen, J., Yuan, X., Moges, M.: Performance Analysis of Data Aggregation in Wireless Sensor Mesh Networks. In: 11th International Conference on Engineering, Science, Construction, and Operations in Challenging Environments, pp. 1–8. IEEE Press, New York (2008)
5. Choi, K., Robertazzi, T.G.: Divisible Load Scheduling in Wireless Sensor Networks with Information Utility Performance. In: 27th IEEE International Performance Computing and Communications Conference, pp. 9–17. IEEE Press, New York (2008)
6. Zeng, Z., Liu, A., Li, D.: A Highly Efficient DAG Task Scheduling Algorithm for Wireless Sensor Networks. In: 9th International Conference for Young Computer Scientists, pp. 570–575. IEEE Press, New York (2008)
7. Lin, J., Xiao, W., Lewis, F.L.: Energy-Efficient Distributed Adaptive Multisensor Scheduling for Target Tracking in Wireless Sensor Networks. IEEE Transactions on Instrumentation and Measurement 58(6), 1886–1896 (2009)
8. Yang, Y., Van Der Raadt, K., Casanova, H.: Multiround algorithms for scheduling divisible loads. IEEE Trans. on Parallel and Distributed Systems 16(11), 1092–1102 (2005)
9. Yeim-Kuan, C., Jia-Hwa, W., Chi-Yeh, C., Chih-Ping, C.: Improved Methods for Divisible Load Distribution on k-Dimensional Meshes Using Multi-Installment. IEEE Transactions on Parallel and Distributed Systems 18(11), 1618–1629 (2007)
10. Heinzelman, W., Chandrakasan, A.: An application-specifid protocol architecture for wireless microsensor networks. IEEE Transaction on Wireless Communications 1(4), 660–670 (2002)

Comparing Fuzzy Algorithms on Overlapping Communities in Networks

Jian Liu

LMAM and School of Mathematical Sciences, Peking University,
Beijing 100871, P.R. China
dugujian@pku.edu.cn

Abstract. Uncovering the overlapping community structure exhibited by real networks is a crucial step toward an understanding of complex systems that goes beyond the local organization of their constituents. Here three fuzzy c-means methods, based on optimal prediction, diffusion distance and dissimilarity index, respectively, are test on two artificial networks, including the widely known ad hoc networks and a recently introduced LFR benchmarks with heterogeneous distributions of degree and community size. All of them have an excellent performance, with the additional advantage of low computational complexity, which enables one to analyze large systems. Moreover, successful applications to real world networks confirm the capability of the methods.

Keywords: Overlapping community structure, Fuzzy c-means, Optimal prediction, Diffusion distance, Dissimilarity index.

1 Introduction

The modern science of networks has brought significant advances to our understanding of complex systems [1,2]. One of the most relevant features of networks representing real systems is community structure, i.e. the organization of nodes in clusters, with many edges joining vertices of the same cluster and comparatively few edges joining vertices of different clusters. Such communities can be considered as fairly independent compartments of a network, playing a similar role like the tissues or the organs in the human body. Detecting communities is of great importance in sociology, biology and computer science, disciplines where systems are often represented as networks [3,4,5,6,7,8,9,10,11,12,13,14].

In a previous paper [11], an approach to partition the networks based on optimal prediction theory is derived. The basic idea is to associate the network with the random walker Markovian dynamics [15], then introduce a metric on the space of Markov chains (stochastic matrices), and optimally reduce the chain under this metric. The final minimization problem is solved by an analogy to the traditional fuzzy c-means algorithm in clustering analysis [16]. Another work [7] is also along the lines of random walker Markovian dynamics, then introduce the diffusion distance on the space of nodes and identify

R. Zhu et al. (Eds.): ICICA 2010, LNCS 6377, pp. 269–276, 2010.

the geometric centroid in the same framework. This proximity reflects the connectivity of nodes in a diffusion process. Under the same framework [6], a dissimilarity index for each pair of nodes is proposed, which one can measure the extent of proximity between nodes of a network and signify to what extent two nodes would like to be in the same community. They can motivate us to solve the partitioning problem also by fuzzy c-means algorithms [16] under these two measures.

We will compare the above three algorithms in fuzzy c-means formulation based on optimal prediction, diffusion distance and dissimilarity distance, respectively. From the numerical performance to the artificial networks: the ad hoc network and the LFR benchmark, we can see that the three methods identify the community structure during with a high degree of accuracy, while they also produce little different. Moreover, application to a real word social network, the karate club network, confirms the differences among them.

The rest of the paper is organized as follows. In Section 2, we briefly introduce the three type of fuzzy c-means algorithms and the corresponding framework. In Section 3, we apply the algorithms to the representative examples mentioned before. Finally we make the conclusion in Section 4.

2   The Framework of Fuzzy c-Means Algorithms for Network Partition

2.1   The Fuzzy c-Means Based on Optimal Prediction

We will start with the probabilistic framework for network partition [12]. Let $G(S, E)$ be a network with n nodes and m edges, where S is the set of nodes, $E = \{e(x, y)\}_{x,y \in S}$ is the weight matrix and $e(x, y)$ is the weight for the edge connecting the nodes x and y. We can relate this network to a discrete-time Markov chain with stochastic matrix p whose entries are given by $p(x, y) = \frac{e(x,y)}{d(x)}$, where $d(x) = \sum_{z \in S} e(x, z)$ is the degree of the node x. This Markov chain has stationary distribution $\mu(x) = \frac{d(x)}{\sum_{z \in S} d(z)}$ and it satisfies the detailed balance condition with respect to μ. The basic idea in [12] is to introduce a metric for p with the form $\|p\|_\mu^2 = \sum_{x,y \in S} \frac{\mu(x)}{\mu(y)} |p(x, y)|^2$ and find the reduced Markov chain $\tilde{p}$ by minimizing the distance $\|\tilde{p} - p\|_\mu$. For a given partition of S as $S = \cup_{k=1}^N S_k$ with $S_k \cap S_l = \emptyset$ if $k \neq l$, let $\hat{p}_{kl}$ be the coarse grained transition probability from S_k to S_l on the state space $\mathbb{S} = \{S_1, \ldots, S_N\}$ which satisfies $\hat{p}_{kl} \geq 0$ and $\sum_{l=1}^N \hat{p}_{kl} = 1$. Let $\rho_k(x)$ be the probability of the node x belonging to the k-th community which needs the assumption that $\rho_k(x) \geq 0$ and $\sum_{k=1}^N \rho_k(x) = 1$. Naturally the matrix $\tilde{p}$ can be lifted to the space of stochastic matrices on the original state space S via

$$\tilde{p}(x, y) = \sum_{k,l=1}^N \rho_k(x) \hat{p}_{kl} \mu_l(y), \qquad x, y \in S, \tag{1}$$

where $\mu_k(x) = \frac{\rho_k(x)\mu(x)}{\hat{\mu}_k}$ and $\hat{\mu}_k = \sum_{z \in S} \rho_k(z)\mu(z)$. Given the number of the communities N, we optimally reduce the random walker dynamics by considering the following minimization problem

$$\min_{\rho,\hat{p}} J_{OP} = \|p - \tilde{p}\|_\mu^2 = \sum_{x,y \in S} \mu(x)\mu(y)\left| \sum_{m,n=1}^{N} \rho_m(x)\rho_n(y)\frac{\hat{p}_{mn}}{\hat{\mu}_n} - \frac{p(x,y)}{\mu(y)} \right|^2 \quad (2)$$

subject to the constraints described before. To minimize (2), we define $\hat{p}_{kl}^* = \sum_{x,y \in S} \mu_k(x)p(x,y)\rho_l(y) = \frac{1}{\hat{\mu}_k}\sum_{x,y \in S} \mu(x)\rho_k(x)p(x,y)\rho_l(y)$. Then the Euler-Lagrange equations of (2) are derived as

$$\left(I_{\hat{\mu}}^{-1} \cdot \hat{\mu}\right) \cdot \hat{p} \cdot \left(I_{\hat{\mu}}^{-1} \cdot \hat{\mu}\right) = \hat{p}^*, \quad (3a)$$

$$\rho = I_{\hat{\mu}}\hat{p}^{-1}\hat{\mu}^{-1}\rho p^T, \quad (3b)$$

where $\hat{\mu} = \rho \cdot I_\mu \cdot \rho^T$. The diagonal matrices I_μ, $I_{\hat{\mu}}$ choose $\mu(x)$ and $\hat{\mu}_k$ as their diagonal entries, respectively. To ensure the nonnegativity and normalization for $\hat{p}$ and ρ, we add a projection step after each iteration and change (3) to

$$\hat{p} = \mathcal{P}\left(\hat{\mu}^{-1} \cdot I_{\hat{\mu}} \cdot \hat{p}^* \cdot \hat{\mu}^{-1} \cdot I_{\hat{\mu}}\right), \quad (4a)$$

$$\rho = \mathcal{P}\left(I_{\hat{\mu}}\hat{p}^{-1}\hat{\mu}^{-1}\rho p^T\right). \quad (4b)$$

Here $\mathcal{P}$ is a projection operator which maps a real vector into a vector with nonnegative, normalized components.

2.2 The Fuzzy c-Means Based on Diffusion Distance

The main idea of [7] is to define a system of coordinates with an explicit metric that reflects the connectivity of nodes in a given network and the construction is also based on a Markov random walk. The transition matrix p has a set of left and right eigenvectors $\{\psi_i\}_{i=0}^{n-1}$, $\{\varphi_i\}_{i=0}^{n-1}$ and a set of eigenvalues $1 = \lambda_0 \geq |\lambda_1| \geq \cdots \geq |\lambda_{n-1}| \geq 0$. Let $q(t)$ be the largest index i such that $|\lambda_i|^t > \delta|\lambda_1|^t$ and if we introduce the diffusion map

$$\Psi_t : x \longmapsto \begin{pmatrix} \lambda_1\varphi_1^t(x) \\ \vdots \\ \lambda_{q(t)}\varphi_{q(t)}^t(x) \end{pmatrix}, \quad (5)$$

then the diffusion distance $D_t(x,y)$ between x and y is defined as the weighted L^2 distance and can be approximated to relative precision δ using the first $q(t)$ non-trivial eigenvectors and eigenvalues

$$D_t^2(x,y) = \sum_{z \in S} \frac{(p(x,z) - p(y,z))^2}{\mu(z)} \sim \sum_{i=1}^{q(t)} \lambda_i^{2t}\left(\varphi_i(x) - \varphi_i(y)\right)^2 = \|\Psi_t(x) - \Psi_t(y)\|^2,$$

where the weight $\mu(z)^{-1}$ penalize discrepancies on domains of low density more than those of high density. The centroid $c(S_k)$ of community S_k is defined as $c(S_k) = \sum_{x \in S_k} \frac{\mu(x)}{\hat{\mu}(S_k)} \Psi_t(x)$, where $\hat{\mu}(S_k) = \sum_{x \in S_k} \mu(x)$. Similar as before, given the number of clusters N, we optimally reduce the random walker dynamics by

$$\min_{\rho,c} J_{\mathrm{DD}} = \sum_{k=1}^{N} \sum_{x \in S} \rho_k^2(x)\mu(x)\|\Psi_t(x) - c(S_k)\|^2 \tag{6}$$

subject to $\sum_{k=1}^{N} \rho_k(x) = 1$. To minimize (6), we define $\hat{\mu}_k = \sum_{z \in S} \rho_k^b(z)\mu(z)$. The Euler-Lagrange equations are given by

$$c = I_{\hat{\mu}}^{-1} \rho^b I_\mu \Psi_t, \tag{7a}$$

$$\rho = W I_{1 \cdot W}^{-1}, \tag{7b}$$

where $\rho^b = (\rho_k^b(x))_{k=1,\ldots,N, x \in S}$ and W is with entries $W_k(x) = \frac{1}{\|\Psi_t(x) - c(S_k)\|^{\frac{2}{b-1}}}$.

2.3 The Fuzzy c-Means Based on Dissimilarity Index

In [6], a dissimilarity index between pairs of nodes is defined and can measure the extent of proximity between nodes in graphs. Suppose the random walker is located at node x. The mean first passage time $t(x, y)$ is the average number of steps it takes before it reaches node y for the first time, which is given by

$$t(x,y) = p(x,y) + \sum_{j=1}^{+\infty} (j+1) \cdot \sum_{z_1, \cdots, z_j \neq y} p(x, z_1)p(z_1, z_2) \cdots p(z_j, y). \tag{8}$$

It has been shown that $t(x, y)$ is the solution of the linear equation in [6]. The difference in the perspectives of nodes x and y about the network can be quantitatively measured. The dissimilarity index is defined by the following expression

$$\Lambda(x,y) = \frac{1}{n-2}\left(\sum_{z \in S, z \neq x, y}\left(t(x,z) - t(y,z)\right)^2\right)^{\frac{1}{2}}. \tag{9}$$

Then fuzzy c-means is considered to address the optimization issue

$$\min_{\rho,m} J_{\mathrm{DI}} = \sum_{k=1}^{N}\sum_{x \in S} \rho_k^2(x)\Lambda^2(m(S_k), x), \tag{10}$$

which guarantees convergence towards a local minimum [16]. The Euler-Lagrange equation for (10) with constraints $\sum_{k=1}^{N} \rho_k(x) = 1$ is given by the following

$$\rho_k(x) = \frac{1/\Lambda^2(m(S_k), x)}{\sum_{l=1}^{N} 1/\Lambda^2(m(S_l), x)}, \quad x \in S, \quad k = 1, \cdots, N, \tag{11a}$$

$$m(S_k) = \arg\min_{x \in S_k} \frac{1}{|S_k|} \sum_{y \in S_k, y \neq x} \Lambda(x, y), \quad k = 1, \cdots, N, \tag{11b}$$

where $|S_k|$ is the number of nodes in S_k and we set $x \in S_k$ if $k = \arg\max_l \rho_l(x)$.

3 Experimental Results

3.1 Ad Hoc Network with 128 Nodes

We apply our methods to the ad hoc network with 128 nodes. The ad hoc network is a typical benchmark problem considered in many papers [4,6,11,12,13,14]. Suppose we choose $n = 128$ nodes, split into 4 communities containing 32 nodes each. Assume pairs of nodes belonging to the same communities are linked with probability p_{in}, and pairs belonging to different communities with probability p_{out}. These values are chosen so that the average node degree, d, is fixed at $d = 16$. In other words p_{in} and p_{out} are related as $31p_{in} + 96p_{out} = 16$. Here we naturally choose the nodes group $S_1 = \{1 : 32\}, S_2 = \{33 : 64\}, S_3 = \{65 : 96\}, S_4 = \{97 : 128\}$. Testing an algorithm on any graph with built-in community structure also implies defining a quantitative criterion to estimate the goodness of the answer given by the algorithm as compared to the real answer that is expected. We change z_{out} from 0.5 to 8 and look into the normalized mutual information [8,9,10] produced by the three methods. From Figure 1, we can see that OP fuzzy c-means performs better than the two others, especially for the more diffusive cases when z_{out} is large.

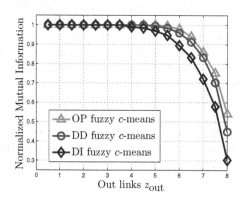

Fig. 1. Test of the three fuzzy c-means algorithms on the ad hoc network with 128 nodes with the normalized mutual information defined in [8]. Each point corresponds to an average over 20 graph realizations.

3.2 The LFR Benchmark

The LFR benchmark [9,10] is a special case of the planted partition model, in which groups are of different sizes and nodes have different degrees. The

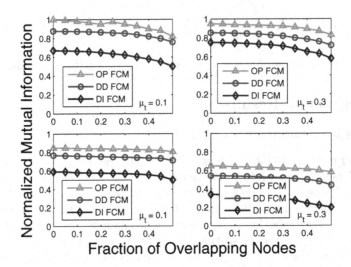

Fig. 2. Test of the three fuzzy c-means methods on the LFR benchmark for undirected and unweighted network with overlapping communities. The plot shows the variation of the normalized mutual information between the planted and the recovered partition, in its generalized form for overlapping communities [10]. The number of nodes $n = 1000$ and the average degree $\langle k \rangle = 20$, the other parameters are $\gamma = 2, \beta = 1$. For the upper two $s_{\min} = 10, s_{\max} = 50$ and for the lower two $s_{\min} = 20, s_{\max} = 100$. Each point corresponds to an average over 20 graph realizations.

node degrees are distributed according to a power law with exponent γ; the community sizes also obey a power law distribution, with exponent β. It is more practical to choose as independent parameter, the mixing parameter μ, which expresses the ratio between the external degree and the total degree of a node. In Figure 2, we show what happens if one operates the three fuzzy c-means methods on the benchmark, for $n = 1000$ and the average degree $\langle k \rangle = 20$. The other parameters are $\gamma = 2, \beta = 1$. We have chosen combinations of the extremes of the exponents' ranges in order to explore the widest spectrum of network structures. Each curve shows the variation of the normalized mutual information with the fraction of overlapping nodes. In general, we can infer that the fuzzy c-means type methods give good results.

3.3   The Karate Club Network

This network was constructed by Wayne Zachary after he observed social interactions between members of a karate club at an American university [17]. Soon after, a dispute arose between the clubs administrator and main teacher and the club split into two smaller clubs. It has been used in several papers to test the algorithms for finding community structure in networks [3,4,5,6,11,12,13,14]. The partitioning results are shown in Figure 3 and Table 1.

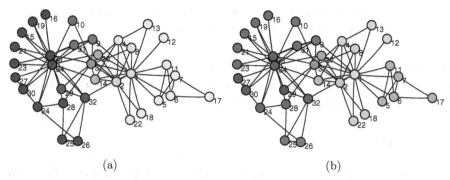

| | (a) | (b) |

Fig. 3. The fuzzy community structure for the karate club network, corresponding to two overlapping communities represent by the weighted color average described in [12]. (a)OP fuzzy c-means; (b)DD fuzzy c-means.

Table 1. The association probability of each node belonging to different communities for the karate club network. ρ_R or ρ_Y means the probability belonging to red or yellow colored community, respectively.

Nodes	1	2	3	4	5	6	7	8	9	10	11	12
OP ρ_R	0.0386	0.0782	0.4396	0	0	0	0	0.0037	0.6746	0.7640	0	0
ρ_Y	0.9614	0.9218	0.5604	1.000	1.0000	1.0000	1.0000	0.9963	0.3254	0.2360	1.0000	1.0000
DD ρ_R	0.1766	0.2510	0.3330	0.1942	0.3935	0.4356	0.4356	0.2095	0.5455	0.5318	0.3935	0.1962
ρ_Y	0.8234	0.7490	0.6670	0.8058	0.6065	0.5644	0.5644	0.7905	0.4545	0.4682	0.6065	0.8038

Nodes	13	14	15	16	17	18	19	20	21	22	23	24
OP ρ_R	0	0.2271	1.0000	1.0000	0	0	1.0000	0.3030	1.0000	0	1.0000	1.0000
ρ_Y	1.0000	0.7729	0	0	1.0000	1.0000	0	0.6970	0	1.0000	0	0
DD ρ_R	0.1864	0.2426	0.6029	0.6029	0.4674	0.2227	0.6029	0.3191	0.6029	0.2227	0.6029	0.6054
ρ_Y	0.8136	0.7574	0.3971	0.3971	0.5326	0.7773	0.3971	0.6809	0.3971	0.7773	0.3971	0.3946

Nodes	25	26	27	28	29	30	31	32	33	34
OP ρ_R	1.0000	1.0000	1.0000	0.9651	0.8579	1.0000	0.7339	0.9103	1.0000	0.9631
ρ_Y	0	0	0	0.0349	0.1421	0	0.2661	0.0897	0	0.0369
DD ρ_R	0.5329	0.5472	0.7456	0.5569	0.6391	0.7353	0.5517	0.5734	0.7270	0.7287
ρ_Y	0.4671	0.4528	0.2544	0.4431	0.3609	0.2647	0.4483	0.4266	0.2730	0.2713

4   Conclusions

In this paper, we test three fuzzy c-means methods, based on optimal prediction, diffusion distance and dissimilarity index, respectively, on two artificial networks, including the widely known ad hoc network with same community size and a recently introduced LFR benchmarks with heterogeneous distributions of degree and community size. All of them have an excellent performance, with the additional advantage of low computational complexity, which enables one to analyze large systems. They identify the community structure during iterations with a high degree of accuracy, with producing little different. Moreover, successful applications to real world networks confirm the capability among them and the differences and limits of them are revealed obviously.

Acknowledgements. This work is supported by the National Natural Science Foundation of China under Grant 10871010 and the National Basic Research Program of China under Grant 2005CB321704.

References

1. Albert, R., Barabási, A.L.: Statistical mechanics of complex networks. Rev. Mod. Phys. 74(1), 47–97 (2002)
2. Newman, M., Barabási, A.L., Watts, D.J.: The structure and dynamics of networks. Princeton University Press, Princeton (2005)
3. Girvan, M., Newman, M.: Community structure in social and biological networks. Proc. Natl. Acad. Sci. USA 99(12), 7821–7826 (2002)
4. Newman, M., Girvan, M.: Finding and evaluating community structure in networks. Phys. Rev. E 69(2), 026113 (2004)
5. Newman, M.: Modularity and community structure in networks. Proc. Natl. Acad. Sci. USA 103(23), 8577–8582 (2006)
6. Zhou, H.: Distance, dissimilarity index, and network community structure. Phys. Rev. E 67(6), 061901 (2003)
7. Lafon, S., Lee, A.: Diffusion Maps and Coarse-Graining: A Unified Framework for Dimensionality Reduction, Graph Partitioning, and Data Set Parameterization. IEEE Trans. Pattern. Anal. Mach. Intel. 28, 1393–1403 (2006)
8. Danon, L., Diaz-Guilera, A., Duch, J., Arenas, A.: Comparing community structure identification. J. Stat. Mech. 9, P09008 (2005)
9. Lancichinetti, A., Fortunato, S., Radicchi, F.: Benchmark graphs for testing community detection algorithms. Phys. Rev. E 78(4), 046110 (2008)
10. Lancichinetti, A., Fortunato, S.: Benchmarks for testing community detection algorithms on directed and weighted graphs with overlapping communities. Phys. Rev. E 80(1), 016118 (2009)
11. E.W., Li, T., Vanden-Eijnden, E.: Optimal partition and effective dynamics of complex networks. Proc. Natl. Acad. Sci. USA 105(23), 7907–7912 (2008)
12. Li, T., Liu, J., E.W.: Probabilistic Framework for Network Partition. Phys. Rev. E 80, 026106 (2009)
13. Liu, J.: Detecting the fuzzy clusters of complex networks. Patten Recognition 43, 1334–1345 (2010)
14. Liu, J., Liu, T.: Detecting community structure in complex networks using simulated annealing with k-means algorithms. Physica A 389, 2300–2309 (2010)
15. Lovasz, L.: Random walks on graphs: A survey. Combinatorics, Paul Erdos is Eighty 2, 1–46 (1993)
16. Hastie, T., Tibshirani, R., Friedman, J.: The Elements of Statistical Learning: Data Mining, Inference, and Prediction. Springer, New York (2001)
17. Zachary, W.: An information flow model for conflict and fission in small groups. J. Anthrop. Res. 33(4), 452–473 (1977)

Color Image Segmentation Using Swarm Based Optimisation Methods

Salima Nebti

Department of computer science, Ferhat Abbas University
Setif. 19000, Algeria
snebti@live.fr

Abstract. The present paper places specific swarm based optimization methods that are the predator prey optimizer, the symbiotic algorithm, the cooperative co-evolutionary optimizer and the bees' algorithm in color image segmentation framework to offer global pixels clustering. The Predator prey optimiser is mainly designed to create diversity through predators to permit better segmentation accuracy. The symbiotic one is proposed to allow finer search through a symbiotic interaction with varying parameters. The cooperative co-evolutionary optimizer which results in a good quality of image segmentation through interaction between three species where each of them evolves in an independent color space through a standard particle swarm optimizer and the bees algorithm which is proposed to offer the most accurate results based on a neighborhood search.

Keywords: Image segmentation, particle swarm optimisation, cooperative co-evolution, the bees algorithm.

1 Introduction

Image segmentation is in fact a low level task which consists in image division into coherent regions (sets of pixels) pertaining to the same structure (object or scene). This task is the basis of many applications such as diseases detection in medical imagery or regions location in satellite imagery. The segmentation quality measured by its precision of regions' partition has a direct influence on the performance of the later applications. Many methods have been proposed by adapting existing techniques to remove some limitations for some applications. However the search for an optimal image segmentation method remains a problem in image analysis and processing. In general, segmentation methods can be distinguished in three main classes: pixel based methods (clustering), region based methods and contour based methods.

Clustering is a hard and difficult task in unsupervised pattern recognition; it consists in pixels grouping into coherent clusters according to their similarity. Clustering applications cover various fields such as: Data-mining, pattern recognition, image segmentation, handwritten character recognition and machine learning. In this

R. Zhu et al. (Eds.): ICICA 2010, LNCS 6377, pp. 277–284, 2010.

paper our interest is focused on image clustering i.e. the unsupervised image classification.

The proposed work is an image clustering approach with specific prior knowledge, we must here precise in advance the number of classes, and it begins with a population of vectors composed of randomly chosen clusters centres. The vectors move into the search space according to new strategies resembling the dynamic behaviour of predators' attack, preys' evasion, symbiosis interactions and swarm bees when searching for food sites. In fact, these methods can be regarded as an enhancement of the already applied image classification method presented in [1] which is based on the particle swarm optimizer (PSO). In PSO method, particles trajectories oscillate between their own best positions and the best ones found in their neighbourhood. Thus, particles adhere to the best-found particles positions by moving from better to better ones, ending up into local optima [2]. Consequently, the obtained results are not to be considered the most accurate. The proposed approach aims at improving image classification through modified PSO methods: called the Predator Prey Optimiser (PPO). The adaptable particle swarm optimizer (APSO), the cooperative particle swarm optimizer (CPSO) and the bees' algorithm (BA).

The rest of this paper is organized as follows. Sections 2, 3, 4 and 5 describe the basic concepts underlying the presented hybridizations using PPO, APSO, CPSO and BA. Section 6 gives some experimental results. Finally, a conclusion is drawn.

2 The Predator Prey Based Approach

The Predator Prey Optimiser (PPO) has the ability to escape local optima by additional particles called predators which serve to heighten the search space by fleeing the other particles called preys tending to converge in new directions, permitting them to improve their fitness. At the initial stages of the evolutionary process, the predators' effect is overlooked, thus, each prey moves in a similar way to the Particle Swarm Optimiser i.e. according to the following equations [3]:

$$\begin{cases} V_{id} = wV_{id} + c_1 \times r_1 \times (p_{id} - x_{id}) + c_2 \times r_2 \times (p_g - x_{id}) \\ \\ x_{id} = x_{id} + v_{id} \end{cases} \tag{1}$$

Where: X: is the particle position into the search space, V: represents its velocity, **Pid** and **Pg** are respectively its personal best position and the best found position in its neighborhood, C_1 and C_2: are respectively the cognitive and social factors that control its individual and collective behaviors, r_1 and r_2: are randomly varying values between [0,1] to improve the search exploration and **w**: is the inertia weight that controls the exploration properties.

Once the particles start to converge, the predators' effect appears by evading particles and in a significant way the nearest particles towards new and perhaps better areas in the search space. The behaviour of a predatory particle is very simple; it aims at tracking the best particle into the swarm according to the following rules [4]:

$$\begin{cases} V_{pred}=C_1\times(X_g-X_{pred}) \\ X_{pred}=X_{pred}+V_{pred} \end{cases} \qquad (2)$$

Where: C_1 is a randomly varying value between 0 and an upper limit. It serves to control the predator's speed towards the best particle. The speed of any prey may be changed in one or more dimensions according to an escape probability. If the alteration of the velocity V in the dimension d of the prey i is permitted according to the avoidance probability then the velocity and consequently the position of this prey are to be updated using the following equations [4]:

$$\begin{cases} V_{id}=wV_{id}+c_1\times r_1\times(p_{id}-x_{id})+c_2\times r_2\times(p_g-x_{id})+c_3\times D(dist) \\ x_{id}=x_{id}+V_{id} \end{cases} \qquad (3)$$

Where: $D(dist)$ is an exponentially varying function that has as argument the distance between the predators and preys.

In the other case, the preys' movement remains similar to the movement of particles in PSO [4].

In image segmentation a particle either a prey or a predator is a vector of clusters centers. It aims to find the set of cluster centers that minimizes the sum-of-squared-error criterion given by equation (4) :

$$SSE = \sum_{i=1}^{M} \sum_{x \in C_i}^{N} \left\| x - \overline{C}_i \right\|^2 \qquad (4)$$

Where: M: is the number of clusters, N is the number of pixels per cluster and $\overline{C}_i$: are the gravity centers of image classes.

The color image segmentation problem using PPO can be solved using the following scheme [13]:

{Initialise a population of preys with a known number of randomly chosen clusters centers

Initialise the predators with a known number of randomly chosen clusters centers

   Repeat

   {For each prey do

        {Compute the distance of each pixel from each center

          Assign each pixel to the nearest center

          Evaluate the prey performance according to (4)

      Update P_{best} t and G_{best}

      For each dimension do

          {If the change is allowed by the avoidance probability then

          Update position and velocity according to (3)

          Else

            Update position and velocity according to (1)   }}

  Update the predators' position and velocity according to (4)

  Until a Maximum number of iterations is reached}

P_{best} and G_{best} denote respectively the Personal and Global best solutions.

---

3   The Symbiotic Based Approach

The main objective of parameters adaptation in image segmentation using the co-evolutionary symbiotic algorithm described in [5] is for both allowing a finer search with flexible (i.e. varying parameters) and providing the user by the set of parameters that has caused accuracy. In this work, for each solution particle either a predator or a prey, It is associated a parameter particle encoding the seven parameters used for adjusting solution positions. Co-evolution takes place when the parameters obtain their fitness from their companion solutions, enabling the parameters to adapt to their solutions using the standard PSO. On the other side, solutions (centres' positions) change by taking into account the evolutionary progress of their associated parameters.

Parameter fitness is the improvement that has produced to its solution which is the following amount [6]:

Improvement (fitness of a parameter) = (old fitness - new fitness) of its solution.

The best parameter is the parameter having the greatest improvement among the other parameters and the action of parameters fitness assignment only happens after ten iterations, unless they are kept unchanged increasing solutions accuracy [6].

4   The Cooperative Co-evolutionary Based Approach

Co-evolution is the process of reciprocal influences between two or more populations [7], often termed as species. These species evolve simultaneously through interaction between them so that the evaluation of one species depends on the evolutionary progress of the other living species [7]. The idea behind this novel notion is thus: a system will be able to better evolve through reciprocal performances [7],[8].

There are two main forms of co-evolution [7]: the *competitive co-evolution*; where the co-adapted species are guided by the opposing objective, i.e. the individual performances of one species is inversely proportional to the individual performances of the other species [5], and *cooperative co-evolution* where species evolve together in order to solve various elements of the same problem [7]. *Cooperative co-evolution* has been proved to be an effective tool for solving separable problems made up of distinct sub-problems, in order to make the task of resolution easier [7], mainly for function optimization [9].

Image segmentation using the Cooperative Particle Swarm Optimizer is a new hybridization basically inspired by the work of [10] which is applied here to image segmentation task. In this work the CPSO algorithm is used to solve the image clustering problem, It consists of three sub-populations where each of them search for better solutions in a given color space, these sub-populations are considered as dissimilar species where each of them evolves using relatively an independent particle swarm optimizer. To evaluate the particles of one species, the other particles of the other species are kept frozen. The fitness of each particle in each species is measured by combining the current particle of the current species with randomly chosen particles from the other species and then with the best ones found in the other species.

According to this new strategy, the behavior of particles within color image segmentation framework can be controlled by the following algorithm:

Initialize three species with random centres in the three color spaces (R, G and B)
For each species do
    {**for** each particle P do
  {Compute the distance of each pixel from each centre
  Assign each pixel to the nearest center
  Evaluate the particle by combination with random particles from
  the other species using   (4)}
  Save the best particles}
Repeat {**for** each species do
  {For each particle P do
  {Compute the distance of each pixel from each centre
   Assign each pixel to the nearest center
   Combine the current particle with the best ones found in the other species
   Evaluate its first fitness using the criterion function (4)
   Combine the current particle with random collaborators from the other
species
   Evaluate its second fitness using the criterion function (4)
   Assign the best found value of fitness to the current particle
   Update P_{best} t and G_{best} }}
Apply a standard PSO for each species.
Until maximum number of iterations is reached}

---

5   The Bees Based Approach

The Bees Algorithm is a recent meta-heuristic that imitates the foraging behavior of honey bees when searching for food sites. This algorithm achieves a neighborhood search in joint with random search for combinatorial or functional optimization [11]. To find an optimal solution' a proportion of the population is specified as representative bees (sites) searching for best patches and the remaining bees scout randomly from one patch to another during exploration [11], [12].

The following is the bees algorithm for colour image segmentation:

Initialise a swarm of bees with a known number of randomly chosen clusters centers
Repeat
For P= 1:NumberOfscout do
  { Compute the distance of each pixel from each center
  Assign each pixel to the nearest center
  Evaluate the scout fitness according to (4)

For F= 1: aroundelite do
{Determine the elite bee in the neighbourhood of the current scout bee.
Evaluate the elite fitness according to (4)
{If the elite fitness is better then, replace the current scout bee by the elite
bee}}.
For F = (aroundelite+1): aroundsite do
{Determine the site bee in the neighbourhood of the current scout bee.
Evaluate the site fitness according to (4)
{If the site fitness is better then, replace the current scout bee by the site
bee}}}.
For F = (aroundsite+1): NumberOfscout
{Initialize the rest of scout bees in a random way}
For F = 1: NumberOfscout
{Evaluate the scout bees and determine the best bee}
Until Maximum number of iterations is reached.
Compute the distance of each pixel from each centre in the best bee
Image segmentation by partition of pixels to their nearest centers.

6   Experimental Results and Discussion

To assess the performance of the proposed methods some obtained results using PSO, PPO, APPO, CPSO and BA are shown (see figures: fig2, fig3, fig4, fig5 and fig6).

Table 1. Parameters setting

PSO	*A decreasing inertia weight from 0.9 to 0.4, C1=C2 =2, population size=20, Nb of iterations =100.*
PPO	A decreasing inertia weight from 0.9 to 0.4, C1=C2 =2, population size=20, Nb of iterations =100, a=10, b=2, The fear probability = 0.06.
APPO	A decreasing inertia weight from 0.9 to 0.4, C1=C2 =2, population size=20, Nb of iterations =100, a= varies into the range [0 , 15], b= belongs to the range [0, 3.2], The fear probability = varies into the range [0, 1].
CPSO	A decreasing inertia weight from 0.78 to 0.1, C1=C2 =1.49, population size for each species =20, Nb of iterations =50.
BA	The number of scout bees = 400, The number of elite bees = 40, The number of sites = 40, The number of bees around elite bee = 100, The number of bees around site bee =50, The size of neighbourhood = 1, Nb of iterations =50.

Fig. 1. Original image

The following are some obtained results on fig1 where the number of clusters = 5.

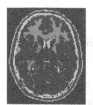 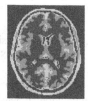 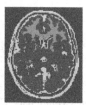 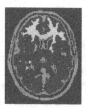 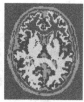

Fig. 2. Result using PSO Fitness= 2.83e+007

Fig. 3. Result using PPO Fitness= 2.16e+007

Fig. 4. Result using APPO Fitness = 2.168e+007

Fig. 5. Result using CCPSO Fitness= 2.167e+007

Fig. 6. Result using BA Fitness = 2.15e+007

Table 2. Comparative results on image Fig.1 after ten runs

	The Sum of squared error
PSO	2.8227e+007 ± 2399000
APPO	2.1682e+007 ± 11000
PPO	2.1626e+007 ± 16000
CCPSO	2.1673e+007 ± 193000
BA	2.1581e+007 ± 0001
Kmeans	2.16e+007 ± 253000

When the social neighborhood is considered, all these algorithms will be greedy in time and give almost the same results or slightly worst. From these obtained results, itis seen that: The BA gives the best results in terms of speed and accuracy. The PPO, APPO and CPSO give better results than the standard PSO. PPO and CPSO give slightly better results than the APPO, while PPO gives comparable performance to CPSO and kmeans, However the proposed approach offers an extensible platform where other fitness functions can be investigated to obtain better results.

7 Conclusions

The present paper proposes four swarm optimisers to deal with the unsupervised color image segmentation problem. Incorporating ideas of co-evolutionary interactions observed in nature, these algorithms were applied to maintain diversity and thus allowing better segmentation accuracy. The results quality has been estimated and compared to k-means method. Results show that the bees' algorithm has a good potential in handling image segmentation problem. In this work, image segmentation is performed cooperatively among a set of particles having an intrinsic parallelism based on the cooperation of autonomous agents (particles). These particles have limited knowledge where the collective intelligence is only arisen by emergency. This mainly give us the opportunity to advance our capability about how to build better models based on reactive agents that only communicate with simple rules, allowing in this way considerable improvement in term of robustness and flexibility.

References

1. Omran, M., Salman, A., Engelbrecht, A.P.: Image classification using particle swarm optimization. In: Proceedings of the 4th Asia-Pacific Conference on Simulated Evolution and Learning 2002 (SEAL 2002), pp. 370–374 (2002)
2. Kennedy, J.: The particle swarm: Social adaptation of knowledge. In: Proceedings of the 1997 International Conference on Evolutionary Computation, Indianapolis, Indiana, pp. 303–308. IEEE Serice Center, Piscataway (1997)
3. Eberhart, R.C., Shi, Y.: Comparing Inertia Weights and Constriction Factors in Particle Swarm optimization. In: Proceedings of the Congress on Evolutionary Computation, pp. 84–88 (2000)
4. Silva, A., Neves, A., Costa, E.: Chasing The Swarm: A Predator Prey Approach To Function Optimisation. In: Proc. of Mendal 2002 - 8th International Conference on Soft Computing. Brno, Czech Republic, June 5-7 (2002)
5. van den Bergh, F., Engelbrecht, A.P.: A Cooperative Approach to Particle Swarm Optimisation. IEE transactions on evolutionary computation 8(3) (June 2004)
6. Silva, A.F., Silva, A.P., Costa, E.: SAPPO: A Simple, Adaptive, Predator Prey Optimiser. In: Pires, F.M., Abreu, S.P. (eds.) EPIA 2003. LNCS (LNAI), vol. 2902, pp. 59–73. Springer, Heidelberg (2003)
7. Wiegand, P.: Analysis of Cooperative Coevolutionary Algorithms.: Ph.D. thesis, George Mason University (2004)
8. Cartlidge, J.: Rules of Engagement: Competitive Coevolutionary Dynamics in Computational Systems. PhD thesis, University of Leeds (2004)
9. Potter, M., DeJong, K.: A cooperative coevolutionary approach to function optimisation. In: Davidor, Y., Männer, R., Schwefel, H.-P. (eds.) PPSN 1994. LNCS, vol. 866, pp. 249–257. Springer, Heidelberg (1994)
10. Paredis, J., Westra, R.: Coevolutionary Computation for Path Planning. In: Proceedings of 5th European Congress on Intelligent Techniques and Soft Computing, pp. 394–398. Verlag Mainz, Aachen (1997)
11. Pham, D.T., Ghanbarzadeh, A., Koç, E., Otri, S., Rahim, S., Zaidi, M.: The Bees Algorithm, Technical Note. Manufacturing Engineering Centre, Cardiff University, UK (2005)
12. Pham, D.T., Ghanbarzadeh, A., Koç, E., Otri, S., Rahim, S., Zaidi, M.: The Bees Algorithm – A Novel Tool for Complex Optimisation Problems. In: Proceedings of IPROMS 2006 Conference, pp. 454–461 (2006)
13. Meshoul, S., Nebti, S., Batouche, M.: Predator-Prey Optimiser for unsupervised Clustering in image segmentation. In: Proceedings of the 2005 International ARAB Conference on Information Technology (ACIT 2005), Amman-Jordan, pp. 317–324 (2005)

Adaptive Seeded Region Growing for Image Segmentation Based on Edge Detection, Texture Extraction and Cloud Model

Gang Li and Youchuan Wan

School of Remote Sensing and Information Engineering, Wuhan University, Wuhan
430079, China
whulg@163.com

Abstract. Considering the segmentation results of region growing depend on two key factors: seed selection and growing strategy, this paper proposed a method of adaptive seeded region growing based on edge detection, texture extraction and cloud model. Our work included two aspects. Firstly, we proposed a new method to extract region seeds automatically based on spectrum features, edge information and texture features. According to two conditions defined by us, region seeds could be extracted as accurately as possible. Secondly, we proposed an adaptive region growing strategy based on cloud model. Our strategy consisted of three major stages: expressing region by cloud model, calculating the qualitative region concept based on the backward cloud generator, and region growing based on cloud synthesis. The experiment results demonstrate seed extraction based on spectrum features, edge information and texture features has a good accuracy, and almost all of the extracted seeds are located at the homogeneous objects inner. The experiment results also demonstrate the adaptive region growing strategy based on cloud model makes regions grow not only in a simultaneous way but also with inner homogeneity.

Keywords: seeded region growing; adaptive edge detection; gray level co-occurrence matrix; cloud model; backward cloud generator; cloud synthesis; adaptive region growing strategy.

1 Introduction

Image segmentation is an important step for image analysis, and it is also a classical problem in image processing. It can be described as a process of pixel clustering. Pixels which are of space adjacency and spectrum similarity are assembled to form homogenous regions. Homogenous regions may provide more features such as spectrum features, texture features, shape features for further processing. With the development of high-resolution remote sensing image analysis, image segmentation has been a basis of higher-level applications such as image classification, thematic information extraction, and target measurement.

The traditional segmentation methods can be categorized into two different approaches, such as edge-based technique or region-based technique. By using either

R. Zhu et al. (Eds.): ICICA 2010, LNCS 6377, pp. 285–292, 2010.
© Springer-Verlag Berlin Heidelberg 2010

edge-based or region-based technique alone, segmentation results may not be accurate. Adams and R. Adams [1] proposed seeded region growing method. Region grows first from an assigned seed, and later to its neighboring pixels. In region growing process, we must consider two issues as follows. The first one is how to choose seeds which should be relevant to the interesting objects. The second one is how to make regions grow in a simultaneous way with inner homogeneity as more as possible. Because region growing result is sensitive to the initial seeds, the accurate seed selection is very important for image segmentation. As we know, seeds can't fall on noise points or edge points. The "true" seeds must be relevant to the meaningful objects and be located at the homogeneity objects inner. It is still difficult to obtain accurate seeds automatically from image [2] [3] [4]. Region growing has two inherent dependencies on pixel order and region order that can cause different resulting segments [5].

To solve the above two issues, we propose a method of adaptive seeded region growing based on edge detection, texture extraction and cloud model. Firstly, considering that a gray-level image consists of three main features, namely region, edge, and texture, we propose a new method of automatic seed selection taking into account spectrum features, texture features and edge information synthetically. Secondly, considering that region growing has inherent pixel order dependency, we propose an adaptive region growing strategy based on cloud model. Firstly, we use cloud model to express region and calculate the qualitative region concepts based on the backward cloud generator. Secondly, for these region concepts expressed by cloud model, we make them grow not only in a simultaneous way but also with inner homogeneity by using cloud synthesis.

2   Automatic Seed Selection Based on Edge Detection and Texture Extraction

2.1 Adaptive Edge Detection and Map of Distance from Edge

Edges can provide the major geometric structures in an image [6]. Traditional edge detection operators such as robert, sobel, prewitt, kirsch and laplacia are very sensitive to noises and can't provide highly accurate results in practice. Some robust edge detection techniques have also been proposed [7] [8], but it is complex and difficult to set proper parameters for them. In 1986, John Canny developed the optimal edge detection operator: Canny edge detection operator [9]. Because canny operator has good detection, good localization and only one response to a single edge, it is more suitable for edges detection. Canny operator has a difficulty in double-threshold selection. It is difficult to set proper high threshold value and low threshold value automatically. In this paper we adopt an adaptive double-threshold selection method to detect the edges.

Supposing that the gradient image is divided into L-level gray and pixels which have local maximum gradient magnitudes are partitioned to three clusters C_0, C_1 and C_2. C_0 is collection of non-edge pixels which's gradient magnitudes are in range[0,l], and C_2 is collection of edge pixels which's gradient magnitudes are in range[h+1,L]. C_1 contains the pixels which's gradient magnitudes are in range[l+1,h], and they may be the edge pixels, or not the edge pixels. Let N denote total number of pixels in the image, n_i denote the number of pixels which's gradient magnitudes equal to i, and p_i denote the ratio of n_i to N, so

$$p_i = \frac{n_i}{N}, \sum_{i=0}^{L-1} p_i = 1. \tag{1}$$

The average gradient value $\mathrm{Aver_L}$ is calculated by using

$$\mathrm{Aver_L} = \sum_{i=0}^{L-1} ip_i. \tag{2}$$

Let $p(0)$, $p(1)$ and $p(2)$ denote the probability of all the pixels in C_0, C_1 and C_2 respectively, we can calculate them as followings

$$p(0) = \sum_{i=0}^{l} p_i, p(1) = \sum_{i=l+1}^{h} p, p(2) = \sum_{i=h+1}^{L} p_i. \tag{3}$$

Let $s(0)$, $s(1)$ and $s(2)$ denote the sum of gradient values of all the pixels in C_0, C_1 and C_2 respectively, they can be calculated by using

$$s(0) = \sum_{i=0}^{l} ip_i, s(1) = \sum_{i=l+1}^{h} ip_i, s(2) = \sum_{i=h+1}^{L} ip_i. \tag{4}$$

Let $\mathrm{Aver}(0)$, $\mathrm{Aver}(1)$ and $\mathrm{Aver}(2)$ denote the mean gradient value of all the pixels in C_0, C_1 and C_2 respectively, they can be calculated by using

$$\mathrm{Aver}(0) = \frac{s(0)}{p(0)}, \mathrm{Aver}(1) = \frac{s(1)}{p(1)}, \mathrm{Aver}(2) = \frac{s(2)}{p(2)}. \tag{5}$$

We calculate the deviation $\mathrm{Dev}(0)$, $\mathrm{Dev}(1)$ and $\mathrm{Dev}(2)$ as

$$
\begin{aligned}
\mathrm{Dev}(0) &= \frac{\sum_{i=0}^{l}(i-\mathrm{Aver}(0))^2 p_i}{s(0)} \\
\mathrm{Dev}(1) &= \frac{\sum_{i=l+1}^{h}(i-\mathrm{Aver}(1))^2 p_i}{s(1)} \\
\mathrm{Dev}(2) &= \frac{\sum_{i=h+1}^{L}(i-\mathrm{Aver}(2))^2 p_i}{s(2)}
\end{aligned}
\tag{6}
$$

Obviously, where l is the low threshold value and h is the high threshold value. We consider that the optimal low threshold value and high threshold value must make within-class variance smallest. So we define evaluation function $J(l,h)$ as

$$J(l,h) = \mathrm{Arg\,min}(s(0)\mathrm{Dev}(0)+s(1)\mathrm{Dev}(1)+s(2)\mathrm{Dev}(2)). \tag{7}$$

The equation (7) can also be described as

$$J(l,h) = \int_0^l (i - Aver(0))^2 p_i di + \int_{l+1}^h (i - Aver(1))^2 p_i di$$
$$+ \int_{h+1}^{L-1} (i - Aver(2))^2 p_i di. \tag{8}$$

In order to obtain the optimal solution of the evaluation function $J(l,h)$, we can solve the equation (8) as follows

$$\frac{\partial J(l,h)}{\partial l} = 0, \frac{\partial J(l,h)}{\partial h} = 0. \tag{9}$$

From the equation (9), we can infer that the optimal low threshold value and high threshold value must satisfy the following condition

$$2l - Aver(0) - Aver(1) = 0$$
$$2h - Aver(1) - Aver(2) = 0 \tag{10}$$

With the adaptive double-threshold, the canny operator can detect and connect all edges of image. From these edges, for each pixel, we can compute its smallest distance from the nearest edge point and obtain the map of distance from edge. From the distance map, we can see that the greater the distance is, the more likely the pixel is located at the centroid of a region.

2.2 Neighborhood Similarity Based on Spectrum Feature and Texture Feature

Texture contains important structure information of image surface. Gray level co-occurrence matrix (GLCM) has been proved to be an efficient method to compute texture features [10]. Measures of texture features can be calculated based on GLCM. In our scheme, three measures are used, they are energy, homogeneity and Entropy, denoted by Ener , Hom and Ent respectively.

By combination of spectrum feature and texture feature, we calculate the similarity of a pixel to its neighbor as follows. For each pixel (x, y), considering a 3x3 window centered on it, the standard deviation of gray component is calculated by using

$$\sigma_{gray} = \sqrt{\frac{1}{9} \sum_{i=1}^{9} (gray_i - \overline{gray})^2} \tag{11}$$

Where $\overline{gray}$ is the mean value of gray component in the window, the standard deviations of three texture components are calculated by using

$$\sigma_{Ener} = \sqrt{\frac{1}{9} \sum_{i=1}^{9} (Ener_i - \overline{Ener})^2}$$
$$\sigma_{Hom} = \sqrt{\frac{1}{9} \sum_{i=1}^{9} (Hom_i - \overline{Hom})^2} \tag{12}$$
$$\sigma_{Ent} = \sqrt{\frac{1}{9} \sum_{i=1}^{9} (Ent_i - \overline{Ent})^2}$$

Where $\overline{\text{Ener}}$, $\overline{\text{Hom}}$ and $\overline{\text{Ent}}$ are the mean values of three texture components. The total standard deviation $\sigma_{(x,y)}$ of pixel (x, y) is defined as

$$\sigma_{(x,y)} = W_{gray} \times \sigma_{gray} + W_{Ener} \times \sigma_{Ener} + W_{Hom} \times \sigma_{Hom} + W_{Ent} \times \sigma_{Ent} \tag{13}$$

Where W_{gray} , W_{Ener} , W_{Hom} , W_{Ent} are the weights of four components. The total standard deviation $\sigma_{(x,y)}$ is normalized as

$$n\sigma_{(x,y)} = \frac{\sigma_{(x,y)}}{\sigma_{max}} \tag{14}$$

Where σ_{max} is the maximum of the standard deviations of all the pixels, then we define the similarity of pixel (x, y) to its neighbor as follow

$$s_{(x,y)} = 1 - n\sigma_{(x,y)} \tag{15}$$

2.3 Seeds Selection Based on Map of Distance from Edge and Neighborhood Similarity

By using the adaptive edge detection, most edges of image can be detected and connected. From these edges, we can compute the smallest distance of each pixel from the nearest edge point, thus we can obtain the map of distance from edge. Based on the distance map, we define the first condition for the region centroids as follow.

Condition1. The region centroid must have minimum distance from the nearest edge greater than a distance threshold.

In our scheme, we use Otsu's method to choose automatically the distance threshold for Condition 1. The threshold is determined by choosing the value that maximizes the ratio of between-class variance to within-class variance.

Condition2. The region centroid must have maximum similarity to its neighbor, compared with any other pixels in its neighborhood.

3 Adaptive Region Growing Based on Cloud Model

The segmentation results of region growing depend on two key factors: seed selection and growing strategy. After extracting out a set of strict seeds, which in fact are true region centroids, region will grow first from each centroid later to its neighboring pixels which have similar features with the centroid. Region growing has inherent pixel order dependency. It leads that regions can't grow in a simultaneous way. That is to say, some regions grow excessively and others are suppressed. So the sizes of all regions are not of comparable scale. In this paper we propose an adaptive region growing strategy based on Cloud Model.

The cloud model theory is a new theory about formal expression and analysis of concept. It can reflect randomness and fuzziness of concept in subjective world and human cognitive science, express the correlation between randomness and fuzziness, and establish mapping between qualitative concept and quantitative numeric value. Cloud model uses three numerical characteristics to reflect the features of the concept, they are expected value (Ex), entropy (En), and hyper-entropy (He). The expected value Ex is the central value of the concept expressed by cloud model. It can most effectively represent the qualitative concept, and reflect the center of the concept of cloud droplet group. The entropy En measures comprehensively the fuzziness and probability of concept. It reflects the dispersion degree of cloud droplet group. The hyper-entropy He is a measure of entropy uncertainty, that is to say, it is the entropy of entropy (En), and reflects the discrete degree of cloud droplet group [11].

The backward cloud generator is a model of transition from quantitative numeric values to qualitative concepts [11]. We can achieve the transition from cloud droplet group to a region concept by using backward cloud generator.

By using backward cloud generator, for each cloud droplet group, we have extracted the qualitative concept of the region and established its cloud model. Next, we implement the process of cloud synthesis to make the concept expand and make the region expressed by cloud model grow. Our algorithm is described mainly as follows.

(1)By using the forward cloud generator, the memberships of any untreated pixel to its neighboring cloud models are calculated.

(2)By comparing different memberships of the pixel to different cloud models, the pixel is merged to the region expressed by the cloud model to which the pixel's membership is the greatest.

Here, we need pay attention to one issue, if a pixel has the same memberships to several neighboring cloud models, then we adopt the strategy that the pixel is assigned to the cloud model with the greatest size.

4   Experimental Data and Result

As an example for adaptive seeded region growing, consider the original high-resolution remote sensing image (of size 355 x264, Figure 1(a)). Adaptive edge detection result is shown in Figure 1(b). From Figure 1(b), we can see proposed adaptive method can detect and connect most edges. The map of distance from edge is shown in Figure 1(c). From Figure 1(c), we can see the greater the distance is, the more likely the pixel is located at the centroid of a region. The result of extracting seeds based on distance map is shown in Figure 1(d), and the result of extracting seeds based on neighbor similarity is shown in Figure 1(e). The result of extracting seeds based on the distance map and neighbor similarity is shown in Figure 1(f). Figure 1(g) shows the result of cloud drop groups. The segmentation result based on proposed method is shown in Figure 1(h). From the experiment, we see that our method can produce good segmentation result.

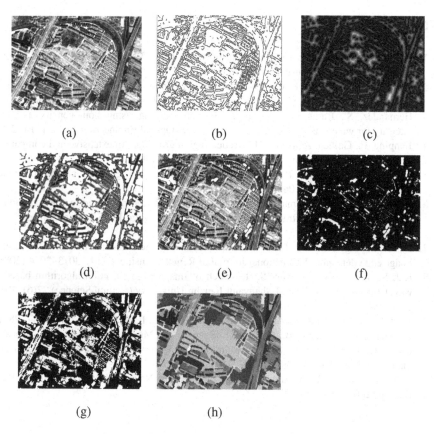

Fig. 1. (a)original image (b)the result of adaptive edge detect (c)the map of distance from edge (d)extracting seeds based on distance map (e)extracting seeds based on neighbor similarity (f)extracting seeds based on the distance map and neighbor similarity (g)the result of cloud drop groups (h)the segmentation result by using our method

5 Conclusions

Image segmentation is an important part in the remote sensing applications. In this paper, we propose the method of adaptive seeded region growing based on edge detection, texture extraction and cloud model. Considering that land covers are very complex in the remote sensing image, artificial targets and natural surfaces are in co-existence, texture-dominant regions and spectrum-dominant regions are in co-existence, it is insufficient and inaccurate to segment the image only by spectrum and texture. The spatial features should be considerable to improve the segmentation accuracy. A more improved method is that we can adopt a strategy of regions merging and take into account the spectrum features, texture features and shape features synthetically to make adjacent homogeneity regions merged.

References

1. Adams, R., Bischof, L.: Seeded region growing. IEEE Transactions on Pattern Analysis and Machine Intelligence 16, 641–647 (1994)
2. Pan, Z., Lu, J.: A Bayes-Based Region-Growing algorithm for medical image segmentation. Computing in Science and Engineering 9, 32–38 (2007)
3. Hernandez, S., Barner, K., Yuan, Y.: Region merging using homogeneity and edge integrity for watershed-based image segmentation. Optical Engineering 44(1), 1–14 (2005)
4. Jianping, F., Guihua, Z., Body, M.: Seeded region growing: An extensive and comparative study. Pattern Recognition Letters 26(8), 1139–1156 (2005)
5. Mehnert, A., Jackway, P.: An improved seeded region growing algorithm. Pattern Recognition Letters 18, 1065–1071 (1997)
6. Fan, J., Yau, D.K.Y., Elmagarmid, A.K., Aref, W.G.: Automatic image segmentation by integrating color-edge extraction and seeded region growing. IEEE Transactions on Image Processing 10, 1454–1466 (2001)
7. Jubai, A., Jing, B., Yang, J.: Combining fuzzy theory and a genetic algorithm for satellite image edge detection. International Journal of Remote Sensing 27(14), 3013–3024 (2006)
8. Kai, S., Jianwei, J., Xiaoyan, S.: Research of image edge detection algorithm based on wavelet transform. Journal of Shenyang Jianzhu University (Natural Science) 22(6), 1012–1014 (2006)
9. John, C.: A Computational Approach to Edge Detection. IEEE-PAMI 8, 679–698 (1986)
10. Xuewei, L., Chenguang, B., Guibao, Q., Shengfu, Z., Meilong, H.: Relationship between texture features and mineralogy phases in iron ore sinter based on gray-level co-occurrence matrix. ISIJ International 49(5), 709–718 (2009)
11. Li D.-Y., Du, Y.: Uncertainty artificial intelligence. National Defence Industrial Press, Beijing (2005) (in Chinese)

A New Optimization Algorithm for Program Modularization

Saeed Parsa, Amir Mehrabi-Jorshary, and Mohammad Hamzei

Department of Computer Engineering, Iran University of Science and Technology
Tehran, Iran
Parsa@iust.ac.ir, Mehrabi@comp.iust.ac.ir, Hamzei@iust.ac.ir

Abstract. The aim has been to achieve the highest degree of possible concurrency in the execution of distributed program modules. To achieve this, a new invocation reordering algorithm is offered in this paper. The algorithm attempts to increase the time interval between each remote call instruction and the very first instructions using the values effected by the remote call. In order to increase the time distance, the algorithm reshuffles invocations, when possible, such that local invocations move in between remote calls and the instructions applying the results of the calls. The evaluation results indicate that the proposed algorithm provides higher degree of concurrency compared with the existing instruction reordering algorithms.

Keywords: Concurrency, Distributed Computing, Instruction Reordering, Modularization, Parallelization.

1 Introduction

Today dedicated networks of low cost computers are replacing expensive super-computers for running some computationally intensive code [1] [2] [3]. The question is how to optimize distributed code for higher performance in term of execution time. Applying Actor model [4] for distributing programs the execution time maybe reduced by increasing the concurrency in the execution of distributed modules of programs [5] [6].

A barrier against the concurrency is the need for the return values by the caller before the termination of the callee. Instruction scheduling technique could be applied to reshuffle the instructions in such a way that the time distance between each remote call instruction and the instructions dependent on the call results are increased [5] [7]. Apparently, program instructions could be reshuffled as long as their data and control inter-dependencies are not violated.

A major difficulty with automatic translation of sequential to distributed code is that the sequential programmers are used to apply the results of any invocation immediately after the invocation instruction. When applying the results of a call immediately after the call there will be no chance for the parallel execution of the caller and the callee. To resolve, the use of instruction re-ordering algorithms has been suggested [1] [5] [8]. A major difficulty with the existing instruction re-ordering

R. Zhu et al. (Eds.): ICICA 2010, LNCS 6377, pp. 293–300, 2010.

algorithm is that they do not consider the type of the calls to be local or remote. The main reason is that the instruction reordering algorithm is applied to the sequential code and before partitioning the code into distribsutable modules.

In this article a new instruction re-ordering algorithm, SIR (*Synchronous Invocation Reordering*), is presented. The algorithm attempts to increase the time distance between each remote method call and the very first instructions applying any value affected by the call. This is achieved by moving local invocation instructions between each remote call instruction and the instruction dependent on the call results, as many as possible.

The remaining parts of this paper organized as follows: in Section 2, instruction reordering and its drawback is presents. In Section 3 a new optimization algorithm is described and in Section 4, three case studies are presents to evaluate our algorithm. Finally concluding remarks are the topic of Section 5.

2   Distributed Code Optimization

In order to optimize a distributed program, in the first position data and control dependencies between the program instructions has to be determined. The resultant dependency graph is then applied as a mean for controlling the validity of moving instructions within the code.

In the second step, after the dependency graph is built, the algorithm presented in [5] is applied to move instructions between each call instruction and its dependent instruction conditioned that the dependencies are not violated. Apparently, the program semantics will be preserved if the dependencies between the instructions are not violated.

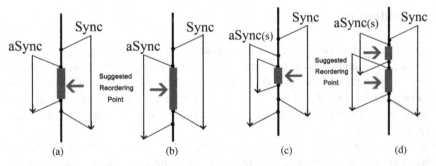

Fig. 1. Different positions of asynchronous invocations which could occur after each synchronous invocation

A major difficulty with instruction re-ordering algorithm presented in [8] is that it attempts to increase the time distance between both the local and remote call instructions and their dependent instructions. For instance, in Fig. 1.a, a remote or asynchronous call and its dependent instruction are both located within a local call and its dependent instruction. To increase the concurrency the local call instruction and its dependent statement could be moved between the remote call and its dependent instruction provided that the remote call instruction is not dependent on the local call and also the instruction dependent on the remote call is not dependent on the local call. Similarly different conditions are shown in Fig. 1.b to 1.d. all these invocations could be reshuffled to increase the concurrency in the execution of the remote calls.

3 Synchronous Invocation Reordering Algorithm

A method must exist to evaluate a modularization of a program. In this section before the re-ordering algorithms will have been presented, a relation for evaluating a modularization presented. For the first time in [1], a new relation presented for evaluating a program. The new relation named EET (*Estimated Execution Time*). Concurrent execution of distributed modules considered in the EET. The EET is a parametric relation to evaluate every modularization which made based on Actor Model. The EET could have generated by a static analysis of program source code and consist of two equation which shows in equation (1) and (2).

$$EET_m(r) = \sum w_i + \sum a_i * EET_{Ii}(r) + \sum (1 - a_i) * T(S_i) \tag{1}$$

$$T(S_i) = \max((EET_{Ii}(r) + O_i) - t_i, 0) \tag{2}$$

The w_i variable in the equation (1) is calculated summery of instructions without considering invocations. The EET considers two probabilities for each invocation instruction. If an invocation instruction is synchronous the a_i coefficient will set to 1 otherwise set to 0. The variable of t_i in equation (2) is time delay for invocation instruction I_i. The O_i variable is communication overhead for remote calls. Indeed $T(S_i)$ in equation (2) is the concurrent execution time of I_i. In these equations the r variable is modularization structure. The estimated execution time of each instruction has calculated based on JOP standard [9]. The JOP estimates the execution time of byte-codes which run on sample hardware like the Java virtual machine. This estimation could be a good approximation. In [9] showed the estimation was near to real measurement.

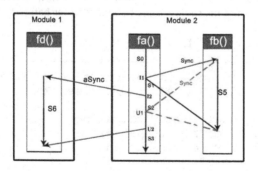

Fig. 2. A modularization instance which a synchronous invocation instruction occurs before an asynchronous invocation instruction

There are some methods in Fig. 2 which noted f_a and f_b that exist in module 2 and a method noted f_d which exists in module 1. The invocation instruction which occurs in I_1, will execute synchronously and invocation instruction which occurs in I_2, asynchronously. The EET will calculate as follows:

$$EET_{fa}(r) = S0 + S1 + S2 + S3 + EET_{fb}(r) + T(fd)$$

$$EET_{fb}(r) = S5$$

$$T(S2) = Max(S6 - (S2),0)$$

Executing of f_d must delayed until invocation instruction of f_b finished, but by invocation reordering of f_b between I_2 to U_2, method noted f_d and f_b could execute concurrently, but in normal execution of I_1, the asynchronous method call has fewer degree of concurrency. Suppose I_1 invocation re-ordered to a location between I_2 and U_2. The re-ordered position calculates as follows:

$$EET_{fa}(r) = S0 + S1 + S2 + S3 + EET_{fb}(r) + T(fd)$$

$$EET_{fb}(r) = S5$$

$$T(S2) = Max(S6 - (S2 + EET_{fb}(r)),0)$$

The concurrency in executing method noted f_d with method noted f_a could increase. This situation can be evaluated for every possible situation which some asynchronous invocations occur between synchronous invocation point and its result's use point.

The synchronous reordering algorithm shows in table 1 which works on modularization structure of program. In each module, the algorithm tries to find synchronous invocations and its delay time to very instructions which use invocation result. The algorithm tries to find some asynchronous invocation instruction which exist in delay time distance. The SI.top variable and SI.end used to show begin and the end of delay time distance. The algorithm searches from SI.top to SI.end for any asynchronous invocation instruction which could re-order before SI.top.

Table 1. The SIR algortihm

```
Synchronous Invocation Reordering Algorithm
(Modularization RM) OUT : Optimized RM
Begin
1. In each module M do evaluating
2.  for each  method m that exists in M do
3.   for each Sync invocation SI do
4.      set Top=SI.top
5.      set End=SI.end
6.      set ActiveASyncInvocation = null
7.      for each aSync invok. aSI that not scheduled
from SI.top to SI.end
```

Table 1. (*continued*)

```
8.          if(aSI.top>Top and aSI.end>End) then
9.            if(waitTime(aSI)>waitTime(Last async
invoc.)) then
10.              set Top=aSI.top
11.              set End=Min(SI.end,aSI.end)
12.              for each aSync Invocation I in
ActiveASyncInvocation
13.                  Label I as Not Scheduled
14.              End for
15.              set ActiveASyncInvocation to aSI
16.            end if
17.          else
18.              add aSI to ActiveASyncInvocation
19.                set Top=Max(Top,aSI.top)
20.                set End=Min(End,aSI.end)
21.                Label aSI as scheduled
22.          end if
23.        end for
24. Calculate Cost/Beneft relation for moving SI to
top
25. If it improve concurrency of executing other
aSync invocation then
26.                Move SI to top
27.        end if
28.      end for
29.    end for
30. end of Module Evaluation
End
```

If there is more than one asynchronous invocation, the algorithm tries to find suitable shared position for synchronous invocation which can improve concurrency of almost asynchronous invocations which exist in delay time distance of synchronous invocation otherwise place synchronous invocation point after an asynchronous invocation point which has shortest delay time. At the end by evaluating new reordered method, if this reordering could improved concurrency of parent method then reordering fixed. These operations applied for each module in program modularization to improve all modules concurrency.

4 Evaluation

Practical evaluation of algorithm in this section presents. Three case studies selected to evaluate the algorithm which wrote in Java. Case studies are different by number of invocations and number of objects in its object graphs. One of case studies is a small program named TestBed1 which is a small program and wrote by us to evaluate the algorithm. TestBed2 is another program which is larger than TestBed1 in size of methods and number of invocations which exists in method's body to reflect program's size affect on the algorithm. TSP is the last case study which is a popular program to calculating Hamiltonian paths in graphs.

The object graph of each case study extracted by static analyzer tool which has wrote by us in Java. The object graph extracting method is like the method mentioned in [10]. Execution time of instruction in case studies estimated based on JOP standard which is base on CPU clock cycles. The EET generation process for each case study done by traversing the object graph. The method of generating the EET is like the method mentioned in [1]. The EET relation used as evaluating function in genetic a algorithm to evaluate modularizations [11]. The genetic algorithm used to find proper modularization of program. At the end of each iteration's calculation, in the genetic algorithm executing, the SIR algorithm applied to genetic algorithm's chromosome to improve its speedup if the algorithm can improve speedup, the new chromosome replaced by older chromosome. This kind of manipulating of genetic algorithm can increase time of completion of genetic algorithm extremely, but for a program that the calculation does once and runs many, this overhead could be tackled. Result of evolutions for different modularization before and after applying SIR algorithm shows in table 2 and 3. Communication overhead for remote invocation instruction is considered 10^7 clock cycles.

Case studies in size of objects and number of invocations in its object graph are different. The kind of choosing case studies is because of showing effect of method's size and number of invocations in the SIR algorithm. Poor effect expected in small program. Proof of this situation displayed in fig 4.a which shows TestBed1 in some iteration of genetic algorithm with and without applying the SIR algorithm.

TestBed2 in comparison to TestBed1 has larger method and number of invocations is each method is more than TestBed1. As regards to number of invocations and size of methods we expected that the algorithm must have a better result. As seen in Fig. 4.b, improvement of the algorithm in TestBed2 is evident.

Travel Salesman Problem (TSP) is a popular problem in distributed computing and has used in many articles to evaluate algorithms. TSP is not a behaved-well program because it calculates a loop for a many times and contains many small methods which frequently execute. In distributed computing, a program with fewer large methods is better than a program with many small methods due to great communication overhead. Hence TSP is a suitable case study to evaluate the SIR algorithm.

Although TSP is not a behaved-well program for distributed computing but the SIR algorithms shows that could improve speedup which shows is Fig. 4.c. Results of applying the SIR algorithm show the improvement of performance in term of execution time. The algorithm can improve performance of every program which has more than two invocations in each method's body. By increasing of method size or number of invocations in each method's body, effect of the SIR algorithm will increase. Table 2 shows that effect of the SIR algorithm in TestBed1 is fewer than other case studies and this due to its method's size and number of invocation in method's body but in TestBed2 by increasing method's size and number of invocations in method's body, the algorithm produce better result than TestBed1.

Effect of the SIR algorithm depends on location of synchronous invocations and other asynchronous invocation that occurs in domain of each synchronous invocation. Therefore it is possible that two different modularization that have same evaluation, after applying the SIR algorithm, different improvements gain. This situation can be seen in fig 4.d that occurred in iteration 6 and 8 or 9 and 10. Evaluation in iteration 6 and 8 almost near but after applying the SIR algorithm, results are different and in iteration 9 and 10 respectively.

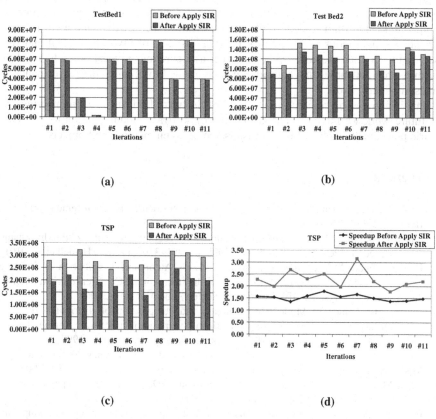

(a)   (b)

(c)   (d)

Fig. 3. Evaluations results

Table 2. The SIR algorithm affect in case studies

Case Study	EET - Serial Execution (cycles)	EET- Before Apply SIR (cycles)	EET- After Apply SIR (cycles)
TestBed1	93139260	69009620	66718805
TestBed2	2406602288	1580848044	1431494488
TSP	432216784	282494630	170164288

Table 3. Speedup of the algorithm

Case Study	Speedup after applying SIR	Speed without applying SIR
TestBed1	1.39%	1.34%
TestBed2	1.68%	1.52%
TSP	2.54%	1.53%

5 Conclusions

In this paper by introducing a new algorithm for performance improvement we extend program modularization. For this at first by extracting object graph and using genetic algorithm to find best modularization, structure of modularization specified then by applies this algorithm speedup of modularization increased. This algorithm by relocating synchronous invocation to decrease distance of invocation point and first use point try to increase concurrency of other asynchronous invocations. The result of our measurement shows this algorithm can be applied to improve the performance of almost modularization.

This is an ongoing research in the field of Software Performance Engineering. As the future work we intend to extend domain of software modularization to spot data centric program and delay of data transmission between methods and objects.

References

1. Parsa, S., Bushehrian, O.: Performance-driven object-oriented program remodularisation. IET 2, 362–378 (2008)
2. Parsa, S., Hamzei, M.: An Improved Technique for Program Remodularization. In: Zhang, W., et al. (eds.) HPCA 2009. LNCS, vol. 5938, pp. 305–310. Springer, Heidelberg (2010)
3. Deb, D., Fuad, M.M., Oudshoorn, M.J.: Towards Autonomic Distribution of Existing Object Oriented Programs. In: Proceedings of the International Conference on Autonomic and Autonomous Systems. IEEE Computer Society, Los Alamitos (2006)
4. Astley, M., Agha, G.: Modular construction and composition of distributed software architectures. In: Proceedings of the International Symposium on Software Engineering for Parallel and Distributed Systems. IEEE Computer Society, Washington (1998)
5. Parsa, S., Bushehrian, O.: The Design and Implementation of a Framework for Automatic Modularization of Software Systems. The Journal of Supercomputing 32, 71–94 (2005)
6. Fuad, M.M.: AdJava: Automatic Distribution of Java. Department of Computer Science, MSc Thesis. Adelaide University, Adelaide (2002)
7. Parsa, S., Khalilpour, V.: Automatic Distribution of Sequential Code Using JavaSymphony Middleware. In: Wiedermann, J., Tel, G., Pokorný, J., Bieliková, M., Štuller, J. (eds.) SOFSEM 2006. LNCS, vol. 3831, pp. 440–450. Springer, Heidelberg (2006)
8. Parsa, S., Bushehrian, O.: On the Optimal Object-Oriented Program Re-modularization. In: Shi, Y., van Albada, G.D., Dongarra, J., Sloot, P.M.A. (eds.) ICCS 2007. LNCS, vol. 4487, pp. 599–602. Springer, Heidelberg (2007)
9. Schoeberl, M.: JOP: A Java Optimized Processor for Embedded Real-Time Systems. Fakultat fur Informatik, PhD Thesis. Technischen Universitat Wien, Wien (2005)
10. Spiegel, A.e.: Pangaea: An Automatic Distribution Front-End for Java. In: Rolim, J.D.P. (ed.) IPPS-WS 1999 and SPDP-WS 1999. LNCS, vol. 1586, pp. 93–99. Springer, Heidelberg (1999)
11. Parsa, S., Bushehrian, O.: A framework to investigate and evaluate genetic clustering algorithms for automatic modularization of software systems. In: Bubak, M., van Albada, G.D., Sloot, P.M.A., Dongarra, J. (eds.) ICCS 2004. LNCS, vol. 3037, pp. 699–702. Springer, Heidelberg (2004)

Self-organizing Learning Algorithm for Multidimensional Non-linear Optimization Applications

C.H. Zhou[1,2], A.S Xie[1,3], and B.H. Zhao[2]

[1] School of Management Science and Engineering, Anhui University of Technology,
Maanshan 243002, P.R. China
[2] Department of Computer Science and Technology,
University of Science and Technology of China, Hefei 230026, P.R.China
[3] Institute of Policy and Management, Chinese Academy of Sciences,
BeiJing, 100190, P.R. China
chzhou863@ustc.edu, shermanxas@163.com

Abstract. In order to cope with the multidimensional non-linear optimization problems which involved a great number of discrete variables and continuous variables, a self-organizing learning algorithm (SOLA) was proposed in this paper, in which the parallel search strategy of genetic algorithm(GA) and the serial search strategy of simulated annealing (SA) were involved. Additionally, the learning principle of particle swarm optimization(PSO) and the tabu search strategy were adopted into the SOLA, wherein the integrated frame work was different from traditional optimization methods and the interactive learning strategy was involved in the process of random searching. SOLA was divided into two handling courses: self-learning and interdependent-learning. The local optimal solution would be achieved through self-learning in the process of local searching and the global optimal solution would be achieved via the interdependent learning based on the information sharing mechanism. The search strategies and controlled parameters of SOLA were adaptively fixed according to the feedback information from interactive learning with the environments thus SOLA is self-organizing and intelligent. Experiments for the multidimensional testbed functions showed that SOLA was far superior to traditional optimization methods at the robustness and the global search capability while the solution space ranged from low-dimensional space to the high-dimensional space.

Keywords: self-organizing, learning principle, high-dimensional space, genetic algorithm.

1 Introduction

Almost all the practical application problems in the real world always have much to do with some large-scale system which generally involved with a great deal of discrete variables and continuous variables. The traditional math-based optimization methods, which always have very strict requirements in the certainty and accuracy of datasets involved, are unable to cope with these multidimensional non-linear

R. Zhu et al. (Eds.): ICICA 2010, LNCS 6377, pp. 301–308, 2010.

optimization problems. Thus, the intelligent optimization methods, represented by genetic algorithm[1] (GA), have been proposed. Glover proposed tabu search algorithm[2,3](TS). In 1983, Kirkpatrick proposed simulated annealing algorithm[4,5] (SA). Into the nineties, Kennedy and Eberhart proposed particle swarm optimization algorithm[6,7](PSO).

These optimization methods have been improved a lot respectively since they were proposed. A hybrid niche genetic simulated annealing algorithm (HNGSA) was proposed [8], and a multigroup parallel genetic algorithm based on simulated annealing method (SAMPGA) is discussed[9]. A new genetic algorithm based on simulated annealing mechanism is proformed[10]. The chaotic parallel genetic algorithm with feedback mechanism was addressed[11].

2   Self-organizing Learning Algorithm (SOLA)

the SOLA proposed in this paper blended the parallel search strategy of GA with the serial search strategy of SA. What is more, the learning principle of PSO and the tabu search strategy were involved in SOLA, thus, SOLA is self-organizing and intelligent. The integrated frame work of SOLA consists of two circles: the outer circle is a simulated annealing (SA) process, and the inner circle is composed of both self-learning process and interdependent-learning process. The local optimal solution will be achieved through the self-learning in the process of local searching and the global optimal solution will be achieved via the interdependent learning based on the information sharing mechanism(ISM). The search strategies and controlled parameters of the SOLA are adaptively fixed according to the feedback information from interactive learning with the environment.

2.1   Selection Strategy

Because the outer layer of SOLA is an iterative simulated annealing process based on Monte-Carlo, the guidelines for the use of Metropolis acceptance criteria is accepted naturally in the process of seeking for the optimal solution.

Let $f(i)$ be the current value of the fitness function, and $f(j)$ be one of the neighborhood solutions, and T be the current temperature, $\xi \in U[0,1]$. Selection rule of SOLA can be given as below:

$$
\min f(x): \quad p = \begin{cases} \exp(\dfrac{f(i)-f(j)}{T}) & if \quad f(j) > f(i) \\ 1 & if \quad f(j) \le f(i) \end{cases}
$$

$$
\max f(x): \quad p = \begin{cases} \exp(\dfrac{f(j)-f(i)}{T}) & if \quad f(j) \le f(i) \\ 1 & if \quad f(j) > f(i) \end{cases} \tag{1}
$$

If $p \geq \xi, f(j)$ will be accepted as the current value of the fitness function, or else, $f(j)$ will be abandoned.

2.2 Interdependent-Learning Process Design

In SOLA, the information sharing mechanism(ISM) consists of both the information-exchange process and the information-sharing process. The information-exchange process drives the individuals in the population to exchange their historical information and current information, including the state space that had been scaned and the corresponding solutions. The interdependent learning process based on ISM can be divided into two phases: one-to-one learning and one-to many learning

2.2.1 One-to-One Learning

Let the i th individual`s coordinate in the state space be $X_i$, and the $j$ th individual`s coordinate in the state space be X_j. Let $f(X_i)$ be the fitness of the i th individual, and f_{avg}^k be the average fitness of the current population. Then, the i th individual`s coordinate in the state space will be updated according to the rule (2) as below:

> *while* X_i^{k+1} has not yet reached the aspiration level or
>
>   still remains on the tabu list
>
> $$X_i^{k+1} = \theta X_i^k + (1-\theta) X_j^k \tag{2}$$
>
> *end*

Wherein, $\theta \in \begin{cases} (0.5,1) & if \quad f(X_i^k) \succ f_{avg}^k \\ (0,0.5] & otherwise \end{cases}$," $\succ$ " here stands for non-inferiority. Here, θ reflects that how much the indivilual followed in its search scheme at last generation. That is to say, if its fitness at last generation was improved, the individual will inherit its parent in a large part. Or else, the individual will carry on its parent in a small part and exchange imformation with its partner more.

2.2.2 One-to-Many Learning

Let the i th individual`s coordinate in the state space be X_i, whose composite index of the search direction and search intensity is U_i. Let the number of individuals in its neighbourhood be n (here n need to be determined due to the topology structure of the neighborhood); Let the coordinates of the individuals be $X_1, X_2, X_3, \cdots X_n$ respectively, and the weights of the individuals be $\omega_1, \omega_2, \omega_3, \cdots \omega_n$ respectively, and $\omega_1 + \omega_2 + \omega_3 + \cdots + \omega_n = 1$. Let $f(X_i)$ be the fitness of the i th individual, and f_{avg}^k be the average fitness of the current population. Then, the i th individual`s coordinate in the state space will be updated according to the rule (3) as below:

$$X = [X_1, X_2, X_3, \cdots X_n] \quad W = [\omega_1, \omega_2, \omega_3, \cdots \omega_n],$$

while X_i^{k+1} has not yet reached the aspiration level or

still remains on the tabu list

$$\begin{cases} U_i^{k+1} = \eta U_i^k + W \left(X - repmat(X_i, 1, n) \right)^T \\ X_i^{k+1} = \theta X_i^k + (1-\theta)U_i^{k+1} \end{cases} \tag{3}$$

end

Wherein, the demain and function of θ are as the same as that in *2.2.1. One-to-one*

Learning, $\eta \in \begin{cases} (0.5,1) & if \quad f(X_i^k) \succ f(X_i^{k-1}) \\ (0,0.5] & otherwise \end{cases}$ here, η is the inertia

weight, which reflects the extent that the indivilual followed in its search direction and search intensity at last generation. Additionally, η can be used to balance the exploration and exploitation of each individual`s search activity.

2.3 Self-learning Process Design

Let N be the size of population. Let the i th individual`s coordinate in the state space be $X_i$. Let the $i$ th individual`s composite index of the search direction and search intensity be V_i, and the optimal solution it had achieved so far be P_i. Let $f(X_i)$ be the fitness of the i th individual, and f_{avg}^k be the average fitness of the current population. Then, the i th individual`s coordinate in the state space will be updated according to the rule (4) as below:

while X_i^{k+1} has not yet reached the aspiration level or

still remains on the tabu list

$$\begin{cases} V_i^{k+1} = \eta V_i^k + (1-\eta)(P_i - X_i) \\ X_i^{k+1} = \theta X_i^k + (1-\theta)V_i^{k+1} \end{cases} \tag{4}$$

end

Wherein, the demain and function of θ and η are as the same as that in *2.2.2. One-to-many Learning*,

2.4 Pseudocode

Let T_0 be the initial temperature, $\lambda \in (0,1)$ be the cooling coefficient, T_f be terminal temperature, K be the number of iterations to reach thermal equilibrium, N be the size of population, P_g be the current global optimal solution of the population so far, P_i be the current optimal solution the ith individual has achieved so far, C_i be the i th individual`s coordinate, $I_i$ the $i$th individual`s local tabu imformation, I_g be the global tabu imformation, F_i be the ith individual`s fitness, $M_i$ be the $i$th individual`s neighbourhood.

{(**Initialization Stage**)

Set T_0, λ, T_f, K, N and other parameters }

$for \quad (T = T_0, T > T_f, T = \lambda \cdot T)$ {

(**Interdependent-Learning Process**)

Update I_g and P_g;

$for \quad i = 1 : N \quad do$ {

$for \quad (j = 0, j < K, j = j + 1)$ {

(**One-to-one Learning**)

Update C_i according to rule(2); Accepte C_i according to rule(1); Update I_i }

Updating P_i; If F_i did not be improved, it will go into the next stage

$for \quad (j = 0, j < K, j = j + 1)$ {

(**One-to-many learning**)

Define M_i; Update C_i according to rule(3); Accepte C_i according to rule(1); Update I_i }

Update P_i; If F_i didn't be improved, it will go into the next stage

$for \quad (j = 0, j < K, j = j + 1)$ {

(**Self-Learning Process**)

Update C_i according to rule(4); Accepte C_i according to rule(1); Update I_i} Update P_i }

Update I_g; Update P_g }

3 Experiment

To compare with other optimization methods including SAMPGA[9] and SHPSO[12], SOLA was used to optimize the complex high dimensional functions using the testbed functions shown in Table 1.

Table 1. Testbed functions

$Function$		x_i
$F1$	$\min f(x) = \sum_{i=1}^{n} [-x_i \sin(\sqrt{|x_i|})]$	$x_i \in [-500, 500]$
$F2$	$\min f(x) = \sum_{i=1}^{n} [100(x_{i+1} - x_i^2)^2 + (1 - x_i)^2]$	$x_i \in [-2.048, 2.048]$
$F3$	$\min f(x) = \sum_{i=1}^{n} [x_i^2 - 10\cos(2\pi x_i) + 10]$	$x_i \in [-5.12, 5.12]$
$F4$	$\min f(x) = \sum_{i=1}^{n} \frac{x_i^2}{4000} - \prod_{i=1}^{n} \cos(\frac{x_i}{\sqrt{i}}) + 1$	$x_i \in [-600, 600]$

To verify the adaptability for high-dimensional space, the mean best fitness(MBF) and the standard deviation(SD) were took as evaluating indicator to evaluate the performance of methods mentioned above.

A set of evolutionary algorithm toolbox was developed based on the intrinsic function of MATLAB 7.6 for the optimization methods mentioned above. It is difficult and unnecessary to describe all the controlled parameters, since there are as many as 52 parameters involved in the above-mentioned methods. To ensure the comparison as fair as possible, some main controlled parameters involved in SOLA are identical with that in the other methods. For instance, the population size was set as 100, the maximal evolution iteration number was set as 3000, the Euclidean distance was adopted as the measurement units of neighborhood radius and the real number code was involved in all the optimization methods. The following data are the average value of running 100 times.

Table 2. Test result of 2-dimensional space(n =2)

function	indicator	SAMPGA	SHPSO	SOLA
F1	MBF	-766.8156	-837.6568	-837.9650
	SD	431.3605	30.7334	30.2818
F2	MBF	0.5016	0	0.0649
	SD	2.7703	0	4.3623
F3	MBF	0.0482	0	0
	SD	0.2852	0	0
F4	MBF	0.0023	25086.0	0
	SD	0.0178	0.0126	0

Table 3. Test result of 50-dimensional space(n =50)

function	indicator	SAMPGA	SHPSO	SOLA
F1	MBF	-5511.2	-6757.0	-8325.8
	SD	10452.0	6178.7	9493.6
F2	MBF	101.9048	119.9541	15.2504
	SD	208.6150	164.3125	180.8025
F3	MBF	220.0835	307.4070	0
	SD	605.3467	217.7965	0
F4	MBF	25.7381	15.5640	0
	SD	62.9570	26.7626	0

Table 4. Test result of 100-dimensional space(n =100)

function	indicator	SAMPGA	SHPSO	SOLA
F1	MBF	-9430.8	-12076.0	-14694.0
	SD	18191.0	11496.0	17122.0
F2	MBF	227.0052	279.1849	27.7685
	SD	471.6492	328.8235	414.6865
F3	MBF	475.410	746.7863	0
	SD	1525.2	397.3802	0
F4	MBF	48.9408	38.3174	0
	SD	76.0427	56.0452	0

4   Conclusions

In order to cope with the multidimensional non-linear optimization problems which involve a great number of discrete variables and continuous variables, a self-organizing learning algorithm (SOLA) was proposed in this paper, in which the parallel search strategy of GA and the serial search strategy of SA were involved. Additionally, the learning principle of PSO and the tabu search strategy were also integrated. The SOLA consisted of the self-learning stage and the interdependent learning stage. The search strategies and controlled parameters of the SOLA are adaptively fixed according to the feedback information from interactive learning with the environments, thus the SOLA is self-organizing and intelligent. Experiments for the multidimensional testbed functions showed that SOLA had great robustness and global search capability though the solution space was high-dimensional.

At present, the algorithm proposed in this paper mainly deals with the case of real-number encoding. As a matter of fact, the real-number encoding method is not suitable for some practical application problems, so how to apply the intelligent learning strategy to the case of nonreal number coding is our next research subject.

Acknowledgement

This work is supported by the Major Program of the Natural Science Foundation of the Anhui Higher Education Institutions of China (Grant No. ZD200904).

References

1. Holland, J.H.: Adaptation in Natural and Artificial Systems. University of Michigan Press (1975)
2. Glover, F.: Tabu search-PartI. ORSA Journal on Computing 1(3), 190–206 (1989)
3. Glover, F.: Tabu search-PartII. ORSA Journal on Computing 2(1), 4–32 (1990)
4. Metroplis, N., Rosenbluth, A., Rosenbluth, M., et al.: Equation of state calculation by fast computing machines. Journal of Cherimal Physics 21, 1087–1092 (1953)
5. Kirkpatrick, S., Gelatt Jr., C.D., Vecchi, M.P.: Optimization by simulated Annealing. Science 220, 671–680 (1983)
6. Kennedy, J., Eberhart, R.C.: Particle Swarm Optimization: Proc. IEEE International Conference on Neural Network, pp. 1942–1948. IEEE Service Center, Riscataway (1995)
7. Eberhart, R.C., Kennedy, J.: A New optimizer using particle swarm theory. In: Proc. on 6th International Symposium on Micromachine & Human Science, pp. 39–43. IEEE Service Center, Riscataway (1995)
8. Sun, Y., Sun, Z.: Application of Hybrid Niche Genetic Simulated Annealing Algorithm to Dynamic Traffic Assignment. Journal of Highway & Transportation Research & development 25(5), 95–99 (2008) (in Chinese)
9. Wu, H.-y., Chang, B.-g., Zhu, C.-c., Liu, J.-h.: A Multigroup Parallel Genetic Algorithm Based on Simulated Annealing Method. Journal of Software 11(4), 416–420 (2000) (in Chinese)

10. Fan, Y.-m., Yu, J.-j., Fang, Z.-m.: Hybrid Genetic Simulated Annealing Algorithm Based on Niching for QoS multicast routing. Journal of Communications 29(5), 65–71 (2008) (in Chinese)
11. Sun, Y.-F., Zhang, C.-K., Gao, J.-G., Deng, F.-Q.: For Constrained Non-Linear Programming:Chaotic Parallel Genetic Algorithm with Feedback. Chinese Journal of Computers 30(3), 424–430 (2007) (in Chinese)
12. Ratnaweera, A., Halgamuge, S.K., Watson, H.C.: Self-organizing hierarchical particle swarm optimizer with time-varying acceleration coefficients. IEEE Trasaction on Evolutionary Computation 8(3), 240–255 (2004)

Research on Set Pair Cognitive Map Model

Chunying Zhang[1,2] and Jingfeng Guo[1]

[1] College of Information Science and Engineering,Yanshan University,
Qin Huangdao, Hebei, China, 066004
[2] College of Science, Hebei Polytechnic University, Tang Shan, Hebei, China, 063009
zchunying@heut.edu.cn,
jfguo@ysu.edu.cn

Abstract. Aiming at the disadvantage of cognitive map which expressed the concept causality in one direction now, Set Pair Cognitive Map Model is proposed which compromise three-dimensional measurement methods (positive, negative and uncertain) of Set Pair and the cognitive map. First, considering the time factor in the premise, Set Pair Cognitive Map Time Three Dimensional Model which is analysis dynamic model with time trend is given; then, further considering the spatial characteristics that impact on the concept, Set Pair Cognitive Map Space-Time Multi-Dimensional Model is given. Using Set Pair Situation Table, it can be obtained the development trend of causal relationship between concepts with multi-state; Finally, Analysis indicates that two basic theorems of Set Pair Cognitive Map Model-Concepts Equivalent transformation Theorem and Set Pair dynamic measurement equivalence theorems play an active role in guiding between the system conversion and identification of the new system.

Keywords: Fuzzy Cognitive Map, Set Pair Cognitive Map, Set Pair Cognitive Map Space-Time Multi-Dimensional Model, Set Pair dynamic measurement equivalence.

1 Introduction

Causality representation and reasoning is very important in artificial intelligence research. In 1948, Tloman proposed cognitive map(CM)[1]which is the graph model that express causality of concepts in representation and reasoning system, nodes and edges express causality of concepts the respectively. Concept (indicated with a node) can be expressed as moves, causes, results, goals, feelings, tendencies and trends of the system. It reflects the properties, performance, quality and state of the system. The relationship between the concepts expresses the affect relations, (it's expressed as arc with arrows and directions of arrow express the direction of influence). The association strength is the weight of arc[2] with numerical value. Cognitive map can be expressed dynamic causal system with feedback that is difficult expressed by tree structure, Bayes networks, Markov and so on. Cognitive map model can only be expressed increase and decrease states of the relationship between concepts and not quantify the degree of change for causal relationship, so Kosko proposed the Fuzzy Cognitive Map (FCM)[3]

R. Zhu et al. (Eds.): ICICA 2010, LNCS 6377, pp. 309–316, 2010.

using Fuzzy Set Theory of Zadeh and Cognitive Map Theory of Alexrod. The fuzzy measure is introduced from causal relationships between concepts, three-valued logic relation {-1, 0, 1} is extended to the fuzzy relation in the interval [-1, 1]. It's used for expression and reasoning for the concepts of fuzzy causal relationship. Fuzzy logic can carry more information than three-valued logic clearly; the concept value and the weight of arc in FCM can be fuzzy values, the knowledge representation and reasoning are stronger. Recently, FCM theory is widely applied in the political, economic, medical, military, social relations, information systems, network management and fault analysis, multi-Agent systems, industrial control, virtual reality and other fields [3, 4]. In 2003, Chinese scholar Xiangfeng Luo proposed Probabilistic Fuzzy Cognitive Map Model[5] that introduces the conditional probability measure in the causality between concepts for the first time. This model can express Qualitative of concepts and Fuzzy causality, also express Conditional probability causality and can degenerate into Fuzzy Cognitive Map. Probabilistic Fuzzy Cognitive Map model is simple, better robustness and practical. It has more realistic simulation capabilities than FCM Model in real world.

However, Fuzzy Cognitive Map and Probabilistic Fuzzy Cognitive Map consider causality between concepts only from single side, that positive or negative, or no influence. In fact, causality between concepts is changed as change of time and the development of events. Two concepts with positive influence may change into negative for any reason, and vice versa. Therefore, it is incomplete that consider the causality between concepts only from a single direction. Based on this, combine Set Pair and Cognitive Map, Set Pair Cognitive Map Time Three Dimensional Model (SPCMTTDM) and Set Pair Cognitive Map Space-Time Multi-Dimensional Model (SPCMSTMDM) are proposed. The two sets are integrated as Set Pair Cognitive Map (SPCM) model and applied research

2 Basic Concepts

2.1 Fuzzy Cognitive Map

The concept value of Fuzzy Cognitive Map [3, 4] is Fuzzy value, can be two values, reflect the node occurs for the concept in some degree or express the concept's state is off or open. The causality between concepts is fuzzy relation; its intensity of association is Fuzzy value too. FCM store the knowledge into the relation between concepts, thought it to express Fuzzy Reasoning. The output of the concept's node relates to the level of two types, that is the intensity between the state of concept's node and external causal link. It's an unsupervised model which simulates system behavior through interaction of concept nodes.

Definition 1: the Topology of a basic FCM is a three sequence $U = (V, E, W)$, where $V = \{v_1, v_2, \dots v_n\}$ is expressed as the set of concept nodes, $E = \{<v_i, v_j> | v_i, v_j \in V\}$ is causal association directed arc (directed arc $<v_i, v_j>$ is expressed that node v_i has causal association or influence to v_j), $W = \{w_{ij} | w_{ij}$ is the weight of directed arc $<v_i, v_j> \}$, (w_{ij} is expressed that the node c_i has the relevance or impact strength to c_j). Each node has a state space, $V_{c_i}(t)$ is expressed state value the node c_i is at the time of t.

Proof

Assume $V_{c_i}(t) \in [-1,1]$, $w_{ij} \in [-1,1]$, otherwise it can do Fuzzy Standardization. In most of the current literature, most of $V_{c_i}(t)$ is 1 and 0 where 1 is expressed the node is activated, 0 is inactive or stationary.

If $w_{ij} > 0$, then w_{ij} is the degree of change in the same direction that the change of c_j is caused by c_i;

If $w_{ij} < 0$, then w_{ij} is the degree of change in the opposite direction that the change of c_j is caused by c_i;

If $w_{ij} = 0$, then w_{ij} is expressed that c_i and c_j has no relation.

Only the initial vertex is active, the impact is effective. In other words, if the initial vertex is stationary, its impact is very strong in the activities, but also that there is no effect on the terminal vertex.

State space of FCM is originally decided by the initial conditions, then automatic transmission through vertex function with the threshold value until up to a static model. When the FCM is up to steady limited circulation state or fixed point, we completed the causal inference. The mathematical model of FCM reasoning follows as:

$$V_{c_j}(t+1) = f(\sum_{\substack{i \neq j \\ j \in E}} V_{c_i}(t) w_{ji}) . \tag{1}$$

In this equation, $V_{c_i}(t)$ is the state value of reason concept node c_i at the time of t; $V_{c_j}(t)$ is the state value of reason concept node c_j at the time of $t+1$; E is the concept node set which has adjacent relations with c_j; f is threshold function, it can be two values, S-type, Fuzzy set or Probability Function.

2.2 The Basic Idea of Set Pair Analysis

Set Pair is the pair that is composed by two sets has certain link. It is to analysis the characteristics of set pair. Establish IDC connection degree expression as:

$$\mu = a + bi + cj . \tag{2}$$

In this formula, a is the identity degree of two sets; b is the discrepancy degree of two sets; c is the contrary degree of two sets. I is difference notations or the corresponding coefficient, $i \in [-1,1]$. By definition, a, b, c satisfy the normalization condition:

$$a + b + c = 1 . \tag{3}$$

This description is a quantitative description of certainty and uncertainty[3], where: a, c is relatively certain, while b is relatively uncertain. This is due to the complexity and variability of objective objects and subjectivity and ambiguity of understanding and characterization. Therefore equation (2) reflects opposition and unity relation of uncertain system. It has a more profound significance using Set pair connection degree to analyze the system.

3 Mathematical Models of Set Pair Cognitive Map

3.1 Set Pair Cognitive Map Time Three Dimensional Model (SPCMTTDM)

Cognitive maps and fuzzy cognitive map theory see references [8-13]. From these conferences we can see, although FCM has many advantages, it can't express dynamic dependency of the concept state value to casualty between concepts and the uncertain of the concept state value. Shown in Fig. 1, affect on learning achievement as a class cadre and the Internet, it can't simply say it's a positive or negative impact. The weight of w_b and w_n is related to the attitude of learners as a class cadre and the Internet and their selves. At the same time, learner's attitude and understanding are constantly changed over time, the results and extent of affects are certainly very different, considering this only from a single direction among three is not in line of reality.

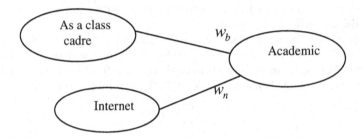

Fig. 1. The uncertainty of concept relation

To solve the above shortcomings, introduced Set Pair Analysis Thought in FCM, Set Pair Cognitive Map Model is proposed. Eugene et al (1994) proved that the direction of time is joined in the ring; concepts of ring will not appear interdependence [14]. Stylios et al introduced time variable in Fuzzy Cognitive Map Model of Kosko. It laid a theoretical foundation in Fuzzy Cognitive Map for introduction of Set Pair Analysis Thought [12-13].

FCM with the time and memory proposed by stylios can be expressed as:

$$V_{c_j}(t) = f\left[\sum_{\substack{i=1 \\ i \neq j}}^{N} V_{c_i}(t)w_{ij} + \gamma V_{c_j}(t-1)\right]. \qquad (4)$$

In this equation, $V_{c_j}(t)$ is the state value of concept c_j at the time t, γ is the impact factor of the state value the last time to the next time.

If Set Pair Analysis formula $a_{ij}(t) + b_{ij}(t)I + c_{ij}(t)J$ replace w_{ij} in equation (4), we have Set Pair Cognitive Map Time Three Dimensional Model (SPCMTTDM) with memory function and dynamic properties:

$$V_{c_j}(t) = f\left[\sum_{\substack{i=1 \\ i \neq j}}^{N} V_{c_i}(t)(a_{ij}(t) + b_{ij}(t)I + c_{ij}(t)J) + \mathcal{W}_{c_j}(t-1)\right].$$ (5)

In this equation, $a_{ij}(t)$ is the positive impact degree of the concept c_i to c_j in time t, $c_{ij}(t)$ is the negative impact degree of the concept c_i to c_j in time t, $b_{ij}(t)$ is the uncertain impact degree of the concept c_i to c_j in time t, $I \in [-1,1]$, $j = -1$. Therefore, $a_{ij}(t) + b_{ij}(t)I + c_{ij}(t)J$ is expressed as certain-uncertain of causality between concepts in time t, $a_{ij}(t)$ and $b_{ij}(t)$ are the certain degrees, $c_{ij}(t)$ is the uncertain degree. The value of I may change over time, the positive or negative impact degree will increase or decrease.

When $c_{ij}(t) = b_{ij}(t) = 0$ and do not consider the time characteristics, the equation (5) degenerate to (4) and the impact degree is positive, $w_{ij} = a_{ij}(t) > 0$.

When $a_{ij}(t) = b_{ij}(t) = 0\!\!\!\!\!\!$ and do not consider the time characteristics, the equation (5) degenerate to (4) and the impact degree is negative, $w_{ij} = c_{ij}(t) < 0$.

For Fig. 1, $a_{ij}(t) + b_{ij}(t)I + c_{ij}(t)J$ is easy to solve the problem of FCM. Because of the introduction of w, $w(t)$ not only show certain-uncertain of causality between concepts as "on duty cadres" and "student achievement", but also the dynamic characteristic of causality so that it can establish a time three-dimensional dynamic measure relational degree of dynamic causality. Therefore, SPCMTTD not only inherits the advantages of FCM, but also extends the ability that FCM simulate causality.

3.2 Set Pair Cognitive Map Space-Time Multi-dimensional Model

SPCMTTDM established dynamic causality over time. In fact, in addition to change over time, the relations of concepts are related to the concept's state in space. From Fig. 1, "Internet" is to affect learning or to promote learning, it is related to the browsed site, Network Configuration (If set to prohibit access to harmful Web site) and the network degree (Control degree). Based on considering the time characteristics of causality, we further consider the spatial characteristics of causality, and then we can have Set Pair Cognitive Map Space-Time Multi-Dimensional Model (SPCMSTMDM):

$$V_{c_j}(t) = f\left[\sum_{\substack{i=1 \\ i \neq j}}^{N} \sum_{k=1}^{M} V_{c_i}(t)(a_{ij}(t) + b_{ij}(t)I + c_{ij}(t)J)(a_{ik}(t) + b_{ik}(t)I + c_{ik}(t)J) + \mathcal{W}_{c_j}(t-1)\right].$$ (6)

The equation (6) has effective conformity of the time characteristics in cognitive map. In Fig. 1, w_n, the affect degree of "Internet ", is not only related to the state of the Internet, but also to the cumulate state, is expressed as the time characteristics. w_n, is related to the browsed site, Network Configuration (If set to prohibit access to harmful Web site) and the network degree (Control degree), is expressed as the space characteristics.

w_n is not only solved the defects of Fig. 1 using FCM, but also can has effective conformity of the connection between time and space in the causality of concepts, so that the cognitive map can solve the uncertain of measure of causality between concepts, also has effective conformity of the connection between time and space in the causality of concepts. This puts the uncertainty and the time characteristics of causality into Fuzzy Cognitive Map that further expand the fuzzy cognitive map.

In equation (6), without considering the spatial characteristics, it degenerate to Set Pair Cognitive Map Time Three Dimensional Model; if it does not consider the time characteristics, it degenerate to the ordinary Fuzzy Cognitive Map.

In SPCMSTMDM, according to the Set Pair Analysis Situation Table[16], it can look up which situation the affect degree is: $a_{ij}(t) > c_{ij}(t)$ means the same direction of c_j caused by c_i is stronger; $a_{ij}(t) < c_{ij}(t)$ means the opposite direction of c_j caused by c_i is stronger; $a_{ij}(t) = c_{ij}(t)$ means the concepts between c_i and c_j have no causality, or the causality is weak, it can be ignored.

4 The Nature of SPCM

SPCMTTDM and SPCMSTMDM are Set Pair Cognitive Map (SPCM).

For the equation (5) and (6), f is two value set or S-type functions, or Fuzzy Set, or Probability Relation or Set Pair Relation. Set Pair Relation $a_{ij}(t) + b_{ij}(t)I + c_{ij}(t)J$ is generalized. It can express dynamic measurement of causality between concepts; also express subjective certainty and uncertainty for a thing by exporters.

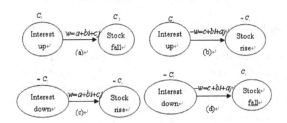

Fig. 2. Equivalent transformations of concepts

In SPCM, If "Interest up" impacts "Stock fall", interest rates is different, the affect degree of "Stock down" is different. While affected by other factors, the impact of "Interest up" to "Stock down" has certainty and uncertainty. When their impacts are stable, as the affect degree of "Interest up" to "Stock down" is $w = a + bi + cj$ (for Fig. 2), then according to reference [12] and [13], we can obtain Fig. 2 (b), 2 (c), 2 (d). When the relation of concepts is extended to SPCM model.

We can obtain Equivalent transformation Theorem of the relation between concepts as follows:

Let C is all concepts in SPCM, V is all state values of concepts in SPCM, and R is the measure of all concepts with directed causality, then R is as formula (7):

$$R= \sum_{\substack{i=1 \\ i \neq j}}^{N} \sum_{k=1}^{M} V_{c_i}(t)(a_{ij}(t)+b_{ij}(t)I+c_{ij}(t)J)(a_{ik}(t)+b_{ik}(t)I+c_{ik}(t)J) \ . \tag{7}$$

B is the confidence of all concepts with directed causality.

Theorem 1 (Equivalent transformation Theorem of the relation between concepts in SPCM)

In SPCM, if $\sim C_i \in C$, $\sim V_i \in V$, $-w_{ij} \in R$ $C_i \xrightarrow{w_{ij}} C_j$, we have $C_i \xrightarrow{-w_{ij}} \sim C_j$ or $\sim C_i \xrightarrow{-w_{ij}} C_j$ or $C_i \xrightarrow{w_{ij}} \sim C_j$.

Theorem 2 (Equivalence Theorem of Set Pair dynamic measurement between concepts in SPCM)

In SPCM, if $\sim C_i \in C$, $\sim V_i \in V$, $-w_{ij} \in R$, and $w_{ij}(t) = a_{ij}(t)+b_{ij}(t)I+c_{ij}(t)J$ we have $-w_{ij}(t) = c_{ij}(t)+b_{ij}(t)I+a_{ij}(t)J$.

That is, in $-w_{ij}$, the positive effect degree is the negative in w_{ij}, the negative effect degree is the positive in w_{ij}.

The two theorems have a very important practical significance. It can obtain a new one from a SPCM, guide us to know a new causality and reduce the workload.

5 Conclusion

Against to the defects in FCM, Set Pair Cognitive Map model is proposed. It can express certain and uncertain causality of concepts and has the Integration of time and space while analysis its nature, give Equivalent transformation Theorem of the relation and Equivalence Theorem of Set Pair dynamic measurement between concepts in SPCM. Set Pair Cognitive Map model is described from certain and uncertain affect degree in the positive and negative. It has more holistic view, more realistic to examine the relation from a single direction. Theoretical study of SPCM, in particular, how to better express the time and multi-state space, the application of SPCM in pattern recognition and image understanding, is the next researcher.

References

1. Chaib-draa, B., Desharnais, J.: A relational model of cognitive maps, http://citeseer.nj.nec.com/
2. Axelrod, R.: Structure of Decision: The Cognitive Maps of Political Elites. Princeton University Press, Princeton (1976)
3. Kosko, B.: Fuzzy cognitive maps. Int. J. Man-machine Studies 24, 65–75 (1986)
4. Kosko B.:Adaptive inference in fuzzy knowledge networks. In: Proc. 1st Int. Conf. Neural Networks. pp. 261–268 (1987)
5. Luo, X.F., Gao, J.: Probabilistic Fuzzy Cognitive Map. J. China University of Science and Technology 33, 26–33 (2003)

6. Zhao, K.Q.: Set pair analysis and its preliminary application. Zhejiang Science and Technology Press, Hangzhou (2000)
7. Liu, Z.Q., Miao, Y.: Fuzzy cognitive map and its causal inference. In: Proc. IEEE Int. Conf. Fuzzy Systems Seoul Korea, pp.1540–1545 (1999)
8. Kosko, B.: Fuzzy Engineering. Prentice-Hall, Englewood Cliffs (1997)
9. Liu, Z.Q., Satur, R.: Contextual fuzzy cognitive map for decision support in geographic information systems. IEEE Transactions on Fuzzy Systems, 495–502 (1999)
10. Satur, R., Liu, Z.Q.: A contextual fuzzy cognitive map framework for geographic information systems. IEEE Transactions on Fuzzy Systems 7, 481–494 (1999)
11. Thierry, M.: Theory and methodology cognitive maps and fuzzy implications. European Journal of Operational Research 114, 626–637 (1999)
12. Liu, Z.Q., Miao, Y.: Fuzzy cognitive map and its causal inferences. In: IEEE International Fuzzy Systems Conference Proceedings, Korea, Seoul, pp. 22–25 (1999)
13. Stylios, C.D., Groups, P.: Fuzzy cognitive maps: a soft computing technique for intelligent control. In: Proc. IEEE International Sym-posium on Intelligent Control, Italy Patras, pp. 97–102 (2000)
14. Santor Jr., E.: Probabilistic temporal networks: A unified framework for reasoning with time and uncertainty, http://citeseer.nj.nec.com/
15. Zhao, K.Q.: The uncertain analysis and classification of IDC network planning. J. Systems Engineering and Electronics. 22, 72–74 (2000)

The Development of Improved Back-Propagation Neural Networks Algorithm for Predicting Patients with Heart Disease

Nazri Mohd Nawi, Rozaida Ghazali, and Mohd Najib Mohd Salleh

Faculty of Information Technology and Multimedia, University Tun Hussein Onn Malaysia
86400, Batu Pahat, Johor, Malaysia
{nazri,rozaida,najib}@uthm.edu.my

Abstract. A study on improving training efficiency of Artificial Neural Networks algorithm was carried out throughout many previous papers. This paper presents a new approach to improve the training efficiency of back propagation neural network algorithms. The proposed algorithm (GDM/AG) adaptively modifies the gradient based search direction by introducing the value of gain parameter in the activation function. It has been shown that this modification significantly enhance the computational efficiency of training process. The proposed algorithm is generic and can be implemented in almost all gradient based optimization processes. The robustness of the proposed algorithm is shown by comparing convergence rates and the effectiveness of gradient descent methods using the proposed method on heart disease data.

Keywords: We would like to encourage you to list your keywords in this section.

1 Introduction

The back-propagation algorithm has been the most popular and most widely implemented algorithm for training these types of neural network. When using the back-propagation algorithm to train a multilayer neural network, the designer is required to arbitrarily select parameter such as the network topology, initial weights and biases, a learning rate value, the activation function, and a value for the gain in the activation function. Improper selection of any of these parameters can result in slow convergence or even network paralysis where the training process comes to a virtual standstill. Another problem is the tendency of the steepest descent technique, which is used in the training process, can easily get stuck at local minima.

Recently, improving training efficiency of back-propagation neural network based algorithm is an active area of research and numerous papers have been proposed in the literature. Early research on back propagation algorithms saw improvements on: (i) selection of better error functions [1-8]; (ii) different choices for activation functions [3, 9] and, (iii) selection of dynamic learning rate and momentum [10-12].

Later, as summarized by Bishop [13], various optimization techniques were suggested for improving efficiency of the error minimization process or in other words

R. Zhu et al. (Eds.): ICICA 2010, LNCS 6377, pp. 317–324, 2010.

the training efficiency. Among these are methods of Fletcher and Powel [14] and the Fletcher-Reeves [15] that improve the conjugate gradient method of Hestenes and Stiefel [16] and the family of Quasi-Newton algorithms proposed by Huang [17].

This research suggests that a simple modification to the gradient based search direction used by almost all optimization method that has been summarized by Bishop [13] can substantially improve the training efficiency.

The remaining of the paper is organized as follows: Section two states the research objectives. Section three illustrates the proposed method and the implementation of the proposed method in gradient descent optimization process. In Section four, the robustness of proposed algorithm is shown by comparing convergence rates for gradient descent methods on Cleveland Heart Disease data. The paper is concluded in the final section along with short discussion on further research.

2   The Proposed Method

In this section, a novel method for improving the training efficiency of back propagation neural network algorithms is proposed. The proposed method modifies the initial search direction by changing the gain value adaptively for each node. The following subsection describes the method. The advantages of using an adaptive gain value have been explored. Gain update expressions as well as weight and bias update expressions for output and hidden nodes have also been proposed. These expressions have been derived using same principles as used in deriving weight updating expressions.

The following iterative algorithm has been proposed for changing the gradient based search direction using a gain value.

Initialize the initial weight vector with random values and the vector of gain values with unit values. Repeat the following steps 1 and 2 on an epoch-by-epoch basis until the given error minimization criteria are satisfied.

> *Step 1*   *By introducing gain value into activation function, calculate the gradient of error with respect to weights by using Equation (5), and gradient of error with respect to the gain parameter by using Equation (7)*
>
> *Step 2*   *Use the gradient weight vector and gradient of gain vector calculated in step 1 to calculate the new weight vector and vector of new gain values for use in the next epoch.*

2.1   Derivation of the Expression to Calculate Gain Value

Consider a multilayer feed-forward network, as used in standard back propagation algorithm[13]. Suppose that for a particular input pattern o^0, the desired output is the teacher pattern $t = [t_1 ... t_n]^T$, and the actual output is o_k^L, where L denotes the output layer. The error function on that pattern is defined as,

$$E = \frac{1}{2}\sum_k (t_k - o_k^L)^2 \tag{1}$$

Let o_k^s be the activation values for the kth node of layer s, and let $o^s = [o_1^s ... o_n^s]^T$ be the column vector of activation values in the layer s and the input layer as layer 0. Let

w_{ij}^s be the weight values for the connecting link between the ith node in layer $s-1$ and the jth node in layer s, and let $w_j^s = [w_{1j}^s...w_{nj}^s]^T$ be the column vector of weights from layer $s-1$ to the jth node of layer s. The net input to the jth node of layer s is defined as $net_j^s = (w_j^s, o^{s-1}) = \sum_k w_{j,k}^s o_k^{s-1}$, and let $net^s = [net_1^s...net_n^s]^T$ be the column vector of the net input values in layer s. The activation value for a node is given by a function of its net inputs and the gain parameter c_j^s;

$$o_j^s = f(c_j^s net_j^s),$$ (2)

where f is any function with bounded derivative.

This information is now used to derive an expression for modifying gain values for the next epoch. Most of gradient based optimization methods use the following gradient descent rule:

$$\Delta w_{ij}^{(n)} = -\eta^{(n)} \frac{\partial E}{\partial w_{ij}^{(n)}}$$ (3)

where $\eta^{(n)}$ is the learning rate value at step n and the gradient based search direction at step n is $d^{(n)} = -\frac{\partial E}{\partial w_{ij}^{(n)}} = g^{(n)}$.

In the proposed method the gradient based search direction is modified by including the variation of gain value to yield

$$d^{(n)} = -\frac{\partial E}{\partial w_{ij}^{(n)}} (c_j^{(n)}) = g^{(n)}(c_j^{(n)})$$ (4)

The derivation of the procedure for calculating the gain value is based on the gradient descent algorithm. The error function as defined in Equation (1) is differentiated with respect to the weight value w_{ij}^s. The chain rule yields,

$$\frac{\partial E}{\partial w_{ij}^s} = \frac{\partial E}{\partial net^{s+1}} \cdot \frac{\partial net^{s+1}}{\partial o_j^s} \cdot \frac{\partial o_j^s}{\partial net_j^s} \cdot \frac{\partial net_j^s}{\partial w_{ij}^s}$$

$$= [-\delta_1^{s+1}...-\delta_n^{s+1}] \begin{bmatrix} w_{1j}^{s+1} \\ \vdots \\ w_{nj}^{s+1} \end{bmatrix} . f'(c_j^s net_j^s) c_j^s . o_j^{s-1}$$ (5)

where $\delta_j^s = -\frac{\partial E}{\partial net_j^s}$. In particular, the first three factors of Equation (5) indicate that the following equation holds:

$$\delta_1^s = (\sum_k \delta_k^{s+1} w_{k,j}^{s+1}) f'(c_j^s net_j^s) c_j^s$$ (6)

It should be noted that, the iterative formula as described in Equation (6) to calculate δ_1^s is the same as used in the standard back propagation algorithms [13] except for the appearance of the gain value in the expression. The learning rule for calculating weight values as given in Equation (3) is derived by combining (5) and (6).

In this approach, the gradient of error with respect to the gain parameter can also be calculated by using the chain rule as previously described; it is easy to compute as

$$\frac{\partial E}{\partial c_j^s} = (\sum_k \delta_k^{s+1} w_{k,j}^{s+1}) f'(c_j^s net_j^s) net_j^s \tag{7}$$

Then the gradient descent rule for the gain value becomes,

$$\Delta c_j^s = \eta \delta_j^s \frac{net_j^s}{c_j^s} \tag{8}$$

At the end of every epoch the new gain value is updated using a simple gradient based method as given by the following formula,

$$c_j^{new} = c_j^{old} + \Delta c_j^s \tag{9}$$

2.2 Implementation of the Proposed Method with Gradient Descent Method

In gradient descent method, the search direction at each step is given by the local negative gradient of the error function, and the step size is determined by a learning rate parameter. Suppose at step n in gradient descent algorithm, the current weight vector is w^n, and a particular gradient based search direction is d^n. The weight vector at step n+1 is computed by the following expression:

$$w^{(n+1)} = w^n + \eta^n d^n \tag{10}$$

where, η^n is the learning rate value at step n. By using the proposed method namely as Back-propagation Gradient Descent Method with Adaptive Gain Variation (BPGD/AG) [18], the gradient based search direction is calculated at each step by using Equation (4).

3 Results and Discussions

3.1 Preliminaries

The performance criteria used to asses the result of proposed method focuses on; (i) the speed of convergence, measured in number of iterations as well as the corresponding CPU time and (ii) the effectiveness of models that gave the highest percentage of correct predictions for diagnosing patients with heart disease.

A total of 909 records with 15 attributes (factors) were obtained from the Cleveland Heart Disease database [19]. The records were split equally into two datasets: training dataset (545 records) and testing dataset (364 records). The records for each set were selected randomly in order to avoid bias. For consistency, only categorical attributes are used for neural networks model. All the medical attributes in Table 1 were transformed from numerical to categorical data. The attribute "Diagnosis" was identified as the predictable attribute with value '1' for patients with heart disease and value '0' for patients with no heart disease. The attribute 'PatientID' was used as the key, the rest were used as input attributes. It is assume that missing, inconsistent and duplicate data have been resolved.

Table 1. Description of attributes

Predictable Attribute	
1.	Diagnosis (Value 0: <50% diameter narrowing (no heart disease); value 1:> 50% diameter narrowing (has heart disease))
Key Attribute	
1.	PatientID – Patient's identification number
Input Attributes	
1.	Sex (value 1: Male; Value 0: Female)
2.	Chest Pain Type (Value 1: Typical type 1 angina, Value 2: typical type angina, Value 3: non-angina pain; Value 4: asymptomatic)
3.	Fasting Blood Sugar (Value 1:> 120 mg/dll; value 0: < 120 mg/dll)
4.	Restecg – resting electrographic results (value0: normal; value 1: 1 having ST-T wave abnormality; value 2: showing probable or define left ventricular hypertrophy)
5.	Exang – exercise induced angina (value 1: YES; value 0: NO)
6.	Slope – the slope of the peak exercise ST segment (value 1: unsloping; value 2: flat; value 3: downsloping)
7.	CA – number of major vessels colored by floursopy (value 0-3)
8.	Thal (value 3: normal; value 6: fixed defect; value 7: reversible defect)
9.	Trest Blood Pressure (mm Hg on admission to the hospital)
10.	Serum Chlolestoral (mg/dll)
11.	Thalach – maximum heart rate achieved
12.	Oldpeak – ST depression induced by exercise relative to rest
13.	Age in Year

The simulations have been carried out on a Pentium IV with 3 GHz PC, 1 GB RAM and using MATLAB version 6.5.0 (R13). The following three algorithms were analyzed and simulated on the datasets.

1) The standard gradient descent with momentum (*traingdm*) from 'Matlab Neural Network Toolbox version 4.0.1'.
2) The standard Gradient descent with momentum (GDM)
3) The Gradient descent with momentum and Adaptive Gain (GDM/AG)

For comparison with other standard optimization algorithms from the MATLAB neural network toolbox, network parameters such as network size and architecture (number of nodes, hidden layers etc), values for the initial weights and gain parameters were kept same. The research only focused on the neural network with one hidden layer with five hidden nodes and sigmoid activation function was used for all nodes. All algorithms were tested using the same initial weights that were initialized randomly from range [0, 1] and received the input patterns for training in the same sequence. For gradient descent algorithm, the learning rate value was 0.3 and the momentum term value was 0.7. The initial value used for the gain parameter was one.

3.2 Validating Algorithm Effectiveness

The effectiveness of each algorithm was tested using Classification Matrix which displays the frequency of correct and incorrect predictions by comparing the actual values in the test dataset with the predicted values in the trained algorithm. In the example, the test dataset contained 208 patients with heart disease and 246 patients without heart disease. Figure 1 shows the results of the classification matrix for all three algorithms. The rows represent predicted values while the columns represent actual values ('1' for patients with heart disease, '0' for patients with no heart disease). The left most columns show the values predicted by the algorithms. The diagonal values show correct predictions.

Counts for *traingdm*		
Predicted	0 (Actual)	1 (Actual)
0	220	62
1	26	146
Counts for *GDM*		
Predicted	0 (Actual)	1 (Actual)
0	211	24
1	35	184
Counts for *GDM/AG*		
Predicted	0 (Actual)	1 (Actual)
0	211	20
1	35	188

Fig. 1. Results of Classification Matrix for the three algorithms

Table 2 summarizes the results of all three algorithms. The proposed algorithm (GDM/AG) appears to be most effective as it has the highest percentage of correct prediction (90.3%) for patients with heart disease, followed by GDM with difference of less than 2%) and *traingdm*. However, *traingdm* appears to be most effective for predicting patients with no heart disease (89.4%) compared to other algorithms.

Table 2. Algorithms Results

Model		No. of cases	Prediction
traingdm	Patients with heart disease, predicted as having heart disease	146	correct
	Patients with no heart disease, predicted as having heart disease	26	Incorrect
	Patients with no heart disease, predicted as having no heart disease	220	Correct
	Patients with heart disease, predicted as having no heart disease	62	Incorrect
GDM	Patients with heart disease, predicted as having heart disease	184	correct
	Patients with no heart disease, predicted as having heart disease	35	Incorrect
	Patients with no heart disease, predicted as having no heart disease	211	Correct
	Patients with heart disease, predicted as having no heart disease	24	Incorrect
BPGD/AG	Patients with heart disease, predicted as having heart disease	188	correct
	Patients with no heart disease, predicted as having heart disease	35	Incorrect
	Patients with no heart disease, predicted as having no heart disease	211	Correct
	Patients with heart disease, predicted as having no heart disease	20	Incorrect

3.3 Verification Algorithms Convergence Speed

For each training datasets, 100 different trials were run, each with different initial random set of weights. For each run, the number of iterations required for convergence is reported. For an experiment of 100 runs, the mean of the number of iterations, the standard deviation, and the number of failures are collected. A failure occurs when the network exceeds the maximum iteration limit; each experiment is run to one thousand iterations except for back propagation which is run to ten thousand iterations; otherwise, it is halted and the run is reported as a failure. Convergence is achieved when the outputs of the network conform to the error criterion as compared to the desired outputs.

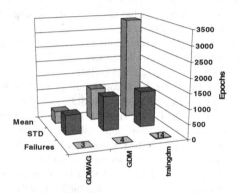

Fig. 2. Heart disease summary chart

Fig. 2 shows the 3D plot for the results of the Heart Disease classification problem. The proposed algorithms (GDM/AG) show better results because it converges in smaller number of epochs as suggested by the low value of the mean. Furthermore, the number of failures for GDM/AG is lower as compared to other two algorithms. This makes the GDM/AG algorithm a better choice for this problem since it had only 3 failures for the 100 different runs.

4   Conclusion

A novel approach is presented in this paper for improving the training efficiency of back propagation neural network algorithms by adaptively modifying the initial search direction. The proposed algorithm uses the gain value to modify the initial search direction. The proposed algorithm is generic and has been implemented in all commonly used gradient based optimization processes. Classification Matrix methods are used to evaluate the effectiveness and the convergence speed of the proposed algorithm. All three algorithms are able to extract patterns in response to the predictable state. The most effective algorithm to predict patients who are likely to have a heart disease appears to the proposed method (GDM/AG) followed by others two algorithms. The results showed that the proposed algorithm is robust and has a potential to significantly enhance the computational efficiency of the training process.

Acknowledgment

The authors would like to thank Universiti Tun Hussein Onn Malaysia for supporting this research under the Short Term Research Grant.

References

1. Ooyen, A.V., Nienhuis, B.: Improving the convergence of the back-propagation algorithm. Neural Networks 5, 465–471 (1992)
2. Ahmad, M., Salam, F.M.A.: Supervised learning using the cauchy energy function. In: International Conference on Fuzzy Logic and Neural Networks, vol. 1 (1992)
3. Pravin, C., Yogesh, S.: An activation function adapting training algorithm for sigmoidal feedforward networks. Neurocomputing 61, 429–437 (2004)
4. Krzyzak, A., Dai, W., Suen, C.Y.: Classification of large set of handwritten characters using modified back propagation model. In: Proceedings of the International Joint Conference on Neural Networks, vol. 3, pp. 225–232 (1990)
5. Sang, H.O.: Improving the Error Backpropagation Algorithm with a Modified Error Function. IEEE Transactions on Neural Networks 8(3), 799–803 (1997)
6. Hahn, M.L., Tzong, C.H., Chih, H.C.: Learning Efficiency Improvement of Back Propagation Algorithm by Error Saturation Prevention Method. IJCNN 3, 1737–1742 (1999)
7. Sang, H.O., Youngjik, L.: A Modified Error Function to Improve the Error Back-Propagation Algorithm for Multi-Layer Perceptrons. ETRI Journal 17(1), 11–22 (1995)
8. Shamsuddin, S.M., Darus, M., Sulaiman, M.N.: Classification of Reduction Invariants with Improved Back Propagation. IJMMS 30(4), 239–247 (2002)
9. Ng, S.C.: Fast convergence for back propagation network with magnified gradient function. In: Proceedings of the International Joint Conference on Neural Networks 2003, vol. 3, pp. 1903–1908 (2003)
10. Jacobs, R.A.: Increased rates of convergence through learning rate adaptation. Neural Networks 1, 295–307 (1988)
11. Weir, M.K.: A method for self-determination of adaptive learning rates in back propagation. Neural Networks 4, 371–379 (1991)
12. Yu, X.H., Chen, G.A., Cheng, S.X.: Acceleration of backpropagation learning using optimized learning rate and momentum. Electronics Letters 29(14), 1288–1289 (1993)
13. Bishop, C.M.: Neural Networks for Pattern Recognition. Oxford University Press, Oxford (1995)
14. Fletcher, R., Powell, M.J.D.: A rapidly convergent descent method for minimization. British Computer J., 163–168 (1963)
15. Fletcher, R., Reeves, R.M.: Function minimization by conjugate gradients. Computer. Journal. 7(2), 149–160 (1964)
16. Hestenes, M.R., Stiefel, E.: Methods of conjugate gradients for solving linear systerns. J. Research NBS 49, 409 (1952)
17. Huang, H.Y.: A unified approach to quadratically convergent algorithms for function minimization. J. Optim. Theory Appl. 5, 405–423 (1970)
18. Nawi, N.M., Ransing, M.R., Ransing, R.S.: An improved Conjugate Gradient based learning algorithm for back propagation neural networks. International Journal of Computational Intelligence 4(1), 46–55 (2007)
19. Blake, C. L.: UCI Machine Learning Databases, http://mlearn.ics.uci.edu/database/heart-disease/

Two-Stage Damage Detection Method Using the Artificial Neural Networks and Genetic Algorithms

Dan-Guang Pan, Su-Su Lei, and Shun-Chuan Wu

Department of Civil Engineering, University of Science and Technology Beijing, 100083,
Beijing, P. R. China
pdg@ustb.edu.cn, moonlss1988@163.com,
wushunchuan@ustb.edu.cn

Abstract. To identify the location and extent of structural damage, a new two-stage approach was developed, which combined the artificial neural networks (ANN) and genetic algorithms (GA). The changes in the dynamic characteristics of a structure as the input parameters of ANN were used for the interval estimation of damage element. Subsequently, the estimation interval is considered as a feasible region of GA to obtain the accurate estimate of damage location and damage extent. One advantage of the proposed approach is that it would decrease the size of ANN and form a small feasible region of GA. Another one is that only a few frequencies and associated modal shapes are needed to accurately assess the location and extent of damage. So it is suitable for damage detection of large and complex structure of civil engineering.

Keywords: structures of civil engineering; artificial neural networks; genetic algorithms; damage localization; estimate of the damage extent.

1 Introduction

Our daily lives rely on the civil infrastructures, such as bridges, buildings, offshore platforms. A lot of existing infrastructures have been in service for decades, even more than 100 years [1]. The accumulation of damage and aging etc. of structures, which would reduce the safety and even result in the structural failures, are inevitable. Therefore, it is necessary to detect the damage of structures before it broken.

As well known, the dynamic characters are easily measured, so vibration-based damage detection techniques have received considerable attention. The basic idea is that the modal parameters (frequencies and mode shapes etc.) vary with the physical properties (mass and stiffness etc.). Therefore, using the changes in modal parameters to detect the damage of structures is the basis for various vibration-based damage detection methods [3], [4], [5], [6].

In fact, the damage detection is the solution of inverse problems by using the post-damage information. In recent years, the computational intelligence methods have been applied to the structural damage detection. For example neural networks and genetic algorithms, the computational intelligence methods have shown more effective and robust characteristics than mathematical methods for uncertainly, insufficient

R. Zhu et al. (Eds.): ICICA 2010, LNCS 6377, pp. 325–332, 2010.

information. Neural networks are universal function approximators for functions of arbitrary complexity. Many researchers (Kaminski [6], Ni *et al*. [7], Lee *et al*. [8], Mehrjoo *et al*. [9], Oliver *et al*. [10], María *et al*. [11]) applied neural networks to study the damage detection. Another group formulated the damage problem as an optimization problem by using genetic algorithms (Mares and Surace [12], Friswell *et al*. [13]). For the civil infrastructures, there are lots of elements, and the degree of freedom could be very large. Directly using ANN to locate damage will result in the problem of sample combination explosion and network volume too big. And directly using GA will cause individual's chromosome too long. These problems make the accuracy of damage estimates rarely reliable. Substructural technique [14] and multi-stage approach [15] for damage detection are promising methods to identify the damage in a large structural system.

In this paper, a new two-stage approach for damage detection is proposed under the assumption that the first few lower-order modal parameters have been extracted. At first, a back-propagation neural network is used to estimate the potential damage region. Then, in the second stage, an assessment of damage severity based on GA is performed on the potentially damaged members identified in the previous stage. At last, a numerical example analysis is presented to demonstrate the effectiveness of the proposed method.

2 Formulation of Artificial Neural Networks

In the paper, a BP neural networks model was used to estimate the damage region. The ANN consists of an input layer, a hidden layer and an output layer. The relationship between input and output can be expressed as:

$$O_k = f_2 \left[\sum_{j=1}^{m} w_{jk} f_1 (\sum_{i=1}^{n} x_i v_{ij} - v_{0j}) - w_{0k} \right], \ (k = 1, 2, \cdots l). \tag{1}$$

Where, v_{ij} is the weight factor of connection between input layer mode i and hidden layer mode j, w_{jk} is the weight factor of connection between hidden layer mode j and output layer mode k . To output layer, x_i is input data, O_k is output data, f_1 and f_2 are transfer function from input layer to hidden layer and from hidden layer to output layer. Sigmoid functions are used as nonlinear activation functions for all layers.

The ANN is increasingly used in vibration-based damage detection. Reliably predicting the location and extent of damage in complex structures required selecting reasonable input and output data. Frequency-based input data is popular employed, but different damage locations can produce the same degree of the frequency shift. Therefore, using only frequency changes might not be sufficient to uniquely determine damage location. In this study, the frequencies and mode shape data at a few selected points are used as the input data to the neural networks.

For the case of output layer, we utilized location and extent of damage of elements. As the probability of occurrence of structural damage in different parts is different, and failure tree analysis shows that the structure will collapse if the number of damage elements rise to a certain number, we can estimate the number of structural damage element as m, and then design a neural network of $2m$ nodes:

$$\{O\} = \{l_1 \quad d_1 \quad l_2 \quad d_2 \quad \cdots \quad l_m \quad d_m\}. \tag{2}$$

Where, $l_i = n_i / n_s$ represents damage location, n_i is damage element number, n_s is total number of elements, d_i represents the damage extent of l_i.

When the ANN is trained by simulation data, it can be an effective tool for the damage assessment. From another perspective, ANN can be considered as a form of non-linear regression, then for any sample O_k, the ANN estimation result $\hat{O}_k$ will be satisfy with:

$$O_k = \hat{O}_k + \varepsilon. \tag{3}$$

Assumption that the calculation error ε obeys normal distribution, $\varepsilon \sim N(0, \sigma^2)$, then for a given input $\mathbf{X}_0$ and the confidence level $1 - \alpha$, the prediction interval of output $\hat{O}_k$ is approximate as [16]:

$$(\hat{O}_k - \delta, \ \hat{O}_k + \delta). \tag{4}$$

Where $\delta = \sigma k$, k is the quantile under certain confidence level. For the case that the confidence levels are 97.5%, 99.8%, 99.99%, the associated values of k are 2, 3 and 4, respectively. σ is the variance of ANN estimation error ε .and its value can be calculated by:

$$\sigma \approx \sqrt{E'/m}. \tag{5}$$

$$E' = \frac{1}{2n} \sum_p \left(\varepsilon^p\right)^2 = \frac{1}{2n} \|\varepsilon\|^2. \tag{6}$$

Where, n is ANN training sample number, E' is the convergence error of the neural network.

3   Formulation of Genetic Algorithms

The feasible region of the GA in this paper is defined by the results of ANN, so the feasible region is far less than the whole domain, which can reduce the population size and the times of iterations to improve convergence speed.

In the following calculation, the GA using real-coded, if the number of elements of structural damage is m, then the chromosome of each individual $\mathbf{x}$ is $2m$-dimensional vector.

$$\mathbf{x} = \{x_1, x_2, \cdots, x_{2m-1}, x_{2m}\} = \{n_1, d_1, \cdots, n_m, d_m\}. \tag{7}$$

Where, n_i is damage element number, d_i the damage extent of n_i. Genetic operations adopt proportional selection, linear crossover and Gaussian mutation to optimize the calculation.

The objective function of GA can be defined by the natural frequency and mode before and after the structural damage, that is,

$$F = W_\omega F_\omega + W_\phi F_\phi .$$ (8)

Where, F_ω is the difference between measured frequency and calculated frequency, F_ϕ is the difference between measured mode and the calculated mode. W_ω and W_ϕ are the weight coefficient. F_ω and F_ϕ can be calculated by:

$$F_\omega = \sqrt{\sum_{j=1}^{r}\left(\frac{\omega_{mj} - \omega_{aj}}{\omega_{mj}}\right)^2} .$$ (9)

$$F_\phi = \sqrt{\sum_{j=1}^{r}\sum_{i=1}^{s}\Delta\phi_{ij}^2} , \quad \Delta\phi_{ij} = \begin{cases} \left(\phi_{mij} - \phi_{aij}\right)/\phi_{mij} & (\phi_{mij} \neq 0) \\ \phi_{mij} - \phi_{aij} & (\phi_{mij} = 0) \end{cases} .$$ (10)

Where ω_j and ϕ_j are the j order frequency and associated mode shape. Subscript m denotes the calculated results and a denotes the measured results.

The objective function reflects the error between the calculation and the measurement, and its value is as small as possible. Therefore, the optimization process of GA is the process of $F \rightarrow \min(F)$. The fitness of individual $\mathbf{x}_i$ is defined as:

$$f(\mathbf{x}_i) = F_{\max} - F(\mathbf{x}_i) .$$ (11)

Where $F_{\max} = \max\{F(\mathbf{x}_1), F(\mathbf{x}_2), \cdots, F(\mathbf{x}_n)\}$ represents the maximum value of all of the individual objective functions.

4 Verification and Examples

A numerical example analysis was performed on a three-dimension frame structure to demonstrate the effectiveness of the proposed method. The frame is modeled using beam elements for beams and columns as shown in Fig. 1. The model is composed of 16 elements. We assume that beams of the following numerical example are homogeneous and isotropic, rectangular cross-section with cross-section area 0.01 m². Young's modulus E is 2.06×10^{12}Pa and density is 7850Kg/m³.

The first three frequencies and partial mode shape data which include the horizontal displacement of 8 nodes (1,2,4,5,7,8,10,11) are used as the input data for damage detection.

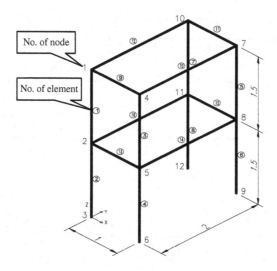

Fig. 1. Finite element model of framework (unit: m)

The element-level damage severity d_i is defined as [17]

$$d_i = 1 - S_i.$$ (12)

Where S_i is the element-level stiffness indices identified as

$$\left[k_i^d\right] = S_i\left[k_i^u\right].$$ (13)

Superscripts u and d represent intact and damaged states, respectively.

4.1 Artificial Neural Network Analysis

Learning. Take the damage extent of learning samples as 30%, 60% and 90%.There is a total of 49 samples including undamaged case. Neural network structure is taken as $51 \times 6 \times 2$. Convergence of the error limit is 0.005. Convergence of the network is so fast that the real convergence error of the network is 0.0049 when learning is successful.

Test. Sixteen samples are used to simulate the situation that the damage extent of each element is 50% during the test. Fig. 2 shows the results of test examples. As illustrated, the expected output of neural network is within the range of estimates, which shows that the trained neural network can reflect the actual damage well and can be applied to the actual forecasting analysis.

Application. After ANN is trained by simulation data, it can be an effective tool for damage assessment.

After the frequency and mode of damage structure are obtained, import them into trained neural network and forecast. Table 1 shows part of the predicted results and the estimative interval of each element for $k = 3$ by the trained ANN. The results show that ANN can be a good interval estimates which contain the true damage location and damage extent for a successful trained network.

Table 1. Predicted results and interval by the trained ANN

the expected output		estimation results of ANN		estimation interval of ANN	
No. of element	damage extent	No. of element	damage extent	element	damage extent
1	0.44	3	0.4609	1-6	0.2509-0.6709
2	0.44	1	0.4467	1-4	0.2367-0.6567
9	0.44	9	0.3165	5-12	0.1065-0.5265
14	0.44	13	0.5553	10-16	0.3453-0.7653

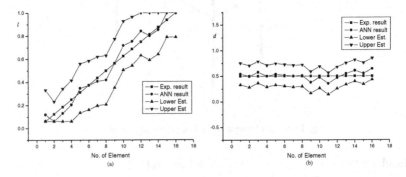

Fig. 2. The test results of ANN(a) Damage location prediction,(b) Damage extent estimation

4.2   The Estimation Results of GA

The parameters in GA are set as follows: crossover probability is 1.0, mutation probability is 0.05, and population size is 50. Stop the genetic manipulation by controlling the generations of evolution. The largest evolutionary generation is set as 20, the weight of objective function $W_\omega = 2$ in the calculation. For different damage conditions, the results of GA are shown in Table 2. The results show that GA can accurately determine the location of damage while the estimative error of damage extent within 2%.

Table 2. The estimation results of GA

Actual damage scenario		Estimation results of GA	
Damage element	Damage extent	Damage element	Damage extent
1	0.44	1	0.439
2	0.44	2	0.438
9	0.44	9	0.436
14	0.44	14	0.434

5   Conclusions

The paper proposes a new two-stage approach to solve large-scale civil engineering structure damage location and damage estimation. In the first stage, the estimative interval of damage location and damage extent is obtained by combining nonlinear mapping ability of ANN and interval estimation of mathematical statistics. In the second stage, the estimative interval of ANN is considered as a feasible region of GA, from which precise damage location and damage extent is obtained. A numerical example analysis is performed on a three-dimension frame structure. The results show that the method has the characteristics of high calculation efficiency, small calculation error, which is suitable for large and complex structure damage detection.

Acknowledgments. The research is supported by the 863-project of China (Program Number 2009AA11Z105). This support is gratefully acknowledged.

References

1. Gao, Y.: Structural Health Monitoring Strategies for Smart Sensor Networks. Doctoral Dissertation, University of Illinois at Urbana-Champaign (2005)
2. Doebline, S.W., Farrar, C.R., Prime, M.B., et al.: Damage Identification and Health Monitoring of Structural and Mechanical Systems from Changes in the Vibration Characteristics: A Literature Review. Los Alamos National Laboratories. Report LA-13070-MS (1996)
3. Li, H.J., Wang, J.R., Hu, S.L.J.: Using Incomplete Modal Data for Damage Detection in Offshore Jacket Structures. Ocean Engineering 35, 1793–1799 (2008)
4. Anjan, D., Talukdar, S.: Damage Detection in Bridges Using Accurate Modal Parameters. Finite Elements in Analysis and Design 40, 287–304 (2004)
5. Gentile, C., Saisi, A.: Ambient Vibration Testing of Historic Masonry Towers for Structural Identification and Damage Assessment. Construction and Building Materials 21, 1311–1321 (2007)
6. Kaminski, P.C.: The Approximate Location of Damage through the Analysis of Natural Frequencies with Artificial Neural Networks. Journal of Process Mechanical Engineering 209, 117–123 (1995)
7. Ni, Y.Q., Wang, B.S., Ko, J.M.: Constructing Input Vectors to Neural Networks for Structural Damage Identification. Smart Materials and Structures 11, 825–833 (2002)
8. Lee, J.J., Lee, J.W., Yi, J.H., Yun, C.B., Jung, H.Y.: Neural Networks-Based Damage Detection for Bridges Considering Errors in Baseline Finite Element Models. Journal of Sound and Vibration 280, 555–578 (2005)
9. Mehrjoo, M., Khaji, N., Moharrami, H., Bahreininejad, A.: Damage Detection of Truss Bridge Joints Using Artificial Neural Networks. Expert Systems with Applications 35, 1122–1131 (2008)
10. Oliver, R.D.L., Piotr, O.: Prediction of Seismic-induced Structural Damage Using Artificial Neural Networks. Engineering Structures 31, 600–606 (2009)
11. María, P.G., José, L.Z.: Seismic Damage Identification in Buildings Using Neural Networks and Modal Data. Computers and Structures 86, 416–426 (2008)
12. Mares, C., Surace, C.: An Application of Genetic Algorithms to Identify Damage in Elastic Structures. Journal of Sound and Vibration 195, 195–215 (1996)
13. Friswell, M.I., Penny, J.E.T., Garvey, S.D.: A Combined Genetic Eigensensitivity Algorithm for the Location of Damage in Structures. Computers and Structures 69, 547–556 (1998)
14. Yun, C.B., Bahng, E.Y.: Substructural Identification Using Neural Networks. Computers and Structures 77, 41–52 (2000)

15. Ko, J.M., Sun, Z.G., Ni, Y.Q.: Multi-Stage Identification Scheme for Detecting Damage in Cable-Stayed Kap Shui Mun Bridge. Engineering Structures 24, 857–868 (2002)
16. Pan, D.G., Gao, Y.H., Song, J.L.: Multi-Level Interval Estimation for Locating damage in Structures by Using Artificial Neural Networks. In: Proceedings of the 2nd International Symposium on Computational Mechanics and the 12th International Conference on the Enhancement and Promotion of Computational Methods in Engineering and Science, pp. 442–447. AIP Press, New York (2010)
17. Cawley, P., Adams, R.D.: The Location of Defects in Structures from Measurements of Natural Frequencies. Journal of Strain Analysis 14, 49–57 (1979)

Designing an Artificial Immune System-Based Machine Learning Classifier for Medical Diagnosis

Hui-Ping Cheng[1], Zheng-Sheng Lin[1], Hsiao-Fen Hsiao[2], and Ming-Lang Tseng[1]

[1] Department of Business Innovation and Development, MingDao University,
Peetow, Changhua 52345, Taiwan
[2] Department of Finance, MingDao University, Peetow, Changhua 52345, Taiwan
myjasmine129@hotmail.com, sheng@mdu.edu.tw, fen@mdu.edu.tw,
hpcheng@mdu.edu.tw

Abstract. The purpose of this paper is to develop an efficient approach to improve medical diagnosis performance of breast cancer. First, the medical dataset of breast cancer is selected from UCI Machine Learning Repository. After that, the standardization and normalization of datasets are pre-processing procedure. Secondly, the proposed approach combines support vector machine with artificial immune system as the medical diagnosis classifier. The results of diagnosis are identified and the rates of classification accuracy are evaluated. A simple artificial immune algorithm with various affinity criteria is investigated for comparison. Furthermore, the grid-search with 10-fold cross-validation is applied to choose two parameters of C and γ for AIS-based machine learning classifier. Through grid-search technique, the proposed classifier could yield the best results.

Keywords: Artificial immune algorithm, support vector machine, grid-search, distance measure, medical diagnosis.

1 Introduction

Breast cancer is a very usual type of diagnosed cancers among women in the world. Today, more women are living with breast cancer than any other cancer (excluding skin cancer). However, many women are living with breast cancer but they do not yet know they have the disease. The last, more than 80% of women who receive suspicious results from a screening mammogram do not have breast cancer. That is, the false positive results may lead to unnecessary, intrusive surgical interventions, while false negative results will not find cancerous tumors. National Cancer Institute [1] reported that a woman's cumulative risk for a false positive result after ten mammograms is almost 50%. Therefore, the primary objective of this investigation is to develop a computer-aid classification system in order to solve medical problems, and further, the efficiency and benefit by the proposed classification system will be explored and compared. Various approaches, including artificial neural networks [2-3], and data mining [4-6] have been applied to this issue with varying

R. Zhu et al. (Eds.): ICICA 2010, LNCS 6377, pp. 333–341, 2010.

degrees of success. In respect of artificial immune systems (AISs), AISs are adaptive soft computing paradigm that inspired by biological immunity theory and outlined several principles, models, and applications. The natural immune system is a pattern recognition system with various functional components positioned in strategic locations throughout the body. The most important task of immune system is to provide the body staying in homeostasis with neural and endocrine system. Immune system regulates defense mechanism of the body by means of innate and adaptive immune responses. Therefore, adaptive immune response is greatly important for humans because it contains diverse function like recognition, memory acquisition, diversity, and self-regulation. The architects of adaptive immune response are lymphocytes, which can be divided into two classes as B and T lymphocytes (cells). Particularly, B cells keep a great significance because of their secreted antibodies that take critical roles in adaptive immune response [7]. Timmis *et al.* [8] studied the advantages of AISs algorithm, including clone selection, immune network, and negative selection algorithms. Furthermore, Hart and Timmis [9] summarized the application areas of AISs and suggested a set of problem features for AISs development, and defined a unique niche for AISs. For that reason, the AISs are successful techniques to solve problem fields such as classification, regression, clustering, and pattern recognition. Recently, support vector machines (SVMs) have been proposed as popular tools for learning from experimental datasets [10-14]. Besides, an SVM obtains high generalization performance without the need to add a priori knowledge even when the input dimension space is high. Therefore, the main concern of this paper is to develop an efficient approach which can improve medical performance for diagnosis of breast cancer. In our classification tasks are comprised of three primary strategies. (i) the medical dataset of breast cancer is selected as the input vector. After that, the standardization and normalization of datasets are pre-processing procedure. (ii) the proposed approach combines support vector machine with artificial immune system as the medical diagnosis classifier is introduced. The clinical instances of breast cancer are the subjects of this investigation. In Particular, the AIS is responsible for clustering, cloning, and mutation the disease patterns. A simple artificial immune algorithm with various distance criteria are evaluated for affinity degrees, such as Euclidean distance, Manhattan distance, Minkowski distance, and statistical correlation coefficient. And then, the SVM focuses on identifying the different disease patterns promptly and accurately. Furthermore, the grid-search with 10-fold cross-validation is applied to choose two optimal parameters of C and γ for SVM. Through grid-search technique, the AIS-based machine learning classifier could yield the best results. (iii) the results of diagnosis are identified and the rates of classification accuracy are evaluated. For the case of breast cancer, each instance has one of two classes, that is, benign and malignant. Fig. 1 describes a framework of proposed AIS-based machine learning classifier for diagnosis of breast cancer.

In numerical experiments, our proposed approach is quantitatively compared to several classifiers and affinity criteria in a 10-fold cross-validation procedure. An

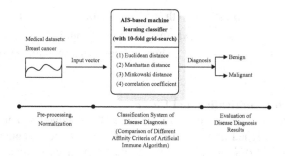

Fig. 1. A framework of the medical diagnosis system is presented. The classification tasks are comprised of three primary phases, including preparation phase, classification phase, and evaluation phase.

adopted real-world dataset is chosen as the input vector to the proposed classifier The Wisconsin Breast Cancer Dataset (WBCD) is a patient's clinical dataset that obtained from the University of California Irvine (UCI) Machine Learning Repository [15]. This dataset consists of 683 instances that were acquired by Dr. W. H. Wolberg from University of Wisconsin Hospitals. Properties of cancer cells were collected for 683 instances, with 444 benign (65.01%) and 239 (34.99%) malignant instances of cancer. Each of these patterns consists of nine attributes taken from fine needle aspirates from a patient's breast. These attributes are characterized as follows. (i) clump thickness; (ii) uniformity of cell size; (iii) uniformity of cell shape; (iv) marginal adhesion; (v) single epithelial cell size; (vi) bare nuclei; (vii) bland chromatin; (viii) normal nucleoli; (ix) mitoses. These attributes were coded 1 to 10 integer value with 1 being the closest to benign and 10 indicating the most anaplastic. The problem is to distinguish between malignant and benign breast cancer cells.

2   AIS-Based Machine Learning Classifier

2.1   AIS Algorithm

(a) Initialization

First, all of the input datasets are normalized to make certain that the Euclidean distance between two dataset is in the interval of [0, 1]. The training samples are named as Ag_s (antigens) while composed memory units which will be then used as classifying units are called as Ab_s (antibodies) in this algorithm. Cell memory Ab_s of that class from the memory Ab matrix and calculate the distance between Ag_i and these memory Ab_s. The D denotes Euclidean distance which is described for both affinity and stimulation level, it can be expressed by the following equation.

$$D = \sqrt{\sum_{p=1}^{M}\left(Ab_{j,p} - Ag_{i,p}\right)^2} \tag{1}$$

where $Ab_{j,p}$ and $Ag_{i,p}$ express the p th attribute in the datasets of Ab_j and Ag_i, respectively. Here, the $i = 1,2,3,...,n$, which i denotes the number of Ag_s (the number of input vector), and the $j = 1,2,3,...,mc$, which j represents the number of memory Ab_s in the class c_s.

(b) Memory Cell Identification and Clone

The feature vectors presented for training and test are named as antigens while the system units are designed as B cells. Similar B cells are represented with artificial recognition balls (ARB_s) and these ARB_s compete with each other for a fixed resource number. In this step, Immune algorithm begins to train antigen for iteration. Antigen could memorize cell and the most stimulated memory cell by that antigen is cloned. Consequentially, the number of clones is determined according to the most affinity between memory cell and antigen. The appraisals of affinity values and stimulation are defined below.

$$affinity(x, y) = 1 - D \tag{2}$$

$$stimulation(x, y) = \begin{cases} affinity(x,y) & \text{if class of } x = \text{class of } y \\ 1 - affinity(x,y) & \text{otherwise} \end{cases} \tag{3}$$

The certain value results in higher affinities for lower Euclidean distances. In practical, AIS clones and mutates B cells to promote a memory of B cells that can identify similar patterns to the one that caused the cloning.

(c) Test for Stimulation Threshold

In test stage, the lower affinity ARB_s begin to eliminate and this step continues until the required number is equal to the allowed number of resources. The stimulation levels of the remaining ARB_s are tested and the certain value of these levels is decided for each class. If the certain value is lower than a stimulation threshold, this ARB belonging to this class are mutated and the clones are added to the ARB pool. This step progresses until average stimulation of all classes is bigger than the stimulation threshold that can be written as follows.

$$ST_i = \frac{\sum_{j=1}^{|ARB_i|} sl_j}{|ARB_i|} \tag{4}$$

where ST_i is the stimulation threshold for i th class. $|ARB_i|$ is the number of ARB_s belonging to i th class. The sl_j is the stimulation level of j th ARB pool of i th class.

(d) Candidate Memory Cell Merged with Initial Memory Cell

After all of the stimulation value in all classes reaches stimulation threshold, the best ARB in the same class with training antigen is taken as a candidate memory cell. Here, the AIS population consists of two sub-populations, that is, the initial population and the clone population.

(e) Building the Immune Network

Once the AIS have gone through one training cycle, the weakest 5% of the B cells are removed from the AIS. Therefore, the network of B cells expressed more robust than before, and the artificial immune network has been established.

2.2 Criteria of Distance Measure

In terms of AIS, the D represents the distance which is described for both affinity and stimulation level that can be expressed by four criteria as follows. Euclidean distance measurement criterion is used for traditional AIS as the measurement of affinity. In this study, many different criteria to estimate the affinity are presented and investigated among the artificial immune algorithm. (i) Euclidean distance. The dissimilarity (or similarity) between the objects described by interval-scaled variables is typically computed based on the distance between each pair of objects. (ii) Manhattan distance. Another well-known metric is Manhattan (or city-block) distance which can be written as $D = \sum_{p=1}^{M} |Ab_{j,p} - Ag_{i,p}|$. (iii) Minkowski distance. Minkowski distance is a generalization of both Euclidean distance and Manhattan distance, which can be expressed by the following equation $D = \left(|Ab_{j,1} - Ag_{i,1}|^q + |Ab_{j,2} - Ag_{i,2}|^q + ... + |Ab_{j,p} - Ag_{i,p}|^q \right)^{1/q}$, where q is a positive integer. It represents the Manhattan distance when $q = 1$, and Euclidean distance when $q = 2$. (iv) Statistical correlation coefficient. The statistical correlation coefficient between two vectors x and y is defined as

$$r = \frac{\sum_{i=1}^{n}(x_i - \bar{x})(y_i - \bar{y})}{\sqrt{\sum_{i=1}^{n}(x_i - \bar{x})^2}\sqrt{\sum_{i=1}^{n}(y_i - \bar{y})^2}} \tag{5}$$

The principal concept of the statistical correlation coefficient is to measure the normalized consistency in the signs of the remainders of two vectors x and y about their sample means. Here, the value of $1 - r$ is evaluated for this distance criterion.

2.3 Support Vector Machine and Kernel Functions

Support vector machine is a powerful technique for solving problems in nonlinear classification, function estimation and density that proposed by [10]. In general, a classification work usually involves with training and testing datasets which consists of some data instances. Considering a training datasets $\{\mathbf{x}_k, y_k\}$, $k = 1,2,3,...,N$ where $\mathbf{x}_k \in R^d$ is the k th input vector, d denotes the dimension of the input space, and $y_k \in \{-1,+1\}$ is its corresponding target value (class label). Assume the training datasets are linearly separable after mapped into a higher dimensional feature space by a nonlinear function $\Phi(\cdot)$. The classifier is represented by $f(x) = \text{sgn}(\Phi(\mathbf{x})) \cdot \mathbf{w} + b)$, where $\text{sgn}(\cdot)$ is the sign function, $\mathbf{w}$ is the vector perpendicular to the hyperplane, and b is a constant. In order to classify the datasets correctly with best generalization capability, a separable hyperplane with largest margin have to construct, the $\Phi(\mathbf{x}_k) \cdot \mathbf{w} + b \geq 1$ for the positive points and $\Phi(\mathbf{x}_k) \cdot \mathbf{w} + b \leq -1$ for the negative points. The optimal hyperplane is required to satisfy the following constrained minimization.

$$
\begin{aligned}
\min \quad & \tau(\mathbf{w}) = \frac{1}{2}\|\mathbf{w}\| \\
\text{s.t.} \quad & y_k(\Phi(\mathbf{x}_k) \cdot \mathbf{w} + b) \geq 1 \\
& k = 1,2,3,...,N
\end{aligned}
\tag{6}
$$

In practice, the training datasets are usually not linearly separable even mapped into a high dimensional feature space. A soft margin is introduced to incorporate the possibility of violation. This leads to the following optimization problem with regard to the primal variables $\mathbf{w}$ and b,

$$
\begin{aligned}
\min \quad & \tau(\mathbf{w}) = \frac{1}{2}\|\mathbf{w}\| + C\sum_{k=1}^{N}\xi_k \\
\text{s.t.} \quad & y_k(\Phi(\mathbf{x}_k) \cdot \mathbf{w} + b) \geq 1 - \xi_k \\
& \xi_k \geq 0, k = 1,2,3,...,N
\end{aligned}
\tag{7}
$$

where C is the penalty parameter of the error term, It is important to note that the variables ξ_i are introduced to allow for misclassifications in the inequalities. It can be viewed as a tuning parameter which can be used to control the trade-off between maximizing the margin and the classification error. It should be noted that the C should be chosen carefully to avoid over-fitting. By defining a kernel function $K(\mathbf{x}_i,\mathbf{x}_j) = \Phi(\mathbf{x}_i)^T\Phi(\mathbf{x}_j)$, the explicit computing of $\Phi(\cdot)$ is avoided. Consequently, the decision function as follows is obtained.

$$
f(x) = \text{sgn}(\sum_{i=1}^{N}\alpha_i y_i K(\mathbf{x}_i,\mathbf{x}) + b)
\tag{8}
$$

where α_i are called support vectors which represent nonzero values. The advantage of the kernel function is which tries to make the training datasets linearly separable in the high dimension feature space. Thus, it could achieve non-linearly separable in the input space. Some well-known kernel functions including linear kernel, polynomial kernel, sigmoid and radial basis function (RBF) kernels are defined in [11].

3 Numerical Experiments

3.1 Quantitative Performance Evaluation

The rate of correct classification (ROCC) is calculated to estimate performance of classifier. Table 1 summarizes the overall performances of different classifiers in terms of the classification accuracy. It is available in some packages of software [16, 17]. Classification rates were approximated based on 100000 runs in each training phase using 10-fold cross-validation. The pairs of (C, γ) are regulated for (15, 0.00111) in this study by experiment. The results indicate that proposed classifier uniformly performs better than the other classifiers from literatures. The proposed classifier with various affinity criteria are discussed, as shown in Table 2. Between different affinity criteria, Euclidean distance and Minkowski distance ($q = 3$) perform marginally better than remaining criteria. It is evident that AIS-based machine learning classifier yield quite stable results.

Table 1. Comparison of different classifiers for WBCD classification problem is presented. The results of the first twelve are cited from [5].

Author (Year)	Method	ROCC (%)
Quinlan (1996)	C4.5 (10-fold cross-validation)	97.74
Hamilton (1996)	RIAC (10-fold cross-validation)	94.99
Ster and Dobnikar (1996)	LDA (10-fold cross-validation)	96.80
Bennett and Blue (1997)	SVM (5-fold cross-validation)	97.20
Nauck and Kruse (1999)	NEFCLASS (10-fold cross-validation)	95.06
Rena-Reyes and Sipper (1999)	Fuzzy-GA1 (train: 75%; test: 25%)	97.36
Setiono (2000)	Neuro-Rule 2a (train: 50%; test: 50%)	98.10
Goodman *et al.* (2002)	Optimized-LVQ (10-fold cross-validation)	96.70
Goodman *et al.* (2002)	Big-LVQ (10-fold cross-validation)	96.80
Goodman *et al.* (2002)	AIRS (10-fold cross-validation)	97.20
Abonyi and Szeifert (2003)	Supervised fuzzy clustering (10-fold cross-validation)	95.57
Şahan *et al.* (2005)	Fuzzy-AIRS (10-fold cross-validation)	98.51
Cheng *et al.* proposed approach (2010)	AIS-based machine learning classifier (10-fold cross-validation)	99.14

Table 2. AIS-based machine learning classifier with various affinity criteria

Affinity Criteria	ROCC (%)
Euclidean distance	99.14
Manhattan distance	98.50
Minkowski distance	99.14
correlation coefficient	99.04

3.2 Grid- Search on C and γ for SVM and Performance Evaluation

For SVMs classification issue, the proper parameters setting can improve the SVMs classification accuracies. The parameters that should be optimized include penalty parameter C and the kernel parameters such as the gamma γ for the RBF kernel. The grid algorithm is an alternative to finding the best C and γ when using the RBF kernel. Thus, we applied a grid-search approach on the range of $C = 2^{-5}, 2^{-3}, ..., 2^{15}$ and $\gamma = 2^{-15}, 2^{-13}, ..., 2^{5}$ using 10-fold cross-validation in order to fulfill the classification model, as shown in Fig. 2. After searching on the grid, we can observe that the optimal pairs of (C, γ) are found at middle left edge. The figure also reveals that the proposed approach is very robust against parameter selections.

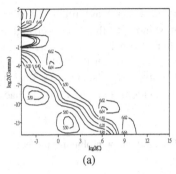
(a)

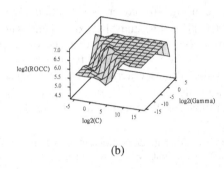
(b)

Fig. 2. (a) A contour plot of grid-search is formed. After searching on the grid, an optimal parameter region can be constructed. We can notice that the optimal pairs of (C, γ) are found at a middle left field. (b) A surface plot is shaped, and the classification accuracy is displayed on the vertical axis. The optimal pairs of (C, γ) are the same as contour plot.

4 Conclusions

The finding of their investigation was that too large or too small of (C, γ) will lead to over-fitting or under-fitting, respectively. This paper is to develop an AIS-based machine learning classifier which can improve performance of breast cancer diagnosis. The results demonstrated that proposed classifier can give considerable classification improvements. It also states that the proposed approach using different combinations of parameters yield quite stable results.

References

1. National Cancer Institute, http://www.cancer.gov/ (last accessed: March 30, 2010)
2. Setiono, R., Liu, H.: Neural-Network Feature Selector. IEEE Trans. Neural Network 8(3), 654–662 (1997)
3. Abbass, H.A.: An Evolutionary Artificial Neural Networks Approach for Breast Cancer Diagnosis. Artif. Intell. Med. 25, 265–281 (2002)
4. Polat, K., Şahan, S., Güneş, S.: A Novel Hybrid Method Based on Artificial Immune Recognition System (AIRS) with Fuzzy Weighted Pre-Processing for Thyroid Disease Diagnosis. Expert Syst. Appl. 32, 1141–1147 (2007)
5. Polat, K., Şahan, S., Kodaz, H., Güneş, S.: Breast Cancer and Liver Disorders Classification Using Artificial Immune Recognition System (ARIS) with Performance Evaluation by Resource Allocation Mechanism. Expert Syst. Appl. 32, 172–183 (2007)
6. Şahan, S., Polat, K., Kodaz, H., Güneş, S.: A New Hybrid Method Based on Fuzzy-Artificial Immune System and K-NN Algorithm for Breast Cancer Diagnosis. Comput. Biol. Med. 37, 415–423 (2007)
7. Timmis, J., Neal, M., Hunt, J.: An Artificial Immune System for Data Analysis. BioSystems 55, 143–150 (2000)
8. Timmis, J., Hone, A., Stibor, T., Clark, E.: Theoretical Advances in Artificial Immune Systems. Theor. Comput. Sci. 403, 11–32 (2008)

9. Hart, E., Timmis, J.: Application Areas of AIS: the Past, the Present and the Future. Appl. Soft Comput. 8, 191–201 (2008)
10. Vapnik, V.N.: The Nature of Statistical Learning Theory. Springer, Heidelberg (1995)
11. Burges, C.J.C.: A Tutorial on Support Vector Machines for Pattern Recognition. Data Min. Knowl. Disc. 2, 121–167 (1998)
12. Hsu, C.W., Lin, C.J.: A Comparison of Methods for Multiclass Support Vector Machines. IEEE Trans. Neural Network 13, 415–425 (2002)
13. Hsu, C.W., Chang, C.C., Lin, C.J.: A Practical Guide to Support Vector Classification. Technical Report, Department of Computer Science and Information Engineering, National Taiwan University (2003),
    http://www.csie.ntu.edu.tw/~cjlin/papers/guide/guide.pdf
14. Huang, C.L., Lee, Y.J., Lin, D.K.J., Huang, S.Y.: Model Selection for Support Vector Machines via Uniform Design. Comput. Stat. Dat. Anal. 52, 335–346 (2007)
15. University of California Irvine Machine Learning Repository,
    http://archive.ics.uci.edu/ml/ (last accessed: March 30, 2010)
16. MathWorks: MATLAB 7.0 User's Guide. MathWorks, Natick (2004)
17. Statistica: Statistica Data Miner. StatSoft, Oklahoma (2004)

Human-Oriented Image Retrieval of Optimized Multi-feature via Genetic Algorithm

Mingsheng Liu[1], Jianhua Li[2], and Hui Liu[2]

[1] School of Information Engineering, Handan College, Handan, China
liums601001@sina.com
[2] School of Information Science and Technology
Shijiazhuang TieDao Univercity, Shijiazhuang, China
{lijh,liuh}@sjzri.edu.cn

Abstract. There have been two problems in the implementation of a content-based image retrieval (CBIR) system in web. One is the absence of a standardized way to describe image content, the other is the disregard for the special needs of individual users To address these two problems, in this paper, a human-oriented CBIR system is presented which is implemented by applying MPEG-7 descriptors. In the new system, a multi-feature space is established and both homogeneous texture descriptor and color layout descriptor are used. Since there are difference in human perceptions of color and texture, in order to successfully retrieve an image which caters to the users, PGA (parallel genetic algorithm) is employed to adjust the weight of each feature space. The experimental evidence shows that the system is robust in general format by using MPEG-7 and it is capable of matching the user profile as well.

Keywords: content-based image retrieval, human preference, MPEG-7, parallel genetic algorithm.

1 Introduction

The research of CBIR usually focuses on visual feature extraction, multi-dimensional indexing, and retrieval system design. As the basis of CBIR, the features are usually discussed. Within the visual feature scope, the features can be further classified as general features and domain-specific features. The former category includes color, texture and shape feature while the latter is application dependent and may include, for example, human faces and fingerprints. Many methods of extracting image features have been developed [1], [2]. Those methods can be used to establish a CBIR system in their own right. However, when a single person uses the CBIR system, problems emerge. The first, a web based CBIR system must provide different way of interpretation, which universally can be passed onto, or accessed by an application or an interface whether they are from CBIR system own or from outer. The second, for an individual, high level query and perception subjectivity cannot be represented by single low-level feature. It is unseemliness to use a single feature to match human demands. The third, a particular person is interested in particular features. How can we satisfy different people's needs?

R. Zhu et al. (Eds.): ICICA 2010, LNCS 6377, pp. 342–349, 2010.

In this paper, the multi-feature space is proposed and implemented in our image retrieval system, and by adjusting the weight of different features in the retrieval, the optimal result can be obtained. We first extract features of the homogeneous texture descriptor and color layout descriptor in MPEG-7 standard, and then we use the genetic algorithm to obtain the relevance weight of features, finally we establish a human-oriented image retrieval system.

2 The Features Based on MPEG-7

2.1 The MPEG-7 Homogeneous Texture Descriptor (HTD)

The homogeneous texture descriptor is composed by the average brightness f_{dc}, the brightness deviation f_{sd}, the average energy and energy deviation. The descriptor is written as $TD = \{f_{dc}, f_{sd}, e_1, \cdots, e_{30}, d_1, \cdots, d_{30}\}$ [3].

The texture descriptor can be represented at two different layers: base layer and enhancement layer. The texture descriptor only consists of f_{dc}, f_{sd}, and 30 energy values (e_i) of the Fourier transform of the image. In the enhancement layer, the texture descriptor (additionally or) adds 30 (or additional) energy deviation values of the Fourier transform of the image in the texture descriptor vector. The layering scheme of the texture descriptor provides scalability of representing image texture depending upon applications. For the delivery of limited bandwidths, only texture descriptor components at the base layer may be transmitted. In addition, fast matching can be performed at the base layer if retrieval accuracy can be guaranteed.

The similarity measured by calculating the distance between the two feature vectors is as follows

$$D_{HTD}(i, j) = dis(TD_i, TD_j) = \sum_k \left| \frac{w(k)[TD_i(k) - TD_j(k)]}{\alpha(k)} \right| \tag{1}$$

$w(k)$ is the weighting factor and $\alpha(k)$ are the standard deviations of k-th descriptor values of all the images in the database.

2.2 The MPEG-7 Color Layout Descriptor (CLD)

This descriptor effectively represents the spatial distribution of the color of the visual signals in a very compact form. This compactness ensures efficient visual signal matching at very low computational costs. It provides image-to-image matching as well as ultra high-speed sequence-to-sequence matching, which requires so many repetitions of similarity calculations. It also provides very friendly user interface using hand-written sketch queries since these descriptors capture the layout information of color feature. The sketch queries are not supported in other color descriptors.

The similarity measured by calculating the distance between the two feature vectors is as follows

$$D_{CLD}(CLD_1, CLD_2) = \sqrt{\sum_i W_{yi}(DY_i - DY_i')^2} + \sqrt{\sum_i W_{bi}(DCb_i - DCb_i')^2} + \sqrt{\sum_i W_{ri}(DCr_i - DCr_i')^2}. \tag{2}$$

Where, $\{DY_i, DCb_i, DCr_i\}$ is the i-th coefficient of DCT, W_{yi}, W_{bi}, W_{ri} is the weighting factor of i-th descriptor value. The weights of low frequencies are larger than the high frequencies.

2.3 Establishing the Composite Feature-Space

The similarity measured by calculating the distance between the two features is as follows

$$D_{Un} = W_{HTD} \times D_{HTD} + W_{CLD} \times D_{CLD}. \tag{3}$$

Where, D_{HTD} is the distance of homogeneous texture description, the D_{CLD} is the distance of color layout description, W_{HTD} and W_{CLD} are the weight of two description in the composite feature-space corresponding.

3 The Feature Optimization Based on Genetic Algorithm

The homogeneous texture descriptor and color layout descriptor can present the texture feature and the color feature of an image. People may observe one image from different visual angles because of the affection of human visual system, due to which we adjust the weight of features to meet the user's satisfaction. We employ the parallel genetic algorithm to realize the user's demand [4],[5],[6],[7].

3.1 The Implementation of PGA

At first, we obtain the correlative image set by automatically or manually. They are the basis of calculate fitness value, for an image Q_0, the image set shown as below.

$$I_{set} = \{Q_0, Q_1, Q_2, \cdots, Q_n\}. \tag{4}$$

The genetic algorithm is listed below.
   Step 1: Initial the population.
   Present the weights of homogeneous texture descriptor and color layout descriptor corresponding by real number of 0 to 1. The real coded genes of the HTD shown as

$$GA_{W(i)} = \overbrace{\underbrace{0.23}_{W(1)}, \underbrace{0.53}_{W(2)}, \cdots, \underbrace{0.34}_{W(62)}}^{62}. \tag{5}$$

The real coded genes of the CLD have the same formation with the HTD.
   The outer weight, W_{HTD} and W_{CLD} has been encoded by binary gene, shown a
$$\sigma$$

$$GA_{W_{HTD}} = \overbrace{01010101}^{8} \quad GA_{W_{CLD}} = \overbrace{10101010}^{8} \tag{6}$$

The mount of genes is $64 \times 3 + 62 + 2 \times 8$, totally 270. The population size M normally set 100 to 200. When we get the initial generation, divide the population into 5 subspace and the selection, crossover and mutation are all operated in its own subspace.

Step 2: Calculate individual fitness.

Use the distance formulation of composite feature-space by the genes of HTD and CLD to the weight corresponding, and calculate the distance of two features by (1) and (2). Then we calculate the sum of two distances by outer weight with (3).

We get the order of the result by the distance in each subspace. For the relative images in (4), calculate the fitness value according to their sequence in the result by (7). The more ahead the image is the better fitness value it is. The $Score_i$ is to give a grade to the relative image by user. That is the key factor to present user's profile.

$$F = \sum_{i=0}^{N} \left[\frac{1}{Sequence_{Q_i}} \right]^2 \times Score_i. \tag{7}$$

For example, if we take the image in Fig.1 as the target image, we get the queue of the image set and the score of each image shown as Fig.2.

Fig. 1. The example picture

Fig. 2. User graded image sequence

Step 3: Selection operator.

We use the method that combines reserving the max fitness value individual with roulette wheel selection to make sure the best individual can be reproduced to the next generation. It means reserving the best individual unconditionally, replacing the worst individual with the best one, and then using the roulette wheel selection to determine whether the individual will be reproduced to the next generation.

Step 4: Crossover operator.

The genes are made up with two kinds of weight, two inner weights and one outer weight. We employ thrice single-point crossover for the genes. It means the employment of the crossover operator for genes of weights of HTD, CLD and outer respectively. The crossover rate P_c normally set 0.5 to 0.9.

Step 5: Mutation operator.

We employ thrice single-point mutation for the genes as well. The mutation rate P_m normally set 0.0001 to 1.

Step 6: Migration operation

We use the island model to realize the PGA. It runs several single population genetic algorithms in parallel. Each island is an SGA with its own subpopulation. Migration between islands uses grid topology, and two best individuals are chosen for migration. The two best random individuals from the other subpopulation replace the lost individual. After the migration, each subpopulation has the new good gene to do next evolution.

Step 7: The end of evolution.

Terminate the evolution if conditions permitting, or go to the step (2) to continue the algorithm. Normally, the termination condition T normally set 100 to 500.

3.2 Genetic Algorithm Parameters

In the genetic algorithm, there are 4 parameters should be set carefully to make sure we can get the best genes, and they are population size, termination condition, crossover rate and mutation rate. How to determinate the current parameters are still a problem, we must perform some experiments to get the best parameters.

We use the orthogonal experiment approach to determinate those parameters [8], [9]. In order to simplify the orthogonal design, we take the population size, crossover rate and mutation rate as the factors and set them as 5 levels, then get a $L_{15}(5^3)$ table, shown as Table 1.

Table 1. Experiment Project orthogonal test

Levels	Factors		
	M	P_c	P_m
1	20	0.0001	0.5
2	40	0.001	0.6
3	60	0.01	0.7
4	80	0.1	0.8
5	100	1	0.9

After the experiment, we get the genetic algorithm parameters: M=60, P_c =0.1. , P_m =0.9, T=100. By the way, the weight of feature must be confirmed by experiments several times.

4 Analysis of the Experiment Result

The icpr2004 image set which contains 1243 images from university of Washington D.C. was used to conduct the experiments. A number of experiments were conducted on the image set by taking Fig.1 as sample. The experiments can be summarized as follows in terms of the feature sets used.

1) MPEG-7 Homogeneous Texture Descriptor (HTD) only.

2) MPEG-7 Color Layout Descriptor (CLD) only.

3) Combination of two MPEG-7 features and set W_{HTD} and W_{CLD} as 1 in (3) and calculate the distance.

4) Combination of two MPEG-7 features and using the MARS [10] as an optimization method.

5) Combination of two MPEG-7 features and using the PGA as an optimization method.

The retrieval result sets by using before-mentioned feature sets shown as Fig.3, one row of images means using one term of feature sets above.

Fig. 3. The retrieval result by different feature sets

Using efficient content-based image retrieval (ECBIR) from university of Washington D.C performs retrieval by color and texture feature result shown as Fig.4, the first row is the result of 512bin color histogram and wavelet texture, the second row is the result of 214bin asymmetry color histogram and wavelet texture, and the third row is the result of color histogram, Sobel edge and wavelet texture.

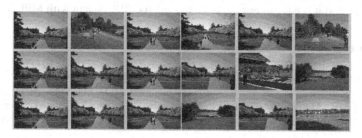

Fig. 4. The result sets by ECBIR

Experimental results clearly show that the method of only using CLD or HTD also has a pretty good retrieval result. Nevertheless, it cannot fully match the perfect result set based on user preference as Fig.2. If we do not consider the weight factor in (3), the equation becomes a simple sum of the distance of two descriptors. The retrieval performance improves to some degree, since we quantify each value of the two features from 0 to 255.

Finally, Table 2 summarizes the average recall rate and precision for these experiments and it is observed that the retrieval performance can be improved by combining different feature set properly. The weight script file shows those using genetic algorithms adjust the weights of the feature space. The value of feature weight of the correlative image set is amplified, and vice versa. The optimized results are better than those using single features. The retrieval results optimized by PGA not only include all the pertinent images but also those which have the same sequence with the user marked image order shown in the Fig. 2.

Table 2. The efficiency comparison

	Only CLD	Only HTD	ECBIR	Using Mars	Using PGA
recall(%)	66	63	66	75	83
precision(%)	60	61	61	71	80

5 Conclusion

A human-oriented image retrieval system must match the user interest. Therefore, we employed multi feature-space, which is one of the high efficiency approaches to meet human visual system. In this paper, the homogeneous texture descriptor and color layout descriptor from MPEG-7 are implemented. Furthermore, since different people may have different visual angles, we employ the parallel genetic algorithm to adjust the weight of multi feature-space to obtain the best possible result set. In addition, with the development of WEB, we must provide different access interface to satisfy versatility request. The MPEG-7 standard is capable of describing image feature with the defined syntax and semantics of descriptors and description schemes, so that it may be used as fundamental tools for multimedia content description, it has a favorable performance to make the retrieval universal. The experiments result show that the composite feature-space description and optimization method well match the users' profile, and it is easy to implement a universal CBIR system with MPEG-7.

References

1. Xiang-yang, L., Yue-ting, Z., Yun-he, P.: Technique and Systems of Content-based Image Retrieval. Journal of Computer Research Development 38(3), 344–354 (2001)
2. Müller, H., Müller, W., Squire, D.M., Marchand-Maillet, S., Pun, T.: Performance evaluation in content-based image retrieval: Overview and proposals. Pattern Recognition Letters 22(5), 593–601 (2001)
3. Multimedia Content Description Interface - Part 3: Visual, Final Draft for International Standard, ISO/IEC/JTC1/SC29/WG11, Doc. N4358 (2001)
4. Affenzeller, M., Winkler, S., Wagner, S., Beham, A.: Genetic Algorithms and Genetic Programming: Modern Concepts and Practical Applications (Numerical Insights). CRC Press Inc., Boca Raton (2009)

5. Man, K.F., Tang, K.S., Kwong, S.: Genetic Algorithms: Concepts and Applications. IEEE Transaction on Industrial Electronics 43(5), 519–534 (1996)
6. Seo, K.-K.: Content-Based Image Retrieval by Combining Genetic Algorithm and Support Vector Machine. In: de Sá, J.M., Alexandre, L.A., Duch, W., Mandic, D.P. (eds.) ICANN 2007, Part II. LNCS, vol. 4669, pp. 537–545. Springer, Heidelberg (2007)
7. Zeng, X.-p., Cheng, Y.-f., Li, Y.-m.: Real Adaptive genetic algorithm with parallel operators. Application Research of Computers 25(6), 1687–1689 (2006)
8. Ma, h., Sun, W., Dai, J.-s., Wen, b.-c.: Bearing parameter optimization of a large-scale centrifugal compressor based on orthogonal experiment. Computer Integrated Manufacturing Systems 16(2), 390–395 (2010)
9. Zhou, X.-g., Li, W.-m., Liu, Y.: Modeling of UAV Search Strategy Based on Nearly Orthogonal Latin Hypercube Experiment. Computer Engineering 36(9), 1–3 (2010)
10. Squire, D.M., Müller, H., Müller, W., Marchand-Maillet, S., Pun, T.: Design and Evaluation of a Content-based Image Retrieval System. In: Design & Management of Multimedia Information Systems: Opportunities & Challenges, pp. 125–151. IGI Publishing, Hershey (2001)

Genetic Algorithm Based on Activities Resource Competition Relation for the RCPSP

Shiman Xie, Beifang Bao, and Jianwei Chen

College of Mechanical Engineering, Hebei Polytechnic University,
Tangshan Hebei 063009, China
xie_s@126.com

Abstract. Chromosome encoded by the matrix of activities resource competition relation (ARCR) in Genetic algorithm (GA) is used to solve the resource constrained project scheduling problem (RCPSP). The relevant code length and code data structure etc. are studied. Decoding, the fitness computation, selection, crossover and mutation algorithms based on ARCR encoding method are proposed. Finally, the standard data collection download from PSPLIB is used to test the algorithm, the results show the algorithm is effective and feasible.

Keywords: RCPSP, GA, chromosome encoding, ARCR.

1 Introduction

Along with the increasing complexity and constraint of the project, it is difficult for project scheduling personnel to work out a more reasonable project plan to balance resource requirements and schedule conflicts in a short time to solve resource constrained project scheduling problems (RCPSP).

Genetic Algorithm (GA) simulates the natural selection and replication, crossover and mutation[1-3]. Starting from any initial population, GA makes groups evolve into better area in the search space, and converges to a group of individuals which best adapted to the environment. Finally the satisfied solution could be obtained.

2 Resource Constrained Project Scheduling Model

Suppose the count of the activity in project is n+2 and the count of the resource kind is m. (Activity 0 and Activity n+1 are void activities which mean the start and end of the project)[4]. T_i denotes the start time of activity i; d_i denotes the duration of activity i; r_{ik} denotes the demand on resource k of activity i; R_k denotes the daily supply of resource k[5]. A_i denotes all the predecessor activities of activity i. The model of RCPSP optimization can be get as follows:

R. Zhu et al. (Eds.): ICICA 2010, LNCS 6377, pp. 350–356, 2010.

Constraints:

$$d_i \geq 0 \tag{1}$$

$$T_i \geq T_j + d_j, \forall j \in A_i \tag{2}$$

$$\sum_{i=1}^{n} r_{ik} \leq R_k, k = 1, 2, \cdots, m \tag{3}$$

Objective function: There are a variety of optimization goals, and this is one of the advantages of genetic algorithm[6-8]. The shortest duration target:

$$\min T_{n+1} \tag{4}$$

3 Implementation of GA Based on Activities Resource Competition Relation

To solve the RCPSP problem, the order constraint of activities and the resource constraints of project are necessary to be considered. Chromosome encoding is a foundation of the genetic algorithms.

3.1 Introduction of RCPSP Traditional Encoding

Traditional encoding methods of genetic algorithm to solve RCPSP problem usually ignored order and resource constraints, randomly generated active sorting string[9]. The project network chart as shows in Figure 1 randomly generated codes as shown in Figure 2.

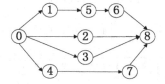

Fig. 1. Project network diagram

a) | 0 | 1 | 5 | 3 | 4 | 2 | 6 | 7 | 8 |

b) | 0 | 2 | 1 | 3 | 5 | 4 | 6 | 7 | 8 |

c) | 0 | 5 | 1 | 2 | 3 | 4 | 6 | 7 | 8 |

Fig. 2. Project Scheduling code sample based string sorting

This is a special string encoding method. Its' advantages are those coding results is simple, decoding algorithm implement easily.

Disadvantage of this encoding: firstly, it possibly produces the wrong chromosome which do not meet the order constraint. Activity 5 and Activity 1 as shown in Figure 2: c). Secondly, more importantly, this encoding will result in that the follow-up crossover and mutation process are difficult to achieve, such as single-point cross in a) and b), they inevitably product activity 5 and activity 2's invalid offspring duplication.

3.2 Encoding Based on Activities Resource Competition Relation Matrix

After detailed analysis of the root causes of project scheduling problems, it can be found that the entire process of scheduling is a process of activities to compete with limited resources[10]. This article designs an encoding method based on Activities Resource Competition Relation (ARCR) matrix. Resources competition between activity i and activity j means that project scheduling arrived at a certain time when activity i and activity j need scheduling options.

The activities competition relations include binary relations (The competition between two activities) and multi-relations (The competition among various activities). Let K_{ij} denotes the competition winner that activity i and activity j to compete with limited resources, $K_{(1...n)}$ denotes the competition winner that the activities of a total of n to compete with limited resources. To simplify the algorithm, the multi-relations will be broken down into some sequence of binary relations. The $K_{(1...n)}$ is the last winner between adjacent competitive activities, expressed by the adjacency matrix[11]. With the around restriction between the project network activities, and the principle that the label of predecessor activity is less than the label of successor activity, it needed only store the upper triangular matrix. As figure 3 shows, the matrix expressed the basic binary relations of competition between activities in figure 1 project network. In this paper, this matrix will be named Activities Resource Competition Relation (ARCR) matrix.

In the ARCR matrix:

$$a_{ij} \begin{cases} = 0, \text{there is not competition between Activity i and Activity j} \\ > 0, \text{there is competition between Activity i and Activity j} \end{cases}$$

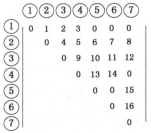

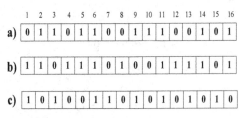

Fig. 3. Activities Resource Competition Relation Matrix

Fig. 4. Sample of chromosome coding based on Activities Resource Competition Relation Matrix

When all activities do not have the sequence relationship, the maximum of competition relations are N_{max},

$$N_{max} = \frac{n(n-1)}{2} \tag{5}$$

By analyzing competition relations, it can be proved that the necessary and sufficient condition of the existence between the activity i and activity j is that there is not precedence relation. Therefore, by calculating the accessibility of project network, the preliminary ARCR matrix can be obtained.

Numbering the nonzero elements of preliminary ARCR matrix in order of top to bottom, left to right, the final ARCR matrix can be got. The maximum number of ARCR matrix is marked N_R. In this case $N_R = 16$. Chromosome structure can be constructed based on the final ARCR matrix as shown in Figure 4, It is a linear string of binary numbers, and its length of N_R.

$$B_n \begin{cases} = 0 & , K_{ij} = i \\ = 1 & , K_{ij} = j \end{cases} \tag{6}$$

This encoding method can be shown to meet the chromosome coding principle of completeness and integrity, but it does not satisfy the principle of non-redundant, which is each point (candidate solution) in the space of problems corresponds to at least one point (chromosome) in the space of genetic algorithm, while one chromosome in the space of genetic algorithm corresponds only one candidate solution in the space of problems.

3.3 Coding Algorithm and Generate the Initial Population Algorithm

Chromosome encoding algorithm based on (ARCR) matrix as shown in Figure 5:

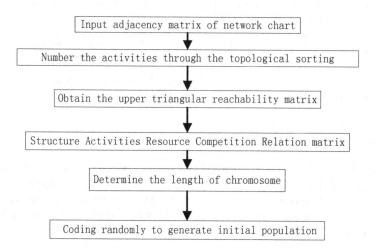

Fig. 5. Coding Algorithm and Generate the initial population Algorithm

The original input of encoding process is the adjacency matrix about relationship between the project activities. First, it needs convert the adjacency matrix into the upper triangular matrix through encoding number for activities; then obtain the upper triangular reachability matrix; the third step, structure Activities Resource Competition Relation (ARCR) matrix and obtain its chromosome length; finally, Randomly code and generate the initial population according to initial population size.

3.4 Decoding and Fitness Algorithm

Chromosome decoding algorithm and calculation of fitness algorithm are shown in Figure 6. Using the Activities Resource Competition Relation (ARCR) matrix encoding algorithm generated, and topological sorting, it can obtain an activities' scheduling sequence; then based on the resource constraints, it can calculate a project scheduling target; finally, it converted this to fitness value according to the objective function. The process that generated the scheduling sequence is shown in Figure 7.

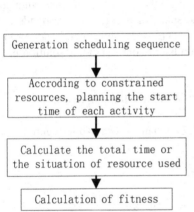

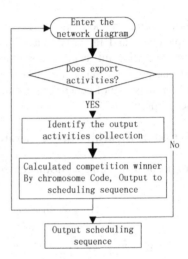

Fig. 6. Chromosome decoding algorithm and calculation of fitness algorithm

Fig. 7. Generation scheduling sequential algorithm

3.5 Other Genetic Operations

Because ARCR-based encoding method is a binary code, follow-up of the selection, crossover and mutation operation can use a variety of sophisticated algorithms. In this article we choose roulette method, crossover operation using two point crossover, Mutation operation using simple mutation. Cause of universality, so this article will not describe these algorithms.

4 Programming Verification

Genetic algorithm is a kind of intelligent evolution algorithm, mainly rely on group continuously evolved to confirm the best individuals. So a manual method will be more complicated, can not meet the actual project needs of project scheduling program optimized. This article uses C# for programming the algorithm and selects the shortest possible time adaptability priority.

Experimental data is selected from the well-known Project Scheduling Problem Library (PSPLIB), These problems are generated by the Instance generator ProGen developed by Kolish etc. widely used to assess the method for solving RCPSP in optimal operation of the project. Each experimental data was run 50 times, and the resulting data shown in Table 1.

Table 1. PSPLIB test data

Experimental data	Number of activities	Chromosome digits	Target time	Maximum evolution	Average evolution
J301-1	30	291	45	55	4
J301-2	30	313	52	65	24
J601-1	60	1362	85	51	20
J601-2	60	1312	81	62	25
X1-1	120	5841	125	86	31
X1-2	120	5755	135	56	33

5 Conclusion

During researching the genetic algorithm for the resource constrained project scheduling problem (RCPSP), the algorithm proposed remedies the traditional RCPSP coding method in application. A kind of chromosome encoding based on Activities Resource Competition Relation (ARCR) matrix is put forward. This algorithm makes it easier to solve the problem of crossover and mutation, meanwhile the code length and data structure of the coding method are studied. Since this is a binary code, so it can use mature operations in genetic evolution. With the PSPLIB experiment data, finally, the results show the feasibility and effectiveness of the genetic algorithm using the coding method.

References

1. Guan, C., Ren, H., Jiang, L.: Based on multi-resource constrained project scheduling model and algorithm. Machine Tools and Hydraulic 36(7), 65–68 (2008)
2. Mendes, J.J.M., Goncalves, J.F., Resende, M.G.C.: A random key based genetic algorithm for the resource constrained project scheduling problem. Computers & Operations Research 36(1), 92–109 (2009)
3. Vincent, V.P., Mario, V.: A genetic algorithm for the preemptive and nonpreemptive multi-mode resource-constrained project scheduling problem. European Journal of Operational Research 201(2), 409–418 (2010)
4. Khaled, M., Jacques, A.F.: Activity list representation for a generalization of the resource-constrained project scheduling problem. European Journal of Operational Research 199(1), 46–54 (2009)
5. Vicente, V., Francisco, B., Sacramento, Q.: A hybrid genetic algorithm for the resource-constrained project scheduling problem. European Journal of Operational Research 185(2), 495–508 (2008)

6. Goncalves, J.F., Mendes, J.J.M., Resende, M.G.C.: A genetic algorithm for the resource constrained multi-project scheduling problem. European Journal of Operational Research 189(3), 1171–1190 (2008)

7. Babak, A., Shahram, S., Jamal, A.: Bi-objective resource-constrained project scheduling with robustness and makespan criteria. Applied Mathematics and Computation 180(1), 146–152 (2006)

8. Chang, C., Jiang, H., Di, Y., Zhu, D., Ge, Y.: Time-line based model for software project scheduling with genetic algorithms. Information and Software Technology 50(11), 1142–1154 (2008)

9. Mohammad, R.R., Fereydoon, K.: Solving the discrete time/resource trade-off problem in project scheduling with genetic algorithms. Applied Mathematics and Computation 191(2), 451–456 (2007)

10. Kwan, W.K., Mitsuo, G., Genji, Y.: Hybrid genetic algorithm with fuzzy logic for resource-constrained project scheduling. Applied Soft Computing 2(3), 174–188 (2003)

11. Rainer, K., Arno, S.: PSPLIB - A project scheduling problem library: OR Software - ORSEP Operations Research Software Exchange Program. European Journal of Operational Research 96(1), 205–216 (1997)

A New Flatness Pattern Recognition Model Based on Variable Metric Chaos Optimization Neural Network

Ruicheng Zhang and Xin Zheng

College of Computer and Automatic Control, Hebei Polytechnic University, Hebei Tangshan
063009, China
rchzhang@yahoo.com.cn

Abstract. Aim at the problems occurring in a least square method model and a neural network model for flatness pattern recognition, a new approach of flatness pattern recognition based on the variable metric chaos optimization neural network is proposed to meet the demand of high-precision flatness control for cold strip mill. The model is shown to fit the actual data pricisely and to overcome several disadvantages of the conventional BP neural network. Namely:slow convergence, low accuracy and difficulty in finding the global optimum. A series of tests have been conducted based on the data of the actual flatness pattern. The simulation results show that the speed and accuracy of the flatness pattern recognition model are obviously improved.

Keywords: flatness; pattern recognition; variable metric chaos optimization; neural network.

1 Introduction

Flatness (defect) pattern recognition is an important part of flatness theory and an important constituent of flatness control system. Its task and purpose is that according to transversely distributed (width orientation) discrete values of measured or calculated residual stress (or residual strain), the values of flatness pattern parameters or characteristic parameters are obtained after calculation, which can supply bases for corresponding flatness control strategy.

Early flatness pattern recognition method was a polynomial regression method based on the least square method [1,2]. The defects of the method were that the magnitude of approximation factorial n could not be fixed on and its approximation precision was limited. The main reason was that the method had principle approximation, which put flatness pattern recognition on the crossroad to look for optimal approximation polynomial and ignored that the ultimate task of flatness pattern recognition was to recognize flatness patterns, to compress the number of characteristic variables, and to serve for on-line control. Later, the orthodoxy polynomial regression recognition method [3, 4] based on the least square method was proposed. This method overcame the defect of early least square regression method, but the integral value of its even polynomial by width did not equal zero and it did not meet the qualification that residual stress was self-canceling; thus, it had its defect in theory and did not conform to the essence of flatness distribution. In recent years, artificial neural network model

R. Zhu et al. (Eds.): ICICA 2010, LNCS 6377, pp. 357–364, 2010.

[5] has been proposed, but the orthodoxy polynomial it selected still has these defects mentioned above. In Ref. [6, 7], flatness basic patterns are expressed with Legendre orthodoxy polynomial, overcoming these defects mentioned above, but the large learning assignment, slow convergence, and local minimum in the neural network are observed.

For the problems in those flatness pattern recognition models mentioned above, in this study, a new flatness pattern recognition model, variable metric chaos optimization neural network model, is proposed, which integrates chaos optimization and neural network, learns from others' strong points to offset one's weakness, and considerably improves precision, velocity, and anti-interference ability.

2 Legendre Orthodoxy Polynomial for Flatness Basic Patterns

The flatness after rolling is the transverse distribution of the longitudinal residual stress. The residual stress meets self-canceling qualification that the integral value by width equals zero. There are six kinds of common flatness patterns on engineering: left wave, right wave, middle wave, double side wave, quarter wave, and side-middle wave. Residual stress of every pattern still meets self-canceling qualification. The residual stress distributions of six kinds of patterns mentioned above are defined as flatness basic patterns after being normalized. Simple, quadratic, and quartic Legendre orthodoxy polynomials $p_1(y)$, $p_2(y)$, $p_3(y)$ are chosen to express residual stress distributions of three pairs of anticlastic basic flatness patterns, and then the normalized equations of left wave, right wave, middle wave, double-side wave, quarter wave, and side-middle wave are as follows:

$$Y_1 = p_1(y) = y \,, \tag{1}$$

$$Y_2 = -p_1(y) = -y \,, \tag{2}$$

$$Y_3 = p_2(y) = \frac{3}{2}y^2 - \frac{1}{2} \,, \tag{3}$$

$$Y_4 = -p_2(y) = -(\frac{3}{2}y^2 - \frac{1}{2}) \,, \tag{4}$$

$$Y_5 = p_3(y) = \frac{1}{8}(35y^4 - 30y^2 + 3) \,, \tag{5}$$

$$Y_6 = -p_3(y) = -\frac{1}{8}(35y^4 - 30y^2 + 3) \,. \tag{6}$$

Where Y_k (k=1, 2, ..., 6) are flatness standard samples or basic samples.

It is easily proved that the flatness basic pattern equations of Equation (1) to Equation (6) all meet self-canceling qualification. Thus, it is rational to express flatness with Legendre orthodoxy polynomial.

Generally, the flatness after rolling σ can be expressed as the linear combination of flatness basic patterns:

$$\sigma = a_1 p_1(y) + a_2 p_2(y) + a_3 p_3(y) , \tag{7}$$

where a_1, a_2 and a_3 are the flatness characteristic coefficients.

It is obvious that flatness pattern recognition is actually to extract flatness basic pattern coefficients or characteristic coefficients a_1, a_2 and a_3 according to practically measured or calculated $\sigma(\xi)$ ($\xi=1,2, ...,n$, where ξ is the transverse coordinate point and n is the number of the points measured or calculated) after mathematical manipulation. Since a_1, a_2 and a_3 can be positive or negative, they can represent the magnitudes of six kinds of flatness pattern components mentioned above.

3 Variable Metric Chaos Optimization Neural Network Model for Flatness Pattern Recognition

3.1 Multilayer Neural Network

The multilayer neural network is one of the networks to be studied largely. The multilayer neural network possessing strong function has been proved. For simplicity there is one layer in the hidden layer. The multilayer neural network is composed with a input layer that the number of the input layer nodes is M, a hidden layer that the number of the hidden layer nodes is L, a output layer that the number of the output layer nodes is N. The connection weight between the intput layer and the hidden layer is W_1. The connection weight between the hidden layer and the output layer is W_2. The threshold of the hidden layer is B_1, The threshold of the output layer is B_2. The output of the multilayer neural network is:

$$Y = F_2(W_2 * F_1(W_1 * X + B_1) + B_2) , \tag{8}$$

where F_1 is the transfer function of the hidden layer, F_2 is the transfer function of the output layer.

3.2 Variable Metric Chaos Optimization Algorithm

Chaos is a normal phenomenon in the nonlinear systems. Although it looks like a chaotic transform proeess, in fact it contains inherent regularities. A chaos variable in certain range has some features as follows: randomness, ergodic property and regularity. Randomness is its disorder superficies as random variable. Ergodic property is that it may undergo non-repeatedly all states in the metric space. Regularity is that the variable is obtained by certain iterative equation [8].

The basic idea of the chaos optimization algorithm is that the chaos variables are linear mapping on the intervals of the optimization variables and the optimal values are searched with chaos variables[9]. A variable-metric chaos optimization algorithm to optimize the variables is presents in Ref[10]. Its main feature is to reduce continuously the search intervals of optimization variables and to adjust the coefficients of the secondary search according to the search proeess. This method overcomes the defects of the conventional chaos optimization algorithm which obtains different results to search in the big intervals and multi-variables.

The chaos variable arises by Logistic model.

$$x_{k+1} = \mu * x_k (1 - x_k) \quad x_k \in [0,1] , \tag{9}$$

where μ is control parameter.

When $\mu=4$, the equation turns into chaos state. For optimizing n parameters, n dissimilar initial values in interval [0,1] should be defined, but the values are not the fixed points (0.25, 0.5, 0.75). In this way, n dissimilar tracks of the chaos variables will be botained.

The optimization of the global minimum for the continuous object is

$$\min f(x_1, x_2 \cdots, x_n) \quad x_i = [a_i, b_i], i = 1, 2, \cdots, n . \tag{10}$$

The concrete algorithm step are as follows:

(1) Initialization: n chaos variable values in interval [0, 1] are obtained by equation (9). The chaos variable values being as initializations are linear mapping on the intervals of the optimization variables. N is a biggish integer.

(2) Iterative operation is performed with the chaos variables and the optimal variable values of the iterative operation are put into the object function to operation.

(3) If the current object function values are less than last optimal values, then the optimal values are replaced with the current object function values and the optimal variables are replaced with the current variables. Otherwise, the next iterative operation goes on.

(4) After N steps iterative operations, if the optimal function values and the optimal variables values are not change, the iterative operation goes to step (1). Otherwise, the iterative opration goes on.

(5) The optimization interval of each variable is reduced. The optimal variables are $\{x_1^*, x_2^*, \cdots, x_n^*\}$, r is the sign of the search, m is a constant in interval [0, 0.5], $[a_i^{r+1}, b_i^{r+1}]$ ($i=1,2,\ldots,n$) is the optimization interval of each transformed variable. The transformation equations are as follows:

$$\begin{cases} a_i^{r+1} = x_i^* - m^r (b_i^r - a_i^r) \\ b_i^{r+1} = x_i^* + m^r (b_i^r - a_i^r) \end{cases} \tag{11}$$

In order to the new values be in certain ranges, the values needs disposal as follows:

If $a_i^{r+1} < a_i^r$ then $a_i^{r+1} = a_i^r$

If $b_i^{r+1} < b_i^r$ then $b_i^{r+1} = b_i^r$

(6) The iterative operation goes to step (1) and goes on the next search.

(7) If the results satisfy the halt conditions, the search stop, or else the iterative operation goes to step (2), goes on the next operation.

The optimization intervals of the paper gradually reduce with exponential speed. The iterative operation searches the optimal values in the small intervals, and the purpose of the speediness optimization is attained. The method is effective especially in the big interval in particular.

3.3 Variable-Metric Chaos Optimization Neural Network

The purpose of the chaos optimization algorithm being used in the parameters estimation of the multilayer neural network is to search the optimal connection weight vector W and neuron threshold B, makes the error least between the output of the neural network and the output of the object.

The connection weight vector W and the neuron threshold B compose the variables of the optimization problem. The sample is represented with $[X_k, D_k]$ $(k=1,2, ...,p)$. The real output Y_k is obtained by equation (8) for each sample. The error square sum of the each operation is

$$E = \sum_{k=1}^{p} (Y_k - D_k)^2 . \tag{12}$$

The above equation is the object function of the neural network optimization too.

The intervals of the chaos variables are linear mapping on the intervals of the connection weight vector W and the neuron threshold B. The optimal values are gained and the error E is made least by using variable-metric chaos optimization algorithm.

3.4 Flatness Pattern Recognition Model and Steps

In order to reduce input nodes, simplify network structure, and meet different width, six inputs (nodes) based on the Euclidean distances between practical samples and standard samples are used. Fig.1 shows the topological structure of neural network. The first layer is input layer whose nodes are directly connected to each component of input vector. Its function is to transmit input to the next layer. Each component of the input vector is Euclidean distance D_k between flatness stress deviation and six kinds of flatness basic samples, i. e. ,

$$D_k = \sqrt{\sum_{\xi=1}^{n} [\sigma(\xi) - \sigma_k(\xi)]^2} \quad k = 1, 2, \cdots 6 , \tag{13}$$

where $\sigma_k(\xi)$ is the residual stress of a basic sample.

Standard in-out samples are shown in Table 1, where "*" is a random nonzero constant between 0 and 1, expressing normalized Euclidean distance between flatness deviation to be recognized and standard flatness patterns of left wave, right wave, middle wave, double-side wave, quarter wave and side-middle wave.

Table 1. Standard input-output samples

Standard input samples D_k $(k=1,2,...,6)$						Standard output samples $u_i(i=1,2,3)$		
0	*	*	*	*	*	1	0	0
*	0	*	*	*	*	-1	0	0
*	*	0	*	*	*	0	1	0
*	*	*	0	*	*	0	-1	0
*	*	*	*	0	*	0	0	1
*	*	*	*	*	0	0	0	-1

Recognition steps

The steps of flatness recognition by trained network are as follows:

(1) Measure or calculate forward tensile stress distribution $\sigma_{1\xi}(\xi = 1,2,\cdots,n)$.

(2) Calculate practical residual stress, i.e., $\sigma_\xi^R = \sigma_{1\xi} - \overline{\sigma_1}$, where $\overline{\sigma_1}$ is measured or calculated mean forward tensile stress.

(3) Calculate flatness deviation, i.e., $\Delta\sigma_\xi = \sigma_\xi^R - \sigma_\xi^T$, where σ_ξ^T is stress value of target flatness.

And then calculate maximal flatness deviation $\max\left|\Delta\sigma_\xi\right|$.

(4) Normalize flatness deviation,i.e. $\Delta\sigma_\xi^0 = \dfrac{\Delta\sigma_\xi}{\max\left|\Delta\sigma_\xi\right|}$.

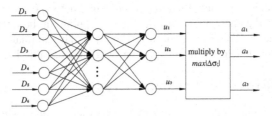

Fig. 1. Structure of optimal flatness pattern recognition network

(5) Calculate Euclidean distance D_k which is between $\Delta\sigma_\xi^0$ and six kinds of standard patterns Y_k, $(k=1,2,3,4,5,6)$.

(6) Optimize neural network by variable-metric chaos optimization algorithm and get corresponding network output u_1,u_2, and u_3. namely, flatness membership grade.

(7) Deoxidize flatness membership grade to practical flatness characteristic parameter values, i.e., $a_i = u_i \cdot \max\left|\Delta\sigma_\xi\right|$ $i = 1,2,3$.

4   Recognition Examples

For previous, network structure is 6-6-3. Then the solution is quickly done by variable-metric chaos optimization algorithm where the convergence condition of object function is $J \leq 10^{-7}$. 10 working sample books with known results were input into the model and the known results and recognition results were compared. The known results and recognition results were shown in Table 2. In Table 2, the first eight working sample books have been trained, and the last two have not been trained. It can be seen from the trained results that on the premise of well training of neural network, using this network to make pattern recognition can get high recognition precision. For trained working sample books, the error is not beyond 0.05% between the recognition result and known result. Whereas, the error is relatively bigger for untrained working sample books. Fig.2 showed the corresponding curves of the recognition result and

Table 2. Comparison of known results and recognition results

	Input samples	Standard outputs			Network outputs		
1	$Y=Y_1$	$u_1=1$	$u_2=0$	$u_3=0$	$u_1=0.9999$	$u_2=0$	$u_3=0.0001$
2	$Y=Y_2$	$u_1=-1$	$u_2=0$	$u_3=0$	$u_1=-0.9998$	$u_2=0$	$u_3=0$
3	$Y=Y_3$	$u_1=0$	$u_2=1$	$u_3=0$	$u_1=0.0002$	$u_2=0.9992$	$u_3=0$
4	$Y=Y_4$	$u_1=0$	$u_2=-1$	$u_3=0$	$u_1=0$	$u_2=-0.9988$	$u_3=0.0003$
5	$Y=Y_5$	$u_1=0$	$u_2=0$	$u_3=1$	$u_1=0$	$u_2=0.0011$	$u_3=0.9999$
6	$Y=Y_6$	$u_1=0$	$u_2=0$	$u_3=-1$	$u_1=0.0004$	$u_2=0$	$u_3=-1$
7	$Y=0.8Y_1+0.2Y_3$	$u_1=0.8$	$u_2=0.2$	$u_3=0$	$u_1=0.8020$	$u_2=0.2010$	$u_3=-0.0001$
8	$Y=0.2Y_2+0.5Y_4+0.3Y_5$	$u_1=0.2$	$u_2=-0.5$	$u_3=0.3$	$u_1=0.1999$	$u_2=-0.5010$	$u_3=0.3008$
9	$Y=0.4Y_2+0.5Y_3+0.1Y_6$	$u_1=-0.4$	$u_2=0.5$	$u_3=-0.1$	$u_1=-0.4002$	$u_2=0.4991$	$u_3=-0.0998$
10	$Y=0.4Y_1+0.1Y_3+0.5Y_6$	$u_1=0.4$	$u_2=0.1$	$u_3=-0.5$	$u_1=0.4102$	$u_2=0.1050$	$u_3=-0.4958$

known result of the two untrained working sample books. The curves in Fig.2 (a) are the working sample book No.9 (in Table 2) and the curves in Fig.2 (b) are the working sample book No.10 (in Table 2). The two curves in Fig.2 (a) or Fig.2 (b) are very close. This showed that the recognition effectiveness of this neural model is very good, meanwhile it means that it is important to learn working sample books for variable-metric chaos optimization neural network.

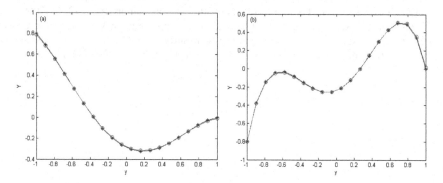

Fig. 2. Known objects and recognition objects of sample books

5   Conclusions

A BP neural network model combining variable-metric chaos optimization algorithm and BP algorithm is used to flatness pattern recognition. The model is shown to fit the data precisely and to overcome several disadvantages of the conventional BP neural networks, namely: slow convergence, low accuracy and difficulty in finding the global optimum. A series of tests have been conducted based on the samples. It has been shown that the variable-metric chaos optimization neural network model is an effective intelligent recognition method. After the network is trained, it becomes simple, fast, and precise, with strong self-adaptability and anti-interference ability to dispose data while recognizing flatness.

References

1. Jian-xin, H., Ze-yan, Z.: Polynomial Regression and Mathematical Model of Flatness Defect for Cold Strip. Iron and Steel 27(3), 27–31 (1992)
2. Jin, L.: Expression Regression and Mathematical Model of Flatness Defect for Cold Strip. Steel Rolling (5), 5–8 (1996)
3. Hong-shuang, D., Xiao-feng, Z., Xiang-hua, L., et al.: Orthogonal Polynomial Decomposition and Mathematical Model for Measured Signals of Thin Strip Flatness in Cold Rolling. Iron and Steel 3(9), 33–36 (1995)
4. Xu-dong, Z., Guo-dong, W.: Orthogonal Polynomial Decomposition Model for the Flatness of Cold-Rolled Strip. Iron and Steel 32(8), 46–47 (1997)
5. Jun-fei, Q., Ge, G., Tian-you, C., et al.: Application of Neural Network in Flatness Measurement. The Chinese Journal of Nonferrous Metals 8(3), 551–556 (1998)
6. Hong-xing, Z., Hai-jun, S., Hong-yan, L.: An Improved Approach of Neural Network Flatness Pattern Recognition. Microcomputer Information 23(2-1), 273–274 (2007)
7. Chun-yu, J., Xiu-ying, S., Hong-min, L., et al.: Fuzzy Neural Model for Flatness Pattern Recognition. Journal of Iron and Steel Research, International 15(6), 33–38 (2008)
8. Bao-zeng, Z.: Application of Chaos Mappings in Optimization calculation. Geomatics and Information Science of Wuhan University 32(11), 998–1000 (2007)
9. Qing-wu, S., Hong-yuan, G., Yu-xiao, C.: Application of Chaotic Optimization in the TDOA-based Location. Techniques of Automation & Applications 28(7), 42–45 (2009)
10. Feng-xiang, G., Chang-song, W., Yu-bao, Z., et al.: Application of Variable-metric Chaos Optimization Neural Network in Predicting Slab Surface Temperature of the Continuous Casting. In: Chinese Control and Decision Conference, pp. 2296–2299 (2009)

Comparison between BP Neural Network and Multiple Linear Regression Method

Guoli Wang, Jianhui Wu, Sufeng Yin, Liqun Yu, and Jing Wang

Hebei Province Key Laboratory of Occupational Health and safety for Coal Industry,
Division of Epidemiology and Health Statistics, North China Coal Medical College, Tang Shan
063000, China
wgl3726393@yahoo.com.cn

Abstract. BP neural network and multiple linear regression model can be used for multi-factor analysis and forecasting, but the data of the multiple linear regression required to meet independence, normality and other conditions, while the data of the BP neural network do not need to. This article uses the same set of data to established BP neural network model and multiple linear regression model, then compare the ability of fitting and forecasting of the two kinds of models finding that BP neural network has a strong fitting ability and a stable ability of prediction, which can be further used and promoted in the anglicizing and forecasting of the continuous data factors.

Keywords: BP neural network; multiple linear regression; OSS algorithm; coefficient of determination; forecast.

1 Introduction

BP neural network is currently the most widely used neural network model for one of its multi-layer feed forward neural network by error back propagation, widrow-Hoff learning rule will be extended to the multi-layer networks and nonlinear differentiable activation function resulting from neural network, can form a continuous non-linear mapping of any arbitrary approximation. In the continuous multi-factor analysis of data, the most commonly used is the multiple linear regression analysis, however, since many factors affecting the information model is a typical multi-factor combined effect of the model, the mode of action between the factors is very complex, Output factor that may exist between some of the relationships themselves interfere with the efficiency of the existing statistical model fitting, such as confounding factors, such as multi-collinearity, the existing linear model of such interference corrective measures are very limited, nor is a good way to handle this information with the interference method [1,2]. Application of neural networks to deal with the problem of nonlinear regression models to overcome the weaknesses, which is characterized by the distribution of information storage and parallel co-processing, and highly fault-tolerance and ability to learn, can be fitted close to the real model [3].

R. Zhu et al. (Eds.): ICICA 2010, LNCS 6377, pp. 365–370, 2010.

2 BP Neural Network Theory

2.1 Basic Principle

BP neural network is a multi-layer networks [4], "back stepping" learning algorithm, by an input layer, one or several hidden layers and an output layer, the learning process, including positive communication and signal error back-propagation. Forward propagation, the input samples imported from the input layer, layer by layer through the hidden layer to output layer mass after treatment. If the output layer does not match the actual output and desired output, then the errors carry out back-propagation.

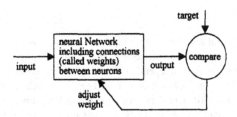

Fig. 1. Neural network processes

Error back-propagation is the output error to some form of input layer through hidden layer to layer by layer back-propagation, and error apportioned to all the units on each floor in order to obtain layers of error signal, This error signal that, as the right to amend the value of each unit basis. The signal being transmitted and the error back-propagation of the layers of the right to carry out the value of the adjustment process cycle until the output error to reach an acceptable level, or to a pre-set number of times until the study.

2.2 Learning Algorithm of BP Neural Network

BP algorithm is a learning algorithm proposed for MLP, the BP neural network of hidden transfer function USES is continuously differentiable nonlinear function, usually used Sigmoid function. The output layer of transmission function can use linear function or Sigmoid function, is based on the distribution of vector of output layer.

The basic steps of Algorithm [5]:

(1)For each of the threshold value or the initial value: $\theta_j(0)$ and $w_{ji}(0)$ are small numbers.

(2)Provide training samples: the input vector X_k, k = 1, 2, ..., P; expected output d_k: k = 1, 2, ..., P; For each input sample iteration below 3-5 step.

(3)To calculate the real output of network and hidden layer of the unit:

$$o_{kj} = f_j(\sum_i w_{ji} o_{ki} + \theta_j).$$

(4)Calculate error of training:

$$\delta_{kj} = o_{kj}(1 - o_{kj})(t_{kj} - o_{kj}), \qquad \text{(output layer)}$$

$$\delta_{kj} = o_{kj}(1 - o_{kj})\sum_m \delta_{km} w_{mj}. \qquad \text{(hidden layer)}$$

(5)Fixed weights and threshold

$$w_{ji}(t+1) = w_{ji}(t) + \eta \delta_j o_{ki} + \alpha[w_{ji}(t) - w_{ji}(t-1)],$$

$$\theta_j(t+1) = \theta_j(t) + \eta \delta_j + \alpha[\theta_j(t) - \theta_j(t-1).$$

(6)When k every experience after $1 - p$, Judge index whether meet the precision requirement:

$$E \le \varepsilon; \quad \varepsilon : accuracy.$$

(7)End.

3 BP Neural Network and Multiple Linear Regression Model

3.1 Introduction Examples

The past, a large number of studies on hospital costs are based on multiple linear regressions, analysis of variance and other methods required satisfying the independence assumption [6]. However, due to the same cost categories of cases in the hospital charges are often similarities, their observations are not completely independent [7, 8], therefore, multiple linear regression, analysis of variance and other methods, in the absence of such information in the data, taking into account the existence of the hierarchy, resulting in analysis of the factors of their effects is not accurate, or even come to completely opposite conclusions [9]. In this paper, hospitalization costs as the dependent variable, influencing factors as independent variables, namely the establishment of BP neural network model and multiple linear regression models.

3.2 BP Neural Network Model Results

The use of OSS algorithm BP neural network model building, model parameters are as follows.

Table 1. Hospitalization costs BP neural network model parameter table

Structure parameters	Training parameters	Simulation results	Training set fitting results
Hidden layers: a layer:	Training Algorithm: OSS algorithm	$R = 0.86504$	$R = 0.84747$
Hidden layer neurons: 15	A total cessation of training iterations: 27	$R^2 = 0.74829$	$R^2 = 0.7182$
Input layer neurons: 8	Learning speed: 0.01	$R^2_{adj} = 0.51195$	$R^2_{adj} = 0.5387$
Output layer neron: 1	Performance function: SSE	$SSE = 4.9944e+009$	$SSE = 2.0119e+010$
	Stop training $SSE^* = 1.2857$	$MSE = 1.7046e+007$ $RMSE = 4128.6$	$MSE = 1.7036e+007$ $RMSE = 4127.5$

* The SSE for the normalized [0, 1] in terms of data.

3.3 Multiple Linear Regression Model Results

Multiple linear regression showed that the impact on hospital costs in descending order of availability of emergency treatment, hospital days, treatment outcome, first hospital admission, payment methods, gender, and hospitalization costs of hospitalization days the greatest impact.

Table 2. Hospitalization cost implications of the results of multiple linear regression analysis of factors

Variable	B	Beta	t	Sig
Constant term	2963.03966	-	5.36	0.0000
Gender	-590.04777	-0.05364	-3.54	0.0004
First-time hospitalization	-559.67022	-0.04671	-3.06	0.0022
Rescue	1761.84145	0.09233	6.06	0.0000
Payment methods	-679.39106	-0.03747	-2.43	0.0150
Hospitalization days	413.46664	0.69922	45.91	0.0000
Treatment outcome	404.21294	0.03804	2.47	0.0135

4 Model Comparison

4.1 Comparison of Model Fitting Capabilities

BP neural network model to establish the use of OSS algorithm, put the data set is divided into test set and training set, multiple linear regression model using the same data is divided into test set and training set, the two models fit indicators are as follows:

Table 3. Model fit index

Indicators	Multiple linear regression model		BP neural network model	
	Test set	Training set	Test set	Training set
R^2	0.50	0.49	0.75	0.72
R^2_{adj}	0.50	0.48	0.51	0.54

Comparative Fit Index of the two models can be seen, both the test set or training set, BP neural network model fitting capabilities are superior to multiple linear regression model, with some scholars agreed conclusions of the study [10].

4.2 Performance Comparison of Model Prediction

In general, in accordance with the principle of randomization randomly selected 500 samples, respectively, using two kinds of models to predict and calculate the real value of the relative error comparison, paired t-test to compare the two models to predict the performance of the pros and cons of the following results:

Table 4. Multiple linear regression and BP neural network prediction performance comparison

Methods	case	mean ($\overline{x} \pm s$)	difference ($\overline{x} \pm s$)	t	P
Multiple linear regression	500	0.52 ± 0.47	0.21 ± 0.22	12.33	0.000
BP neural network	500	0.31 ± 0.24			

Table 4: Multiple linear regression model the relative mean error of 0.52, BP neural network model for the mean relative error of 0.31 yuan, $t = 12.33$, $P < 0.001$. The results show that differences between the two methods, through the relative error of the mean size of the two groups can be seen that BP neural network has good predictive ability.

5 Conclusion

This article uses the impact factors of hospitalization costs and the data were set up BP neural network model and multiple linear regression model Type, obtained two kinds of model goodness of fit index R^2 , R^2_{adj}, and forecasting performance of the model were compared and found that BP neural network stability and predictive power is superior to multiple linear regression model, and because of BP neural network Models do not need to consider whether the independent association between variables, the dependent variable is normally distributed to meet the conditions, and therefore the projections of continuous data, we recommend the use of BP neural network model.

References

1. Wei, G., Shaofa, N., Lvyuan, S.: Neural Networks in Application of Survival Analysis. Chinese Journal of Health Statistic 23(4), 76–78 (2006)
2. Na, W., Xianping, M.: Application of BP Neural Network in Creating Modeling of Non-liner System. Guangzhou Chemical 37(3), 43–45 (2009)
3. Wei, H., Junshan, T., Chuzheng, W., et al.: Improved Algorithm and Application of BP Neural Network. China Computer & Communication (10), 56–57 (2009)
4. Cariboni, J., Catelli, D., Liska, R., et al.: The role of sensitivity analysis in ecological modeling. Ecological Modelling 203(1-2), 167–182 (2007)
5. Zhenyu, S., Qiuyan, W., Xiaofeng, D.: The BP neural network training of practical problems to solve. Journal of Naval Aeronautical and Astronautical University 24(6), 704–706 (2009)
6. Erol, F.S., Uysal, H., Ergiun, U., et al.: Prediction of Minor Head Injured Patients Using Logistic Regression and MLP Neural Network. Journal of Medical Systems 29(3), 205–215 (2005)
7. Chunmei, M., Zongzan, N., Chunyan, H.: The Problem and Improvement about Multiple Linear Regression Model to Analyze the Influent Factor of the Cost of Inpatient. Modern Preventive Medicine 29(1), 33–34 (2002)
8. Biyao, L., Yi, S., Fan, H., et al.: Research of Establishing Hospitalization Charge Fitting Model by Using BP Neural Network. Zhejiang Prev. Med. 21(9), 77–78 (2009)
9. Bartfay, E., Mackillop, W.J., Peter, J.L.: Comparing the predictive value of neural network models to Logistic regression models on the risk of death for small-cell lung cancer patients. Eur. J. Cancer Care (Engl.) 15(2), 115–124 (2006)
10. Lifeng, Z., Ersheng, G., Pihuan, J.: Comparison Between Neural Networks And Multivariate Linear Regression Method. Modern Preventive Medicine 25(3), 272–274 (1998)

Research of Granularity Pair and Similar Hierarchical Algorithm*

Chunfeng Liu and Li Feng

College of Science, Hebei Polytechnic University
Tangshan Hebei 063009, China
liucf403@163.com, fengli3@126.com

Abstract. The hierarchical model reflects different awareness from different levels. Combining the property of certainty-uncertainty of set pair and the hierarchy of granularity, a new concept is proposed in this paper, that is granularity pair, which is the definition of granularity in set pair, connects the granular computing and the set pair analysis, pairs with object sets and attribute sets, owns the properties of dynamics, limits and similarity. And a similar hierarchical algorithm is designed about the similarity. The example shows that the algorithm is feasible.

Keywords: Granularity Pair, Hierarchy, Set Pair, Distance, Quotient space.

1 Introduction

Human understanding of the world is in depth constantly, so, from a develop view; our understanding will always be imprecise and ambiguous. But from a point of view it is accurate and clear in a certain level (or stage). The hierarchy (or more simple classification) model can reflect the delicate relationship better between the ambiguous and clear, the certainty and uncertainty, and describe people's understanding and analyze from different levels and requirements of things [1]. Many scholars put forward their ideas and algorithms for hierarchical model to realize things better from all levels. Baoxiang Liu has made layers from the angle of the set pair, using fuzzy clustering method [2]; Feng Ye's calculation based on fuzzy sets, which is a model of granular computing, can reduce computational complexity [3].

Taking into account that the set pair deals with certainty-uncertainty system and hierarchical computing solves the problem with hierarchy, this paper will integrate the two sides, proposes a concept of granularity pair. Granularity pair is the definition of granularity to set pair, pairs with object sets and attribute sets, inherits the collection on the nature of set pair and granularity. This article will design the hierarchical algorithm by the use of the similarity of granularity pair.

---

* Supported by the Natural Scientific Fund Project in Hebei Province (No.A2009000735), Scientific Technology Research and Development Plan Project of Tangshan(No.09130202C).

R. Zhu et al. (Eds.): ICICA 2010, LNCS 6377, pp. 371–378, 2010.

2 Related Concepts

Suppose U is a domain, R is an equivalence relation on U, also called knowledge, R'quotient sets on U is marked

$$U/R = \{X_1, X_2, \cdots, X_n\}, R \subseteq U \times U \qquad (1)$$

then the granularity of X_i is defined as:

$$p(X_i) = \frac{|X_i|}{|U|} \qquad (2)$$

$p(X_i)$ is the probability of X_i in the U, there $|\cdot|$ is the base number of sets. There are three Granular Computing[4] models currently: word computing model[5,6,7], rough set model[8,9,10] and quotient space theory [1,11,12].

Word computing model is a standard of the birth of Granular Computing, aims to solve Fuzzy Intelligent Control according to the nature language by making use of fuzzy inference and judgment.

Rough set theory has a strong qualitative analysis, can express the uncertain or imprecise knowledge effectively. The core idea is to divide into the disjoint equivalent classes using equivalent relations on the domain U, quotient set $U/R = \{[X]_R \mid X \in U\}$ represents granularities of the domain, and describes rough sets with the up and down approximation operators of subset X.

The question (X, f, T), where X is the domain, f is an attribute set, T is the topological structure on the X, we say that the question (X, f, T) is considered from the different granularity (angle, level), which is to say an equivalent relation R on the certain X, and generates quotient set $[X]$ by R, corresponds to the triple group $([X],[f],[T])$, which is called the quotient space corresponding to R.

Academician Zhang Bo and Professor Zhang Ling spread the quotient space model to the fuzzy granular world, and gave two basic conclusions [11]. One conclusion is that the four expressions following are equivalent:

(1) Given a fuzzy equivalent relation on the domain X;
(2) Given a normalized isosceles distance in the quotient space of X;
(3) Given a hierarchical structure on the domain X;
(4) Given a fuzzy knowledge base on the domain X.

A fuzzy equivalent relation on X corresponds to a distance space on $[X]$, corres ponds to the a hierarchical structure. Suppose $\underset{\sim}{R}$ be a fuzzy equivalent relation on X, and definite following

$$\forall x, y \in X, \quad x \sim y \Leftrightarrow \underset{\sim}{R}(x,y) = 1, \quad d(a,b) = 1 - \underset{\sim}{R}(x,y) \qquad (3)$$

$$\forall x \in a, y \in b$$

We say $d(a,b)$ is the distance function on $[X]$ [1].

Set pair analysis(SPA) is a type of system theory and method to deal with uncertainty with a connection degree proposed by Keqin Zhao in 1989, which is due to deal with fuzzy, random, intermediate and incomplete information centrally. It is characterized it admits objective recognition of uncertainty of a objective, and makes certainty-uncertainty characters be an identity-difference-opposite (IDO) system to do dialectical analysis and mathematical treatment.

Set pair analysis is an effective method to deal with certain-uncertain systems. The so-called set pair [13, 14], that is, a pair with a certain link between the two sets. The basic idea of set pair is to carry on the analysis under a certain issue characters to pairs, and establish two sets' IDO connection degree expression $\mu = a + bi + cj$ in the specific problems, there a is called the identity degree, b is called the difference degree, c is called opposite degree, and satisfies $a + b + c = 1$.

3   The Advancement of Granularity Pair

3.1   The Definition of Granularity Pair

Granularity pair connects the granular computing and the set pair analysis, is the definition of granularity to set pair. The specific definitions are as follows.

Definition 1. (granularity pair) Suppose object set X and attribute set Y constitute a set pair $H = (X, Y)$, R is the equivalent relation on $H = (X, Y)$, we call set pair $H = (X, Y)$ as a granularity pair on equivalent relation R.

Definition 2. (connection degree) In a specific information system, analyze the linkages of set pair $H = (X, Y)$ under the equivalent relation R. Suppose the base number of object sets is $| X |= m$, the base number of the attribute sets is $| Y |= n$, then the base number of the granularity pair is $| H |= mn = N$ composited by X and Y.

When the object has the properties definitely, make the pairing $S(X, Y)$, the identity degree is $\dfrac{| S |}{N}$.

When the object does not have the properties definitely, make the pairing $P(X, Y)$, the opposite degree is $\dfrac{| P |}{N}$.

When the objects and attributes have no clear relationship, make the pairing $F(X, Y)$, the difference degree is $\dfrac{| F |}{N}$, and $| F |= N - | S | - | P |$.

There $S(X, Y), P(X, Y), F(X, Y) \subseteq H(X, Y)$.

Then the connection degree of granularity pair is

$$\mu = \frac{| S |}{N} + \frac{| F |}{N} i + \frac{| P |}{N} j \tag{4}$$

3.2   The Properties of the Granularity Pair

Granularity pair integrates granularity and set pair, which inherits the characteristics each other, and produces a number of its own natures. T structure of connection degree μ makes things shape continuously and have a dynamic nature; When it reaches the limit state, shows the concept lattice form in data mining; and on the link of fuzzy clustering and granularity pair , it receives its similarity also.

1) Dynamic

The instability of bi makes the whole system is in a precarious state. When part of b tends to a, the certainty of system increases, the base number of the certain granularity increases correspond. Then the system is close to a center, layers are upgraded. The higher the same degree, the higher the level.

2) Limits

When the identity degree is 1 of granular pair, it achieves the limit state. Then, $H = (X,Y)$ is changed into $R(O,D)$, there O presents extension, D presents intension, that is the concept lattice. This is a special form of granular pair.

3) Similarity

Similarity is a right inherent of set pair, a fuzzy similarity relation about granularity pair connection degree can be gotten by the use of a particular function. Then use the distance function in quotient space to realize the hierarchy of the granularity pair H (object set, attribute set).

This paper will be aimed at similarity to hierarchy. Be different from the traditional transfer closure method, this paper uses a conclusion in fuzzy quotient space--distance function, which makes the layers effective. The smaller the distance, the lower level of granularity.

4 Similar Hierarchical Algorithm

4.1 Algorithm Idea

The paper will use the similarity of granularity with the help of IDO coefficient method in SPA, get a fuzzy similar matrix, and then have a quotient space with distance. The quotient space is a hierarchical structure.

4.2 Algorithm Design

Step 1 Establish the specific granularity pair (m,n), m presents object, n presents property;

Step 2 Analyzing and combining with the actual situation to establish a information system with the granularity pair connection vectors;

Step 3 The weights are different because of the different importance of various attributes to individuals, suppose $\omega = (\omega_1, \omega_2, \cdots, \omega_n)$ and $\sum_{i=1}^{n} \omega_i = 1$, then the connection degree expression of granularity pair made up individuals and attributes is:

$$u_k = a_k + b_k i + c_k j = \sum_{i=1}^{n} \omega_i u_k^t \tag{5}$$

$$k = 1, 2, \cdots, n$$

Step 4 Use IDO coefficient method, get a fuzzy similar matrix

$$\rho(i,j) = \begin{cases} \dfrac{\max(|a_i - a_j|, |b_i - b_j|, |c_i - c_j|)}{\sqrt{|a_i - a_j|^2 + |b_i - b_j|^2 + |c_i - c_j|^2}} & i \neq j \\ 1 & i = j \end{cases} \tag{6}$$

$$i = 1,2,\cdots,n$$
$$j = 1,2,\cdots,m$$

And the fuzzy similar matrix elements are

$$r_{ij} = \rho(i,j) = \rho(j,i) = r_{ji} \tag{7}$$

Step 5 Based on the fuzzy quotient space theory , hierarchical structure $\{X(\lambda)\}$ is obtained on X by distance

$$d_{ij} = 1 - r_{ij} \tag{8}$$

When all the objects belong to the same set, the hierarchy ends.

5 Application

Table 1 is a knowledge representation system of cars. Establish the granularity pair with (object, attribute), such as (2 car, white) to be a granularity pair.

Table 1. A knowledge representation system of cars

U	attributes				
	a	b	c	d	e
cars	interior design	model	color	speed	accelerated performance
1	moderate	diesel	silver	middle	poor
2	crowd	gasoline	white	high	excellent
3	spacious	diesel	black	high	good
4	moderate	gasoline	black	middle	excellent
5	moderate	diesel	silver	low	good
6	spacious	propane	black	high	good
7	spacious	gasoline	white	high	excellent
8	crowd	gasoline	white	low	good

Make the reference standard according to (spacious, propane, black, high, excellent), suppose large = 3, moderate = 2, crowd = 1, propane = 5, gasoline = 3, diesel = 1, black = 3, silver = 2 , white = 1, high = 3, middle = 2, low = 1, excellent = 5, good = 4, poor = 1, calculate the connection degree of (auto, property), establish the information system with the granularity pair connection vectors(Table 2).

Table 2. Connected vectors' information system of the granularity pair (auto, property)

A	interior design	model	color	speed	accelerated performance
Cars	w(a)=0.18	w(b)=0.2	w(c)=0.1	w(d)=0.22	w(e)=0.3
1	(2/3,1/6,1/6)	(1/5,1/8,27/40)	(2/3,1/6,1/6)	(1/2,1/3,1/6)	(1/5,1/5,3/5)
2	(1/3,1/6,1/2)	(3/5,1/6,7/30)	(1/3,1/6,1/2)	(1,0,0)	(1,0,0)
3	(1,0,0)	(1/5,1/4,11/20)	(1,0,0)	(1,0,0)	(4/5,1/8,3/40)
4	(2/3,1/5,2/15)	(3/5,1/9,13/45)	(1,0,0)	(1/2,1/6,1/3)	(1,0,0)
5	(2/3,1/20,17/60)	(1/5,1/7,23/35)	(2/3,1/20,17/60)	(1/4,2/15,37/60)	(4/5,1/6,1/30)
6	(1,0,0)	(1,0,0)	(1,0,0)	(1,0,0)	(4/5,1/40,7/40)
7	(1,0,0)	(3/5,1/40,3/8)	(1/3,1/6,1/2)	(1,0,0)	(1,0,0)
8	(1/3,1/6,1/2)	(3/5,1/8,11/40)	(1/3,1/6,1/2)	(1/4,1/3,5/12)	(4/5,3/40,1/8)

Set the weight $\omega = (0.18, 0.2, 0.1, 0.22, 0.3)$ according to consumer preferences for cars of various attributes, use the method of Step 3, easy to get

$$u_1 = 0.39 + 0.21i + 0.4j,$$
$$u_2 = 0.68 + 0.16i + 0.16j,$$
$$u_3 = 0.78 + 0.0875i + 0.1325j,$$
$$u_4 = 0.7 + 0.01i + 0.29j,$$
$$u_5 = 0.455 + 0.0122i + 0.423j,$$
$$u_6 = 0.94 + 0.0075i + 0.0525j,$$
$$u_7 = 0.85 + 0.025i + 0.125j,$$
$$u_8 = 0.505 + 0.102i + 0.393j.$$

According to Step4, just use a small program y=max(abs(X-Y))/norm(X-Y) in fact, you can get the fuzzy similar matrix as follows:

$$
\begin{pmatrix}
1 & & & & & & & \\
0.76 & 1 & & & & & & \\
0.80 & 0.79 & 1 & & & & & \\
0.81 & 0.75 & 0.82 & 1 & & & & \\
0.79 & 0.76 & 0.73 & 0.82 & 1 & & & \\
0.81 & 0.81 & 0.82 & 0.71 & 0.78 & 1 & & \\
0.81 & 0.77 & 0.74 & 0.74 & 0.78 & 0.77 & 1 & \\
0.73 & 0.78 & 0.73 & 0.82 & 0.81 & 0.78 & 0.78 & 1
\end{pmatrix}
$$

Use distance $d_{ij} = 1 - r_{ij}$, it is easy to have

$$X(0) = \{1,2,\cdots,8\},$$

$$X(0.18) = \{\{1\},\{2\},\{7\},\{3,4,5,6,8\}\},$$

$$X(0.19) = \{\{1,2,\cdots,8\}\},$$

$$X(1) = \{\{1,2,\cdots,8\}\},$$

Get the quotient space

$$X(0) < X(0.18) < X(0.19) = X(1)$$

Then the similar hierarchical algorithm is completed with the granularity pair.

6 Conclusion

In fact, the fuzzy equivalent relation can get not only with seeking quotient space, but also can use the traditional transitive closure method to achieve the fuzzy equivalent matrix. In comparison, the former has a smaller calculation and gets the layered structure directly. From this point, the hierarchical structure can make the computation time less than fuzzy equivalent relations.

References

1. Zhang, B., Zhang, L.: Problem Solving Theory and Application. Tsinghua University Press, Beijing (1990)
2. Liu, B., Tan, Y.: Application and fuzzy clustering analysis method based on SPA. Statistics and Decision (2006)
3. Ye, F.: Applications and research in the hierarchical fuzzy control based on granular computing of fuzzy sets. Guangdong University Master's degree thesis (2008)
4. Homenda, W.: Optical music recognition: the case of granular computing, pp. 151–160. Granular computing Physica-Verlag GmbH, Germany (2001)
5. Zadeh, L.A.: Fuzzy Logic = Computing with Words. On Fuzzy Systems 2, 103–111 (1996)
6. Yao, Y.Y., Zhao, Y.: Attribute reduction in decision-theoretic rough set models. Information Sciences 178(17), 3356–3373
7. Li, H.X., Yao, Y.Y., Zhou, X.Z., Huang, B.: Two-Phase Rule Induction from Incomplete Data. In: Wang, G., Li, T., Grzymala-Busse, J.W., Miao, D., Skowron, A., Yao, Y. (eds.) RSKT 2008. LNCS (LNAI), vol. 5009, pp. 47–54. Springer, Heidelberg (2008)
8. Pawlak, Z.: Rough sets. Intl. Journal of Computer and Information Science. 11, 341–356 (1982)
9. Wang, G.Y., Zhang, Q.H.: Uncertainty of rough sets in different knowledge granularities. Chinese Journal of Computers 31(9), 1588–1598 (2008)
10. Liu, Q.: Rough Sets and Rough Reasoning. Science Press, Beijing (2001)

11. Zhang, L., Zhang, B.: Fuzzy quotient space theory (Fuzzy Granular Computing). Journal of Software 14(4), 770–776 (2003)
12. Zhang, B., Zhang, L.: Theory and applications of problem solving. Elsevier Science Publishers B.V, North-Holland (1992)
13. Zhao, K.: Set Pair Analysis and Its Application. Zhejiang Science Technology Press, Hangzhou (2000)
14. Bing, Z., Hongfang, W., et al.: Analysis of relation between flood peak and volume based on set pair. Journal of Sichuan University: Engineering Science Editon 39(3), 29–33 (2007)

The Research and Application of Parallel Generalized Minimal Residual Algorithm Based on Grid MPI Parallel Running Framework

Yun Tang[1], Junsong Luo[1], and Yajuan Hao[2]

[1] College of Information Engineering, Chengdu University of Technology,
Chengdu, China, 610000
[2] College of Science, Yanshan University,
Qinhuangdao, China, 066004
ty@cdut.edu.cn

Abstract. Through the research of MPI's theory and features, the G-MPI parallel program design and running framework have been constructed. Afterwards the design and communication cost of GMRES (m) Algorithm has been studied, so one parallel numerical algorithm, with coarse granularity and low communication cost which is applied to solving the large elastic problems by using boundary element method, has been presented. Through the comparison with the result of the traditional parallel GMRES (m) in MPI, the new parallel algorithm in G-MPI has comparatively higher calculation accuracy and calculation efficiency.

Keywords: G-MPI, Parallel Running Framework, Boundary Element, GMRES (m) Algorithm, Parallel Algorithm, Communication Cost.

1 Introduction

In recent decades, large-scale parallel machines has a rapid development, because of various reasons, developers provide the necessary support to users, such as their proprietary messaging packages NC EUI PVM etc, it has a very superior performance on a specific platform, but the view from the application, transplant is poor. On the meeting of Supercomputing'92, the MPI forum which based on establish a platform for standard messaging had set up in November 1992, the forum not only includes developer of PVM, Express etc and the user of parallel programs, also drew representatives from many well-known computer manufacturers. Forum announced the MPI standard in May 1994. MPI is a widely used standard and base on developed for the messaging, it provides portable, efficient and flexible standards for messaging, and aroused the concern of a large number of research workers, especially the design of the parallel programming and running framework of MPI became a focus. This paper, which base on the Grid, research the MPI parallel programming [1-4] , and build a G-MPI operating framework ,finally, parallel Gmres (m) algorithm is studied and base on grid-based G-MPI environment ,it applied to boundary element calculations.

R. Zhu et al. (Eds.): ICICA 2010, LNCS 6377, pp. 379–386, 2010.

2   The Principles and Characteristics of MPI

MPI is a function library, rather than a language, it is a message passing model, its ultimate aim that is serve the inter-process communication. MPI as a development platform of parallel library, it provides facilities to write and run programs for users. Because MPI is built based on message passing system, it has a broad application of space in architecture to distributed Memory Parallel Machines; it can be applied to a variety of homogeneous and heterogeneous network platform. The programming language can be divided into Fortran77∕90 and C∕C++. In the language of Fortran77∕90 and C∕C++, the MPI function can be called, it as parallel programming environments of message passing model, MPI parallel program requires division of tasks, and start the implementation of multiple processes at the same time, the various processes achieve messaging transfer by MPI library functions. Compared with other parallel programming environment, MPI remarkable features are:

(1) Strong transplantable, and can support both homogeneous and heterogeneous parallel computing;

(2)Strong flexible, and allow increase or decrease of the node to parallel structure;

(3) Support the way of point and collective communication

(4) On the C language and Fortran language support, in order that it can meet the needs of the various large-scale scientific and engineering computing.

Then, to MPI as parallel applications program of a public message passing and connect $t = 1$ which can refuse to make any changes to the transplant to different types and models parallel machines, and can normally running, or move to grid environment.

3   G-MPI Library Base on Grid

G-MPI parallel design library provides MPI programming interface for programmers of parallel program in G-MPI framework. Users can easily call these interfaces in program, Program written language can be C or C + +.The MPI standard proposes interface explanation and the binding mode of C language. In order to the existing MPI programs move to the grid platform, the various interface of functions and standards of G-MPI require to maintain consistency. The design principle of G-MPI library is fully compatible with MPI-1.1 standard, the aim is:

(1) For programmers of having MPI parallel programming experience, he does not learn and directly write the MPI parallel program of the grid environment;

(2) For the current parallel program of MPI by C/C, it changes without too many and can normally running to move under grid environment.

3.1   The Overall Designed Structure of G-MPI Library

For MPI's design, two issues be concerned, the first one is manage the parallel process of the nodes by system services; the second is implementation of MPI library, the staff of parallel programming called library function to complete messag –passing, the actual communication working is accomplished by another layer. Naturally, G-MPI library design was divided into two layers.

MPI-API layer provides MPI programming interface for programmers of parallel program; programmers can directly call the interface to complete the message transmission and the transmission, etc. The design form of MPI-API layer has a certain influence to the performance of MPI, for example, news organizations and accession, if the way of index is created with a pointer, the access memory operations may required several times on message inquiry process , the spending will be relatively large.

MPI communication service layer is used to implement some features associated with data communications, these are included that other communication-related functions for message buffer in this layer. The design of MPI service layer has also a relatively large impact on the overall performance of the MPI, because this layer involves the establishment of communication lines, communication processing and communication error processing, the cost of communication agreement should also consider.

3.2 The Implementation of G-MPI Library

3.2.1 The Status of Message Passing
Currently, the MPI G-MPI framework is still very simple to the achieve way of MPI standard, some improve and optimize work will done. MPI has an important data structure- MPI Status, after calling MPI communication interface, various states and errors can be checked by MPI Status.

3.2.2 The Status of Message Passing
According to the MPI standard, MPI send is divided into two types about blocking and non-blocking. When non-blocking sends message, message is stored in the buffer at first, function calling immediately returns and not has to wait the implementation before sending successful. Nonblocking send calling which return a request object, message is sent after the contents of this object need to be detected. General, after the non-blocking send calling, procedures need to check the send operation has completed or not. MPI programs may send multiple messages, these request objects need to managed.

In the design of G-MPI parallel program running, request compose into several domains, type is different domains with message_type, message is used to send or receive, dust express message destination; source express source address; tag domain is used to identify and distinguish multiple messages; completed mark express whether complete the operation of message or not; mode express communication mode, it is used to distinguish the standard communication, ready communication and synchronous communication; message points to the location of information, it is application of the user or system buffer address [5, 6, 7].

The way is that G-MPI library deals with non-blocking request: a transceiver request object is established, and then this object joined in the appropriate queue. Non-blocking communication calling completed, queue processing proceed as well as MPI code. Communication request for processing, sending and receiving is completed in the queue processing function.

3.2.3 The Basic Operation of Design G-MPI
The returning status of G-MPI calling:

MPI SUCCESS: Function calls succeed, the error don't occur;
MPI ERR COMM: This value represents invalid communicator;

MPI ERR COUNT: Invalid count argument;

MPI ERR TYPE: Invalid parameter data type.

Sending and receiving operation of G-MPI [8]

For sending and receiving messages, Users calls the MPI, but the actual message is sent and received which is completed the communication service layer by the G-MPI library. Send and receive operation is the most complicated and difficult operation in the G-MPI library, its complexity is a wide kinds of sending and receiving provisions in the MPI standards, the differences vary from type to type, and the way organization of communication buffer and the expending of communication operating has a major impact in G-MPI framework, these will give G-MPI library to bring some difficulties. Following, it is a description for the typical sending and receiving functions.

(1) Non-blocking send;

(2) Blocking send: blocking communication can be completed by the non-blocking communication, difference lies in blocking communication call haven't return until communications request is disposed, the actual send or receive operation that is completed;

(3) Non-blocking receive: Non-blocking messages received regardless of whether the desired reached, Calling will immediately return, user program can perform non-blocking to call program code. The way of G-MPI's achieve which is the request object of the non-blocking request insert into receive queue, and check to receive the message queue.

(4) Blocking receive: compared to non-blocking receive, blocking receive is relatively simple to achieve. When user program calls the blocking receive function, communication service layer need to check whether the desired message has arrived in the receiving message queue, if it arrives and directly transmitted to the user, the calling returns; if the message does not arrive, you need to wait until the required information has been received, then the calling return.

Cluster operation: Cluster operations show that all must participate in the parallel sub-tasks such as sending and receiving operations, these functions include the MPI Bcast (), MPI Gather () and so on.

4   The Research of Parallel GMRES (m) Algorithm Based on Grid MPI Parallel Environment

4.1   The Analysis of GMRES (m) Parallel Algorithm

GMRES (m) algorithm major include: computing vector inner product, matrix and vector multiplication, matrix and matrix multiplication, using QR decomposition to solve least squares problems and so on. The algorithm is implemented by message passing programming model for distributed memory parallel systems, each processor has local storage, so every local storage stored row matrix and the components of a vector. Communications requirements by Parallel arising mainly stem from matrix and vector multiplication, matrix and matrix multiplication, iterative process of using QR decomposition to solve least squares problems. Each component is calculated for each process in parallel, so it needs to process global operations for process group, it need to collect the component of the new vector before every new iteration process, and enable each process to get new vector, so it need to process operation of data aggregation communication for many-to-many, after fulfillment iteration, and need to process operation of data aggregation communication for one-to-many in the master-slave mode, in order to collect the solution vectors of final iteration. In the two-dimensional grid connection networks and Wormhole-type communication mode, one to many communication time complexity is $O(n \log_2 P)$.

4.2 The Analysis Parallel Communication for G-MPI Environment

Cluster communication is a communication operations to participation of all processes together. Compared with point to point communications(SEND⫠RECV),matching requirements the sender and receiver of data types is more strict, and is more efficient, for the various processes, coordination and communication of receive and send requests is managed by the internal of the cluster communication operations. G-MPI offers a rich cluster communication function, and the operation can be divided into four categories:

(1) Communication operations is one to many, the root process sends the same data to all processes or distribute data to all processes in different. Such as G-MPI-BCAST() and G-MPI-SCATTER( ).

(2) Communication operations are many to one, root process receive data from all the process. Such as G-MPI-GATHER( ).

(3) Communication operations is many to many, any process receive data from any process for process group, or every process distribute data to each process and to receive data from each process. Such as G-MPI-ALLGATHER() and G-MPI-ALLTOALL( ).

(4) All process conduct global data computation, results of operation are returned to the root process or all processes. Such as G-MPI-REDUCE( ) of many to one and G-MPI-ALLREDUCE( ) of many to many.

Figure 1 show that several operations are supported G-MPI cluster communication, a, b, c, respectively express the process 0,1,2,in the figure.

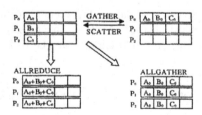

Fig. 1. Communication operation

4.3 Parallel GMRES(m) Algorithm and Communication

Considering the problem of GMRES (m) algorithm realization on parallel clusters, it must have been started from several designed parallel algorithms, and then parallel

GMRES (m) algorithm of fitting cluster system is constructed. For large linear problem, They are the most part of GMRES (m) algorithm to calculate, including the establishment of precondition, preconditioned computation and decomposition to solve least squares problem with QR, so parallel working is necessary, the parallel GMRES (m) algorithm is the three parts of the organic combination of parallel.

On the basis of the parallel analysis, GMRES (m) parallel algorithm achieved based on application of MPI Collective Communication's broadcast operations, data gathering operation and the global data-sharing computing operation programming, major components achieve as following [9]:

(1) In the process of orthogonal for the formation of V and H matrix, it calls parallel inner product algorithms and parallel matrix-vector product algorithm and so on;

(2) In the course of solving least squares problems, it will call the parallel QR decomposition, parallel matrix-vector and matrix multiplication algorithm, etc. Order $A = (A_1^T, A_2^T, \cdots, A_P^T)^T$, $b = (f_1^T, f_2^T, \cdots, f_P^T)^T$, the type is the block form of equations, each block can be distributed to different processors, and use parallel GMRES (m) algorithm for solving linear equations, parallel iterative solution complete. In order to quickly get the convergence solution, it re-formed matrix in each iteration $\overline{H}_k$, and its order is increasing. In the calculation, the following questions should also be paid attention:

1) When calculating f_k with the $Q_k R_k$ decomposition of $\overline{H}_k$ (plane rotation transformation); this transformation acts on βe_1 can be g_k, to determine whether x_k meet the precision requirements, if met ,it can quickly get back on behalf of solving y_k, and then calculate x_k.

2) The approximate solution meet: $n \to \infty$, $\| r_m \| < \xi$ (to ensure accuracy), $\max \| v_i \| \le \alpha$ (to ensure orthogonally of v_i), $\max \| \| r_k \| - \| r_i \| \| \le \beta$ (to ensure stability of the process).

On the pseudo code of algorithm, global product communications and computing operations were completed by calling the G-MPI message passing library functions about G-MPI-ALLREDUC(),G-MPI-ALLGATHERV() and G-MPI-GATHERV() .Main statement is:

i) Message send statement
G-MPI_SEND(BUF, COUNT, DATATYPE, DEST, TAG, COMM, IERROR)
<type> BUF(*)
INTEGER COUNT, DATATYPE, DEST, TAG, COMM, IERROR

The call will be sent in the count buffer data type data type of the data were sent to the destination process, logo of purpose process is dust in the communications domain, the message marked is the tag, using this logo which can distinguish between them, for sending this message and purpose of this process, send messages to the same process.

ii) Message received statement
G-MPI_RECV(BUF, COUNT, DATATYPE, SOURCE, TAG, COMM, STATUS, IERROR)
<type> BUF(*)
INTEGER COUNT, DATATYPE, SOURCE, TAG, COMM, STATUS (G-MPI_STATUS_SIZE), IERROR

The call receive messages from the specified source process , the data type of the message consistent data type with tag, and receiving process of the specified data type and the tag line, the received message contains the number of data elements can not exceed a maximum count.

5 Calculating Examples

When the boundary element method solve elasticity problems, the object's boundary surface need to determined at first, then separated into a number of quadrilateral elements linear units or other types units, and the unit is given nodes and node coordinates. Element node number is counterclockwise, and the outer unit vector point the outside boundary. According to the known boundary conditions of force and displacement, determine the boundary conditions of nodes and elements. Then enter the iterative solution, methods used in parallel GMRES (m) algorithm. Eventually, it constructs a new approximate solution. If the approximate solution meets the accuracy requirements, iteration stop, otherwise, to get the approximate solution for the early solution continue iteration, until we set up precision [10].

With a single elastic empty body A (20m×20m×2.5m, 3m×2.5m), the calculation model of the fixed side by the pull. A object's elastic modulus $E = 210GPa$, Poisson's ratio is $v = 0.3$, pressure of uniform load $P = 10^4 MPa$.

In parallel computing GMRES (m), $m = 20$, $P = 8$ and the error were:

RK1=2.37868678562411454E-005.
RK2=-6.125687455632444E-004.

When RK=1.000000087924568E-006, it stops to calculate, under Parallel MPI environment GMRES (m) algorithm, the total computing time for solving boundary element is 7h25m43s9 ms, in this paper, under Parallel G-MPI environment GMRES (m) algorithm, the total computing time for solving boundary element is:6h0m6s13ms.

6 Conclusion

On the base of parallel computing and traditional boundary element method, in the boundary element method for solving the process, the idea of parallel algorithm is introduced, the G-MPI parallel program design and running framework have been constructed, thus the parallel GMRES (m) algorithm was designed based on the study, updated the parallel Gmres(m) algorithm based on traditional MPI, the new form of calculation of the parallel boundary element method is established, then a single elastomer hole as a model, combined with the application of GMRES (m) algorithm in Boundary Element, the calculation process is given. Numerical results show that the boundary element method in the G-MPI-based parallel GMRES (m) algorithm, which has the higher the speedup, computational efficiency and accuracy and stability.

References

1. Du, Z.H.: High Performance Computing of Parallel Programming. Tsinghua University Press, Beijing (2001)
2. Wang, C.H., Zhao, C., Xu, X.G.: Distributed Parallel Computing Environment. Computer Science 30(1), 25–26 (2003)
3. Chen, G.L.: Parallel Algorithm Design and Analysis. Science and Technology Press, Beijng (1993)
4. Bian, X.F.: Message passing parallel programming environment. Fujian PC 6, 28–29 (2003)
5. Yang, A.M., Chen, Y.M.: MPI parallel programming environment and the research of program design. Hebei Institute of Technology 3, 41–44 (2005)
6. Zhang, Y.J.: The design and implementation based on MPI parallel program running framework. Master Thesis of Beijing University of Posts and Telecommunications (2008)
7. MPI-2: Extension to the Message Passing Interface, http://www.mpi-forum.org
8. http://www.lam-mpi.org
9. Yang, A.M., Liu, C.F.: The Research and Application of the Parallel Algorithm for QR Decomposition of Matrix. In: Dcabse 2006 Proceedings, pp. 29–32 (2006)
10. Yu, C.X.: The Krylov subspace-based FMM IGMRES (m) the new algorithm and its application. Technology of Hebei University 9, 448–455 (2006)

A New Family of Methods for Nonlinear Equations*

Yuxin Zhang, Hengfei Ding**, Wansheng He, and Xiaoya Yang

School of Mathematics and Statistics, Tianshui Normal University, Tianshui 741001,
P.R. China
dinghf05@163.com

Abstract. In this paper, a family of seventh-order iterative methods
for solving nonlinear equation is presented and analyzed. This family
of seventh-order methods contains the Bi's seventh-order methods and
many other seventh-order iterative methods as special cases. In terms of
computational cost, per iteration the new methods require three evaluations of the function and one evaluation of its first derivative. Therefore
their efficiency index is 1.627. The convergence of this family of methods
is analyzed to establish its seventh-order convergence.

Keywords: Non-linear equations; Seventh-order iterative methods; Efficiency index; Order of convergence; Numerical results.

1 Introduction

One of the most important and challenging problems in scientific and engineering
applications is to find the solutions of the nonlinear equations. The boundary
value problems appearing in Kinetic theory of gases, elasticity and other applied
areas are reduced to solving these equations. Many optimization problems also
lead to such equations. With the advancements in computer H/W and S/W, this
problem has gained added importance.

This paper is concerned with the iterative methods for finding a simple root
r, i.e., $f(r) = 0$ and $f'(r) \neq 0$ of $f(x) = 0$, where $f : I \subset R \to R$, be the continuously differentiable real function. Newton's method is the well-known iterative
method for finding r, which converges quadratically in some neighborhood of r
[1]. It is given by

$$x_{n+1} = x_n - \frac{f(x_n)}{f'(x_n)}, \quad n = 0, 1, 2 \cdots.$$

To improve the local order of convergence, some fourth-order iterative methods
have been proposed and analyzed for solving nonlinear equations which improve
Newton's method in a number of ways, see [2-5] and the references therein. These

* The project Supported by 'QingLan' Talent Engineering Funds and SRF(TSA0928)
by Tianshui Normal University.
** Corresponding author.

R. Zhu et al. (Eds.): ICICA 2010, LNCS 6377, pp. 387–394, 2010.
© Springer-Verlag Berlin Heidelberg 2010

methods can also be viewed as obtained by taking an appropriate approximation to $f'(w_n)$ in the following iteration scheme:

$$x_{n+1} = w_n - \frac{f(w_n)}{f'(w_n)}, \quad n = 0, 1, 2 \cdots, \tag{1}$$

where $w_n = \phi(x_n)$, $\phi(x)$ is usually an iteration function such as the Newton iteration function. In [2], Chun approximate $f'(w_n)$ given in (1) as follows:

$$f'(w_n) = f'(x_n)h(u_n), \tag{2}$$

where $u_n = \frac{f(w_n)}{f(x_n)}$ and $h(t)$ is a real valued function. So that, the two-step iteration scheme presented by Chun is given by

$$\begin{cases} w_n &= x_n - \frac{f(x_n)}{f'(x_n)}, \\ x_{n+1} &= w_n - \frac{f(w_n)}{f'(x_n)h(u_n)}, \end{cases} \tag{3}$$

which contains the well-known King's fourth-order family [3] as a particular case. Recently, based on King's methods or Ostrowski's method, Grau et.al [6], Sharma et.al [7] and Chun et.al [8] developed some sixth-order iteration methods. Kou et.al [9] presented a family of variants of Ostrowskis method with seventh-order convergence. Next, in [10], Bi et.al proposed a new family of seventh-order methods for nonlinear equations. It is given by

$$\begin{cases} w_n = x_n - \frac{f(x_n)}{f'(x_n)}, \\ z_n = w_n - \frac{f(w_n)}{f'(x_n)} \frac{f(x_n) + \beta f(w_n)}{f(x_n) + (\beta - 2)f(w_n)}, \\ x_{n+1} = z_n - \frac{f(z_n)}{f[z_n, w_n] + f[z_n, x_n, x_n](z_n - w_n)}. \end{cases} \tag{4}$$

The aim of this paper is to develop a family of three-step seventh-order methods for solving nonlinear equation $f(x) = 0$ based on the Chun's fourth-order methods and Bi's seventh-order methods. This family of seventh-order methods contains Bi's seventh-order family and many other seventh-order iterative methods as special cases. Starting with a suitably chosen x_0, the new methods generate a sequence of iterates converging to the root. In terms of computational cost, per iteration the new methods require three evaluations of the function and one evaluation of its first derivative. Therefore their efficiency index equals to $\sqrt[4]{7} \approx 1.627$.

This paper is organized as follows. In section 2, a family of seventh-order iterative methods for solving single nonlinear equation is presented. In section 3, the convergence of this family of methods is analyzed to establish its seventh-order convergence. Section 4 gives some known methods and many other seventh-order iterative methods which are special cases of our seventh-order family. Conclusions are given in section 5.

2   Iterative Methods

In order to construct new methods, we need the knowledge of the divided difference. Let $f(x)$ be a function defined on I, where I is the smallest interval containing $k+1$ distinct nodes $x_0, x_1, ..., x_k$. The divided difference $f[x_0, x_1, \cdots, x_k]$ with kth-order is defined as follows [10,11]:

$$f[x_0] = f(x_0),$$
$$f[x_0, x_1] = \frac{f[x_1] - f[x_0]}{x_1 - x_0},$$
$$\cdots$$
$$f[x_0, x_1, ..., x_k] = \frac{f[x_1, x_2, ..., x_k] - f[x_0, x_1, ..., x_{k-1}]}{x_k - x_0}. \tag{5}$$

It is clear that the divided difference $f[x_0, x_1, ..., x_k]$ is a symmetric function of its arguments $x_0, x_1, ..., x_k$. Moreover if we assume that $f \in C^{k+1}(I_x)$, where I_x is the smallest interval containing nodes $x_0, x_1, ..., x_k$ and x, then

$$f[x_0, x_1, ..., x_k, x] = \frac{f^{k+1}(\xi)}{(k+1)!}, \tag{6}$$

for a suitable $\xi \in I_x$. In particular, if $x_0 = x_1 = \cdots = x_k = x$, then

$$f\underbrace{[x, x, \cdots, x, x]}_{k+2} = \frac{f^{k+1}(x)}{(k+1)!}. \tag{7}$$

Now, consider the three-step iterative method

$$\begin{cases} w_n = x_n - \frac{f(x_n)}{f'(x_n)}, \\ z_n = w_n - \frac{f(w_n)}{f'(x_n)h(u_n)}, \\ x_{n+1} = z_n - \frac{f(z_n)}{f'(z_n)}, \end{cases} \tag{8}$$

where $u_n = \frac{f(w_n)}{f(x_n)}$ and $h(t)$ is a real valued function.

Using Taylor expansion, $f(z_n)$ and $f'(z_n)$ in (8) can be approximated by

$$f(z_n) \approx f(w_n) + f'(w_n)(z_n - w_n) + \tfrac{1}{2}f''(w_n)(z_n - w_n)^2, \tag{9}$$

$$f'(z_n) \approx f'(w_n) + f''(w_n)(z_n - w_n). \tag{10}$$

Then

$$f'(z_n) \approx \frac{f(z_n) - f(w_n)}{z_n - w_n} + \tfrac{1}{2}f''(w_n)(z_n - w_n) = f[z_n, w_n] + \tfrac{1}{2}f''(w_n)(z_n - w_n). \tag{11}$$

In order to avoid the computation of the second derivative, we approximate $f''(w_n)$ as follows

$$f''(w_n) \approx 2f[z_n, x_n, x_n] = 2\frac{(f[z_n, x_n] - f'(x_n))}{z_n - x_n}, \tag{12}$$

where z_n and x_n are sufficiently close to w_n when n is a sufficiently big integer. So, from (11) and (12), we get

$$f'(z_n) \approx f[z_n, w_n] + f[z_n, x_n, x_n](z_n - w_n). \tag{13}$$

Replacing $f'(z_n)$ with the approximation in (13), we can construct a new family of methods by (8) and (13) as follows:

$$\begin{cases} w_n = x_n - \frac{f(x_n)}{f'(x_n)}, \\[2mm] z_n = w_n - \frac{f(w_n)}{f'(x_n)h(u_n)}, \\[2mm] x_{n+1} = z_n - \frac{f(z_n)}{\lambda}, \end{cases} \tag{14}$$

where $u_n = \frac{f(w_n)}{f(x_n)}$, $h(t)$ is a real valued function and $\lambda = f[z_n, w_n] + f[z_n, x_n, x_n]$ $(z_n - w_n)$.

3   Analysis of Convergence

In this section, we will prove that the new family of methods defined by (14) has seventh-order convergence. The following definition is used for the convergence of our methods.

Definition 3.1. Let $r \in R$, $x_n \in R$, $n = 0, 1, 2 \cdots$. Then the sequence $\{x_n\}$ is said to converge to r if

$$\lim_{n \to \infty} |x_n - r| = 0.$$

If in addition, there exists a constant $c \geq 0$, an integer $n_0 \geq 0$ and $p \geq 0$ such that for all $n > n_0$

$$|x_{n+1} - r| \leq c|x_n - r|^p,$$

then $\{x_n\}$ is said to converge to r with order at least p. If $p = 2$ or 3, the convergence is said to be quadratic or cubic, respectively.

When $e_n = x_n - r$ be the error at the nth iterate, the relation

$$e_{n+1} = ce_n^p + O(e_n^{p+1})$$

is called the error equation. The value of p is called the order of this method.

Theorem 3.2. *Let $r \in I$ be a simple zero of sufficiently differentiable function $f : I \subset R \to R$ for an open interval I and h any function with $h(0) = 1$, $h'(0) = -2$ and $|h''(0)| < \infty$. If x_0 is sufficiently close to r, then the three-step iterative method defined by (14) is of seventh-order, and satisfies the error equation*

$$e_{n+1} = c_3 c_2^2 [(2 + h''(0))c_2^2 - 2c_3]e_n^7 + O(e_n^8),$$

where $c_k = \frac{1}{k!}\frac{f^{(k)}(r)}{f'(r)}$, $k = 1, 2, \dots$ and $e_n = x_n - r$.

Proof. Let r be a simple zero of f and h a function with $h(0) = 1$, $h'(0) = -2$ and $|h''(0)| < \infty$. We let $u_n = \frac{f(w_n)}{f(x_n)}$. Then by expanding $f(x_n)$ and $f'(x_n)$ about r, we have

$$f(x_n) = f'(r)[e_n + c_2 e_n^2 + c_3 e_n^3 + c_4 e_n^4 + c_5 e_n^5 + c_6 e_n^6 + \cdots], \tag{15}$$

and

$$f'(x_n) = f'(r)[1 + 2c_2 e_n + 3c_3 e_n^2 + 4c_4 e_n^3 + 5c_5 e_n^4 + 6c_6 e_n^5 + \cdots], \tag{16}$$

where $c_k = \frac{1}{k!}\frac{f^{(k)}(r)}{f'(r)}$, $k = 1, 2, \ldots$ and $e_n = x_n - r$. By a simple calculation, we get

$$\frac{f(x_n)}{f'(x_n)} = e_n - c_2 e_n^2 + 2(c_2^2 - c_3)e_n^3 + (7c_2 c_3 - 4c_2^3 - 3c_4)e_n^4 + \tag{17}$$
$$(8c_2^4 - 20c_3 c_2^2 + 6c_3^2 + 10c_2 c_4 - 4c_5)e_n^5 + \cdots,$$

so that

$$w_n = r + c_2 e_n^2 - 2(c_2^2 - c_3)e_n^3 - (7c_2 c_3 - 4c_2^3 - 3c_4)e_n^4 - (8c_2^4 - \tag{18}$$
$$20c_3 c_2^2 + 6c_3^2 + 10c_2 c_4 - 4c_5)e_n^5 + \cdots.$$

Expanding $f(w_n)$ about r and from (18), we have

$$f(w_n) = f'(r)[c_2 e_n^2 + 2(c_3 - c_2^2)e_n^3 + (5c_2^3 - 7c_2 c_3 + 3c_4)e_n^4 + \tag{19}$$
$$(4c_5 - 12c_2^4 + 20c_3 c_2^2 - 6c_3^2 + 10c_2 c_4)e_n^5 + \cdots].$$

Dividing (19) by (15) gives us

$$u_n = \frac{f(w_n)}{f(x_n)} = c_2 e_n + (2c_3 - 3c_2^2)e_n^2 + O(e_n^3). \tag{20}$$

From the assumption on h and (20), we have

$$h(u_n) = h(0) + h'(0)u_n + \frac{h''(0)}{2}u_n^2 + O(u_n^3)$$
$$= 1 - 2c_2 e_n + [-4c_3 + (6 + \frac{h''(0)}{2})c_2^2]e_n^2 + O(e_n^3), \tag{21}$$

whence, we easily obtain from (16) and (21)

$$f'(x_n)h(u_n) = f'(r)[1 + ((2 + \frac{h''(0)}{2})c_2^2 - c_3)e_n^2 + O(e_n^3)]. \tag{22}$$

From (18), (19) and (22), we now have

$$z_n = w_n - \frac{f(w_n)}{f'(x_n)h(u_n)}$$
$$= r + c_2[(1 + \frac{h''(0)}{2})c_2^2 - c_3]e_n^4 + O(e_n^5). \tag{23}$$

Again expanding $f(z_n)$ about r and from (23), we have

$$f(z_n) = f'(r)[z_n - r + c_2(z_n - r)^2 + \cdots]$$
$$= f'(r)[c_2[(1 + \frac{h''(0)}{2})c_2^2 - c_3]e_n^4 + O(e_n^5)]. \tag{24}$$

So, from (15), (16), (18), (23) and (24), we get

$$f[z_n, x_n, x_n] = f'(r)[c_2 + 2c_3 e_n + 3c_4 e_n^2 + O(e_n^3)], \tag{25}$$

and

$$f[z_n, y_n]) = f'(r)[1 - 2c_2 c_3 e_n^3 + O(e_n^4)]. \tag{26}$$

Furthermore, from (18), (23), (25) and (26), we have

$$\begin{aligned}
\lambda &= f[z_n, y_n] + f[z_n, x_n, x_n](z_n - y_n) \\
&= f'(r)[1 + c_2^2 e_n^2 - 2c_2(c_2^2 - c_3)e_n^3 + O(e_n^4)].
\end{aligned} \tag{27}$$

Thus, from (14), (24) and (27), we obtain

$$e_{n+1} = z_n - r - \frac{f(z_n)}{\lambda} = c_3 c_2^2 [(2 + h''(0))c_2^2 - 2c_3]e_n^7 + O(e_n^8), \tag{28}$$

which shows that (14) is seventh-order convergent. This completes the proof.

4   Some Examples

Some known methods and many other seventh-order iterative methods are special cases of Theorem 3.2. In particular, the following methods are obtained as particular cases.

Example 4.1. For h given by

$$h(t) = \frac{1 + (\beta - 2)t}{1 + \beta t} = 1 - 2t + 2\beta t^2 - 2\beta^2 t^3 + 2\beta^3 t^4 + \cdots, \tag{29}$$

we obtain (4), that is, Bi's seventh-order family.

Example 4.2. For h given by

$$h(t) = 1 - 2t + \beta t^2 + \gamma t^3,$$

we obtain the new two-parameter seventh-order family

$$\begin{cases}
w_n = x_n - \frac{f(x_n)}{f'(x_n)}, \\
z_n = w_n - \frac{f(w_n)}{f'(x_n)[1 - 2\frac{f(w_n)}{f(x_n)} + \beta\frac{f^2(w_n)}{f^2(x_n)} + \gamma\frac{f^3(w_n)}{f^3(x_n)}]}\frac{f(x_n)}{f'(x_n)}, \\
x_{n+1} = z_n - \frac{f(z_n)}{\lambda}, \quad n = 0, 1, 2, \cdots,
\end{cases} \tag{30}$$

where $\lambda = f[z_n, y_n] + f[z_n, x_n, x_n](z_n - y_n)$.

Example 4.3. For h given by

$$h(t) = \frac{1}{1 + 2t} = 1 - 2t + 4t^2 - \cdots,$$

we obtain the new seventh-order method

$$
\begin{cases}
w_n = x_n - \dfrac{f(x_n)}{f'(x_n)}, \\[2mm]
z_n = x_n - [1 + \dfrac{f(w_n)}{f(x_n)} + 2\dfrac{f^2(w_n)}{f^2(x_n)}]\dfrac{f(x_n)}{f'(x_n)}, \\[2mm]
x_{n+1} = z_n - \dfrac{f(z_n)}{\lambda}, \quad n = 0, 1, 2, \cdots,
\end{cases}
\tag{31}
$$

where $\lambda = f[z_n, y_n] + f[z_n, x_n, x_n](z_n - y_n)$.

Example 4.4. For h given by

$$
h(t) = (1 + t)^{-2} = 1 - 2t + 3t^2 - 4t^3 + \cdots,
$$

we get the following new seventh-order method

$$
\begin{cases}
w_n = x_n - \dfrac{f(x_n)}{f'(x_n)}, \\[2mm]
z_n = x_n - [1 + \dfrac{f(w_n)}{f(x_n)} + 2\dfrac{f^2(w_n)}{f^2(x_n)} + \dfrac{f^3(w_n)}{f^3(x_n)}]\dfrac{f(x_n)}{f'(x_n)}, \\[2mm]
x_{n+1} = z_n - \dfrac{f(z_n)}{\lambda}, \quad n = 0, 1, 2, \cdots,
\end{cases}
\tag{32}
$$

where $\lambda = f[z_n, y_n] + f[z_n, x_n, x_n](z_n - y_n)$.

Now, we consider the efficiency index of the new methods. If we consider the definition of efficiency index as $\sqrt[w]{p}$ [2], where p is the order of the method and w is the number of functions evaluations required by the method (units of work per iteration), then the efficiency index of the present methods is $\sqrt[4]{7} \approx 1.627$.

5   Conclusions

In this paper, we have obtained a family of seventh-order iterative methods for solving nonlinear equation. This family of seventh-order methods contains Bi's seventh-order family and many other seventh-order iterative methods as special cases. From Theorem 3.2, we prove that the order of convergence of this family of methods is seven. Analysis of efficiency shows that these methods are preferable to King's method, Grau's method in high-precision computations.

References

1. Ostrowski, A.M.: Solution of Equations in Euclidean and Banach Space. Academic Press, New York (1973)
2. Chun, C.: Some fourth-order iterative methods for solving nonlinear equations. Appl. Math. Comput. 195, 454–459 (2008)
3. King, R.: A family of fourth-order methods for nonlinear equations. SIAM J. Numer. Anal. 10, 876–879 (1973)
4. Kou, J., Li, Y., Wang, X.: Fourth-order iterative methods free from second derivative. Appl. Math. Comput. 184, 880–885 (2007)

5. Noor, M.A., Ahmad, F.: Fourth-order convergent iterative method for nonlinear equation. Appl. Math. Comput. 182, 11149–11553 (2006)
6. Grau, M., Díaz-Barrero, J.L.: An improvement to Ostrowski root-finding method. Appl. Math. Comput. 173, 450–456 (2006)
7. Sharma, J.R., Guha, R.K.: A family of modified Ostrowski methods with accelerated sixth-order convergence. Appl. Math. Comput. 190, 111–115 (2007)
8. Chun, C., Ham, Y.M.: Some sixth-order variants of Ostrowski root-finding methods. Appl. Math. Comput. 193, 389–394 (2007)
9. Kou, J.S., Li, Y.T., Wang, X.H.: Some variants of Ostrowski's method with seventh-order convergence. J. Comput. Appl. Math. 209, 153–159 (2007)
10. Bi, W.H., Ren, H.M., Wu, Q.B.: New family of seventh-order methods for nonlinear equations. Appl. Math. Comput. 203(1), 408–412 (2008)
11. Quarteroni, A., Sacco, R., Saleri, F.: Numerical Mathematics. Springer, New York (2000)
12. Gautschi, W.: Numerical Analysis: An Introduction. Birkhäuser, Basel (1997)

A Filter Method to Solve Nonlinear Bilevel Programming Problems

Jean Bosco Etoa Etoa

Senior Lecturer, Department of economic and management sciences,
University of Yaounde II BP 15 Soa Cameroon
jbetoa_etoa@hotmail.com, jbetoa3101@rogers.com
Current address: Cameroon High Commission, 170 Clemow Avenue,
Ottawa (ON) K1S 2B4 Canada
Tel.: 1 613 238 7252; Fax: 1 613 238 4318

Abstract. Filter methods, introduced by Fletcher and Leyffer for nonlinear programming are characterized by the use of the dominance concept of multiobjective optimization, instead of a penalty parameter whose adjustment can be problematic. This paper presents a way to implement a filter based approach to solve a nonlinear bilevel programming problem in a linear approximations framework. The approach presented is based on the trust region idea from nonlinear programming, combined with filter-SQP algorithm, smooth and active sets techniques. The restoration procedure introduced in our algorithm consists in computing a rational solution.

Keywords: Filter methods, bilevel programming, nonlinear programming, trust region methods, approximation solution.

1 Introduction

Bilevel programming problems (BLP) are hierarchical optimization problems in the sense that their constraints are defined in part by a parametric optimization problem, describing practical situations: management (network facility location, credit allocation, and energy policy), economic planning (agricultural, tax policies, electric pricing, and bio-oil production), transportation planning and modeling, engineering design and optimal control (see [10]). Comprehensive overview of the historical development of BLP can be found in [5], [8], [9]. In this paper, the BLP considered takes the following form:

$$\min_{x,y} F(x,y)$$
$$s.t. \begin{cases} x \in X, \\ y \in \operatorname{argmin}_{y'} f(x,y') \\ s.t. \ \{g(x,y') \le 0, \ h(x,y') = 0, \end{cases} \tag{1.1}$$

where $X = \{x \in \mathbb{R}^{n_1} : G(x) \le 0\}$ is nonempty and compact, $G : \mathbb{R}^{n_1} \to \mathbb{R}$, a continuously differentiable function, $(x,y) \in \mathbb{R}^{n_1 \times n_2}$, $F : \mathbb{R}^{n_1 \times n_2} \to \mathbb{R}$, $f : \mathbb{R}^{n_1 \times n_2} \to \mathbb{R}$, $g : \mathbb{R}^{n_1 \times n_2} \to \mathbb{R}^p$

R. Zhu et al. (Eds.): ICICA 2010, LNCS 6377, pp. 395–406, 2010.

and $h: \mathbb{R}^{n_1 \times n_2} \to \mathbb{R}^q$ are twice continuously differentiable functions. The cases where the functions F, f, G, g and h are linear or convex have been addressed extensively; (see the survey papers [8]). For the cases where F, f, G, g and h are nonlinear and nonconvex, to date, only a few algorithms exist for the problem with any degree of success [1], [6]. Penalty methods constitute another important classes of algorithms for solving non linear BLP (see [5] for a review). Colson et al. [6] consider the approximation of nonlinear BLP by solvable programs of the same type, as well as a quadratic approximation of the lower-level objective function. The lower level problem is defined by

$$\min_y f(x,y)$$
$$s.t. \ \{g(x,y) \le 0, \ h(x,y) = 0. \tag{2.2}$$

Of course, the choice of a value of the upper level variable x will not violate the lower level feasible region. The lower level rational solution set for $x \in X$ is defined by $M(x) = \text{Argmin}_y \{f(x,y): y \in \Omega(x)\}$. In the formulation (1.1), when the functions F, f, G, g and h are linear or convex, several algorithms have been proposed computing an optimal solution using enumeration scheme (see [11]), and some recent methods exist also (see [1]). One of a solution approach to BLP is to transform the original two level problems into a single level problem by replacing the lower level problem with its Karush-Kuhn-Tucker (KKT) optimality conditions; based on this transformation, other methods containing branch--and--bound algorithms were developed (see [3], [9]). Local optimization procedures were also developed (see [2]).

Our algorithm uses the KKT conditions on the lower level problem (1.2) as constraints on the upper-level problem, thus turning the BLP into a nonconvex single mathematical problem, known as a mathematical program with equilibrium constraints (MPEC). In this work, we focus on how to implement filter based method in the context of nonlinear bilevel programming. The approach we propose is closed to a specialization to bilevel programs of the smoothing method introduced in [4], [12], [14] to solve MPECs.

The rest of the paper is organized as follows. In the next section, we present some basic assumptions. We use smooth techniques to reformulate the KKT formulation of BLP as an equivalent series of smooth nonlinear programs. Some important properties of the smoothed problems are investigated. In section 3, we describe our algorithm: we use a filter-SQP framework to solve the series of smooth nonlinear programs described in section 2. The convergence of our algorithm is then stated. Finally in section 4, few indications are given for computational experiences on a MATLAB environment.

2 Preliminaries

2.1 Formulations and Properties

We make the following blanket assumptions:

A1. The set of feasible solution Ω is nonempty and bounded.

A2. $\Omega(x) \ne \varnothing$ for all $x \in A$, where $A \subseteq X$ is an open set, and $\Omega(x)$ is uniformly compact on A, i.e. there exists an open set $B \subseteq \mathbb{R}^{n_2}$ such that for all $x \in A$, $\Omega(x) \subseteq B$.

A3. F and f are uniformly strongly monotone with respect to y on $A \times B$

Some simple consequences of these assumptions follow. The assumption A1 is stated in order for the problem (1.1) to be well posed. From assumptions A2 and A3, for every $x \in X$, there exists one and only one solution for the lower level program defined by (1.2). For fixed $x \in X$, the following regularity conditions for (1.2) will be used in the sequel for the lower level problem.

R1) The linear independence condition (LI) holds at y.

R2) the Strict Complementary Slackness condition (SCS) holds at y with respect to (λ, μ) if $\lambda_i > 0$ for every $i \in I(x,y) = \{i : g_i(x,y) = 0\}$.

R3) The Second--Order Sufficient Condition (SSOSC) holds at y with respect to (λ, μ) if $d^T \nabla_y^2 L(x,y,\lambda,\mu) d > 0$ for all $d \neq 0$ such that $d^T \nabla_y g_i(x,y) = 0$ if $u_i > 0$, $d^T \nabla_y h_j(x,y) = 0$, $j = 1,2,...,q$.

R4) The Mangasarian-Fromowitz constraint qualification (MFCQ) holds at y with respect to some KKT multipliers of the lower level problem (λ, μ).

Necessary conditions for y to solve (1.2) are that y is a feasible point and, if MFCQ holds, that then the set of directions

$$\{d : d^t f(x,y) < 0,\ d^t h_j(x,y) = 0,\ j = 1,2,...,q,\ d^t g_i(x,y) < 0,\ i \in I(x,y)\}$$

is empty. From assumption R1, for fixed $x \in X$, every solution y of the lower level program must satisfy the KKT conditions defined by

$$\begin{cases} \nabla_y L(x,y,\lambda,\mu) = 0, \\ g(x,y) + u = 0,\ h(x,y) = 0, \\ \lambda^t u = 0,\ u, \lambda \geq 0, \end{cases} \tag{2.1}$$

where $L(x,y,\lambda,\mu) = f(x,y) + \lambda^T g(x,y) + \mu^T h(x,y)$ is the Lagrangian associate with (1.2), $(\lambda, \mu) \in \mathbb{R}_+^p \times \mathbb{R}^q$ are multipliers of (1.2) which by assumption R1, are uniquely determined and bounded according to assumption R4. We have seen that, for each $x \in X$, we can associate the unique solution of the lower level program (1.2) and the corresponding multipliers. On the other hand, if (x,y,λ,μ) satisfies the KKT conditions (2.1), then y belongs to $M(x)$. Therefore, under our assumptions, the second level program and its KKT conditions are equivalent. It then follows from the definition that a necessary condition that (x^*, y^*) is a local solution to the BLP is that there exists $(\lambda^*, \mu^*) \in \mathbb{R}_+^p \times \mathbb{R}^q$ such that $(x^*, y^*, \lambda^*, \mu^*)$ is feasible to the following KKT formulation of problem (1.1) :

BLP$_{\text{KKT}}$

$$\min_{x,y,\lambda,\mu} F(x,y)$$

$$s.t. \begin{cases} \nabla_y L(x,y,\lambda,\mu) = 0,\ g(x,y) + u = 0, \\ h(x,y) = 0,\ \lambda^T u = 0,\ \lambda, u \geq 0,\ x \in X, \end{cases} \tag{2.2}$$

where $(\lambda,\mu)\in \mathbb{R}_+^p \times \mathbb{R}^q$. Considering problem BLP_{KKT} as an MPEC, if a feasible solution $w^* =(x^*,y^*,\lambda^*,\mu^*)$ of BLP_{KKT} satisfies the regularity conditions R1-R2, then w^* is a stationary point of BLP_{KKT} if and only if there exist MPECs multipliers $(\beta_G',\beta_L',\beta_g',\beta_h',\beta_{\lambda u}')\in \mathbb{R}^{n_1+n_2+p+q+p}$. We use in the sequel the following notation: let $V\in \mathbb{R}^n$, $J=\{1,2,...,n\}$. For $E\subseteq J$, V_E consists of components V_i, $i\in E$.

The following result is an application of the basic sensitivity theorem in [15]. It states that under nondegenerate conditions SCS, the local optimal solution of the lower level problem corresponding to a value of an upper level variable depends only locally and uniquely on the value of that upper level variable.

Proposition 1. Consider problem BLP and $\overline{x}\in X$; assume that KKT, SCS and MFCQ hold at $\overline{y}$ with multipliers $(\overline{\lambda},\overline{\mu})$ for (1.2) with, and the problem functions f, g and h are C^3 in a neighborhood of $(\overline{x},\overline{y})$. Let $I(\overline{x},\overline{y})$ be the active set of indexes of the set of constraints $\{g_i, i=1,2,...,p\}$ at $(\overline{x},\overline{y})$, and let $I^c(\overline{x},\overline{y})=\{1,2,..,p\}\setminus I(\overline{x},\overline{y})$ be the complementary of $I(\overline{x},\overline{y})$. Then,

a) $\overline{y}$ is a locally unique solution of (1.2) and b) the Jacobian $M(\overline{x})$ of the system of equations defined by

$$\left\{\nabla_y L(\overline{x},\overline{y},\overline{\lambda},\overline{\mu})=0;\ g_{I(\overline{x},\overline{y})}(\overline{x},\overline{y}))=0;\ h(\overline{x},\overline{y})=0 \text{ and } g_{I^c(\overline{x},\overline{y})}(\overline{x},\overline{y})+u_{I^c(\overline{x},\overline{y})}=0, \right. \tag{2.3}$$

with respect to $(\overline{y},\overline{\lambda},\overline{\mu})$ is locally nonsingular.

Proof. For a) see [15].

b) After rearranging the rows corresponding to the binding constraints $g_{I(\overline{x},\overline{y})}$ and the nonbinding constraints $g_{I^c(\overline{x},\overline{y})}$ at $(\overline{x},\overline{y})$, let $J(\overline{x})$ be the Jacobian of system (2.3); after removing the last row and the last column in $J(\overline{x})$, according to Fiacco [16], the resulting Jacobian matrix is locally nonsingular. The conclusion follows.   □

Now, we consider the KKT formulation of the BLP problem defined by (2.2). As in [9], [13], [14], the algorithm proposed in this paper makes the use of the perturbed version of Fischer-Burmeister functional $\psi:\mathbb{R}^2\times]0,\infty]\to \mathbb{R}$ defined by: $\psi(a,b,\eta)=a+b-\sqrt{a^2+b^2+2\eta}$. For all $\eta>0$, the functional ψ satisfies the following property:

$$\psi(a,b,\eta)=0 \Leftrightarrow a\geq 0,\ b\geq 0,\ ab=\eta \tag{2.4}$$

We now consider the following perturbed problem associated with problem (2.2) where the active set of constraints is taken into account:

$BLP_{KKT}(\eta)$

$$\min_{x,y,u,\lambda,\mu} F(x,y)$$

$$s.t.\begin{cases} H_\eta(x,y,\lambda,\mu,u)=0, \\ \lambda,\ u\geq 0, x\in X. \end{cases} \tag{2.5}$$

H_η is defined on $\mathbb{R}^{n_1+n_2+p+q+|f^c_{(x,y)}|}$ by $H_\eta(w)=H_\eta(x,y,\lambda,\mu,u)=\left(\nabla_y L(x,y,\lambda,\mu),\ g_{I(x,y)}(x,y),\right.$

$\left. g_{f^c_{(x,y)}}(x,y)+u_{f^c_{(x,y)}},\ h(x,y),\ \Psi(\lambda_{f^c_{(x,y)}},u_{f^c_{(x,y)}},\eta)\right)^T$ and $\Psi(u,\lambda,\eta)^t=(\psi(u_1,\lambda_1,\eta),...,\psi(u_p,\lambda_p,\eta))$. According to (2.4), problem (2.5) may be considered as an approximation to the problem (2.2) when $\eta>0$ is small. For $\eta=0$, (2.5) and (2.2) are equivalent. For $\eta>0$ problem (2.5) is an ordinary differentiable nonlinear program.

We may view η as a parameter when η is a subscript. But in proofs, η will be considered as an independent variable. Hence, from this point of view, the function $H\equiv H_\eta$ depends on the six variables (x,y,λ,μ,u,η) .

Remark 1. For a fixed value of the parameter η and a fixed value of $x\in X$, under the assumptions of proposition 1. , the nonlinear programming problem $BLP_{KKT}(\eta)$ is locally regular and has a locally unique solution since the Jacobian of H_η with respect to the variables (y,λ,μ,u) is nonsingular (see proposition 3 [14]).

The following lemma will be used several times in the sequel.

Lemma 1. Let $\bar{x}\in X$ be given. Then, for every η there exists a unique point in $\mathfrak{F}_\eta$ such that it x-parts is equal to $\bar{x}$. This point is denoted by $\bar{w}_\eta=(\bar{x},y_\eta(\bar{x}),\lambda_\eta(\bar{x}),\mu_\eta(\bar{x}),u_\eta(\bar{x}))$. Furthermore, $\bar{w}_\eta$ is continuous as a function of η .

Proof. Let $\bar{x}\in X$ be given. If $\eta=0$, then the existence and the uniqueness follow from Proposition 1 and its assumptions. If $\eta\neq0$, see Remark 1. For the continuity property, let $\bar{x}\in X$ and η be given. By the first part of the lemma, there exists a unique point $w_\eta=(\bar{x},y_\eta(\bar{x}),\lambda_\eta(\bar{x}),\mu_\eta(\bar{x}),u_\eta(\bar{x}))$ such that $H_\eta(w_\eta)=0$. Let $(\bar{\eta},\bar{x},\bar{y},\bar{\lambda},\bar{\mu},\bar{u})$ be such that $H_\eta(\bar{x},\bar{y},\bar{\lambda},\bar{\mu},\bar{u})=0$. From the application of the implicit function theorem for continuous equations, to the system of equations $H_\eta(x,y,\lambda,\mu,u)=0$, we conclude that there exists a neighborhood Θ of $(\bar{\eta},\bar{x})$ and a continuous function $(y,\lambda,\mu,u):\Theta\to\mathbb{R}^{n_2+p+q+|f^c_{(x,y)}|}$ such that, for each $(\eta,x)\in\Theta$, $H_\eta(x,y(x,\eta),\lambda(x,\eta),\mu(x,\eta),u(x,\eta))=0$.

Since by the uniqueness proved in the first part of the lemma, $y_\eta(\bar{x})=y(\bar{x},\eta)$, $\lambda_\eta(\bar{x})=\lambda(\bar{x},\eta)$, $\mu_\eta(\bar{x})=\mu(\bar{x},\eta)$, $u_\eta(\bar{x})=u(\bar{x},\eta)$.

The continuity assertion is also proved. □

Now a useful result is proved for further analysis which asserts that the feasible region of the perturbed problem $BLP_{KKT}(\eta)$ are uniformly compact.

Theorem 1. For every $\hat{\eta}$ and for $(x,y)\in X\times\mathbb{R}^{n_2}$, there exists a compact set $C(\hat{\eta})\subseteq\mathbb{R}^{n_1+n_2+p+q+|f^c_{(x,y)}|}$ such that $\mathfrak{F}_\eta\subseteq C(\hat{\eta})$ for every $\eta\in]0,\hat{\eta}]$.

Proof. We first notice that, for every $\eta > 0$ and for every $w = (x,y,\lambda,\mu,u) \in \mathfrak{F}_\eta$, by hypothesis x belongs to a compact set X. We also have by $u = g(x,y)$ and by (2.4), that $g(x,y) \leq 0$ and $h(x,y) = 0$, which in view of assumption A2 implies that y belong to the bounded set B. This, in turn taking into account the continuity of the function g and $u = g(x,y)$ implies that u belongs to a compact set.

The KKT multipliers λ and μ are also bounded according to assumption R4. The conclusion follows.   □

Corollary 1. $\mathfrak{F}_\eta$ is nonempty and compact as long as η is bounded.

Proof. The nonemptiness of $\mathfrak{F}_\eta$ follows from Lemma 1. Furthermore $\mathfrak{F}_\eta$ is closed by the continuity of the function and bounded by Theorem 1.   □

By Corollary 1 and the continuity of F, it is easy to see that the BLP (1.1) and all the problems $\text{BLP}_{KKT}(\eta)$ have a solution.

2.2 Optimality Properties

The optimality properties considered in this subsection for the problem ($\text{BLP}_{KKT}(\eta)$) show that the perturbed problems ($\text{BLP}_{KKT}(\eta)$) always satisfy the KKT conditions and are fairly locally regular, as oppose to problem (BLP_{KKT}). Furthermore, in case $\eta \cong 0$, optimality conditions for the MPEC problem (BLP_{KKT}) shall be derived and related these conditions to those of the perturbed problem. Our goal in deriving optimality conditions for the problem (BLP_{KKT}) is to construct a suitable stopping criteria for the SQP algorithm framework to be described in farther. The constraints qualification for the problem (BLP_{KKT}) are then easily derived from the regularity conditions R1-R4 (see [17]). η is now considered as a parameter in (2.5). To simplify the notation, we assume that the active set of indices $I(x^{k_t}, y^{k_t}) = \varnothing$ for all k_t, i.e. $|I^c(x^{k_t}, y^{k_t})| = p$. In a SQP algorithm, assume that for a fixed value $0 < \eta_t < 1$, the sequence $\{w^{k_t} = (x^{k_t}, y^{k_t}, \lambda^{k_t}, \mu^{k_t})\}$ is defined by $w^{k_t} = w^{k_t - 1} + d^{k_t}$ where $w^{k_t} \in \mathfrak{F}_{\eta_t}$ for all $k_t = 0, 1, 2...$ and $d^{k_t} \in \mathbb{R}^{n_1 + n_2 + 2^* p + q}$ is a feasible displacement direction. The constraints in the problem $(\text{BLP}_{KKT}(\eta_t))$ are regular (see Remark 1). It easy to show that the stationary points of the series of approximate problems $\{\text{BLP}_{KKT}(\eta_t)\}$ converges to a stationary point $w^* = (x^*, y^*, \lambda^*, \mu^*)$ of BLP_{KKT} when $\eta_t \to 0$. We use a filter-SQP method to solve the series of smooth nonlinear programming problems $\text{BLP}_{KKT}(\eta)$, with $\eta \to 0$.

3 A Filter-SQP Method for Bilevel Programming Problems

In this section, we describe a filter-SQP algorithm, for solving the series of perturbed KKT formulation of the nonlinear bilevel programming problems (1.1), considered as regular nonlinear programming programs.

3.1 Description of the Algorithm

We now consider the perturbed problem $\mathrm{BLP}_{KKT}(\eta_t)$ associated with problem (2.2) and, we assume that an initial solution $w^{k_t} = (x^{k_t}, y^{k_t}, \lambda^{k_t}, \mu^{k_t}, u^{k_t})$ is available. We build a quadratic programming model of problem (2.5) with linear constraints around local linear approximations of f, g, h, $\nabla_y L$, G and Ψ, and a quadratic approximation of the upper-level objective function F. For a given value of $\eta_{k_t} > 0$, if w^{t_0} is the current iterate we need to compute $d = (dx, dy, d\lambda, d\mu, du)$ such that $w^{k_t+1} = w^{k_t} + d \in \mathfrak{F}_{\eta_t}$. We incorporate a trust region constraint with respect to the upper-level variable x. Let $L_x = \nabla^2_{yx} f(x^{k_t}, y^{k_t}) + \nabla^2_{yx} g(x^{k_t}, y^{k_t}) \lambda^{k_t} + \nabla^2_{yx} h(x^{k_t}, y^{k_t}) \mu^{k_t}$, and

$$D_{u_i^{k_t}} \equiv \mathrm{diag}\left(\frac{\partial \psi(\lambda_i^{k_t}, u_i^{k_t}, \eta_t)}{\partial u_i^{k_t}}\right) \text{ and } D_{\lambda_i^{k_t}} \equiv \mathrm{diag}\left(\frac{\partial \psi(\lambda_i^{k_t}, u_i^{k_t}, \eta_t)}{\partial \lambda_i^{k_t}}\right), \; i \in I^C(x^{k_t}, y^{k_t}). \cdot$$

Let $z^{k_t} = (x^{k_t}, y^{k_t})$; to compute the next iterate, we solve the following quadratic programming problem:

$$\mathrm{LBLP}_{KKT}(w^{k_t}, \eta_t, \rho)$$

$$\min_{dx, dy, du, d\lambda, d\mu} q(d) = \nabla_x F(z^{k_t})^T dx + \nabla_y F(z^{k_t})^T dy + \frac{1}{2}(dx, dy)^T \nabla^2_{(x,y)} F(z^{k_t})(dx, dy)$$

$$s.t. \begin{cases} \|dx\|_\infty \le \rho, \\ L_x^T dx + \nabla^2_y L(z^{k_t}, \lambda^{k_t}, \mu^{k_t})^T dy + \nabla_y g(z^{k_t})^T d\lambda + \nabla_y h(z^{k_t})^T d\mu = -\nabla_y L(z^{k_t}, \lambda^{k_t}, \mu^{k_t}), \\ \nabla_x g_{I(z^{k_t})}(z^{k_t})^T dx + \nabla_y g_{I(z^{k_t})}(z^{k_t})^T dy = -g_{I(z^{k_t})}(z^{k_t}), \\ \nabla_x g_{I^C(z^t)}(z^{k_t})^T dx + \nabla_y g_{I^C(z^{k_t})}(x^t, y^t)^T dy + du_{I^C(z^t)} = -g_{I^C(z^t)}(z^{k_t}) - \bar{u}_{I^C(z^{k_t})}, \\ \nabla_x h(z^{k_t})^T dx + \nabla_y h(z^{k_t})^T dy = -h(z^{k_t}); \; D_{\lambda_i^{k_t}} d\lambda_{I^C(z^{k_t})} + D_{\lambda_i^{k_t}} du_{I^C(z^{k_t})} = -\Psi(\bar{u}_{I^C(z^{k_t})}, \bar{\lambda}_{I^C(z^{k_t})}, \eta_t), \\ x^{k_t} + dx \in X, \; d\lambda_i \ge -\lambda_i^{k_t}, \; d_i u \ge -u_i^{k_t}, \; i \in I^C(z^{k_t}). \end{cases} \quad (3.1)$$

The above model takes into account the active set of indices $I(z^{k_t})$ of the constraints $g(x, y) \le 0$ at the current iterate w^{k_t}. $\|dx\|_\infty \le \rho$ represents the trust region constraint. In the series $\{\eta_t\}$, we set $\eta_{t+1} = \beta \eta_t$ where $0 < \beta < 1$. We then check both for optimality and infeasibility. Checking infeasibility for each value of η_t used to solve $\mathrm{LBLP}_{KKT}(\eta_t, \rho)$ may be time consuming. In our algorithm, infeasibility is checked only when we have $\eta_t \cong 0$, or when one of the subproblem $\mathrm{LBLP}_{KKT}(\eta_t, \rho)$ do not have a solution. The measure of constraint infeasibility is $e(x, y) = \|g^+(x, y)\|_1 + \|h(x, y)\|_1$.

Let $w^{k_t} = (x^{k_t}, y^{k_t}, \lambda^{k_t}, \mu^{k_t}, u^{k_t})$ be the current solution of the given subproblem $\mathrm{BLP}_{KKT}(\eta_t)$. For a solution w^{k_t} computed in the restoration phase to be acceptable to the filter, w^{k_t} should also be a solution of the given perturbed subproblem $\mathrm{BLP}_{KKT}(\eta_t)$.

We update the set of indexes $I(x^{k_t}, y^{k_t})$ and $I^C(x^{k_t}, y^{k_t})$ and we consider the following subsets of indexes:

$$I_g(x^{k_t}, y^{k_t}) = \{i : g_i(x^{k_t}, y^{k_t}) \le 0\}, \ I_h(x^{k_t}, y^{k_t}) = \{i : h_i(x^{k_t}, y^{k_t}) = 0\},$$

for constraints infeasibility and $I_{g^+}(x^{k_t}, y^{k_t}) = \{i : g_i(x^{k_t}, y^{k_t}) > 0\}, \ I_{h^\pm}(x^{k_t}, y^{k_t}) = \{i : h_i(x^{k_t}, y^{k_t}) \ne 0\}$ for constraints feasibility. For the restoration phase, we propose to solve the following nonlinear programming problem:

$\text{RBLP}_{\text{KKT}}(\eta_t)$

$$\min_{x,y,u,\lambda,\mu} RF(x,y) = \sum_{i \in I_{g^+}(x^{k_t}, y^{k_t})} \| g_i(x,y) \|^2 + \sum_{i \in I_{h^\pm}(x^{k_t}, y^{k_t})} \| h_i(x,y) \|^2$$

$$s.t. \begin{cases} \nabla_y L(x,y,\lambda,\mu) = 0, \ g_{I_g(x^{k_t}, y^{k_t})}(x,y) + u_{I_g(x^{k_t}, y^{k_t})} = 0, \\ h_{I_h(x^{k_t}, y^{k_t})}(x,y) = 0, \ \Psi(u_{I_g(x^{k_t}, y^{k_t})}, \lambda_{I_g(x^{k_t}, y^{k_t})}, \eta_t) = 0, \\ \lambda_{I_g(x^{k_t}, y^{k_t})}, u_{I_g(x^{k_t}, y^{k_t})} \ge 0. \end{cases} \tag{3.2}$$

The objective function of ($\text{RBLP}_{\text{KKT}}(\eta_t)$) consists of violated constraints at the current solution computed by the algorithm. If the program ($\text{RBLP}_{\text{KKT}}(\eta_t)$) does not have a solution or its solution $w^{k_t} = (x^{k_t}, y^{k_t}, u^{k_t}, \lambda^{k_t}, \mu^{k_t})$ is such as $RF(x^{k_t}, y^{k_t}) > \varepsilon$ where $\varepsilon > 0$, then Ω the set of solutions of the BPL problem (1.1) may be empty. If the restoration phase is successful, then a rational and optimal solution of the original BLP problem (1.1) is computed when $\eta_t \cong 0$.

At iteration with index k, let d_{k_t} be the solution of the quadratic programming problem $\text{LBLP}_{\text{KKT}}(\eta_t, \rho)$. If w^{k_t} is the current solution of program $\text{BLP}_{\text{KKT}}(\eta_t)$ then, we have $w^{k_t+1} = w^{k_t} + d_{k_t}$ and $F(x,y) = F(x^{k_t}, y^{k_t}) + q(d_{k_t})$. Iterations of our algorithm compute the series $\{w^{k_t}\}$ where $w^t = \lim_{k_t \to \infty} w^{k_t}$ is a solution of $\text{BLP}_{\text{KKT}}(\eta_t)$ and $\eta_t \to 0$. If the procedure **Filter-SQP** $(F, w^*, \text{BLP}_{\text{KKT}}(\eta_t), \text{LBLP}_{\text{KKT}}(w^{k_t}, \eta_t, \rho))$ computes a solution $w^* = \infty$, then we conclude that the original BLP may not have a solution. When $\eta_t \cong 0$, w^* is an optimal solution of $\text{BLP}_{\text{KKT}}(\eta_t)$. We update the active set of indexes $I(x^*, y^*)$ of the constraints $g(x,y) \le 0$ at w^*. The optimality is achieved when the complementarity constraints $u_i^* \lambda_i^* = 0$ for any $i \in I^C(x^*, y^*)$. We now describe the complete algorithm.

1. Initialization. Initial values are provided for the trust region radius $\rho^0 = 10^{-4}$, as well as constants β; set $\beta = 0.5$. k_{max} is the maximum number of iterations allowed and ε is the allowed precision. We solve the following nonlinear programming problem using a filter-SQP algorithm to compute an initial feasible solution of BLP_{KKT}:

SLBLP

$$\min_{x,y} f(x,y)$$
$$s.t.\{g(x,y) \le 0, \ h(x,y) = 0.$$

(3.3)

The procedure **Filter-SQP** $(F, z^0, \text{SLBLP}, QP(z^k,\rho), k_{max})$ is executed. Let $z^0 = (x^0, y^0)$ be a solution of (3.3) with KKT multiplies (λ^0, μ^0) corresponding to constraints $g(x,y) \le 0$ and $h(x,y) = 0$ respectively. $I(x^0, y^0)$ represents the active set of indices of constraints $g(x,y) \le 0$ at $w^0 = (x^0, y^0, \lambda^0, \mu^0, u^0)$ where $u_i^0 = -g_i(x^0, y^0), i \in I^C(x^0, y^0)$. w^0 is the initial solution of BLP_{KKT}. Let $\{d_{k_t}\}$ be a sequence, such that, d_{k_t} is a "solution" of problem ($LBLP_{KKT}(\eta_t,\rho)$); then $w^{k_t+1} = w^{k_t} + d_{k_t}$.

2. Solving the series of subproblems { $BLP_{KKT}(\eta_t)$ }, $\{\eta_t\} \to 0$. Set $k=1$, $\eta_t = 0.6$, $w^{k_t} = w^0$.

Step1: Execute the procedure **Filter-SQP** $(F, w^t, BLP_{KKT}(\eta_t), LBLP_{KKT}(w^{k_t},\eta_t,\rho))$ to compute the solution of
$BLP_{KKT}(\eta_t)$. If $w^t = \infty$, stop; the original problem BLP may not have a solution. Else, go to Step 2.

Step2: Set $k_t = k_t + 1$. If $k_t \ge k_{max}$, then stop; the maximal number of iterations is exceeded.
Else, set $\eta_{k_t} = \beta \eta_{k_t-1}$, $w^* = w^k$. Go to Step3.

Step3: (Optimality). If $\eta_t \ge \varepsilon$, update $I(x^t, y^t)$ and go to step1. Else stop; $z^* = (x^*, y^*) = (x^t, y^t)$ is
a local optimal solution of the problem BLP.

3.2 Convergence of the Algorithm

Using the assumptions of proposition 2.2, we show that the subproblem $LBLP_{KKT}(w^{k_t},\eta_t,\rho)$ is always solvable.

Proposition 2. Consider problem BLP and $x^{k_t} \in X$; suppose that KKT, SSOSC, SCS and MFCQ hold at y^{k_t} with multipliers $(\lambda^{k_t}, \mu^{k_t})$ for (1.2). Let $I(x^{k_t}, y^{k_t})$ be the active set of indices of the set of constraints $\{g_i, i=1,2,...,p\}$ at (x^{k_t}, y^{k_t}) , and consider the smoothed approximation of the KKT formulation of BLP defined by (2.5). Then, for $0 \le \eta_t < 1$, the problem $LBLP_{KKT}(w^{k_t},\eta_t,\rho)$ has a unique optimal solution.

Proof: Let $0 \le \eta_t < 1$; the nonlinear programming problem $BLP_{KKT}(\eta_t)$ is locally regular and has a locally unique solution. For a fixed value $x^{k_t} \in X$, let $J(x^{k_t})$ be the

Jacobian of H_{η_t} in (2.5). According to Remark 1, $J(x^{k_t})$ is nonsingular; thus, using the substitution:

$$
\begin{pmatrix}
dy \\
d\lambda_{I(z^{k_t})} \\
d\lambda_{I^C(z^{k_t})} \\
d\mu \\
du_{I(z^{k_t})} \\
du_{I^C(z^{k_t})}
\end{pmatrix}
= J(x)^{-1}\left[
\begin{pmatrix}
-\nabla_y L(w^{k_t}) \\
-g_{I(z^{k_t})}(z^{k_t}) \\
-g_{I^C(z^{k_t})}(z^{k_t})+\overline{u}_{I^C(z^{k_t})} \\
-h(z^{k_t}) \\
-\Psi(\lambda^t_{I^C(z^{k_t})},u^t_{I^C(z^{k_t})},\eta_t)
\end{pmatrix}
+
\begin{pmatrix}
L_x^T dx \\
\nabla_x g_{I(z^{k_t})}(z^{k_t})^T dx \\
\nabla_x g_{I^C(z^{k_t})}(z^{k_t})^T dx \\
\nabla_x h(z^{k_t})^T dx \\
0
\end{pmatrix}
\right],
$$

we can reduce $\text{LBLP}_{KKT}(w^{k_t},\eta_t,\rho)$ to an equivalent strictly convex program in the variable dx and with the constraints $\|dx\|_\infty \le \rho$, $x^t+dx\in X$, $d\lambda_i \ge -\lambda_i^{k_t}$, $du_i \ge -u_i^{k_t}$, $i\in I^C(z^{k_t})$. Since $dx=0$ satisfies trivially the constraints $\|dx\|_\infty \le \rho$ and $x^{k_t}+dx\in X$ because $x^{k_t}\in X$, it follows that $\text{LBLP}_{KKT}(w^{k_t},\eta_t,\rho)$ has a unique optimal solution. □

In the procedure **Filter-SQP** $(F, w^t, \text{BLP}_{KKT}(\eta_t), \text{LBLP}_{KKT}(w^{k_t},\eta_t,\rho))$, to compute a stationary solution w^t of the program $\text{BLP}_{KKT}(\eta_t)$, a SQP method is used: at the iteration number k_t of such method and from the current solution w^{k_t}, the displacement direction d_{k_t} is computed by solving the quadratic programming problem $\text{LBLP}_{KKT}(w^{k_t},\eta_t,\rho)$. Then we have $w^{k_t+1}=w^{k_t}+d_{k_t}\in \mathfrak{F}_{\eta_t}$. From Corollary 1, $\mathfrak{F}_{\eta_t}$ is a compact set. The accumulation point w^t of the sequence $\{w^{k_t}\}$ exists and is a stationary point of the program $\text{BLP}_{KKT}(\eta_t)$. Moreover, the sequence $\{\eta_t\}$ is such that $\eta_t \to 0$. According to proposition 2.3 and from the hypothesis, the sequence $\{w^t\}$ contained in a compact set, and each limit points $w^*=(x^*,y^*,\lambda^*,\mu^*,u^*)$ of the main iteration of our algorithm is a stationary point of problem (BLP_{KKT}) and $z^*=(x^*,y^*)$ is a local optimal solution of BLP (1.1). But the filter-SQP algorithm is globally convergent [18]. Hence, our algorithm is globally convergent. □

4 Conclusion

The filter-SQP algorithm can be coded in MATLAB for solving problem of type (1.1), based on the above described methodology. The software should be designed around tools for addressing subproblems $\text{BLP}_{KKT}(\eta_t)$. Programming effort should be focus on SQP method for solving $\text{BLP}_{KKT}(\eta_t)$ using the filter framework. The nonlinear programming problem SLBLP defined by (3.3) can be solved using the MATLAB routine *fmincon* to compute an initial feasible solution of BLP_{KKT}. This routine uses SQP procedure in the MATLAB Optimization Toolbox; it is an active set strategy. To solve the series of the perturbed problems $\{\text{BLP}_{KKT}(\eta_t)\}$ associated with problem (2.2), the MATLAB routine *quadprog* may be used to compute a solution to the quadratic programming problem $\mathsf{LBLP}_{KKT}(w^{k_t}, \eta_t, \rho)$. For the restoration phase, let w^{k_t} be the current solution of the given subproblem $\mathsf{BLP}_{KKT}(\eta_t)$. The nonlinear programming problem $\mathsf{RBLP}_{KKT}(\eta_t)$ defined by (3.2) should be solved using the MATLAB routine *fmincon* with the starting point w^t. In a further research, we will focus on some numerical experiments of the SQP-filter algorithm described in this paper.

References

1. Amouzegar, M.: A global Optimization Method for Nonlinear Bilevel Programming Problems. IEEE Transactions on System, Man and Cybernetics-Part B: Cybernetics 29, 1–6 (1999)
2. Audet, C., Savard, G., Zghal, W.: A new Branch-and-cut Algorithm for the Bilevel Programming. Journal of Optimization Theory and Applications 134, 353–370 (2007)
3. Bard, J.F., Moore, J.T.: A branch and Bound Algorithm for the Bilevel Programming Problems. SIAM J. Sci. Stat. Comput. 11, 281–292 (1990)
4. Chin, C.M., Fletcher, R.: On the Global Convergence of an SLP-filter Algorithm that takes EQP Steps. Mathematical Programming 96(1), 161–177 (2003)
5. Colson, B., Marcotte, P., Savard, G.: Bilevel Programming: a Ssurvey. 4OR 3, 87–107 (2005)
6. Colson, B., Marcotte, P., Savard, G.: A Trust Region Method for Nonlinear Bilevel Programming: Algorithm and Computational Experience. Computational Optimization and Application 30, 211–227 (2005)
7. Conn, A.R., Gould, M., Toint, P.L.: Trust Region Methods. Siam Publications, Philadelphia (2000)
8. Dempe, S.D.: Annoted Bibliography on Bilevel Programming and Mathematical Programs with Equilibrium Constraints. Optimization 52, 333–359 (2003)
9. Etoa Etoa, J.B.: Contribution à la résolution des programmes mathématiques à deux niveaux et des programmes mathématiques avec contraintes d'équilibre, PhD Thesis. École Polytechnique de Montréal (2005)
10. Etoa Etoa, J.B.: Optimisation Hiérarchique: Théorie, Algorithmes et ApplicationS. Éditions Publibook (Sciences Mathématiques) 14, rue des Volontaires, 75015 Paris (2007)
11. Etoa Etoa, J.B.: Solving Convex Quadratic Bilevel Programming Problems using an Enumeration Sequential Quadratic Programming Algorithm. Journal of Global Optimization (to appear)
12. Etoa Etoa, J.B.: An Enumeration Sequential Linear Programming Algorithm for Bilevel Programming with Linear Constraints. Journal of Pacific Optimization (to appear)
13. Etoa Etoa, J.B.: A Globally Convergent Sequential Linear Programming Algorithm for Mathematical Programs with Linear Complementarity Constraints. Journal of Information and Optimization Sciences (to appear, No 0903006)
14. Facchinei, F., Jiang, H., Qi, L.: A Smoothing Method for Mathematical Programs with Equilibrium Constraints. Mathematical Programming 85, 107–133 (1999)
15. Falk, J.E., Liu, J.: On Bilevel Programming part I: General Nonlinear Case. Mathematical Programming 70, 47–72 (1995)

16. Fiacco, A.F.: Introduction to Sensitivity Analysis in Nonlinear Programming. Academic Press, New York (1983)
17. Flegel, M.L., Kanzow, C.: Abadie-type Constraint Qualification for Mathematical Programs with Equilibrium Constraints. Journal of Optimization Theory and Applications 124(3), 595–614 (2005)
18. Fletcher, R., Leyffer, S., Toint, P.L.: On the Global Convergence of a Filter-SQP Algorithm. SIAM Journal on Optimization 13(1), 44–59 (2002)

Convergence of the Semi-implicit Euler Method for Stochastic Age-Dependent Population Equations with Markovian Switching

Wei-jun Ma and Qi-min Zhang*

School of Mathematics and Computer Science, Ningxia University, Yinchuan,
750021, China
zhangqimin64@sina.com

Abstract. A class of semi-implicit methods is introduced for stochastic age-dependent population equations with Markovian switching. In general, most of stochastic age-dependent population equations do not have explicit solutions. Thus numerical approximation schemes are invaluable tools for exploring their properties. It is proved that the numerical approximation solutions converge to the exact solutions of the equations under the given conditions.

Keywords: Stochastic age-dependent population equations; Markovian switching; Semi-implicit Euler method; Convergence.

1 Introduction

Stochastic modeling has been widely used to model the phenomena arising in many branches of science and industry such fields as biology, economics, mechanics, electronics and telecommunications [1-2]. Most stochastic modeling with Markovian switching are nonlinear and cannot have explicit solutions, so the construction of efficient computational methods is of great importance. For example, Wang et. al [3] discussed the convergence of numerical solutions to stochastic differential delay equations with Poisson jump and Markovian switching. A. Rathinasamy et.al [4] studied mean square stability of semi-implicit Euler method for linear stochastic differential equations with multiple delays and Markovian switching. Zhou et.al [5] investigated the convergence of numerical solutions to neutral stochastic delay differential equations with Markovian switching under the local Lipschitz condition. Zhou et.al [6] studied the stability and boundedness of the solution for stochastic functional differential equation with infinite delay. The equations they considered are stochastic delay differential equations with Markovian switching.

However, to the best of our knowledge, there are not any numerical methods available for stochastic population equations with Markovian switching. O. Angulo et.al [7] gave a numerical method for nonlinear age-structured population models with finite maximum age. Zhang studied the existence, uniqueness

---

* Corresponding author.

R. Zhu et al. (Eds.): ICICA 2010, LNCS 6377, pp. 407–414, 2010.

and exponential stability of a stochastic age-dependent population equation [8]. Numerical analysis of a stochastic age-dependent population equation has been studied by Zhang [9]. In this paper, we shall consider the numerical solutions convergence of the semi-implicit Euler method for stochastic age-dependent population equations with Markovian switching.

2   Preliminaries and Semi-implicit Approximation

Throughout this paper, let $(\Omega, \mathcal{F}, \{\mathcal{F}_t\}_{t \geq 0}, P)$ be a complete probability space with a filtration $\{\mathcal{F}_t\}_{t \geq 0}$ satisfying the usual conditions(i.e., it is increasing and right continuous while $\mathcal{F}_0$ contains all P-null sets).

Let $\{r(t), t \geq 0\}$ be a right-continuous Markov chain on the probability space taking values in a finite state $S = \{1, 2, ..., N\}$ with the generator $\Gamma = (\gamma_{ij})_{N \times N}$ given by

$$P\{r(t + \Delta) = j | r(t) = i\} = \begin{cases} \gamma_{ij}\Delta + o(\Delta) & \text{if } i \neq j, \\ 1 + \gamma_{ij}\Delta + o(\Delta) & \text{if } i = j, \end{cases}$$

where $\Delta > 0$. Here $\gamma_{ij} \geq 0$ is the transition rate from i to j if $i \neq j$ while $\gamma_{ii} = -\sum_{i \neq j} \gamma_{ij}$. We assume that the Markov chain $r(\cdot)$ is independent of the Brownian motion W_t. It is well known that almost every sample path of $r(t)$ is a right-continuous step function with a finite number of simple jumps in any finite subinterval of R_+.

Let

$$V = H^1([0, A]) \equiv \{\varphi | \varphi \in L^2([0, A]), \frac{\partial \varphi}{\partial x_i} \in L^2([0, A]),$$

$$\text{where} \frac{\partial \varphi}{\partial x_i} \text{is generalized partial derivatives}\}.$$

V is a Sobolev space. $H = L^2([0, A])$ such that $V \hookrightarrow H \equiv H' \hookrightarrow V'$. V' is the dual space of V. We denote by $\| \cdot \|$, $| \cdot |$ and $\| \cdot \|_*$ the norms in V, H and V' respectively; by $\langle \cdot, \cdot \rangle$ the duality between V, V', and by $(\cdot, \cdot)$ the scalar product in H. Let W_t be a Wiener process defined on $(\Omega, \mathcal{F}, P)$ and taking its values in the separable Hilbert space K, with increment covariance W. For an operator $B \in \mathcal{L}(K, H)$ be the space of all bounded linear operators from K into H, we denote by $\|B\|_2$ the Hilbert-Schmidt norm, i.e. $\|B\|_2^2 = \text{tr}(BWB^T)$.

Let $C = C([0, T]; H)$ be the space of all continuous function from $[0, T]$ into H with sup-norm $\|\psi\|_C = \sup_{0 \leq s \leq T} |\psi|(s)$, $L_V^p = L^p([0, T]; V)$ and $L_H^p = L^p([0, T]; H)$.

Consider the following stochastic age-dependent population equations with Markovian switching

$$\begin{cases} d_t P = [-\frac{\partial P}{\partial a} - \mu(t, a)P + f(r(t), P)]dt + g(r(t), P)dW_t, & \text{in } Q, \\ P(0, a) = P_0(a), r(0) = i_0, & \text{in } [0, A], \\ P(t, 0) = \int_0^A \beta(t, a)P(t, a)da, & \text{in } [0, T], \end{cases} \quad (1)$$

where $T > 0, A > 0, Q = (0, T) \times (0, A), d_t P = \frac{\partial P}{\partial t}$. $P = P(t, a)$ denotes the population density of age a at time t, $\beta(t, a)$ denotes the fertility rate of females of age a at time t, $\mu(t, a)$ denotes the mortality rate of age a at time t and state $r(t)$. $f(r(t), P)$ denotes effects of external environment for population system. $g(r(t), P)$ is a diffusion coefficient. $f(i, \cdot) : S \times L_H^2 \to H$ be a family of nonlinear operators, $\mathcal{F}_t$-measurable almost surely in t. $g(i, \cdot) : S \times L_H^2 \to \mathcal{L}(K, H)$ is the family of nonlinear operator, $\mathcal{F}_t$-measurable almost surely in t. $P_0 \in L_H^2$.

The integral version of Eq. (1) is given by the equation

$$P_t = P_0 - \int_0^t \frac{\partial P_s}{\partial a} ds - \int_0^t \mu(s, a) P_s ds + \int_0^t f(r(s), P_s) ds$$

$$+ \int_0^t g(r(s), P_s) dW_s, \tag{2}$$

here $P_t = P(t, a)$.

For system (1) the semi-implicit approximate solution on $t = 0, h, 2h, \dots, Nh$ is defined by the iterative scheme

$$Q_t^{k+1} = Q_t^k + (1 - \theta)[-\frac{\partial Q_t^{k+1}}{\partial a} - \mu(t_k, a)Q_t^k + f(r_k^h, Q_t^k)]h$$

$$+ \theta[-\frac{\partial Q_t^{k+1}}{\partial a} - \mu(t_k, a)Q_t^{k+1} + f(r_k^h, Q_t^{k+1})]h + g(r_k^h, Q_t^k)\triangle W_k, \tag{3}$$

with initial value $Q_t^0 = P(0, a), Q^k(t, 0) = \int_0^A \beta(t, a)Q_t^k da, r_k^h = r(kh), k \geq 1$. Here, Q_t^k is the approximation to $P(t_k, a)$, for $t_k = kh$, the time increment is $h = \frac{T}{N} \ll 1$, Brownian motion increment is $\triangle W_k = W(t_{k+1}) - W(t_k)$.

For convenience, we shall extend the discrete numerical solution to continuous time. We first define the step functions

$$Z_1(t) = Z_1(t, a) = \sum_{k=0}^{N-1} Q_t^k 1_{[kh,(k+1)h)},$$

$$Z_2(t) = Z_2(t, a) = \sum_{k=0}^{N-1} Q_t^{k+1} 1_{[kh,(k+1)h)},$$

$$\bar{r}(t) = \sum_{k=0}^{N-1} r_k^h 1_{[kh,(k+1)h)}(t),$$

where 1_G is the indicator function for set G. Then we define

$$Q_t = P_0 + \int_0^t (1 - \theta)[-\frac{\partial Q_s}{\partial a} - \mu(s, a)Z_1(s) + f(\bar{r}(s), Z_1(s))]ds$$

$$+ \int_0^t \theta[-\frac{\partial Q_s}{\partial a} - \mu(s, a)Z_2(s) + f(\bar{r}(s), Z_2(s))]ds$$

$$+ \int_0^t g(\bar{r}(s), Z_1(s))dW_s, \tag{4}$$

with $Q_0 = P(0,a)$, $Q(t,0) = \int_0^A \beta(t,a)Q_t da$, $Q_t = Q(t,a)$, $\bar{r}(0) = i_0$. It is straightforward to check that $Z(t_k,a) = Q_t^k = Q(t_k,a)$.

Assume the following conditions are satisfied:

(i)$f(i,0) = 0, g(i,0) = 0, i \in S$;

(ii) (Lipschitz condition) there exists positive constants K_i such that $x,y \in C, i \in S$,

$$|f(i,x) - f(i,y)| \vee \|g(i,x) - g(i,y)\|_2 \leq K_i \|x-y\|_C, a.e.t;$$

(iii) $\mu(t,a), \beta(t,a)$ are continuous in $\bar{Q} = Q + \partial Q$ such that

$$0 \leq \mu_0 \leq \mu(t,a) \leq \bar{\alpha} < \infty, \quad 0 \leq \beta(t,a) \leq \bar{\beta} < \infty.$$

In an analogous way to the corresponding proof presented in [8], we may establish the following existence and uniqueness conclusion: under the conditions (i)-(iii), Eq.(1) has a unique continuous solution $P(t,a)$ on $(t,a) \in Q$.

3   The Main Results

As for $r(t)$, the following lemma is satisfied (see [10]).

Lemma 1. Given $h > 0$, then $\{r_n^h = r(nh), n = 0,1,2....\}$ is a discrete Markov chain with the one-step transition probability matrix,

$$P(h) = (P_{ij}(h))_{N \times N} = e^{h\Gamma}. \tag{5}$$

Lemma 2. Under the conditions (ii)-(iii), there are constants $k \geq 2$ and $C_1 > 0$ such that

$$E[\sup_{0 \leq t \leq T} |P_t|^k] \leq C_1. \tag{6}$$

The proof is similar to that in[6].

Lemma 3. Under the conditions (ii)-(iii), there exists a constant $C_2 > 0$ such that

$$E[\sup_{0 \leq t \leq T} |Q_{t \wedge v_n}|^2] \leq C_2, \tag{7}$$

where $\tau_n = \inf\{t \geq 0 : |P_t| \geq n\}, \sigma_n = \inf\{t \geq 0 : |Q_t| \geq n\}, v_n = \tau_n \wedge \sigma_n$.

Proof.   From (4), one can obtain

$$dQ_t = -\frac{\partial Q_t}{\partial a} dt + (1-\theta)[f(\bar{r}(t), Z_1(t)) - \mu(t,a)Z_1(t)]dt$$
$$+\theta[f(\bar{r}(t), Z_2(t)) - \mu(t,a)Z_2(t)]dt + g(\bar{r}(t), Z_1(t))dW_t.$$

Applying Itô formula to $|Q_{t \wedge v_n}|^2$ yields

$$|Q_{t \wedge v_n}|^2 = |Q_0|^2 + 2 \int_0^{t \wedge v_n} \langle -\frac{\partial Q_s}{\partial a}, Q_s \rangle ds + \int_0^{t \wedge v_n} \|g(\bar{r}(s), Z_1(s))\|_2^2 ds$$

$$+ 2 \int_0^{t \wedge v_n} ((1 - \theta) f(\bar{r}(s), Z_1(s)) + \theta f(\bar{r}(s), Z_2(s)), Q_s) ds$$

$$- 2 \int_0^{t \wedge v_n} (\mu(s, a)[(1 - \theta) Z_1(s) + \theta Z_2(s)], Q_s) ds$$

$$+ 2 \int_0^{t \wedge v_n} (Q_s, g(\bar{r}(s), Z_1(s)) dW_s)$$

$$\leq |Q_0|^2 + A\bar{\beta}^2 \int_0^{t \wedge v_n} |Q_s|^2 ds + 2 \int_0^{t \wedge v_n} |Q_s| |(1 - \theta) f(\bar{r}(s), Z_1(s))$$

$$+ \theta f(\bar{r}(s), Z_2(s))| ds + 2\mu_0 \int_0^{t \wedge v_n} |Q_s| |(1 - \theta) Z_1(s) + \theta Z_2(s)| ds$$

$$+ \int_0^{t \wedge v_n} \|g(\bar{r}(s), Z_1(s))\|_2^2 ds + 2 \int_0^{t \wedge v_n} (Q_s, g(\bar{r}(s), Z_1(s)) dW_s).$$

Using condition (ii), for any $t \in [0, T]$

$$E \sup_{0 \leq s \leq t} |Q_{s \wedge v_n}|^2 \leq E|Q_0|^2 + (A\bar{\beta}^2 + 1 + 5\mu_0) \int_0^{t \wedge v_n} E \sup_{0 \leq s \leq t} |Q_s|^2 ds$$

$$+ 5K_i^2 \int_0^{t \wedge v_n} E\|Q_s\|_C^2 ds$$

$$+ 2E \sup_{0 \leq s \leq t} \int_0^{s \wedge v_n} (Q_u, g(\bar{r}(u), Z_1(u)) dW_u). \tag{8}$$

Applying Burkholder-Davis-Gundy's inequality, we have

$$E \sup_{0 \leq s \leq t} \int_0^{s \wedge v_n} (Q_u, g(\bar{r}(u), Z_1(u)) dW_u)$$

$$\leq \frac{1}{4} E[\sup_{0 \leq s \leq t} |Q_{s \wedge v_n}|^2] + K_1 K_i^2 \int_0^{t \wedge v_n} E\|Z_1(s)\|_C^2 ds, \tag{9}$$

for some positive constant $K_1 > 0$. Thus, it follows from (8) and (9)

$$E \sup_{0 \leq s \leq t} |Q_{s \wedge v_n}|^2 \leq 2(A\bar{\beta}^2 + 1 + 5\mu_0 + 5K_i^2 + 2K_1 K_i^2) \int_0^t E \sup_{0 \leq u \leq s} |Q_{u \wedge v_n}|^2 ds$$

$$+ 2E|Q_0|^2, \quad \forall t \in [0, T].$$

Applying Gronwall's lemma, one can get

$$E \sup_{0 \leq s \leq t} |Q_{s \wedge v_n}|^2 \leq 2e^{2T(A\bar{\beta}^2 + 1 + 5\mu_0 + 5K_i^2 + 2K_1 K_i^2)} E|Q_0|^2 = C_2, \quad \forall t \in [0, T].$$

Lemma 4. For any $t \in [0, T]$

$$E \int_0^{t \wedge v_n} |f(\bar{r}(s), Q_s) - f(r(s), Q_s)|^2 ds \leq C_3 h + o(h), \tag{10}$$

$$E \int_0^{t \wedge v_n} \|g(\bar{r}(s), Q_s) - g(r(s), Q_s)\|_2^2 ds \leq C_4 h + o(h). \tag{11}$$

The proof is similar to that in [5].

Lemma 5. Under the conditions (ii)-(iii), there exist constants $k \geq 2$ and $C_5 > 0$ such that

$$E[\sup_{0 \leq t \leq T} |Q_t|^k] \leq C_5. \tag{12}$$

The proof is similar to that of Lemma 2.

Lemma 6. Under the conditions (ii)-(iii) and $E|\frac{\partial Q_s}{\partial a}|^2 < \infty$, then

$$\int_0^{t \wedge v_n} E|Q_s - Z_1(s)|^2 ds \leq C_6 h, \tag{13}$$

$$\int_0^{t \wedge v_n} E|Q_s - Z_2(s)|^2 ds \leq C_7 h. \tag{14}$$

Theorem 7. Under the conditions (i)-(iii), then

$$E \sup_{0 \leq t \leq T} |P_{t \wedge v_n} - Q_{t \wedge v_n}|^2 \leq C_8 h + o(h). \tag{15}$$

Proof.   Combining (2) with (4) has

$$P_t - Q_t = -\int_0^t \frac{\partial(P_s - Q_s)}{\partial a} ds - \int_0^t \mu(s, a)[(1 - \theta)(P_s - Z_1(s))$$

$$+\theta(P_s - Z_2(s))]ds + \int_0^t [(1 - \theta)(f(r(s), P_s) - f(\bar{r}(s), Z_1(s)))$$

$$+\theta(f(r(s), P_s) - f(\bar{r}(s), Z_2(s)))]ds$$

$$+ \int_0^t (g(r(s), P_s) - g(\bar{r}(s), Z_1(s)))dW_s.$$

Therefore using Itô formula, along with the Cauchy-Schwarz inequality yields,

$$|P_t - Q_t|^2$$

$$= -2 \int_0^t \langle P_s - Q_s, \frac{\partial(P_s - Q_s)}{\partial a} \rangle ds + \int_0^t \|g(r(s), P_s) - g(\bar{r}(s), Z_1(s))\|_2^2 ds$$

$$-2 \int_0^t (P_s - Q_s, \mu(s, a)[(1 - \theta)(P_s - Z_1(s)) + \theta(P_s - Z_2(s))])ds$$

$$+2 \int_0^t (P_s - Q_s, (1 - \theta)(f(r(s), P_s) - f(\bar{r}(s), Z_1(s))) + \theta(f(r(s), P_s)$$

$$-f(\bar{r}(s), Z_2(s)))ds + 2\int_0^t (P_s - Q_s, (g(r(s), P_s) - g(\bar{r}(s), Z_1(s)))dW_s)$$

$$\leq [A\bar{\beta}^2 + 9\bar{\alpha} + 1]\int_0^t |P_s - Q_s|^2 ds + 10K_i^2\int_0^t \|P_s - Q_s\|_C^2 ds$$

$$+4\bar{\alpha}\int_0^t |Q_s - Z_1(s)|^2 ds + 4\bar{\alpha}\int_0^t |Q_s - Z_2(s)|^2 ds$$

$$+16\int_0^t |f(\bar{r}(s), Q_s) - f(r(s), Q_s)|^2 ds + 12K_i^2\int_0^t \|Q_s - Z_1(s)\|_C^2 ds$$

$$+4\int_0^t \|g(\bar{r}(s), Q_s) - g(r(s), Q_s)\|_2^2 ds + 8K_i^2\int_0^t \|Q_s - Z_2(s)\|_C^2 ds$$

$$+2\int_0^t (P_s - Q_s, (g(r(s), P_s) - g(\bar{r}(s), Z_1(s)))dW_s).$$

Hence, by Lemmas 4 and 6, for any $t \in [0, T]$,

$$E \sup_{0\leq s\leq t} |P_{s\wedge v_n} - Q_{s\wedge v_n}|^2$$

$$\leq (A\bar{\beta}^2 + 1 + 9\bar{\alpha} + 10K_i^2)\int_0^t E\sup_{0\leq u\leq s} |P_{u\wedge v_n} - Q_{u\wedge v_n}|^2 ds$$

$$+4(\bar{\alpha} + 3K_i^2)\int_0^{t\wedge v_n} E|Q_s - Z_1(s)|^2 ds$$

$$+16E\int_0^{t\wedge v_n} |f(\bar{r}(s), Q_s) - f(r(s), Q_s)|^2 ds$$

$$+4(\bar{\alpha} + 2K_i^2)\int_0^{t\wedge v_n} E|Q_s - Z_2(s)|^2 ds$$

$$+4E\int_0^{t\wedge v_n} \|g(\bar{r}(s), Q_s) - g(r(s), Q_s)\|_2^2 ds$$

$$+2E\sup_{0\leq s\leq t}\int_0^{s\wedge v_n} (P_s - Q_s, (g(r(s), P_s) - g(\bar{r}(s), Z_1(s)))dW_s)$$

$$\leq (A\bar{\beta}^2 + 1 + 9\bar{\alpha} + 10K_i^2)\int_0^t E\sup_{0\leq u\leq s} |P_{u\wedge v_n} - Q_{u\wedge v_n}|^2 ds$$

$$+4(\bar{\alpha} + 3K_i^2)C_6 h + 16C_3 h + 4(\bar{\alpha} + 2K_i^2)C_7 h + 4C_4 h + o(h)$$

$$+2E\sup_{0\leq s\leq t}\int_0^{s\wedge v_n} (P_s - Q_s, (g(r(s), P_s) - g(\bar{r}(s), Z_1(s)))dW_s).$$

Applying Burkholder-Davis-Gundy's inequality, we have

$$E \sup_{0\leq s\leq t}\int_0^{s\wedge v_n} (P_s - Q_s, (g(r(s), P_s) - g(\bar{r}(s), Z_1(s)))dW_s)$$

$$\leq \frac{1}{4}E[\sup_{0\leq s\leq t} |P_{s\wedge v_n} - Q_{s\wedge v_n}|^2] + \gamma\int_0^{t\wedge v_n} E\|P_s - Q_s\|_C^2 ds + \gamma C_4 h + o(h),$$

where γ is a positive constant. Applying Gronwall inequality, the result then follows with

$$C_8 = 2[4(\bar{a}+3K_i^2)C_6+4(\bar{a}+2K_i^2)C_7+16C_3+4C_4+2\gamma C_4]e^{2T(A\bar{\beta}^2+1+9\bar{a}+10K_i^2+2\gamma)}.$$

Theorem 8. Under the conditions (i)-(iii), then

$$E\sup_{0\leq t\leq T}|P_t - Q_t|^2 \leq C_9h + o(h). \tag{16}$$

The proof is similar to that in [5].

Theorem 9. Under the conditions (i)-(iii), the numerical approximate solution (4) will converge to the exact solution to Eq.(1) in the sense

$$\lim_{h\to 0} E[\sup_{0\leq t\leq T}|P_t - Q_t|^2] = 0. \tag{17}$$

Acknowledgments. The research was supported by Ministry of Education of the People's Republic of China key Research Foundation(208160); also was supported by NingXia Natural Science Foundation(NZ0835)(China).

References

1. Dong, M., Zhang, H., Wang, Y.: Dynamics analysis of impulsive stochastic Cohen-Grossberg neural networks with Markovian jumping and mixed time delays. J. Neurocomputing 72, 1999–2004 (2009)
2. Svishchuk, A.V., Kazmerchuk, Y.I.: Stability of stochastic delay equations of Ito form with jumps and Markovian switchings and their applications in finance. Theor. Probab. Math. Stat. 64, 167–178 (2002)
3. Wang, L., Xue, H.: Convergence of numerical solutions to stochastic differential delay equations with Poisson jump and Markovian switching. J. Appl. Math. Comput. 188, 1161–1172 (2007)
4. Rathinasamy, A., Balachandran, K.: Mean square stability of semi-implicit Euler method for linear stochastic differential equations with multiple delays and Markovian switching. J. Appl. Math. Comput. 206, 968–979 (2008)
5. Zhou, S., Wu, F.: Convergence of numerical solutions to neutral stochastic delay differential equations with Markovian switching. J. Comput. Appl. Math. 229, 85–96 (2009)
6. Zhou, S., Wang, Z., Feng, D.: Stochastic functional differential equations with infinite delay. J. Math. Anal. Appl. 357, 416–426 (2009)
7. Angulo, O., Lopez-Marcos, J.C., Lopez-Marcos, M.A., Milner, F.A.: A numerical method for nonlinear age-structured population models with finite maximum age. J. Math. Anal. Appl. 361, 150–160 (2010)
8. Zhang, Q., Liu, W., Nie, Z.: Existence, uniqueness and exponential stability for stochastic age-dependent population. J. Appl. Math. Comput. 154, 183–201 (2004)
9. Zhang, Q., Han, C.: Numerical analysis for stochastic age-dependent population equations. J. Appl. Math. Comput. 169, 278–294 (2005)
10. Anderson, W.J.: Continuous-time Markov Chains. Springer, Berlin (1991)

Interior Point Algorithm for Constrained Sequential Max-Min Problems[*]

Xiaona Fan and Qinglun Yan

College of Science, Nanjing University of Posts and Telecommunications
Nanjing, Jiangsu 210046, P.R. China

Abstract. To trace the aggregate homotopy method for constrained sequential max-min problems, a new interior point algorithm is proposed, and its global convergence is established under some conditions. The residual control criteria, which ensures that the obtained iterative points are interior points, is given by the condition that ensures the β-cone neighborhood to be included in the interior of the feasible region. Hence, the algorithm avoids judging whether the iterative points are the interior points or not in every predictor step and corrector step of the Euler-Newton method so that the computation is reduced greatly.

Keywords: nonsmooth optimization, aggregate function, path following algorithm, homotopy method, global convergence.

1 Introduction

In this paper, we consider the following constrained sequential maximin problem (CSMMP for short):

$$\min_{x \in R^n} \left\{ \Phi(x) = \max_{1 \le i \le m} \min_{1 \le j \le l_i} \{ f_{ij}(x) \} \right\} \tag{1}$$

$$s.t. \quad \Psi(x) = \max_{1 \le i \le k} \min_{1 \le j \le p_i} \{ g_{ij}(x) \} \le 0,$$

where $x \in R^n$, $f_{ij}(x)(1 \le i \le m,\ 1 \le j \le l_i)$, $g_{ij}(x)(1 \le i \le k,\ 1 \le j \le p_i)$ are all continuously differentiable. Denote $\Omega = \{x \in R^n : \Psi(x) \le 0\}$ and $\Omega^0 = \{x \in R^n : \Psi(x) < 0\}$.

Maximin problems arise from engineering design [2,14], computer-aided design [11] and circuit design [9,13] and optimal control [12]. For a complete treatment of the maximin problems, see the books [3,4]. Generally speaking, maximin functions are nonconvex and nonsmooth even if the functions are smoothly convex functions even linear functions. Therefore, it is difficult to solve it in theory as well as in numerical test. Up to now, the literatures on maximin problems are relatively small.

[*] This work is supported by Foundation of the Natural Science Foundation of China under Grant No. 70972083, NJUPT under Grant No. NY208069 and the Natural Sciences Foundation for Colleges and Universities in Jiangsu Province of China under Grant No. 09KJD110004.

R. Zhu et al. (Eds.): ICICA 2010, LNCS 6377, pp. 415–422, 2010.
© Springer-Verlag Berlin Heidelberg 2010

Originally, Kort and Bertsekas [5] proposed the exponential penalty function to solve the following constrained optimization problem

$$\min f(x)$$
$$\text{s.t. } g_i(x) \leq 0, \ i = 1, 2, \cdots, m.$$

The exponential penalty function $g(x, \mu) = \mu ln \Sigma_{i=1}^{m} exp(g_i(x)/\mu)$ with a penalty parameter μ transforms the above problem into the unconstrained optimization problem as an exponential penalty item. The function $g(x, \mu)$ provides a good approximation to the function $g(x)$ in the sense that

$$g(x) \leq g(x, \mu) \leq g(x) + \mu ln m$$

for $\mu > 0$. The function is sometimes called the exponential penalty function [1] or aggregate function [5,6], and has been used to solve nonlinear programming problems [1,6], the generalized linear complementarity problems [10] and constrained sequential max-min problem [7,8].

Yu, Liu and Feng [16] followed the idea of Li [6] to develop aggregate function method to sequential maximin problems, and provided a theoretical basis for optimization problem of this type. They proposed a continuation method for solving the CSMMP based on twice aggregate function. Based on the approximation of aggregate function to max-function, they constructed the following smooth functions for $\Phi(x)$ and $\Psi(x)$

$$\Phi(x, \mu) = \mu ln \Sigma_{i=1}^{m} \left(\Sigma_{j=1}^{l_i} exp \left(-\frac{f_{ij}(x)}{\mu} \right) \right)^{-1}$$

$$\Psi(x, \mu) = \mu ln \Sigma_{i=1}^{k} p_i \left(\Sigma_{j=1}^{p_i} exp \left(-\frac{g_{ij}(x)}{\mu} \right) \right)^{-1},$$

where $\mu > 0$ is a control parameter. $\Phi(x, \mu)$ and $\Psi(x, \mu)$ are called twice aggregate functions of $\Phi(x)$ and $\Psi(x)$.

We denote

$$I(x) = \left\{ i \in \{1, 2, \cdots, m\} : \Phi(x) = \phi_i(x) = \min_{1 \leq j \leq l_i} \{f_{ij}(x)\} \right\},$$

$$II(x) = \left\{ i \in \{1, 2, \cdots, k\} : \Psi(x) = \psi_i(x) = \min_{1 \leq j \leq p_i} \{g_{ij}(x)\} \right\},$$

$$J_i(x) = \{j \in \{1, 2, \cdots, l_i\} : \phi_i(x) = f_{ij}(x)\},$$

$$JJ_i(x) = \{j \in \{1, 2, \cdots, p_i\} : \psi_i(x) = g_{ij}(x)\}.$$

Conjecture 1. Ω^0 is nonempty (Slater condition) and Ω is bounded.

Conjecture 2. For any $x \in \partial\Omega = \Omega \setminus \Omega^0$, $\{\nabla g_{ij}(x) : i \in II(x), j \in JJ_i(x)\}$ are positively independent, i.e.

$$\Sigma_{i \in II(x)} \rho_i \Sigma_{JJ_i(x)} \eta_{ij} \nabla g_{ij}(x) = 0, \rho_i \geq 0, \ \eta_{ij} \geq 0$$

implied that $\rho_i = 0$, $\eta_{ij} = 0$ (regularity of $\partial\Omega$).

A smooth homotopy, called aggregate homotopy, is constructed on the basis of twice aggregate functions of maximin functions as follows:

$$H(w, w^{(0)}, \mu) = \begin{pmatrix} (1 - \mu)(\nabla_x \Phi(x, \mu) + y \nabla_x \Psi(x, \theta\mu)) + \mu(x - x^{(0)}) \\ y\Psi(x, \theta\mu) - \mu y^{(0)} \Psi(x^{(0)}, \theta) \end{pmatrix} = 0, \quad (2)$$

where $w = (x, y) \in R^{n+1}$, $w^{(0)} = (x^{(0)}, y^{(0)}) \in \Omega^0 \times R^1_{++}$, and $\theta \in (0, 1]$ is given in advance.

Besides Conjecture 1 and Conjecture 2, in order to obtain the globally convergent analysis for the proposed algorithm, the authors make some additional conjectures.

Conjecture 3. $f_{ij}(x)$, $g_{ij}(x)$ are all r-times $(r > 2)$ continuously differentiable.

Conjecture 4. There exists a closed subset $\hat{\Omega} \subset \Omega^0$ with nonempty interior $\hat{\Omega}^0$ such that, for any $x \in \partial \Omega = \Omega \setminus \Omega^0$, Ω satisfies the weak normal cone condition with respect to $\hat{\Omega}$, namely,

$$\{x + \Sigma_{i \in II(x)} \mu_i \Sigma_{j \in JJ_i(x)} \nu_{ij} \nabla g_{ij}(x) : \mu_i \geq 0, \nu_{ij} \geq 0, \Sigma_{i \in II(x)} \mu_i > 0,$$

$$\Sigma_{j \in JJ_i(x)} \nu_{ij} > 0, i \in II(x), j \in JJ_i(x)\} \cap \hat{\Omega} = \phi.$$

In this paper, based on [15], we obtain a path following algorithm for tracing the homotopy pathway which is globally linearly convergent. On the other hand, in terms of the technique of the β-cone neighborhood, the obtained iterative points $\{(w^{(k)}, \mu_k)\} \subset \Omega_\theta(\mu)^0 \times R^1_{++} \times (0, 1]$ and the limit point of the sequence $\{x^{(k)}\}$ exists and is the solution of (1).

2 Algorithm

First, we give the definition of the β-cone neighborhood. Letting $\mathcal{C} = \{(w, \mu) : H(w, w^{(0)}, \mu) = 0, \mu \in (0, 1]\} \subset \Omega_\theta(\mu)^0 \times R^1_{++} \times (0, 1] \triangleq D$, we call $\mathcal{C}$ the smoothly central path which is to be followed. We next define a β-cone neighborhood around the central path $\mathcal{N}(\beta) = \{(w, \mu) : \|H(w, w^{(0)}, \mu)\| \leq \beta\mu, \mu \in (0, 1]\}$, where $\beta > 0$ is called the width of the neighborhood.

Lemma 1. *If $\beta_0 = |y^{(0)} \Psi(x^{(0)}, \theta)|$ and $\beta \in (0, \beta_0)$, we have $\mathcal{N}(\beta) \subset \Omega_\theta(\mu)^0 \times R^1_{++} \times (0, 1]$.*

Proof. From the definition of the β-cone neighborhood, we know when $\|H(w, w^{(0)}, \mu)\| \leq \beta\mu$, the following inequality holds,

$$\mu y^{(0)} \Psi(x^{(0)}, \theta) - \beta\mu \leq y\Psi(x, \theta\mu) \leq \mu y^{(0)} \Psi(x^{(0)}, \theta) + \beta\mu$$

For $\beta \in (0, \beta_0)$, in terms of $\beta_0 = -y^{(0)} \Psi(x^{(0)}, \theta)$, we have

$$y\Psi(x, \theta\mu) < (y^{(0)} \Psi(x^{(0)}, \theta) + \beta_0)\mu = 0.$$

Since $(x^{(0)}, y^{(0)}, 1) \in D$, so $\mathcal{N}(\beta) \subset \Omega_\theta(\mu)^0 \times R^1_{++} \times (0,1]$.
Let

$$G(w, w^{(0)}, \mu) = \begin{pmatrix} H(w, w^{(0)}, \mu) \\ \mu \end{pmatrix}. \tag{3}$$

For convenience, in the rest paper, we write $G(w, w^{(0)}, \mu)$ and $H(w, w^{(0)}, \mu)$ as $G(w, \mu)$ and $H(w, \mu)$, respectively.

Algorithm 2.1 (the path following algorithm)

Step 0 (Initialization)
Set $k = 0$, $\mu_0 = 1$. Take the width of β-cone neighborhood $\beta \in (0, \beta_0)$, $(w^{(0)}, 1) \in \mathcal{N}(\beta)$, $\alpha \in (0,1)$, $\delta \in (0,1)$, $\epsilon > 0$.
Step 1 (Termination Criterion)
If $\mu_k < \epsilon$, stop, and $w^{(k)} := (x^{(k)}, y^{(k)})$ solves approximately the homotopy equation (2).
Step 2 (Computation of the Newton Direction)
Let $(\triangle w^{(k)}, \triangle \mu_k)$ solve the equation

$$G(w^{(k)}, \mu_k) + \nabla G(w^{(k)}, \mu_k)^T \begin{pmatrix} \triangle w^{(k)} \\ \triangle \mu_k \end{pmatrix} = \begin{pmatrix} 0 \\ (1-\alpha)\mu_k \end{pmatrix}. \tag{4}$$

Step 3 (Backtracking Line Search)
Let λ_k be the maximum of the values $1, \delta, \delta^2, \cdots$ such that

$$\|H(w^{(k)} + \lambda_k \triangle w^{(k)}, (1 - \alpha\lambda_k)\mu_k)\| \leq (1 - \alpha\lambda_k)\beta\mu_k. \tag{5}$$

Set $w^{(k+1)} := w^{(k)} + \lambda_k \triangle w^{(k)}$, $\mu_{k+1} := (1 - \alpha\lambda_k)\mu_k$, $k := k+1$, and go to Step 1.

Conjecture 5. For any $\mu \in (0,1]$ and $(w, \mu) \in \mathcal{N}(\beta)$, $H'_w(w, \mu)$ is nonsingular.

3   Global Linear Convergence

Before the global linear convergence analysis, we discuss the property of the mapping $G(w, \mu)$.

Lemma 2. Assume that $G(w, \mu)$ is defined by Eq. (3). Given the bounded convex set $\mathcal{M} \subset R^{n+m}$, for $\forall w \in \mathcal{M}$ and $\mu \in (0,1]$, there exists a positive constant $C > 0$ such that

$$\left\| \frac{\partial^2 G_i(w, \mu)}{\partial(w, \mu)^2} \right\| \leq C, \quad i = 1, 2, \cdots, n + m + 1.$$

Conjecture 6. Given $\mu \in (0,1]$ and the point $(w, \mu) \in \mathcal{N}(\beta)$, there exists $M > 0$ such that $\|\nabla G(w, \mu)^{-1}\| \leq M$.

Theorem 1. *If $\mu_k > \epsilon$, then for all $k \geq 0$, $\lambda_k \geq \hat{\lambda} = \delta\bar{\lambda}$, where*

$$\bar{\lambda} = \min\left\{1, \frac{2(1-\alpha)\beta}{C\sqrt{n+m}M^2(\beta+\alpha)^2}\right\}.$$

Hence, the backtracking procedure for evaluating λ_k in Step 3 is finitely terminating.

Proof. Let $(w^{(k)}, \mu_k) \in \mathcal{N}(\beta)$ be chosen to satisfy the Newton equation (4). It follows from Conjecture 5 and after some simple computation, we have

$$\begin{pmatrix} \triangle w^{(k)} \\ \triangle \mu_k \end{pmatrix} = \nabla G(w^{(k)}, \mu_k)^{-1} \begin{pmatrix} -H(w^{(k)}, \mu_k) \\ -\alpha\mu_k \end{pmatrix},$$

then

$$\left\| \begin{pmatrix} \triangle w^{(k)} \\ \triangle \mu_k \end{pmatrix} \right\| \leq M(\|H(w^{(k)}, \mu_k)\| + \alpha\mu_k)$$

$$\leq M(\beta + \alpha)\mu_k.$$

On the other hand, recalling the relation between the mappings G and H, we have

$$\begin{pmatrix} H(w^{(k)} + \lambda\triangle w^{(k)}, (1-\alpha\lambda)\mu_k) \\ 0 \end{pmatrix}_i$$

$$= \left(G(w^{(k)} + \lambda\triangle w^{(k)}, (1-\alpha\lambda)\mu_k) - \begin{pmatrix} 0 \\ (1-\alpha\lambda)\mu_k \end{pmatrix} \right)_i$$

$$= G_i(w^{(k)}, \mu_k) + \lambda\frac{\partial G_i(w^{(k)}, \mu_k)}{\partial(w^{(k)}, \mu_k)}\begin{pmatrix} \triangle w^{(k)} \\ \triangle \mu_k \end{pmatrix} - \begin{pmatrix} 0 \\ (1-\alpha\lambda)\mu_k \end{pmatrix}_i$$

$$+ \frac{1}{2}\lambda^2 \begin{pmatrix} \triangle w^{(k)} \\ \triangle \mu_k \end{pmatrix}^T \frac{\partial^2 G_i(\tilde{w}^{(k)}, \tilde{\mu}_k)}{\partial(w^{(k)}, \mu_k)^2}\begin{pmatrix} \triangle w^{(k)} \\ \triangle \mu_k \end{pmatrix}$$

$$= (1-\lambda)\begin{pmatrix} H(w^{(k)}, \mu_k) \\ 0 \end{pmatrix}_i + \frac{1}{2}\lambda^2\begin{pmatrix} \triangle w^{(k)} \\ \triangle \mu_k \end{pmatrix}^T \frac{\partial^2 G_i(\tilde{w}^{(k)}, \tilde{\mu}_k)}{\partial(w^{(k)}, \mu_k)^2}\begin{pmatrix} \triangle w^{(k)} \\ \triangle \mu_k \end{pmatrix},$$

where

$$(\tilde{w}^{(k)}, \tilde{\mu}_k) = (w^{(k)} + \lambda\theta_i\triangle w^{(k)}, \mu_k + \lambda\theta_i\triangle\mu_k), \theta_i \in (0,1),$$

and the second equality follows from (4). Let

$$A = \left(\frac{\partial^2 G_1}{\partial(w^{(k)}, \mu_k)^2}, \cdots, \frac{\partial^2 G_{n+m}}{\partial(w^{(k)}, \mu_k)^2} \right), \tag{6}$$

then $\|A(\tilde{w}^{(k)}, \tilde{\mu}_k)\| \leq \sqrt{n+m}C$. From the deduction given above, we have

$$\|H(w^{(k)} + \lambda\triangle w^{(k)}, (1-\alpha\lambda)\mu_k))\|$$

$$\leq (1-\lambda)\|H(w^{(k)}, \mu_k)\| + \frac{1}{2}\lambda^2\|A(\tilde{w}^{(k)}, \tilde{\mu}_k))\|\|(\triangle w^{(k)}, \triangle\mu_k)\|^2$$

$$\leq (1-\lambda)\beta\mu_k + \frac{\sqrt{n+m}}{2}\lambda^2 CM^2(\beta+\alpha)^2\mu_k^2$$

$$\leq (1-\lambda)\beta\mu_k + \frac{\sqrt{n+m}}{2}\lambda^2 CM^2(\beta+\alpha)^2\mu_k.$$

It is easy to verify that

$$(1 - \lambda)\beta\mu_k + \frac{\sqrt{n + m}}{2}\lambda^2 CM^2(\beta + \alpha)^2\mu_k \leq (1 - \alpha\lambda)\beta\mu_k$$

whenever

$$\lambda \leq \frac{2(1 - \alpha)\beta}{C\sqrt{n + m}M^2(\beta + \alpha)^2}.$$

Therefore, taking

$$\bar{\lambda} = \min\left\{1, \frac{2(1 - \alpha)\beta}{C\sqrt{n + m}M^2(\beta + \alpha)^2}\right\},$$

we have $\lambda_k \geq \hat{\lambda}$ with $\hat{\lambda} = \delta\bar{\lambda}$,

We are now in the position to show that the algorithm is well defined.

Theorem 2. *The above algorithm is well defined, that is to say, if $(w^{(k)}, \mu_k) \in \mathcal{N}(\beta)$ with $\mu_k > 0$, we have that $(w^{(k+1)}, \mu_{k+1})$ is well defined with the backtracking routine in Step 3 finitely terminating. And we have $(w^{(k+1)}, \mu_{k+1}) \in \mathcal{N}(\beta)$, where $0 < \mu_{k+1} \leq \mu_k$.*

Proof. Let $(w^{(k)}, \mu_k) \in \mathcal{N}(\beta)$, where $\mu_k \in (0, 1]$. $\mu_k < \epsilon$ if and only if $w^{(k)}$ solves approximately Eq.(2). If $w^{(k)}$ does not solve Eq.(2). Let $(w^{(k+1)}, \mu_{k+1}) = (w^{(k)} + \lambda_k\Delta w^{(k)}, (1 - \alpha\lambda_k)\mu_k)$. By Theorem 1, we have the backtracking routine in Step 3 is finitely terminating. Hence, (4) can also be regarded as an instance of a standard backtracking line search routine and is finitely terminating with $0 < \mu_{k+1} \leq \mu_k$. (4) implies $(w^{(k+1)}, \mu_{k+1}) \in \mathcal{N}(\beta)$. This completes the proof.

Assume that the algorithm does not terminate finitely, we are now in the position to state and prove the global linear convergence result for the algorithm described in the preceding section.

Theorem 3. *Suppose that Conjecture 6 holds for the infinite sequence $\{(w^{(k)}, \mu_k)\}$ generated by the algorithm. Then*

(i) *For $k = 0, 1, 2, \cdots$,*

$$(w^{(k)}, \mu_k) \in \mathcal{N}(\beta), \tag{7}$$

$$(1 - \alpha\lambda_{k-1}) \cdots (1 - \alpha\lambda_0) = \mu_k. \tag{8}$$

(ii) *For all $k \geq 0$, $\lambda_k \geq \hat{\lambda} = \delta\bar{\lambda}$, where*

$$\bar{\lambda} = \min\left\{1, \frac{2(1 - \alpha)\beta}{C\sqrt{n + m}M^2(\beta + \alpha)^2}\right\}.$$

Therefore, μ_k converges to 0 at a global linear rate.

(iii) *The sequence $\{(x^{(k)}, y^{(k)})\}$ converges to a solution of (2), i.e., $\{x^{(k)}\}$ converges to a solution of the CSMMP (1).*

Proof

(i) We establish (7) and (8) by induction on k. Clearly these relations hold for $k = 0$. Now assume that they hold for some $k > 0$. By Theorem 2, the algorithm is well defined and so (7) and (8) hold with k replaced by $k + 1$. Hence, by induction, (7) and (8) hold for all k.

(ii) By Theorem 1, we have $\lambda_k \geq \hat{\lambda} = \delta\bar{\lambda}$, which combines with (8) implying $\mu_k \leq (1-\alpha\hat{\lambda})^k\mu_0 = (1-\alpha\hat{\lambda})^k$, for all k sufficiently large. Thus $\{\mu_k\}$ converges globally linearly to zero.

(iii) Let $(\triangle w^{(k)}, \triangle\mu_k)$ be chosen to satisfy the Newton equation (4). Then,

$$\left\| \begin{pmatrix} w^{(k+1)} \\ \mu_{k+1} \end{pmatrix} - \begin{pmatrix} w^{(k)} \\ \mu_k \end{pmatrix} \right\| = \lambda_k \left\| \begin{pmatrix} \triangle w^{(k)} \\ \triangle\mu_k \end{pmatrix} \right\| \leq \left\| \begin{pmatrix} \triangle w^{(k)} \\ \triangle\mu_k \end{pmatrix} \right\|$$

$$\leq M(\beta + \alpha)\mu_k \leq M(\beta + \alpha)(1 - \alpha\hat{\lambda})^k.$$

Therefore, $\{w^{(k)}\}$ is a Cauchy sequence and converges to a point w^*. It follows from $(w^{(k)}, \mu_k) \in \mathcal{N}(\beta)$ that $w^* \in \Omega \times R_+^1$. Hence, $(w^*, 0)$ is a solution of the homotopy equation (2) and correspondingly, the point x^* solves the CSMMP (1).

4 Complexity Analysis

Theorem 4. *Let $\epsilon > 0$ be an accuracy parameter. The algorithm has a complexity bound of iterations $O(\sqrt{n}L)$ and the total complexity bound of the algorithm is $O(n^{3.5}L)$, where $L = log\frac{1}{\epsilon}$.*

Proof. Following from Theorem 1 and Theorem 3, we have

$$\mu_k \leq (1 - \alpha\hat{\lambda})^k\mu_0 = \left(1 - \frac{2\alpha\delta(1 - \alpha)\beta}{C\sqrt{n} + mM^2(\beta + \alpha)^2}\right)^k.$$

Assume that there exists a constant $p > 0$ such that $m = pn$. To ensure $\left(1 - \frac{2\alpha\delta(1-\alpha)\beta}{C\sqrt{n}+mM^2(\beta+\alpha)^2}\right)^k \leq \epsilon$, it suffices to take logarithms in both sides above and use the following inequality

$$log\left(1 - \frac{2\alpha\delta(1 - \alpha)\beta}{C\sqrt{n} + mM^2(\beta + \alpha)^2}\right) \leq -\frac{2\alpha\delta(1 - \alpha)\beta}{C\sqrt{n} + mM^2(\beta + \alpha)^2} = -\frac{2\alpha\delta(1 - \alpha)\beta}{C\sqrt{1 + p}\sqrt{n}M^2(\beta + \alpha)^2}.$$

Let $L = log\frac{1}{\epsilon}$, then at most $K = \left\lceil \frac{C\sqrt{1+p}M^2(\beta+\alpha)^2}{2\alpha\delta(1-\alpha)\beta}\sqrt{n}log\epsilon^{-1} \right\rceil = O(\sqrt{n}log\frac{1}{\epsilon}) = O(\sqrt{n}L)$ iterations in the algorithm, we can obtain a ϵ-solution of (2). However, in every step, the complexity bound of computing the linear system is $O(n^3)$. Therefore, the total complexity bound of the algorithm is $O(n^{3.5}L)$.

References

1. Bertsekas, D.P.: Minimax methods based on approximation. In: Proceeding of the 1976 Johns Hopkins, Conference on Information Sciences and Systems (1976)
2. Bhowmik, R.: Building design optimization using sequential linear programming. Journal of Computers 3, 58–64 (2008)
3. Demyanov, V.F., Molozemov, V.N.: Introduction to Minimax. Wiley, New York (1974)
4. Du, D.Z., Pardalos, P.M. (eds.): Minimax and Applications. Kluwer Academic Publishers, Dordrecht (1995)
5. Kort, B.W., Bertsakas, D.P.: A new penalty function algorithm for constrained minimization, New Orlean, Louisiana (1972)
6. Li, X.S.: An aggregate function method for nonlinear programming. Science in China (A) 34, 1467–1473 (1991)
7. Liu, Q., Wang, X., Tan, J.: Homotopy method for constrained sequential max-min problem with a bounded feasible field (2009), http://www.paper.edu.cn
8. Wang, X., Jiang, X., Liu, Q.: The aggregate constraint shiffting homotopy method for constrained sequential max-min problem (2009), http://www.paper.edu.cn
9. Ogryczak, W., Sliwinski, T.: Sequential algorithms for max-min fair bandwidth allocation. Lecture Notes in Electrical Engineering 27, 511–522 (2010)
10. Peng, J.-M., Lin, Z.: A non-interior continuation method for generalized linear complementarity problems. Mathematical Programming 86, 533–563 (1999)
11. Polak, E., Higgins, J.E., Mayne, D.Q.: A barrier function method for minimax problems. Mathematical Programming 64, 277–294 (1994)
12. Rockafellar, R.T.: Linear-quadratic programming and optimal control. SIAM Journal on Control and Optimization 25, 781–814 (1987)
13. Sussman-Fort, S.E.: Approximate direct-search minimax circuit optimization. International Journal for Numerical Methods in Engineering 28, 359–368 (1989)
14. Warren, A.D., Lasdon, L.S., Suchman, D.F.: Optimization in engineering design. Proc. IEEE 55, 1885–1897 (1967)
15. Xu, S.: The global linear convergence of an infeasible noninterior path-following algorithm for complementarity problems with uniform P-functions. Math. Program. Ser. A 87, 501–517 (2000)
16. Yu, B., Liu, G.X., Qi, L.Q.: The aggregate homotopy method for constrained sequential max-min problems (submitted)

Representations for the Generalized Drazin Inverse of Bounded Linear Operators

Li Guo[1,2] and Xiankun Du[1]

[1] School of Mathematics, Jilin University, Changchun 130012, China
[2] School of Mathematics, Beihua University, Jilin 132013, China
http://www.springer.com/lncs

Abstract. To investigate the generalized Drazin invertible of a 2×2 operator matrix M, representations for the generalized Drazin inverse of M in terms of its individual blocks are presented under some conditions and some recent results are extended.

Keywords: generalized Drazin inverse; Banach space; operator matrix; quasi-nilpotent.

1 Introduction

Let X and Y be complex Banach spaces. The set of all bounded linear operators from X into Y will be denoted by $\mathbf{B}(X, Y)$. We abbreviate $\mathbf{B}(X, X)$ to $\mathbf{B}(X)$. An operator $T \in \mathbf{B}(X)$ is said to be quasi-nilpotent if the spectrum $\sigma(T)$ consists of the set $\{0\}$[1]. It is easy to check that T is quasi-nilpotent if and only if the spectral radius $r(T) = 0$.

An operator $T \in \mathbf{B}(X)$ is said to be Drazin invertible if there exists an operator $T^D \in \mathbf{B}(X)$ such that

$$TT^D = T^D T, \ T^D T T^D = T^D, \ T - T^2 T^D \ \textit{is nilpotent.}$$

The concept of the generalized Drazin inverse in a Banach algebra is introduced by Koliha[2]. Koliha[3] and Rakočević[4] studied the generalized Drazin inverse for the bounded linear operators. An operator $T \in \mathbf{B}(X)$ is said to be Drazin invertible if there exists an operator $T^D \in \mathbf{B}(X)$ such that

$$TT^D = T^D T, \ T^D T T^D = T^D, \ T - T^2 T^D \ \textit{is quasi-nilpotent.} \tag{1}$$

The Drazin inverse and the generalized Drazin inverse of a operator matrix and its applications are very important in various applied mathematical fields like singular differential equations, singular difference equations, Markov chains, iterative methods and so on [5,6,7,8,9].

A related topic is to obtain the representation for the generalized Drazin inverse of the operator matrix $M = \begin{pmatrix} A & B \\ C & D \end{pmatrix}$ in terms of the individual blocks, where $A \in \mathbf{B}(X)$ and $D \in \mathbf{B}(Y)$ are generalized Drazin invertible[10,12,15,16].

R. Zhu et al. (Eds.): ICICA 2010, LNCS 6377, pp. 423–430, 2010.

Djordjević and Stanimirović [10] firstly gave the formula of the generalized Drazin inverse for block triangular operator matrices. This result is generalized in several directions [10,11,13]. In this paper, we give explicit expressions for the generalized Drazin inverse of 2×2 operator matrix M under some conditions and then Several results[10,11,12,13,14] are generalized. For notational convenience, we define a sum to be 0, whenever its lower limit is bigger than its upper limit. We write $T^{\pi} = I - TT^{D}$.

2 Main Results

Lemma 1. *[5]. If $P, Q \in \mathbf{B}(X)$ are generalized Drazin invertible and $PQ = 0$, then $P + Q$ is generalized Drazin invertible and*

$$(P + Q)^{D} = Q^{\pi} \sum_{i=0}^{\infty} Q^{i}(P^{D})^{i+1} + \sum_{i=0}^{\infty} (Q^{D})^{i+1} P^{i} P^{\pi}.$$

Lemma 2. *[6]. If $P, Q \in \mathbf{B}(X)$ are quasi-nilpotent and $PQ = 0$, then $P + Q$ is quasi-nilpotent.*

Let $A \in \mathbf{B}(X)$ and $D \in \mathbf{B}(Y)$ are generalized Drazin invertible, and $B \in \mathbf{B}(Y, X)$ and $C \in \mathbf{B}(X, Y)$. Throughout this paper, we will use the symbol Σ_n and S_n to denote two sequences of matrices. For any nonnegative integer n, let

$$\Sigma_n = \sum_{i=0}^{\infty} (D^{D})^{i+n+2} C A^{i} A^{\pi} + D^{\pi} \sum_{i=0}^{\infty} D^{i} C (A^{D})^{i+n+2} - \sum_{i=0}^{n} (D^{D})^{i+1} C (A^{D})^{n-i+1},$$

$$(2)$$

$$S_n = \sum_{i=0}^{n} A^{i} B D^{n-i}. \tag{3}$$

Lemma 3. *For any nonnegative integer k, let Σ_k be as in Eq. (2). Then we have*

(1) $\Sigma_k = D\Sigma_{k+1} + C(A^{D})^{k+2}$.
(2) $\Sigma_k = \Sigma_{k+1} A + (D^{D})^{k+2} C$.
(3) $\Sigma_{k+1} = D^{D} \Sigma_k + \Sigma_0 (A^{D})^{k+1}$.

Moreover, if $BD^{i}C = 0$, $i = 0, 1, \ldots, n, BD^{n+1} = 0$ for some nonnegative integer n, then $BD^{D} = 0$ and $BD^{i}\Sigma_k = 0$ for any $i \geq 0, k \geq 0$.

Proof. (1) Let k is any nonnegative integer. By Eq. (2) of the expression of Σ_k, we have

$$D\Sigma_{k+1} = \sum_{i=0}^{\infty} (D^{D})^{i+k+2} C A^{i} A^{\pi} + D^{\pi} \sum_{i=1}^{\infty} D^{i} C (A^{D})^{i+k+2}$$

$$-DD^{D} C (A^{D})^{k+2} - \sum_{i=0}^{k} (D^{D})^{i+1} C (A^{D})^{k+1-i},$$

$$= \Sigma_k - C(A^{D})^{k+2}.$$

(2) It can be obtained following similar to the property (1).

(3) By the expression of Σ_k, we can get

$$\Sigma_{k+1} = D^D[\sum_{i=0}^{\infty}(D^D)^{i+k+2}CA^iA^\pi - \sum_{i=1}^{k+1}(D^D)^iC(A^D)^{k-i+2}]$$

$$+[-D^DCA^D + D^\pi \sum_{i=0}^{\infty}D^iC(A^D)^{i+2}](A^D)^{k+1}$$

$$= D^D\Sigma_k + \Sigma_0(A^D)^{k+1}.$$

Since $BD^{n+1} = 0$, $BD^D = BD^{n+1}(D^D)^{n+2} = 0$. Noting that $BD^iC = 0$, $i = 0, 1, \ldots, n$ and $BD^D = 0$, we have that $BD^i\Sigma_k = 0$ for any $i \geq 0, k \geq 0$.

Lemma 4. For any nonnegative integer k, let S_k be as in Eq. (3). We have

(1) $S_{k+1} = AS_k + BD^{k+1}$.

(2) $S_{k+1} = S_kD + A^{k+1}B$.

Moreover, if $BD^iC = 0$, $i = 0, 1, \ldots, n, BD^{n+1} = 0$ for some nonnegative integer n, then $S_nD^iC = 0$ for any $i \geq 0$ and

(3) $AS_n = S_nD + A^{n+1}B$.

Theorem 1. Let $M = \begin{pmatrix} A & B \\ C & D \end{pmatrix}$ be a 2×2 block operator matrix where $A \in \mathbf{B}(X)$ and $D \in \mathbf{B}(Y)$ are generalized Drazin invertible, $B \in \mathbf{B}(Y, X)$ and $C \in \mathbf{B}(X, Y)$. If there exists a nonnegative integer n such that

$$BD^iC = 0, \quad i = 0, 1, \ldots, n, \quad and \quad BD^{n+1} = 0. \tag{4}$$

Then M is generalized Drazin invertible and

$$M^D = \begin{pmatrix} A^D & \Gamma \\ \Sigma_0 & D^D + \Delta \end{pmatrix}, \tag{5}$$

where Σ_n as in Eq. (2) and S_n as in Eq. (3) and

$$\Gamma = (A^D)^{n+2}S_n, \Delta = \sum_{i=0}^{n-1}(D^D)^{i+3}CS_i + \Sigma_{n+1}S_n. \tag{6}$$

Proof. Let M^D be defined as in Eq. (5). By Eq. (4) and Eq. (6), we have for any nonnegative integer k,

$$\Gamma D^kC = 0, BD^k\Delta = 0, \Delta D^kC = 0. \tag{7}$$

We first prove that $MM^D = M^DM$. Noting that $B\Sigma_0 = 0$, $\Gamma C = 0$, $B\Delta = 0$ and $\Delta C = 0$, we have

$$MM^D = \begin{pmatrix} AA^D & A\Gamma \\ CA^D + D\Sigma_0 & C\Gamma + DD^D + D\Delta \end{pmatrix},$$

$$M^DM = \begin{pmatrix} A^DA & A^DB + \Gamma D \\ \Sigma_0A + D^DC & \Sigma_0B + D^DD + \Delta D \end{pmatrix}.$$

By using the properties (1) and (2) of Lemma 3, we get the following relation:

$$CA^D + D\Sigma_0 = \Sigma_0 A + D^D C.$$

By Eq. (4) and the property (3) of Lemma 4, we have

$$A\Gamma = (A^D)^{n+2} A S_n = (A^D)^{n+2}(S_n D + A^{n+1}B) \tag{8}$$
$$= (A^D)^{n+2} S_n D + A^D B = \Gamma D + A^D B. \tag{9}$$

Now, we have to prove the lower right blocks of MM^D and $M^D M$ are equal. We compute

$$DA + C\Gamma = \sum_{i=0}^{n-1}(D^D)^{i+2}CS_i + D\Sigma_{n+1}S_n + C\Gamma$$

$$= \sum_{i=0}^{n}(D^D)^{i+2}CS_i + (D\Sigma_{n+1} - (D^D)^{n+2}C)S_n + C\Gamma.$$

It follows $D\Sigma_n + C(A^D)^{n+1} = \Sigma_n A + (D^D)^{n+1}C$ by Lemma 3, we have

$$DA + C\Gamma = \sum_{i=0}^{n}(D^D)^{i+2}CS_i + (\Sigma_{n+1}A - C(A^D)^{n+2})S_n + C\Gamma$$

$$= \sum_{i=0}^{n}(D^D)^{i+2}CS_i + \Sigma_{n+1}AS_n.$$

By the property (3) of Lemma 4, we have

$$\Delta D + \Sigma_0 B = \sum_{i=0}^{n-1}(D^D)^{i+3}CS_i D + \Sigma_{n+1}AS_n - \Sigma_{n+1}A^{n+1}B + \Sigma_0 B.$$

By the property (2) of Lemma 3 by an induction on n, it can be proved that

$$\Sigma_{n+1}A^{n+1} = \Sigma_0 - \sum_{i=0}^{n}(D^D)^{i+2}CA^i. \tag{10}$$

Substituting Eq. (10) into $\Delta D + \Sigma_0 B$ and by the property (2) of Lemma 4, we have

$$\Delta D + \Sigma_0 B = \sum_{i=0}^{n-1}(D^D)^{i+3}CS_i D + \Sigma_{n+1}AS_n + \sum_{i=0}^{n}(D^D)^{i+2}CA^i B$$

$$= \sum_{i=0}^{n}(D^D)^{i+2}CS_i + \Sigma_{n+1}AS_n.$$

Therefore $C\Gamma + DD^D + DA = \Sigma_0 B + D^D D + \Delta D$. Thus we conclude that $MM^D = M^D M$.

Since for any integer $i \geq 0$, $\Gamma D^i C = 0$, $\Delta D^i C = 0$ and $BD^D = 0$ by Lemma 3 and $\Sigma_0 A^D + D^D \Sigma_0 = \Sigma_1$, we have

$$(M^D)^2 M = \begin{pmatrix} A^D & (A^D)^2 B + A^D \Gamma D \\ \Sigma_1 A + (D^D)^2 C & \Sigma_1 B + \Sigma_0 \Gamma D + D^D + D^D \Delta D \end{pmatrix}.$$

Since $A\Gamma = A^D B + \Gamma D$ by (8), we have

$$(A^D)^2 B + A^D \Gamma D = AA^D \Gamma = \Gamma.$$

By the property (2) of Lemma 3, $\Sigma_1 A + (D^D)^2 C = \Sigma_0$.

By the properties (2) and (3) of Lemma 3, it can be proved that

$$D^D \Sigma_{n+1} A = \Sigma_{n+1} - (D^D)^{n+3} C - \Sigma_0 (A^D)^{n+1}. \tag{11}$$

By the property (2) and (3) of Lemma 4, we see that

$$D^D \Delta D = \sum_{i=0}^{n-1} (D^D)^{i+4} C S_i D + D^D \Sigma_{n+1} S_n D$$

$$= \sum_{i=0}^{n-1} (D^D)^{i+4} C (S_{i+1} - A^{i+1} B) + D^D \Sigma_{n+1} A S_n - D^D \Sigma_{n+1} A^{n+1} B.$$

Substituting Eq. (10) and Eq. (11) into $D^D \Delta D$, we get

$$D^D \Delta D = \sum_{i=0}^{n-1} (D^D)^{i+3} C S_i + \Sigma_{n+1} S_n - \Sigma_0 (A^D)^{n+1} S_n - D^D \Sigma_0 B$$

$$= \Delta - \Sigma_0 (A^D)^{n+1} S_n - D^D \Sigma_0 B.$$

Then by the property (3) of Lemma 3, we have

$$D^D \Delta D + \Sigma_1 B + \Sigma_0 \Gamma D$$
$$= \Delta - \Sigma_0 (A^D)^{n+1} S_n - D^D \Sigma_0 B + \Sigma_1 B + \Sigma_0 (A^D)^{n+2} S_n D$$
$$= \Delta - (\Sigma_1 - \Sigma_0 A^D) B + \Sigma_1 B - \Sigma_0 A^D B = \Delta.$$

Thus $M^D = (M^D)^2 M$.

Finally, we will prove $M - M^2 M^D$ is quasi-nilpotent. By Eq. (4), for any nonnegative integer k, by an induction on k, a calculation yields

$$M^{n+k+1} = \begin{pmatrix} A^{n+k+1} & A^k \sum_{i=0}^{n} A^i B D^{n-i} \\ \sum_{i=0}^{n+k} D^{n+k-i} C A^i & D^{n+k+1} + N_{n+k+1} \end{pmatrix},$$

where $N_{n+k+1} = \sum_{i=0}^{n+k-1} D^{n+k-1-i} C \sum_{j=0}^{i} A^j B D^{i-j}$. Noting that for any integer $i \geq 0$, $BD^i \Delta = 0$, $BD^i \Sigma_0 = 0$ and $BD^D = 0$, we compute

$$M^{n+1} - M^{n+2} M^D = \begin{pmatrix} A^{n+1} A^\pi & \sum_{i=0}^{n} A^i B D^{n-i} - A^{n+2} \Gamma \\ \sum_{i=0}^{n} D^{n-i} C A^i - \Phi & D^{n+1} D^\pi + N_{n+1} - \Lambda \end{pmatrix}$$

where

$$\Phi = \sum_{i=0}^{n} D^{n-i} C A^i A^D + D^{n+1} \Sigma_0, \Lambda = \sum_{i=0}^{n} D^{n-i} C A^i \Gamma + D^{n+1} \Delta.$$

Since A and D are generalized Drazin invertible, $A^{n+1} A^\pi$ and $D^{n+1} D^\pi$ are quasi-nilpotent. By the expressions of N_{n+1} and Λ, we know $N_{n+1} - \Lambda$ is nilpotent. Let

$$P = \begin{pmatrix} A^{n+1} A^\pi & \sum_{i=0}^{n} A^i B D^{n-i} - A^{n+2} \Gamma \\ 0 & N_{n+1} - \Lambda \end{pmatrix},$$

and

$$Q = \begin{pmatrix} 0 & 0 \\ \sum_{i=0}^{n} D^{n-i} C A^i - \Phi & D^{n+1} D^\pi \end{pmatrix}.$$

Then P and Q are quasi-nilpotent and $PQ = 0$. Hence by Lemma 2, $P + Q = M^{n+1} - M^{n+2} M^D$ is quasi-nilpotent and so $r(M^{n+1} - M^{n+2} M^D) = 0$. Since we have prove that $MM^D = M^D M$ and $M^D = (M^D)^2 M$, we see that MM^D is idempotent. Hence $(M - M^2 M^D)^{n+1} = [M(I - MM^D)]^{n+1} = M^{n+1}(I - MM^D) = M^{n+1} - M^{n+2} M^D$ and so $r((M - M^2 M^D)^{n+1}) = r(M^{n+1} - M^{n+2} M^D) = 0$. By $Theorem1.3.4[1]$, $r(M - M^2 M^D) = 0$ and so $M - M^2 M^D$ is quasi-nilpotent. This completes the proof.

By taking $n = 0$ in Theorem 1, we obtain the following corollary.

Corollary 1. [13] Let $M = \begin{pmatrix} A & B \\ C & D \end{pmatrix}$ be a 2 × 2 block operator matrix where $A \in \mathbf{B}(X)$ and $D \in \mathbf{B}(Y)$ are generalized Drazin invertible, $B \in \mathbf{B}(Y, X)$ and $C \in \mathbf{B}(X, Y)$. If $BC = 0$ and $BD = 0$, then

$$M^D = \begin{pmatrix} A^D & (A^D)^2 B \\ \Sigma_0 & D^D + \Sigma_1 B \end{pmatrix}.$$

The following result is a generalization of Theorem2.2 in [14].

Theorem 2. Let $M = \begin{pmatrix} A & B \\ C & D \end{pmatrix}$ be a 2×2 block operator matrix where $A \in \mathbf{B}(X)$ and $D \in \mathbf{B}(Y)$ are generalized Drazin invertible, $B \in \mathbf{B}(Y, X)$ and $C \in \mathbf{B}(X, Y)$. If $BC = 0, BDC = 0$ and $BD^2 = 0$, then

$$M^D = \begin{pmatrix} A^D & (A^D)^3 (AB + BD) \\ \Sigma_0 & D^D + (D^D)^3 CB + \Sigma_2 (AB + BD) \end{pmatrix}.$$

Theorem 3. Let $M = \begin{pmatrix} A & B \\ C & D \end{pmatrix}$ be a 2 × 2 block operator matrix where $A \in \mathbf{B}(X)$, $D \in \mathbf{B}(Y)$ and BC are generalized Drazin invertible, $B \in \mathbf{B}(Y, X)$ and $C \in \mathbf{B}(X, Y)$. If $ABC = 0, BD = 0$, then

$$M^D = \begin{pmatrix} XA & XB \\ \Sigma_0' A + YC & \Sigma_0' B + YD \end{pmatrix},$$

where

$$X = \sum_{i=0}^{\infty}((BC)^D)^{i+1}A^{2i}A^{\pi} + (BC)^{\pi}\sum_{i=0}^{\infty}(BC)^i(A^D)^{2i+2} \tag{12}$$

$$Y = \sum_{i=0}^{\infty}(D^D)^{2i+2}(CB)^i(CB)^{\pi} + D^{\pi}\sum_{i=0}^{\infty}D^{2i}((CB)^D)^{i+1} \tag{13}$$

$$\Sigma_0' = \sum_{i=0}^{\infty}Y^{i+2}(CA + DC)(A^2 + BC)^iA^{\pi} \tag{14}$$

$$+((CB)^{\pi} - D^2Y)\sum_{i=0}^{\infty}(CB + D^2)^i(CA + DC)X^{i+2} - YCA^D - D^DCX \tag{15}$$

Proof. It is easy to see, from the hypothesis of the theorem, that

$$M^2 = \begin{pmatrix} A^2 + BC & AB \\ CA + DC & CB + D^2 \end{pmatrix}.$$

Noting that $ABC = 0$ and $BD = 0$, by Lemma 1, we have $A^2 + BC$ and $CB + D^2$ are generalized Drazin invertible. Let X, Y be defined as Eq. (12), then we can see that $X = (A^2 + BC)^D$ and $Y = (CB + D^2)^D$. It is easy to check that M^2 satisfies the conditions in Corollary 1, whence

$$(M^2)^D = \begin{pmatrix} X & X^2AB \\ \Sigma_0' & Y + \Sigma_1'AB \end{pmatrix},$$

where Σ_n' is defined analogously in Eq. (2) with A, C, D replaced by $A^2 + BC, CA + DC, CB + D^2$, respectively, for $n = 0, 1$. Since $(M^2)^D = (M^D)^2$, we have $M^D = (M^2)^DM$.

$$M^D = \begin{pmatrix} X & X^2AB \\ \Sigma_0' & Y + \Sigma_1'AB \end{pmatrix}\begin{pmatrix} A & B \\ C & D \end{pmatrix} = \begin{pmatrix} XA & XB \\ \Sigma_0'A + YC & \Sigma_0'B + YD \end{pmatrix},$$

where X, Y, Σ_0' are as in Eq. (12).

Theorem 3 extend the formula $(ABC = 0, D = 0)$ in [12].

References

1. Murphy, G.J.: C^*-Algebras and operator Theory. Academic Press, San Diego (1990)
2. Koliha, J.J.: A generalized Drazin inverse. Glasgow Math. J. 38, 367–381 (1996)
3. Koliha, J.J., Rakočević, V.: Continuity of the Drazin inverse II. Studia Math. 131, 167–177 (1998)
4. Rakočević, V.: Continuity of the Drazin inverse. J. Operator Theory 41, 55–68 (1999)
5. Djordjević, D.S., Wei, Y.: Additive results for the generalized Drazin inverse. J. Austral. Math. Soc. 73, 115–125 (2002)

6. Cvetković-Ilić, D.S., Djordjević, D.S., Wei, Y.: Additive results for the generalized Drazin inverse in a Banach algebra. Linear Algebra Appl. 418, 53–61 (2006)
7. Ben Israel, A., Greville, T.N.E.: Generalized Inverses: Theory and Applications. Wiley, New York (1974)
8. Campbell, S.L., Meyer, C.D.: Continuity properties of the Drazin inverse Inverse. Linear Algebra Appl. 10, 77–83 (1975)
9. Campbell, S.L.: The Drazin inverse and systems of second order linear differential equations. Linear and Multilinear Algebra 14, 195–198 (1983)
10. Djordjević, D.S., Stanmirovic, P.S.: On the generalized Drazin inverse and generalized resolvent. Czechoslovak Math. J. 51, 617–634 (2001)
11. Deng, C., Cvetković-Ilić, D.S., Wei, Y.: Some results on the generalized Drazin inverse of operator matrices. Linear Multilinear Algebra 14, 1–10 (2008)
12. Deng, C., Wei, Y.: A note on the Drazin inverse of an anti-triangular matrix. Linear Algebra Appl. 431, 1910–1922 (2009)
13. Hartwig, R.E., Li, X., Wei, Y.: Representations for the Drazin inverse of a 2 × 2 block matrix. SIAM J. Matrix. Anal. Appl. 27, 757–771 (2006)
14. Dopazo, E., Matinez-Serrano, M.F.: Further results on the representation of the Drazin inverse of a 2 × 2 block matrix. Linear Algebra Appl. 432, 1896–1904 (2010)
15. Cvetković-Ilić, D.S., Wei, Y.: Representations for the Drazin inverse of bounded operators on Banach space. Electronic Journal of Linear Algebra 18, 613–627 (2009)
16. Deng, C.: A note on the Drazin inverses with Banachiewicz-Schur forms. Appl. Math. Comput. 213, 230–234 (2009)

Uniformity of Improved Versions of Chord

Jacek Cichoń, Rafał Kapelko, and Karol Marchwicki

Institute of Mathematics and Computer Science,
Wrocław University of Technology, Poland
{jacek.cichon,rafal.kapelko,karol.marchwicki}@pwr.wroc.pl

Abstract. In this paper we analyse the uniformity of Chord P2P system and its improved versions defined in [1] - folded Chord. We are interested in the maximal and the minimal areas controlled by nodes in these systems. We recall known results for the classical Chord system and compare it with the new results for its modifications. It is known that the function $n \mapsto n^{-2}$ is a threshold for a number of nodes in Chord controlling small areas (i.e. w.h.p. there exists one node controlling area of length $\leq n^{-2}$ and for every $\varepsilon > 0$ there are no nodes controlling areas of size less than $n^{-2-\varepsilon}$). We show that the function $n \mapsto \sqrt{2}n^{-3/2}$ is a similar threshold for 2-folded Chord. We also discuss the number of nodes controlling large areas and we find upper thresholds for all these P2P systems. All modifications of Chord are very soft and flexible and can be easily applied to P2P systems which use the classical Chord protocol.

Keywords: Peer-to-peer networks, Chord, Asymptotic, Order statistics.

1 Introduction

Uniformity of decentralised P2P systems such as Chord can be analysed either by measuring the concentration of a random variable, which describes the length of intervals controlled by nodes, or by inspecting the spread between minimal and maximal length of these intervals. In this paper we focus on estimating minimal and maximal intervals lengths in Chord and one of its modifications proposed in [1]. Improving the uniformity of decentralised P2P systems plays an important role in many applications since it is directly correlated with the load balance of nodes. For that reason one of our main goals is to find the method of estimating the length of minimal and maximal areas controlled by nodes and show the improvement of uniformity when comparing to the classical Chord P2P protocol.

The classical Chord protocol defined in [2] and developed in [3] and many other papers may be described as a structure

$$\text{Chord} = (\{0,1\}^{160}, H, H_1) ,$$

where H is a hash function assigning position to each node and H_1 is a hash function assigning position of descriptors of documents. The space $\{0,1\}^{160}$ is identified with the set $\{0,1,\ldots,2^{160}-1\}$ considered as the circular space with the ordering $0 < 1 < \ldots < 2^{160} - 1 < 0 < \ldots$. Each new node X obtains a position $H(Id)$ (where Id is an identifier of the node) in the space $\{0,1\}^{160}$ and is responsible for the interval starting

R. Zhu et al. (Eds.): ICICA 2010, LNCS 6377, pp. 431–438, 2010.
© Springer-Verlag Berlin Heidelberg 2010

at point $H(Id)$ and ending at the next point from the set $\{H(Id') : Id' \neq Id\}$. This node is called the successor of the node X. Each document with a descriptor doc is placed at point $H_1(doc)$ in the space $\{0,1\}^{160}$ and the information about this document is stored by the node which is responsible for the interval into which $H_1(doc)$ falls.

In [1] two natural modifications of the classical Chord protocols are defined and analysed from the reliability point of view: folded Chord and direct union of Chord. However our discussion will concentrate on the folded Chords. We describe this protocol in Section 2.

The paper is organised as follows. In Subsection 1.1 we discuss basic facts and notation. In Section 2 we describe the k-folded Chord P2P protocol and analyse cases in which those structures can be used. In Section 3 we inspect how to improve the uniformity of classical Chord and present several theorems for estimating the minimum and maximum length of intervals controlled by nodes in proposed modifications. Finally, Section 4 summaries and concludes our work.

1.1 Basic Facts and Notation

Let $\operatorname{succ}(X)$ be the successor of a node in Chord. In the classical Chord protocol each node controls the subinterval $[X, \operatorname{succ}(X)]$ of the space $\{0,1\}^{160}$.

Let $\mathcal{N}$ denote the set of nodes in the system. Chord protocol (and its modifications as well) has a virtual space Ω and each node $x \in \mathcal{N}$ controls some area $N_x \subset \Omega$. In the Chord protocol $\Omega = \{0,1\}^{160}$ and $(N_x)_{x \in \mathcal{N}}$ is a partition of Ω.

In further discussion we shall identify the Chord virtual space Ω with the interval $[0,1)$ (we think about $[0,1)$ as a circle of unit length): we place one node at point 0 and next points will form a random subset of the interval $[0,1)$. Hence in the case of Chord (in case of folded Chord defined in Section 2 as well) the sets (N_x) are subintervals of $[0,1)$.

Let us fix a number of nodes n. Let d_i denotes the length of area controlled by i-th node. For Chord we have $d_1 + \ldots + d_n = 1$. For and fChord$_k$ described in the next Section we have $d_1 + \ldots + d_n = k$.

For $\delta \geq 0$ we define

$$S_n(\delta) = \operatorname{card}(\{i : d_i < \delta\}), \quad L_n(\delta) = \operatorname{card}(\{i : d_i \geq \delta\}) \qquad (1)$$

and

$$\min_n = \min\{d_1, \ldots, d_n\}, \quad \max_n = \max\{d_1, \ldots, d_n\} \ .$$

Then $S_n(\delta)$, $L_n(\delta)$, $\min_n$ and $\max_n$ are random variables on the space of all possible realizations of considered P2P protocol with n nodes. In this paper we shall investigate asymptotic of average values of these random variables for the case where the number n of nodes is large.

By $\Gamma(z)$ we denote the standard generalisation of the factorial function. The following identities hold: $n! = \Gamma(n+1)$, $z\Gamma(z) = \Gamma(z+1)$.

Let X be a random variable. We denote its expected value by $\mathbf{E}[X]$. We will also use the eulerian function $B(a,b) = \int_0^1 x^{a-1}(1-x)^{b-1}dx$ which is defined for all complex numbers a, b such as $\Re(a) > 0$ and $\Re(b) > 0$. We will use the following basic identity $B(a,b) = \Gamma(a)\Gamma(b)/\Gamma(a+b)$.

Let $X_1, \ldots, X_n$ be independent random variables with the uniform density on $[0, 1)$. The order statistics $X_{1:n}, \ldots X_{n:n}$ are the random variables obtained from $X_1, \ldots, X_n$ by sorting each of their realisations in the increasing order. The probabilistic density $f_{k:n}(x)$ of the variable $X_{k:n}$ equals

$$f_{k:n}(x) = \frac{1}{\mathrm{B}(k, n - k + 1)} x^{k-1}(1 - x)^{n-k} . \tag{2}$$

(see e.g. [4]). Let us recall that these kinds of probabilistic distributions are called Beta distributions.

In the following two theorems we formulate basic properties of the random variables $S_n(\delta)$, $L_n(\delta)$, and their connection with the random variables $\min_n$ and $\max_n$.

Theorem 1. *Let n denote the number of nodes in the P2P system. Then*

1. $S_n(\delta) + L_n(\delta) = n,$
2. $\mathbf{E}\left[S_n(\delta)\right] \geq \Pr[\min_n < \delta],$
3. $\mathbf{E}\left[L_n(\delta)\right] \geq \Pr[\max_n \geq \delta].$

Proof. Let $A = \{i : d_i < \delta\}$ and $B = \{i : d_i \geq \delta\}$. Then $A \cup B = \{1, \ldots, n\}$ and $A \cap B = \emptyset$. Hence $n = \mathrm{card}(A) + \mathrm{card}(B) = S_n(\delta) + L_n(\delta)$. Observe that

$$\mathbf{E}\left[S_n(\delta)\right] = \sum_k k \Pr[S_n(\delta) = k] \geq \sum_{k \geq 1} \Pr[S_n(\delta) = k] = \Pr[S_n(\delta) \geq 1] .$$

Notice finally that $(S_n(\delta) \geq 1) \leftrightarrow (\exists i)(d_i < \delta) \leftrightarrow (\min_n < \delta)$. Therefore,

$$\mathbf{E}\left[S_n(\delta)\right] \geq \Pr[S_n(\delta) \geq 1] = \Pr[\min_n < \delta)] .$$

The last part of Theorem follows directly from part (1) and (2).

Theorem 2. *Let n denote the number of nodes in the P2P system and let $\delta \geq 0$. Then*

1. $\mathbf{E}\left[\min_n\right] \geq \delta(1 - \mathbf{E}\left[S_n(\delta)\right]),$
2. $\mathbf{E}\left[\max_n\right] \leq \delta(1 - \mathbf{E}\left[L_n(\delta)\right]).$

Proof. Let $h(x)$ be the density of the random variable $\min_n$. Then

$$\mathbf{E}\left[\min_n\right] = \int_0^\infty x h(x) dx \geq \int_\delta^\infty x h(x) dx \geq$$

$$\delta \int_\delta^\infty h(x) dx = \delta \Pr[\min_n \geq \delta] = \delta(1 - \Pr[\min_n < \delta]) .$$

From Theorem 1 we get $\mathbf{E}\left[S_n(\delta)\right] \geq \Pr[\min_n < \delta]$, so $\mathbf{E}\left[\min_n\right] \geq \delta(1 - \mathbf{E}\left[S_n(\delta)\right])$. A proof of the second part is similar to the above ones.

Suppose that we have a sequence (δ_n) such that $\mathbf{E}\left[S_n(\delta_n)\right] = o(1)$ when n tends to infinity. From Theorem 1 we deduce that also $\Pr[\min_n < \delta_n] \to 0$ and from Theorem 2 we deduce that $\mathbf{E}\left[\min_n\right] \geq \delta_n(1 - o(1))$. A similar remark holds for the random variables $L_n(\delta_n)$ and $\max_n$.

2 Folded Chord

In [1] two natural modifications of the classical Chord protocols were defined and analysed from the reliability point of view: direct unions of Chord and folded Chord.

Let $succ(X)$ be the successor of a node in Chord. In the classical Chord protocol each node controls the subinterval $[X, succ(X))$ of the space $\{0, 1\}^{160}$. The k-*folded Chord*, denoted as fChord$_k$, is the modification of the Chord protocol in which each node controls the interval $[X, sc^k(X))$, where $sc^1(X) = succ(X)$ and $sc^{k+1}(X) = succ(sc^k(X))$.

Let $\mathcal{N}$ denote the set of nodes in the system. Each of the above P2P protocols has a virtual space Ω and each node $x \in \mathcal{N}$ controls some area $N_x \subset \Omega$. In the Chord protocol $\Omega = \{0, 1\}^{160}$ and $(N_x)_{x \in \mathcal{N}}$ is a partition of Ω. In k-folded Chord $\Omega = \{0, 1\}^{160}$ and $(N_x)_{x \in \mathcal{N}}$ is a k-covering of Ω, i.e.

$$(\forall \omega \in \Omega)(|\{x \in \mathcal{N} : \omega \in N_x\}| = k) \ .$$

The main reason for the introduction of k-folded Chords was to increase the average life-time of documents in the system. Namely in any P2P systems we must pay attention to nodes that leave the system in unexpected ways: they can leave the system without the transfer of collected information back into the system. We call such an event an unexpected departure (see [5]). The classical Chord system is vulnerable in this situation. But if $k \geq 2$ then in k-folded Chord there is a possibility of recover partially lost information items since each information item is stored in k different nodes. This process was discussed in [1]. Let us only mention that for systems with medium number of nodes (of rank 10^5) and realistic performance parameters the average life-time of documents stored in 2-folded Chord is several dozen times longer than in the classical Chord. Moreover, for small values of the parameter k, the communication complexity in k - folded Chord is not essentially larger than in classical Chord. The main cost of this approach is the increase of memory of nodes - nodes in k-folded Chord stores k-times more information items than in the classical Chord.

3 Uniformity of Folded Chord

In this section we analyse the number of nodes in k-folded Chord which control small and large areas.

We denote by $S_n^k(\delta)$ and $L_n^k(\delta)$ the variants of variables $S_n(\delta)$ and $L_n(\delta)$ defined by Equation (1) for the structures fChord$_k$ with n nodes.

In order to analyse properties of areas controlled by nodes in the structure fChord$_k$ we should generate the sequence $0 = \xi_{1:n} \leq \xi_{2:n} \leq \cdots \leq \xi_{n:n} \leq 1$ and investigate the differences $d_1 = \xi_{k+1:n} - \xi_{1:n}$, $d_2 = \xi_{k+2:n} - \xi_{2:n}$ and so on. Notice that the distance d_1 follows $f_{k:n-1}$ distribution. Notice also that all random variables (d_i) have the same distribution as the random variable d_1 (all nodes have the same statistical properties). Hence $\mathbf{E}\left[S_n^k(\delta)\right] = n \int_0^\delta f_{k:n-1}(x)dx$ and $\mathbf{E}\left[L_n^k(\delta)\right] = n \int_\delta^1 f_{k:n-1}(x)dx$ (see Equation 2).

Lemma 1. *Let $c \geq 0$, $k \geq 2$ and $\delta = \frac{(k!)^{\frac{1}{k}}}{n^{1+\frac{1}{k}+c}}$. Then*

$$\mathbf{E}\left[S_n^f(\delta)\right] = \frac{1}{n^{kc}} - \frac{k}{k+1}(k!)^{\frac{1}{k}}\frac{1}{n^{\frac{1}{k}+kc+c}} + O\left(\frac{1}{n^{kc+1}}\right) + O\left(\frac{1}{n^{\frac{2}{k}+kc+2c}}\right).$$

Proof. Notice that $(1-x)^{n-1-k} = 1 - (n-1-k)x + S_{n-1-k}(x)$, where

$$S_{n-1-k}(x) = \sum_{i=2}^{n-1-k}\binom{n-1-k}{i}x^i(-1)^i.$$

Observe that for $x \in (0,\delta)$ we have

$$|S_{n-1-k}(x)| \leq \sum_{i=2}^{n-1-k}\frac{\binom{n-1-k}{i}}{n^i}\frac{(k!)^{\frac{i}{k}}}{n^{\frac{i}{k}+ic}} \leq \frac{1}{2!}\sum_{i=2}^{n-1-k}\frac{(k!)^{\frac{i}{k}}}{n^{\frac{i}{k}+ic}} \leq$$

$$\frac{1}{2!}\frac{(k!)^{\frac{2}{k}}}{n^{\frac{2}{k}+2c}}\frac{1}{1-(\frac{k!}{n})^{\frac{1}{k}}\frac{1}{n^c}}.$$

Using the Equation 2 we get

$$n\int_0^\delta f_{k:n-1}(x)dx =$$

$$\frac{(n-1)!n}{(k-1)!(n-1-k)!}\int_0^\delta (1-(n-1-k)x)\,x^{k-1}dx +$$

$$\frac{(n-1)!n}{(k-1)!(n-1-k)!}\int_0^\delta S_{n-1-k}(x)x^{k-1}dx =$$

$$\frac{1}{n^{kc}} - \frac{k}{k+1}(k!)^{\frac{1}{k}}\frac{1}{n^{\frac{1}{k}+kc+c}} + O\left(\frac{1}{n^{kc+1}}\right) + O\left(\frac{1}{n^{\frac{2}{k}+kc+2c}}\right). \qquad \square$$

A direct consequence of the previous Lemma is the following result:

Theorem 3. *Let $c > 0$. Then*

1. $\lim_{n\to\infty} \mathbf{E}\left[S_n^k\left(\frac{(k!)^{\frac{1}{k}}}{n^{1+\frac{1}{k}}}\right)\right] = 1,$

2. $\lim_{n\to\infty} \mathbf{E}\left[S_n^k\left(\frac{(k!)^{\frac{1}{k}}}{n^{1+\frac{1}{k}+c}}\right)\right] = 0.$

The last theorem implies that s_k

$$s_k(n) = \frac{(k!)^{\frac{1}{k}}}{n^{1+\frac{1}{k}}}$$

is a threshold function for number of small nodes in k-folded Chord. Notice that $s_1(n) = \frac{1}{n^2}$, $s_2(n) = \frac{\sqrt{2}}{n^{\frac{3}{2}}}$ $s_3(n) = \frac{\sqrt[3]{6}}{n^{\frac{4}{3}}}$. In order to properly compare these functions we should divide this function by k, since the average size of controlled intervals in k-folded Chord is equal to $\frac{k}{n}$. Observe that

$$\frac{1}{n^2} < \frac{\sqrt{2}}{2n^{\frac{3}{2}}} < \frac{\sqrt[3]{6}}{3n^{\frac{4}{3}}} < \cdots$$

for sufficiently large n, so the size of „smallest" nodes significantly increases with the increase of k.

We shall investigate now the number of large nodes.

Lemma 2. *Let* $f(n) = O(\ln(n))$, $\delta = \frac{f(n)}{n}$ *and let* $k \geq 2$. *Then*

$$\mathbf{E}\left[L_n^k(\delta)\right] = n(1-\delta)^{n-k}\left(O\left((\ln n)^{k-2}\right) + \frac{\delta^{k-1}n^{k-1}}{(k-1)!}\right) . \tag{3}$$

Proof. The proof will be done by induction. For $k = 2$ we have

$$\int_\delta^1 f_{2:n-1}(x)dx = (1-\delta)^{n-2}(1 - 2\delta + \delta n) = (1-\delta)^{n-2}(O(1) + \delta n) .$$

Let us assume the result holds for the number k. Then we have

$$\int_\delta^1 f_{k+1:n-1}(x)dx = \frac{(n-1)!}{k!(n-1-k)!}\delta^k(1-\delta)^{n-1-k} + \int_\delta^1 f_{k:n-1}(x)dx .$$

Using the inductive assumption we get

$$\int_\delta^1 f_{k+1:n-1}(x)dx = \frac{(n-1)!}{k!(n-1-k)!}\delta^k(1-\delta)^{n-1-k}+$$

$$(1-\delta)^{n-k}\left(O\left((\ln n)^{k-2}\right) + \frac{\delta^{k-1}n^{k-1}}{(k-1)!}\right) =$$

$$(1-\delta)^{n-k-1}\left(O\left((\ln n)^{k-1}\right) + \frac{\delta^k n^k}{k!}\right) ,$$

which gives the claimed equality for $k + 1$. $\qquad\square$

Let us fix a number $c \geq 0$. After putting $\delta = \frac{\ln(n)+\ln\left(\frac{1}{(k-1)!}(\ln n)^{k-1}\right)}{n}(1+c)$ into Equation 3 for $\mathbf{E}\left[L_n^k(\delta)\right]$ we get

$$\mathbf{E}\left[L_n^f(\delta)\right] \approx$$

$$n\left(1 - \frac{\ln(n) + \ln\left(\frac{1}{(k-1)!}(\ln n)^{k-1}\right)}{n}(1+c)\right)^{n-k}\frac{(1+c)^{k-1}(\ln n)^{k-1}}{(k-1)!} \approx$$

$$\frac{1}{n^c}\left(\frac{(k-1)!}{(\ln n)^{k-1}}\right)^c(1+c)^{k-1} .$$

and from this approximation we deduce the next result:

Theorem 4. *Let $c > 0$ and $k \geq 1$. Then*

1. $\lim_{n \to \infty} \mathbf{E}\left[L_n^k\left(\dfrac{\ln(n) + \ln\left((\ln n)^{k-1}\right) - \ln((k-1)!)}{n}\right)\right] = 1,$

2. $\lim_{n \to \infty} \mathbf{E}\left[L_n^k\left(\dfrac{\ln(n) + \ln\left((\ln n)^{k-1}\right) - \ln((k-1)!)}{n}(1+c)\right)\right] = 0.$

Let

$$l_k(n) = \frac{\ln n + (k-1)\ln\ln n - \ln(k-1)!}{n} .$$

From the last theorem we deduce that the function l_k is a threshold function for the number of large nodes in k-folded Chord. In order to properly compare these functions we should remember that the average size of interval controlled by one node in k - folded Chord is equal to $\frac{k}{n}$, hence we should compare the functions

$$l_k^*(n) = \frac{1}{k} l_k = \frac{\frac{1}{k}\ln n + (1 - \frac{1}{k})\ln\ln n - \frac{1}{k}\ln(k-1)!}{n} .$$

4   Conclusions and Further Works

Theorem 1, Theorem 2 and the two theorems from the previous section imply that the lengths of intervals controlled by nodes in k-folded Chord are, with high probability for large n, inside the intervals

$$\left[\frac{(k!)^{\frac{1}{k}}}{n^{1+\frac{1}{k}}}, \frac{\ln(n) + (k-1)\ln\ln n - \ln(k-1)!}{n}\right] .$$

If we divide the upper bound by the lower bound, then we deduce that the measure of concentration of intervals in k - folded Chord is of the order $\Theta(n^{\frac{1}{k}}\ln n)$. This observation gives a precise formula for the influence of the parameter k on the uniformity of the k-folded Chords.

We plan to extend our study to other popular P2P protocols such as CAN (see [6]), Binary-Chord (see [7]), PASTRY (see [8]), KADEMLIA (see [9]) and others.

References

1. Cichoń, J., Jasiński, A., Kapelko, R., Zawada, M.: How to Improve the Reliability of Chord? In: Meersman, R., Tari, Z., Herrero, P. (eds.) OTM-WS 2008. LNCS, vol. 5333, pp. 904–913. Springer, Heidelberg (2008)
2. Stoica, I., Morris, R., Karger, D., Kaashoek, M.F., Balakrishnan, H.: Chord: A Scalable Peer-to-Peer Lookup Service for Internet Applications. In: SIGCOMM 2001, San Diego, California, USA, pp. 149–160 (2001)
3. Liben-Nowell, D., Balakrishnan, H., Karger, D.: Analysis of the Evolution of Peer-to-Peer Systems. In: ACM Conference on Principles of Distributed Computing, Monterey, California, USA, pp. 233–242 (2002)
4. Arnold, B., Balakrishnan, N., Nagaraja, H.: A First Course in Order Statistics. John Wiley & Sons, New York (1992)

5. Derek, L., Zhong, Y., Vivek, R., Loguinov, D.: On Lifetime-Based Node Failure and Stochastic Resilience of Decentralized Peer-to-Peer Networks. IEEE/ACM Transactions on Networking 15, 644–656 (2007)
6. Ratnasamy, S., Francis, P., Handley, M., Karp, R., Shenker, S.: A scalable Content-addressable Network. In: SIGCOMM 2001, San Diego, California, USA, pp. 161–172 (2001)
7. Cichoń, J., Klonowski, M., Krzywiecki, L., Rożański, B., Zieliński, P.: Random Subsets of the Interval and p2p Protocols. In: Charikar, M., Jansen, K., Reingold, O., Rolim, J.D.P. (eds.) RANDOM 2007 and APPROX 2007. LNCS, vol. 4627, pp. 904–913. Springer, Heidelberg (2007)
8. Druschel, P., Rowstron, A.: Pastry: Scalable, Decentralized Object Location and Routing for Large-Scale Peer-to-Peer Systems. In: Guerraoui, R. (ed.) Middleware 2001. LNCS, vol. 2218, pp. 329–350. Springer, Heidelberg (2001)
9. Maymounkov, P., Mazières, D.: Kademlia: A Peer-to-Peer Information System Based on the XOR Metric. In: Druschel, P., Kaashoek, M.F., Rowstron, A. (eds.) IPTPS 2002. LNCS, vol. 2429, pp. 53–65. Springer, Heidelberg (2002)

Aggregate Homotopy Method for Solving the Nonlinear Complementarity Problem*

Xiaona Fan and Qinglun Yan

College of Science, Nanjing University of Posts and Telecommunications,
Nanjing, Jiangsu 210046, P.R. China

Abstract. To solve the nonlinear complementarity problem, a new aggregate homotopy method is considered. The homotopy equation is constructed based on the aggregate function which is the smooth approximation to the reformulation of the nonlinear complementarity problem. Under certain conditions, the existence and convergence of a smooth path defined by a new homotopy which leads to a solution of the original problem are proved. The results provide a theoretical basis to develop a new computational method for nonlinear complementarity problem.

Keywords: nonlinear complementarity problem, homotopy method, smoothing method, global convergence.

1 Introduction

Let $F : R^n \to R^n$ be continuously differentiable. The nonlinear complementarity problem (NCP for abbreviation) is to find a vector $x \in R^n$ such that

$$x \geq 0, \ F(x) \geq 0, \ x^T F(x) = 0. \tag{1}$$

The NCP has many applications in a lot of fields, such as mathematical programming, economic equilibrium models, engineering design, operations research, games theory and so on. It has attracted many researchers since its appearance and numerous methods have been developed to solve the NCP. The survey papers by Harker and Pang [15], Ferris and Pang [9] include a large number of recent development and important applications of the NCP. In algorithm, the NCP has been used as a general framework for linear complementarity problems, some mathematical programming problems and equilibrium problems. Therefore, many different algorithms for solving the NCP have poured out. These solution methods for the nonlinear complementarity problems can be classified into three categories: 1) transforming into nonsmooth or smooth equations (or, fixed point problems) and then being solved by semismooth Newton-type

* This work is supported by Foundation of NJUPT under Grant No. NY208069, the Natural Sciences Foundation for Colleges and Universities in Jiangsu Province of China under Grant No. 09KJD110004 and the Natural Science Foundation of China under Grant No. 70972083.

R. Zhu et al. (Eds.): ICICA 2010, LNCS 6377, pp. 439–446, 2010.

methods, smoothing Newton methods, continuation method or projective methods(see, e.g., [4,5,6,8,11,12,13,14,16,18,19,20,29,31]); 2) reformulating as optimization problems and then being solved by some algorithms for optimization problems(see, e.g., [2,3,10,17,21,27]); 3) solving K-K-T systems of the nonlinear complementarity problems similarly with K-K-T system of constrained optimization (homotopy methods, e.g., [23,24,32]). However, the convergence of many algorithms were established when the mapping F is assumed to have some monotonicity.

For an extensive survey of the NCP, we refer the readers to [26]. Among the presented methods, reformulations of the NCP as a system of nonsmooth equations have been drawn much attention. People often use so called NCP function to reformulate it as a system of equations. To discuss the NCP's reformulation requires the following definition first, which is equivalent to the NCP function defined in [28].

Definition 1. *A function* $\varphi : R^n \rightarrow R$ *is called a NCP function provided* $\varphi(a, b) = 0$ *if and only if* $a \geq 0, b \geq 0, ab = 0$.

The following are two most common equivalent equations referring to the NCP functions to solve the NCP.

(i) $\min(a, b) = 0$, where min operator is taken component-wise;

Another equivalent equation formulation referring to the Fischer-Burmerister function is defined by

(ii) $\phi_{FB}(a, b) = \sqrt{a^2 + b^2} - (a + b) = 0$.

As we know, the two equations are only locally Lipschitz continuous but not differentiable. Hence, many classic methods for smooth equations are not applied directly. In this paper, reformulating (i), we derive its smooth approximation [4]:

$$\varphi(a, b, \mu) = -\mu \ln\{e^{-a/\mu} + e^{-b/\mu}\}. \tag{2}$$

When $\mu \rightarrow 0$, we can yield the approximate solution of the NCP.

In this paper, we aim to apply the homotopy method to solve the NCP based on the smooth equation (2). Homotopy methods established by Kellogg et al. [22], Smale [30] and Chow et al. [7] have become a powerful tool in finding solutions of various nonlinear problems, such as zeros or fixed points of maps and so on. A distinctive advantage of the homotopy method is that the algorithm generated by it exhibits the global convergence under weaker conditions.

For good introductions and surveys about homotopy methods, we refer the readers to the books [1,12].

The remainder of this paper is organized as follows. In Section 2, we introduce some lemmas which from differential topology will be used in our further discussions. In Section 3, the main results of the paper are given. The homotopy equation for the above approximation of the equivalent formulation of the NCP is formulated. And under the assumption which is the same condition as the one in [32], the existence and convergence of a smooth path from any given initial point in R^n_+ to a solution of the NCP are proved. Our results provide a theoretical basis to develop a new computational method for nonlinear complementarity problem.

2   Preliminaries

The following lemmas from differential topology will be used in the following. At first, let $U \in R^n$ be on the open set, and let $\phi : U \to R^p$ be a $C^\alpha(\alpha > \max\{0, n - p\})$ mapping. We say that $y \in R^p$ is a regular value for ϕ, if

$$Range \left[\frac{\partial \phi(x)}{\partial x} \right] = R^p, \; \forall \, x \in \phi^{-1}(y).$$

Lemma 1 (Parameterized Sard Theorem [1]). *Let $V \subset R^n$, $U \subset R^m$ be open sets and let $\phi : V \times U \to R^k$ be a C^α mapping, where $\alpha > \max\{0, m - k\}$. If $0 \in R^k$ is a regular value of ϕ, then for almost all $a \in V$, 0 is a regular value of $\phi_a = \phi(a, \cdot)$.*

Lemma 2 (Inverse Image Theorem [25]). *Let $\phi : U \in R^n \to R^p$ be a C^α $(\alpha > \max\{0, n - p\})$ mapping. If 0 is a regular value of ϕ, then $\phi^{-1}(0)$ consists of some $(n - p)$-dimensional C^α manifolds.*

Lemma 3 (Classification Theorem of One-Dimensional Smooth Manifolds [25]). *A one-dimensional smooth manifold is homeomorphic to a unit circle or a unit interval.*

3   Main Results

For arbitrary given $x^{(0)} \in R^n$ and $\mu \in (0, 1]$, we construct the homotopy equation as follows:

$$H(x, \mu) = \Phi(x, \mu) + \mu x^{(0)} = 0, \tag{3}$$

where

$$\Phi_i(x, \mu) = -\mu ln\{e^{-x_i/\mu} + e^{-F_i(x)/\mu}\}, \; i = 1, 2, \cdots, n.$$

So for every $i = 1, 2, \cdots, n$, there holds the following identity:

$$-\mu ln\{e^{-x_i/\mu} + e^{-F_i(x)/\mu}\} = -\mu x_i^{(0)}. \tag{4}$$

Set

$$H^{-1}(0) = \{(x, \mu) \in R^n \times (0, 1] : H(x, x^{(0)}, \mu) = 0\}.$$

Conjecture 1. For any $\{x^{(k)}\} \subseteq R_+^n$, as $k \to \infty$, $\|x^{(k)}\| \to \infty$ and $F(x^{(k)}) > 0$ when $k > K_0$ for some $K_0 > 0$.

This condition can also be found in [32]. It is different from the ones in the literature, but it is easily verified. Furthermore, in [32], the authors have verified that there exists the mapping F satisfy Conjecture 1, but it is not a P_0 function and it is also not monotone on R^n. This means Conjecture 1 is not stronger than that of function is monotone or P_0.

Theorem 1. *Let F be twice continuously differentiable. Suppose Conjecture 1 holds. Then, for almost all $x^{(0)} \in R_+^n$, the homotopy equation (3) determines a smooth curve $\Gamma \subset R^n \times (0,1]$ starting from $(x^{(0)}, 1)$ and approaches the hyperplane at $\mu = 0$. When $\mu \to 0$, the limit set $T \times \{0\} \subset R^n \times \{0\}$ of Γ is nonempty, and the x-component x^* of every point $(x^*, 0)$ in $T \times \{0\}$ solves (3).*

To prove Theorem 1, we first prove the following lemmas.

Lemma 4. *For almost all $x^{(0)} \in R^n$, 0 is a regular value of $H : R^n \times (0,1] \to R^n$, and $H^{-1}(0)$ consists of some smooth curves. Among them, a smooth curve Γ starts from $(x^{(0)}, 1)$.*

Proof. Taking $x^{(0)}$ also as a variate, we write the homotopy map as $H(x, x^{(0)}, \mu)$. Using $DH(x, x^{(0)}, \mu)$ to denote the Jacobian matrix of $H(x, x^{(0)}, \mu)$. Then

$$DH(x, x^{(0)}, \mu) = \left(\frac{\partial H(x, x^{(0)}, \mu)}{\partial x}, \frac{\partial H(x, x^{(0)}, \mu)}{\partial x^{(0)}}, \frac{\partial H(x, x^{(0)}, \mu)}{\partial \mu} \right).$$

For all $x^{(0)} \in R^n$ and $\mu \in (0,1]$, recalling the homotopy equation (3), we have

$$\frac{\partial H(x, x^{(0)}, \mu)}{\partial x^{(0)}} = -\mu I,$$

where I is the identity matrix. Thus, $DH(x, x^{(0)}, \mu)$ is of full row rank. That is, 0 is a regular value of $H(x, x^{(0)}, \mu)$. By Lemma 1 and Lemma 2, for almost all $x^{(0)} \in R^n$, 0 is a regular value of $H(x, x^{(0)}, \mu)$ and $H^{-1}(0)$ consists of some smooth curves. And since $H(x^{(0)}, x^{(0)}, 1) = 0$, there must be a smooth curve Γ in $H^{-1}(0)$ starting from $(x^{(0)}, 1)$.

The following lemma will play an important role in our discussion.

Lemma 5. *Suppose Conjecture 1 holds. When 0 is a regular value of $H(x, \mu)$, for almost all $x^{(0)} \in R_+^n$, Γ is bounded on $R^n \times (0,1]$.*

Proof. By Lemma 4, we have that 0 is a regular value of $H(x, x^{(0)}, \mu)$. If $\Gamma \subset R^n \times (0,1]$ is an unbounded curve, and because $(0,1]$ is bounded, then there exists a sequence of points $\{(x^k, \mu_k)\} \subset \Gamma$ such that $\| x^k \| \to \infty$, so there exists $i \in \{1, \cdots, n\}$ such that $|x_i^k| \to +\infty$ for such x_i^k satisfying the equation (4), which also can be reformulated as

$$- \mu_k ln\{e^{-x_i^k/\mu_k} + e^{-F_i(x^k)/\mu_k}\} = -\mu_k x_i^{(0)} \tag{5}$$

– For $x_i^k \to -\infty$, we have

$$\begin{aligned}
\Phi_i(x^k, \mu_k) &= -\mu_k ln\{e^{-x_i^k/\mu_k} + e^{-F_i(x^k)/\mu_k}\} \\
&= x_i^k - \mu_k ln\{1 + e^{(x_i^k - F_i(x^k))/\mu_k}\} \\
&\leq x_i^k \\
&\to -\infty
\end{aligned}$$

which is a contradiction to the right side of the equality (5). Hence, this case can not occur.

– For $x_i^k \to +\infty$, we have the following three possible subcases:
  – $\liminf_{k \to +\infty} F_i(x^k) = -\infty$;

In this case, we have

$$\Phi_i(x^k, \mu_k) = -\mu_k ln\{e^{-x_i^k/\mu_k} + e^{-F_i(x^k)/\mu_k}\}$$
$$= F_i(x^k) - \mu_k ln\{1 + e^{(F_i(x^k)-x_i^k)/\mu_k}\}$$
$$\leq F_i(x^k)$$
$$\to -\infty$$

which is also a contradiction to the right side of the equality (5). Hence, this case can not occur.

  – $\limsup_{k \to +\infty} F_i(x^k) = +\infty$;

In this case, we have

$$\Phi_i(x^k, \mu_k) = -\mu_k ln\{e^{-x_i^k/\mu_k} + e^{-F_i(x^k)/\mu_k}\}$$
$$\geq -\mu_k ln\{2e^{\max\{-x_i^k, -F_i(x^k)\}/\mu_k}\}$$
$$= -\mu_k ln2 + \min\{x_i^k, F_i(x^k)\}$$
$$\to +\infty,$$

which contradicts with the equation (5).

  – $\lim_{k \to +\infty} F_i(x^k)$ is finite.

In this case, we have the left side of the equality (5)

$$\Phi_i(x^k, \mu_k) = -\mu_k ln\{e^{-x_i^k/\mu_k} + e^{-F_i(x^k)/\mu_k}\}$$
$$= F_i(x^k) - \mu_k ln\{1 + e^{(F_i(x^k)-x_i^k)/\mu_k}\}.$$

For $x_i^k \to +\infty$ and $\mu_k \in (0, 1]$, we have $(F_i(x^k) - x_i^k)/\mu_k \to -\infty$ and therefore, $\mu_k ln\{1 + e^{(F_i(x^k)-x_i^k)/\mu_k}\} \to 0$. Let $k \to \infty$ take the limit, we derive

$$\lim_{k \to \infty} \Phi_i(x^k, \mu_k) = \lim_{k \to +\infty} F_i(x^k)$$

However, if we take the initial point $x^{(0)}$ such that $x^{(0)} \geq 0$, the right side of the equality (5) less than 0, which contradicts with the Conjecture 1.

Combing the above two cases together, we have that Γ is bounded on $R^n \times (0, 1]$.

Lemma 6. For $x^{(0)} \in R^n$, the equation $H(x, x^{(0)}, 1) = 0$ has a unique solution $(x^{(0)}, 1)$.

Proof. It is obvious when $\mu = 1$, the homotopy equation (3) becomes $x = x^{(0)}$. Hence the conclusion holds.

Proof of Theorem 1. By Lemma 3, Γ must be homeomorphic to a unit circle or a unit interval $(0,1]$. By Lemma 4, for almost all $x^{(0)} \in R_+^n, 0$ is a regular value of $H^{-1}(0)$ and $H^{-1}(0)$ contains a smooth curve $\Gamma \subset R^n \times (0,1]$ starting from $(x^{(0)}, 1)$. By the classification theorem of the one-dimensional smooth manifold, $\Gamma \subset R^n \times (0,1]$ must be homeomorphic to a unit circle or the unit interval $(0,1]$.

Noticing that $\frac{\partial H(x^{(0)}, 1)}{\partial x} = I$ is nonsingular, we have that Γ is not homeomorphic to a unit circle. That is, Γ is homeomorphic to $(0,1]$. The limit points of Γ must lie in $R^n \times [0,1]$. Let (x^*, μ^*) be a limit point of Γ. Only the following two cases are possible:

(i) $(x^*, \mu^*) \in R^n \times \{1\}$;
(ii) $(x^*, \mu^*) \in R^n \times \{0\}$.

For Case (i), since the equation $H(x^{(0)}, 1) = 0$ has only one solution $(x^{(0)}, 1)$ in $R^n \times \{1\}$, Case (i) is impossible. Therefore, Case (ii) is the only possible case. If $(x^*, 0)$ is the limit of Γ, by Lemma 5, we have $x^* \in R^n$, so $(x^*, 0)$ is a solution of (3) and x^* is the solution of the NCP. By Theorem 1, for almost all $x^{(0)} \in R^n_+$, the homotopy equation (3) generates a smooth curve Γ, which is called as the homotopy pathway. Tracing numerically Γ from $(x^{(0)}, 1)$ until $\mu \to 0$, one can find a solution of (3). Letting s be the arc-length of Γ, we can parameterize Γ with respect to s. That is, there exist continuously differentiable functions $x(s), \mu(s)$ such that

$$H(x(s), \mu(s)) = 0, \tag{6}$$

$$x(0) = x^{(0)}, \mu(0) = 1.$$

By differentiating (6), we obtain the following result.

Theorem 2. *The homotopy path Γ is determined by the following initial value problem to the system of ordinary differential equations*

$$DH_{x^{(0)}}(x(s), \mu(s)) \begin{pmatrix} \dot{x} \\ \dot{\mu} \end{pmatrix} = 0,$$

$$x(0) = x^{(0)}, \ \mu(0) = 1.$$

And the x component of the solution point $(x(s^*), \mu(s^*))$ of (6), which satisfies $\mu(s^*) = 0$, is the solution of (3) and $x(s^*)$ is the solution of the NCP.

References

1. Allgower, E.L., Georg, K.: Numerical Continuation Methods: An Introduction. Springer, Berlin (1990)
2. Andreani, R., Friedlander, A., Martínez, J.M.: On the solution of finite-dimensional variational inequalities using smooth optimization with simple bounds. Journal of Optimization Theory and Applications 94, 635–657 (1997)
3. Andreani, R., Friedlander, A., Martínez, J.M.: On the solution of bounded and unbounded mixed complementarity problems. Optimization 50, 265–278 (2001)
4. Birbil, S., Fang, S.C., Han, J.: Entropic regularization approach for mathematical programs with equilibrium constraints. Technical Report, Industrial Engineering and Operations Research. Carolina, USA (2002)

5. Billups, S.C., Speight, A.L., Watson, L.T.: Nonmonotone path following methods for nonsmooth equations and complementarity problems. In: Ferris, M.C., Mangasarian, O.L., Pang, J.-S. (eds.) Applications and Algorithms of Complementarity. Kluwer, Dordrecht (2001)

6. Chen, C., Mangasarian, O.L.: A class of smoothing functions for nonlinear and mixed complementarity problems. Comput. Optim. Appl. 5, 97–138 (1996)

7. Chow, S.N., Mallet-Paret, Y.J.A.: Finding Zeros of Maps: Homotopy methods that are constructive with probability one. Math. Comput. 32, 887–899 (1978)

8. Fan, X., Yu, B.: Homotopy method for solving variational inequalities with bounded box constraints. Nonlinear Analysis TMA 68, 2357–2361 (2008)

9. Ferris, M.C., Pang, J.-S.: Engineering and economic applications of complementarity problems. SIAM Review 39, 669–713 (1997)

10. Friedlander, A., Martínez, J.M., Santos, S.A.: A new strategy for solving variational inequalities on bounded polytopes. Numerical Functional Analysis and Optimization 16, 653–668 (1995)

11. Fukushima, M.: A relaxed projection method for variational inequalities. Mathematical Programming 35, 58–70 (1986)

12. Garcia, C.B., Zangwill, W.I.: Pathways to Solutions, Fixed Points and Equilibria. Prentice-Hall, Englewood Cliffs (1981)

13. Haddou, M.: A new class of smoothing methods for mathematical programs with equilibrium constraints. Pacific Journal of Optimization 5(1), 86–96 (2009)

14. Haddou, M., Maheux, P.: Smoothing Methods for Nonlinear Complementarity Problems (2010), http://arxiv.org/abs/1006.2030v1

15. Harker, P.T., Pang, J.S.: Finite-dimensional variational inequality and nonlinear complementarity problem: a survey of theory, algorithm and applications. Math. Progam. 48, 161–220 (1990)

16. Harker, P.T., Xiao, B.: Newton method for the nonlinear complementarity problem: A B-differentiable equation approach. Math. Progam (Series B) 48, 339–357 (1990)

17. Huang, C., Wang, S.: A power penalty approach to a nonlinear complementarity problem. Operations Research Letters 38, 72–76 (2010)

18. Kojima, M., Megiddo, N., Noma, T.: Homotopy continuation methods for nonlinear complementarity problems. Mathmatics of Operation Research 16, 754–774 (1991)

19. Jiang, H.Y., Qi, L.Q.: A new nonsmooth equations approach to nonliner complementarity problems. SIAM J. Control Optim. 35, 178–193 (1997)

20. Kanzow, C.: Some equation-based methods for the nonlinear complementarity problem. Optimization Methods and Software 2, 327–340 (1994)

21. Kanzow, C.: Nonlinear complementarity as unconstrained optimization. J. Optim. Theory. Appl. 88, 139–155 (1996)

22. Kellogg, R.B., Li, T.Y., Yorke, J.A.: A constructive proof of the Brouwer fixed-piont theorem and computational results. SIAM J. Numer. Anal. 18, 473–483 (1976)

23. Lin, Z., Li, Y.: Homotopy method for solving variational inequalities. Journal of Optimization Theory and Applications 100, 207–218 (1999)

24. Liu, G.X., Yu, B.: Homotopy continuation mathod for linear complementarity problems. Northeast. Math. J. 3, 309–316 (2004)

25. Naber, G.L.: Topological Method in Euclidean space. Cambridge Univ. Press, London (1980)

26. Pang, J.S.: Complementarity problems. In: Horst, R., Pardalos, P. (eds.) Handbook of Global Optimization, pp. 463–480. Kluwer Academic Publishers, Boston (1997)

27. Pang, J.S., Gabriel, S.A.: A robust algorithm for the nonlinear complementarity problem. Math. Programming 60, 295–337 (1993)

28. Qi, L.: Regular pseudo-smooth NCP and BVIP functions and globally and quadratically convergent generalized Newton methods for complementarity and variational inequality problems. Mathematics of Operations Research 24, 440–471 (1999)
29. Qi, L., Sun, D.: A survey of some nonsmooth equations and smoothing Newton methods. In: Eberhard, A., Glover, B., Hill, R., Ralph, D. (eds.) Progress in Optimization: Contributions from Australasia, pp. 121–146. Kluwer Academic Publishers, Boston (1999)
30. Smale, S.: Algorithms for solving equations, Berkeley, California, pp. 172–195 (1986)
31. Watson, L.T.: Solving the nonlinear complementarity problem by a homotopy method. SIAM J. Control Optim. 17, 36–46 (1979)
32. Xu, Q., Dang, C.: A new homotopy method for solving non-linear complementarity problems. Optimization 57(5), 681–689 (2008)

A Biomathematic Models for Tuberculosis Using Lyapunov Stability Functions

Shih-Ching Ou[1], Hung-Yuan Chung[2], and Chun-Yen Chung[3]

[1] Professor, Department of Computer Science and Information Engineering,
Leader University, Tainan 709, Taiwan, R.O.C.
[2] Professor, Department of Electrical Engineering,
National Central University, Jhongli, 32001, Taiwan, R.O.C.
[3] Ph.D. Student, Department of Electrical Engineering,
National Central University, Jhongli, 32001, Taiwan, R.O.C.
chunyen911@gmail.com

Abstract. According the World Health Organization, one third of the world's population is infected with tuberculosis (TB), leading to between two and three million deaths each year. TB is now the second most common cause of death from infectious disease in the world after human immunodeficiency virus/acquired immunodeficiency syndrome (HIV/AIDS). Tuberculosis is a leading cause of infectious mortality. Although anti-biotic treatment is available and there is vaccine, tuberculosis levels are rising in many areas of the world. Mathematical models have been used to study tuberculosis in the past and have influenced policy; the spread of HIV and the emergence of drug-resistant TB strains motivate the use of mathematical models today .In the recent year, the Biomathmetics has become the main important trend of research dirction which has applied to the epidemic models of disease mechanism, spreading, regulation, and stategy of disease preventing in the field of medical and public health. The papers will apply Lyapunov stability function V (x) to construct a dynamic mathematics models for tuberculosis and to meet the above-mentioned TB disease mechanism,spreading regulation, and stategy of disease preventing in the medical field. The theory of Lyapunov stability function is a general rule and method to examine and determine the stability characteristics of a dynamic system. There are two functions of Lyapunov theory: (a) the Lyapunov indirect method which solves the dynamics differential equations of the constructing system then determines its stability properties, and (b) the Lyapunov direct method which determine the system stability directly via constructing a Lyapunov Energy Function V(x) of the dynamic mathematic model for tuberculosis. Here we will analyse the complex dynamic mathematic model of tuberculosis epidemic and determine its stability property by using the popular Matlab/Simulink software and relative software packages.

Keywords: Tuberculosis, Biomathmetics, Lyapunov.

1 Introduction

Tuberculosis (TB) is a bacterial infection that causes more deaths in the world than any other infectious disease. The bacteria are called Mycobacterium tuberculosis and

R. Zhu et al. (Eds.): ICICA 2010, LNCS 6377, pp. 447–453, 2010.

it usually affects the lungs (pulmonary tuberculosis). It can also affect the central nervous system, the lymphatic system, the brain, spine and the kidneys. Only people who have pulmonary TB are infectious. One-third of the world's population is currently infected with the TB bacillus and new infections are occurring at a rate of one per second [6].In the recent year, the Biomathematics has become the main important trend of research direction which has applied to the epidemic models of disease mechanism, spreading regulation, and strategy of disease preventing in the field of medical and public health. Despite many decades of study, the widespread availability of a vaccine, an arsenal of anti-microbial drugs and, more recently, a highly visible World Health Organization effort to promote a unified global control strategy, tuberculosis (TB) remains a leading cause of infectious mortality [3]. It is responsible for approximately two million deaths each year. Although TB is currently well-controlled in most countries, recent data indicate that the overall global incidence of TB is rising as a result of resurgence of disease in Africa and parts Eastern Europe and Asia. In these regions, the emergence of drug-resistant TB and the convergence of the HIV (human immunodeficiency virus) and TB epidemics have created substantial new challenges for disease control.

TB is the most common serious opportunistic infection in HIV positive patients and is the manifestation of AIDS in more than 50% of cases in developing countries3. Also to be noted are the facts that TB shortens the survival of patients afflicted with HIV infection, may accelerate the progression of HIV and is the cause of death in one third of people with AIDS world wide. The higher mortality is due to the progression of AIDS rather than TB probably due to the fact that tuberculosis increases viral replication.

In fact, one third of the 33.2 million people living with HIV world wide are also infected with TB. HIV-positive people have a 60% lifetime risk of developing TB, compared to a 10% lifetime risk in HIV-negative people. The risk of recurring TB is higher in people living with HIV. It is estimated that of the 1.5 million people who died of TB in 2006, about 200,000 were infected with HIV. An increase in TB cases among people living with HIV may lead to an increase in risk of TB transmission to the general population. Increasing rates of TB in the recent decade are directly related to HIV/AIDS.

The Biomathematics has become the main important trend of research dirction which has applied to the epidemic models of disease mechanism, spreading regulation, and strategy of disease preventing in the field of medical and public health. The papers will apply Lyapunov stability function $V(x)$ to construct a dynamic mathematics models for tuberculosis and to meet the above-mentioned TB disease mechanism, spreading regulation, and strategy of disease preventing in the medical field.

In this paper used Lyapunov stability function is a general rule and method to examine and determine the stability characteristics of a dynamic system. In order to simulate the transmissions of vector-borne diseases and discuss the related health policies effects on vector-borne diseases, we combine the social network, and compartmental model to develop an epidemic simulation model.

The research will analyze the complex dynamic mathematic model of tuberculosis epidemic and determine its stability property by using the popular Matlab/Simulink software and relative software packages. Facing to the currently TB epidemic situation, in this project we will investigate the development of TB and its developing trend thought constructing the dynamic biomathematics system model of TB.

2 The History of Tuberculosis

Tuberculosis, once called "consumption" and "white plague," is an ancient disease that may have always been with us. Evidence of tubercular decay found in the skulls and spines of Egyptian mummies, tell us that TB has been plaguing humans for at least 4,000 years. Hippocrates, the ancient Greek physician, noted that "phthisis" (consumption) was the most widespread and fatal disease of his time. It has been estimated that in the two centuries from 1700 to 1900, tuberculosis was responsible for the deaths of approximately one billion (one thousand million) human beings. The annual death rate from TB when Koch made his discovery was seven million people. Although the disease has not been eradicated, there is no doubt that Robert Koch's (Robert Koch, a German physician and scientist, presented his discovery of *Mycobacterium tuberculosis*, the bacterium that causes tuberculosis (TB), on the evening of March 24, 1882)discovery of the tubercle bacillus, subsequent inventions for curing infected and sick individuals as well as the application of measures to prevent the spread of TB, has had a profound impact on human history and has saved many lives.

Tuberculosis is a global disease which is not only specific to humans. There are variants of the TB bacterium that infect cattle (milk was known to transmit the disease from cattle to humans before heat treatment - pasteurization - efficiently removed the risk), birds, fish, turtles and frogs. In humans, symptoms of active TB often include coughing, fever, nightly sweats and wasting of the body. TB usually affects the lungs, but it can also affect the brain, the kidneys or the skeleton. The symptoms of TB of the lungs include persistent coughing, chest pain and coughing up blood. Symptoms involving other areas of the body vary, depending on the affected organ.

Tuberculosis is spread from person to person through the air, in tiny microscopic droplets. When a person with TB in the lungs coughs or sneezes, the bacteria can be inhaled by persons nearby, often family members or co-workers. Tuberculosis is currently increasing across the world at about 1% a year. Population growth, HIV, which renders the human body uniquely susceptible to tuberculosis, and poverty are causing a rapid increase in some parts of the developing world, particularly Sub-Saharan Africa. It is estimated that each year 10 million new cases of tuberculosis occur, of which 2 million die. In 1993 the WHO declared tuberculosis to be a global emergency and advocated DOTS (directly observed therapy) as a means of control.

3 Epidemiological and SEIR Models

The first mathematical model of TB was presented by Waaler et al. (1962).He divides the host population into the following epidemiological classes or subgroups: susceptibles (S), exposed (E, infected but not infectious), and infected (I, assumed infectious) individuals, has given a linear discrete model. Although this model has not promulgated disease's dissemination mechanism truly, but in the model uses data and the determination parameter for the present developing country determined that the tuberculosis popular some parameters the estimate has provided the reference data.

This is sometimes referred to as a rate or ratio. It is one of the most useful threshold parameters, which characterize mathematical problems concerning infectious diseases. It is widely used in mathematical epidemiology models. The basic reproduction number denoted R_0, is the expected number of secondary cases produced, in a completely susceptible population, by a typical infective individual [1, 2]. If $R_0 < 1$, then on average an infected individual produces less than one new infected individual over the course of its infectious period, and the infection cannot grow. Conversely, if $R_0 > 1$, then each infected individual produces, on average, more than one new infection, and the disease can spread in the population. For the case of a single infected compartment, R_0 is simply the product of the infection rate and the mean duration of the infection.

However, for more complicated models with several infected compartments this simple definition of R_0 is insufficient. For a more general situation we can establish this parameter by investigating the stability of the infection-free equilibrium. This parameter identifies critical conditions for an epidemic to grow or die out. Furthermore, it can provide significant insight into the transmission dynamics of a disease and can guide strategies to control its spread.

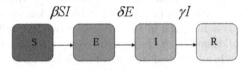

Fig. 1. SEIR model

Some diseases have a long latent period. Once a person is infected, he or she does not become infectious immediately until the incubation period has passed. This is the idea of an SEIR model. The standard form of SEIR epidemic model is given by Eq. (1)

$$\frac{dS}{dt} = -\beta SI \; , \frac{dE}{dt} = \beta SI - \delta E \; ,$$
$$\frac{dI}{dt} = \delta E - \gamma I \; , \frac{dR}{dt} = \gamma I \tag{1}$$

where δ is the incubation rate and E represents the exposed class which means that the population in this class is infected but not infectious. Again a closed population is assumed with $S + E + I + R = N$, where N denotes the total population size.

In the same paper, Feng and Castillo-Chavez present a two-strain model [4] [5], in which the drug-resistant strain is not treated, and latent, infectious and treated individuals may be re-infected with the drug-resistant strain. Each strain has a different R_0, and there are 3 equilibrium points (no disease, coexistence of both strains, and only the drug-resistant strain). Without acquisition of drug resistance, there is an additional equilibrium with only the drug-sensitive strain. The authors discuss stability of the equilibria and find, interestingly, areas of parameter space of postive measure where coexistence of the strains is possible; they report that coexistence is rare when drug resistance is mainly primary (resulting from transmission) but almost certain if the resistant strain is the result of aquisition, for example under poor treatment. Neglecting disease-induced death and setting the transmission parameter equal for the two strains, they are able to prove that the disease-free equilibrium is globally asymptotically stable if both R_0' s are less than 1. These results were extended in Mena-Lorca et al.

4 Lyapunoy Method

We give a survey of results on global stability for deterministic compartmental epidemiological models. Using Lyapunov techniques we revisit a classical result, and give a simple proof. By the same methods we also give a new result on differential susceptibility and infectivity models with mass action and an arbitrary number of compartments. These models encompass the so-called differential infectivity and staged progression models. In the two cases we prove that if the basic reproduction ratio $R_0 \leq 1$, then the disease free equilibrium is globally asymptotically stable. If $R_0 > 1$, there exists an unique endemic equilibrium which is asymptotically stable on the positive orthant.

Lyapunov stability analysis plays a significant role in the stability analysis of molecular systems described by the state-space equation. Since the solution of some nonlinear equations is very difficult to identify, the Lyapunov second method can be adopted to analyze the characteristic that does not require solving differential equations. The stability and period of the system are determined with the qualitative theorem of differential equations. The Lyapunov method is the first efficient technique to solve the solution's stability using differential equations. Hence, the second method is very useful in practice.

Although many significant stability criteria exist for control systems, such as the Jury stability criterion and the Roth-Hurwitz stability criteria, they are constrained to

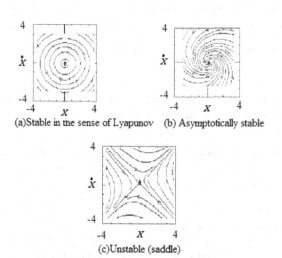

(a)Stable in the sense of Lyapunov   (b) Asymptotically stable

(c)Unstable (saddle)

Fig. 2. Phase portraits for stable and unstable equilibrium points

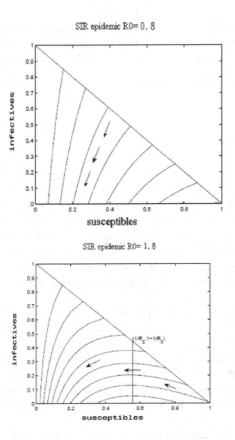

Fig. 3. Phase plane of the susceptibles and the infectives in the SIR epidemic model. All classes
are normalized to the total population. An epidemic occurs if $I(t) > I(0)$ for some time $t > 0$. In
(b), epidemic occurs when the initial value of $u > 1/R_0$; in (a) where $R_0 < 1$, $R_0u - 1$ is
always smaller than 1 because $0 \leq u \leq 1$ and thus the infectives decay for all time so that the
disease dies out.

linear time-invariant systems. The second Lyapunov method is not restrained to linear
time-invariant systems; it is applicable to both linear and nonlinear systems, and time
invariant or time varying.

Theorem 1. Consider a continuously differentiable function V (x) such that V (x) > 0
for all $x \neq 0$ and V (0) = 0 (V is positive definite). We then have the following conditions for the various notions of stability.

If $\dot{V}$ (x) ≤ 0 for all x, then x = 0 is stable. In addition, if $\dot{V}$ (x) < 0 for all $x \neq 0$, then x
= 0 is asymptotically stable. In addition to (1) and (2) above, if V is radially un-
bounded, i.e., $\| x \| \to \infty \Rightarrow$ V (x) $\to \infty$, then x = 0 is globally asymptotically stable.
V is called a Lyapunov function and V must be positive definite.

Stability means that the Lyapunov function decreases along the trajectory of x(t).

Finally, we say that an equilibrium point is unstable if it is not stable. This is less of a tautology than it sounds and the reader should be sure he or she can negate the definition of stability in the sense of Lyapunov to get a definition of instability. In robotics, we are almost always interested in uniformly asymptotically stable equilibria. If we wish to move the robot to a point, we would like to actually converge to that point, not merely remain nearby. Figure 2 illustrates the difference between stability in the sense of Lyapunov and asymptotic stability.

The research will analyse the complex dynamic mathematic model of tuberculosis epidemic and determine its stability property by using the popular Matlab/Simulink software and relative software packages.

5 Conclusions

Facing to the currently TB epidemic situation, in this paper we will investgate the development of TB and its developing trend through constructing the dynamic bio-mathematics system model of TB. The fact that for each of the systems studied here there is a unique solution implies there is some important underlying structure. A more detailed analysis of this phenomenon may yield much more general results.

Furthermore, the coefficients that are used for the Lyapunov function for $R_0 \leq 1$ are a scalar multiple of those used for $R_0 > 1$, but with the coefficient for S set to zero. Again, this points to deeper structure.

Acknowledgment

The authors wish to thank the financial support of the National Science Council, Taiwan, under Contract NSC 98-2221-E-426-007.

References

1. Hethcote, H.W.: The mathematics of infectious diseases. SIAM Rev., 599–653 (2000)
2. Diekmann, O., Heesterbeek, J.A.P.: Heesterbeek.: Mathematical epidemiology of infections disease: Model building, analysis and interpretation. Springer/Wiley, New York (2000)
3. World Health Orgnization.: WHO report 2001: Global tuberculosis control Technical Report, world Health Organization (2001)
4. Castillo-Chavez, C., Feng, Z.: To treat or not to treat: the case of tuberculosis. J. Math. Biol. 35, 629–659 (1997)
5. Castillo-Chavez, C., Feng, Z.: Mathematical Models for the Disease Dynamics of Tuberculosis. In: Axelrod, O.D., Kimmel, M. (eds.) Advances In Mathematical Population Dynamics - Molecules, Cells and Man, pp. 629–656. World Scientific Press, Singapore (1998)
6. World Health Organization.: Tuberculosis, fact sheet no 104 (March 2007)
7. http://www.who.int/mediacentre/factsheets/fs104/en/index.html

Construction of Transition Curve between Nonadjacent Cubic T-B Spline Curves*

Jincai Chang[1,2], Zhao Wang[1], and Aimin Yang[1]

[1] College of Science, Hebei Polytechnic University
Tangshan Hebei, 063009, China
[2] Shanghai Key Laboratory for Contemporary Applied Mathematics,
Shanghai, 200433, China
jincai@heut.edu.cn

Abstract. In this paper, we investigate the geometric continuous connection between the adjacent cubic T-B spline curves, and the construction of transition curve between nonadjacent T-B spline curves. First, we calculate the expression of cubic T-B spline basis function and the expression of cubic T-B spline curve. Then based on the condition of smooth connection between adjacent cubic T-B spline curves, we construct the relations of control points between transition curve and nonadjacent T-B spline curves. Thus we get the geometric continuous connect conditions between transition curve and nonadjacent T-B spline curves.

Keywords: T-B Spline, transition curve, geometric continuity, smooth connection.

1 Introduction

Schoenberg [1] proposed spline function, it is a tool to solve the problem of smooth connection on curve and surface in the early industrial design. As the rapid development of the computer science and technology, the application of curve and surface modeling are widespread in CAD/CAM/CAE, such as the design of car, aircraft and mechanical parts. In recent years, as a key technology in CAD/CAM/ CAE, CAGD (Computer Aided Geometry Design) has developed into an independent subject. In CAGD, we usually used more than one curves. Therefore, smooth connection among curves is the key problem.

This paper studies smooth connection among cubic adjacent T-B splines and construction of transition curve between nonadjacent cubic T-B spline curves. Then calculate the G^0, G^1, G^2 smooth connect conditions about control points. T-B spline curve and B-spline curve have the similar properties. T-B spline curve could express some common quadratic curves accurately such as: circular arc and elliptical arc. But

---

* Project supported by Natural Science Foundation of Hebei Province of China (No. A2009000735, A2010000908), Educational Commission of Hebei Province of China (No.2009448) and Shanghai Key Laboratory for Contemporary Applied Mathematics (09FG067).

R. Zhu et al. (Eds.): ICICA 2010, LNCS 6377, pp. 454–461, 2010.

the rational B-spline curve can't do it accurately. Therefore, We often used T-B spline to fit some quadratic curves in industrial design. So the application of T-B spline curve is extensive[2].

2   The Definition of the T-B Spline Curve

The basis functions $B_{j,n}(t)$ of T-B spline have the properties as follows [3]:

(1)   Positivity

$$B_{j,n}(t) \geq 0 \tag{1}$$

(2)   Normality

$$\sum_{j=0}^{n} B_{j,n}(t) \equiv 1 \tag{2}$$

(3)   Endpoint properties

$$\begin{cases} B_{j,n}(\pi/2) = 0, j = 0 \\ B_{j,n}(0) = 0, j = n \end{cases} \tag{3}$$

$$\begin{cases} B_{j,n}^{(k)}(\pi/2) = 0, j = 0 \\ B_{j,n}^{(k)}(0) = 0, j = n \end{cases}, \quad (j = 1, 2, \cdots, n-1; \ 1 \leq k < n) \tag{4}$$

$$B_{j,n}(0) = B_{j+1,n}(\pi/2), \quad (j = 1, 2, \cdots, n-1) \tag{5}$$

$$B_{j,n}^{(k)}(0) = B_{j+1,n}^{(k)}(\pi/2), \quad (j = 1, 2, \cdots, n-1; \ 1 \leq k < n) \tag{6}$$

When $n = 2$, then

$$B_{i,2}(t) = C_{i,0} + C_{i,1} \sin t + C_{i,2} \cos t \tag{7}$$

When $n \geq 3$, then

$$B_{i,n}(t) = \begin{cases} B_{i,n-1}(t) + C_{i,n} \cos[(n+1)/2]t, & (n \text{ is odd}) \\ B_{i,n-1}(t) + C_{i,n} \sin[n/2]t, & (n \text{ is even}) \end{cases} \tag{8}$$

When $n = 3$, the basis functions $B_{i,3}(t)$ $(i = 0,1,2,3)$ of T-B spline are that:

$$B_{i,3}(t) = C_{i,0} + C_{i,1} \sin t + C_{i,2} \cos t + C_{i,3} \cos 2t, \quad i = 0,1,2,3$$

The basis functions of T-B spline should satisfy the boundary conditions (1)-(8), then

$$\begin{cases} B_0(\pi/2) = 0 \\ B_0^{(1)}(\pi/2) = 0 \\ B_0^{(2)}(\pi/2) = 0 \end{cases} ; \quad \begin{cases} B_0(0) = B_1(\pi/2) \\ B_0^{(1)}(0) = B_1^{(1)}(\pi/2) \\ B_0^{(2)}(0) = B_1^{(2)}(\pi/2) \end{cases} ; \quad \begin{cases} B_1(0) = B_2(\pi/2) \\ B_1^{(1)}(0) = B_2^{(1)}(\pi/2) \\ B_1^{(2)}(0) = B_2^{(2)}(\pi/2) \end{cases}$$

$$\begin{cases} B_2(0) = B_3(\pi/2) \\ B_2^{(1)}(0) = B_3^{(1)}(\pi/2) \\ B_2^{(2)}(0) = B_3^{(2)}(\pi/2) \end{cases} ; \begin{cases} B_3(0) = 0 \\ B_3^{(1)}(0) = 0 \\ B_3^{(2)}(0) = 0 \end{cases}$$

$$B_0(t) + B_1(t) + B_2(t) + B_3(t) \equiv 1$$

Thus, we get an equation system which contains 16 equations and 16 unknowns, solving it with MATLAB [4], and we obtain the expressions of basis functions are that:

$$[B_{0,3}(t), B_{1,3}(t), B_{2,3}(t), B_{3,3}(t)] = \frac{1}{12}[1, \sin t, \cos t, \cos 2t] \begin{bmatrix} 3 & 3 & 3 & 3 \\ -4 & 0 & 4 & 0 \\ 0 & 4 & 0 & -4 \\ -1 & 1 & -1 & 1 \end{bmatrix} \tag{9}$$

If P_0, P_1, P_2, P_3 are the control points, then the expression of cubic T-B spline curve is as follows:

$$T(t) = B_{0,3}(t)P_0 + B_{1,3}(t)P_1 + B_{2,3}(t)P_2 + B_{3,3}(t)P_3 \tag{10}$$

3 The Expression of Cubic T-B Spline Basis Functions and Endpoints Properties

The basis functions $B_{i,3}(t)$ $(i = 0,1,2,3)$ of T-B spline are that [5]

$$\begin{cases} B_{0,3}(t) = (3 - 4\sin t - \cos 2t)/12 \\ B_{1,3}(t) = (3 + 4\cos t + \cos 2t)/12 \\ B_{2,3}(t) = (3 + 4\sin t - \cos 2t)/12 \\ B_{3,3}(t) = (3 - 4\cos t + \cos 2t)/12 \end{cases} \quad t \in [0, \pi/2] \tag{11}$$

(1) The cubic T-B spline curve has the properties at the endpoint $t = 0$:

$$T(0) = P_0/6 + 2P_1/3 + P_2/6 \tag{12}$$

$$T'(0) = (P_2 - P_0)/3 \tag{13}$$

$$T''(0) = (P_0 - P_1)/3 + (P_2 - P_1)/3 \tag{14}$$

(2) The cubic T-B spline curve has the properties at the endpoint $t = \pi/2$:

$$T(\pi/2) = P_1/6 + 2P_2/3 + P_3/6 \tag{15}$$

$$T'(\pi/2) = (P_3 - P_1)/3 \tag{16}$$

$$T''(\pi/2) = (P_1 - P_2)/3 + (P_3 - P_2)/3 \tag{17}$$

4 Smooth Connect Condition

Given two cubic T-B spline curves. The one is

$$T_1(t) = B_{0,3}(t)P_0 + B_{1,3}(t)P_1 + B_{2,3}(t)P_2 + B_{3,3}(t)P_3$$

where P_0, P_1, P_2, P_3 are control points. The other one is

$$T_2(t) = B_{0,3}(t)Q_0 + B_{1,3}(t)Q_1 + B_{2,3}(t)Q_2 + B_{3,3}(t)Q_3$$

where Q_0, Q_1, Q_2, Q_3 are control points. When the endpoint $t = \pi/2$ of $T_1(t)$ and the endpoint $t = 0$ of $T_2(t)$ satisfy the G^0, G^1, G^2 smooth connect condition, The control points P_0, P_1, P_2, P_3 and the control points Q_0, Q_1, Q_2, Q_3 should satisfy the following conditions:

4.1 G^0 Smooth Connect Condition

$T_1(t)$ and $T_2(t)$ should have common point, that is

$$T_1(\pi/2) = T_2(0) \tag{18}$$

$$T_1(\pi/2) = P_1/6 + 2P_2/3 + P_3/6$$

$$T(0) = Q_0/6 + 2Q_1/3 + Q_2/6$$

Then we can get G^0 smooth connect conditions of $T_1(t)$ and $T_2(t)$ are that:

$$P_1 + 4P_2 + P_3 = Q_0 + 4Q_1 + Q_2 \tag{19}$$

4.2 G^1 Smooth Connect Condition

If the two curves $T_1(t)$ and $T_2(t)$ satisfy G^1 smooth connect conditions. It should meet two conditions as follows:

(a) G^0 smooth connect conditions.
(b) The two curves have the same tangent direction on the common point (Fig.1).

It should satisfy (19), and it also need to meet that:

$$T_1'(\pi/2) = mT_2'(0) \tag{20}$$

$$T_1'(\pi/2) = (P_3 - P_1)/3$$

$$T_2'(0) = (Q_2 - Q_0)/3$$

Then G^1 smooth connect conditions of $T_1(t)$ and $T_2(t)$ are that:

$$P_3 - P_1 = m(Q_2 - Q_0) \tag{21}$$

According to (21), we can obtain $P_1P_3 \,/\!/\, Q_0Q_2$ .Due to the two curves $T_1(t)$ and $T_2(t)$ have a common point, so the points P_1, P_3 and Q_0, Q_1, Q_2 are coplanar. Similarly the points Q_0, Q_2 and P_1, P_2, P_3 are coplanar, so the six control points $P_1, P_2, P_3, Q_0, Q_1, Q_2$ are coplanar.

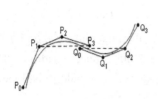

Fig. 1. G^1 Smooth Connection   **Fig. 2.** G^2 Smooth Connection

4.3 G^2 Smooth Connect Condition

If the two curves $T_1(t)$ and $T_2(t)$ satisfy G^2 smooth connect conditions. It should meet two conditions as follows [6]:

(a) G^1 smooth connect conditions.
(b) Two curves have the same curvature on the common point.
(c) Two curves have the same binormal vector on the common point. (Fig. 2)

It should satisfy (21), the curvature of $T_1(\pi/2)$ is $k_1(\pi/2)$, and the curvature of $T_2(0)$ is $k_2(0)$. Where

$$T_1''(\pi/2) = (P_1 - P_2)/3 + (P_3 - P_2)/3$$

$$T_2''(\pi/2) = (Q_0 - Q_1)/3 + (Q_2 - Q_1)/3$$

According to the curvature equations, we can get the equations as follows:

$$k_1(\pi/2) = k_2(0) \tag{22}$$

$$k_1(\pi/2) = \left|T_1'(\pi/2) \times T_1''(\pi/2)\right| / \left|T_1'(\pi/2)\right|^3 = 6\left|(P_3 - P_1) \times (P_1 - P_2)\right| / \left|(P_3 - P_1)\right|^3 \tag{23}$$

$$k_2(0) = \left|T_1'(0) \times T_1''(0)\right| / \left|T_1'(0)\right|^3 = 6\left|(Q_2 - Q_0) \times (Q_0 - Q_1)\right| / \left|(Q_2 - Q_0)\right|^3 \tag{24}$$

$$S_{\Delta P_1 P_2 P_3} = \left|(P_3 - P_1)(P_1 - P_2)\right|/2$$

$$S_{\Delta Q_0 Q_1 Q_2} = \left|(Q_2 - Q_0) \times (Q_0 - Q_1)\right|/2$$

Take (23), (24) into (22), then

$$S_{\Delta P_1 P_2 P_3} / S_{\Delta Q_0 Q_1 Q_2} = m^3 \tag{25}$$

5 Construction of Transition Curve between Nonadjacent Cubic T-B Spline Curves

If the cubic T-B spline curves are nonadjacent, where

$$T_1(t) = B_{0,3}(t)P_0 + B_{1,3}(t)P_1 + B_{2,3}(t)P_2 + B_{3,3}(t)P_3$$

$$T_2(t) = B_{0,3}(t)Q_0 + B_{1,3}(t)Q_1 + B_{2,3}(t)Q_2 + B_{3,3}(t)Q_3$$

We can smooth connect nonadjacent cubic T-B spline curves through a transition curve, and the transition curve will maintain a certain smooth degree. Then we can calculate the control points of transition curve by the control points of $T_1(t)$ and $T_2(t)$. The method of transition curve construction between nonadjacent cubic T-B spline curves is that [7]: (Fig. 3)

Set the transition curve $T_3(t)$ is a cubic T-B spline curve. The expression is that:

$$T_3(t) = B_{0,3}(t)R_0 + B_{1,3}(t)R_1 + B_{2,3}(t)R_2 + B_{3,3}(t)R_3$$

(R_0 , R_1 , R_2 , R_3 are the control points of $T_3(t)$). We can determine control points R_0, R_1, R_2, R_3 by the control points P_0, P_1, P_2, P_3 and the control points Q_0, Q_1, Q_2, Q_3. Due to the control points R_0, R_1, R_2, R_3 are four unknowns, so we need find a equation system which contain four equations.

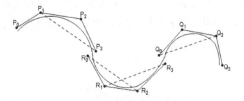

Fig. 3. G^1 Smooth Connection

The endpoint points properties of $T_1(\pi/2)$ and $T_3(0)$ should satisfy G^0, G^1 smooth connect conditions. And we can get the two equations as follows:

$$R_0 + 4R_1 + R_2 = P_1 + 4P_2 + P_3 \tag{26}$$

$$R_2 - R_0 = m(P_3 - P_1) \tag{27}$$

The endpoint points properties of $T_3(\pi/2)$ and $T_1(0)$ should satisfy G^0, G^1 smooth connect conditions. And we can get the two equations as follows[8]:

$$R_1 + 4R_2 + R_3 = Q_0 + 4Q_1 + Q_2 \tag{28}$$

$$R_3 - R_1 = n(Q_2 - Q_0) \tag{29}$$

From (26), (27), (28), (29), in order to simplify the calculation, we set

$$A = P_1 + 4P_2 + P_3$$

$$B = m(P_3 - P_1)$$

$$C = Q_0 + 4Q_1 + Q_2$$

$$D = n(Q_2 - Q_0)$$

Then, we can obtain the expressions of R_0, R_1, R_2, R_3 as follows,

$$\begin{cases} R_0 = -A/6 - 7B/6 + C/3 - D/3 \\ R_1 = A/3 + B/3 - C/6 + D/6 \\ R_2 = -A/6 - B/6 + C/6 - D/6 \\ R_3 = A/3 + B/3 - C/6 + 7D/6 \end{cases} \tag{30}$$

When the control points R_0, R_1, R_2, R_3 satisfy the constraints (30), then $T_3(t)$ is a transition curve which connected $T_1(t)$ and $T_2(t)$ about G^1 smooth connect conditions.

In the fig.3, where $P_1P_3 \mathbin{/\mkern-5mu/} R_0R_2$, $R_1R_3 \mathbin{/\mkern-5mu/} Q_0Q_2$, and the control points P_1, P_2, P_3, R_0, R_1, R_2, R_3, Q_0, Q_1, Q_2 are coplanar[9].

If the transition curve $T_3(t)$ which connected $T_1(t)$ and $T_2(t)$ about G^2 smooth connect conditions, it should satisfy the two constraints as follows:

$$S_{\Delta R_0 R_1 R_2} \big/ S_{\Delta P_1 P_2 P_3} = m^3 \tag{31}$$

$$S_{\Delta R_1 R_2 R_3} \big/ S_{\Delta Q_0 Q_1 Q_2} = n^3 \tag{32}$$

Combined equations (26) - (29), (31), (32), we can get an equation system which contains 6 equations and 6 unknowns. We can obtained the specific expressions of R_0, R_1, R_2, R_3, m, n. Because the calculation is very complicated, so we don't deduce the solutions[10].

6 Conclusion and Outlook

This paper describes the cubic T-B spline curve which is commonly used in computational geometry, we discussed the G^0, G^1, G^2 smooth connect conditions between the cubic T-B spline curves. Based on it, we focus on the nonadjacent cubic T-B spline curves. And give the G^1 smooth connect condition between transition curve and nonadjacent cubic T-B spline curves. The conclusion are that the transition curve which satisfy the constraints of G^1 smooth connect conditions are a group of curves. And the transition curve which satisfy the constraints of G^2 smooth connect conditions is only one curve, regulatory factors m, n is a certain constant in the expression. In the future work, we will consider smooth connection between adjacent cubic T-B spline surfaces. And the transition surface construction between nonadjacent bicubic T-B spline surfaces, and get the relationship about corresponding control points.

References

1. Schoenberg, I.J.: Contributions to the problem of approximation of equidistant data by analytic function. Quart. Appl. Math. 4, 45–99, 112–141 (1946)
2. Wang, R.H., Li, C.J., Zhu, C.G.: Textbook of Computational Geometry. Science Press, Beijing (2008)
3. Su, B.Y., Huang, Y.D.: Construction of trigonometric polynomial curves in CAGD and its application. J. of Hefei University of Technology 28, 105–108 (2005)
4. Ren, Y.J.: Numerical Analysis and MATLAB Implementation. Higher Education Press, Beijing (2008)
5. Ma, S.J., Liu, X.M.: Research of uniform T-B-spline curves. Computer Engineering and Applications 44, 88–91 (2008)
6. Feng, R.Z., Wang, R.H.: G^2 continuous conditions between cubic B spline curve. Journal of Dalian University of Technology 43, 407–411 (2003)
7. Che, X.J., Liu, D.Y., Liu, Z.X.: Construction of joining surface with G^1 continuity for two NURBS surfaces. Journal of Jilin University 37, 838–841 (2007)
8. Zhu, C.G., Wang, R.H., Shi, X.Q., et al.: Functional splines with different degrees of smoothness and their applications. Computer-Aided Design 40(5), 616–662 (2008)
9. Zhu, C.G., Li, C.Y., Wang, R.H.: Functional Spline Curves and Surfaces with Different Degrees of Smoothness. Journal of Computer-aided Design & Computer Graphics 21(7), 930–935 (2009)
10. Ma, S.J., Liu, X.M.: Cubic TC-Bézier Curves With Shape Parameter. Computer Engineering and Design 30(5), 1151–1153 (2009)

Finite Element Simulation of Reinforce-concrete Frame Beam to Resist Progressive Collapse

Jiarui Qi[1], Youpo Su[2], Yahui Sun[1], Yousong Ding[1], and Lihui Ma[2]

[1] College of Light Industry; [2] College of Civil and Architectural Engineering, Hebei Polytechnic University 46 West Xinhua Road, Tangshan 063009, P.R. China
qi_jiarui@163.com

Abstract. The finite element model for reinforced-concrete frame beam to resist progressive collapse was established by ADINA program, which geometrical and material non-linearity considered. Axial forces are often present in reinforced- concrete beam at the ultimate load as a result of the boundary conditions and geometry of deformation of the beam segments. So the ultimate load-carrying capacity of reinforced-concrete frame beam was increased because of the arching and cable action (compressive and tensile membrane action). The influence of the beam to resist progressive collapse has been discussed such as steel ratio, span-depth ratio. It shows that the finite element model presented is feasible and can be applied to further research on engineering practice for reinforced-concrete frame structure to resist progressive collapse.

Keywords: Arching action, cable action, reinforce-concrete frame's beam, ADINA, nonlinear finite element.

1 Introduction

Structures, potentially suffer abnormal loads such as air blast pressure generated by an explosion or impact by vehicles, etc. Buildings or structure systems under accumulated abnormal loads was analyzed to the risk of partial failure due to accidental event. If energy produced by the abnormal loads couldn't be depleted or failure in the structure couldn't be controlled, the vertical or level progressive failure would occur in the structure, which was called progressive collapse. Progressive collapse occurs when a structure has its loading pattern, or boundary conditions changed such that structural elements are loaded beyond their capacity and fail. The residual structure is forced to seek alternative load paths to redistribute the load applied to it. As a result, other elements may fail, causing further load redistribution. The process will continue until the structure can find equilibrium either by shedding load, as a by-product of other elements failing, or by finding stable alternative load paths. So the most important to resist progressive collapse is how to find new alternative load paths when the girders or columns fail in local structure. Considered arching and cable action, the ultimate load-carrying capacity of reinforced-concrete beam is more greatly improved than the computation according to the rule of pure bending. In recent years, the arching and cable action hasn't been considered in the alternate path approach for resisting

R. Zhu et al. (Eds.): ICICA 2010, LNCS 6377, pp. 462–469, 2010.

progressive collapse is uneconomical and unpractical. In this paper, a reinforced-concrete frame beam with damage or failure of a vertical support, i.e. a column, was simulated. The beam changed from one span to two because of the default of the column, at the same time it carried upper load instantaneously. Due to the arching action and cable action, the two-span beam sought alternative load paths to redistribute the load applied on it and the failure was controlled in local region to achieve resisting vertical progressive collapse of frame structures.

2 Numerical Model for Reinforced-Concrete Frame Beam

2.1 Geometrical Model

In order to study the frame's capacity on resisting progressive collapse under arching and cable action, some tests have been done in references [1, 2]. The cross section characteristic and the main parameters of the specimen were given in Fig. 1 and Table 1. Combined with the experimental results, the capacity of resisting progressive collapse about reinforced-concrete frame beam is discussed by ADINA.

Table 1. Geometrical parameter of frame beam

beam	Cross-section size b x h mm	span mm	Concrete strength f_{cu} Mpa	Longitudinal reinforcement ratio (%)				Longitudinal reinforcement strength f_y (MPa)	Stirrup
				Support		Mid-span			
				Top	Bottom	Top	Bottom		
KLJ-8	150x300	3000	26.8	1.11	1.11	1.11	1.11	360	Φ8@100

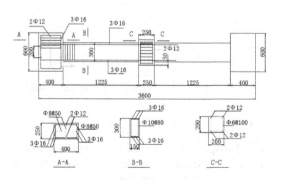

Fig. 1. Geometrical model

2.2 Material Model

Concrete model. Concrete stress-strain relationship for monotonic load is mapped as Saenz model [3, 4, 5] and inputted as nonlinear elasticity material model shown as Fig.2. The relation shows that are three strain phases, namely $\varepsilon \geq 0$, $0 \geq t \varepsilon \geq \varepsilon c$

and $\varepsilon c \geq \varepsilon \geq \varepsilon u$, where εc is the strain corresponding to the minimum (crushing) stress σc that can be reached, and εu is the ultimate compressive strain. The concrete failure criterion adopts failure envelopes to identify whether tensile or crushing failure of the material.

Steel bar model. Bilinear model is used in longitudinal and stirrup reinforcement, and the stress-strain curve is divided into two stages linear elasticity and pre-peak nonlinear hardening as shown in Fig.3. Because of the cable action of reinforced-concrete frame beam, the failure criterion of the beam is the longitudinal steel snapped, and when the tensile strain reached 0.25 considers the steel snapped.

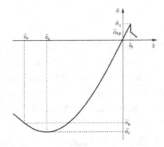

Fig. 2. Uniaxial stress-strain relation used in the concrete model

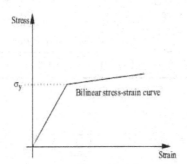

Fig. 3. Bilinear stress-strain relation used in steel

2.3 Load and Constraint

Using the techniques of displacement control and continuously loading, load is applied on the mid-span joints of the beam in order to simulate the failure of the column. The supports at two ends use ideal full constraint.

2.4 Element Type and Meshing

The there-dimensional 8-node hexahedral solid element model of the beam (shown as Fig.4) is developed by the integral dividing method. In order to ensure the integrity of the beam, it is jointed in common nodes in the interface of the two bodies. Truss rebar element is developed to simulated steel and interacted with concrete element.

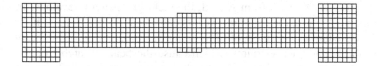

Fig. 4. Analysis model of the beam

2.5 Iteration Method and Definition

The solution to the nonlinear static analysis of the reinforce-concrete beam can be obtained in ADINA using Modified Newton iterations, the BFGS method and full Newton iterations. STOL [3] is the convergence tolerance, smaller the value exacter the solution.

2.6 Birth and Death Element

All-element model is established firstly with finite element method. But some elements should be 'killed' in a certain calculation time after it is inexistent in construction. In this paper, when mid-span displacement achieved some degree, concrete in compressed area has been crushed, then define the concrete element as death element continue to calculate until the longitudinal steel snapped.

3 Analysis of Resisting Progressive Collapse

Based on the test results in references [1,4], the effects of steel ratio and span-depth ratio are considered. Then 16 finite element models are established using ADINA program. Loaded after setting control parameters and computational steps, well convergence of these RC beams is proved.

3.1 Arching and Cable Action

Figs 5 and 6 show the load-deflection curve of a two-way reinforced concrete beam with laterally restrained edges.

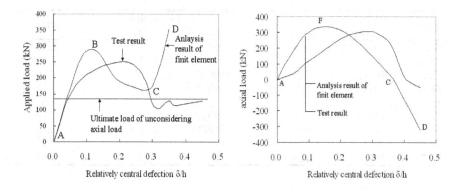

Fig. 5. Mid vertical load-central deflection curve   **Fig. 6.** Axial load-central deflection curve

As the load is increased from A to B, the yield line pattern develops, and with the help of arching action, the beam reaches its enhanced ultimate load at B. The arching action in the beam can be thought of as being due to jamming of the beam segments between the boundaries restraints, which cause the beam to arch from boundary to boundary. The induced arching action in the beam results in an enhancement of flexural strength of beam sections due to the action of axial force. The ultimate load increases 2.21 times compared with beam not considering the existence of axial force. Then, it doesn't reach maximum axial force but arrived late at F (see Fig. 6) from ultimate load.

As the deflection increases beyond B (see Fig. 5), the load carried by the beam decreases because of concrete crushed and it decreases rapidly beyond F because of a reduction in the compressive axial force (arching action). As C is approached to, the axial force in the beam changes from compression to tension. Beyond C the beam carries load by the reinforcement acting as a cable with full-depth crack of the concrete over the plastic zone of the beam. The beam continues to carry further load with an increase in deflection until at D the reinforcement begins to fracture. The load-carrying capacity increases 1.22 times compared with the ultimate capacity.

Compared with the test results, ultimate capacity and central deflection in finite element computational result is 45kN larger and 30mm smaller, due to the restriction of test condition. The constraint in test couldn't as ideal as in finite element analysis software, which makes the supports at two ends is rigid completely, that is the reason of the discrepancy. Therefore, the model established using ADINA program is correct and can be applied to analyze progressive collapse resistance in engineering practice.

3.2 Effect of Steel Ratio

As one of the most important performance of the beam's load-carrying capacity, the steel ratio influences the capacity of resisting progressive collapse of RC frame beam. Based on the test model in reference [6], finite element model is established by ADINA.

Table. 2. Steel ratio rate with Mid-span and support cross section in list of the finite element analysis results

beam	Mid-span cross section		Support cross section		Pu/Pj
	$\rho T - \rho C$	$\rho T/\rho C$	$\rho T'-\rho C'$	$\rho T'/\rho C'$	
KLJ-1	-0.0017	0.69	0.0017	1.45	3.52
KLJ-2	0	1	0	1	3.42
KLJ-3	0.0016	0.69	0.0016	0.69	3.36
KLJ-4	-0.0027	0.67	0.0027	1.5	3.11
KLJ-5	0	1	0	1	2.97
KLJ-6	0.003	1.37	-0.003	0.73	2.86
KLJ-7	-0.003	0.66	-0.0028	1.37	2.52
KLJ-8	0	1	0	1	2.21
KLJ-9	0.0031	1.39	-0.0031	0.78	2.13

Table 2 shows the relationship of increasing coefficient of load-carrying capacity (P_u/P_j) and rate with longitudinal tensile and compressive reinforcement ratio, where ρ_T, ρ_C are steel ratio of longitudinal tensile and compressive reinforcement in mid-span section of the beam, and $\rho_T{}'$, $\rho_C{}'$ are steel ratio of longitudinal tensile and compressive reinforcement in the supports of the beam at two ends. Finite element analysis shows that, when the ratio of longitudinal tensile and compressive reinforcement ratio being the same, along with the increasing of the steel ratio, the P_u/P_j decreasing, which illuminated the arching action is inconspicuous (as shown in Fig.7).

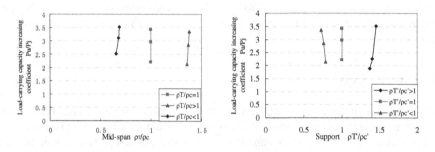

Fig. 7. Compare of relationship between increasing coefficient of load-carrying capacity and Rate of longitudinal tensile and compressive reinforcement ratio

3.3 Effect of Span-Depth Ratio

Based on the boundary conditions and geometric shape of the beam, axial force exists in the RC frame beam. As one of the most important performance of the beam's geometric size, the span-depth ratio influences the capacity of resisting progressive collapse of RC frame beam. According to the test model in reference [2], finite element model is established through changing the span by ADINA.

Fig. 8 shows the relationship between load-carrying capacity and span-depth ratio of the beams with the existence of the axial force. Variety of increasing factor of load-carrying capacity in arching action phase is shown as Fig. 8 (a), and cable action phase shown as Fig. 8 (b).

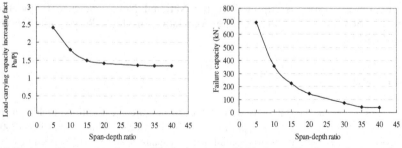

(a) Variety of increasing factor of load-carrying   (b) Variety of load-carrying capacity
    capacity in arching action phase   in cable action phase

Fig. 8. Effect of span-depth ratio

With the increase of the span-depth ratio at ultimate load-carrying capacity phase, the relatively central defection of the beam increased, namely the ductility improved. But the increasing factor of load-carrying capacity will decrease with the increase of the span-depth ratio because of the decreasing of the axial force. The decrease of the arching action is finite as shown in Fig.8(a), the span-depth ratio increases from 5 to 20, the increasing factor of load-carrying capacity decreases obviously, but beyond 20, the curve change slow at 1.4.

The axial force experienced from pulling to bearing after concrete is crushed, when the load is undertaken by reinforcement acting as a cable until it is snapped. At this time the failure load is defined, which decreases with the increase of the span-depth ratio. Namely, the cable action is inconspicuous with the increase of span-depth ratio.

4 Conclusions

Based on the finite element analysis of the reinforced-concrete frame beam, some conclusions are obtained in progressive collapse resistance of RC frame beam:

The ultimate load-carrying capacity of reinforced-concrete beam with laterally restrained edges can be improved greatly about 2 times more than beams not considering the existence of axial force. After the concrete over the plastic zone of the beam full-depth cracked, the beam carries load by the reinforcement acting as a cable until the reinforcement begins to fracture, that reduce the possibility of progressive collapse.

When the rate of longitudinal tensile and compressive reinforcement ratio of being the same, along with the increase of the steel ratio, the increasing coefficient of load-carrying capacity decreasing, namely the arching action is inconspicuous, but conspicuous the cable action.

The arching action will decrease with the increase of the span-depth ratio, but it is finite. When the span-depth ratio more than 20, the ratio-factor curve tend to slow at 1.4.

Acknowledgments

Funding for this work is supplied by the National Nature Science Foundation of China (No.50478078) and the Science Foundation of Hebei Polytechnic University (No. z200911).

References

1. Minghui, C.: Experimental study on influence of reinforcement ratio on arching action of reinforced concrete frame beams, pp. 17–19. Hebei Polytechnic University, Hebei (2007)
2. Xiaosheng, S.: Experimental study on influence of span-thickness ratio on Arching action of reinforced concrete frame beams, pp. 37–41. Hebei Polytechnic University, Hebei (2009)
3. ADINA R&D.: ADINA Theory and Modeling Guide. Watertown, pp. 263–270 (2001)

4. Guice, L.K., Edward, J.: Rhomberg. Membrance Action in partially Restrained Slab. ACI Structural Jounrnal, 365–373 (2008)
5. Guice, L.K.: Effects of Edge Restraint on Slab Behavior. Technical Report No.86-2, U.S. Army Engineer Waterways Experiment Station, pp. 180–185 (1996)
6. Park, Robert, Gamble: Reinforced Concrete Slabs, pp. 575–578. John Wiley & Sons, New York (1990)

Recognition of Linkage Curve Based on Mathematical Morphology*

Liyan Feng, Teng Liu, Xuegang Li, and Mingyu Tian

School of Mechanical Engineering, Hebei Polytechnic University,
Hebei, Tangshan 063009, China

Abstract. Based on the mathematical morphological image analysis theory, the research has established a kind of description method about the character parameters of linkage curves which is not associated with the graphic's location, scale and rotation. The research has summarized the internal relationships between the types of linkage curves and their corresponding shape spectrums, and proposed a new idea that the narrow degree of a linkage curve graphic determines its position of the shape spectrum's crest. Furthermore, for two linkage curves, their similarity function value mainly depends on the distance between their shape spectrums' crests. According to that, the linkage curve regional electronic atlas that is divided into several characteristic regions of linkage curves is constructed. This kind of electronic atlas can bring some advantages. For instance, it has a higher inquiry and recognition speed of similar linkage curves, and can reduce the data redundancy and so on.

Keywords: Linkage curve, mathematical morphology, shape spectrum, crest, regional electronic atlas.

1 Introduction

In the actual field, the special tracks (linkage curves) produced by some linkage mechanisms are widely used in the innovative mechanism design. As is illustrated in Fig. 1, the track produced by point E, on link BC of the blender, must be adapted to the shape of the container, so as to complete the stirring action. Obviously, in the four-bar mechanism ABCDE, with the position of point E or the changing of four bars' measurements, the linkage curves will vary dramatically. However, how to synthesize the mechanical size parameters according to the scheduled track, is always a heated discussion in the academia of mechanism, because it is difficult to cope with it.

By means of the computer's massive storage capacity and quick searching capacity, the indirect synthesis[1] achieving scheduled track has been widely recognized by academics. We can adopt the following steps: "scheduled track→track matching→mechanism type and components' lengths→mechanism evaluation". That is to say, we search the matching track from the linkage curve electronic atlas constructed

---

* The research is supported by Hebei Education Department (grant No.:2007119).

R. Zhu et al. (Eds.): ICICA 2010, LNCS 6377, pp. 470–477, 2010.

before, and pick up the corresponding mechanism type and measurements parameters. Finally, we gain the best mechanism by the evaluation to this synthesis. The most vital step of the indirect synthesis is to create a linkage curve electronic atlas involving the known mechanism types and their measurements. And the critical technical problem to be solved in this task is how to extract the linkage curve a parametric characterization to describe its shape features accurately, as well as how to get the similar linkage curve quickly and definitely.

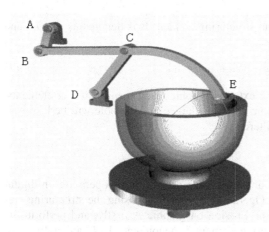

In this paper, we have studied in depth the mathematical morphological image analysis theory, then found out how to make use of the shape spectrum, which has nothing to do with the linkage curves' location, scale and rotation, to describe the shape features of linkage curves. We have analyzed the relationship between the narrow degree of a linkage curve graphic and the position of its shape spectrum's crest. We have researched the function of two linkage curves' similarity evaluation, proposed

Fig. 1. The application of linkage curve in blender

a new method to finish the division of the characteristic regions of linkage curves, constructed the linkage curve regional electronic atlas.

2   Mathematical Morphology Fundamentals

Currently, domestic and foreign scholars are making massive researches on parametric description about the linkage curves' shape feature. They have adopted some methods, such as Coordinate Transformation and Fast Fourier Transformation (FFT)[2,3]etc., to calculate the characteristic parameters, but none of them was satisfactory. The main problems of these methods were that they don't have a high stability and the identification accuracy is influenced by the operation etc. Mathematical morphology is a new digital image processing theory, exerting a series of structural transformations on the graphics using the structuring elements of different shapes, doing the analysis, processing and description on the digital image.

Mathematical morphology has two basic operations, which are Erosion and Dilation.

2.1   Erosion Operation

The Erosion on graphic A using the structuring element B is denoted as $A\Theta B$, and defined as:

$$A \ominus B = U \left\{ a - b : a \in A, b \in B \right\} \tag{1}$$

The Erosion signifies to lessen the internal graphic using the structuring elements, the effect being that the target graphic will be lessened and the hole will be enlarged. Thus, the internal graphic will be filtered.

2.2 Dilation Operation

The Dilation on graphic A using the structuring element B is denoted as $A \oplus B$, and defined as

$$A \oplus B = U \left\{ a + b : a \in A, b \in B \right\} \tag{2}$$

The Dilation signifies to enlarge the external graphic using the structuring elements, the effect being that the target graphic will be enlarged and the hole will be lessened. Thus, the external graphic will be filtered.

2.3 Open Operation

Based on the two basic operations above, we can draw another operation on digital image: Open Operation. The Open Operation on graphic A using the structuring element B, which means to perform the Erosion on graphic A firstly, and perform the Dilation on it, using the same structuring element, is denoted as AoB, and defined as

$$AoB = (A \ominus B) \oplus B \tag{3}$$

2.4 Shape Spectrum

By means of the Open Operation, we can calculate the shape spectrum[4-7], which can describe the shape of a given plane graphic accurately. Generally, the shape spectrum of graphic X can be defined as

$$S_X(r) = \frac{1}{A(X)} \frac{-dA(X \circ \sqrt{A(X)}rO)}{dr}, \quad r \geq 0 \tag{4}$$

In the equation above, $A(X)$ is defined as the area of graphic X; O stands for the unit circle(radius=1); $\sqrt{A(X)}rO$ represents the circle whose radius is $\sqrt{A(X)}r$; and $Xo\sqrt{A(X)}rO$ means to perform the Open Operation on graphic X, using the structuring element $\sqrt{A(X)}rO$.

3 Evaluation of Linkage Curves' Similarity

Based on shape spectrum, we can use the following similarity function to evaluate the similarity of any two linkage curves.

$$C(X,Y) = \frac{2\sum_r S_x(r)S_Y(r)}{\sum_r (S_x(r))^2 + \sum_r (S_Y(r))^2} \tag{5}$$

In the equation above, X and Y are two planar graphics, $S_x(r)$ and $S_Y(r)$ are the shape spectrums of graphic X and graphic Y respectively[8]. If they have an overall same shape, the similarity $C = 1$; If their shapes are distinct, the similarity $C < 1$; the more similar two graphics are, the closer to 1 the similarity C is.

4   Research on Linkage Curve's Shape Spectrum

Fig.2(a).shows a water droplet-shaped linkage curve. We have used Matlab to calculate its shape spectrum $S(r)$ values, which are shown in Table 1, according to the equation 4[9,10]. We have drawn the shape spectrum graph shown in Fig.2(b), with r being the horizontal axis and $S(r)$ being the vertical axis.

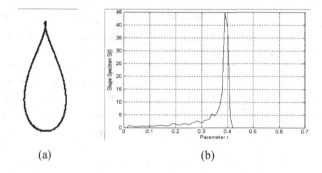

(a)   (b)

Fig. 2. Water droplet-shaped linkage curve and its shape spectrum

It can be seen from Table 1.that, the shape spectrum will reach the peak (S(r)= 47.7763), when r is 0.37. The black part of Fig.3(a). is the rest part of the Erosion and the Dilation on the linkage curve in Fig.2(a). using the structuring element when r is 0.37. Nevertheless, when r is 0.38, the linkage curve graphic will be completely eroded. Therefore, the remaining area of the Dilation is still zero, which is shown in Fig.3(b). We can concluded that it is the structuring element with a certain r ranging from 0.37 to 0.38 that results in the largest area changing rate ,and brings the shape spectrum's crest.

We can come to the conclusion that, the cause of the shape spectrum's crest of a linkage curve is attributable to that the diameter of structuring element will exactly reach or exceed the maximum inscribed circle radius of the linkage curve graphic. Under this condition, if we perform the Erosion on the linkage curve graphic using the

Table 1. The values of the shape spectrum of Water droplet-shaped linkage curve

r	0.01	0.02	0.03	0.04	0.05	0.06	0.07	0.08
S(r)	0.6160	0.6680	0.4294	0.3352	0.4866	0.6739	0.5179	0.4328
r	0.09	0.1	0.11	0.12	0.13	0.14	0.15	0.16
S(r)	0.6553	0.6596	0.5941	0.8759	0.8667	0.8109	0.6514	0.6347
r	0.17	0.18	0.19	0.2	0.21	0.22	0.23	0.24
S(r)	1.2125	1.6923	1.4156	0.9095	0.9635	1.4485	1.5457	1.2872
r	0.25	0.26	0.27	0.28	0.29	0.3	0.31	0.32
S(r)	1.7149	1.9003	2.5213	2.6209	1.9118	2.8124	3.0569	3.3696
r	0.33	0.34	0.35	0.36	0.37	0.38	0.39	0.4
S(r)	5.2132	4.5492	6.2031	12.6483	47.7763	44.7777	4.9412	0
r	0.41	0.42	0.43	0.44	0.45	0.46	0.47	0.48
S(r)	0	0	0	0	0	0	0	0
r	0.49	0.50	0.51	0.52	0.53	0.54	0.55	
S(r)	0	0	0	0	0	0	0	

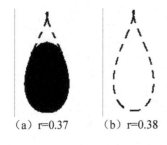

(a) r=0.37   (b) r=0.38

Fig. 3. The remaining area of Open Operations which are exerted on water droplet-shaped linkage curves

structuring element $\sqrt{A(X)r}O$, the linkage curve graphic will be completely eroded, and the remaining area is zero. Owing to that the Erosion, in the Open Operation, is the first step of the Dilation, the remaining area of the Dilation will still be zero. And all above will give rise to $A(X o \sqrt{A(X)r}O)$,in equation 4, is zero, and bring the largest area changing rate—the shape spectrum's crest. On the other hand, $A(X o \sqrt{A(X)r}O)$ refers to the remaining area of the Open Operation on graphic X using the structuring element $\sqrt{A(X)r}O$. Therefore, the r value corresponding its shape spectrum's crest is the r that can generate a structuring element $\sqrt{A(X)r}O$,with which a linkage curve graphic will be completely eroded.

5 Internal Relationships between the Shapes of Linkage Curves and Their Shape Spectrums

Through a comprehensive analysis about various types of linkage curves, we have summarized the internal relationships between the types of linkage curves and their corresponding shape spectrums. Some common types of linkage curves and their corresponding shape spectrums, obtained by Matlab, are shown in Fig.4.

According to equation 5, we have obtained the similarities, shown in Table 3, of any two of those linkage curves below.

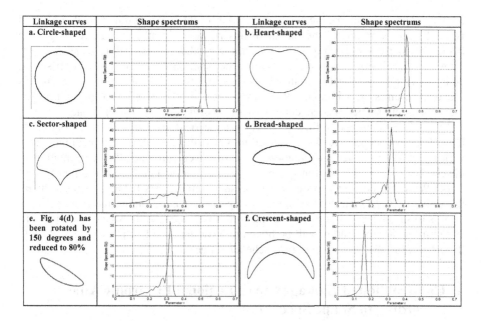

Fig. 4. Various kinds of linkage curves and their shape spectrums

Table 2. The similarity C of different linkage curves

Similarity / Linkage curve	a	b	c	d	e	f
a	1.0000	0.0070	0.0142	0.0094	0.0077	0.0001
b	0.0070	1.0000	0.1709	0.0168	0.0114	0.0040
c	0.0142	0.1709	1.0000	0.2079	0.1869	0.0380
d	0.0094	0.0168	0.2079	1.0000	0.9952	0.0303
e	0.0077	0.0114	0.1869	0.9952	1.0000	0.0467
f	0.0001	0.0040	0.0380	0.0303	0.0467	1.0000

According to Fig.4.and Table 2, we have drawn the conclusions as follows:

(1) The linkage curves in Fig.4(d).and Fig.4(e).have the same shape, and their similarity is 0.9952(close to 1). The minor deviation mainly results from the discretion of structuring element (unit circle).This indicates that the shape spectrum has nothing to do with a linkage curve graphic's location, scale and rotation. On the other hand, it can also be seen from Table 2. that, the similarity of two linkage curves whose shapes vary greatly, is extraordinarily low. It shows that the shape spectrum characterizes the difference between any two distinct graphics, and distinguishes two different curves effectively. Therefore, we can, by the shape spectrum, establish the linkage curve electronic atlas that can reduce the data redundancy and improve the inquiry speed.

(2) The position of a shape spectrum's crest is associated with the radius of the maximum inscribed circle of the linkage curve graphic. The more slender the shape of

a linkage curve graphic is, the smaller the radius of the maximum inscribed circle of it is. And with the radius of the maximum inscribed circle of a linkage curve graphic being growingly low, such as the crescent, the r value corresponding its shape spectrum's crest is becoming increasingly low, the position of its shape spectrum's crest being more left; While the r value corresponding the circle-shaped linkage curve's shape spectrum's crest is higher than any others. In other words, the position of the crest of a circle-shaped linkage curve's shape spectrum is the most right one.

(3) As far as any type of linkage curves is concerned, the r values corresponding to their shape spectrums' crests are divided into a small interval, even though they have various locations, scales and rotations. This discovery provides the segmentation of the characteristic regions of linkage curves with a significant theoretical support.

(4) With the location gap of two shape spectrum's crests being growingly small, the similarity C of their corresponding linkage curves is becoming increasingly high. That is to say, when we perform the track matching inquiry, the shape spectrum, obtained from electronic atlas, will be bound to have the crest that is extremely close to the crest of the shape spectrum of the scheduled track.

6 Construction of Linkage Curve Regional Electronic Atlas According to Shape Spectrum

According to the conclusions we got, we have finished the division of the characteristic regions of linkage curves, and constructed the linkage curve regional electronic atlas on the basis of the narrow degree of linkage curve graphics (the r values corresponding their shape spectrums' crests)

We have known that the r value, which is in [0.5, 0.55], corresponding the crest of the shape spectrum of the circle-shaped linkage curve is higher than any others. In addition, $r \geq 0$, which is known from equation 4. As a consequence, we affirm that the r values corresponding the shape spectrums' crests are in [0, 0.55].

According to the types of linkage curves and the r values corresponding the shape spectrums' crests, we have distributed [0, 0.55] into 11 subintervals, whose ranges depend on the changing steps of mechanical parameters and the density of the database. In every inquiry, the shape spectrum and the r value corresponding the shape spectrum's crest will be calculated automatically, then the searching will be located to a certain subinterval. All the records in this subinterval will be matched, and their similarities with the scheduled track will be calculated respectively. Then, the records that meet the similarity requirements will be sorted by similarity. Comparing with the traditional inquiry, this method improves the inquiry and recognition efficiency.

7 Conclusions

Based on mathematical morphology, we adopt the shape spectrum, which has nothing to do with the graphic's location, scale and rotation, to describe the shape of a given plane graphic accurately. This method can be adapted to the description about any linkage curve. It has been the most effective and accurate method so far. The narrow degree of a linkage curve graphic determines the position of the shape spectrum's crest of this linkage curve. And different types of linkage curves have different r values corresponding to their shape spectrums' crests. It goes without saying that this regulation has some theoretical significance. Meanwhile, the establishment and application of the linkage curve regional electronic atlas provides the synthesis of planar linkage mechanism for scheduled tracks with a rapid and effective design method.

References

1. Yong, L.: Research on Computer-Aided Creative Design Method Based on Planar Mechanism Path Synthesis [D]. Huazhong University of Science & Technology PhD thesis, 4: 9-30 (2005)
2. Li-yan, F., Yong-qiang, H., Xue-gang, L.: Research on Extracting Characteristic Parameter From Linkage Curves. Machinery Design and Manufacture 6(6), 154–155 (2007)
3. Xinchun, G.: Analyses of the Four-bar Coupler Curve Based on the Algorithm of BP Neural Network. Hefei University of Technology Master Dissertation 11, 24–34 (2007)
4. Chatzis, V., Pitas, I.: A Generalized Fuzzy Mathematical Morphology and its Application in Robust 2-D and 3-D Object Representation. IEEE Transaction Image Processing 9(10) (October 2000)
5. Hui, Y.: Design of Flapping Mechanism for a Micro Air Vehicle Based on Mathematical Morphology. Southwest Jiaotong University Master Degree Thesis 3, 9–19 (2007)
6. Xiaochen, W.: Mathematical Morphology Theory and its Application in Color Image Processing. Harbin Engineering University Master Degree Thesis 6, 16–20 (2008)
7. Jutao, Z.: Based on Shape Spectrum Characteristic Parameters Database of Six-bar Mechanism. Huazhong Agricultural University Master's Degree Dissertation 6, 22–25 (2009)
8. Shengtao, S.: Study on the Hybrid-driven and Controlled Seven-bar Mechanism. Sun Yat-Sen University Master Degree Thesis 4 (2008)
9. Ying, X., Katsumi, W.: Classification Method of Coupler Curves of Nongrashof Mechanisms by an Algebraic Characteristic. Mechanical Science and Technology for Aerospace Engineering 23(5), 602–604 (2004)
10. Huizhen, Z., Liyan, F., Jutao, Z.: The Construction of the Database for Curve's Shape Spectrum of Six-bar Mechanism. Machinery Design and Manufacture 2(2), 80–82 (2010)

Interval Implicitization of Parametric Surfaces*

Ning Li[1,2,**], Jing Jiang[3], and Wenfeng Wang[4]

[1] School of Statistics and Mathematics, Shandong Finance University, Jinan 250002, China
[2] Department of Mathematics, Shanghai University, Shanghai 200444, China
lnsdfi@163.com
[3] Department of Mathematics, Qilu Normal College, Jinan 250013, China
[4] Department of Automatic, Research Center of Automatic Control, Binzhou College,
Binzhou 256603, China

Abstract. The interval implicit representations of parametric surfaces have wide applications in Computer Graphics, Geometric Modelling, and others. Based on the properties of interval algebraic surfaces, barycentric coordinates and Bernstein basis functions, this paper presents an algorithm to compute the interval implicit representation of a rational Bézier surface by solving an optimal problem with a quadratic object function and linear constraints. This problem is equivalent to finding the two bounding surfaces of the interval implicit surface. An example is provided to demonstrate the algorithm.

Keywords: Interval arithmetic, Interval algebraic surfaces, Interval implicitization.

1 Introduction

Representation of surface is one of the topics of very active research in computational mathematics, and has been widely applied in various areas. We know that parametric surfaces and implicit surfaces are two common types of representations of surfaces in CAGD, which are very useful in mathematics, engineering problems, and others. Both of the representations of parametric surfaces and implicit surfaces have their own advantages and disadvantages. So investigating the conversion of the two representations should be significant and interesting.

A large number of papers have focused on the problem of how to find the accurate implicit representations of rational surfaces [1]-[6]. However, the practical usefulness of accurate implicitization is hampered by the complex representations of the implicit equations of rational surfaces, so it is valuable to find the approximate implicit representations. Several approaches have been proposed to solve this problem recently [7] [8]. One problem with approximate implicitization is how to deal with the numerical gap between the parametric equation and the implicit representation, which

* This research was supported by the Research Fund Special Contract of Binzhou College (BZXYKJ0802), and the Binzhou College Field Grade Bilingual Curriculum Project (2008 No. 01).
** Corresponding author.

R. Zhu et al. (Eds.): ICICA 2010, LNCS 6377, pp. 478–485, 2010.

may result in unreliability in geometrical computation such as boundary evaluation and intersections. One possible approach to solve this problem is to use interval representation of geometric objects [9] [10]. The interval representation can embody a complete description of coefficient errors and transfer the errors to applications in other systems. The recent works on the applications of interval arithmetic in geometric modeling suggest that such representation greatly helps to increase the numerical stability in geometric computations [11]. Based on the interval representations of implicit equations, [12] put forward a new concept called interval implicitization of rational curves and propose an algorithm to compute the interval implicit representation of a rational curve by solving some optimal problems.

Motivated by the work mentioned above and keeping applications of interval arithmetic in view, we in this paper generalize the interval implicitization of rational curves to the situation of rational surfaces, that is finding an interval algebraic surface of lower degree which bounds the given rational Bézier surface such that an object function involving the width and the tension term (as we have defined in this paper) of the interval algebraic surface is minimized.

2 Interval Arithmetic and Interval Algebraic Surfaces

Definition 1. An interval is a set of real numbers defined by: $[a,b]=\{x \mid a \leq x \leq b\}$. The width of interval $[a,b]$ is $\omega([a,b])=b-a$, and the center of $[a,b]$ is $c([a,b])=(a+b)/2$. If $A=[a,b]$ and $B=[c,d]$ are two intervals, and $o \in \{+,-,\times,\div\}$ is an operator, then $A o B=\{x o y \mid x \in A, y \in B\}$.

Definition 2. An interval algebraic surface is an algebraic surface with interval coefficient:

$$[f](x,y,z) := \sum_{0 \leq i+j+k \leq m} [f_{ijk}] x^i y^j z^k = [0], \qquad (1)$$

where $[f_{ijk}]$ are intervals, and $[0]$ stands for any interval which contains zero. The width of the interval algebraic surface is

$$\omega([f]) := \sqrt{\sum_{0 \leq i+j+k \leq m} \omega^2([f_{ijk}]) / ((m+3)(m+2)(m+1)/6)} \cdot$$

And the center surface of the interval algebraic surface is

$$c([f]) := \sum_{0 \leq i+j+k \leq m} c([f_{ijk}]) x^i y^j z^k = 0 \cdot$$

An interval algebraic surface can be interpreted as the set of points defined by

$$IAS := \{(x,y) \mid \sum_{0 \leq i+j+k \leq m} g_{ijk} x^i y^j z^k = 0, g_{ijk} \in [f_{ijk}]\}.$$

A surface S lies inside IAS, if $S \in IAS$.

Definition 3. An interval algebraic surface segment is an interval algebraic surface defined inside a tetrahedron, the Bernstein-Bézier representation of which is

$$[f](u,v,w,q) := \sum_{i+j+k+l=m} [f_{ijkl}] B_{ijkl}^m (u,v,w,q) = [0] ,$$

where $B_{ijkl}^m (u,v,w,q) = \dfrac{m!}{i!\,j!\,k!\,l!} u^i v^j w^k q^l, i+j+k+l = m$ are the Bernstein basis functions, $[f_{ijkl}]$ is an interval, and (u,v,w,q) are the barycentric coordinates of a point with respect to the base tetrahedron $T = \Delta T_1 T_2 T_3 T_4$. The width of the algebraic surface segment is defined to be

$$\omega([f]) := \sqrt{\sum_{i+j+k+l=m} \omega^2 ([f_{ijkl}]) / ((m+3)(m+2)(m+1)/6)} \cdot$$

Its center surface is defined to be

$$c([f]) := \sum_{i+j+k+l=m} c([f_{ijkl}]) B_{ijkl}^m (u,v,w,q) = 0.$$

Since $B_{ijkl}^m (u,v,w,q) \geq 0$, the two boundary algebraic surfaces of the interval algebraic surface segment are

$$ub([f]) := f_{ijkl}^2 B_{ijkl}^m (u,v,w,q) = 0, lb([f]) := f_{ijkl}^1 B_{ijkl}^m (u,v,w,q) = 0,$$

where $[f_{ijkl}] = [f_{ijkl}^1, f_{ijkl}^2]$. $ub([f])$ and $lb([f])$ are called the upper boundary surface and lower boundary surface respectively.

The boundary surfaces of the interval algebraic surface can be very complicated. This is the main reason why we define an interval algebraic surface segment inside a tetrahedron and employ Bernstein-Bézier representations.

3   Interval Implicitization of Rational Bézier Surfaces

Let $B(u,v)$ be a rational Bézier surface of degree $n_1 \times n_2$ in parametric form:

$$B(u,v) = (x(u,v), y(u,v), z(u,v)) = \frac{\displaystyle\sum_{i=0}^{n_1} \sum_{j=0}^{n_2} \omega_{ij} P_{ij} B_{i,n_1}(u) B_{j,n_2}(v)}{\displaystyle\sum_{i=0}^{n_1} \sum_{j=0}^{n_2} \omega_{ij} B_{i,n_1}(u) B_{j,n_2}(v)}, \quad (2)$$

where $P_{ij}, i=0,1,..., n_1, j=0,1,..., n_2$ are the control points, $\omega_{ij} \geq 0, (\sum_{i=0}^{n_1} \sum_{j=0}^{n_2} \omega_{ij} > 0)$ are the weights of the rational Bézier surface, $B_{i,n_1}(u), B_{j,n_2}(v)$ are the Bernstein basis functions.

The problem of interval implicitization of the rational surface $B(u,v)$ can be stated as follows:

Find an interval algebraic surface IAS such that $B(u,v) \in IAS$ and an objective function involving the width of the interval algebraic surface and a tension term is minimized.

We will find the interval algebraic surface IAS through an optimal problem.

Optimal objective function. We denote the width of the algebraic surface segment $L := \omega^2([f])$ and the tension term $G := \iiint_T (g_{xx}^2 + g_{yy}^2 + g_{zz}^2 + 2g_{xy}^2 + 2g_{xz}^2 + 2g_{yz}^2)dxdydz$. We set $F=L+\omega G$ as the optimal objective function of the optimal problem, where ω is a non-negative weight.

Bounding conditions. For a given base tetrahedron $T = \Delta T_1 T_2 T_3 T_4$, the rational Bézier surface $B(u,v)$ can be rewritten in Bernstein-Bézier form over T:

$$B(u,v) = (U(u,v), V(u,v), W(u,v), Q(u,v)), 0 \le u \le 1, 0 \le v \le 1, \tag{3}$$

where $U(u,v), V(u,v), W(u,v), Q(u,v)$ are the barycentric coordinates of point $B(u,v)$ with respect to the base tetrahedron T. If the parametric surface (2) lies inside tetrahedron T, then $U(u,v), V(u,v), W(u,v), Q(u,v)$ are all nonnegative for any $0 \le u \le 1, 0 \le v \le 1$.

The Bernstein-Bézier form of the rational surface (3) and the parametric form (2) are related by

$$\begin{cases} U(u,v) = c_{11}x(u,v) + c_{12}y(u,v) + c_{13}z(u,v) + c_{14} \\ V(u,v) = c_{21}x(u,v) + c_{22}y(u,v) + c_{23}z(u,v) + c_{24} \\ W(u,v) = c_{31}x(u,v) + c_{32}y(u,v) + c_{33}z(u,v) + c_{34} \\ Q(u,v) = c_{41}x(u,v) + c_{42}y(u,v) + c_{43}z(u,v) + c_{44} \end{cases}, \tag{4}$$

where $\begin{pmatrix} c_{11} & c_{12} & c_{13} & c_{14} \\ c_{21} & c_{22} & c_{23} & c_{24} \\ c_{31} & c_{32} & c_{33} & c_{34} \\ c_{41} & c_{42} & c_{43} & c_{44} \end{pmatrix} = \begin{pmatrix} X_1 & X_2 & X_3 & X_4 \\ Y_1 & Y_2 & Y_3 & Y_4 \\ Z_1 & Z_2 & Z_3 & Z_4 \\ 1 & 1 & 1 & 1 \end{pmatrix}^{-1}$ and (X_i, Y_i, Z_i) are the

Cartesian coordinates of $T_i, i = 1, 2, 3, 4$.

If $B(u,v)$ lies inside $[f](u,v,w,q) = [0]$, which is an interval algebraic surface segment of degree m, then for any $0 \le u \le 1, 0 \le v \le 1$,

$[f](U(u,v), V(u,v), W(u,v), Q(u,v)) =$

$\sum_{i+j+k+l=m} [f_{ijkl}]B_{ijkl}^m(U(u,v), V(u,v), W(u,v), Q(u,v)) = [0]$, which is equivalent to:

$$\sum_{i+j+k+l=m} f^1_{ijkl} B^m_{ijkl}(U(u,v),V(u,v),W(u,v),Q(u,v)) \leq 0$$

$$\sum_{i+j+k+l=m} f^2_{ijkl} B^m_{ijkl}(U(u,v),V(u,v),W(u,v),Q(u,v)) \leq 0.$$

From (4), we get:

$$\sum_{i+j+k+l=m} f^1_{ijkl} B^m_{ijkl}(U(u,v),V(u,v),W(u,v),Q(u,v)) = \sum_{r=0}^{mn_1n_2} h^1_r B^{mn_1n_2}_r(u,v)/\omega(u,v)^m$$

$$\sum_{i+j+k+l=m} f^2_{ijkl} B^m_{ijkl}(U(u,v),V(u,v),W(u,v),Q(u,v)) = \sum_{r=0}^{mn_1n_2} h^2_r B^{mn_1n_2}_r(u,v)/\omega(u,v)^m,$$

where $\omega(u,v) = \sum_{i=0}^{n_1}\sum_{j=0}^{n_2} \omega_{ij} B_{i,n_1}(u) B_{i,n_2}(v); h^1_r = \sum_{i+j+k+l=m} c^r_{ijkl} f^1_{ijkl}, h^2_r = \sum_{i+j+k+l=m} c^r_{ijkl} f^2_{ijkl},$

$r = 0,1,\ldots, mn_1n_2; c^r_{ijkl}, r = 0,1,\ldots, mn_1n_2$ are constants.

Theorem. The interval algebraic surface (1) bounds rational surface (2) if

$$\sum_{i+j+k+l=m} c^r_{ijkl} f^1_{ijkl} \leq 0 \text{ and } \sum_{i+j+k+l=m} c^r_{ijkl} f^2_{ijkl} \geq 0, r = 0,1,\ldots, mn_1n_2.$$

Noticing $B^{mn_1n_2}_r(u,v) \geq 0, r = 0,1,\ldots, mn_1n_2$, we know the theorem is obvious.

Optimal problem: the optimal objective function F=L+ωG is a quadratic function with f^1_{ijkl}, f^2_{ijkl}.

Now the interval implicitization problem is converted to the following optimal problem:

Min   F

s.t. $\sum_{i+j+k+l=m} c^r_{ijkl} f^1_{ijkl} \leq 0, \sum_{i+j+k+l=m} c^r_{ijkl} f^2_{ijkl} \geq 0, r = 0,1,\ldots, mn_1n_2,$

$$\sum_{\substack{i+j+k+l=m \\ r=1,2}} f^r_{ijkl} = 2, f^2_{ijkl} \geq f^1_{ijkl}, i+j+k+l = m.$$

The restrict condition $\sum_{i+j+k+l=m; r=1,2} f^r_{ijkl} = 2$ is from the normalize condition

$$\sum_{i+j+k+l=m} c[f_{ijkl}] = 1.$$

We can solve the optimal problem through matlab.

If we couldn't get a correct shape for the interval implicit representation, a higher degree interval implicit surface could be tried.

For a given tolerance $\varepsilon > 0$, if the width of the interval implicit representation is greater than ε, we can recursively subdivide the rational surface until the width of the interval implicit representation for each surface segment is less than ε. From the following example, we can see that the width of each interval implicit representation is much smaller than that of the interval implicit representation which bounds the whole parametric surface.

The choice of the base tetrahedron has some influence to the result. In the practical computation, we should choose the base tetrahedron to be a tighter bound of the rational surface.

4 Numerical Example

Given a rational Bézier surface of degree 2×2 with control points and weights as follows:

$$(P_{00}, \omega_{00}) = (1,1,1,1), (P_{01}, \omega_{01}) = (3,1,4,2), (P_{02}, \omega_{02}) = (6,1,1,1),$$
$$(P_{10}, \omega_{10}) = (1,3,1,1), (P_{11}, \omega_{11}) = (3,3,4,2), (P_{12}, \omega_{12}) = (5,3,1,1),$$
$$(P_{20}, \omega_{20}) = (5,5,1,1), (P_{21}, \omega_{21}) = (3,5,3,2), (P_{22}, \omega_{22}) = (5,5,1,1).$$

The vertices of the base tetrahedron are given by

$$T_1 = (4,2,5), T_2 = (2.5,11,1), T_3 = (-3,0,1), T_4 = (10,0,1).$$

Solving the optimal problem, we can get the interval implicit representation:

$$[f](u,v,w,q) = [1.3159,1.3816]B^2_{0002}(u,v,w,q) + [-1.8698,-1.8036]B^2_{0011}(u,v,w,q)$$

$$+[1.3800,1.4196]B^2_{0020}(u,v,w,q) + [-0.0740,0.0042]B^2_{0101}(u,v,w,q)$$

$$+[-0.4342,-0.3556]B^2_{0110}(u,v,w,q) + [0.0686,0.1295]B^2_{0200}(u,v,w,q)$$

$$+[0.2989,0.3272]B^2_{1001}(u,v,w,q) + [-0.1953,-0.1335]B^2_{1010}(u,v,w,q)$$

$$+[0.1628,0.2218]B^2_{1100}(u,v,w,q) + [0.0629,0.0931]B^2_{2000}(u,v,w,q) = [0]$$

Its width is $\omega([f]) = 0.187836$.

Figure 1 shows the rational Bézier surface and the interval implicit surface in the same system of coordinates.

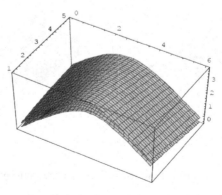

Fig. 1. Rational Bézier surface and the interval implicit surface in the same system of coordinates

Then we subdivide the rational surface into four pieces, the parameters of which respectively are

$$u \in (0,1/2), v \in (0,1/2); u \in (0,1/2), v \in (1/2,1);$$
$$u \in (1/2,1), v \in (0,1/2); u \in (1/2,1), v \in (1/2,1).$$

The vertices of the corresponding base tetrahedron are given by

$$T_{11} = (0,1,3), T_{12} = (-1,2,-1.5), T_{13} = (4,-1,3.5), T_{14} = (4,6,3.5); T_{21} = (6,2,4),$$
$$T_{22} = (7,6,-0.5), T_{23} = (7,-2,-0.5), T_{24} = (0,2,4.75); T_{31} = (0,4,3), T_{32} = (0,-1,0),$$
$$T_{33} = (0,7,0), T_{34} = (6,4,4); T_{41} = (4,4,4), T_{42} = (0,4,5), T_{43} = (7,0,-2), T_{44} = (7,7,-2).$$

We can solve the optimal problems respectively, and get four interval implicit surfaces. Their widths are:

$$\omega([f]_1)=0.102241, \ \omega([f]_2)=0.10742, \ \omega([f]_3)=0.113 \text{ and } \omega([f]_4)=0.0915259.$$

Fig. 2 shows the four pieces of the rational Bézier surface and the corresponding interval implicit surfaces.

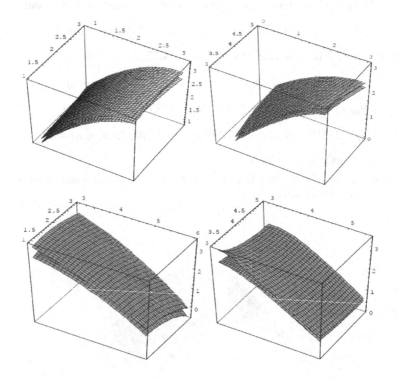

Fig. 2. Four pieces of the rational Bézier surface and the corresponding interval implicit surfaces

The algebraic surface usually has several branches. In this example, we take the one that is the closest to the original surface. This example shows that the interval implicit representation is a nice approximation to a given parametric surface and the width decreases rapidly after the subdivision.

References

1. Hoffmann, C.M.: Implicit Curves and Surfaces in CAGD. IEEE Computer Graphics and Applications 13, 79–88 (1993)
2. Perez, D.S., Sendra, J.R.: A Univariate Resultant-based Implicitization Algorithm for Surfaces. Journal of Symbolic Computation 43, 118–139 (2008)
3. Wang, X.H., Chen, F.L., Deng, J.S.: Implicitization and Parametrization of Quadratic Surfaces with One Simple Base Point. In: 21st Annual Meeting of the International Symposium on Symbolic Computation, pp. 31–38. ACM Press, New York (2008)
4. Chionh, E.W.: Shifting Planes Always Implicitize a Surface of Revolution. Computer Aided Geometric Design 26, 369–377 (2009)
5. Wu, J.M., Wang, R.H.: Approximate Implicitization of Parametric Surfaces by Using Compactly Supported Radial Basis Functions. Computers and Mathematics with Applications 56, 3064–3069 (2008)
6. Dohm, M.: Implicitization of Rational Ruled Surfaces with Mu-bases. Journal of Symbolic Computation 44, 479–489 (2009)
7. Dokken, T.: Approximate Implicitization. In: Lyche, T., Schumaker, L. (eds.) Mathematical Methods in CAGD, pp. 81–102. Vanderbilt University Press, Oslo (2001)
8. Sederberg, T.W., Zheng, J., Klimaszewski, K., Dokken, T.: Approximate Implicitization Using Monoid Curves and Surfaces. Graphical Models and Image Processing 61, 177–198 (1999)
9. Mudur, S.P., Koparkar, P.A.: Interval Methods for Processing Geometric Objects. IEEE Computer Graphics and Applications 4, 7–11 (1984)
10. Sederberg, T.W., Farouki, R.T.: Approximation by Interval Bézier Curves. IEEE Computer Graphics and Applications 15, 87–95 (1992)
11. Chen, F.L., Low, W.P.: Degree Reduction of Interval Bézier Curves. Computer-Aided Design 32, 571–582 (2000)
12. Chen, F.L., Deng, L.: Interval Implicitization of Rational Curves. Computer Aided Geometric Design 21, 401–415 (2004)

Calculation Method of Indirect Accident Loss Based on Life Value

Shuzhao Chen[1,2], Qingxiang Cai[2], Yanchao Yang[3], and Cangyan Xiao[3]

[1] State Key Laboratory of Coal Resources and Mine Safety, China University of Mining and
Technology, Xuzhou, Jiangsu 221008 China
[2] School of Mining Engineering, CUMT, Xuzhou, Jiangsu 221008, China
[3] College of Light Industry, Hebei Polytechnic University, Tangshan, hebei 063020, China
Chshzh052@163.com, qxcai@vip.sohu.com, ancerromeo@sina.com,
Qingsong315@126.com

Abstract. In view of the widespread serious phenomenon of safety loans among
domestic coal mines, this paper puts forward a calculation method of indirect
accident loss in the hope of raising the awareness of coal mines on safety input
thorough analysis. This paper studies the validity of the calculation method based
on the fatalities caused by coal mine accidents and puts forward the method of
indirect accident loss through studying the number of death and severe injuries,
and therefore builds a corresponding optimization model of Safety input. Value
of life, created by a miner through his whole life can be determined as much as
5million Yuan with reference to foreign standard of compensation in coal mine
accidents. Approximate solution, figured out through the model, can help the
enterprise examine the reasonable safety input and find the method to calculate
the economic benefits under a certain amount of input. This paper analyzes the
validation of the model with a case study of a mining group with different input
parameters on coal mine safety standards and a reasonable level of ultimate
benefit.

Keywords: Value of life, Accident damage, Calculation, Indirect losses, Safety
input.

1 Introduction

China is the world's largest coal producer and consumer countries, also the most frequent occurrence coal mine fatalities countries, million tons coal mine death rate is not
only the United States, Australia and other developed countries the number of times,
but also several times more than India and other developing countries [1]. Safety input
shortage to coal mine accidents in China is the major reason [2] [3]. Official statistics
show that, only state-owned key coal mines in safety engineering, safety equipment and
safety facilities, reach loans of 50 billion yuan [4]. Due to this situation has two main
reasons, one is incapable of company itself [5], second, investment in corporate security benefits (accident damage) lack of knowledge [6].Paper based the existing re-
search- accident, proposed a calculation method of indirect losses of the accident, hope

R. Zhu et al. (Eds.): ICICA 2010, LNCS 6377, pp. 486–492, 2010.

though the loss of the accident to improve safety fully into account the degree of attention investment. Heinrich and other studies suggest that indirect losses are direct losses four times, this conclusion as the International Labor Union (ILO) adopted [1]. Thus, the loss of indirect losses is the main accident.

People in the study of the formation mechanism of the accident, gradually realize that the "decision-making, management, system" and other corporate behavior in accident causation and the role of the formation mechanism [7]. To prevent and reduce the occurrences of security enterprise security into the underlying motivation [8], safety input is coal an important part of enterprise security act. From a psychological point of view, behavior is the subject under certain external stimuli, the response to so "business behavior is essentially outside the enterprise structure and the internal interaction of the stimulus fundamental constraint for the realization of a goal and make a realistic response [9]. Therefore, strengthen the stimulation and improving the expectation of accident loss, is beneficial to improving the safety input level.

2 Optimization Model

2.1 Foundation Calculated of Indirect Losses

Using the number of deaths as calculated indirect losses accident is a reasonable basis mainly embodied the following areas. First of all, high incidence of fatal accidents in coal mines. Two decades, the death toll in China has accounted for more than half of the world, table 1 show coal mine safety production since 2000 to today. Second, fatal accidents are widespread in coal mines. Although the township coal mines is the subject accident deaths, but the large state-owned coal enterprises also occur, even the safe and efficient mine is no exception [10]. Finally, direct response to casualties can be part of indirect losses. In China, the number of casualties to define the most important indicator of the accident level, but also with the loss of labor resources, cut-off time (output reduction), etc. There is a direct relationship between the content of indirect losses.

Table 1. 2000-2009 coal mine safety conditions

Years	Productivity(Mt)	Deaths(people)	Million tons mortality
2000	1314	5797	4.41
2001	1459	5670	3.89
2002	1380	6716	4.87
2003	1668	6434	3.86
2004	1956	6027	3.08
2005	2190	5986	2.73
2006	2381	4746	1.99
2007	2524	3786	1.5
2008	2716	3092	1.18
2009	2850	2700	0.95
Total	20438	50954	2.49

Based on the above analysis, study the number of deaths and serious injuries caused by accident the number of indirect losses as a basis for calculating the accident, namely:

$$S = S_z + S_j = S_z + (a + b \times \eta) \times c , \tag{1}$$

where: S —Accident damage, Million. S_z —Direct economic loss accident, Million ; S_j—Indirect economic losses caused by the accident, Million ; a —The number of deaths caused by the accident, people. b —The number of serious injuries caused by the accident, people. η —The proportion of seriously injured workers loss of life value. c —Value of human life, Million /people.

2.2 Optimization Model of Safety Input

Business goal is to achieve profits maximize, but the safety and economic efficiency is the unity of opposites [11], Companies must invest a balance between security and strike profit maximization. Suppose the relation between mine casualty rate and security exists a certain functional: $P = f(Q)$. To the problem we make the following assumptions simplify.

The accident rate and inversely proportional to safety input, that: $\dfrac{dP}{dQ} < 0$. But with the rising cost of security investment, easy to control less and less insecurity, much additional safety input control effect of decreased safety incidents [12], expressed as $\dfrac{d^2 P}{d^2 Q} > 0$.

Assuming an average of one accident deaths caused by n_1, n_2 of them seriously, then put into a certain level of security incidents caused by the number of deaths and serious injuries, respectively: $a = n_1 \times f(Q)$, $b = n_2 \times f(Q)$.

Suppose one casualty and caused direct economic losses average S_z, $S_z = s_z \times f(Q)$.

In normal coal production based profit C_0.

Based on the above assumption that a certain safety level of coal production into profit:

$$\begin{aligned} C = C_0 - S - Q = C_0 - \{s_z \times f(Q) \\ + [n_1 \times f(Q) + n_2 \times f(Q) \times \eta] \times c\} - Q \end{aligned} \tag{2}$$

Arranged:

$$C = C_0 - [s_z + (n_1 + n_2 \times \eta) \times c] \times f(Q) - Q . \tag{3}$$

$$-[s_z + n_1 \times c + n_2 \times \eta \times c] \times f'(Q) - 1 = 0 . \tag{4}$$

Arranged:

$$\frac{dP}{dQ} = -\frac{1}{s_z + (n_1 + n_2 \times \eta) \times c} \tag{5}$$

To facilitate the analysis, based on the assumption 1, and further assume that $P = f(Q) = \dfrac{m}{Q}$, Where m is a constant. By equation (5) available:

$$\frac{dP}{dQ} = -\frac{m}{Q^2} = -\frac{1}{s_z + (n_1 + n_2 \times \eta) \times c} \tag{6}$$

Accordingly, a reasonable solution, and the level of safety input into the security level of the economic benefits of mine development are:

$$Q^* = \sqrt{m[s_z + (n_1 + n_2 \times \eta) \times c]} \tag{7}$$

$$C^* = C_0 - [s_z + (n_1 + n_2 \times \eta) \times c] \times \frac{m}{Q} - Q \tag{8}$$
$$= C_0 - 2Q = C_0 - 2\sqrt{m[s_z + (n_1 + n_2 \times \eta) \times c]}$$

From (7) can see, mine with a reasonable level of security into the value of life also increased.

2.3 Life Value Determine

China has not improved the value of life calculation of compensation in many casualties as often as death compensation but there are other reasons capabilities of different pricing for the same life, so this may be no reference. Current state to the mine killed at least 20 million workers compensation standards should be regarded as part of direct economic losses, rather than the identification value of life, so the research proposed to mine the output value will be created as a standard to calculate the value of life.

$$c = \frac{25 \times 250 \times 4 \times 200}{1000000} = 5 \text{ (million yuan)}, \tag{9}$$

where: 25 - expected working hours, a; 250 - the number of years working, d/a; 4 - effect of coal mine employees, t/work; 200 - collected the raw coal output, Yuan/t.

In addition, the United States in 1995, assessed the lives of persons killed in industrial accidents average price of 75 million, Japan's per capita compensation for work injuries and death for the 70 million yen [4]. The current exchange rate about 5.2 million yuan.

Thus, to determine the value of life of 500 million is reasonable. Thesis that, although seriously injured workers loss of working capacity, but still alive, the family and society resulting from the negative psychological impact of small, so the proportion of seriously injured workers loss of value of life, of taking.

3 Case Study

3.1 Basic Information

Design a total production capacity of mining group 12.6Mt/a, sales profit 180yuan/t. Assuming 420 million yuan investment in security conditions, 8 cases of casualties, direct economic losses of 3million yuan/play, the death toll of 1.6 people/play starting number of 2.5 people seriously injured/play. Based on these assumptions determine the parameters of Table 2, mine safety.

Table 2. Safety parameters

Symbol	Unit	Value	Symbol	Unit	Value
C_0	Million	2268	n_1	people/play	1.6
S_z	Million /play	3	n_2	people/play	2.5
Q	Million	420	c	Million	5
P	per	8	η		0.6

According to Table 2 parameters and the type (7) calculate the probability function of the group casualty value of the parameter m=3360. By substituting (7) and type (8) solution was: reasonable level of safety input Q*=231.86, and economic benefits C*=1804.28.

Table 3 shows the comparison of the mining group security, indicators and model optimization value.

Table 3. Comparison index

Index	Symbol	Unit	Actual value	Theoretical optimal value	Relative proportions/%
Safety input	Q	Million	420	231.86	181.14
Economic benefits	C	Million	1720	1804.28	95.33
Casualties	P	per	8	15	53.33
Deaths	a	people	13	23	56.52
serious injuries	b	people	20	36	55.56
Million tons mortality	n	people/Mt	1.0	1.8	55.56

Comparison of results from the Table 3 shows that by improving the safety of the mining group to invest in cost reduction is only less than 5% of the index case production safety improvement of 40% or more.

3.2 Parameter

Recognition the value of life is not only reflect the level of value for human life, c, but also the proportion of serious injuries, loss of human life value, the sensitivity analysis shown in Table 4.

Table 4. Value of life and reasonable safety input

c \ η	0	0.2	0.4	0.6	0.8	1
0	10039.9	10039.9	10039.9	10039.9	10039.9	10039.9
200	14433.3	15553.8	16598.8	17581.8	18512.7	19399.0
400	17771.9	19571.4	21218.9	22747.3	24179.3	25531.2
600	20575.7	22894.5	24999.2	26939.9	28750.0	30452.6
800	23040.8	25793.0	28278.6	30562.7	32687.6	34682.6
1000	25266.6	28397.2	31215.4	33799.4	36199.4	38450.0

The direct economic losses related the fatalities S_z and production conditions, accident type, loss calculation methods and other factors. China in recent years, statistics show that fatal accidents in the direct economic loss of 20-150 million / person, and was gradually rising trend [1]. Thus, the direct economic losses of different accident are very different. Figure 1 shows the relationship between the direct economic losses and the casualty reasonable level of security.

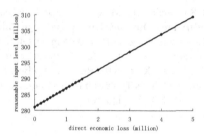

Fig. 1. Relationship between the direct economic losses and reasonable safety investment level

4   Conclusions

Indirect loss is the major component of the losses caused by accident. For the calculation of indirect accident losses rationally determines the level of security is important significance. Study proposed the number of casualties caused by the accident as the basis for calculating indirect losses accidents and to analyze its rationality. Based on the number of casualties in the accident calculation of indirect losses, to establish a reasonable safety into the optimization model and solution method. Mine life to create the basis for calculating the output value, and with reference to foreign work accident compensation standards, determine the value of human life is 5 million yuan. For a mining group as example in verification of the model, analyze the different parameters on the coal into a reasonable level of safety.

References

1. Xueqiu, H., Li, S., Baisheng, N.: Basic characteristics of China's Law of Safety. China Safety Science Journal 18(1), 5–12 (2008)
2. Jiacai, Z.: On Coal Mine Safety Accident-prone Problems. Coal Technology (4), 41–42 (2005)
3. Shimin, S., Di, W.: Coal Mine Safety and Health Economic Impact Study. China Safety Science Journal 16(6), 60–64 (2006)
4. Hanqiu, W.: Coal Mine Safety Analysis of the Relationship between Input and Cost-effective. Coal 31(5), 60–61 (2005) (in Chinese)
5. Hongyi, X.: With the Economic Perspective of State-owned Coal Mine Production Safety. Coal Economic Research 11, 58–59 (2003) (in Chinese)
6. Jinxian, L.: Security Cost-effective Quantitative Simulation of High-risk Industries. Friends of Science 10, 134–136 (2009) (in Chinese)
7. Qingguo, Y., Yuyang, H.: Behavior and Economic Analysis of Enterprise Security. Coal Economic Research 7, 67–69 (2005) (in Chinese)
8. Hong, C., Hui, Q.: Safe Behavior of Coal Enterprises Selected for Study of Dynamic. China Mining 18(9), 79–82 (2009) (in Chinese)
9. Anning, W., Li, J., Xiangming, Y.: Review on Corporate Behavior. Tianjin Social Sciences (6), 31–35 (1998)
10. Chief, W.X. (ed.): 2008 China's Coal Mine Construction Industry Safe and Efficient Annual Report. Coal Industry Press, BeiJing (January 2009) (in Chinese)
11. Chunxiang, W.: On the economic benefits of coal mine safety production inputs and the relationship between. Coal Project 6, 14–15 (2007) (in Chinese)
12. Yongkun, Q., Hong, X., Jianbo, X.: Into the Relationship Between Security and Economic Benefits - as an Example of China's Township Coal Mines. Quantitative & Technical Economics Research 8, 40–45 (2004) (in Chinese)

Hazard Source Identification of Mined-Out Area Based on Grey System Theory

Haibo Zhang[1,2] and Weidong Song[1]

[1] Beijing University of Science and Technology Beijing 10083
[2] Hebei polytechnic University Tangshan 063009 China
zhbts@heut.edu.cn

Abstract. In order to avoid or reduce the mined-out area of instability, we should monitor these hazards in situation so as to achieve the purpose of disaster prevention and mitigation, using the monitoring results predicted and timely protective measures. Due to rock with nonlinear dynamic instability disasters and time series data, the theory of grey system was suitable for disaster of identification. So the method on the modeling of grey prediction model was researched in this paper , the grey system theory was put into application in mined-out area with instability of rock, the identification model was established with the characteristics of rock acoustic emission. The data sequence of acoustic emission monitoring was forecasted by the established model of mine in field. Forecasting results in the actual situation had shown relatively close to the grey prediction model, It was indicated that the grey prediction model was feasible.

Keywords: grey system theory; rock mass failure; acoustic emission.

1 Introduction

Method on the modeling of grey prediction created by Professor Deng julong is an important part of the Theory of Grey System. From its first appearance in the year 1982, method on the modeling of grey prediction has been used for about 20 years. It is based on the Grey Dynamic Model, GM for short. In the recent years, the Theory of Grey System has drawn lots of scholars' attention home and abroad. Meanwhile, the Theory of Grey System has been successfully used in the following aspects, such as social sciences, management of the economy, meteorology, environment, systematic engineering and so on. Also the Theory of Grey System can be used in the area of safety engineering, for example, the prediction of abundance of methane, the prediction of abundance of ground water as well as the prediction of roof weighting [1, 2, 3, 4, 5, 6, 7].

2 The Model of Grey Prediction

In the Theory of Grey System, the completely distinct relationship is called "white", while, the completely unknown and indistinct relationship is called "black". The part

R. Zhu et al. (Eds.): ICICA 2010, LNCS 6377, pp. 493–500, 2010.

between "white" and "black" is called "grey"[8]. Apparently, the mine safety system or mine accident system is typically grey system. Up to now, the certainty of mine's safe condition and relationships among different factors during the mine accident are not clear. Thus, the mine safety system is treated as grey system. That is to say, the theory and methodology of grey prediction can be applied to solve the problem of safety prediction. The method of grey prediction has the advantages of less original data and characteristics of weakening its randomness by reprocessing the information that is already generated. Thus, the model of grey prediction can be transformed into a new sequence, which has the typical nonlinear character.

So far, a number of grey prediction models have been created among which GM(1,1) is used most frequently and effectively in the safety engineering. This model is a single argument of a linear differential equation, suitable for array of strong exponential law. Meanwhile, it can only describe the dull change process. The sequence of original data generally has no exponential law, but after one or several accumulated generations, the data series usually can meet requirements of modeling.

2.1 The Predictive Modeling of Grey GM(1,1)

The prediction of grey GM(1,1) can be divided into two different series predictions, namely, series signals with the equal interval and series signals with non-equal interval. The latter can be divided into weak random prediction of series signals with non-equal interval and strong random prediction of series signals with non-equal interval [9]. Since the test time interval, the distance between the tests points are not equally spaced, the practical monitoring results may be series signals with the equal interval or series signals with non-equal interval. However, the original data monitoring from unstable Mined-out area are usually series signals with the equal interval instead of series signals with non-equal interval. When encountered series signals with non-equal interval, we can adopt interpolation to transform the series signals with non-equal interval into series signals with the equal interval [1]. In addition, there is the grey modeling suitable for series signals with non-equal interval [9]. Here we only discussed the modeling method of series signals with the equal interval. When the precision of the GM(1,1) model does not meet the demand, the residual sequence can be used to establish the residual GM(1,1) model to correct the original residual model in order to improve the precision. Following is the respective introduction based on these two different models.

2.1.1 Modeling Steps of GM(1,1)

Step 1: Establish the original data series. Give or measure the original data series $X^{(0)}$, and make sure it is non-negative. It is usually the absolute indexes gotten during the field monitoring, such as rock acoustic emission index, and rock surrounding displacement pressure value [10]:

$$X^{(0)} = \left\{ x^{(0)}(1), x^{(0)}(2), \cdots, x^{(0)}(n) \right\} \tag{1}$$

Step 2: Change the original data sequence by the method of r order, then we can get a new data series

$$X^{(1)} = \left\{ x^{(1)}(1), x^{(1)}(2), \cdots, x^{(1)}(n) \right\} \tag{2}$$

$$x^{(1)}(k) = x^{(0)}(1) + x^{(0)}(2) + \cdots, x^{(0)}(k) \tag{3}$$

Step 3: Make smooth test to $X^{(0)}$. If the data series meets the following demand,

$$\rho(k+1)/\rho(k) < 1$$

$$\rho(k) = x^{(0)}(k)/x^{(1)}(k-1) \in [0, 0.5], \quad k = (3, 4, \cdots, n),$$

Then, we call this data series smooth series.

Step 4: The test of $X^{(1)}$'s the index of law. If the series meets the following requirements:

$$\rho^{(1)}(k) = x^{(1)}(k)/x^{(1)}(k-1) \in [1, 1.5], \quad (k = 3, 4, \cdots, n)$$

then, the series has allowed the index.

Step 5 : Make the $X^{(1)}$ on the test of average, and establish a first-order nonlinear differential equation of bleaching

$$dx^{(1)}/dt + ax^{(1)} = b \tag{4}$$

a and b are undetermined parameters.

Step 6: Use the least square method and extreme principle to get the matrix form, and use a and b to illustrate them respectively.

$$\hat{a} = [a, b]^T = [B^T B]^{-1} B^T Y_N \tag{5}$$

$$B = \begin{pmatrix} -0.5[x^{(1)}(1) + x^{(1)}(2)] & 1 \\ -0.5[x^{(1)}(2) + x^{(1)}(3)] & 1 \\ -0.5[x^{(1)}(n-1) + x^{(1)}(n)] & 1 \end{pmatrix} \tag{6}$$

$$Y_N = [x^{(0)}(2), x^{(0)}(3), \cdots, x^{(0)}(n)]^T$$

Step 7: Establish the modeling and its time response

$$\hat{x}^{(1)}(k+1) = \left(x^{(0)}(1) - b/a\right) e^{-ak} + b/a \tag{7}$$

Step 8: Find $X^{(1)}$'s analog value, and obtain the generated sequence series using the above formula:

$$\hat{X}^{(1)} = \left\{ \hat{x}^{(1)}(1), \hat{x}^{(1)}(2), \cdots, \hat{x}^{(1)}(n) \right\}$$

Step 9: Restore and find the $X^{(0)}$'s analog value, through IAGO , then we can get the predictive sequence series.

$$\hat{X}^{(0)} = \left\{ \hat{X}^{(0)}(1), \hat{X}^{(0)}(2), \cdots, \hat{X}^{(0)}(n) \right\} \tag{8}$$

$$\hat{x}^{(0)}(k) = \hat{x}^{(1)}(k) - \hat{x}^{(1)}(k-1)$$

Step 10: Test the accuracy of this modeling, the residual calculation and relative error are as follows:

$$\varepsilon(k) = x^{(0)}(k) - \hat{x}^{(0)}(k) \tag{9}$$

$$\Delta_k = |\varepsilon(k)| / x^{(0)}(k) \tag{10}$$

In the process of prediction analysis, if the accuracy can meet the requirements, then we can use the (7) to predict the systematic behavior characteristic value at any time in the future. If the accuracy is not enough, we need to establish the residual model GM(1,1) to correct the original model so as to further improve the model's prediction accuracy.

2.1.2 Residual Modeling Steps of GM(1,1)

Step 1: Construct $X^{(0)}$'s and $\hat{X}^{(0)}$'s residual paragraph,

$$\varepsilon^{(0)} = \left\{ \varepsilon^{(0)}(k_0), \varepsilon^{(0)}(k_0 + 1), \cdots, \varepsilon^{(0)}(n) \right\}$$

Step 2: If the above residual sequence has negative, then we should adopt the non-negative processing so as to form a non-negative residual sequence $\dot{\varepsilon}^{(0)}$.

Step 3: Do the accumulation process to the non-negative residual sequence $\dot{\varepsilon}^{(0)}$ and establish GM(1,1) model, and get $\dot{\varepsilon}^{(0)}$'s time response in 1-AGO.

Step 4: Find the time response's derivative reducing value in the above formula: $\hat{\varepsilon}^{(0)}(k+1)$.

Step 5: According to the different ways of reduction, we can get different residual fixed time response.

$$\hat{x}^{(0)}(k+1) = \hat{x}^{(1)}(k+1) - \hat{x}^{(1)}(k) = (1-e^a)\left(x^{(0)}(1) - b/a\right)e^{-ak}$$

The corresponding residual fixed time response is

$$\hat{x}^{(0)}(k+1) = \begin{cases} (1-e^a)\left(x^{(0)}(1) - b/a\right)e^{-ak}, k < k_0 \\ (1-e^a)\left(x^{(0)}(1) - b/a\right)e^{-ak} \pm \hat{\varepsilon}^{(0)}(k+1), k \ge k_0 \end{cases}$$

$$\hat{x}^{(0)}(k+1) = (-a)\left(x^{(0)}(1) - b/a\right)e^{-ak}$$

The corresponding residual fixed time response is

$$\hat{x}^{(0)}(k+1) = \begin{cases} -a(1-e^a)\left(x^{(0)}(1) - b/a\right)e^{-ak}, k < k_0 \\ -a\left(x^{(0)}(1) - b/a\right)e^{-ak} \pm \hat{\varepsilon}^{(0)}(k+1), k \ge k_0 \end{cases}$$

Step 6: According to the steps mentioned above, go on to find the residual. And test whether the result meets the requirements. If the result does not meet the requirement, the second residual modeling is needed until it reaches accuracy required. Finally we can select the model with the least error extent to make the prediction.

3   GM(1,1)'s Application to Goaf's Hazard Identification

Relevant parameters can be obtained through the application to goaf's hazard identification of GM(1,1), such as rock-mass acoustic emission index, the pressure value of the surrounding rock and the displacement value of rock mass. Also we can use the GM(1,1) grey modeling to do the prediction. For example, now let's look at how to apply the GM(1,1) model to the acoustic emission prediction.

During the technical research of pressure monitoring of a mine stope, the acoustic emission technology is used to monitor the safety of the stope stability. Following is the table which illustrates data (NT: the total events of the acoustic emission) collected under the shaft. All the figures are the respondent average figures of different monitoring points.

Table 1. The Original Data of the Acoustic Emission Monitoring

Date	Oct, 11	Oct, 12	Oct, 13	Oct, 14	Oct, 15	Oct, 16	Oct, 17
NT	7.5	8.3	9.6	11.2	13.0	14.2	15.9

According to Table3-1, establish the $GM(1,1)$ prediction model of the acoustic emission. Here are the main steps.

Step 1: Establish the original data series

$$x^{(0)} = \left\{ x^{(0)}(1), x^{(0)}(2), \ldots x^{(0)}(7) \right\} = \{7.5, 8.3, 9.6, 11.2, 13.0, 14.2, 15.9\}$$

Step 2: Do the first adding process to the original data and obtain the get sequence.

$$X^{(1)} = \left\{ x^{(0)}(1), x^{(0)}(2), \ldots x^{(0)}(7) \right\} = \{7.5, 15.8, 25.4, 36.6, 49.6, 63.8, 79.7\}$$

Step 3: Make smooth test to $X^{(0)}$

$$\rho(k) = x^{(0)}(k) / x^{(1)}(k-1) \ ; \ k = (3, 4, \cdots, n)$$

$$\rho(3) = 0.61, \rho(4) = 0.44, \rho(5) = 0.36, \rho(6) = 0.29, \rho(7) = 0.25$$

When $k > 4, \rho(k) < 0.5$, then, it meets the smooth demand.

Step 4: The test of $X^{(1)}$'s the index law.

$$\rho^{(1)}(k) = x^{(1)}(k) / x^{(1)}(k-1)$$

$$\rho^{(1)}(3) = 1.61, \rho^{(1)}(4) = 1.44, \rho^{(1)}(5) = 1.36, \rho^{(1)}(6) = 1.29, \rho^{(1)}(7) = 1.25$$

When $k > 4, \rho^{(1)}(k) \in [1, 1.5]$, then, it meets the demand of the index law. Thus, we can establish $X^{(1)}$'s GM(1,1)model

Step 5: Make $X^{(1)}$'s test of average, this is the series generated:

$$\{11.65, 20.6, 31.0, 43.1, 56.7, 71.75\}$$

$$B = \begin{bmatrix} -11.65 & -20.6 & -31.0 & -43.1 & -56.7 & -71.7 \\ 1.000 & 1.000 & 1.000 & 1.000 & 1.000 & 1.000 \end{bmatrix}^T$$

$$Y_N = [8.3 \quad 9.6 \quad 11.2 \quad 13.0 \quad 14.2 \quad 15.9]$$

Step 6: Use the least square method and extreme principle to get the matrix form (a and b)

$$\hat{a} = [a, b]^T = [B^T B]^{-1} B^T Y_N = \begin{bmatrix} -0.1263 \\ 7.0903 \end{bmatrix}$$

Step 7: Finally establish the model

$$dx^{(1)}/dt - 0.1263x^{(1)} = 7.0903$$

$$\hat{x}^{(1)}(k+1) = \left(x^{(0)}(1) - b/a\right)e^{-ak} + b/a = 63.6385e^{0.1263k} - 53.13856$$

Step 8: Find the $X^{(1)}$'s analog value

$$\hat{X}^{(1)} = \left\{\hat{x}^{(1)}(1), \hat{x}^{(1)}(2), \cdots, \hat{x}^{(1)}(7)\right\} = \{7.500, 16.067, 25.788, 36.817, 49.331, 63.529, 79.639\}$$

Step 9: Restore and find the $X^{(0)}$'s analog value

$$\hat{x}^{(0)}(k) = \hat{x}^{(1)}(k) - \hat{x}^{(1)}(k-1)$$

$$\hat{X}^{(0)} = \left\{\hat{x}^{(0)}(1), \hat{x}^{(0)}(2), \cdots, \hat{x}^{(0)}(7)\right\} = \{7.500, 8.567, 9.721, 11.029, 12.514, 14.198, 16.110\}$$

Step 10: Test the accuracy of this modeling: Table 2
Average relative error:

$$\Delta = \frac{1}{6}\sum_{k=2}^{7}\Delta_k = 1.85\%$$

Table 2. Test Error of Data

Number	Actual Data	Analog data	Residual error	Relative error
2	8.3	8.567	-0.267	3.22%
3	9.6	9.721	-0.121	1.26%
4	11.2	11.029	0.171	1.53%
5	13.0	12.514	0.486	3.74%
6	14.2	14.198	0.002	0.0001%
7	15.9	16.110	-0.210	1.32%

From this table, we can get that the average relative error is 1.85%, the maximum relative error is 3.74%. Both of them are less than 5.0% (the limit of the fine grade is 5.0%). Thus, this model is effective and it can be used to do the prediction.

Step 11: Establish the further prediction

According to the established model to do the acoustic emission prediction based on the data collected on Oct, 18 and Oct, 19. Table 3-3 illustrates the error condition.

Table 3. The Prediction Result of NT

Date	Actual Data	Predictive Data	Absolute Error	Relative Error
Oct,18	17.7	18.28	0.58	3.3%
Oct,19	22.0	20.74	1.26	5.7%

4 Conclusion

From the above table, it is clear that both on the date of Oct, 18 and Oct, 19, the actual data and predictive data are close to each other. The maximum error is 5.7%. Thus, it means that the model established before is feasible. According to the detailed condition of this mine, we have selected NT=20 as the prediction index. Since on the date of Oct, 19, NT=20.74, so we immediately set the instable prediction to the management staff of this mine. Then, they asked the working staff under the ground to move away and remove those equipments there. Actually, at the 6 am of the Oct, 20 this stope area had an inbreak accident. The inbreak area is 200 m^2. Even though this accident is not very serious, anyway, it happens. Thus, according to the prediction result, we have reduced the loss to some extent.

On the other hand, according to the grey model prediction, the predicted value of the acoustic emission is changing constantly. This value may increase based on the exponential law or decrease based on the negative-exponential law. Apparently, this result is not suitable to the reality. Thus, we conclude that the grey prediction model is only feasible in a short-term. Thus, in order to further improve its effectiveness, we need to correct it constantly with newly collected data.

This example shows that the acoustic emission technology is quite effective in the stability monitoring process of the mine stope. It is possible to make the short-term prediction to the acoustic emission by using the GM(1,1) grey prediction model.

References

1. Gui, X.Y., Yu, Z.M.: Based on the grey system theory of coal gas flow-volume prediction research. J. of Guizhou University of Technology 36(6), 9–13 (2007)
2. Guo, D.Y., Li, N.Y., Pei, D.W., Zheng, D.F.: Coal and gas outburst prediction of grey theory- the neural network method. J. of Beijing University of Science and Technology 29(4), 354–359 (2007)
3. Zhao, J.B., Li, L., Gao, Q.: Slope deformation prediction of grey theory and application research. J. of Rock Mechanics and Engineering 24(2), 5800–5802 (2005)

4. Cheng, X.J., Hu, W.J., Cai, M.F.: Acoustic emission and nonlinear theory in forecasting the rock instability application. J. of Beijing University of Science and Technology 20(5), 409–411 (1998)
5. Jiao, J.B., Li, J.F., Cao, J.J.: GM(1,1) model based drill-hole abnormal gas dynamic grey forewarning and predication for catastrophe. J. of China Coal 35(12), 86–89 (2009)
6. Tian, Q.Y., Fu, H.L.: Failure time predication of slope collapse of block rockmass based on gray and catastrophic theories. J. of South China University of Technology 37(12), 122–124 (2009)
7. Yan, R.B., Niu, Y.L., Li, J.S., Lian, Y.X.: Determining sensitive indexes of coal and gas outburst forecasting based on grey theory. J. of Henan Institute of Engineering 21(4), 5–7 (2009)
8. Deng, J.L.: The grey system theory. Huazhong University of Science and Technology Press, Wuhan (1990)
9. Yuan, J.Z.: Grey system theory and its application. Science Press, Beijing (1991)
10. Liu, S.F., Guo, T.B.: The gray system theory and its application. Science Press, Beijing (2002)

Consistency Analysis of Dynamic Evolution of Software Architectures Using Constraint Hypergraph Grammars

Hongzhen Xu[1,2], Bin Tang[1,2], and Ying Gui[1]

[1] Department of Computer Science and Technology, East China Institute of Technology,
Fuzhou, Jiangxi Province, 344000, China
[2] Application of Nuclear Technology Engineering Center of Ministry of Education,
East China Institute of Technology, Nanchang, Jiangxi Province, 330013, China
xhz_97@163.com

Abstract. With increasing demands and changing environment on software systems, a major challenge for those systems is to evolve themselves to adapt to these variations, especially during their running, where dynamic evolution of software architectures has been a key issue of software dynamic evolution research. Most current research in this direction focuses on describing dynamic evolution process of software architectures, and lack consistency analysis of dynamic evolution of software architectures. In this paper, we propose to represent software architectures with constraint hypergraphs, model dynamic evolution of software architectures with constraint hypergraph grammars, and discuss the consistency condition and corresponding consistency decision method of dynamic evolution of software architectures. Our approach provides a formal theoretical basis and a user-friendly graphical representation for consistency analysis of dynamic evolution of software architectures.

Keywords: Software architecture; dynamic evolution; constraint hypergraph grammars; consistency.

1 Introduction

With the continuing development of software technologies such as pervasive computing, mobile computing and cloud computing, software systems become more and more open and complex. A major challenge for those systems is to evolve themselves to adapt to variable requirements and other environment, especially during their running. Software dynamic evolution means that the evolution of software systems occurs during the execution of those systems, which can be implemented dynamically either by hot-swapping existing components or by integrating newly developed components without the need for stopping those systems [1].

The software architecture provides design-level models and guidelines for composing the structure, interaction, and key properties of a software system. It helps to understand large systems, supports reuse at both component and architecture levels,

R. Zhu et al. (Eds.): ICICA 2010, LNCS 6377, pp. 501–508, 2010.

indicates major components, their relationships, constraints, and so on [2]. Dynamic evolution of software architectures [3] means that software architectures can be modified and those changes can be enacted during the system's execution. The typical evolution operations for dynamic evolution of software architectures include adding/removing/updating components or connectors, changing the architecture topology.

In this paper, we focus on constraints and consistency analysis of dynamic evolution of software architectures. We depict software architectures with constraint hypergraphs, model dynamic evolution of software architectures using constraint hypergraph grammars, and discuss the consistency condition and corresponding consistency decision method of dynamic evolution of software architectures.

2 Related Works

Many research works are focusing on dynamic evolution of software architectures at present and they can be sub-divided into three categories. The first uses UML and its extended models [4, 5] to design software architectures and describe their dynamic evolution. The second uses ADLs (Architectural Description Languages) to model and analyze software architectures and their dynamic evolution. Some of those ADLs like Darwin [6], dynamic Wright [7] and π-ADL [8] can model dynamic evolution of software architectures with formal methods. However, they do not offer any graphical approaches to display these models. Some others such as AADL [9] provide graphical tools for modeling dynamic evolution of software architectures, but they don't give mechanisms for validating these models. The third uses formal techniques such as graph-based techniques [10, 11, 12, 13], logic-based techniques [14] and algebra-based techniques [15]. Métayer [10] proposed to describe software architecture evolution using graph grammars. Bruni et al. [11] presented to model dynamic software architectures using typed graph grammars. Ma et.al [12] proposed to model dynamic software architectures with attributed typed graph grammar. Bucchiarone et al. [13] presented to model self-repairing systems using dynamic software architectures formalized as T-typed hypergraph grammars. Aguirre et al. [14] proposed a formal specification language for dynamically reconfigurable component-based systems based on temporal logic. Canal et al. [15] described the refinement of components and architectures of dynamic software systems using π-calculus.

Although researchers have done many works in dynamic evolution of software architectures, few works mention architecture constraints and relevant consistency analysis of dynamic evolution of software architectures.

3 Basic Notations

Definition 3.1 (Hypergraphs). A hypergraph is a tuple $H = (V, E, s, t)$, where V and E are disjoint finite sets of nodes and hyperedges respectively, $s, t : E \rightarrow V^*$ are two mappings indicating the source and the target of a hyperedge, where $*$ denotes that each hyperedge can be connected to a list of nodes.

Definition 3.2 (Total Hypergraph Morphisms). Let $H_1=(V_1, E_1, s_1, t_1)$, $H_2=(V_2, E_2, s_2, t_2)$ be two hypergraphs. A total hypergraph morphism $f: H_1 \rightarrow H_2$ between H_1 and H_2, or f for short, consists of a pair of functions $f_V: V_1 \rightarrow V_2$ and $f_E: E_1 \rightarrow E_2$ such that (1) $s_2 °f_E = f^*_V ° s_1$; (2) $t_2 °f_E = f^*_V ° t_1$.

f is called injective (surjective) if both f_V and f_E are injective (surjective). f is an isomorphism if it is both injective and surjective. In the sequel, we also call a total hypergraph morphism as a hypergraph morphism.

Definition 3.3 (Partial Hypergraph Morphisms). A partial hypergraph morphism $f: H_1 \rightarrow H_2$ between H_1 and H_2 is a pair $< H_{1f}, f'>$, where H_{1f} is a subgraph of H_1, and $f': H_{1f} \rightarrow H_2$ is a total hypergraph morphism.

Definition 3.4 (Hypergraph Production Rules). A hypergraph production rule $p= (L, R)$, commonly written $p: L \rightarrow R$, is a partial hypergraph morphism from L to R, where L is called the left-hand side, and R is called the right-hand side.

Definition 3.5 (Hypergraph Grammars). A hypergraph grammar is a tuple $G = (\mathcal{H}, P, H_0)$, where $\mathcal{H}$ is a finite set of hypergraphs, P is a finite set of hypergraph production rules and H_0 is the initial hypergraph.

Definition 3.6 (Hypergraph Constraints). An atomic hypergraph constraint is a hypergraph morphism $c: G \rightarrow C$, where G, C are hypergraphes. A hypergraph constraint is a series of atomic hypergraph constraints combining by logical connectives.

Definition 3.7 (Satisfiability of Atomic Hypergraph Constraints). Given an atomic hypergraph constraint $c: G \rightarrow C$, a hypergraph H satisfies c if for each injective hypergraph morphism $g: G \rightarrow H$, there is an injective hypergraph morphism $q: C \rightarrow H$, such that $q ° c=g$, denoted by $H \vDash c$. $H \vDash c$ specifies that H must include C if it includes G, denoted $\forall(c: G \rightarrow C)$. When $G = \varnothing$, it means H must include C, denoted $\exists(c: C)$, where $\forall$ is the universal logical quantifier "all", $\exists$ is the existential logical quantifier "exists".

The underlying idea of a hypergraph constraint is that it can specify that certain structures must (or must not) be present in a given hypergraph. In this paper, we express hypergraph constraints in a graphical way. For example, a hypergraph H satisfies a hypergraph constraint c shown in Fig. 1, which means that if there are two hyperedges in H to respectively connect nodes v_1 and v_2, v_2 and v_3, then there is a hyperedge to connect v_1 and v_3 in H.

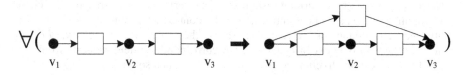

Fig. 1. Example of hypergraph constraints

4 Modeling Dynamic Evolution of Software Architectures

In order to visually model dynamic evolution of software architectures, we represent software architectures using hypergraphs with constraints (we call them constraint hypergraphs), model dynamic evolution of software architectures with constraint hypergraph grammars.

Definition 4.1 (Software Architectures Based on Constraint Hypergraphs). A software architecture based on constraint hypergraphs is a tuple $SA=(E_{SA}, V_{SA}, s_{SA}, t_{SA}, C_{SA})$, where E_{SA} is a set of hyperedges, corresponding to the set of components and connectors of the software architecture; V_{SA} is a set of nodes, corresponding to the set of communication ports between components and connectors of the software architecture, which denote link relations between components and connectors; $s_{SA}, t_{SA:}$ $E_{SA}->V^*_{SA}$ are two mappings indicating source nodes and target nodes of a hyperedge, which denote interactive relations between components and connectors of the software architecture; C_{SA} is a set of hypergraph constraints, corresponding to software architecture constraints. The corresponding hypergraph is called the software architecture hypergraph.

Definition 4.2 (Constraint Hypergraph Grammars of Dynamic Evolution of Software Architectures). A constraint hypergraph grammar of dynamic evolution of software architectures is a tuple $\hat{G} = (\mathcal{H}, P, H_0, C)$, where $\mathcal{H}$ is a finite set of software architecture hypergraphs without constraints, P is a finite set of evolution rules of software architectures and H_0 is the initial software architecture hypergraph, C is a set of software architecture hypergraph constraints.

Using constraint hypergraph grammars, we can formally model the dynamic evolution process of software architectures based on grammars similar to our approach of [16].

5 Consistency Analysis of Dynamic Evolution of Software Architectures

In order to illustrate consistency analysis of dynamic evolution of software architectures using constraint hypergraph grammars, we introduce the following scenario, whose architecture hypergraph is shown as Fig. 2. In the system, there are three types of components: client(c), control server (cs) and server (s); two types of connectors: client connector (cc) and sever connector (sc). Clients can access system resources by making a request to the server through the control server. The control server is responsible for returning responses of the server to the corresponding client. In the architecture, c_i are client entities, cs is the control server entity, s are the server entity, cc_i are connector cc entities, sc is the connector sc entity, Pc_i are communication ports between c_i and cc_i, CR correspond to client requests from c_i to cc_i, and CA correspond to client answers from cc_i to c_i, and so on.

In our paper, nodes are represented by black dots. Component hyperedges are drawn as rectangles while connector hyperedges as rounded boxes, which are connected to their attached nodes by their tentacles.

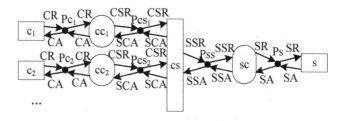

Fig. 2. Architecture hypergraph of a client/server system

5.1 Hypergraph Constraints

In addition to the architectural composition and interaction, the system can have some specific constraints which must be satisfied during dynamic evolution of its architectures. In this paper, we consider following constraints: 1) There are at most one server and one control server during dynamic evolution of the system; 2) Each component of the system can be connected to a connector through only one communication port; 3) If there is a client, there must be a server in the system.

We represent these system architecture constraints with hypergraph constraints, which are shown respectively in Fig. 3(1)-(7).

5.2 Constraint Hypergraph Grammar

Similar to our approach of [16], we can define adding/removing/updating component, adding/removing/updating connector evolution rules of our system. For lack of space, we don't give out these evolution rules. For more detail about evolution rules of dynamic evolution of software architectures, please refer to the literature [16].

Supposed the initial architecture of the system is $\varnothing$, we can define a constraint hypergraph grammar of dynamic evolution of the system software architectures as $\hat{G} = \{\{CS_0, CS_1, ..., CS_t\}, P, CS_0, C\}$, where CS_0, CS_1, ..., CS_t are finite software architecture hypergraphs, P is the set of all evolution rules, $CS_0 = \varnothing$ is the initial software architecture hypergraph, C is the set of architecture constraints as mentioned in section 5.1. According to the constraint hypergraph grammar, the system architectures can be evolved dynamically as the process of [16], where the system must judge the corresponding constraint during dynamic evolution process of the system software architectures when applying to these evolution rules here. For lack of space, we don't give out the corresponding evolution process.

5.3 Consistency Analysis

The consistency condition of dynamic evolution of software architectures describes properties of software architectures which are preserved by all software architectures during the system dynamic evolution, for example, the existence or uniqueness of certain elements or link relations in software architectures. To depict the consistency of dynamic evolution of software architectures, we propose the following definition,

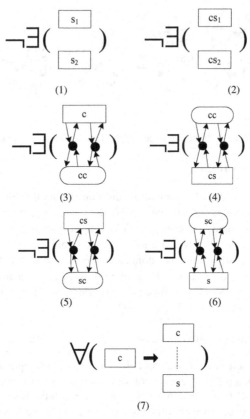

Fig. 3. Hypergraph constraints of dynamic evolution of software architectures

Definition 5.1 (The Consistency Condition of Dynamic Evolution of Software Architectures). Supposed $\mathcal{H}$ is the set of software architecture hypergraphs during dynamic evolution of a system, given a constraint c, if any software architecture hypergraph $H \in \mathcal{H}$, such that $H \models c$, then c is called a consistency constraint of dynamic evolution of the system software architectures. The consistency condition of dynamic evolution of software architectures is the set of all consistency constraints of dynamic evolution of software architectures. If all software architectures during the system dynamic evolution satisfy the consistency condition, we say that dynamic evolution of the system software architectures is consistent.

Proposition 5.1 (Constraint Satisfiability of Dynamic Evolution of Software Architectures). Given a hypergraph constraint $c: G \rightarrow C$, $p: L \rightarrow R$ is an evolution rule of software architectures, and the software architecture hypergraph H can be evolved to H' in one step through p, i.e. $H \xrightarrow{p} H'$. If $H \models c$ and $R \models c$, then $H' \models c$.

Proposition 5.2 (Consistency Decision of Dynamic Evolution of Software Architectures). Given a set of hypergraph constraints C, and a constraint hypergraph grammar $\hat{G} = (\mathcal{H}, P, H_0, C)$ of dynamic evolution of a system software architectures, if the initial software architecture hypergraph H_0 satisfies all constraints in C, and each right-hand side of evolution rules in P satisfies all constraints in C, then all evolved software architectures according to the constraint hypergraph grammar satisfy these constraints, i.e. all constraints in C are consistency constraints. If C is the set of all consistency constraints of the system, i.e. C is the consistency condition, and then dynamic evolution of the system software architectures is consistent.

In our scenario, We can get that all constraints of section 5.1 are consistency constraints. We take the constraint (1) as an example to prove that it is a consistency constraint, and the consistency of other constraints is similar. The initial software architecture hypergraph $CS_0 = \varnothing$, satisfy the constraint (1). It is obviously that all right-hand sides of evolution rules defined according to our approach [16] satisfy the constraint (1). So the the constraint (1) is a consistency constraint of dynamic evolution of the system software architectures according to the proposition 5.1.

We define these consistency constraints as the consistency condition of the system, then the dynamic evolution of software architectues of our system satisfies the consistency condition according to the proposition 5.2, i.e. the dynamic evolution of the system software architectures is consistent.

6 Conclusion

The development of software technology in software engineering field makes it a growing concern on the dynamic nature of software evolution, especially dynamic evolution of software architectures. However, most of research works of at present do not care about constraints and consistency analysis of dynamic evolution of software architectures. In this paper, we represent software architectures with constraint hypergraphs, model dynamic evolution of software architectures with constraint hypergraph grammars, and discuss the consistency condition definition and corresponding consistency decision method of dynamic evolution of software architectures. Following these constraints and hypergraph grammars, it can ensure the consistency of software architectures before and after their evolution, and make sure the correctness of software dynamic evolution.

Acknowledgment

The authors wish to thank the support by the National High-Tech Research and Development Plan of China (863 Program) under Grant No. 2007AA06Z111; the National Grand Fundamental Research Program of China (973 Program) under Grant No. 2006CB708409; the Scientific Research Plan Projects of Education Department of Jiangxi province of China under Grant No. GJJ09263.

References

1. Mens, T., Buckley, J., Zenger, M., Rashid, A.: Towards a taxonomy of software evolution. In: Proceedings of the International Workshop on Unanticipated Software Evolution, pp. 309–326 (2003)
2. Gang, H., Hong, M., Fuqing, Y.: Runtime software architecture based on reflective middleware. Science in China Ser. F Information Sciences 47(5), 555–576 (2004)

3. Gomaa, H., Hussein, M.: Software reconfiguration patterns for dynamic evolution of software architectures. In: Proceedings of the Fourth Working IEEE/IFIP Conference on Software Architecture, pp. 79–88 (2004)
4. Miladi, M.N., Jmaiel, M., Kacem, M.H.: A UML profile and a fujaba plugin for modelling dynamic software architectures. In: Proceedings of the Workshop on Model-Driven Software Evolution, pp. 20–26 (2007)
5. Kacem, M.H., Kacem, A.H., Jmaiel, M., Drira, K.: Describing dynamic software architectures using an extended UML model. In: Proceedings of Symposium on Applied Computing, pp. 1245–1249 (2006)
6. Magee, J., Kramer, J.: Dynamic structure in software architectures. In: Proceedings of the Fourth ACM SIGSOFT Symposium on Foundations of Software Engineering, pp. 3–14 (1996)
7. Allen, R., Douence, R., Garlan, D.: Specifying and analyzing dynamic software architectures. In: Astesiano, E. (ed.) ETAPS 1998 and FASE 1998. LNCS, vol. 1382, pp. 21–37. Springer, Heidelberg (1998)
8. Oquendo, F.: π-ADL: an architecture description language based on the higher-order typed π-calculus for specifying dynamic and mobile software architectures. ACM Sigsoft Software Engineering Notes 29(4), 1–14 (2004)
9. Vergnaud, T., Pautet, L., Kordon, F.: Using the AADL to describe distributed applications from middleware to software components. In: Vardanega, T., Wellings, A.J. (eds.) Ada-Europe 2005. LNCS, vol. 3555, pp. 67–78. Springer, Heidelberg (2005)
10. Métayer, D.L.: Describing software architecture styles using graph grammars. IEEE Transactions on Software Engineering 24(7), 521–533 (1998)
11. Bruni, R., Bucchiarone, A., Gnesi, S., Melgratti, H.: Modelling dynamic software architectures using typed graph grammars. Electronic Notes in Theoretical Computer Science 213(1), 39–53 (2008)
12. Ma, X.X., Cao, C., Yu, P., Zhou, Y.: A supporting environment based on graph grammar for dynamic software architectures. Journal of Software 19(8), 1881–1892 (2008)
13. Bucchiarone, A., Pelliccione, P., Vattani, C., Runge, O.: Self-Repairing systems modeling and verification using AGG. In: Proceedings of the Joint Working IEEE/IFIP Conference on Software Architecture & European Conference on Software Architecture, pp. 181–190 (2009)
14. Aguirre, N., Maibaum, T.: A temporal logic approach to the specification of reconfigurable component-based systems. In: Proceedings of the 17th IEEE International Conference on Automated Software Engineering, pp. 271–278 (2002)
15. Canal, C., Pimentel, E., Troya, J.M.: Specification and Refinement of Dynamic Software Architectures. In: Proceedings of the TC2 First Working IFIP Conference on Software Architecture, pp. 107–126 (1999)
16. Xu, H.Z., Zeng, G.S.: Description and verification of dynamic software architectures for distributed systems. Journal of Software 5(7), 721–728

Scalable Model for Mining Critical Least Association Rules

Zailani Abdullah[1], Tutut Herawan[2], and Mustafa Mat Deris[3]

[1] Department of Computer Science, Universiti Malaysia Terengganu
[2] Department of Mathematics Education, Universitas Ahmad Dahlan, Indonesia
[3] Faculty of Information Technology and Multimedia, Universiti Tun Hussein Onn Malaysia
zailania@umt.edu.my, tutut81@uad.ac.id, mmustafa@uthm.edu.my

Abstract. A research in mining least association rules is still outstanding and thus requiring more attentions. Until now; only few algorithms and techniques are developed to mine the significant least association rules. In addition, mining such rules always suffered from the high computational costs, complicated and required dedicated measurement. Therefore, this paper proposed a scalable model called Critical Least Association Rule (CLAR) to discover the significant and critical least association rules. Experiments with a real and UCI datasets show that the CLAR can generate the critical least association rules, up to 1.5 times faster and less 100% complexity than benchmarked FP-Growth.

Keywords: Least association rules; Scalable; Model.

1 Introduction

Mining association rules or patterns has attracted much research interest for a past decade. The main purposes of association rules mining are to find out the interesting correlations, associations or casual structures among sets of items in the data repositories. It was first introduced by Agrawal *et al.* [1] and still attracts many attentions from knowledge discovery community. In association rules, a set of item is defined as an itemset. The itemset is said to be frequent, if it occurs more than a predefined minimum support. Besides that, confidence is another alternative measurement used in pair in association rules. The association rules are said to be strong if it meets the minimum confidence.

Least itemset is a set of item that is rarely found in the database but may produce an interesting result for certain application domains. For example, to detect the air pollution, network intruders, critical faulty and many more [2]. However, the tradition association rule mining [3-10] is not able to classify such important least itemset due to disregard of the domain knowledge. The low minimum support can be set to capture the least itemset. The trade off is it may generate the huge number of association rules. As a result, it is enormously difficult to identify which association rules are most significant and critical. In addition, the low minimum support will also proportionally increase the computational performance and its complexity.

R. Zhu et al. (Eds.): ICICA 2010, LNCS 6377, pp. 509–516, 2010.

The current measurements for evaluating the least association rules whether it is significant or interesting are very limited [4]. In fact, nearly all of measurements are embedded with standard Apriori-like algorithm [3-10]. Therefore, the performance issue is not become their main concern and silently ignored. But in real-world cases, the database size is beyond an expectation and may not cope with typical algorithm.

In order to alleviate the mentioned above problems, a new Critical Least Association Rules (CLAR) model is proposed and experimented based on a real world and UCI datasets [11]. CLAR model contains enhanced version of existing prefix tree and frequent pattern growth algorithm called LP-Tree and LP-Growth algorithm, respectively. Hash-based approach [12] is employed to reduce the complexities and increase the computational performance of the algorithm. Both least and frequent items will be merged (union) and only itemset in transaction that consist both of them will be applied into LP-Tree. By doing this, any unwanted itemset will be ignored at the beginning phase and classified as not really important.

A novel measurement called Critical Relative Support (CRS) is proposed to discover the desired critical least association rules. A range of CRS is always in 0 and 1. The more CRS value reaches to 1, the more significant and critical those particular rules. To ensure only significant rules are selected, a predefined minimum CRS (min-CRS) is introduced. The rule that appears equal or more than min-CRS is classified as critical least association rules. Domain expert is employed to confirm the criticality and usefulness of these types of rules.

The rest of the paper is organized as follows. Section 2 describes the related work. Section 3 explains the basic concepts and terminology of association rule mining. Section 4 discusses the proposed method. This is followed by performance analysis in section 5. Finally, conclusion and future direction are reported in section 6.

2 Related Work

Relatively, there are only few attentions have been paid to mine interesting least patterns as compared to frequent patterns. Three dominant factors of discouraging research in this field are computational performance, complexity and appropriate measurement. The least itemset might contribute to a significant implication for certain domain applications. The question is, how to include those least itemset with the frequent one, especially when the range between them is very high? In addition, how to verify and prove that the significances of criticality among the rules?

Several researches have been focused in least association rules for the past decades such as Dynamic-Collective Support Apriori [13], Improved Multiple Support Apriori Algorithm [3], (IMSApriori), Matrix-based Scheme (MBS) and Hash-based scheme (HBS) [4], Apriori-Inverse [5], Relative Support Apriori Algorithm (RSAA) [6], Multiple Support Apriori (MSA) [7] Adaptive Apriori [8], Weighted Association Rule Mining (WARM) [9] and Transactional Co-Occurrence Matrix (TCOM) [10] in order to discover the significant itemset.

In overall, the basic concept underlying the proposed approaches [3-9] is based on the Apriori-like algorithm. The test-and-generate strategy is still the main concerns and outstanding issues. If the varied minimum support threshold is set close to zero, these approaches will take similar amount of time as taken by Apriori. Most of previous approaches are required to set up a minimum support to be very low in order to capture the least items. As a result, enormous mixed of rules will be generated.

Therefore, any approach to discover either least or frequent association rules should try to evade from employing Apriori-like algorithms. However, implementation wise for others than tradition Apriori-like algorithm is not straight forward. Currently, FP-Growth [14] is considered as one of the fastest approach and benchmarked algorithm for frequent itemset mining. This algorithm can break two bottlenecks of Apriori-like algorithms. Yet, this algorithm is not scalable enough in mining the least patterns and due to its limitation of static minimum support threshold.

3 Proposed Method

Throughout this section the set $I = \{i_1, i_2, \cdots, i_{|A|}\}$, for $|A| > 0$ refers to the set of literals called set of items and the set $D = \{t_1, t_2, \cdots, t_{|U|}\}$, for $|U| > 0$ refers to the data set of transactions, where each transaction $t \in D$ is a list of distinct items $t = \{i_1, i_2, \cdots, i_{|M|}\}$, $1 \le |M| \le |A|$ and each transaction can be identified by a distinct identifier TID.

3.1 Definition

Definition 1. (Least Items). *An itemset X is called least item if* $\alpha \le \text{supp}(X) \le \beta$, *where* α *and* β *is the lowest and highest support, respectively.*
The set of least item will be denoted as Least Items and

$$\text{Least Items} = \{X \subset I \mid \alpha \le \text{supp}(X) \le \beta\}$$

Definition 2. (Frequent Items). *An itemset X is called frequent item if* $\text{supp}(X) > \beta$, *where* β *is the highest support.*
The set of frequent item will be denoted as Frequent Items and

$$\text{Frequent Items} = \{X \subset I \mid \text{supp}(X) > \beta\}$$

Definition 3. (Merge Least and Frequent Items). *An itemset X is called least frequent items if* $\text{supp}(X) \ge \alpha$, *where* α *is the lowest support.*
The set of merging least and frequent item will be denoted as LeastFrequent Items and

$$\text{LeastFrequent Items} = \{X \subset I \mid \text{supp}(X) \ge \alpha\}$$

LeastFrequent Items will be sorted in descending order and it is denoted as

$$\text{LeastFrequent Items}^{\text{desc}} = \left\{ \begin{array}{l} X_i \mid \text{supp}(X_i) \ge \text{supp}(X_j), \ 1 \le i, j \le k, \ i \ne j, \\ k = |\text{LeastFrequent Items}|, \ x_i, x_j \subset \text{LeastFrequent Items} \end{array} \right\}$$

Definition 4. (Ordered Items Transaction). *An ordered items transaction is a transaction which the items are sorted in descending order of its support and denoted as* t_i^{desc} *, where*

$$t_i^{desc} = \text{LeastFrequentItems}^{desc} \cap t_i, 1 \le i \le n, \left|t_i^{least}\right| > 0, \left|t_i^{frequent}\right| > 0.$$

An ordered items transaction will be used in constructing the proposed model, so-called LP-Tree.

Definition 5. (Significant Least Data). *Significant least data is one which its occurrence less than the standard minimum support but appears together in high proportion with the certain data.*

Definition 6. (Critical Relative Support). *A Critical Relative Support (CRS) is a formulation of maximizing relative frequency between itemset and their Jaccard similarity coefficient.*

The value of Critical Relative Support denoted as CRS and

$$\text{CRS}(I) = \max\left(\left(\frac{\text{supp}(A)}{\text{supp}(B)}\right), \left(\frac{\text{supp}(B)}{\text{supp}(A)}\right)\right) \times \left(\frac{\text{supp}(A \Rightarrow B)}{\text{supp}(A) + \text{supp}(B) - \text{supp}(A \Rightarrow B)}\right)$$

CRS value is between 0 and 1, and is determined by multiplying the highest value either supports of antecedent divide by consequence or in another way around with their Jaccard similarity coefficient. It is a measurement to show the level of CRS between combination of the both Least Items and Frequent Items either as antecedent or consequence, respectively.

3.2 Algorithm Development

Determine Interval Least Support. Let I is a non-empty set such that $I = \{i_1, i_2, \cdots, i_n\}$, and D is a database of transactions where each T is a set of items such that $T \subset I$. An itemset is a set of item. A k-itemset is an itemset that contains k items. From Definition 3, an itemset is said to be least if it has a support count within a range of α and β, respectively. In brevity, a least item is an itemset that satisfies the predefined Interval Least Support (*ILSupp*).

Construct LP-Tree. A Least Pattern Tree (LP-Tree) is a compressed representation of the least itemset. It is constructed by scanning the dataset of single transaction at a time and then mapping onto a new or existing path in the LP-Tree. Items that satisfy the ILSupp are only captured and used in constructing the LP-Tree.

Mining LP-Tree. Once the LP-Tree is fully constructed, the mining process will begin using bottom-up strategy. Hybrid 'Divide and conquer' method is employed to decompose the tasks of mining desired pattern. LP-Tree utilizes the strength of hash-based method during constructing itemset in descending order. Intersection technique from definition 4 is employed to increase the computational performance and reduce the complexity.

Construct Critical Least Association Rules (CLAR). The rule is classified as critical least association rules (CLAR) if it fulfilled two conditions. First, CRS of association rule must be greater than predefined minimum CRS. The range of min-CRS is in between 0 and 1. Second, the antecedent and consequence of association rule must be either Least Items or Frequent Items, respectively. The computation of CRS of each association rule is employed from Definition 6. Figure 1 shows a complete procedure to construct the CLAR algorithm.

```
CLAR Algorithm
```

$$
\begin{array}{ll}
1: & \text{Specify } CRS^{\min} \\
2: & \textbf{for } \left(CI_a \in CriticalItemset\right) \textbf{ do} \\
3: & \quad \textbf{for}\left(CFI_i \in CI_a \cap FrequentItems\right) \textbf{ do} \\
4: & \quad\quad \textbf{for}\left(CLI_i \in CI_a \cap LeastItems\right) \textbf{ do} \\
5: & \quad\quad\quad \text{Compute } CRS\left(CFI_i, CLI_i\right) \\
6: & \quad\quad\quad \textbf{if } \left(CRS\left(CFI_i, CLI_i\right) > CRS^{\min}\right) \textbf{ do} \\
7: & \quad\quad\quad\quad \text{Insert } CLAR\left(CFI_i, CLI_i\right) \\
8: & \quad\quad\quad \textbf{end if} \\
9: & \quad\quad \textbf{end for loop} \\
10: & \quad \textbf{end for loop} \\
11: & \textbf{end for loop}
\end{array}
$$

Fig. 1. CLAR Algorithm

4   Comparison Tests

In this section, we do comparison tests between FP-Growth and LP-Growth algorithms. The performance analysis is made by comparing the processing time and number of iteration required. We used one simple dataset and two benchmarked datasets. These experiments have been conducted on Intel® Core™ 2 Quad CPU at 2.33GHz speed with 4GB main memory, running on Microsoft Windows Vista. All algorithms have been developed using C# as a programming language.

4.1   A Dataset from [15]

We evaluate the proposed algorithm to air pollution data taken in Kuala Lumpur on July 2002 as presented and used in [15]. The ARs of the presented results are based on a set of air pollution data items, i.e. $\{CO_,O_,PM_{10},SO_,NO_\}$. The value of each item is with the unit of part per million (*ppm*) except PM_{10} is with the unit of micro-grams (μgm). The data were taken for every one-hour every day. The actual data is presented as the average amount of each data item per day. For brevity, each data item is mapped to parameters 1,2,3,4 and 5 respectively, as shown in Table 1.

Table 2 shows selected 5 ARs and its weight values. Top 2 association rules have a CRS equal to 1.00 with the least item 2 is a consequent. In addition, all CRS values for association rules with least item 2 as a consequent are 1.00. These values are at par with RS values as performed by RSAA. According to domain expert, the item

$2(O_3)$ is the most dominant factor in determining the criticality status of air pollution. Once data item (O_3) appears, the criticality level of air pollution at that particular area is very high and classified as unsafe to us. The values of both CRS and RS are not similar if those measurement values are less than 1.00. Generally, there are no different values of RS whether item 2 as an antecedent or as a consequent in association rules. However, the values of CRS are different when the position of antecedent and consequence are changed. For other association rules where consequence is not item 2, the RS values are more than CRS values. Therefore, CRS are more scalable and precise as compared to RS.

Table 1. The mapped air pollution data

Data	Items
$CO_2 \geq 0.02$	1
$O_3 \leq 0.007$	2
$PM_{10} \geq 80$	3
$SO_2 \geq 0.04$	4
$NO_2 \geq 0.03$	5

Table 2. ARs with different weight schemes

ARs	Supp	Conf	MSA	RSA	CRS
$143 \rightarrow 2$	10.00	23.08	10.00	1.00	1.00
$453 \rightarrow 2$	10.00	23.08	10.00	1.00	1.00
$15 \rightarrow 3$	50.00	71.43	53.33	0.94	0.89
$5 \rightarrow 3$	50.00	71.43	53.33	0.94	0.89
$1 \rightarrow 4$	70.00	75.00	76.67	0.91	0.85

4.2 UCI Dataset from [11]

The second and third benchmarked datasets are Retails and Mushroom. The Retail dataset is retail market-basket data from an anonymous Belgian retail store with 88,136 transactions and 16,471 items. For Mushroom dataset, it consists of 23 species of gilled mushroom in the Agaricus and Lepiota Family. The dataset has 8,124 transactions and 120 items. Variety of interval supports and standard minimum supports were used for both dataset. Here, α is set to equavelant to minimum support and β is set to 100%. For computational complexity, the interval values were setting up to a range of 5, 10 and 20 percent, respectively.

Figure 2 and 3 shows the computational performance and complexity of mining Retail dataset for both algorithms, respectively. The average time taken for pattern sets using LP-Growth was 1.51 times faster than FP-Growth. The average number of iterations taken to construct LP-Tree was 99.40% times lesser than FP-Tree. Computational performance and complexity of both algorithms for Mushroom dataset are shown in Figure 4 and 5, respectively. In average, the time taken for mining pattern sets using LP-Growth was 1.48 times faster than FP-Growth. In term of computational

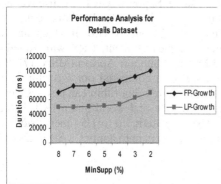

Fig. 2. Computational Performance for Mining Retail dataset

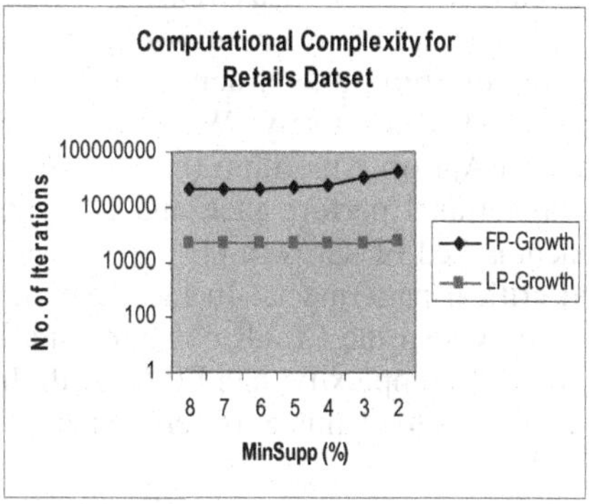

Fig. 3. Computational Complexity for Mining Retail dataset

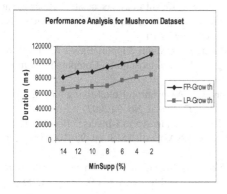

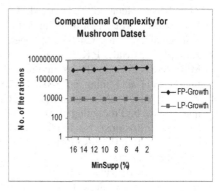

Fig. 4. Computational Performance of Mining the Mushroom dataset

Fig. 5. Computational Complexity of Mining the Mushroom Dataset

complexity, LP-Growth was 100% lesser than FP-Tree. For both datasets and algorithms, the processing time is decreasing once the MinSupp are increasing.

5 Conclusion

Mining the least association rules is a very important study especially when dealing with rare events but its appearance may contribute to a high implication and seriousness. This study is very complicated; computationally expensive and very limited exploration. Most of the existing measurements and algorithms are not scalable enough and always suffer from "rare item problem". In addition, the benchmarked FP-Growth algorithm is also facing the computational problem when the minimum support threshold is set to very low. In this paper, we have proposed a new and scalable model for Mining Critical Least Association Rules (CLAR). CLAR model implements a new measurement, Critical Relative Support (CRS) to discover the significant and critical relationship of least data items. For scalability issue, enhanced version of prefix-tree structure [14], LP-Tree and efficient LP-Growth algorithm are developed, respectively. We have compared our measurement, CRS with Relative Support Apriori Algorithm (RSAA) [6] and Multiple Support Apriori (MSA) [7]. For computational performance and complexity, we have compared our algorithm with benchmarked FP-Growth [14]. The results show that our algorithm can discover least and critical pattern sets. In fact, experiments with the real world and a UCI dataset [11] show that the CLAR can generate the desired pattern, up to 1.5 times faster and less 100% complexity than FP-Growth. In a future, we plan to apply CLAR to another real datasets to evaluate its performance.

References

1. Agrawal, R., Imielinski, T., Swami, A.: Database Mining: A Performance Perspective. IEEE Transactions on Knowledge and Data Engineering 5(6), 914–925 (1993)
2. Abdullah, Z., Herawan, T., Deris, M.M.: Mining Significant Least Association Rules using Fast SLP-Growth Algorithm. In: Kim, T.-h., Adeli, H. (eds.) AST/UCMA/ISA/ACN. LNCS, vol. 6059, pp. 324–336. Springer, Heidelberg (2010)
3. Kiran, R.U., Reddy, P.K.: An Improved Multiple Minimum Support Based Approach to Mine Rare Association Rules. In: Proceeding of IEEE Symposium on Computational Intelligence and Data Mining, pp. 340–347 (2009)
4. Zhou, L., Yau, S.: Assocation Rule and Quantative Association Rule Mining among Infrequent Items. In: Proceeding of ACM SIGKDD 2007, Article No. 9 (2007)
5. Koh, Y.S., Rountree, N.: Finding Sporadic Rules using Apriori-Inverse. In: Ho, T.-B., Cheung, D., Liu, H. (eds.) PAKDD 2005. LNCS (LNAI), vol. 3518, pp. 97–106. Springer, Heidelberg (2005)
6. Yun, H., Ha, D., Hwang, B., Ryu, K.H.: Mining Association Rules on Significant Rare Data using Relative Support. The Journal of Systems and Software 67(3), 181–19 (2003)
7. Liu, B., Hsu, W., Ma, Y.: Mining Association Rules with Multiple Minimum Supports. In: Proceeding of ACM SIGKDD 2007, pp. 337–341 (1999)
8. Wang, K., Hee, Y., Han, J.: Pushing Support Constraints into Association Rules Mining. IEEE Transactions on Knowledge and Data Engineering 15(3), 642–658 (2003)
9. Tao, F., Murtagh, F., Farid, M.: Weighted Association Rule Mining using Weighted Support and Significant Framework. In: Proceeding of ACM SIGKDD 2003, pp. 661–666 (2003)
10. Ding, J.: Efficient Association Rule Mining among Infrequent Items. Ph.D. Thesis, n University of Illinois at Chicago (2005)
11. http://fimi.cs.helsinki.fi/data/
12. Park, J.S., Chen, M.-S., Yu, P.S.: An Effective Hash based Algorithm for Mining Association Rules. In: Carey, M.J., Schneider, D.A. (eds.) Proceedings of the 1995 ACM SIG-MOD International Conference on Management of Data, pp. 175–186. San Jose, California (1995)
13. Selvi, C.S.K., Tamilarasi, A.: Mining association rules with dynamic and collective support thresholds. International Journal on Open Problems Computational Mathematics 2(3), 427–438 (2009)
14. Han, J., Pei, H., Yin, Y.: Mining Frequent Patterns without Candidate Generation. In: Proceeding of the 2000 ACM SIGMOD, pp. 1–12 (2000)
15. Mustafa, M.D., Nabila, N.F., Evans, D.J., Saman, M.Y., Mamat, A.: Association Rules on Significant Rare Data using Second Support. International Journal of Computer Mathematics 88(1), 69–80 (2006)

Research on the Spatial Structure and Landscape Patterns for the Land Use in Beijing Suburb Based on RS & GIS

Yuyuan Wen

Institute of Regional & Urban Economics, School of Public Administration,
Renmin University of China, Beijing 100872, China
wenyuyuan@126.com

Abstract. Based on the TM/ETM imagines in 2004, administration district map and related social and economic statistical data in Beijing, China, based on RS/GIS, the land use information for Beijing suburbs is extracted and consolidated, and by employing the theories and methodologies of spatial structure and landscape pattern, the land use situations in Beijing suburb are analyzed quantitatively. The result shows, (1) the diversity is not high and the influences differ in various areas caused by human activities and natural factors. (2) The combination type of land use is simple, forest land and cropland are the main land use types. (3)As for the landscape pattern, the degree of dominance and evenness is rather low while that of diversity and fragmentation is rather high for the land use in Beijing suburb, which is regional differentia. (4) The reserved land resources are very limited in their development potentials, which will lead more serious contradictions between the demands and the supplies for land. So the present land used is desiderated to be developed more deeply.

Keywords: land utilization; RS & GIS; spatial structure; landscape pattern; Beijing suburb.

1 Introduction

The rationality of its spatial pattern is always a hot one in the land-use research fields. Research projects related to the spatial pattern changing in land-use have been launched in many international organizations and countries [1]. Many achievements have been reached in this field and three schools, i.e. of North America, Japan and Europe have been formed. Since 1990s, the scholars in China have begun to focus on the changes in spatial pattern of land-use [2, 3, 4, 5, 6, 7, 8]. As for Beijing, there are also some researches, for example, the macro spatial characteristics of the land-use changes [9] and the spatial characteristic analysis for separate districts or counties [10]. However, there is rare quantitative research on the land-use changes in the suburb of Beijing by employing the theories of spatial structure and landscape science. This paper attempts to do this research based on GIS and RS technologies.

R. Zhu et al. (Eds.): ICICA 2010, LNCS 6377, pp. 517–524, 2010.

2 Data and Technical Route

The data in this paper include the TM/ETM satellite image that covers Beijing territory in 2004, Beijing's administration map with scale of 1:100,000, the data of cadastre changes and social economy statistic data in recent years. The technical route of the research is as follows, first, to correct the TM/ETM imagines spatially and make them match the administration map in the software Erdas 8.6. Second, to obtain the land-use maps of the 14 suburb districts or counties of Beijing by interpreting the images and being verified by the cadastre statistic data. Third, under support of the software ArcGIS 9.0, to extract and combine related land-use information from the images and then to obtain 8 types of land-use spatial distribution maps including cropland, forest land, lawn, water, urban land, countryside residential land and other built-up land as well as unused land. Last, to quantitatively analyze the land-use information by employing the theories and methodologies of spatial structure and the landscape science.

3 Quantitative Analysis of the Land-Use Spatial Structure in Beijing Suburb

3.1 Diversification Analysis of Land-Use Spatial Structure

The land spatial structure diversification can be measured by using Gibbs - Martin index whose aim is to analyze the degree of completion and diversification of all types of land uses in the observed area. The model is as follows.

$$GM = 1 - \sum f_i^2 / (\sum f_i)^2 \qquad (1)$$

Where GM is the diversification index, f_i is the area of land-use type i. If somewhere has only one land-use type then GM is zero while GM is one when the land uses distribute evenly in each type. Therefore, GM can be employed to analyze the completion and diversification degree of the land-use in a region.

GM indices calculated according to formula (1) for the various districts and counties in Beijing in 2004 are listed in Table 1. As shown in Table 1, the impacts of human activities on the diversification of land uses are great. There are 6 districts and counties' GM indices are more than 0.6, which shows land use diversification in these areas. Among these areas, Haidian, Fengtai, Fangshan and Changping are close or neighbor to the capital core zone and are influenced deeply by accelerated urbanization. In these regions, the local economic development level is rather high, the proportion of urban or built-up land increases while the proportion of cropland and forest land decreases relatively, which makes their diversification indices higher. But the diversification indices are high in Miyun and Pinggu. Why? Because the two districts are influenced not only by human activities but also by terrain and other natural conditions, which makes all types of land-uses (especially cropland, forest land and lawn) be relatively distribution in the areas. The diversification index in Mentougou is the lowest. Its forest land proportion reaches 84.52% and occupies the major part of the land resources, which is consistent with low built-up land rate and backward economic condition. Other districts' diversification indices are in the medium ranks, their indices are not very different, but it does not indicate these districts having analogous land-use structures. For example, the diversification indices are nearly equal in Chaoyang and Yanqing, but the urban land surpasses 50% for the former while forest land reaches 60% for the latter, which are related to their terrain types and economic development condition. As for the whole, Beijing's land use diversification degree, i.e. the completion degree of all types of land uses, is not high overall.

Table 1. Indices of diversity, centralization and combination and combination types for Beijing suburbs

Region	Diversity	Centralization	Combination	# of combi-nation types	Combination types
Changping	0.6127	0.279116	609.9748	2	forest land-cropland
Chaoyang	0.5898	0.412734	382.3407	2	built-up land-cropland
Daxing	0.4355	0.494101	871.7017	1	cropland
Fangshan	0.6429	0.174968	784.3867	2	forest land-cropland
Fengtai	0.6194	0.200472	733.5795	2	built-up land-cropland
Haidian	0.7277	-0.05864	278.9101	3	built-up land-cropland -forest land
Huairou	0.5074	0.460252	1474.7024	1	forest land
Mentougou	0.2782	0.710315	314.0155	1	forest land
Miyun	0.6543	0.157429	968.4159	3	forest land-cropland-lawn
Pinggu	0.6689	0.129975	422.2232	2	forest land-cropland
Shijingshan	0.4773	0.600436	921.8644	2	built-up land-forest land
Shunyi	0.5223	0.317334	1446.1357	1	cropland
Tongzhou	0.4533	0.518093	1058.9315	1	cropland
Yanqing	0.5874	0.368936	943.0248	2	forest land-cropland
Beijing suburb	0.6875	0	558.7160	2	forest land-cropland

3.2 Spatial Centralization Analysis of Land Use

The spatial centralization (or decentralization) can be described and measured with Lorentz curve and centralization index. Lorentz curves' plotting: Firstly, to calculate the area percentage of each land-use type of the total area in a certain region according to the land investigation data, and make them indexed in non-decreasing order and calculate the cumulative percentage of land-use area on the vertical axis and the proportion of land-use type on the horizontal axis, we may plot the cumulative percentage to obtain the Lorentz curve as shown in Figure 1. Looking at the several typical curves of the districts or counties as show in the figure, we know Shijingshan and Mentougou are the districts with the highest centralization degree, but they centralize in different land-use type, the former is focus on urban or built-up land (67.49%) with quite developed economy while the latter is on forest land (84.52%) with less developed economy. Haidian, Pinggu, Miyun, Fangshan and Changping are the districts or counties with low centralization degree, among them Haidian is the lowest, which is related to their speeding up urbanization progress and their relatively balancing various land-use types.

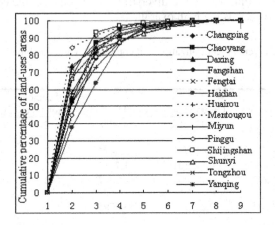

Fig. 1. The Lorenz curve for the land utilization distribution in Beijing suburbs

To measure the spatial centralization more precisely, centralization index can be employed here and its formula is as below.

$$I_i = (A_i - R)/(M - R) \tag{2}$$

where I_i is the ith region's land centralization index, A_i is the ith region's cumulative percentage of all types of land-uses, M is the sum of the cumulative percentage when the land use centralizes in one type, R is the sum of the cumulative percentage of all types of land-use in a higher level region (here is the Beijing suburbs) and is the base benchmark to measure centralization degree. Here, M =800, R =688.72, and we can get the centralization indices for all districts and counties in Beijing as shown in Table 1. In Table 1, we know that the result drawn from centralization indices is consistent with that getting from Lorentz curve.

3.3 Combination Type Analysis of Land Use Spatial Structure

Combination type analysis can confirm the prevalent types and its characteristics of the land use structure in an area. Employing Weaver-Tomas combination coefficient is able to solve the judgment problem of the combination type of the land use structure. This method is to compare the actual distribution (the actually relative area percentage) to the assumed distribution (the assumedly relative area percentage), and then approach the actual distribution step by step and reach an approximate distribution close to the actual distribution, which is the combination type that we search for. The combination coefficients and types of the districts and counties in Beijing are calculated as shown in Table 2.

As shown in Table 1, the completeness degree of the land-use types in Beijing sub-urb is rather low as a whole and there are only two combination types of land-use. Haidian and Miyun have only three combination types even they have the highest completeness degree among the suburbs. Mentougou, Shunyi, Tongzhou, Huairou and Daxing have the least land-use types among the suburbs for they have only one combination type. Except the suburbs above, the other have 2 combination types. Obviously, the land uses in Beijing suburbs display a characteristic of relative high centralization. But along with the speedy urbanization and the increase of the urban or built-up land, this centralization will be broken gradually while a characteristic of land-use diversity will be emerging.

4 The Landscape Pattern Analysis of Land-Use in Beijing

The distribution of large and small patches in a land-use map is called land-use land-scape pattern. Land-use landscape pattern can be measured with diversity, dominance, evenness and fragmentation that originated from landscape ecology [11]. All these indices are called landscape pattern indices.

(1) Land-use diversity index (H) describes the richness and complexity of land-use types and reflects the number and their proportions of the land-use types. When the difference of the proportions of various land-uses reduces, the diversity index will increase. The formula is:

$$H = -\sum (p_i) \log_2 (p_i) \tag{3}$$

(2) Land-use dominance index (D) measures the value of dominance of one land cover over the others. Its formula is:

$$D = H_{max} + \sum (p_i) \log_2 (p_i) \tag{4}$$

$$H_{max} = \log_2 (m) \tag{5}$$

(3) Land-use evenness index (E) describes the deviance between a maximum equipartition of the land-use types into a collection and the distribution observed. It can be calculated with relative Romme evenness degree. It is proposed:

$$E = (H / H_{max}) 100\% \tag{6}$$

$$H = -\log_2 [\sum (p_i)^2] \tag{7}$$

(4) Land-use fragmentation index (C) measures the degree of fragmentation of land-use. Its formula is:

$$C = \sum n_i / A \tag{8}$$

In the above formulas, p_i is the percentage of the area of the ith land-use to the total area, m is the number of land-use types, H is the revised Simpson index, H_{max} is the largest possible evenness, n_i is the total number of patches for all land-use types, A is the total land area (km^2).

The landscape pattern index can reflect the degree of the impacts of the human activities on the land use in a region. If the intensity of impact increases the diversity, evenness and fragmentation of land-uses would also increase while the dominance would decrease. The landscape pattern indices are calculated as shown in Table 2.

Table 2. Landscape pattern indices of the land uses for the suburbs in Beijing

region	diversity H	dominance D	evenness E	fragmentation C
Changping	1.7826	1.2174	0.4563	0.6085
Chaoyang	1.5635	1.4365	0.4285	0.4283
Daxing	1.3640	1.6360	0.2750	0.5335
Fangshan	1.8959	1.1041	0.4951	0.4184
Fengtai	1.8432	1.1568	0.4646	0.3911
Haidian	2.0819	0.9181	0.6256	0.3976
Huairou	1.4699	1.5301	0.3405	0.8099
Mentougou	0.9338	2.0662	0.1568	0.3265
Miyun	1.9087	1.0913	0.5108	0.7444
Pinggu	1.9237	1.0763	0.5316	0.8868
Shijingshan	1.2659	1.7341	0.3120	0.1631
Shunyi	1.6287	1.3713	0.3552	0.6499
Tongzhou	1.3675	1.6325	0.2904	0.7137
Yanqing	1.6531	1.3469	0.4257	0.5688
Beijing suburb	2.0539	0.9461	0.5594	0.6030

As seen in Table 2, the overall dominance of the land-use in Beijing suburbs is rather low and the regional distribution is not balanced. The district with largest dominance is Mentougou, which is related to most of its land-use being forest land. The districts with the second largest dominance are Shijingshan, Daxing, Tongzhou and Huairou, among which Shijingshan has a high dominance for its overwhelming proportion in urban or built-up land while the latter three have high dominance for their high proportion in some agricultural land. Haidian has the lowest dominance obviously because that all land-use types are relatively even in it.

Diversity index is just opposite to dominance index. The overall diversity index is rather high in the whole city. Among the suburbs, Haidian is the one with the highest diversity index, followed by Miyun, Pinggu, Fangshan and Fengtai, and Mentougou is the last one. The reasons are the same as the situation of dominance because the conceptions of these two indices are just right in the opposite. The evenness indices are low for all the suburbs, but speaking relatively, the evenness indices are higher in Haidian, Miyun and Pinggu while lower in Mentougou, Daxing and Tongzhou. As for the fragmentation indices, according to the data calculated in the map in 2004, the highest ones are Pinggu, Huairou and Miyun and the lowest are Shijingshan and Mentougou.

5 Conclusions and Comments

After quantitatively analyzing the spatial structures and landscape patterns of the land-uses in Beijing suburbs, the following conclusions can be drawn:

(1) The overall diversity is not high in Beijing suburbs, which indicates the completion degree is not high for their land-uses, but as far as the impacts from human activities are concerned, it is irregular across various regions. Those close to the core area of the capital are influenced more deeply by human activities while those located in the west of the capital and the northern ecological function areas are affected more by the terrain and landform and other natural conditions.

(2) For the land-use structure, forest land cropland and lawn occupy the largest proportion (83.61%), which is much higher than the national average level 68.42% [1], of the land-uses in Beijing suburb. The centralization for agricultural land is relative high in Beijing suburb. Among various agricultural lands, the location meaning for forest land and cropland is quite significant.

(3) The combination of the land-use types is rather simple in Beijing suburbs. Actually, the combination types are so few and limited to agricultural lands basically that the overall function of the land-use is constrained.

(4) Either the absolute area or the proportion of the unused land in Beijing suburb is very low. The unused land patches are scattered and in an improper location and environment. So the development potential of the reserved land resource available is very limited for Beijing.

(5) Seen from the land-use landscape patterns, the dominance and evenness are lower while the diversity and fragmentation are higher in Beijing suburb as a whole. But for the influences from human activities and natural conditions are different in the degree, various landscape patterns are regional disparity.

Acknowledgments

Research funds were granted by two projects: The 3rd sub-program "211 Project" granted by Education Ministry of PRC and The Project granted by Renmin University of China (No. 10XNB013).

References

1. Hongmei, W., Xiaoyu, W., Hong, L.: Land utilization situation in Heilongjiang Province based on quantitative geography model. Transactions of the Chinese Society of Agricultural Engineering 22(7), 70–74 (2006)
2. Xueli, C.: The study of relationship between the process of desertification and the landscape pattern in Bashang region, Hebei province. Journal of Desert Research 16(3), 222–227 (1996)
3. Yu, C., Wengui, S., Ruiping, G.: Changes of land use pattern in eastern Shenyang. Chinese Journal of Applied Ecology 8(4), 421–425 (1997)
4. Xiangnan, L., Hongmei, X., Fang, H.: Study on Graphic Information Characteristics of Land Use Spatial Pattern and Its Change. Scientia Geographica Sinica 22(1), 79–84 (2002)

5. Yusheng, S., Jieying, X.: Spatial variation in land use and landscape pattern. Chinese Journal of Eco-Agriculture 18(2), 416–421 (2010)
6. Qing, Q., Jixi, G., Wei, W.: Effect of terrain features on the land use pattern in Chuan-dian farming pastoral ecotone. Resources and Environment in the Yangtze Basin 18(9), 812–818 (2009)
7. Fengwu, Z., Buzhuo, P., Jianzhong, D., Yan, Z.: Study on the spatial pattern of land use in Wenzhou. Economic Geography 21(1), 101–104 (2001)
8. Zhijie, Q., Lin, H., Xiaoli, M., et al.: A Study on the dynamic remote sensing of landscape spatial pattern in view of GIS. Agricultural Research in the Arid Areas 15(4), 93–98 (1997)
9. Dafang, Z., Xiangzheng, D., Jinyan, Z., Tao, Z.: A study on the spatial distribution of land use change in Beijing. Geographical Research 21(6), 667–677 (2002)
10. Xiaojun, C., Hongye, Z., Qingsheng, L.: Spatial Pattern of Non-Agricultural Land in the Urban Fringe of Beijing. Resources Science 26(2), 129–137 (2004)
11. O'Neill, R.V., Krummel, J.R., Gardner, R.H., et al.: Indices of landscape pattern. Landscape Ecology 1, 153–162 (1988)

Adaptive Filter and Morphological Operators Using Binary PSO

Muhammad Sharif, Mohsin Bilal, Salabat Khan, and M. Arfan Jaffar

National University of Computer & Emerging Sciences, Islamabad, Pakistan
{m.sharif,mohsin.bilal,salabat.khan,arfan.jaffar}@nu.edu.pk

Abstract. Mathematical morphology is a tool for processing shapes in image processing. Adaptively finding the specific morphological filter is an important and challenging task in morphological image processing. In order to model the filter and filtering sequence for morphological operations adaptively, a novel technique based on binary particle swarm optimization (BPSO) is proposed. BPSO is a discrete PSO, where the components values of a particle position vector are either zero or one. The proposed method can be used for numerous types of applications, where the morphological processing is involved including but not limited to image segmentation, noise suppression and patterns recognition etc. The paper illustrates a fair amount of experimental results showing the promising ability of the proposed approach over previously known solutions. In particular, the proposed method is evaluated for noise suppression problem.

Keywords: Mathematical morphology, Structuring element, Binary PSO, Noise suppression.

1 Introduction

Mathematical morphology (MM) is a powerful methodology for the quantitative analysis of geometrical structures, based on set-theory. For numerous images processing problems, MM is a unified and powerful image analysis approach. Mathematical morphology was originated in the late 1960s by G. Matheron and J. Serra [2]. MM is mathematical in the sense that the analysis is based on set theory, topology, lattice algebra, random functions, etc. The proposed technique uses four types of morphological operations: dilation, erosion, opening and closing. In the proposed method these operations are combined together in different sequence orders to find adaptive filtering sequence. MM is hardly depending upon the filter. The structuring element (SE) is a sub image use as a filter in morphological operation. The size, shape and orientation of the SE are specific to the problem. SE can be horizontal, vertical or center symmetric. The symmetric SE doesn't give good solution for many image processing problems, like noise suppression and image segmentation. The morphological operators generate certain problems by using fixed sized and shaped filters [3][4]. On the basis

R. Zhu et al. (Eds.): ICICA 2010, LNCS 6377, pp. 525–532, 2010.

of local characteristics the filter changes its shape [3]. On the basis of the orientation of the patterns the filter changes its shape [1]. The global cost function is minimized to find the optimal filter [6][11][12]. The evolutionary techniques are used to find the shape and design of the filters adaptively [6][11][12]. Terebes et al. use genetic algorithm to find the adaptive optimal filter and the filtering sequence of the operators [6]. Terebes et al. combines the classical and adaptive morphological operators in order to find the a global, optimum morphological filter for noise reduction task [6]. The optimal filter using classical and adaptive operators [6]. Such an optimal filter is related to a certain sequence of operations, a given structuring element (for classical operators) and/or the size of the adaptive operational window (for adaptive operators) [6]. The structure of chromosome reflects all these parameters [6]. Center Symmetric window filter is the main short coming of the proposed technique in [6]. The genetic algorithm approach is also slow in finding the adaptive filters and operators. Fuzzy mathematical morphology used for segmentation purpose [14]. Adaptive SE and fixed SE are considered as a main difference between traditional mathematical morphology and fuzzy mathematical morphology [14]. The fuzzy structuring element is restricted to cone shaped in paper [14] that does not produce optimal results for multiple applications. A generalized fuzzy mathematical morphology is discussed that is based on fuzzy inclusion indicator [15]. In image processing a generalized mathematical morphology provides flexible and powerful approach and provides better results than mathematical morphology [15]. A generalized mathematical morphology is also restricted to the shape of structure element. The shape of the structure element in this approach is not dynamically changed but must be predefined in generalized mathematical morphology. Similarly in paper [16] the fuzzy type's operators are introduced but the shape of SE are predefined still.

In the proposed approach non-symmetric filter window is obtained by using the binary PSO. The maximum size of SE window is 5 by 5 for testing the proposed BPSO. The PSO is used effectively for solving complex and difficult optimization problems [7][8][9]. In evolutionary computation this is a new methodology, it is more effective for wide range of engineering problems [10]. The standard binary PSO as presented in [13] is modified with inertial factor in the proposed method. The velocity of a particle is updated with cognitive factor, social factor and inertia factor. The inertia factor is multiplied with the previous velocity along with addition of cognitive and social factors, to find the new velocity. The detail of proposed approach is explained in section 3. The proposed method can be used for numerous types of applications like boundary extraction, segmentation, objects detection, watermarking and noise removal etc.

The proposed method is tested for impulse noise removal for multiple standard images, which gives good results. Section 1 describes a brief introduction about morphological image processing, section 2 introduces the discrete PSO and section 3 describes the detail of the proposed technique. The results of proposed method are discussed in section 4 in detail and finally section 5 describes the conclusion of the proposed approach.

2   Binary PSO

Particle swarm optimization (PSO) finds a solution to an optimization problem in a search space. PSO algorithms are especially useful for parameter optimization in continuous, multi-dimensional search spaces. The particle swarm optimization in its basic form is best suited for continuous variables. The method has been adapted as a binary PSO to optimize binary variables which take only one of two values. In binary PSO (BPSO) the search space is discrete and contains binary values, gives that the dimensions values can be 0 or 1. BPSO is introduced by Kennedy and Eberhart in [13], which is applied to discrete binary variables. In proposed method the velocity is updated as in [13], with addition to inertia factor. In BPSO each particle maintains a record of the position of its previous best performance as in standard PSO. The stochastic adjustment of each particle velocity is performed in the direction of particle local best previous position and the best global position of any particle in the neighborhood [13]. The original particle position is modified by the following equation:

$$V_{id}(new) = W \times V_{id}(old) + c_1 \times r_1 \times (P_{id} - X_{id})$$
$$+ c_2 \times r_2 \times (P_{gd} - X_{id}) \tag{1}$$

Where W is inertia factor, $c_1 r_1$ is cognitive acceleration, $c_2 r_2$ is social acceleration, P_{id} is local best position, P_{gd} is the global best position, and X_{id} is the current original position of particle i. i represent the particle number and d represent the dimension of particle position. The cognitive acceleration and social acceleration are same for all dimensions of particle i. The new position of the particle is:

$$X_{id}(new) = X_{id}(old) + V_{id} \tag{2}$$

Instead of using the continues values of V_{id} in the above equation the logistic transform value of V_{id} is used to modify the value of X_{id}, as: If (rand() < logsig(V_{id})) then X_{id}=1; Else X_{id}=0; The detail of the proposed BPSO algorithm is explained in the following proposed method section.

3   Proposed Method

We propose a binary PSO to adaptively find the shape of filter and the sequence of filtering operators. The proposed BPSO finds optimize and effective filter for the specific application.

3.1   Problem Encoding

Using BPSO the SE and filtering sequence is encoded in binary format. Let the filter size = $m \times n$, the possible number of values of a filter = v, and the number of operators in filtering sequence = p. In this case, the number of bits required to encode a particle position = $m \times n \times \lceil \log(v) \rceil \times \lceil \log(p) \rceil$. The experimental results shown in section 4 are based on 5×5 structuring element. The values range of SE are of 0 to 7. The value 7 in structuring element represents that the corresponding pixel value in the underlying image does not take part in filtering process. For each of these pixels value, 3 bits are required. So $5 \times 5 \times 3 = 75$ bits are required to find structuring element. Similarly in the experimental result filtering sequence consist of four operations. Each of these four operations can be any basic operators like dilation, erosion, opening, closing or do-nothing. As there are five possibilities for each operation, so 3 bits are required for each operation encoding. This implies that $4 \times 3 = 12$ bits are required to encode the filtering sequence. Therefore $75 + 12 = 87$ bits are required for each particle position. Each particle position is randomly initialized and then passed through the learning process which is described in section 3.2.

3.2   Training Algorithm

The particles positions in the BPSO algorithm represent variant solutions [13] . The input parameters to this algorithm are swarm size, initial particle positions, fitness evaluation function, and inertia factor. Swarm size is the number of particles in the swarm. More particles means larger initial diversity of swarm & hence larger parts of the search space can be covered per iteration. However, having more particles increases the per iteration computational complexity. We suggest that the swarm sizes of 10 to 50 are used for more problems. The particle positions are randomly initialized within the constrained of the binary search space. Fitness evaluation function is used to compare the accuracy of multiple solutions. Fitness evaluations are the most computationally expensive component in an iteration. The inertia factor in the proposed algorithm for exploration. Simple binary PSO perform exploitation in local environment. Binary PSO combines with inertia factor, performs exploitation as well as exploration in entire search space. The output of the propose algorithm is global best particle position. The algorithm is terminated until some stopping criteria is true. Different stopping criteria can be used like: the number of iterations, function evaluations have been exceeded, an acceptable solution has been found, and no improvement is observed over a number of iterations. We choose the stopping criteria as the number of iterations. The velocities are modified according to equation 1. After changing the velocities the logistic sigmoid function is used to range the values of velocities between 0 and 1. The positions of particles are modified as shown in equation 2. In equation 2 logistic sigmoid value of velocity is compared with random value (0-1). If the random value is less than the logistic value, the corresponding position value is 1, otherwise 0. Similarly the above process is repeated until some stopping criteria meet.

3.3   Fitness Evaluation Functions

Different types of evaluations functions can be used. Here we use three types of measurement functions: Mean Error, Mean Squared Error, and Peak Signal to Noise Ratio. The proposed BPSO is used to minimize the Mean Error and Mean Squared Error, and to maximize the Peak Signal to Noise Ratio.

Table 1. Average measurement values with GA and BPSO for different stopping criteria(iterations)

Images / Iterations		Aeroplane	Boat	Couple	House	Jetplane	Lena	Peppers	Trees
	ME	6.86	19.76	15.32	19.12	18.59	25.04	17.83	18.77
10	MSE	120.55	559.06	266.07	491.47	780.45	583.93	532.21	834.16
	PSNR	24.52	16.00	17.77	30.75	12.41	13.84	16.38	18.52
	ME	6.20	17.28	17.01	20.95	20.53	26.01	18.35	19.97
20	MSE	128.63	530.17	341.42	424.93	760.18	599.09	650.12	786.42
	PSNR	25.23	17.64	10.64	12.55	14.54	14.84	16.61	17.48
	ME	5.39	**17.09**	20.23	20.96	14.68	18.21	17.53	20.82
30	MSE	110.15	511.12	**220.23**	432.26	699.52	597.95	679.34	790.19
	PSNR	26.2	**18.10**	19.43	17.61	17.05	15.92	15.99	17.83
	ME	5.69	20.35	10.44	**14.70**	13.35	**16.32**	15.84	17.25
40	MSE	114.46	583.65	240.98	441.54	610.32	**485.64**	549.31	760.2
	PSNR	**26.49**	15.29	**20.99**	18.02	16.56	16.90	17.51	18.49
	ME	**5.30**	20.13	**10.38**	18.85	**8.92**	19.34	**14.85**	**16.00**
50	MSE	**100.61**	**500.94**	238.78	400.24	**650.35**	578.58	490	**725.51**
	PSNR	26.96	17.38	14.96	**15.36**	**17.50**	**17.54**	**18.01**	**18.73**

(a) Using Genetic Algorithm, where population size=20, salt and pepper noise ratio=30%, mutation rate=3%, elitism=3, and number of operators=4

Images / Iterations		Aeroplane	Boat	Couple	House	Jetplane	Lena	Peppers	Trees
	ME	5.64	13.76	8.32	9.91	12.59	12.04	12.83	15.7
10	MSE	113.51	539.36	226.07	391.27	648.35	485.93	532.34	834.16
	PSNR	27.52	20.98	24.77	21.75	20.14	21.8	21.08	18.52
	ME	4.88	12.88	7.21	9.95	11.53	11.44	11.35	14.97
20	MSE	109.6	508.77	211.42	384.93	560.58	467.09	554.12	786.663
	PSNR	27.99	21.26	24.6	22.35	20.17	21.84	20.71	19.48
	ME	4.39	**12.09**	6.44	9.69	11.68	11.21	11.53	13.82
30	MSE	104.15	491.12	**192.26**	332.26	576.52	397.95	507.04	694.19
	PSNR	28.2	**21.41**	24.79	22.61	20.51	21.94	21.09	19.48
	ME	4.43	12.35	6.44	**8.37**	11.35	**9.56**	10.84	13.25
40	MSE	104.26	487.65	214.28	341	588.32	**385.96**	418.11	708.2
	PSNR	**28.29**	21.29	**24.99**	23.02	20.56	22	21.2	119.49
	ME	**4.31**	12.13	**6.38**	8.85	11.09	9.93	**10.78**	**13.08**
50	MSE	**90.6**	**458.94**	198.78	**316.24**	**533.55**	414.58	409	**620.41**
	PSNR	28.06	21.38	24.96	**23.36**	20.59	**22.11**	**22.01**	**19.75**

(b) Using Proposed Binary PSO, where swarm size=20, salt and pepper noise ratio=30%, inertia factor=3, and number of operators=4

4 Experimental Results

The binary PSO is a probability based algorithm, so the results it would generate will be different on the same instance of a problem. So in order to generate simulations results, we run it twenty times and then average of the generated outputs is reported in the tables. The proposed technique is implemented in Matlab and simulation is carried on Intel P-IV processor with 1 GB of RAM. The proposed algorithm is applied to noise reduction problem where the salt and

Table 2. Average measurement values with GA and BPSO for different swarm sizes

Images / Swarm Size		Aeroplane	Boat	Couple	House	Jetplane	Lena	Peppers	Trees
	ME	8.55	18.59	12.2	12.65	14.44	15.56	17.63	19.51
10	MSE	220.42	673.16	296.92	500.28	700.13	558.11	670.18	985.98
	PSNR	22.23	18.21	20.6	19.18	16.56	20.82	16.64	15.23
	ME	9.45	19.59	12.81	12.94	13.76	16.31	16.89	**18.73**
20	MSE	190.43	618.71	314.3	478.15	683.6	538.22	561.56	850.87
	PSNR	24.74	17.35	20.79	18.26	17.52	20.93	17.36	17.48
	ME	7.56	18.07	12.76	11.4	12.96	15.17	17.14	19.14
30	MSE	**180.25**	599.17	303.3	**412.58**	**627.21**	527.61	578.7	812.38
	PSNR	24.94	16.99	**21.12**	19.16	18.6	20.99	**18.75**	18.47
	ME	**7.12**	17.28	12.67	10.26	12.98	14.56	16.88	19.87
40	MSE	195.91	**560.15**	**292.16**	428.28	678.76	**490.00**	540.95	838.16
	PSNR	**25**	**18.34**	20.93	**20.98**	**18.92**	21.05	17.29	**18.82**
	ME	8.26	**15.17**	10.41	**10.00**	12.41	14.1	**16.75**	20.16
50	MSE	190.16	581.91	300.07	450.11	649.36	499.95	**500.74**	**732.37**
	PSNR	24.53	17.21	19.03	18.98	17.77	**21.35**	16.34	18.62

(a) Using Genetic Algorithm, where number of iterations=30, salt and pepper noise ratio=30%, mutation rate=3%, elitism=3, and number of operators=4

Images / Swarm Size		Aeroplane	Boat	Couple	House	Jetplane	Lena	Peppers	Trees
	ME	4.52	13.09	7.2	9.6	11.44	10.5	11.63	14.51
10	MSE	101.42	533.16	196.92	384.28	591.51	448.11	556.18	805.98
	PSNR	27.79	20.96	24.6	22.18	20.41	21.82	20.64	19.23
	ME	4.53	12.59	6.81	8.94	11.76	11.31	10.89	**13.71**
20	MSE	101.4	518.71	214.3	362.15	583.6	428.22	461.56	750.87
	PSNR	27.74	21.05	24.79	22.26	20.52	21.93	21.36	19.48
	ME	4.56	12.07	6.76	8.74	11.06	10.17	11.14	14.18
30	MSE	**99.65**	499.17	203.3	**312.58**	**527.21**	417.61	459.7	698.38
	PSNR	27.94	21.14	**25.41**	23.16	20.6	21.99	**21.7**	19.47
	ME	**4.23**	11.88	6.67	8.26	10.98	9.16	10.58	13.87
40	MSE	105.91	**460.55**	**194.76**	328.28	578.2	**390.51**	455.95	708.16
	PSNR	27.9	**21.34**	24.93	**23.19**	**20.92**	22.05	21.29	**19.68**
	ME	4.26	**11.17**	**6.41**	**7.25**	10.41	**9.1**	**10.45**	14.16
50	MSE	103.16	481.94	198.07	330.11	544.39	391.95	**452.74**	**687.37**
	PSNR	**28**	21.23	25.03	23	20.77	**22.13**	21.34	19.62

(b) Using Proposed Binary PSO, where number of iterations=30, salt and pepper noise ratio=30%, inertia factor=3, and number of operators=4

pepper noise is suppressed efficiently as compare to other evolutionary technique e.g. genetic algorithm proposed in [6]. Both of these methods are compared through multiple evaluation criteria for eight standard images.

Figure 1(a) shows the original standard image of Baboon, corrupted with 40% salt and pepper noise, shown in Figure 1(b). The filtered resultant image using genetic algorithm and the proposed method are shown in Figure 1(c) and in Figure 1(d), respectively. For genetic algorithm the parameters are kept as: iterations = 30, population size = 30, mutation rate = 3%, and elitism = 3 . In binary PSO the parameters are: stopping criteria(iterations) = 30, swarm size = 30, and inertia factor = 3. The center symmetric filter is obtained by using GA for the standard

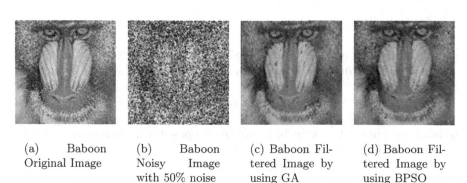

(a) Baboon Original Image

(b) Baboon Noisy Image with 50% noise

(c) Baboon Filtered Image by using GA

(d) Baboon Filtered Image by using BPSO

Fig. 1. Results Comparison of Filtered Baboon Image using GA and BPSO

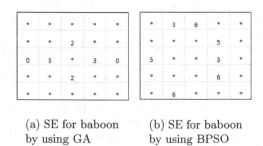

(a) SE for baboon by using GA

(b) SE for baboon by using BPSO

Fig. 2. SE Comparison for Baboon Image using GA and BPSO

Baboon image is illustrated in figure 2(a). The filter obtained by the BPSO is illustrated in figure 2(b). The morphological filtering sequence obtained for peppers image by using GA is *opening − dilate − closing − opening*, and the filtering sequence for standard peppers image by using the proposed approach is *erode − opening − opening − closing*. The mean error, mean squared error, and the PSNR values between the original image and the filtered image obtained by GA are: 25.05, 680.75, and 14.85 respectively. The mean error, mean squared error, and the PSNR values between the original image and the filtered image obtained by the proposed binary PSO are: 19.62, 550.05, and 19.50 respectively. For Baboon the proposed binary PSO outperforms GA in this case also.

The main parameters which are used in the proposed technique are: stopping criteria, swarm size and noise rate. In table 1, the stopping criteria is varying and the other parameters are kept constant. The evaluation functions values for GA and proposed binary PSO for eight standard images are shown in table 1. In table 2, the swarm size and the population size are varied and the other parameters are constant for GA and BPSO respectively. The results shown in these tables are average values with confidence factor of twenty. The results show that the proposed binary PSO outperforms GA in all parametric variations.

The proposed method is applied for eight standard images: aeroplane, boat, couple, house, jetplane, lena, peppers, and trees. The quantitative and visual results of the proposed approach are better than literature genetic approach.

5 Conclusion

The presented technique is used to find the structuring element and filtering sequence of operators, adaptively. Proposed method can be used for multiple types of applications like noise removal, segmentation, boundary extraction and objects detection etc. Impulse noise is removed effectively as compared to genetic algorithm. The main focus of the proposed method is the design of the filter and filtering sequence, adaptively. In future the proposed method may be enhanced by using hybrid evolutionary techniques.

References

1. Terebes, R., Lavialle, O., Baylou, P.: Adaptive Directional Morphological Operators. In: Proceedings of Eusipco, Tampere, Finland (2000)
2. Serra, J.: Image Analysis and Mathematical Morphology, vol. 1. Academic Press, New York (1992)
3. Cheng, F., Venetsanouploulos, A.N.: Adaptive Morphological Operators, fast Algorithm and their Application. Pattern Recognition 33, 917–933 (2000)
4. Pits, I., Venetsanopoulos, A.N.: Non Linear Digital Filters. Kluwer Academic Publishers, Dordrecht (1990)
5. Lavialle, O., Baylou, P.: Morphologie mathematique adaptive d'inspiration coulombienne. In: Proceedings RFIA, vol. 1, pp. 209–216 (1998)
6. Terebes, R., Borda, M., Baozong, Y., Lavialle, O., Baylou, P.: Adaptive Filtering using Morphological Operators and Genetic Algorithm. In: ACM SIGCOMM (2005)
7. Clerc, M., Kennedy, J.: The Particle Swarm-Explosion, Stability, and Convergence in a Multidimensional Complex Space. IEEE Transactions on Evolutionary Computation 6(1) (2002)
8. Kennedy, J., Eberhart, R.C.: Swarm Intelligence. Morgan Kaufmann/Academic Press (2001)
9. Kennedy, J., Eberhart, R.: Particle Swarm Optimization. In: IEEE International Conference (1995)
10. Yang, S., Wang, M., Jiao, L.: A Quantum Particle Swarm Optimization. In: IEEE International Conference, vol. 4, pp. 1942–1948 (2004)
11. Harvey, N.R., Marshall, S.: The use of Genetic Algorithms in Morphological Filter design. Image Communication (1996)
12. Nong, Y., Yushu, L., Qifu, X.: Genetic Training Algorithm for Morphological Filters. In: Proceeding of the International Conference in Signal Processing, Beijing, vol. 1, pp. 476–479 (2000)
13. Kennedy, J., Eberhart, R.C.: A Discrete Binary Version of the Particle Swarm Algorithm. In: IEEE International Conference, vol. 5, pp. 4104–4108 (1997)
14. Bouchet, A., Pastore, J., Ballarin, V.: Segmentation of Medical Images using Fuzzy Mathematical Morphology. JCS and T 7(3) (2007)
15. Chatzis, V., Pitas, I.: A Generalized Fuzzy Mathematical Morphology and its Application in Robust 2-D and 3-D Object Representation. IEEE Transaction on Image Processing 9(10) (2000)
16. Htun, Y.Y., Aye, K.K.: Fuzzy Mathematical Morphology Approach in Image Processing. World Academy of Science, Engineering and Technology 42 (2008)

Driving Factors' Identification Based on Derivative Process of Subjective Default Credit Risk

Jiajun Li, Jia Zhao, and Liping Qin

Northwestern Polytechnical University of Humanities, Economics and Law, P.R. China
jiajiaky@126.com

Abstract. As a system of credit risk, it has subjective complexity equally. In previous studies of credit risk, especially from the perspective of a large system, the subjective complexity of the credit risk system is often overlooked, while the identification of the driving factors of the derivative process directly restricts the inference of credit risk. By establishing a set of indicating factors of the driving factors, this paper has done a fuzzy comprehensive analysis related to the driving factors, and tested the set of driving factors of the pre-stage credit risk. The results indicate that: the index set to the default risk has a strong subjective relationship, which means the selected driving factors are of rationality to infer the risk derivative process.

Keywords: Driving factors; subjective default; derivative process; identification.

1 Introduction

Generally speaking, the risks of financial institutions are divided into there categories: risks which can be eliminated or avoid by businesses, risks which can be transferred to the other side, risks which must manage actively (Oldfield and Sentomero, 1996). Also, risks can be divided into controllable and uncontrollable risks (Lin Kwan-Yue, 2001). It is noteworthy that uncontrollable risks are often passive. There are literatures in which credit risks are divided into subjective and objective ones. Standard & Poor's, Moody's in USA, International Banking and credit analysis companies of United Kingdom, have set up a detailed rating index system. But this rating system ignores the differences of the causes of risks and can not effectively evaluate the malicious (subjective) default risks in the condition of imperfect market.

Based on the existence and mechanism of credit risk, credit risk in this paper will be grouped into two categories: one is the objective of default (that is, the loss of the objective ability to repay) credit risk; the other is subjective default (that is, the lack of subjective will to repay) credit risk. Here the default of credit risk is from the trading interests and endogenous of the participated people, not in the characteristic of observability. And the malicious subjective default caused the loss of credit risk of the other party (Li Jiajun, 2006: 126 pages). Identifying the driving factors in the derivative process of subjective default of credit risk, that is studying the key factors as motivation and prerequisite. For the unique complexity, uncertainty and ambiguity, the stage characteristics of credit risk based on subjective default are studied.

R. Zhu et al. (Eds.): ICICA 2010, LNCS 6377, pp. 533–540, 2010.

Subjective default can be measured by two indicators, that is the credit of operators and personal credit of legal person (senior decision-makers).Based on the subjective ambiguity of default boundaries of credit risk and in order to better define the subjective credit risk, this paper studies driving factors' identification of credit risk derivative process based on subjective default.

2   Driving Factors Identification in the Derivative Process

In the Mainstream research on the subjective and objective credit risk, there is not a clear distinction between two types. The constraints and challenges is that the identification and boundaries are not clear between the two types of risk, or from the surface, subjective risks are often shown in the characteristics of objective risks. Therefore, the comparison and analysis of the two types of risks, risks consequences, and boundary identification problem are complex. These are the key and difficult point.

The Occurrence of subjective default of general credit risk is caused by asymmetric information between banks and enterprises which reflected in the different stages respectively are beforehand those things, in the credit risk of default and after the subjective default:

2.1   Identification in Prior Stage

Prior stages: The enterprise should have its private information(including corporate trade secrets), such as the initial business natural resources, profitability, management level (entrepreneurial abilities and subjective effort), strategic vision, the possibility of future fluctuations in the possession of wealth, these macroeconomic factors. That is, the prior stage should have information superiority. Therefore, in order to get more low-cost loans and to achieve their profit maximizing, it has motivation to subjectively hide, conceal their own shortcomings. Precisely because of the existence of non-common knowledge, the risk of banks offering century loans is higher than observed risk. In this principal - agent relationship, the client's objective function is: Corporate pay debt service on time. But in the pursuit of maximizing profit, the agent may be taken against the principal objectives of the action, thus there is uncertainty in the future repayment of bank loans, that is, there may be credit risk.

Factor set is a set consists of evaluation indicators, evaluation index set $U=\{U1, U2\}$, in which Ui represent respectively the index set of different nature:

$U=\{U1, U2\}=\{$Credit of operators, legal person's (or senior decision-makers) personal credit$\}$;

$U1=\{u11, u12, u13\}=\{$Enterprise performance, business environment indicators, status of management);

$U11=\{u111, u112, u113, u114\}=\{$Business stability, business assets, business life, reputation$\}$;

$U12=\{u121 , u122, u123\}=\{$Macroeconomic factors, the national industrial policy, industry environment$\}$;

$U13=\{u131, u132, u133\}=\{$Age structure of management, stability of corporate management, capacity of managers$\}$;

U2={u21, u22, u23, u24}={Capability index of legal person, personality of legal person, legal person's character , quality of legal practitioners};

U21={u211, u212, u213}={Desire to succeed, relationships, stress resistance};

U22={u221, u222, u223, u224}={Source of driving force, accepted way of information, style of decision-making, approach of work plan};

U23={u231, u232}={Educational Background, Growth environment};

U24={u241, u242}={The level of professional quality, practical experience}.

2.2 Identification in Stage

In stages: when the banks offer loans, they are difficult to grasp the flow of funds as enterprise and are not clear about the actual investment and capital utilization of project. At the same time, there are non-symmetric information problem on loans use, this is the source of credit risk. And droved by interests, enterprise may be due without the consent of the bank loans for its intended purpose or for speculation at greater risk. When the project loss, they repudiate and transfer risk to banks. From this point of view, companies in stages have a lot of knowledge and secret acts off others, and these are often difficult to grasp clearly by banks, which cause the asymmetric information. The results of these secret operations are often transferring a higher risk to banks.

U={U1, U2}={Credit of operators', legal person's (or senior decision-makers) personal credit}

U1={u11, u12, u13}={Solvency, profitability, operating capabilities};

U11={u111 , u112, u113 , u114, u115 , u116, u117}={Asset-liability ratio, current ratio, total debt / EBITDA, the ratio of total assets, multiple interest earned, quick ratio, net cash flow generated by operating activities / total debt};

U12={u121 , u122, u123 , u124, u125}={ROE, profit margin, return on total assets, cost margins, cash flow from operating activities / Sales};

U13={u131, u132, u133, u134}={Total asset turnover, liquidity asset turnover, inventory turnover, turnover ratio of accounts receivable };

U2={u21, u22, u23}={Corporate business strategy, corporate management style, decision-making mechanism of high-level decision-makers }.

2.3 Identification after Stage

Later stages: in the present, in the consideration of debt security and in order to reduce the risk of loans, banks may often require mortgage, pledge, or third-party guarantees and other measures to prevent credit risks. However, in these measures, what is easy to overlook is that there are still credit risks resulting from hidden asymmetric behavior.

U={U1, U2}={Credit of operators', legal person's (or senior decision-makers) personal credit}

U1={u11, u12}={Business credit environment, state of credit guarantees };

U11={u111 , u112, u113}={Regional credit environment, public concern, media evaluation guide};

U12={u121 , u122, u123}={Enterprise mortgage, the enterprise collateral case, third-party security situation};

U2={u21, u22}={Corporate debt-paid will, level of education}

3 Driving Factors Relative Fuzzy Comprehensive Evaluation

3.1 Establish Standard Weights Set

Note: weight of Uijk on Uij is Wijk, and Wij= Wij=(aij1, aij2, ⋯, aijk); weight of Uij on Ui is Wij, and Wi=(Wi1, Wi2, ⋯, Wi); weight of Ui on U is Wi and W=(W1, W2, ⋯, Wi) (i, j, k is respectively index number of first index layer, second index layer, and third index layer) . Based on expert scoring method, the weight of each index is worked out as follows: W=(0.5, 0.5),W1=(0.4, 0.3, 0.3), W2= (0.1, 0.1, 0.6, 0.2), W11=(0.25,0.31,0.11,0.33),W12=(0.25,0.40,0.35),W13=(0.27,0.45,0.28);   W21= (0.28, 0.31, 0.41),W22=(0.18, 0.28, 0.33, 0.31),W23=(0.42, 0.58), W24=(0.38, 0.62).

3.2 Establish Evaluation Set

Evaluation set is the collection judges' possible judgments to the objects marked with P: P={p1, p2, ⋯, pn}. This article divide these judgments into five grades: P={p1, p2, ⋯ p5}={Weak correlation, weaker correlation, moderate, stronger correlation, strong correlation},corresponding indicators' reviews p1 ∈ (-0.2,0], p2 ∈ [-0.2,-0.4), p3 ∈ [-0.4,-0.6), p4∈[-0.6,-0.8), p5∈[-0.8,-1].

3.3 Determine Matrix

To each index, vector Rijk of the evaluation set is obtained in accordance with predetermined criteria: Rijk=(rijk1, rijk2, ⋯, rijk5), and rijkh=pijkh/n, h=1,2, ⋯, 5; n are the total number of experts, pijkh is the number of experts Uijk belonging to ph grades, Assessment under the matrix:

$$
R_{ij} = \begin{bmatrix} r_{ij1} \\ r_{ij2} \\ \vdots \\ r_{ijk} \end{bmatrix} = \begin{bmatrix} r_{ij11} & r_{ij12} & \cdots & r_{ij15} \\ r_{ij21} & r_{ij22} & \cdots & r_{ij25} \\ \vdots & \vdots & \vdots & \vdots \\ r_{ijk1} & r_{ijk2} & \cdots & r_{ijk5} \end{bmatrix}
$$

Credit rating method can choose financial institutions, expert evaluation team, mutual evaluation or higher agents, this paper chose expert evaluation team (10 experts), and got the scoring matrix attached as follows:

$$
R_{11} = \begin{bmatrix} 0 & 0.1 & 0.3 & 0.5 & 0.1 \\ 0.1 & 0.1 & 0.4 & 0.4 & 0 \\ 0 & 0.2 & 0.3 & 0.4 & 0.1 \\ 0 & 0 & 0.3 & 0.5 & 0.2 \end{bmatrix} \quad R_{12} = \begin{bmatrix} 0 & 0 & 0.4 & 0.5 & 0.1 \\ 0 & 0.1 & 0.3 & 0.4 & 0.2 \\ 0 & 0.1 & 0.4 & 0.5 & 0 \end{bmatrix} \quad R_{13} = \begin{bmatrix} 0.1 & 0.1 & 0.3 & 0.5 & 0 \\ 0 & 0 & 0.3 & 0.5 & 0.2 \\ 0 & 0.2 & 0.3 & 0.4 & 0.1 \end{bmatrix};
$$

$$
R_{21} = \begin{bmatrix} 0.1 & 0.1 & 0.3 & 0.4 & 0.1 \\ 0 & 0 & 0.2 & 0.6 & 0.2 \\ 0 & 0.1 & 0.2 & 0.5 & 0.1 \end{bmatrix}, \quad R_{22} = \begin{bmatrix} 0 & 0.2 & 0.4 & 0.4 & 0 \\ 0 & 0.1 & 0.3 & 0.5 & 0.1 \\ 0 & 0 & 0.3 & 0.5 & 0.2 \\ 0 & 0.1 & 0.4 & 0.4 & 0.1 \end{bmatrix};
$$

$$
R_{23} = \begin{bmatrix} 0 & 0 & 0.3 & 0.5 & 0.2 \\ 0 & 0 & 0.2 & 0.6 & 0.2 \end{bmatrix}, \quad R_{24} = \begin{bmatrix} 0 & 0.2 & 0.3 & 0.4 & 0.1 \\ 0 & 0 & 0.3 & 0.5 & 0.2 \end{bmatrix}.
$$

3.4 Fuzzy Comprehensive Evaluation

First level fuzzy evaluation. Comprehensive evaluation of the second indexes, note:

$$B_{ij} = W_{ij} \cdot R_{ij} = (W_{ij1}, W_{ij2}, \cdots, W_{ijk}) \cdot \begin{bmatrix} r_{ij11} & r_{ij12} & \cdots & r_{ij15} \\ r_{ij21} & r_{ij22} & \cdots & r_{ij25} \\ \vdots & \vdots & \vdots & \vdots \\ r_{ijk1} & r_{ijk2} & \cdots & r_{ijk5} \end{bmatrix} = (b_{ij1}, b_{ij2}, \cdots b_{ijk})$$

$$B_{11}{}' = W_{11} \cdot R_{11} = (0.25, 0.31, 0.11, 0.33) \cdot \begin{bmatrix} 0 & 0.1 & 0.3 & 0.5 & 0.1 \\ 0.1 & 0.1 & 0.4 & 0.4 & 0 \\ 0 & 0.2 & 0.3 & 0.4 & 0.1 \\ 0 & 0 & 0.3 & 0.5 & 0.2 \end{bmatrix}$$

$=(0.1, 0.11, 0.31, 0.33, 0.2).$

$B_{11}{}'$ is normalized into $B_{11} = (0.095, 0.105, 0.295, 0.314, 0.191)$.
Similarly:

$$B_{12}{}' = W_{12} \cdot R_{12} = (0.25, 0.40, 0.35) \cdot \begin{bmatrix} 0 & 0 & 0.4 & 0.5 & 0.1 \\ 0 & 0.1 & 0.3 & 0.4 & 0.2 \\ 0 & 0.1 & 0.4 & 0.5 & 0 \end{bmatrix}$$

$=(0, 0.1, 0.35, 0.4, 0.2)$

$B_{12}{}'$ is normalized into $B_{12} = (0, 0.095, 0.333, 0.381, 0.191)$.

$$B_{13}{}' = W_{13} \cdot R_{13} = (0.27, 0.45, 0.28) \cdot \begin{bmatrix} 0.1 & 0.1 & 0.3 & 0.5 & 0 \\ 0 & 0 & 0.3 & 0.5 & 0.2 \\ 0 & 0.2 & 0.3 & 0.4 & 0.1 \end{bmatrix}$$

$=(0.1, 0.2, 0.3, 0.45, 0.2).$

$B_{13}{}'$ is normalized into $B_{13} = (0.08, 0.16, 0.24, 0.36, 0.16)$.

$$B_{21}{}' = W_{21} \cdot R_{21} = (0.28, 0.31, 0.41) \cdot \begin{bmatrix} 0.1 & 0.1 & 0.3 & 0.4 & 0.1 \\ 0 & 0 & 0.2 & 0.6 & 0.2 \\ 0 & 0.1 & 0.2 & 0.5 & 0.1 \end{bmatrix}$$

$=(0.1, 0.1, 0.28, 0.41, 0.2).$

$B21'$ is normalized into $B_{21} = (0.092, 0.092, 0.257, 0.376, 0.183)$.

$$B_{22}{}' = W_{22} \cdot R_{22} = (0.18, 0.28, 0.33, 0.31) \cdot \begin{bmatrix} 0 & 0.2 & 0.4 & 0.4 & 0 \\ 0 & 0.1 & 0.3 & 0.5 & 0.1 \\ 0 & 0 & 0.3 & 0.5 & 0.2 \\ 0 & 0.1 & 0.4 & 0.4 & 0.1 \end{bmatrix}$$

$=(0, 0.18, 0.31, 0.33, 0.2).$

$B_{22}{}'$ is normalized into $B_{22} = (0, 0.176, 0.304, 0.324, 0.196)$.

$$B_{23}{}' = W_{23} \cdot R_{23} = (0.42, 0.58) \cdot \begin{bmatrix} 0 & 0 & 0.3 & 0.5 & 0.2 \\ 0 & 0 & 0.2 & 0.6 & 0.2 \end{bmatrix}$$

$=(0, 0, 0.3, 0.58, 0.2).$

B_{23}' is normalized into $B_{23} = (0,0,0.278,0.537,0.185)$.

$$B_{24}' = W_{24} \cdot R_{24} = (0.38, 0.62) \cdot \begin{bmatrix} 0 & 0.2 & 0.3 & 0.4 & 0.1 \\ 0 & 0 & 0.3 & 0.5 & 0.2 \end{bmatrix}$$

$= (0, 0.2, 0.3, 0.5, 0.2)$.

B_{24}' is normalized into $B_{24} = (0, 0.167, 0.250, 0.416, 0.167)$.

Second level fuzzy evaluation. According to the first level comprehensive evaluation, the following is its matrix:

$$R_i = \begin{bmatrix} B_{i1} \\ B_{i2} \\ B_{i3} \\ \vdots \\ B_{ik} \end{bmatrix} = \begin{bmatrix} b_{i11} & b_{i12} & \cdots & b_{i1n} \\ b_{i21} & b_{i22} & \cdots & b_{i2n} \\ \vdots & \vdots & \vdots & \vdots \\ b_{ik1} & b_{ik2} & \cdots & b_{ikn} \end{bmatrix}$$

$$R_1 = \begin{bmatrix} 0.095 & 0.105 & 0.295 & 0.314 & 0.191 \\ 0 & 0.095 & 0.333 & 0.381 & 0.191 \\ 0.080 & 0.160 & 0.240 & 0.360 & 0.160 \end{bmatrix} \quad R_2 = \begin{bmatrix} 0.092 & 0.092 & 0.257 & 0.376 & 0.183 \\ 0 & 0.176 & 0.304 & 0.324 & 0.196 \\ 0 & 0 & 0.278 & 0.537 & 0.185 \\ 0 & 0.167 & 0.250 & 0.416 & 0.167 \end{bmatrix}$$

$B_i' = W_i \cdot R_i$ is normalized into B_i, B_i is vector of U_i on P.

$$B_1' = W_1 \cdot R_1 = (0.4, 0.3, 0.3) \cdot \begin{bmatrix} 0.095 & 0.105 & 0.295 & 0.314 & 0.191 \\ 0 & 0.095 & 0.333 & 0.381 & 0.191 \\ 0.080 & 0.160 & 0.240 & 0.360 & 0.160 \end{bmatrix}$$

$= (0.095, 0.160, 0.300, 0.314, 0.191)$.

$B_1 = (0.090, 0.151, 0.283, 0.296, 0.180)$.

$$B_2' = W_2 \cdot R_2 = (0.1, 0.1, 0.6, 0.2) \cdot \begin{bmatrix} 0.092 & 0.092 & 0.257 & 0.376 & 0.183 \\ 0 & 0.176 & 0.304 & 0.324 & 0.196 \\ 0 & 0 & 0.278 & 0.537 & 0.185 \\ 0 & 0.167 & 0.250 & 0.416 & 0.167 \end{bmatrix}$$

$= (0.092, 0.167, 0.278, 0.537, 0.185)$.

$B_2 = (0.073, 0.133, 0.221, 0.426, 0.147)$.

Comprehensive index judgment. According to the second fuzzy comprehensive evaluation, the following is its matrix:

$$R = \begin{bmatrix} B_1 \\ B_2 \end{bmatrix} = \begin{bmatrix} b_{11} & b_{12} & b_{13} & b_{14} & b_{15} \\ b_{21} & b_{22} & b_{23} & b_{24} & b_{25} \end{bmatrix},$$

$$R = \begin{bmatrix} 0.090 & 0.151 & 0.283 & 0.296 & 0.180 \\ 0.073 & 0.133 & 0.221 & 0.426 & 0.147 \end{bmatrix}$$

$$B^{'} = W \cdot R = (0.5, 0.5) \cdot \begin{bmatrix} 0.090 & 0.151 & 0.283 & 0.296 & 0.180 \\ 0.073 & 0.133 & 0.221 & 0.426 & 0.147 \end{bmatrix}$$

=(0.090,0.151,0.283,0.426,0.180).

It is normalized into B, and B is vector of U on P.

B=(0.080,0.134,0.250,0.377,0.159).

Assessment results. Using weighted average method to quantify the various elements in the evaluation set, the final evaluation result is G=BPT.G=BPT= (0.080, 0.134, 0.250, 0.377, 0.159)· (-0.2,-0.4,-0.6,-0.8,-1)T = -0.6094.

4 Conclusion

The current research has always attached importance to the objective analysis of default risk, ignoring credit risk caused by the subjective default. In fact, the subjective derivative process of default risk is much more complex. As the credit risk research system, control methods and models are still kept in an ideal (or relative ideal) level of market assumptions, and are still limited to objective credit risk of breach. Therefore, this paper discusses subjective credit risk of breach, which is often overlooked, from the perspective of credit risk's existence and its formation mechanism. Identify driving factors in stages in accordance with the process of credit risk derivatives, and use evaluation of fuzzy mathematics theory to do correlation test, Showing the theoretical rationality of the driving factors screened through the test.

Acknowledgement

This paper is supported by the National Natural Science Foundation of China (NO: 70803040) and the Social Science Planning Fund of Xi'an (NO: 06J52).

References

1. Twala, B.: Multiple classifier application to credit risk assessment. Expert Systems with Applications 37, 3326–3336 (2010)
2. Khashman, A.: Neural networks for credit risk evaluation: Investigation of different neural models and learning schemes. Expert Systems with Applications (2010)
3. Bei, H.: Research on credit card approval models based on data mining technology. Computer Engineering and Design, 2989–2991 (2008)
4. Jia, L.: Credit risk control and game analysis. Northwestern Polytechnic University (2005)
5. Songyan, L.: On corporate loans to credit-rating index system. Chengde Vocational College (2006)
6. Altman, E.I.: Credit risk measurement: developments over the last 20 yeas. Joumal of Banking and Finance 21, 1721–1742
7. Anderson, F.: Credit risk optimization with conditional value-at-risk criterion. University of Florida, research paper (1999)

8. Jiajun, L., Yaya, L.: The improvement of the customer credit rating Based on subjective. Financial Forum 3, 26–30 (2008)
9. Abdou, H., Pointon, J., Elmasry, A.: Neural nets versus conventional techniques in credit scoring in Egyptian banking. Expert Systems and Applications 35, 1275–1292 (2008)
10. Crouhy, M., Galai, D., Mark, R.: A comparative analysis of current credit risk modles. Journal and Banking & Financial (2004)

Mechanical Behavior Analysis of CDIO Production-Blood Vessel Robot in Curved Blood Vessel

Fan Jiang, Chunliang Zhang, and Yijun Wang

School of Mechanical and Electric Engineering, Guangzhou University, Guangzhou 510006
jiangfan2008@gzhu.edu.cn

Abstract. In order to analyze mechanical behavior of blood vessel robot (student's CDIO production) in curved blood, and provide the data for outline design of robot, the flow field out side of robot is numerical simulated. The results show that the vessel shape has significant influent to flow field out side of robot, in curved blood vessel, the wall shear stress (WSS) is greater obviously than that in the straight blood vessel. The radius of blood vessel has influent to WSS, along the radius increases, the WSS on the surface between robot and the inner ring is closer to agreement that of the outer ring gradually. The WSS distribution is also influent by its position in the blood vessel.

Keywords: blood vessel robot, mechanical behavior analysis, curved blood vessel, numerical simulation.

1 Introduction

Vascular diseases are one of main threat to health of people, and their therapeutic method includes medication and operation, the blood vessel robot could enter into blood vessel, directly eliminate arteriosclerosis, aneurysm, stenosis, is important therapeutic way. The blood vessel robot works in fluid dynamic environment, the blood flow should impact moving of blood vessel robot. M. C. Kim, et al simulate that contractive and dilative motion of micro-hydro robot produces the propulsive force at a low Reynolds number fluid [1]. Y. S. Zhang, et al design a new capsule micro robot, establish kinematics mathematical model of capsule micro robot in pipeline environment, and study the relationship between spiral parameters and swimming speed [2]. B. He, et al study on the influences of environment on a novel kind of micro robot, and investigate the relations between the robot running velocity and its driven forces [3]. Z. W. Hu puts forward a sort of spiral-drive, which enters the pipes to fill with liquid and suspended to move, could enter into intestines for the medical treatment [4]. F. Jiang, et al design new blood vessel robot, and numerical analyze the outside flow field of robot, obtain the lots of flow parameters of robot in straight vessel [5]. But there are little references for mechanical behavior of blood vessel robot in the complicated blood vessel, and is obstacle to design the outline of blood vessel robot. The students (CDIO pilot class) design the robot, its shape need to test whether it meet the requirements, numerical simulation is an effective tool.

R. Zhu et al. (Eds.): ICICA 2010, LNCS 6377, pp. 541–548, 2010.
© Springer-Verlag Berlin Heidelberg 2010

In this paper, in order to provide enough references to design the outline of blood vessel robot, the mechanical behavior of blood vessel robot in curvature artery is analyzed.

2 Governing Equation

Three-dimensional incompressible Navier-Stokes equations were employed as governing equations, blood is assumed as Newtonian fluid, the terms of mass source, gravity and external body forces are ignored, the continuity and momentum conservation equations are written as follows [6-10].

$$\frac{\partial u_i}{\partial x_i} = 0 \tag{1}$$

$$\frac{\partial u_i}{\partial t} + \frac{\partial}{\partial x_j}(\rho u_i u_j) = -\frac{\partial p}{\partial x_j} + \frac{\partial}{\partial x_j}[\mu(\frac{\partial u_i}{\partial x_j} + \frac{\partial u_j}{\partial x_j})] \tag{2}$$

where u is the velocity, p is the pressure, ρ is the density and μ is the dynamic viscosity, the x is coordinate directon.

3 FVM Model

In order to analyze the mechanical behavior of robot in the blood vessel, and investigate the influence of curvature radius of curved blood vessel, five couple models of robot and blood vessel are used, the four blood vessels of that are swept along semicricle, radius of semi-circle are 20, 30, 40, 50, respectively, the other is sweeping along spline, which is shown in Fig. 1. the diameter of cross section is 6mm, the diameter of blood vessel robot is 3.9mm, and length is 8mm, the geometry model are meshed by tetrahedral cells, the spline vessel model has 66864 cells and 14451 nodes, is shown in Fig. 2. The blood vessel is treated as being rigid because the elastic deformation of the large arteries including cerebral artery is generally less than 10% and the influence is second order for the main blood flow [4].

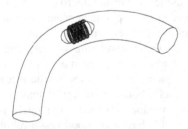

Fig. 1. The geometry model   Fig. 2. The grid model

The computation parameters were set as follows: blood density is 1060 kg/m^3, blood viscosity is 0.004 $Pa \cdot s$, velocity in inlet section is 0.38 m/s, outlet section pressure is 0 Pa, wall is no slip. Commercial software-Fluent 6.3 is used in solving the Navier-Stokes equations (Eqs. (1) and (2)) for the three-dimensional flow.

4 Results and Discussions

4.1 Flow Characteristics Inside of Blood Vessel

Fig. 3 show the pressure distribution at symmetrical profile of curved blood vessel and straight blood vessel, from the pressure results, we can see that pressure drop in straight blood vessel is greater than that in curved blood vessel, and their maximum pressure point is different.

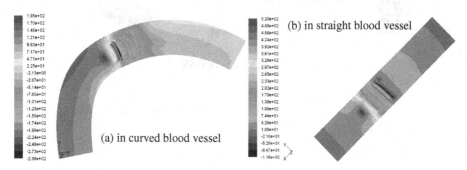

Fig. 3. Results of pressure distribution

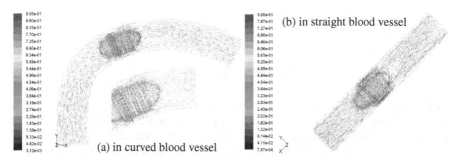

Fig. 4. Results of velocity vector

The results of velocity vector on the symmetric planed of the curved blood vessel and straight blood vessel are shown in Fig. 4, it can be seen that the velocity variation in curved blood vessel is larger than that in straight blood vessel, the maximum velocity positions are similar, is in the side of the robot, due to the blood flows through space between the vessel and the robot, is accelerated to be largest in side region of robot. The vortex position is at tail bottom of robot in curved blood vessel, and the velocity in the out side is greater than that in the inner side.

Fig. 5 shows the results of wall shear stress (WSS) of curved blood vessel and straight blood vessel, the WSS on surface of robot in curved blood vessel is greater obviously than that in straight blood vessel. There are WSS at out side of robot in curved blood vessel, but only at upwind surface in straight blood vessel, these results indicate that the flow is complicated in curved blood vessel, the blood repeatedly acts on the surface of robot, leading to higher shear stress, and the acted region is greater too.

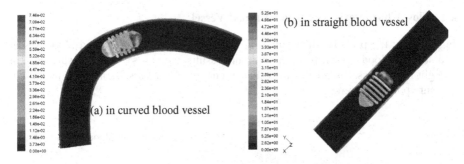

Fig. 5. Results of WSS

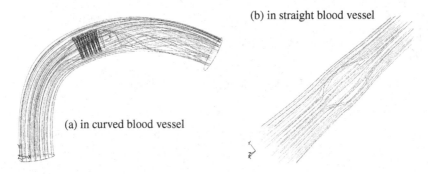

Fig. 6. Results of streamline

Fig. 6 is results of streamline, the streamline expresses the flow path of blood in the blood vessel. From Fig. 6, the streamline is wound in the robot tail as the robot in curved blood vessel, and that is not appeared in straight blood vessel.

Through above analysis, we can see that the shape of blood vessel could be influent to flow field in out side of robot. In the straight blood vessel, the results among of robot is symmetrical, but is asymmetrical in the curve blood vessel.

4.2 Influence of Curvature Radius to WSS

The wall shear stress of robot in different radius vessel (the radius of vessel centerline) is shown in Fig. 7, from these results, with different radius, the WSS on surface of driving screw is significantly different. As the radius is small, the WSS on surface of driving screw relatively small, and the WSS distribution is irregularly, that

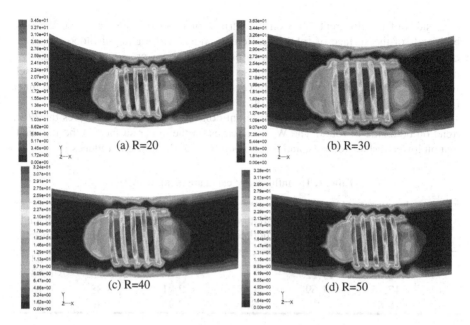

Fig. 7. WSS of different radius vessel

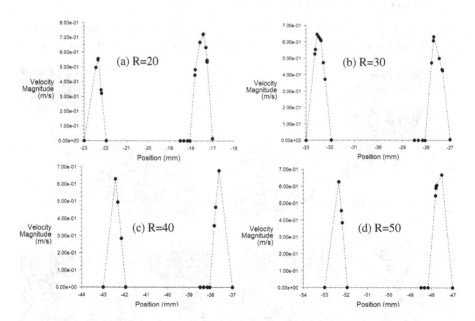

Fig. 8. The velocity distribution between robot and blood vessel

the surface on inner side is large, on outboard is small. Along radius of blood vessel increases, blood flow through the robot directly, the WSS on surface of driving screw tend to well-distributed.

Besides of the different WSS on the surface of robot driving scres, the WSS on both ends of the surface of robot is different. Along with radius of blood vessel increases, the WSS on upper surface increases and that on lower surface decreases.

Fig. 8 shows that velocity distribution on line between robot and blood vessel, from these results, with the increase in vessel diameter, velocity of robot by the inner ring is closer to agreement that of the outer ring.

Table 1 is the WSS value on the different point of robot surface, It gives the WSS trend on both side of robot. The WSS increases on the upper surface of the fore-end, that on lower surface reduces, and that on both side of the rear-end reduces.

Table 1. The influence of curvature radius to WSS

radius	fore-end upper	fore-end lower	bottom middle top	lower middle bottom	rear-end upper	rear-end lower
20	15.86	19.31	3.1	2.41	4.48	7.24
30	16.68	19.22	3.63	2.9	4.35	6.53
40	17.15	21.69	3.88	2.91	3.88	6.15
50	18.68	19	3.6	2.95	3.6	6.55

4.3   Influence of Position to WSS

The robots are placed in different vascular locations of curved vessels, and the impact of the location to WSS on its surface is investigated, the results shown in Fig. 9 and Table 2.

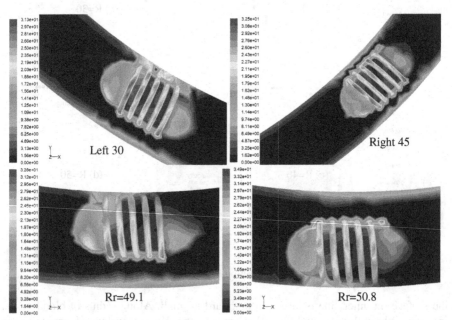

Fig. 9. The influence of position to WSS

Left 30 in Fig. 9, the robot is placed nearby inlet, Right 45 in Fig. 9, the robot is placed nearby outlet, the WSS in position of Left 30 is less than that of Right 45. Rr=49.1 in Fig. 9, the robot is close to the inner ring, the WSS of surface between robot and outer ring is greater. Rr=50.8 in Fig. 9, the robot is close to the outer ring, the WSS of surface between robot and inner ring is greater. These results show that the gap of robot and vessel wall exists, the shear stress on this side is relatively large.

Table 2. The influence of position to WSS

viscosity	fore-end upper	fore-end lower	bottom middle top	lower middle bottom	rear-end upper	rear-end lower
Left 30	14.07	23.14	2.81	2.5	3.44	7.82
Right 45	16.55	21.75	2.92	2.6	4.54	6.8
Rr=49.1	8.2	22.94	3.28	1.64	1.64	9.84
Rr=50.8	20.59	6.97	3.14	0.35	11.16	0.35

From Table 2, the robot is placed different position of vessel centerline, the WSS variation is little, if it is offseted from vessel centerline, the WSS is relatively large on the side of great gap.

5 Conclusions

(1) The flow field characteristics in curve blood vessel is different with that in straight blood vessel, the vascular robot results neared the inner side of vascular is different to external side, but that results in straight vascular is asymmetrical, and the location of the vortex is also changing.

(2) Mechanical behavior of robot is impacted by vascular radius, and it position. As the radius increases, the WSS on the each side of robot should be closed. The position of robot is also impact its WSS, as the robot on the vascular centerline, the influence is little, as it closes inner ring or outer ring, the WSS on gap side is greater.

Acknowledgments

Thanks the support from National Second Feature Major Projection (TS2479), Science and Technology Plan Project of College and University Belonging to Guangzhou (No. 08C062), The Guangdong University Outstanding Young Innovation Talents Cultivation Project.

References

[1] Kim, M.C., Kang, H.K., Chun, H.H., et al.: Simulation for The Propulsion of A Micro-hydro Robot with An Unstructured Grid. Ocean Engineering 35, 912–919 (2008)
[2] Zhang, Y.S., Yu, H.H., Ruan, X.Y., et al.: Kinematics Characteristics of A New Capsule-type Micro Robot in Intestine. Journal of Mechanical Engineering 8, 18–23 (2009)

[3] He, B., Yue, J.G., Zhou, Q., et al.: Study on The Influences of Environment on A Novel Kind of Micro Robot. China Mechanical Engineering 24, 2234–2238 (2005)

[4] Hu, Z.W.: Study on Spiral-drive Mechanism of Micro-robots. Degree Dissertation of Master of Zhejiang University (2005)

[5] Jiang, F., Yu, J., Liang, Z.W.: New Blood Vessel Robot Design and Outside Flow Field Characteristic. Applied Mechanics and Materials 29-32, 2490–2495 (2010)

[6] Jiang, F., Chen, W.P., Li, Y.Y., et al.: Spatial Structure Injection Molding Analysis of Suspended Bio-carriers. Materials Science Forum 575-578, 385–389 (2007)

[7] Jiang, F., Chen, W.P., Li, Y.Y., et al.: Numerical Evalution of Spatial Structure of Suspended Bio-carriers. Journal of South China University of Technology 12, 75–79 (2008)

[8] Jiang, F., Liu, X.C., Wang, C., et al.: Numerical simulation of soot particle flow indoor of automobile. In: Proceedings of the 3rd International Conference on Mechanical Engineering and Mechanics, vol. 1, pp. 1010–1015 (2009)

[9] Jiang, F., Huang, C.M., Liang, Z.W., et al.: Numerical simulation of rotating-cage bio-reactor based on dynamic mesh coupled two-phase flow. In: Zhang, W., Chen, Z., Douglas, C.C., Tong, W. (eds.) HPCA 2009. LNCS, vol. 5938, pp. 206–211. Springer, Heidelberg (2010)

[10] Jiang, F., Yu, J., Xiao, Z.M.: Outside flow field characteristic of biological carriers. Advanced Materials Research 113-114, 276–279 (2010)

The Choice of Neuropathological Questionnaires to Diagnose the Alzheimer's Disease Based on Verbal Decision Analysis Methods

Isabelle Tamanini, Plácido Rogério Pinheiro, and Mirian Calíope D. Pinheiro

University of Fortaleza (UNIFOR) - Graduate Program in Applied Computer Sciences
Av. Washington Soares, 1321 - Bl J Sl 30 - 60.811-905 - Fortaleza - Brazil
isabelle.tamanini@gmail.com, {placido,BBcaliope}@unifor.br

Abstract. There is a great challenge in identifying the early stages of the Alzheimer's disease, which has become the most frequent cause of dementia in the last few years. The aim of this work is to determine which tests, from a battery of tests, are relevant and would detect faster whether the patient is having a normal aging or developing the disease. This will be made applying the method ORCLASS and the Aranaú Tool, a decision support system mainly structured on the ZAPROS method. The modeling and evaluation processes were conducted based on bibliographic sources and on the information given by a medical expert.

Keywords: Verbal Decision Analysis Methods, Diagnosis of Alzheimer's Disease, Neuroimaging, ZAPROS, ORCLASS.

1 Introduction

Demographic studies have shown a progressive and significant increase in the elderly population of developed and developing countries in the last few years [14]. The advances in the medical area have significant importance on the increase of the life expectancy, and, along with this fact, there is a major increase in the number of health problems among the elderly, which, besides being of long duration, require skilled personnel, a multidisciplinary team, equipment and additional expensive tests. Besides, according to studies conducted by the Alzheimer's Association [7], the Alzheimer's disease treatments represent a significant cost, second only to cancer and cardiovascular diseases.

According to [5], the Alzheimer's disease incidence and prevalence double every five years with a prevalence of 40% among people with more than 85 years of age. In the year of 2003, the disease was also recognized as the fifth leading cause of death among those older than the age of 65. Besides, it is an incurable disease and it affects not only the patient, but the whole family involved, impacting on their lives and work.

First described in 1906, the disease is characterized by the presence of senis plaques and tangled neurofibrillaries in the regions of the hippocampus and cerebral cortex, and the neurons appear atrophied in a large area of the brain (Fig.1).

R. Zhu et al. (Eds.): ICICA 2010, LNCS 6377, pp. 549–556, 2010.
© Springer-Verlag Berlin Heidelberg 2010

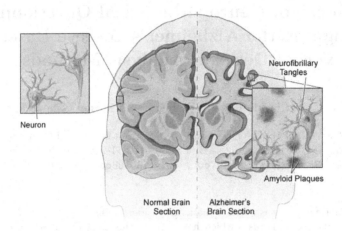

Fig. 1. Normal brain and an Alzheimer's disease brain [13]

The efforts aiming the accuracy of the diagnosis can help identifying conditions potentially reversible or treatable which have contributed to cognitive decline and dementia. Also, based on the accuracy of the diagnosis, family members can plan the future needs of the patient and can also consider the implications of a particular diagnosis regarding their own future.

Even though the only way to have the definitive diagnosis of the disease is by the examination of the brain tissue, a probable diagnosis can be made based on neurological and psychological tests, patient's clinical history, laboratory and neuroimaging tests, etc, being the latter the main focus of this paper. Currently, a great variety of tests with this purpose are available, and one of the major challenges is to find out which test, or which characteristics of a test, would be more efficient to establish the diagnosis of dementia.

The battery of tests from the Consortium to Establish a Registry for Alzheimer's Disease (CERAD) was used in this work, because it encompasses all the steps of the diagnosis and it is used all over the world. The CERAD was founded with the aim of establishing a standard process for evaluation of patients with possible Alzheimer's disease who enrolled in NIA-sponsored Alzheimer's Disease Centers or in other dementia research programs [10]. Some relevant studies have already been developed considering its neuropsychological battery. Among this works, we can cite the ones presented in [1,2,3,4]. This way, the center of interest of this work is the neuropathological battery, which is mainly structured on neuroimaging exams of the patients, and it aims to verify if there are any other problems in the patients' brain, such as vascular lesions, hemorrhages, microinfarcts, etc, that could be relevant to the diagnosis of the disease.

The main focus of this work is to determine the neuropathological questionnaires from this battery that are relevant and would detect faster if the patient is developing the disease. This will be made in two stages: at first, a classification method (ORCLASS [8]) will be applied to determine which questionnaires would, themselves, detect the Alzheimer's disease; then, the questionnaires classified as the ones that could give this diagnosis will be ordered, from the most likely to lead to the diagnosis faster, to the least, considering an ordination methodology mainly structured on the ZAPROS method [8]. The ordering of the questionnaires will be made by means of Aranaú Tool, a decision support system that applies the ordination methodology. This work was based on some other works that apply multicriteria methods aiming the diagnosis of the Alzheimer's disease [16,17,18,19].

2   The Ordinal Classification Method - ORCLASS

The ORCLASS (ORdinal CLASSification) method [8] belongs to the Verbal Decision Analysis framework, and aims at classifying the alternatives of a given set. It enables the verbal formulation of the classification rule obtained for the explanation of decisions, such that any alternatives defined by the criteria and criteria values previously structured can be classified.

One of the characteristics of classification problems is that one does not need to determine the complete preference order of the alternatives: the decision maker only needs that these alternatives are categorized into a decision group, among a few others groups of a set.

In the preferences elicitation process, classification boards will be structured such that each cell is composed by a combination of determined values of all the criteria defined to the problem, which represents a possible alternative to the problem. It will be presented to the decision maker classify only the combinations that, when classified, will reflect this information in a subset of the possible alternatives, so only the alternatives having the most informative index will be presented to decision maker. To determine this alternative, one should calculate, for each cell of the board, the number of alternatives that may be also classified based on the decision maker's response (considering all decision classes). A detailed description of the method's operation is available in [8].

3   An Approach Methodology Based on ZAPROS

A modification to the ZAPROS method [9] is proposed in [15], in order to increase the comparison power of the method. It presents three main stages: Problem Formulation, Elicitation of Preferences and Comparison of Alternatives.

In the preferences elicitation stage, the scale of preferences for quality variations (Joint Scale of Quality Variations - JSQV) is structured. The elicitation of preferences follows the structure proposed in [9]. But, instead of setting the decision maker's preferences based on the first reference situation and, then, establishing another scale of preferences using the second reference situation, we propose that the two substages be transformed in one.

Besides, the preferences elicitation for two criteria, the questions will be made dividing the Quality Variations (QVs) into two items, such that the decision maker will compare possible alternatives instead of quality variations for the criteria. This modification was made because it was observed difficulties on answering the questions when the comparison of two QVs was required.

Also, with the aim of reducing the number of incomparability cases, the alternatives comparison process applies the same structure proposed in [9], but the comparison of pairs of the alternatives' substage was modified: in [12], it is proposed that the vectors of criteria values ranks, which represent the function of quality, are rearranged in an ascending order. Then, the values will be compared to the corresponding position of another alternative's vector of values based on Pareto's dominance rule. Meanwhile, this procedure was modified for implementation because it was proposed to scales of preferences of criteria values, not for quality variation scales.

In cases where the incomparability of real alternatives will not allow the presentation of a complete result, one can evaluate all possible alternatives to the problem in order to rank the real alternatives indirectly. After that, the ranks obtained will be passed on to the corresponding real alternatives.

In order to facilitate the decision process and perform it consistently, observing its complexity and with the aim of making it accessible, a tool implemented in Java was used [15]. At the end of the process, it provides a graph to the user, representing the dominating relations of the alternatives.

4   Multicriteria Models for the Diagnosis of the Alzheimer's Disease

In order to establish which tests would be capable of leading to a diagnosis of the Alzheimer's disease, a multicriterion model was structured based on tests of the CERAD's neuropathological battery.

We can state the classification problem into two groups of questionnaires:

I) The ones that would lead to the diagnosis of Alzheimer's disease; and
II) The ones that would require other data to be able to get the diagnosis.

The criteria established were defined considering parameters of great importance to the diagnosis, based on the analysis of each questionnaire data by the decision maker and in her knowledge. This analysis was carried out following some patterns, such that if a determined data is directly related to the diagnosis of the disease, and this fact can be found based on the number of its occurrences in the battery data, this fact will be selected as a possible value of criteria. For being relevant to the diagnosis, one can notice that questionnaires that are able to detect this occurrence are more likely to give a diagnosis. Regarding the CERAD data, only the results of the tests of patients that had already died and on which the necropsy has been done were selected (122 cases), because it is known that necropsy is essential for validating the clinical diagnosis of dementing diseases. Table 1 shows the criteria defined to the classification model.

The classification was performed based on the analysis of the answers obtained on each questionnaire and the patients' final diagnosis with the medical expert. The facts that were more constant and extremely connected to the patient's final diagnosis were set as preferable over others. This way, it was possible to

Table 1. Criteria for evaluation of the questionnaires capable of leading to the diagnosis

Criteria	Values of Criteria
A: Type of examination performed to answer the questionnaire	A1. Neuroimaging tests were applied A2. Tests concearning the gross characteristics of the brain or abnomalities of meninges A3. Other tests concearning the patient's health
B: The type of the diagnosis (when obtained)	B1. An early diagnosis may be possible considering the questionnaire's answers B2. A diagnosis can be established considering the questionnaire's answers B3. The diagnosis can only be achieved based on post-mortem tests
C: Evaluated clinical history of the patient	C1. A complete study of the patient's clinical history is performed C2. It presents questionings concearning the patient's clinical history C3. No clinical history is evaluated

	B_1	B_2	B_3		B_1	B_2	B_3		B_1	B_2	B_3
A_1	I	I	II	A_1	I	I	II	A_1	I	I	II
A_2	I	I	II	A_2	I	I	II	A_2	II	II	II
A_3	I	I	II	A_3	I	II	II	A_3	II	II	II
	C_1				C_2				C_3		

Fig. 2. Classification board obtained to the model

establish a order of the facts that had a direct relation with the patients' final diagnosis, and so, which of the questionnaires had the questions that were more likely to lead to it. The classification board obtained is presented in Fig. 2, and the questionnaires defined as alternatives to this problem are shown in Table 2.

Then, the questionnaires classified as the ones that itself could lead to the diagnosis were submitted to an ordination method, such that an ordering of these questionnaires would be obtained, from the best one to be applied in order to get to a diagnosis faster, to the least one. This way, the model will be structured based on four questionnaires: the ones classified as belonging to the class I.

The criteria definition followed the same procedure of the previous model. This way, the ones considered relevant to evaluate the CERAD's questionnaires afore mentioned and the values identified for them are exposed in Table 3.

The preferences elicitation was based on the same information sources considered to establish the information of the previous model. This way, the preferences scale obtained is given as follows: $b_1 \equiv c_1 \prec a_1 \prec c_2 \prec b_2 \prec b_3 \prec c_3 \prec a_2 \prec a_3$.

Then, the alternatives were formulated identifying which facts (the values of criteria) would be identified by each questionnaire, considering the tests it would require to be filled. So, we'll have the questionnaires described as criterion values according to the facts verified by each one of them. For example: for the questionnaire *Cerebral Vascular Disease Gross Findings*, we can say that it has

Table 2. The questionnaires represented as criteria values and their respective classes

Alternatives	Criteria Evaluations	Class
Clinical History	A3B2C1	I
Gross Examination of the Brain	A2B1C3	II
Cerebral Vascular Disease Gross Findings	A1B1C3	I
Microscopic Vascular Findings	A1B2C3	I
Assessment of Neurohistological Findings	A2B3C3	II
Neuropathological Diagnosis	A1B2C2	I

Table 3. Criteria for evaluation of the analyzed questionnaires of CERAD

Criteria	Values of Criteria
A: Verification of Other Brain Problems' Existence	A1. There are questions about the severity of other problems A2. There are questions about its existence A3. There are no questions considering its existence
B: Neuroimaging tests: MRI or CT	B1. One or more cerebral lacunes can be detected B2. May detect extensive periventricular white matter changes B3. Focal or generalized atrophy can be detected
C: Clinical Studies	C1. Electroencephalogram C2. Analysis of Cerebrospinal Fluid C3. Electrocardiogram

questions about the severity of the patients' brain problems, that a extensive periventricular white matter change can be detected by the tests required on answering it, and that, as clinical studies, a electroencephalogram would be analyzed to answer some of its questions. The model was applied to the Aranaú Tool [15] and the results presentation screen obtained is presented in Fig. 3.

The order of preference to apply the tests shows that the questionnaire Cerebral Vascular Disease Gross Findings is more likely to detect a possible case of Alzheimer's disease than the others, so, it should be applied first.

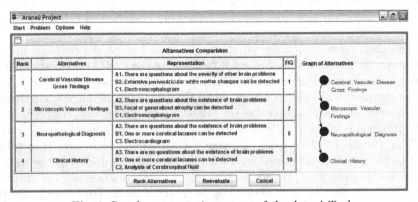

Fig. 3. Results presentation screen of the Aranú Tool

5   Conclusions

The main purpose of this work is to set up an order of questionnaires from the neuropathological battery of CERAD that were more likely to give the diagnosis. To do so, it was presented a model to classify the questionnaires into two groups: the ones that would lead to a diagnosis of the Alzheimer's disease, and the ones that would require further analysis. Then, a model was formulated based on the questionnaires classified in the first group and submitted to Aranaú tool [15], which is structured on the ZAPROS method but with some modifications to improve its comparison power, and the questionnaires order was obtained.

The criteria were defined considering the characteristics of each questionnaire. The preferences were given through the analysis by a medical expert of the questionnaires results and the postmortem diagnosis of each patient, in a way to establish a relation between them. Then, the alternatives were structured according to the facts that could be detected on answering each of these questionnaires. As the contribution of this paper, we had a ranking of the questionnaires, from the one that had the greatest importance on the diagnosis, to the one that had the least. This would enable a faster detection of patients that would develop the disease, increasing the chances of treatment.

As future works, we intend establish a model to rank the questionnaires considering all the characteristics of each one, aiming at a more detailed description of these questionnaires as criteria values; and to verify which stage of the Alzheimer's disease would be detected based on the order established, in order to detect the disease in its earliest stages.

Acknowledgments. The authors are thankful to the National Counsel of Technological and Scientific Development (CNPq) for all the support received and to the Consortium to Establish a Registry for Alzheimer's Disease (CERAD) for making available the data used in this case study.

References

1. Castro, A.K.A., de Pinheiro, P.R., Pinheiro, M.C.D.: A Multicriteria Model Applied in the Diagnosis of Alzheimer's Disease. In: Wang, G., Li, T., Grzymala-Busse, J.W., Miao, D., Skowron, A., Yao, Y. (eds.) RSKT 2008. LNCS (LNAI), vol. 5009, pp. 612–619. Springer, Heidelberg (2008)
2. Castro, A.K.A., de Pinheiro, P.R., Pinheiro, M.C.D.: A Hybrid Model for Aiding in Decision Making for the Neuropsychological Diagnosis of Alzheimer's Disease. In: Chan, C.-C., Grzymala-Busse, J.W., Ziarko, W.P. (eds.) RSCTC 2008. LNCS (LNAI), vol. 5306, pp. 495–504. Springer, Heidelberg (2008)
3. Castro, A.K.A., de Pinheiro, P.R., Pinheiro, M.C.D.: An Approach for the Neuropsychological Diagnosis of Alzheimer's Disease. In: Wen, P., Li, Y., Polkowski, L., Yao, Y., Tsumoto, S., Wang, G. (eds.) RSKT 2009. LNCS, vol. 5589, pp. 216–223. Springer, Heidelberg (2009)
4. Castro, A.K.A., de Pinheiro, P.R., Pinheiro, M.C.D., Tamanini, I.: Towards the Applied Hybrid Model in Decision Making: A Neuropsychological Diagnosis of Alzheimer's Disease Study Case. International Journal of Computational Intelligence Systems (accepted to publication 2010)

5. Fillenbaum, G.G., van Belle, G., Morris, J.C., et al.: Consortium to Establish a Registry for Alzheimers Disease (CERAD): The first twenty years. Alzheimer's & Dementia 4(2), 96–109 (2008)
6. Hughes, C.P., Berg, L., Danzinger, W.L., et al.: A New Clinical Scale for the Staging of Dementia. British J. of Psychiatry 140(6), 566–572 (1982)
7. Koppel, R.: Alzheimer's Disease: The Costs to U.S. Businesses in 2002. Alzheimers Association - Report (2002)
8. Larichev, O., Moshkovich, H.M.: Verbal decision analysis for unstructured problems. Kluwer Academic Publishers, Boston (1997)
9. Larichev, O.: Ranking Multicriteria Alternatives: The Method ZAPROS III. European Journal of Operational Research 131(3), 550–558 (2001)
10. Morris, J.C., Heyman, A., Mohs, R.C., et al.: The Consortium to Establish a Registry for Alzheimer's Disease (CERAD): Part 1. Clinical and Neuropsychological Assessment of Alzheimer's Disease. Neurology 39(9), 1159–1165 (1989)
11. Morris, J.: The Clinical Dementia Rating (CDR): Current Version and Scoring Rules. Neurology 43(11), 2412–2414 (1993)
12. Moshkovich, H., Mechitov, A., Olson, D.: Ordinal Judgments in Multiattribute Decision Analysis. European Journal of Operational Research 137(3), 625–641 (2002)
13. NewYork-Presbyterian Hospital: How the Brain and Nerve Cells Change During Alzheimer's, Internet (March 2010),
   http://nyp.org/health/neuro-alzheim.html
14. Prince, M.J.: Predicting the Onset of Alzheimer's Disease Using Bayes' Theorem. American Journal of Epidemiology 143(3), 301–308 (1996)
15. Tamanini, I., Pinheiro, P.R.: Challenging the Incomparability Problem: An Approach Methodology Based on ZAPROS. Modeling, Computation and Optimization in Information Systems and Management Sciences, Communications in Computer and Information Science 14(1), 344–353 (2008)
16. Tamanini, I., Castro, A.K.A., Pinheiro, P.R., Pinheiro, M.C.D.: Towards an Applied Multicriteria Model to the Diagnosis of Alzheimer's Disease: A Neuroimaging Study Case. In: 2009 IEEE International Conference on Intelligent Computing and Intelligent Systems (ICIS), vol. 3, pp. 652–656 (2009)
17. Tamanini, I., Castro, A.K.A., Pinheiro, P.R., Pinheiro, M.C.D.: Towards the Early Diagnosis of Alzheimer's Disease: A Multicriteria Model Structured on Neuroimaging. Int. J. of Social and Humanistic Computing 1(2), 203–217 (2009)
18. Tamanini, I., Castro, A.K.A., Pinheiro, P.R., Pinheiro, M.C.D.: Verbal Decision Analysis Applied on the Optimization of Alzheimer's Disease Diagnosis: A Study Case Based on Neuroimaging. In: Special Issue: Software Tools and Algorithms for Biological Systems, Advances in Experimental Medicine and Biology (to appear 2010)
19. Tamanini, I., Pinheiro, P.R., Pinheiro, M.C.D.: Analysis of Verbal Decision Analysis Methods Considering a Multicriteria Model to the Diagnosis of Alzheimer's Disease. In: 2010 International Conference on Bioinformatics and Computational Biology (BIOCOMP 2010), Las Vegas, USA (2010) (accepted for publication)

Applying Verbal Decision Analysis on the Choice of Materials to the Construction Process of Earth Dams

Plácido Rogério Pinheiro, Isabelle Tamanini,
Francisco Chagas da Silva Filho, and Moisés Ângelo de Moura Reis Filho[1]

[1] University of Fortaleza (UNIFOR) - Graduate Program in Applied Computer
Sciences, Av. Washington Soares, 1321 - Bl J Sl 30 - 60.811-905 - Fortaleza - Brazil
[2] Federal University of Ceará (UFC) - Department of Hydraulic and Environmental
Engineering, Campus do Pici, Bl 713 - 60451970 - Fortaleza - Brazil
placido@unifor.br, {isabelle.tamanini,fchagasfilho}@gmail.com,
moises_filho@hotmail.com

Abstract. The choice of materials to be used on the construction of
earth dams is made in an empirical way, taking into account previous
projects and the experience of the involved engineers. An engineer often
specifies the materials and their quantities that will be used based on
previous projects, on the geotechnical information about the materials
available and on common sense. In order to improve this process we propose a multicriterion model to aid in the decisions making concerning the
choice of materials on the construction of earth dams with homogeneous
and zoned sections. This will be made by means of the Aranaú Tool,
a decision support system mainly structured on the ZAPROS method.
The case study was applied to the dam Frios project (Ceará, Brazil).

Keywords: Verbal Decision Analysis, Construction of Earth Dams,
ZAPROS.

1 Introduction

The search for places where there was plenty of water has always been a constant.
In places where water was scarce there was a need to create mechanisms that
would guarantee its storage, this gave rise to the need of the construction dams
for its purpose (ICOLD, 1999 in [12]). A dam represents a human intervention
in nature with the aim of adapting the patterns of natural water flow to the
standards demanded by society [2].

In the nineteenth century, around the year 1853, in France, De Sazilly introduces the Engineering of Dams to make its construction something structured
in mathematical calculations in order to prove the efficiency of projects [4].

The construction of earth dams is being enhanced every day due to the
technological development of machinery of implementation and construction
techniques [10]. However, decisions on important aspects such as the type of
material to be used, are taken from an empirical and subjective way, without
the guarantying its construction with the lowest cost.

R. Zhu et al. (Eds.): ICICA 2010, LNCS 6377, pp. 557–564, 2010.

The aim of this paper is to present a modeling process applying a multicriteria method to help in the decision making on the construction of earth dams in order to minimize the materials cost but guarantying a good quality construction.

Multicriteria methodologies help to generate knowledge about the decision context, thus, increasing the confidence of those who make decisions on the results [5]. There are multicriteria methods based either on quantitative ([3,?]) or qualitative ([13,?]) analysis of the problem, and it is a great challenge to choose the approach that best fits the problem to be solved.

This work focuses on the application of a modification of the ZAPROS method [7], which belongs to the Verbal Decision Analysis framework, in order to solve problems in a more realistic way from the decision maker's point of view, since quantitative methods could lead to loss of information when one tries to assign exact measures to verbal values. The ZAPROS method was chosen among other available methods because it fits the characteristics of the contexts questioned, considering the evaluation of the problem, the decision objects and the available information.

2   The Problem of Choosing the Materials for the Construction of Earth Dams

The materials used in the construction of earth dams' process are usually available in mines either in the place of the dam or nearby [16]. The exploration of these mines is not always accessible, since this will generate additional expenses, such as for deforestation or for renting the area (if it is on private property).

Each mine has one or more materials available [1], and the transportation of these materials to the place where the dam is being constructed may require a high cost even though the materials are in the same mine, because of the extraction difficulty. Besides, the volume of material needed on the construction may vary depending on the type used.

After the extraction and transportation, the soils usually loose part of their moisture. To correct these deviations, it is applied a compression process. There are several types of compression that may be applied to soils, and each soil requires a different amount of water, which is obtained and transported from variable cost sources. For each type of compression, the cost dependent directly on the soil to be compacted, because these have different compression curves, requiring, then, a determined compression effort [8].

An earth dam can be classified as homogeneous or zoned, according to the amount and types of materials used in the massive construction [16]. The decision making about which types of materials and compression will be used, which deposits will be explored and if the dam should be zoned or homogeneous is quite complex. Thus, the problem of the construction of a dam can be stated as follows: "To build an earth dam by selecting the deposits, materials, water sources and types of compression that will lead to a lower-cost construction, considering also the transport costs of the material and of water used in the soil compression, the section type of the dam and the compression process used."

3 An Approach Methodology Based on ZAPROS

A modification to the ZAPROS method [7] is proposed on [14], in order to increase the comparison power of the method. It presents three main stages: Problem Formulation, Elicitation of Preferences and Comparison of Alternatives. An overview of the approach is presented bellow.

3.1 Formal Statement of the Problem

The methodology follows the same problem formulation proposed in [7]:
  Given:

  1) $K = 1, 2,..., N$, representing a set of N criteria;
  2) n_q represents the number of possible values on the scale of q-th criterion, $(q \in K)$; for the ill-structured problems, as in this case, usually $n_q \leq 4$;
  3) $X_q = x_{iq}$ represents a set of values to the q-th criterion, which is this criterion scale; $|X_q| = n_q(q \in K)$; where the values of the scale are ranked from best to worst, and this order does not depend on the values of other scales;
  4) $Y = X_1 * X_2 * ... * X_n$ represents a set of vectors y_i, in such a way that: $y_i = (y_{i1}, y_{i2}, ..., y_{iN})$, and $y_i \in Y$, $y_{iq} \in X_q$ and $P = |Y|$, where $|Y| = \prod_{i=1}^{i=N} n_i$.
  5) $A = \{a_i\} \in Y$, i=1,2,...,t, where the set of t vectors represents the description of the real alternatives.

Required: The multicriteria alternatives classification based on the decision maker's preferences.

3.2 Elicitation of Preferences

In this stage, the scale of preferences for quality variations (Joint Scale of Quality Variations - JSQV) is constructed. The elicitation of preferences follows the order of steps shown in Fig. 1 [14]. This structure is the same proposed in [7]; however, substages 2 and 3 (numbered on the left side of the figure) were put together in just one substage.

Instead of setting the decision maker's preferences based on the first reference situation and, then, establishing another scale of preferences using the second reference situation, we propose that the two substages be transformed in one. The questions made considering the first reference situation are the same as the ones made considering the second reference situation. So, both situations will be presented and must be considered in the answer to the question, in order not to cause dependence of criteria. The alteration reflects on an optimization of the process: instead of making 2n questions, only n will be made. The questions to Quality Variations (QV) belonging to just one criteria will be made as follows: supposing a criterion A having $X_A = A_1, A_2, A_3$, the decision maker will be asked about his preferences between the QV $a_1 - a_2$, $a_1 - a_3$ and $a_2 - a_3$. Thus, there is a maximum of three questions to a criterion with three values ($n_q = 3$).

The question will be formulated dividing the QV into two items on the preferences elicitation for two criteria, because there were difficulties in understanding and delay in the decision maker's answers when exposing the QV of different criteria.

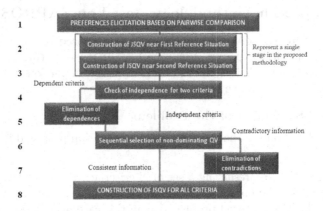

Fig. 1. Elicitation of preferences process

3.3   Comparison of Alternatives

With the aim of reducing the number of incomparability cases, we apply the same structure proposed in [7], but modifying the comparison of pairs of the alternatives' substage according to the one proposed in [9]. Figure 2 shows the structure of the comparison of the alternatives' process.

Each alternative has a function of quality - $V(y)$ [7], depending on the evaluations of the criteria that it represents. In [9], it is proposed that the vectors of ranks of the criteria values, which represent the function of quality, are re-arranged in an ascending order. Then, the values will be compared to the corresponding position of another alternative's vector of values based on Pareto's dominance rule. Meanwhile, this procedure was modified for implementation because it was originally proposed to scales of preferences of criteria values, not for quality variation scales.

So, supposing the comparison between alternatives $Alt1 = A_2, B_2, C_1$ and $Alt2 = A_3, B_1, C_2$, considering a scale of preferences: $a_1 \prec b_1 \prec c_1 \prec a_2 \prec b_2 \prec c_2 \prec a_3 \prec b_3 \prec c_3$, we have the following functions of quality: $V(Alt1) = (0, 0, 2)$ and $V(Alt2) = (0, 3, 4)$, which represents the ranks of, respectively, b_1 and c_1, a_2. Comparing the ranks presented, we can say that Alt1 is preferable to Alt2.

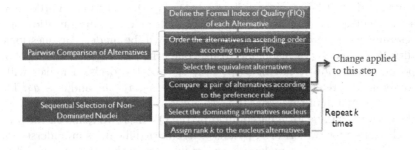

Fig. 2. Alternatives comparison process

However, there are cases in which the incomparability of real alternatives will not allow the presentation of a complete result. These problems require further comparison. In such cases, we can evaluate all possible alternatives to the problem in order to rank the real alternatives indirectly.

3.4   A Tool to the Approach Methodology

In order to facilitate the decision process and perform it consistently, observing its complexity and with the aim of making it accessible, a tool was implemented in Java and it is presented by the following sequence of actions:

- Criteria Definition: The definition of the criteria presented by the problem;
- Preferences Elicitation: Occurring in two stages: the elicitation of preferences for quality variation on the same criteria and the elicitation of preferences between pairs of criteria;
- Alternatives Definition: The alternatives can be defined only after the construction of the scale of preferences;
- Alternatives Classification: After the problem formulation, the user can verify the solution obtained to the problem. The result is presented to the decision maker so that it can be evaluated. The comparison based on all possible alternatives for the problem is possible, but it should be performed only when it is necessary for the problem resolution (for being an elevated cost solution).

4   A Multicriteria Model to Aid in the Choice of Materials to the Construction of Earth Dams

A multicriteria model aiming to define a rank order of the materials that will be used in the dam's construction is presented. The materials and their quantities are determined by an engineer, based on another projects with geotechnical characteristics similar to the ones of the available materials, and their experience in previous projects. Then, the choice of materials and quantities will be facilitated by the ordering obtained after applying the multicriteria model.

The criteria were defined based on the following geometrical characteristics [12]:

1. Compressibility: the capability presented by the soil to decrease its volume when subjected to certain pressure. The criteria values to the compressibility vary from "Very Low" (C1) to "High" (C4);

2. Shear Strength: the capability of soil to resist to shear stress. Due to the frictional nature, the rupture occurs preferentially by shear, becoming an important feature to be observed to guarantee the slope stability. The possible values for this criterion vary from "Very High" (RC1) to "Low" (RC4);

3. Permeability: the facility with which the water flows through the soil. The water may cause unfavorable conditions, affecting the dam's security and

performance when it penetrates in the soil used on the dam. The possible values for this criterion vary from "Very Impermeable" (P1) to "Permeable" (P4);

4. Workability: the convenience of handling and using the material in the construction. It varies from "Very Good" (T1) to "Bad" (T4);

5. Piping Strength: Phenomenon that causes the removal of the soil's particles due to the water flowing through the structure, creating canals that may evolve in an opposite direction to the water flow and it may cause a collapse of the structure. It varies from "High" (RP1) to "Very Low" (P4);

The increasing concern with the environment makes the impact caused by the engineering construction an important criterion. The use of a material that has good geotechnical characteristics may cause a great impact on nature, making its use less interesting than another one with similar characteristics, but causing a minor impact. This way, it was also considered as criteria the features related to the material and the effect of its use:

6. Material Quality, that varies from "Very Good" (QM1) to "Bad" (QM4);

7. Extraction Difficulty: represents the difficulties found in the extraction process considering all material deposits available. The criteria values to the extraction difficulty vary from "Low" (D1) to "Very High" (D4);

8. Environmental Impact: represents the impact caused to the environment when a determined material is used in the construction. It varies from "None" (I1) to "High" (I4).

The preferences' elicitation process was performed by means of interviews with experienced engineers. The information obtained was transformed into the scale of preferences that follows: $rc_1 \prec p_1 \prec c_1 \prec rp_1 \prec rc_2 \prec p_2 \prec rp_2 \prec c_2 \prec q_1 \prec t_1 \prec i_1 \prec d_1 \prec rc_3 \prec p_3 \prec rp_3 \prec c_3 \prec q_2 \prec t_2 \prec i_2 \prec d_2 \prec rc_4 \prec p_4 \prec rp_4 \prec c_4 \prec q_3 \prec t_3 \prec i_3 \prec d_3 \prec rc_5 \prec p_5 \prec rp_5 \prec c_5 \prec q_4 \prec t_4 \prec i_4 \prec d_4 \prec rc_6 \prec p_6 \prec rp_6 \prec c_6 \prec q_5 \prec t_5 \prec i_5 \prec d_5 \prec q_6 \prec t_6 \prec i_6 \prec d_6$.

The case study was applied in the design of zoned dams of Frios reservoir, situated in the same name river, county of Umirim, Ceará, Brazil.

According to the Unified Soil Classification in Araújo (1990 in [12]), the approached dam has zoned section and consists of material from massive type SC (Sand-Clay), SM (Sand-Silt) and residual soil, being these available in eight mines (from J1 to J8). It was included three other types of materials in order to better illustrate the application of the model: M4 (CL - Clay-Low soil), M5 (ML-SC soil) and M6 (ML - Mo-Low soil); also available in the same mines.

The material types were analyzed considering their characteristics based on the criteria previously defined. The values of criteria for the six types of materials, the original classification and the one obtained by the application of the Aranaú tool to the problem are presented in Table 1.

By the application of the proposed methodology, a complete ranking was achieved without being necessary to perform a comparison between all possible alternatives of the problem. Figure 3 shows the graph obtained by the application of the Aranaú Tool to the problem.

Table 1. Material classification for the construction of earth dams

Material	Values of Criteria	Rank
SC (Sand-Clay)	C2 RC2 P2 RP1 T2 Q2 D4 I1	1
SM (Sand-Silt)	C2 RC2 P3 RP2 T3 Q2 D4 I2	3
SM-SC	C2 RC3 P3 RP2 T3 Q2 D4 I2	4
CL (Clay-Low)	C1 RC3 P2 RP1 T2 Q1 D4 I2	2
ML (Mo-Low)	C1 RC4 P2 RP3 T4 Q2 D4 I1	5
ML-CS	C3 RC3 P2 RP2 T3 Q3 D4 I3	6

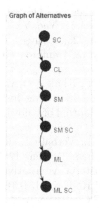

Fig. 3. The graph obtained by the application of the Aranaú Tool to the problem

5   Conclusions

The construction of dams involves a lot of variables, which makes its modeling complex. This work considered some of these variables in order to propose a modeling process, involving multicriteria, with the aim of improving the decision making in the construction of earth dams by observing the lowest cost.

The application of the multicriteria methodology, by means of the Aranaú Tool, aims to facilitate the choice of materials that can be used in the construction of the dam, defining, at the end of the modeling process, a range of minimum and maximum quantities of each material. This way, it was obtained that the best material to be used in the construction is the SC (Sand-Clay).

The work [12] presents an extension to this work, applying non-linear programming in order to determine the best usage of the materials for the construction, the types of compression for the selected materials, the mines of which materials would be extracted and the sources with the volumes of water needed.

As future works, we suggest an improvement of the model, such that the most indicated place to construct a dam, the slope angle and the optimal session would be defined including more evaluation variables. This way, a complete modeling of the problem would be presented.

Acknowledgments. The authors are thankful to the National Counsel of Technological and Scientific Development (CNPq) for all the support received.

References

1. Bordeaux, G.H.M.: Barragens de terra e enrocamento, projeto e construção. Clube de Engenharia, Salvador (1980)
2. Campos, N.B.: Dimensionamento De Reservatórios: O Método Do Diagrama Triangular De Regularização, 51p. Edições UFC, Fortaleza (1996)
3. de Castro, A.K.A., Pinheiro, P.R., Pinheiro, M.C.D.: An Approach for the Neuropsychological Diagnosis of Alzheimer's Disease: A Hybrid Model in Decision Making. In: Wen, P., Li, Y., Polkowski, L., Yao, Y., Tsumoto, S., Wang, G. (eds.) RSKT 2009. LNCS, vol. 5589, pp. 216–223. Springer, Heidelberg (2009)
4. Esteves, V.P.: Barragens de terra. Campina Grande: Escola Politécnica da USP (1964)
5. Evangelou, C., Karacapilidis, N., Khaled, O.A.: Interweaving knowledge management, argumentation and decision making in a collaborative setting: the KAD ontology model. International Journal of Knowledge and Learning 1(1/2), 130–145 (2005)
6. Larichev, O., Moshkovich, H.M.: Verbal decision analysis for unstructured problems. Kluwer Academic Publishers, Boston (1997)
7. Larichev, O.: Ranking Multicriteria Alternatives: The Method ZAPROS III. European Journal of Operational Research 131(3), 550–558 (2001)
8. Machado, S.L., Machado, M.F.C.: Mecânica dos Solos I - Conceitos introdutórios (1997)
9. Moshkovich, H., Mechitov, A., Olson, D.: Ordinal Judgments in Multiattribute Decision Analysis. European Journal of Operational Research 137(3), 625–641 (2002)
10. Narita, K.: Design and Construction of Embankment Dams, Dept. of Civil Eng., Aichi Institute of Technology (2000)
11. Pinheiro, P.R., de Souza, G.G.C., de Castro, A.K.A.: Structuring problem newspaper multicriteria for production. Operational research. Pesqui. Oper., Rio de Janeiro 28(2) (2008), doi:10.1590/S0101-74382008000200002
12. Reis Filho, M.A.M.: A Modeling Process to Optimize the Construction of Earth Dams. In: Master Program in Applied Informatics. University of Fortaleza (2005)
13. Tamanini, I., Machado, T.C.S., Mendes, M.S., Carvalho, A.L., Furtado, M.E.S., Pinheiro, P.R.: A Model for Mobile Television Applications Based on Verbal Decision Analysis. In: Sobh, T. (Org.) Advances in Computer Innovations in Informations Sciences and Engineering, vol. 1, pp. 399–404. Springer, Heidelberg (2008), doi:10.1007/978-1-4020-8741-7_72
14. Tamanini, I., Pinheiro, P.R.: Challenging the Incomparability Problem: An Approach Methodology Based on ZAPROS. Modeling, Computation and Optimization in Information Systems and Management Sciences. Communications in Computer and Information Science 14(1), 344–353 (2008)
15. Tamanini, I., Carvalho, A.L., Castro, A.K.A., Pinheiro, P.R.: A Novel Multicriteria Model Applied to Cashew Chestnut Industrialization Process. Advances in Soft Computing 58(1), 243–252 (2009)
16. Vieira, V.P.P.B., et al.: Roteiro para projeto de pequenos açudes, 160 p. Universidade Federal do Ceará, Fortaleza (1996)

Research on Numerical Analysis of Landslide Cataclysm Mechanism and Reinforcement Treatment Scheme in ShengLi Open-Pit Coal Mine

Yanbo Zhang[1,2], Zhiqiang Kang[1,2], and Chunhua Hou[3]

[1] College of Resources and Environment, Hebei Polytechnic University, Tangshan 063009, Hebei, China
[2] HeBei Province Key Laboratory of Mining Development and Safety Technique, Tangshan 063009, Hebei, China
[3.] Hebei Polytechnic University, Tangshan 063009, Hebei, China
zyb@heut.edu.cn

Abstract. This article according to the ShengLi Open-pit Coal Mine landslide and the slope project special details, used the FLAC numerical calculus analysis software to conduct the research to the landslide cataclysm mechanism, has carried on the optimized analysis to the reinforcement plan.Has obtained the pre-stressed anchor rope frame beam + high pressure splitting grouting reinforcement plan government landslide most superior processing plan through the numerical calculus, thus active control ShengLi Open-pit Coal Mine slope distortion destruction.

Keywords: Numerical calculation; landslide cataclysm mechanism; slope reinforcement plan.

1 Introduction

Along with the coal demand's explosive growth, open pit coal mine's mining scale and the speed obtained the rapid development, the open-air stope deepens year by year, the slope exposition highly, the area as well as the maintenance time unceasingly is also increasing, from this causes the strip mining slope landslide instability accident frequency to send, not only harassed the mine regular production order, the cause country economical property has suffered the heavy loss, moreover also posed the threaten seriously to operating personnel's safety [1, 2, 3].ShengLi No.1 Open-pit Coal Mine located at the ShengLi coal field mid-west, is the ShengLi coal field main mining coal area. Since 2005, east the ShengLi Open-pit Coal Mine the first working area stop the non-work has helped with the northern end gang to have the different scale to fall many times, collapsing, has the enormous influence for the production organization.

Uses the science effective research technique and the method, conducts comprehensively, system's analytical study to the landslide mechanism and the treatment scheme, proposed that essential, practical and feasible prevention countermeasure, is the open pit coal mine carries on the smooth production the safeguard [4, 5, 6, 7]. FLAC (Fast Lagrangian Analysis of Continua, the continuous medium fast Lagrange

R. Zhu et al. (Eds.): ICICA 2010, LNCS 6377, pp. 565–572, 2010.

analysis) is the finite difference numerical calculus procedure which develops by Cundall and American ITASCA Corporation, establishes in the Lagrange algorithm foundation, the especially qualify simulates the big distortion and the distortion. FLAC uses the explicit algorithm obtains the model complete equation of motion (including endomorphism quantity) the time step solution, thus may trace the material the evolution destruction and breaks down falls. This computational method is mainly suitable the soil and rock mechanics analysis, for example ore body landslide, coal mining settlement predict that hydro-junction rock mass stability analyses, mining tunnel investigation into stability and so on.

Therefore, this article utilizes the FLAC numerical simulation software to carry on the cataclysm numerical simulation analysis to the ShengLi Open-pit Coal Mine landslide mechanism [8], through used the research technique which the spot investigation, the numerical simulation and the theoretical analysis unified to conduct the research to the stability of slope, obtained by the time suits the ShengLi Open-pit Coal Mine landslide government some reinforcement treatment scheme, the guarantee ShengLi Open-pit Coal Mine landslide stability.

2   Numerical Calculation and Analysis

(1) The mechanism analysis on slope landslide cataclysm under drying condition

The result of Non-linear large deformation finite different software FLAC as the chart 1 and Figure 2, Loose media slope of quaternary system is presents to be situated the type settlement arc destruction glide[9], on the top of the glide slope presents obvious tensile cracks, When in after the sliding surface lock solid section's marginal value is sheared, displays cuts the destruction form along the toe of slope. This type's slope landslide performance for the upper limb tension fracture, middle locks the triadic cataclysm evolution pattern which solid and the lower limb slipping cuts [10].

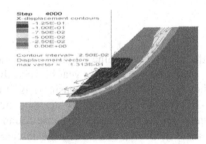   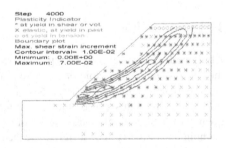

Fig. 1. Horizontal displacement field diagram of quaternary system loose media landslide   **Fig. 2.** Destruction field diagram of quaternary system loose media landslide

(2) The mechanism analysis on slope landslide cataclysm under the effect of rain

From the simulation chart 3 and chart 4, under the infiltration condition of rain, quaternary system loose media full water slope and the dry slope compares, the scope and the displacement quantity of the settlement arc destroys compared to the dry slope settlement arc increases greatly [11], this indicated that under the rain water infiltration ramollescence, it will intensify raise the destruction degree of slope

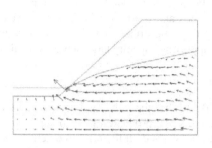
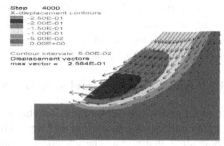

Fig. 3. The diagram of full water slope rain water transfusion field

Fig. 4. The diagram of the full water slope landslide horizontal departure field

May see through the numerical calculus analysis: Upside the ShengLi Open-pit Coal Mine slope work helps fourth is the loose body, (under surface water infiltrates, XiLin river transfusion, toe of slope header capillarity water raising) in the water under the function the after skirt scattered about, is first along fourth is the bottom boundary slips forward, middle and the predestined affinity under the main slippery section thrust force function, cuts the destruction from the toe of slope strong decency putty conglomerate place.

3 Landslide Reinforcement Treatment Scheme Mechanism and Stability Analyses

3.1 The Landslide Reinforcement Treatment Scheme Mechanism Analysis

1. The mechanism of the pre-stressed anchor rope ground beam reinforcing slope
In the pre-stressed anchor rope ground beam structure, the anchor rope and the ground beam combined action, they reinforce the slope the mechanism mainly anchor rope reinforcement slope body's mechanism, namely the anchor rope takes the pre-reinforcement effect through the formidable pre-stressed to the slope body.

2. anchor rope pre-stressed splitting grouting reinforcing mechanism
The anchor rope uses the splitting grouting to be possible to increase anchor rope's anchorage force from many aspects. Uses the splitting grouting technology in the anchor rope note thick liquid working procedure, both can increase the anchoring length and the rock mass contacted area, and can strengthen between both union degree, but can also enhance around the anchoring length the rock mass physical mechanics nature, increases the anchoring length to inlay the solid effect, thus increases the anchorage force.

3. Pre-stressed anchor rope frame beam + high pressure splitting grouting reinforcement mechanism
In the project anchor rope's anchor target weighs by anchor rope's supporting capacity, but anchor rope's supporting capacity is decided by the anchoring length anchorage force. Using the splitting grouting technology is applies the hydraulic fracture principle in the pre-stressed anchor rope grounding project, may enhance the slurry and the rock mass interface limit cohesion strength; simultaneously slurry vein

arteries diffusion, also causes the anchoring length volume and surface area increase, strengthened around the anchoring length the rock and soil mass mechanics characteristic, increased the anchoring length to inlay the solid effect, changed its destruction way, achieved enhances the anchor system supporting capacity large scale the goal.

3.2 Stable Numerical Simulation Analysis

In order to achieve the best reinforcement effect, used the numerical analysis method to simulate the dry condition next three kind of slope protection plan to carry on the contrastive analysis: a. The dry condition has not carried on the reinforcement (to see Figure 5); b. uses pre-stressed anchor rope frame beam to reinforce the technology (to see Figure 6); c. pre-stressed anchor cable frame Liang + the high-pressured splitting grouting reinforcement technology (see Figure 7).

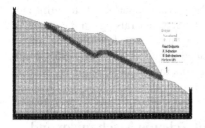

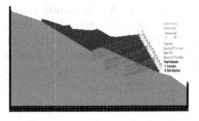

Fig. 5. Mechanical model of drying slope

Fig. 6. Mechanical model of pre-stress frame beam

Fig. 7. Mechanical model of pre-stress frame beam and high press injected slurry

Fig. 8. Displacement vector field distribution diagram of drying slope

2. The calculation results

From figure 8,9,10 we can see, after using the reinforcement measure, the slope displacement vector transforms downward before the reinforcement along the slope face for the vertical slope face is upward, the slope stability is under the obvious control, moreover uses under the high-pressured splitting grouting the slope displacement vector maximum value to be smallest for 3×10-4, the displacement vector field's distribution range adopts under the pre-stressed anchor rope frame beam's displacement vector field distribution to be bigger than purely, showed that uses the splitting grouting , after increasing around the anchoring length the rock and soil mass intensity, may realize the anchoring length bias field proliferation.This is mainly because: Increased the anchor body's volume and the surface area, may under the wide range change landslide body the bedrock intensity, thus increases the anchor effect.

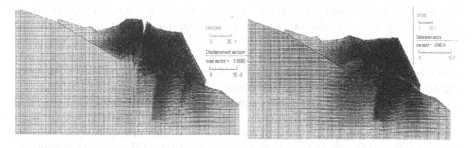

Fig. 9. Displacement vector field distribution diagram of sliding face reinforced by pre-stress frame beam

Fig. 10. Displacement vector field distribution diagram of sliding face reinforced by pre-stress

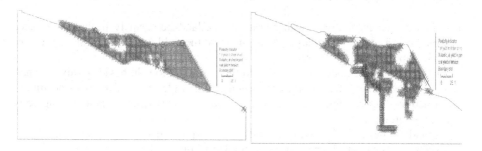

Fig. 11. Broken field distribution diagram of drying slope sliding face

Fig. 12. Broken field distribution diagram of sliding face reinforced by pre-stress frame beam

Fig. 13. Broken field distribution diagram of sliding face reinforced by pre-stress frame beam and high press injected slurry

Figure 11, 12, 13 had demonstrated under three conditions the slope plastic failure area distribution, does not reinforce under the condition the slope destroyed area to be very big, appears in the segmentum anterius pulls the destruction centralism area, is the landside mass, the compartment also appears pulls the destruction, will appear pulls the crack, the after skirt presents the tension fracture to destroy, this with the scene distortion destruction rule will be consistent.Uses under the high-pressured splitting grouting the slope plastic failure scope to reduce obviously, this is mainly because the grouting increases around the anchor body the surrounding rock rock mass intensity, enhances the surrounding rock to pull the destruction which and the shearing failure produces because of anchor rope tension.

Looking from the above numerical calculus analysis result, uses under the pre-stressed anchor rope frame beam + high pressure splitting grouting reinforcement measure the slope mechanics condition to be best[12].This technology both has displayed the pre-stressed anchor rope frame beam's superiority fully, simultaneously and enhanced the anchorage force through the high-pressured splitting grouting, enables the weak gneiss to be able to implement the high tensioning force, the full display opens pulls the function to the gneiss squeezing action, increases the slope skid-resisting capability, to maintained the stability of slope to have the good reinforcement effect.

4 Project Application

For the active control slope, further prevents the landslide cataclysm the occurrence, in the above research's foundation, has conducted the field test research in view of the victory strip mine landslide area.

First sparing water, is being away from the non-work to help bevel certain distance (20~50m), constructs the surface drain; underground elevation 950~960m positions, construction drainage gallery, lowering of ground water level to below dangerous surface or sliding surface.

Second, slope face processing, carries on ramming fill in processing to the land-slide crack of the landside mass surface and behind on the slope face.

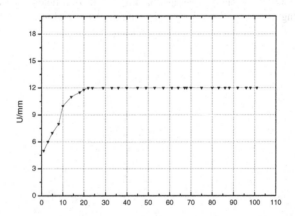

Fig. 14. Test point horizontal departure along with time variation curve

Third, in the landslide predestined affinity pitch, has arranged three row of anchor ropes, length 15~25m, arranges distance 10m, spacing 8m, anchor pole 2×2m, connects with frame beam forms the whole.

Finally the reinforcement plan in the field test process, arranged many intelligent monitor sensor in the slope essential spot to carry on the monitoring target-oriented, the monitor curve see Figure 14. According to the monitoring point monitoring curve, the construction initial period slope has certain displacement under the anchor rope pretightening up force's function, 20 days later the slope stress tends to be balanced, the elastic curve flatten out, does not have the sustained growth change tendency, explained after pre-stressed anchor rope frame beam + high-pressured splitting grouting reinforcement, the slope rock mass is at the safe steady state, the reinforcement effect is good.

5 Conclusion

This article according to the ShengLi Open-pit Coal Mine landslide and the slope project special details, uses method which the numerical simulation and the theoretical analysis unify has carried on to the slope landslide mechanism analysis, mainly draws the following conclusion:

1) In the scene investigation's foundation, utilization theories and so on rock mechanics theory and engineering mechanics, have analyzed the ShengLi strip mine slope landslide major effect factor, and through methods and so on numerical simulation has simulated the landslide cataclysm mechanism;

2) Used the FLAC numerical analysis software to carry on the optimized analysis to the reinforcement plan, proposed that pre-stressed anchor rope frame beam + the high-pressured splitting grouting reinforcement plan might the active control ShengLi Open-pit Coal Mine slope distortion destruction, realize to the glide body's stable control.

Acknowledgements

The authors wish to acknowledge the funding support from HeBei Province Natural Foundation (No E2008000410 and No E2009000782). At the same time, acknowledge the laboratory support from The HeBei Province Key Laboratory of Mining Development and Safety Technique.

References

1. Nianqin, W.: Loess landslides development pattern and the prevention measures. Ph.D. Dissertation of chengdu university of technology (2004)
2. Yourong, L., Huiming, T.: Rockmass mechanics. China University of Geosciences Press, Wuhan (1999)
3. Manchao, H.: Open high slope engineering. Coal Industry Press, Beijing (1991)

4. Changqian, H., Enbao, D.: Slope stability analysis methods. Hydropower Station Design 15(1), 53–58 (1999)
5. Bishop, A.W.: The Use of the Slip Circle in the Stability Analysis of slope. Geotechque 15(1), 7–17 (1995)
6. Janbu, N.: Soil stability computations. In: Hirschfeid, R.C., Poulos, S.J. (eds.) Embankment Dam Engineering, Casagrande Volume, pp. 47–87. John Wiley & Sons, New York (1973)
7. Spencer, E.: A method of analysis for stability of embankment using parallel inters slice force. Geotechnique (17), 11–26 (1967)
8. Jiacheng, Z., Zhangjun, L.: Fuzzy Probability Evaluation and Its Application to Rock Mass Stability Classification. Geological Science and Technology Information 28(1), 109–112 (2009)
9. Li, L., Mingwu, W.: Information entropy-based variable fuzzy sets model for the classification of rock mass stability. Journal of Hefei University of Technology, Natural Science 31(4), 603–607 (2008)
10. Yuhui, D., Hua, X.: Seepage Model and Counting the Parameters on the Rock Mass Stability Analysis. Science Technology and Engineering 9(16), 4709–4713 (2009)
11. Chunmei, D., Jinyu, X.: Extensics in the application of tunnel rock mass stability assessment of underground tunnel engineering. Sichuan Building Science 35(4), 128–130 (2009)
12. Xinping, L., Yifei, D., Jing, H.: Fluid-solid coupling analysis of surrounding rock mass stability and water inflow forecast of a tunnel in a karst zone. Journal of Shandong University, Engineering Science 39(4), 1–6 (2009)

Adaptive Methods for Center Choosing of Radial Basis Function Interpolation: A Review*

Dianxuan Gong[1,**], Chuanan Wei[2], Ling Wang[1],
Lichao Feng[1], and Lidong Wang[3]

[1] College of Sciences, Hebei Polytechnic Universtiy, Tangshan 063009, China
[2] Department of Information Technology, Hainan Medical College, Haikou 571101, China
[3] Department of Mathematics, Dalian Maritime University, Dalian 116026, China
dxgong@heut.edu.cn

Abstract. Radial basis functions provide powerful meshfree method for multivariate interpolation for scattered data. But both the approximation quality and stability depend on the distribution of the center set. Many methods have been constructed to select optimal center sets for radial basis function interpolation. A review of these methods is given. Four kinds of center choosing algorithms which are thinning algorithm, greedy algorithm, arclength equipartition like algorithm and k-means clustering algorithm are introduced with some algorithmic analysis.

Keywords: radial basis function interpolation, greedy algorithm, Native space, thinning algorithm, adaptive method.

1 Introduction

Interpolation by radial basis functions is a well-established method for reconstructing multivariate functions from scattered data. Radial basis function (RBF) methods have been praised for their simplicity and ease of implementation in multivariate scattered data approximation [1]. Since RBF methods are completely meshfree, requiring only interpolation nodes and a set of points called centers defining the basis functions, it leads immediately to the problem of finding good or even optimal point sets for the reconstruction process. Several researchers have incorporated RBF method in several adaptive schemes.

The paper is organized as follows. In section 2 we collect some introductory material and necessary definitions. In section 3, we summarize four kinds of effective center location methods. Some algorithmic analysis also can be found in section 3.

---

* Project supported by Educational Commission of Hebei Province of China (No.2009448), Natural Science Foundation of Hebei Province of China (No.A2009000735) and Natural Science Foundation of Hebei Province of China (No.A2010000908).
** Corresponding author.

R. Zhu et al. (Eds.): ICICA 2010, LNCS 6377, pp. 573–580, 2010.

2 Radial Basis Function

Take a set $X = \{x_1, \cdots, x_N\}$ of N pairwise distinct points coming from a compact subset Ω of R^d. These points $\{x_i\}$ are referred as data sites (or data locations or centers) and the set X as data set. Suppose further that N data values $f_1, \cdots, f_N$ should be interpolated at the data sites. A simple way is to fix a symmetric kernel function $\Phi : \Omega \times \Omega \to R$ and to form an interpolant

$$s_{f,X} = \sum_{j=1}^{N} a_j \Phi(\|x - x_j\|) \tag{1}$$

where $\|\cdot\|$ is the Euclidean norm and the coefficients $\{a_j\}$ are uniquely determined by the interpolation conditions $s_{f,X}(x_j) = f_j$ ($1 \le j \le N$) if the interpolation matrix $A_{\Phi,X} = (\Phi(\|x_i - x_j\|))_{1 \le i, j \le N}$ is invertible. Furthermore, it is sometimes necessary to add the space P_m^d of d-variate polynomials of order not exceeding m to the interpolating function. Call function Φ is conditionally positive definite of order m on R^d, if for all sets X with N distinct points and all vectors $\{a_1, \cdots a_N\}$ satisfying $\sum_{j=1}^{N} a_j p(x_j) = 0$ for all $p \in P_m^d$, the quadratic form $\sum_{i,j=1}^{N} a_i a_j \Phi(\|x_i - x_j\|)$ attains nonnegative values and vanishes only if $a_j = 0$ for all $1 \le j \le N$. Function Φ is called positive definite for the case $m = 0$. Interpolation is uniquely possible under the precondition: If $p \in P_m^d$ satisfies $p(x_j) = 0$ for all $x_j \in X$, then $p = 0$, and Φ is conditionally positive definite of order m [2].

In this paper we focus to the case of positive definiteness, since every conditionally positive definite kernel has an associated normalized positive definite kernel [3].

The kernel Φ defines on the linear space expanded by $\Phi(x, \bullet)$

$$F_\Phi := \left\{ \sum_{j=1}^{M} a_j \Phi(x_j - \bullet) \mid a_j \in R, M \in \mathbb{N}, x_j \in R^d \right\},$$

an inner product via

$$\left(\Phi(x - \bullet), \Phi(y - \bullet) \right)_\Phi = \Phi(x - y), \; x, y \in R^d.$$

The closure of F_Φ with reproducing kernel Φ is called the Native Hilbert space, denoted by $N_\Phi(\Omega)$ [3]. Moreover, there is a Lagrange-type representation of interpolant (1):

$$s_{f,X} = \sum_{j=1}^{N} f(x_j) u_j, \; u_j(x_i) = \delta_{ij}, \; 1 \le i, j \le N.$$

Then the local error estimates have the form

$$\left| f(x) - s_{f,x}(x) \right| \le P_{\Phi,X}(x) \left\| f \right\|_{\Phi}$$

Where $P_{\Phi,X}(x)$ is the power function with explicit form

$$P_{\Phi,X}^2(x) = \Phi(x,x) - 2\sum_{j=1}^{N} u_j(x)\Phi(x,x_j) + \sum_{j=1}^{N} u_j(x)u_k(x)\Phi(x_j,x_k).$$

The power function is bounded in term of fill distance

$$h_{X,\Omega} = \sup_{x \in \Omega} \min_{x_j \in X} \left\| x - x_j \right\|_2$$

and for any function $f \in N_{\Phi}(\Omega)$, the local error of the interpolant is bounded by

$$\left| f - s_{f,X} \right| \le C \cdot h_{X,\Omega}^k \cdot \left\| f \right\|_{\Phi},$$

here $C \in R$ is a constant, k is a natural number and $\left\| f \right\|_{\Phi}$ depends on f and Φ only, details in [4]. On the other hand, as the number of centers grow, RBF method needs to solve a large algebraic system and large condition number of interpolation matrix causing instability makes convergence difficult. Denote separation distance by

$$q_X = \frac{1}{2} \min_{1 \le i \ne j \le N} \left\| x_i - x_j \right\|.$$

Roughly speaking, for a fixed basis function Φ, good approximation quality needs small $h_{X,\Omega}$ and fine stability require large q_X. However one can't minimize $h_{X,\Omega}$ and maximize q_X at same time which is referred to as uncertainty relation.

There are several factors affecting the performance of the RBF interpolation process including kernel function, center distribution, shape parameter and the unknown function. In this paper, we focus to the problem of finding good or even optimal center sets for RBF interpolation process. Many researchers [5, 6, 7, 8, 9, 10] have developed several adaptive schemes. All these algorithms can be roughly divided into two categories: data dependent methods and data independent methods. We will summarize these methods in the next section.

3 Adaptive Methods for Center Locations

In this section, we will display some recent results on selecting near-optimal point sets for interpolation by radial basis functions. Almost all the algorithms are based on theoretical results especially on power function, local error bound and the trade off relation about the point distribution.

According to theoretical research on the error estimate and condition number of RBF interpolation and numerical experiments, a balance between the stability and the approximation quality will be achieved when the point sets is evenly distributed in the domain. By taking the ratio of separation distance q_X and fill distance $h_{X,\Omega}$, Iske A. defined a measure of the uniformity of set X with respect to Ω:

$$\rho_{X,\Omega} = \frac{q_X}{h_{X,\Omega}}.$$

Iske and his cooperator have done a lot of fruitful work on thinning algorithm which removes points from X one by one judging by a pre-selected criterion in order to reach a subset of a certain size. According to the selection of criterion determining which points to be removed, there are several different thinning schemes.

3.1 Thinning Algorithm

Using the uniformity of the subsets as the criterion, we say a point x is removable if the remove of x would maximize the uniformity $\rho_{X,\Omega}$. The following algorithm [5] generates a subset sequence $X = X_N \supset X_{N-1} \supset \cdots \supset X_1$ each of which are chosen to be as evenly distributed in Ω as possible with cardinality $\#(X_i) = i$.

Thinning Algorithm 1

(1) Let $X_N = X$.

(2) For decreasing $i = N, N-1, \cdots, 2,$

    (a) locate a removable point $x \in X_i$,

    (b) let $X_{i-1} = X_i \setminus \{x\}$

(3) Output $X^* = (X_1, X_2, \cdots, X_N)$.

Instead of recursively removing points from $X \subset \Omega$, the inserting algorithm which is the dual of the thinning algorithm recursively iteratively insert points into Ω [6].

Inserting Algorithm

(1) Let $X_0 = \phi$.

(2) For decreasing $i = 0, 1, \cdots, N-1,$

    (a) search for an insertable point $x \in X \setminus X_i$,

    (b) let $X_{i+1} = X_i \cup \{x\}$

(3) Output $X^* = (X_1, X_2, \cdots, X_N)$.

A swapping algorithm also can be found in [6]. On view of algorithmic complexity, for a scattered data set X of N pairwise different centers from general spaces, implement Algorithm 1 requires $O(N^3)$ steps. In planar case, by the method of successive Delaunay triangulations, Algorithm 1 can be improved to be faster requiring only $O(N^2)$ steps.

Thinning Algorithm 2

  (1) Set $X_N = X$ and compute a Delaunay triangulation T_N of X_N.

  (2) For decreasing $i = N, N - 1, \cdots, k + 1$,

    (a) locate a removable point $x \in X_i$,

    (b) let $X_{i-1} = X_i \setminus \{x\}$,

    (c) compute a Delaunay triangulation T_{i-1} from T_i.

  (3) Output $X^* = \left(X_k, X_{k+1}, \cdots, X_N\right)$

Furthermore, by storing the interior nodes of the Delaunay triangulations in a heap and applying the priority queue skill, the computational cost of the thinning algorithm can be reduced to $O(N \log N)$. Algorithm 1 and 2 depends only on the locations of the centers (so it is a non-adaptive thinning) and the numerical result is shown in Fig. 1 from Iske A. [5].

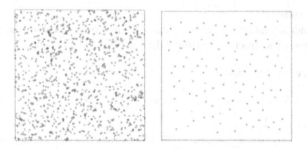

Fig. 1. The center set X and subset X_{100} in Algorithm 1

    All such non-adaptive (data-independent) algorithms produce well distributed sets whose uniformity is large. Moreover, the following theorem is proved in [7]

Theorem 1. Let X be a point set in $\Omega \subset R^d$, then the uniformity of X can be bounded over by

$$\rho_{X,\Omega} \le \sqrt{\frac{(d+1)}{2d}},$$

where equality holds if and only if every simplex of its Delaunay triangulation is regular.

When the criterion, determining whether a point is removable, is chosen to minimize the anticipated error which depends on the function values $\{f(x) : x \in X\}$, the algorithm is called adaptive thinning. Different error measures define different removable points, and lead out different algorithm schemes.

3.2 Greedy Algorithm

In order to minimizing the power function, Marchi S.D., Schaback R. and Wendland H. constructed a numerical greedy algorithm produces near-optimal point sets by recursively adding one of the maxima points of the power function w.r.t. the preceding set [8,9]. Obviously, greedy algorithm is data-dependent and adaptive algorithm.

Greedy Algorithm

(1) Let $X_1 = \{x_1\}$ for $x_1 \in \Omega$ arbitrary.

(2) Do $X_j := X_{j-1} \cup \{x_j\}$ with $P_{\Phi, X_{j-1}}(x_j) = \left\| P_{\Phi, X_{j-1}} \right\|_{L_\infty(\Omega)}$, $j \geq 2$

Until $\left\| P_{\Phi, X_j} \right\|_{L_\infty(\Omega)}$ is small enough.

In practice, the maxima is taken over some large discrete set $X \subset \Omega \subset R^d$. The convergence rate of the above Greedy Algorithm is at least like

$$\left\| P_{\Phi, X_j} \right\|_{L_\infty(\Omega)} \leq C \cdot j^{-1/d}$$

where C is a constant.

Based on numerous numerical experiments of Greedy Algorithm, the same authors suggested a geometric greedy algorithm which is data-independent.

Geometric Greedy Algorithm

(1) Let $\Omega \subset R^d$ be a compact set, and set $X_1 = \{x_1\}$ where x_1 belongs to the boundary of Ω.

(2) For $n \geq 1$, choose $x_{n+1} \in \Omega \setminus X_n$ that its distance to X_n is maximal. Let

$$X_{n+1} := X_n \cup \{x_{n+1}\}.$$

For the sets from Geometric Greedy Algorithm, the following inequalities hold

$$h_{X_n, \Omega} \geq q_{X_n} \geq \frac{1}{2} h_{X_{n-1}, \Omega} \geq \frac{1}{2} h_{X_n, \Omega}.$$

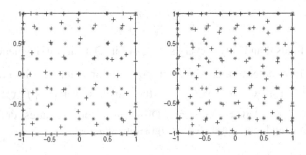

Fig. 2. Points (*) are from Geometric greedy algorithm, (+) are from greedy algorithm

Let X be 10000 random points picked on square $[-1,1] \times [-1,1]$, and the first 65 optimal points for Gaussian (left) and 80 optimal points for Wendland's function (right) by Greedy and Geometric Greedy algorithm are show in Fig. 2 from [8].

3.3 Arc Length Equipartition Like Algorithm

Based on the idea that to display a function with some finite discrete sampling data efficiently, one requires more sampling data where the function is more oscillatory, and less sampling data where the function is more flat, Wu Z.M. [10] and Sarra S.A. [11] both used arclength equipartition algorithm to solve PDEs.

Driscoll T.A. and Heryudono A.R.H. provide a so called residual subsampling method [12]. Take 1D case for example: First, fit the unknown function using a number of equally spaced centers. Second, compute interpolation error at halfway point between the nodes, add the points where the error exceed an upper threshold to the center set, and the centers whose error is below a lower threshold will be removed. An example of Runge function on interval [-1, 1] is shown in Fig. 3.

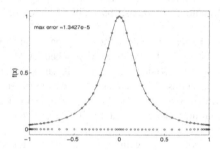

Fig. 3. Numerical example for residual subsampling method

3.4 k-Means Clustering Algorithm

Finally, k-means clustering algorithm commonly used in radial basis function neural networks is easy to implement and of high performance [13]. The working process of k-means: first, choose arbitrary k points as the initial cluster centers. For all other points, compute their Euclidean distances to the k cluster centers, and add each to its nearest cluster. Then recalculate the k cluster centers by taking the geometric center of each cluster, and repeat the above process until the center errors go below a given threshold. This is also a data-independent method.

4 Conclusion

In this paper, focusing on the effect of center locations on RBF interpolation, we introduced the useful RBF method and reviewed four kinds of center choosing algorithms (Thinning Algorithm, Greedy Algorithm, ArcLength Equipartition Like Algorithm and k-Means Clustering Algorithm). This is an important problem as one always want to get higher accuracy with fewer data points. According to the theoretical results of RBF methods, the error estimate relies on both center locations and the unknown function. So, to found the optimal data sets, a data-dependent method is required. We have done preliminary research on this topic, but a rule for the best weight function is still unfound.

References

1. Buhmann, M.D.: Radial Basis Functions: Theory and Implementations. In: Cambridge Monographs on Applied and Computational Mathematics, Cambridge, vol. 12 (2003)
2. Micchelli, C.A.: Interpolation of scattered data: distance matrix and conditionally positive definite functions. Constructive Approximation 2, 11–22 (1986)
3. Schaback, R.: Native Hilbert Spaces for Radial Basis Functions I. International Series of Numerical Mathematics 132, 255–282 (1999)
4. Wu, Z.M., Schaback, R.: Local error estimates for radial basis function interpolation of scattered data. IMA Journal of Numerical Analysis 13, 13–27 (1993)
5. Floater, M.S., Iske, A.: Thinning algorithms for scattered data interpolation. BIT Numerical Mathematics 38(4), 705–720 (1998)
6. Floater, M.S., Iske, A.: Thinning, inserting, and swapping scattered data. In: Surface Fitting and Multi-Resolution Methods, pp. 139–144. Vanderbilt University Press, Nashville (1996)
7. Iske, A.: Optimal distribution of centers for radial basis function methods. Technical Report TUM-M0004, Technische UniversitÄat MÄunchen (2000)
8. Marchi, S.D.: On optimal center locations for radial basis function interpolation: computational aspects. Rend. Splines Radial Basis Functions and Applications 61(3), 343–358 (2003)
9. Marchi, S.D., Schaback, R., Wendland, H.: Near-optimal data-independent point locations for radial basis function interpolation. Advances in Computational Mathematics 23, 317–330 (2005)
10. Wu, Z.M.: Dynamically knots setting in meshless method for solving time dependent propagations equation. Computer Methods in Applied Mechanics and Engineering 193, 1221–1229 (2004)
11. Sarra, S.A.: Adaptive radial basis function methods for time dependent partial differential equations. Applied Numerical Mathematics 54, 79–94 (2005)
12. Driscoll, T.A., Heryudono, A.R.H.: Adaptive residual subsampling methods for radial basis function interpolation and collocation problems. Computers and Mathematics with Applications 53, 927–939 (2007)
13. Preparata, F.P., Shamos, M.I.: Computational Geometry. Springer, New York (1985)
14. Wang, R.H., Li, C.J., Zhu, C.G.: Textbook of Computational Geometry. Science Press, Beijing (2008)
15. Gong, D.X.: Some Research on Theory of Piecewise Algebraic Variety and RBF Interpolation. Dalian, Ph.D. theses of Dalian University of Technology (2009)
16. Tomohiro, A., Sadanori, K., Seiya, I.: Nonlinear regression modeling via regularized radial basis function networks. Journal of Statistical Planning and Inference 138(11), 3616–3633 (2008)
17. Dua, H.P., Nong, Z.G.: Time series prediction using evolving radial basis function networks with new encoding scheme. Neurocomputing 71(7-9), 1388–1400 (2008)
18. Boyd, J.P.: Error saturation in Gaussian radial basis functions on a finite interval. Journal of Computational and Applied Mathematics 234(5), 1435–1441 (2010)
19. Boyd, J.P., Wang, L.: An analytic approximation to the cardinal functions of Gaussian radial basis functions on an infinite lattice. Applied Mathematics and Computation 215(6), 2215–2223 (2009)

Novel Approach for the Design of Half-Band Filter

Xiaohong Huang[1] and Zhaohua Wang[2]

[1] College of information, Hebei Polytech University,
Tangshan, 063009, China
[2] School of Electronic and Information Engineering, Tianjin University,
Tianjin, 300072, China
tshxh@163.com

Abstract. A novel design method of all phase frequency sampling filter are proposed, and can be used to design half-band filter according to the length of filter. Because the amplitude frequency response of this kind of half-band filter is between 0 and 1, no negative, so can be spectral factorized directly to get analysis filter of all phase PR-QMF. The power complementary of the analysis filter is up to 4×10^{-12}dB due to the high spectral factorization accuracy, while the traditional method is only 4×10^{-3}dB.The ratio of signal to noise and the signal reconstruction error of all phase PR-QMF is four times higher and 10^9 lower than traditional PR-QMF respectively.

Keywords: All phase half-band filter; spectral factorization; reconstruction error.

1 Introduction

Half-band filters find several applications in filter banks, wavelets based compression, and multirate techniques. Several designs and implementation tricks have been proposed [1, 2, 11]. By spectral factorization on half-band filter to design PR-QMF (perfect reconstruction-QMF) is proposed in [3], the characteristic of half-band influences the characteristic of PR-QMF deeply. So to design PR-QMF is to design an efficient linear phase half-band filter eventually. There usually has three methods to design half-band filter: Parks-McClellan iterative algorithm [4], lagrange interpolation method [5, 6], single-band filter method [7], but frequency response of the designed half-band filter by all these methods has negative value, so an adjustment is required to make the frequency response are non-negative, the resulting power complementary filter attenuation can only reach 10^{-3} dB due to the choose of adjustment factor. In this paper, all phase half-band filter design methods are put forward, which don't need do optimization and adjustment to do spectral factorization compared with other methods, so the resulting PR-QMF has more better reconstruction property.

2 All Phase DFT Filter

All phase DFT filter design method was introduced in [8, 9]. This filter design method is an excellent method of FIR filter which has the properties both of

R. Zhu et al. (Eds.): ICICA 2010, LNCS 6377, pp. 581–588, 2010.

frequency sampling method and window method. All phase DFT filter has linear phase, less pass-band and stop-band ripples, and higher stop-band attenuation, can control precisely the frequency response at the sampling points. It should be pointed out that: The performance of the filter can be increased by adding a convolution window. It has proved that N-order all phase filter is equivalent to $2N - 1$ order FIR filter with convolution window [10]. The design method of all phase DFT filter is summarized as follows:

(i) According to design requirements, to choose the number of frequency sampling points N, and select the length of all phase DFT filter: $M = 2N - 1$.

(ii) Sampling interval the amplitude frequency response $H_g(\omega)$ of the ideal zero-phase FIR filter in $[0 \ 2\pi]$, $\omega = 2\pi k / N$, or $\omega = 2\pi(k + 1/2)/N, k = 0,1 \cdots N-1$. And the frequency characteristics was even symmetry to $\omega = 0, \pi, 2\pi$.

Let frequency response of the all phase DFT filter is:

$$H_N^1(k) = H_g(2\pi k / N), \ (k \geq 1, \text{is integer}) \qquad (\text{type1}) \qquad (1)$$

$$H_N^2(k) = H_g(2\pi(k + \frac{1}{2})/N), \ (k \geq 1, \text{is integer}) \qquad (\text{type2}) \qquad (2)$$

Substituted $H_N^1(k)$ into the following formula (3) (type1)

$$\begin{cases} h_N(n) = w_N(n)IDFT[H_N^1(k)] \\ h_N(n) = h_N(-n) \end{cases} n, k = 0,1, \cdots N-1. \qquad (3)$$

Substituted $H_N^2(k)$ into the following formula (4) (type 2)

$$\begin{cases} h_N(n) = e^{j\pi(0:N-1)/N} w_N(n)IDFT[H_N^2(k)] \\ h_N(n) = h_N(-n) \end{cases} n, k = 0,1, \cdots N-1 \cdot \qquad (4)$$

Where $w_N(n)$ is the second half of normalized correlation convolution window, that means: $w_N(n) = (f_N(n) * b_N(n))/c$, $c = w_N(0)$ is normalized factor, $f_N(n)$ and $b_N(n)$ are any symmetric windows except rectangular window or both are rectangular window. Obtained the coefficients of all phase filter $h_N(n), n = -N+1, -N+2, \cdots N-2, N-1$.

It is clear that we can get $2N-1$ all phase filter coefficients where traditional sampling method can only get N FIR filter coefficients under the same condition of N sampling points from the above process. The filter property of traditional FIR filter is not good enough even adds the sampling points up to $2N-1$ [8, 9].

3 All Phase Half-Band Filter

All phase half-band filter is a subset of all phase DFT filter, at the same time it meets half-band filter characteristics, namely:

$$H(e^{j\omega}) + H(e^{j(\pi-\omega)}) = 1,$$
(5)

$$\omega_s = \pi - \omega_p,$$
(6)

ω_p and ω_s are respectively pass-band and stop-band cutoff frequency of half-band filter frequency response.

It has pointed that the length of the filter N is even in the complete reconstruction QMF banks [7], the length of half-band filter M is odd, $M = 2N - 1$. N can be divided into two even cases: $N = 4k$, and $N = 4k + 2$, k is a positive integer, so accordingly, there are two kinds of method to design all phase half-band filter.

(i) When $N = 4k$, applying all phase DFT filter type2 design method, the filter response vector of half-band filter $H_N(k)$ is designed as follows:

$$\boldsymbol{H}_N(k) = [\underbrace{1 \ \dots \ 1}_{N/4} \ \underbrace{0 \ \dots \ 0}_{N/2} \ \underbrace{1 \ \dots \ 1}_{N/4}]$$

It can be calculated according to equation (4):

$$h_N(n) = e^{j\frac{\pi}{N}n} w_N(n) \frac{1}{N} \sum_{k=0}^{N-1} H_N(k) W_N^{-kn} = e^{j\frac{\pi}{N}n} w_N(n) \frac{1}{N} (\sum_{k=0}^{\frac{N}{4}-1} W_N^{-kn} + \sum_{k=\frac{3N}{4}}^{N-1} W_N^{-kn})$$

$$= \frac{1}{N} w_N(n) \sum_{k=0}^{\frac{N}{4}-1} [e^{j\frac{\pi n}{N}(2k+1)} (1 + e^{j\frac{3}{2}\pi n})]$$
(7)

Let $n = 0$ in the equation (21), we get $h_N(0) = 0.5$. Let $n = 2m$ ($m \neq 0$) in the equation (7), we get $h_N(2m) = 0$ and $h_N(n) = h_N(-n)$, meeting the definition of half-band filter.

(ii) When $N = 4k+2$, applying all phase DFT filter type1 design method, the filter response vector of half-band filter $H_N(k)$ is design as follows:

$$\boldsymbol{H}_N(k) = [\underbrace{1 \ 1 \dots \ 1}_{N/4} \ \underbrace{0 \ \dots \ 0}_{N/2} \ \underbrace{1 \ \dots \ 1}_{N/4}] \ .$$

It can be calculated according to equation (3):

$$h_N(n) = w_N(n) \frac{1}{N} \sum_{k=0}^{N-1} H_N(k) W_N^{-kn} = w_N(n) \frac{1}{N} [1 + \sum_{k=1}^{\frac{N-2}{4}} W_N^{-kn} + \sum_{k=\frac{3N+2}{4}}^{N-1} W_N^{-kn}] =$$

$$w_N(n) \frac{1}{N} [1 + \sum_{k=1}^{\frac{N-2}{4}} W_N^{-kn} (1 + W_N^{-(\frac{3N+2}{4}-1)n})].$$
(8)

Similarly, satisfy the definition of half-band filter.

Example 1. Design half-band filter with normalized cutoff frequency 0.45(*Rad*).

Choose the length of the filter $M = 39$, the number sampling frequency points $N = 20$, so applying all phase DFT filter type2 design method ,that means :

$$H_{20}(k) = [1\ 1\ 1\ 1\ 1\ 0\ 0\ 0\ 0\ 0\ 0\ 0\ 0\ 0\ 0\ 1\ 1\ 1\ 1\ 1].$$

Substitute DFT filter response into the equation (4) (correlation convolution window is the convolution of double rectangular windows), we get the unit impulse response of all phase half-band filter, as shown in Table 1. Since $h_{20}(n)$ is even symmetry, so only half of the symmetrical coefficients are list.

Table 1. Coefficients of all phase half-band filter h20(n).

n	h20(n)	n	h20(n)
0	0.50000000000000	10	0
1	0.30364152802123	11	-0.02278046533023
2	0	12	0
3	-0.09361429374487	13	0.01964070915860
4	0	14	0
5	0.05303300858899	15	-0.01767766952966
6	0	16	0
7	-0.03647560272312	17	0.01652016948439
8	0	18	0
9	0.02784279095917	19	-0.01598113305375

The solid line in Figure 2 is the frequency response $H_{20}(e^{j\omega})$ designed by this paper's method, no overshoot phenomenon; the amplitude is between 0 and 1. It is steeper than the traditional half-band filter. Dotted lines is the frequency response $H_{20}(e^{j\omega})$ designed by the method of reference [10], the transition band is significantly wider than the solid line because it has add the transition point of 0.5 in the method of reference [10].

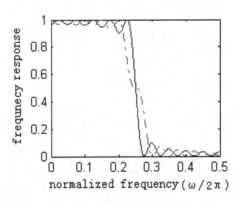

Fig. 2. Comparison of half-band filter amplitude frequency response (Solid line is obtained by the present method, and dashed line is obtained by the literature [10] method)

4 Design of Perfect Reconstruction QMF by All Phase Half-Band Filter Spectral Factorization

We can get low-pass filter in perfect reconstruction QMF bank by half-band filters spectral factorization. Because the half-band filter $H(z)$ has the pairs root $\left\{a_i, \dfrac{1}{a_i}\right\}$, so $H(z)$ can be expressed as the following polynomial form:

$$H(z) = A\prod_{i=1}^{N-1}((1 - a_i z^{-1})(1 - \overline{a_i}z)) \tag{9}$$

If there is a root of $H(z)$ in the unit circle, there will have one outside of the unit circle. Without loss of generality, let $|a_i| < 1$, and let all the roots of $H(z)$ that are less than 1 form $B_0(z)$, namely:

$$B_0(z) = \sqrt{A}\prod_{i=1}^{N-1}(1 - a_i z^{-1}) \tag{10}$$

$B_0(z)$ is the minimum phase spectral factor of $H(z)$, forms the low-pass filter in the perfect reconstruction QMF bank, and then other filters can be obtained easily.

Now do spectral factorization on all phase half-band filter $H_{20}(z)$ designed in example 1. Zeros distribution before and after spectral factorization in the z plane is shown in Figure 3. It is shown that zeros on the unit circle of all phase half-band filter are double zeros, the other roots are conjugate symmetric form in couple, which can ensure that $B_0(z)$ is real-valued function.

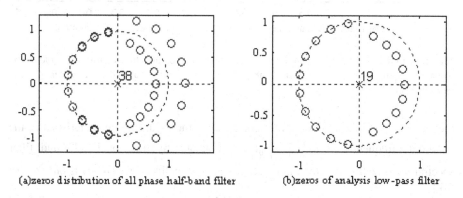

(a)zeros distribution of all phase half-band filter   (b)zeros of analysis low-pass filter

Fig. 3. Zeros distribution in the Z plane

Amplitude frequency response of the analysis filter and the logarithm characteristics of the amplitude frequency of $|B_0(z)|^2 + |B_0(-z)^2|$ are obtained in Figure 4. It can be seen that power complementary characteristics is good, accuracy is 4×10^{-12}dB. In

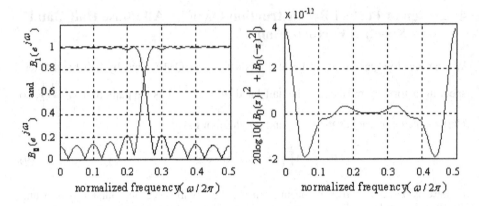

Fig. 4. Amplitude frequency response of the analysis filter and the logarithm characteristic of power complementary of QMF banks obtained by all phase type2 half-band filter spectral factorization

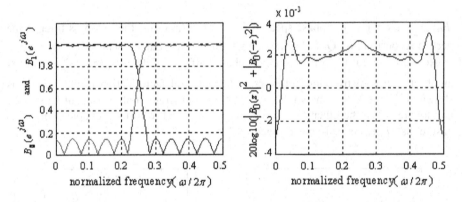

Fig. 5. Amplitude frequency response of the analysis filter and the logarithm characteristic of power complementary of QMF banks obtained by traditional half-band filter spectral factorization

the case of the same length of filter coefficients ,the logarithm characteristics of the amplitude frequency of $|B_0(z)|^2 + |B_0(-z)^2|$ obtained by traditional half-band filter spectral factorization is shown in Fig. 5, it can be seen that the accuracy is only 4×10^3 dB [3].

To measure the reconstruction error of QMF banks obtained by all phase half-band filter and half-band filter in literature [3], we use unit impulse $\delta(n)$ as input signal, the length of filter is $N=20$, all sample number is $L=60$, the delay between input and output signal is 19, We compute the reconstruction error and SNR by the formula (11) and (12):

$$err = \frac{1}{L}\sum_{n=0}^{L-1}\left|y(n) - \delta(n - N - 1)\right| \tag{11}$$

$$SNR = 10\times\log 10(\sum_{n=N}^{N+L} y^2(n) - \sum_{n=N}^{N+L}(y(n - N - 1) - y(n))^2) \tag{12}$$

The comparative result is as Table 2. It shows that QMF banks designed by all phase half-band filter has perfect reconstruction characteristics.

Table 2. Comparison of QMF banks reconstruction error

	err	SNR
Method in this paper	1.0860e-014	249.8078
Method in the literature[3]	2.4392e-005	63.5956

5 Conclusion

A new design method of half-band filter: all phase DFT half-band filter is proposed, and prove that the QMF filter banks obtained by spectral factorization all phase half-band filter has perfect reconstruction characteristics. If changing the window during the design process, the complementary properties will be better.

References

1. Khan, I.R.: Flat magnitude response FIR halfband low/high pass digital filters with narrow transition bands. Digital Signal Processing 20, 328–336 (2010)
2. Patil, B.D., Patwardhan, P.G., Gadre, V.M.: On the Design of FIR Wavelet Filter Banks Using Factorization of a Halfband Polynomial. IEEE Signal Processing Letters 15, 485–488 (2008)
3. Smith, M.J.T., Barnwell, T.P.: Exact reconstruction techniques for tree-structured subband coders. IEEE Trans. Acoust. Speech Signal Processing 34, 434–441 (1986)
4. McClellan, J.H., Parks, T.W., Rabiner, T.W.: A computer program for designing optimum FIR linear phase gigital filters. IEEE Trans. Audio Electroacoust AU-21, 506–526 (1973)
5. Horng, B.R., Willson Jr., A.N.: Lagrange multiplier approaches to the design of two-channel perfect reconstruction linear-phase FIR filter banks. IEEE Trans. on Signal Processing 40, 364–374 (1992)
6. Ansari, R., Guillemot, C., et al.: Wavelet Construction Using Lagrange Halfband Filters. IEEE Trans. CAS 38, 116–118 (1991)
7. Vaidyanathan, P.P.: Multirate Systems and Filter Banks. PrenticeHall, Englewood Cliffs (1993)
8. Xiaohong, H., Jinsheng, S., Zhaohua, W.: FIR Filter Design based on All Phase Symmetric Frequency Sampling Method. In: ICIEA 2006, 1ST IEEE Conference on Industrial Electronics and Applications, pp. 864–868 (May 2006)

9. Xiaohong, H., Zhaohua, W.: Two Kinds of All Phase Half-Band Filter and It's Application in the Filter Banks. Journal of Tianjin University (Science and Technology) 39, 820–826 (2006)
10. Nini, X., Zhengxin, H.: All-phase half-band filter. Journal of Tianjin University (Science and Technology) 38, 206–211 (2005)
11. Nauyen, T.Q., Vaidyanathan, P.P.: Two-channel perfect-reconstruction FIR QMF structure which yield linear-phase analysis and synthesis filters. IEEE Trans. Signal Processing 37, 676–690 (1989)

Key Technique of GMTM for Numerical Analysis Modeling in Geotechnical Engineering: Calculation Region Cutting

Yongliang Lin[1] and Xinxing Li[2]

[1] Civil department of Engineering, Shanghai University, Shanghai, China
[2] R&D Department, Shanghai Tunnel Engineering and Rail Transit Design
& Research Institute, Shanghai, China
{lin_yliang,lxxxinyue}@163.com

Abstract. In order to solve the modeling problem of geotechnical engineering numerical simulation in complex geological condition, a new and practical modeling method (Geologic Model Transforming Method) of numerical analysis by combining geologic model and numerical model has been presented. In GMTM, there are three key techniques be used to realize the model transformation from geological model to numerical model. These techniques include calculation region cutting, surface model reconstructing and finite element automeshing. Calculation region cutting as the first key technique in GMTM is introduced mainly in this paper. The realizing process of the algorithm is exposited in detail. Finally, an example is given to illustrate the application of the technique. By region cutting technique, local model in 3D geological model could be extracted dynamically and the construction process could be simulated conveniently and the excavation boundary must not be defined in advance. Some useful references would be given by the proposed technique to the continuous researches on this subject.

Keywords: Geologic model transforming method; numerical simulation; mesh automatic generation; calculation region cutting.

1 Introduction

With the development of the computer technology, finite element method (FEM) is widely used in geotechnical engineering. As we know, its use usually requires high numerical costs and accurate measurements of the properties of the component materials, which are often difficult to achieve. Then, only the qualitative analysis is carried out by the FEM and the accuracy of result is nearly correlative with the accuracy of numerical model. Nowadays, the numerical model is often constructed following the process of control point, control line, control area and element meshing. So some deficiency is formed [1]. Therefore, preprocessing system is one of the core parts of the finite element analysis and a good preprocessor plays an important role in the

R. Zhu et al. (Eds.): ICICA 2010, LNCS 6377, pp. 589–596, 2010.

success of the method. At present, the geology simulation has the powerful function of 3D geological modeling. 3D strata model can be established by borehole data, and it can reflect the furthest actual geological conditions, especially for complex geological conditions. If the geologic model can be transformed into numerical analysis model and its data can also be directly introduced, the preprocessing system will be consumedly simplified. Many studies were conducted using this method [2, 3, 4, 5]. However, the implementation procedure is rather complex and the man-machine interactive operation is greatly frequent.

Considering the certain similarities in modeling and spatial analysis between geologic model and numerical model, the **GMTM** (Geologic Model Transforming Method) is proposed to transform the geologic model into numerical model rapidly [6, 7, 8]. In this proposed method the technique of calculation region cutting is one of the key techniques and the paper focus on it. Finally, an instance is presented to illustrate the validity of this proposed method.

2   Basic Concepts of GMTM

In this method, the techniques of region cutting, reconstruction of model and finite element meshing automatically are adopted in turn. The initial model is constructed by the techniques of region cutting and reconstruction of model based on geologic model. Then, the automatic generation techniques of surface meshing and solid meshing are utilized and the numerical analysis model for FEM is established. The flowchart of the transforming process is shown in Fig. 1.

3   Calculation Region Cutting Technique

Considering the difference of modeling domain and peripheral shape between geologic model and numerical model, the region cutting technique is proposed. Using the technique, the cutting model can be obtained from the geologic model. In this method, three processes are included: intersection checking before cutting, intersection calculating and model reconstructing. The program of intersection checking estimates the spatial relation (detachment, coplanarity or intersection) between cutting surface and being cut surface. If the intersection relationships exist, the intersection algorithm must be introduced in order to obtain the points or lines of intersection. The topological relations are changed when the region cutting is performed on the original strata surface model. In order to keep the same topological structure of nodes, the cutting model should be reconstructed. This paper focus on the technique of region cutting which includes the techniques of intersection checking and intersection algorithm included.

The GMTM is proposed based on the geologic model which is constructed by the TIN (Triangulated irregular network). To facilitate numerical modeling, it is very important to confirm the region cutting range and cutting surface shape.

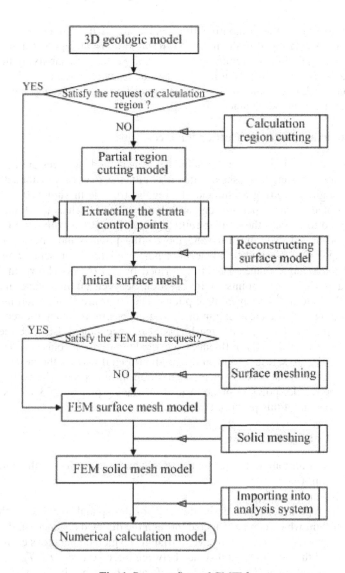

Fig. 1. Program flow of GMTM

3.1 Confirmation for Region Cutting Boundary

According to the engineering geological condition and the survey data, the 3D strata surface model is established with the geological modeling technology. It has the advantages of better accuracy for strata attribute and larger overlying region. For a practical engineer, the numerical model is established aiming at the partial research region instead of the whole area. So it is unnecessary to take the overlying region of the geologic model as the research region of the calculation model.

In order to reduce the computing time and scale of the numerical analysis, the region cutting is performed in the method. The conditions which determine the calculation region usually include removing the boundary effect and satisfying the calculation accuracy. By the region cutting, the partial research region can be arbitrarily acquired on the 3D geologic model. Aiming at different engineering, the reasonable calculation region can be obtained [6].

3.2 Construction of Region Cutting Surface

In 3D geologic modeling, the stratigraphic sections or fault surfaces are described by irregularly spaced triangle meshes. After it is cut, the new curved model is reconstructed through the cutting arithmetic of irregular triangle meshing[10]. The cutting surfaces adopted in this paper are regular polygon planes, such as quadrangles. If the **TIN** is applied to express the regular cutting plane, the cutting arithmetic is the intersection algorithm of different **TIN** and the cutting point is the intersection of two triangles. Fig.2 shows a cutting plane of pentagon plane. It presents 7 intersecting points and the triangle plane of stratum formed by 3 **TIN**. As shown in Fig.2, the points P_3 and P_5 are the points of intersection between cutting plane and stratum plane, but they are not the key control points. The reconstruction of cutting model is implemented through the basic datum of cutting intersections. When the reconstructed model is adopted to calculate, the mesh should be regenerated. Because the quantity of obligatory points directly influences the quality of mesh, only the key control points of stratum are selected to form the mesh efficiently. Thus, the points P_3 and P_5 should be deleted in the process of reconstruction. In this paper, the cutting plane is assumed to be regular polygon plane instead of triangle plane. Fig.3 shows the intersection relationship of this proposed method.

3.3 Region Cutting Technique

The technique of region cutting presented in this paper improves on the conventional cutting algorithm[6].

(1) *Intersection checking*

Before the region cutting, we should confirm the spatial location of the cutting plane and stratum which can be detected through the directed distance. In this method, the polygon plane is dispersed into several triangles which do not cross each other.

It is assumed that the directed distance between three vertices (T_A, T_B, T_C) of triangle (T) and spatial plane (π-plane) are d_1, d_2 and d_3, respectively. It is defined as following:

① when $d_1=0$, $d_2=0$ and $d_3=0$, the triangle is coplanar with the π-plane;

② when $d_1 \times d_2 > 0$ and $d_1 \times d_3 > 0$, the triangle is independent of the π-plane;

Else, the triangle intersects with the π-plane;

(2) *Intersection algorithm*

According to the spatial relationship of the two lines of intersection, the intersecting points and lines can be obtained. If the intersecting line exists, the triangle intersects with polygon. Else, they are detached. After intersection checking and intersection calculating, the control points and lines is obtained.

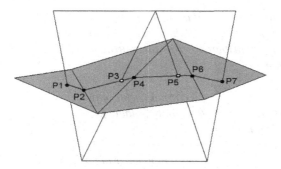

Fig. 2. TIN-TIN intersection

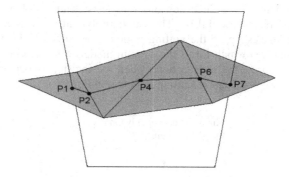

Fig. 3. TIN-Polygon intersection

4 Algorithm Implementation

The basic geometric model which is adopted in this algorithm is divided into 5 classes: Class **Point**, Class **Side**, Class **Triangle**, Class **Plane** and Class **Polygon**. They are defined as following:

```
Class Point
{ Private :
    int  index;        // point number
    double  m_x;       // x-coordinate
    double  m_y;       // y-coordinate
    double  m_z;       // z-coordinate
    int m_attrib(2);   // attribute-marker of two adjacent stratum }
Class Side
{ Private :
    int  index;           // segment number
    Point  m_pt(2);       // two points of segment }
Class Triangle
{ Private :
```

```
    int  index;          // triangle number
    Point  m_pt(3);      // three vertices of triangle
    int  m_triattribute;    //stratum attribution }
Class Plane
{ Private :
    Vector  m_n;         // normal vector of plane
    Point  m_pt;         // a point of plane  }
Class Polygon
{ Private :
    int  m_npts;         // point number of polygon
    PTLIST  m_Ppt;       // vertex list of polygon
    Vector  m_n;         // normal vector of polygon plane }
```

In this method there are three key one–way lists: CuttingPolygonList, Stratum-TrianglelList and IntersectionPtList. The CuttingPolygonList is used to manage the polygons which makes up of the cutting region. The StratumTrianglelList aims at managing the triangles which forms the stratum model. And the IntersectionPtList is introduced to memorize the intersections when the incision is performed. The program flow of Calculation Region Cutting is shown in Fig.4.

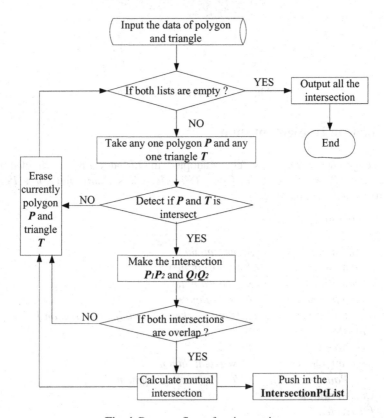

Fig. 4. Program flow of region cutting

5 Verification

To illustrate the application of the region cutting, an example is presented in this section. The information of boreholes is extracted from database. The number of boreholes and strata are 16 and 3, respectively. The total number of the strata control points is 64. The geologic surface model is constructed by the algorithm of the geologic modeling (Fig. 5). The total number of the **TIN** is 144, and the different stratum attribute is indicated with different colors.

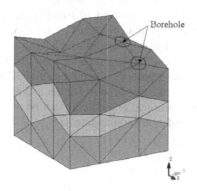

Fig. 5. 3D geologic surface model

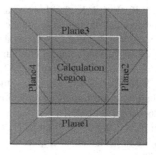

Fig. 6. Cutting region

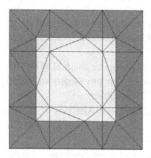

Fig. 7. Topological relations   **Fig. 8.** Model after cutting process

It is assumed the cutting surface is composed of four vertical planes as shown in Fig. 6. And the new topological relations are shown in Fig 7, respectively. And Fig. 8 shows the intersecting points and the lines of intersection after cutting process.

6 Conclusions

This paper focuses on the technique of cutting region of geologic model transforming method. In this method, the intersection calculating with geologic model TIN is performed through the polygon plane instead of triangle plane. It can reduce the frequency of intersection operation and the points of intersection obtained are entirely the control points of stratum. Although introduced here in a polygon plane, it can also be adapted and improved for cutting spatial curved surface. By the region cutting, the partial research region can be arbitrarily acquired on the 3D geologic model. Thus, it is unnecessary to rebuild the calculation model again and again. At the same time, the construction process in geotechnical engineering can be simulated expediently, such as the excavation of the foundation and the tunnel.

References

1. Li, X.X., Zhu, H.H., Chai, Y.C., et al.: An automatic modeling method of numerical analysis in geotechnical engineering based on 3D geologic model. Chinese Journal of Geotechnical Engineering 30, 855–862 (2008)
2. Hou, E.K., Wu, L.X., Li, J.M., et al.: Study on the coupling of 3D geoscience modeling with numerical simulation. Journal of China Coal Society 27, 388–392 (2002)
3. Xu, N.X., Wu, X., Wang, X.G., et al.: Approach to automatic hexahedron mesh generation for rock-mass with complex structure based on 3D geological modeling. Chinese Journal of Geotechnical Engineering 28, 957–961 (2006)
4. Xia, Y.H., Bai, S.W., Ni, C.S.: Study on coupling of 3D visualization with numerical simulation for powerhouse excavation of a certain hydro-junction. Rock and Soil Mechanics 26, 969–972 (2005)
5. Zhou, E.H., Zhu, Y.W., Wang, T.: Transitional-zone method in hexahedral finite element meshing in geotechnical engineering. Engineering Journal of Wuhan University 35, 24–29 (2002)
6. Li X.X.: Study of key techniques on the integration of digital underground space and engineering (DUSE) and numerical analysis. Ph.D dissertation. Tongji University, Shanghai (2008)
7. Li, X.X., Lin, Y.L., Zhu, H.H.: Geologic model transforming technique and its application in foundation pit engineering. Chinese Journal of Geotechnical Engineering 30, 105–111 (2008)
8. Li, X.X., Zhu, H.H., Lin, Y.L.: Geologic model transforming method (GMTM) for numerical analysis modeling in geotechnical engineering. In: 6th Geotechnical Aspects of Underground Construction in Soft Ground, pp. 791–798 (2008)
9. Yong-liang, L., Xin-xing, L.: Application of GMTM for the Analysis of Foundation Pit Engineering. In: 2010 International Conference on Computer Modeling and Simulation, vol. 3, pp. 437–440. IEEE Press, New York (2010)
10. Lindenbeck, C.H.: A program to clip triangle meshes using the rapid and triangle libraries and the visualization toolkit. Computers and Geosciences 28, 841–850 (2002)

Pagerank-Based Collaborative Filtering Recommendation*

Feng Jiang[1,2] and Zhijun Wang[1]

[1] College of Civil Engineering, Chongqing University, Chongqing, China
[2] Construction Engineering Department, Chongqing Technology and Business Institute, Chongqing, China
jiangfeng@cqu.edu.cn, wzj@cqu.edu.cn

Abstract. Item-based collaborative filtering (*CF*) is one of the most popular recommendation approaches. A weakness of current item-based *CF* is all users have the same weight in computing item relationships. In order to solve the problem, we incorporate *userrank* as weight of a user based on *PageRank* into item similarities computing. In this paper, a data model for *userrank* calculation, a user ranking approach, and a *userrank*-based item-item similarities computing approach are proposed. Finally, we experimentally evaluate our approach for recommendation and compare it to traditional item-based Adjusted Cosine recommendation approach.

Keywords: Personalization, Collaboration Filtering, User Rank, PageRank.

1 Introduction

Due to the explosive growth of the Web, recommendation systems have been widely accepted by users [1, 2]. *CFs* are the most popular approaches in recommendation systems [3-5]. Traditional *CF* is named user-based *CF*. It was the most successful used technique for building a recommendation system in past [6, 7]. However, it suffers serious scalability problems. It has been proved experimentally that Item-based *CF* can solve the problem. It is proposed to build offline an item-item similarity matrix for rating prediction. Since it uses a pre-computed model, it will recommend items quickly. Similar to the issue that items have the same weight in user-based *CF* [8], a problem of current item-based *CF* is that all users have the same weight when item-item similarities or differentials are computed. There is a common sense that some users' words are more important than others' in a social group. For item-based *CF* recommendation, that is, some users (and their ratings) will have higher weights than the others.

In this paper a *userrank* approach is proposed to compute the weights of users to solve the problem. The contribution of the paper includes four points. Firstly, a user correlation graph model is presented for *userrank* calculation. Secondly, two rules are

---

* This work is supported by National Social Sciences Foundation of China under Grant No. ACA07004-08, Education Science and Technology Research of Chongqing Municipal Education Commission under Grant No. KJ101602.

R. Zhu et al. (Eds.): ICICA 2010, LNCS 6377, pp. 597–604, 2010.

given for user ranking and then a *userrank* algorithm based on *PageRank* is proposed. Thirdly, we incorporate *user rank* into computing item-item similarity and difference. Fourthly, the *userrank*-based approach is proved experimentally helpful to improve the recommendation results (e.g. MAE, F-measure, and stability) of item-based *CF* approaches.

2   Background and Problem of Item-Based *CF*

In a typical *CF* scenario, there is a rating m*n matrix which includes a list of *m* users *U* (rows) and a list of *n* items *I* (columns) and lots of ratings. Items represented any kind of products. A rating $r_{u,i}$ means how the user *u* likes the item *i*. It is supposed that users mainly interested in high ratings. The key step of *CF* is to extrapolate unknown ratings.

2.1   Item-Based Collaborative Filtering

Item-based *CF* is proposed by Sarwar [9] to compute the similarity between items and then to select the most similar items for prediction. Since it uses a pre-computed model, it recommends items quickly. There are several approaches to compute the similarities between items, such as Adjusted Cosine (See formula 1), and to compute the differences between items, e.g. Slope One.

$$Sim(i, j) = \frac{\sum_{u \in U(i) \cap U(j)} (r_{u,i} - \overline{r_u}) \times (r_{u,j} - \overline{r_u})}{\sqrt{\sum_{u \in U(i) \cap U(j)} (r_{u,i} - \overline{r_u})^2} \sqrt{\sum_{u \in U(i) \cap U(j)} (r_{u,j} - \overline{r_u})^2}} \tag{1}$$

Here $U(i)$ includes all users who have rated on item *i*. Formally, $U(i)=\{u|r_{u,i} \neq 0\}$. $\overline{r_u}$ is the average of user *u's* ratings. And also there are a number ways to estimate a rating, the most important step in a collaborative filtering system, such as weighted sum (See formula 2) and regression (See formula 4). Here $S(i)$ includes all similar items of item *i*.

$$p_{u,i} = \frac{\sum_{j \in S(i)} sim(i, j) \times r_{u,j}}{\sum_{j \in S(i)} |sim(i, j)|} \tag{2}$$

2.2   The Weight Problem of Current Item-Based *CF*

The relationships between items are the basis of the *CF* approaches. Whether in computing similarities between items, the weights of all users are same in current item-based *CF* approaches. That is, they do not consider the weight of users in the approaches. If we take users' weights into consideration in item-base *CF*, the similarity of difference between items will be more in line with the facts.

In the paper, we propose a *Userrank* approach to rank the importance/weights of users. The details of the approach and algorithm will be discussed in the next section.

3 Userrank

In this section, we first propose a data model for *userrank* calculation, then present a *Pagerank*-based user ranking approach, and at last incorporate *user rank* into item similarity/difference computing approaches for further prediction.

3.1 Data Model

Just as there are various relationships between users in any social group, there are different correlation degrees between users in a recommender system. Now we exploit this information for user ranking.

According to literature [10], more the items have been rated by both user u_i and u_j, closer their relationship is. This is the first rule of user correlation relationships.

We define $I(u_i)$ as the set of items which have been rated by the user u_i. $I(u_i, u_j)$ is the set of items which have been rated by both u_i and u_j.

Definition 3.1 *CRM*

CRM is a $(|U| \times |U|)$ correlation rating matrix which records the number of items which have been rated by each pair of users in a rating matrix.

$|U|$ denotes the cardinality of the set of users. *CRM* is formed by all the $I(u_i, u_j)$.

CRM is a symmetric matrix. All $I(u_i, u_j)$ is the same as $I(u_j, u_i)$. However, a fact is that if one of the pair users has rated plenty of items, and another only has rated on small quantity of items, the correlation value should be different between them. This is the second rule. According to this rule, we normalize matrix *CRM* to correlation matrix *CM* by formula (3). Without loss of generality, suppose that $\sum\limits_{u_j \in U} |I(u_i, u_j)| \neq 0$. $|I(u_j)|$ denotes the cardinality of the set $I(u_j)$.

Definition 3.2 *CM*

CM records the relationships between users according to the number of items which they have rated and the numbers of items which are rated by other users.

$$CM_{u_i, u_j} = \frac{CRM_{u_i, u_j}}{\sum\limits_{u_j \in U} CRM_{u_i, u_j}} = \frac{|I(u_i, u_j)|}{\sum\limits_{u_j \in U} |I(u_i, u_j)|} \tag{3}$$

Note that, CM_{u_i, u_j} can be different from CM_{u_j, u_i}, *CM* is an unsymmetrical matrix.

For the user u_j, the sum of his correlation relationship values with the other users will be 1. That is the sum of all CM_{u_i, u_j} for user u_j is 1, where $u_i \in U, u_i \neq u_j$. Formally $\sum\limits_{u_j \in U} CM_{u_i, u_j} = 1$.

CM can be regarded as a weighted connective matrix for a correlation graph G. Nodes in G correspond to users in U and there will be a link (u_i, u_j) from u_i to u_j if

$CM_{u_i,u_j} \neq 0$. The weight of the link (u_i, u_j) is CM_{u_i,u_j}. The graph G is valuable model to further exploit correlation between users.

3.2 *User Rank* Algorithm

The algorithm is to forecast user ranks using the graph model. The ranks of users can spread through the graph. It is important to properly control the rank flow in order to transfer high score to the users that are strongly related to users with high ranks.

The spreading algorithm follows two rules. Firstly, if a user u_i is linked by high ranked users with high weights, then u_i will also have high rank. Secondly, users have to transfer their positive influence through the graph, but this effect decreases its power if it spreads further and further away. Moreover, if the user u_i is connected to two or more nodes, these nodes share the boosting effect according to the weights of the connections as computed in correlation matrix CM.

The rules are just similar to the propagation and attenuation of *Pagerank* algorithm. Thanks to the significant researches for *PageRank* computing [11-13], we can achieve *userrank* and compute *userrank* in an efficient way.

Since *userrank* can be regarded as weighted *PageRank*, the importance value for a node u_k is $UR(u_n) = (1-\alpha) \cdot \dfrac{1}{|V|} \cdot UR(u_n) + \alpha \cdot \displaystyle\sum_{u_k:(u_k,u_n)\in E} \dfrac{UR(u_k)}{O_w(u_k)}$.

Here, $O_w(u_k) = \dfrac{\displaystyle\sum_{u_m:(u_k,u_m)\in E} w_{u_k,u_m}}{w_{u_k,u_n}} = \dfrac{\displaystyle\sum_{u_m:(u_k,u_m)\in E} CM_{u_k,u_m}}{CM_{u_k,u_n}}$ is the weighted sum of the links

to the node u_k divided by the weight of the link (u_k, u_n). Because $\displaystyle\sum_{u_m:(u_m,u_k)\in E} CM_{u_m,u_k}$

always is 1 (See Section 3.1), and the weighted $\dfrac{1}{|V|_w} \cdot UR(u_n)$ is $UR(u_n)$ because

that the sum of the weights of u_n's outputs is 1. So that userrank is
$UR(u_n) = (1-\alpha) \cdot UR(u_n) + \alpha \cdot \displaystyle\sum_{u_k:(u_k,u_n)\in E} UR(u_k) \times CM_{u_k,u_n}$.

3.3 *Userrank*-Based Approach to Item Similarity and Difference Computing

In the research, $UR(u)$ is regard as the weight of user u, $w_u = UR(u)$. Then we combine *userrank* with adjusted cosine (12). Then we apply formula (2) to predict ratings.

$$Sim_{i,j} = \frac{\displaystyle\sum_{u\in U(i)\cap U(j)} (r_{u,i} - \overline{r_u}) \times (r_{u,j} - \overline{r_u}) \times w_u^2}{\sqrt{\displaystyle\sum_{u\in U(i)\cap U(j)} (r_{u,i} - \overline{r_u})^2 \times w_u^2} \sqrt{\displaystyle\sum_{u\in U(i)\cap U(j)} (r_{u,j} - \overline{r_u})^2 \times w_u^2}} \tag{4}$$

4 Experimental Evaluation

4.1 Data Set

In the experiments, we used MovieLens dataset from the well-known MovieLens project (http://MovieLens.umn.edu) to evaluate our approach. MovieLens is a widely used benchmark to evaluate scoring algorithms applied to recommender systems. The data consists of 100,000 ratings (1-5) from 943 users on 1682 movies. Each user has rated at least 20 movies.

4.2 Evaluation Metric

Mean Absolute Error (MAE) is a widely used metric for deviation of predictions from their true values. For all predictions $\{p_1, p_2, ..., p_n\}$ and their real ratings $\{r_1, r_2, ..., r_n\}$. MAE is the average of absolute error between all $\{p_i, r_i\}$ pairs (See formula 5[14]). The lower the MAE, the better the recommendation approach is.

$$MAE = \frac{\sum_{i=1}^{N} |p_i - r_i|}{N} \tag{5}$$

The precision is the percentage of truly "high" ratings (B) among those (A) that were predicted to be "high" by a recommender system, $\dfrac{A \cap B}{A}$.

And the recall is the percentage of correctly predicted "high" ratings among all the ratings known to be "high", $\dfrac{A \cap B}{B}$.

F-measure is a measure of a test's accuracy. It considers both the precision and the recall of the test to compute the score, $F_\beta = \dfrac{(1 + \beta^2) \cdot (precision \cdot recall)}{\beta^2 \cdot precision + recall}$. The parameter β has regular certain values of 0.5, 1, and 2.

4.3 Experimental Procedure and Results

4.3.1 The Comparison of Prediction Results

To compare *userrank*-based Adjusted Cosine with Adjusted Cosine, we performed the experiment where we computed MAE, precision, recall, and f-measure ($F_{0.5}$, F_1, and F_2) for all of them. Our results are shown in Fig.1. The left columns ■ are the metric values for one of *userrank*-based algorithms; the right ones ■ are for typical algorithms. It can be observed from the charts that our *userrank*-based algorithm out performs typical algorithm at MAEF-measure.

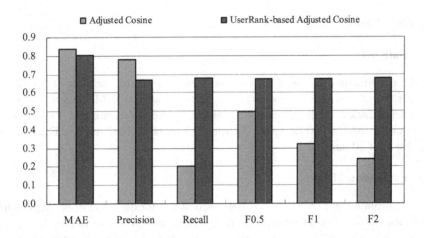

Fig. 1. The experiment results of Adjusted Cosine and userrank-based Adjusted Cosine recommendation algorithms

4.3.2 The Camparision of Algorithm Stability

To compare the stability of the algorithms, we then performed the experiment where we computed MAE, precision, recall, and f-measure of the prediction results for the ratings more than 3 (R3 for short) and more than 4 (R4 for short) in the test set respectively. Fig. 2 to Fig. 3 shows the deviations of the MAE, precision, recall, and f-measure results of *Adjusted Cosine* and *Userrank-based Adjusted Cosine*. The metric values of the prediction for the items in R3 and the items in R4 are shown by the left columns ☐ and the right columns ☷ in the figures. As can be seen from the figures, the prediction stability of *userrank*-based algorithm is better than the typical algorithm.

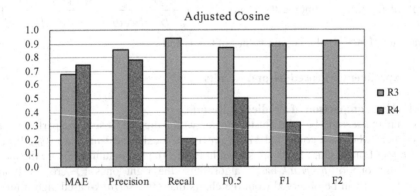

Fig. 2. The results of Adjusted Cosine for R3 and R4

✧ As can be seen from Fig.2, all matric values of the predictions for R3 are better than the predictions for R4. In these metric values, the change of recall is most significant, from 93.6% to 20.3%; secondly, the change of f-measure is great as well, the values of F_2, F_1, and $F_{0.5}$ vary from 91.9%, 89.5%, and 87.1% to 23.9%, 32.2%, and 49.7%; the changements of MAE and precision are the least, from 0.676 and 85.5% to 0.745 and 77.8%.

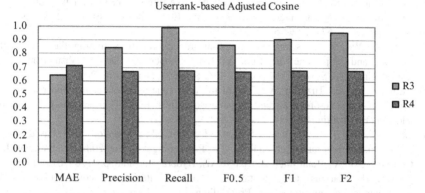

Fig. 3. The results of userrank-based Adjusted Cosine for R3 and R4

✧ As can be seen from Fig.3, the changement trend of all matric values of *userrank*-based Adjust Cosine is similar with Adjust Cosine (Fig.2), but the changement rangeability is lower. The maximum of the changement in Fig.3 is only more than 30%, but it is more than 70% in Fig.2.

In summary, the prediction precision, the prediction accuracy, and the stability of the *userrank*-based algorithm are better than the typical algorithm.

5   Conclusion and Future Work

Currently, item-based collaborative filtering approaches are most popular in recommender systems. The typical Adjusted Cosine is well-known algorithm of them. In this paper we analyzed how to rank users predict ratings for items based on user ranks. Experimental results show that *userrank* information is helpful to improve the prediction results (e.g. MAE, f-measure) and the stability of typical algorithms.

References

1. Gao, M., Liu, K., Wu, Z.: Personalisation in web computing and informatics: theories, techniques, applications, and future research. Information Systems Frontiers (2009)
2. Jiang, F., Gao, M.: Collaborative Filtering Approach based on Item and Personalized Contextual Information. In: Proceedings of the International Symposium on Intelligent Information Systems and Applications Qingdao, P. R. China, pp. 63–66 (2009)

3. Gao, M., Zhongfu, W.: Personalized context-aware collaborative filtering based on neural network and slope one. In: Luo, Y. (ed.) Cooperative Design, Visualization, and Engineering. LNCS, vol. 5738, pp. 109–116. Springer, Heidelberg (2009)
4. Konstan, J.A., Miller, B.N., Maltz, D., Herlocker, J.L., Gordon, L.R., Riedl, J.: GroupLens: applying collaborative filtering to Usenet news. Communications of the ACM 40, 77–87 (1997)
5. Li, Y., Lu, L., Xuefeng, L.: A hybrid collaborative filtering method for multiple-interests and multiple-content recommendation in E-Commerce. Expert Systems with Applications 28, 67–77 (2005)
6. Gao, M., Wu, Z.: Personalized context-aware collaborative filtering based on neural network and slope one. In: Luo, Y. (ed.) Cooperative Design, Visualization, and Engineering. LNCS, vol. 5738, pp. 109–116. Springer, Heidelberg (2009)
7. Adomavicius, G., Tuzhilin, A.: Toward the next generation of recommender systems: a survey of the state-of-the-art and possible extensions. IEEE Transactions on Knowledge and Data Engineering 17, 734–749 (2005)
8. Gori, M., Pucci, A., Roma, V., Siena, I.: Itemrank: A random-walk based scoring algorithm for recommender engines. In: Proceedings of the 20th International Joint Conference on Artificial Intelligence (IJCAI), Hyderabad, India, pp. 778–781 (2007)
9. Sarwar, B., Karypis, G., Konstan, J., Reidl, J.: Item-based collaborative filtering recommendation algorithms. In: Proceedings of the 10th International Conference on World Wide Web Hongkong, pp. 285–295 (2001)
10. Zhang, F.: Research on Trust based Collaborative Filtering Algorithm for User's Multiple Interests. Journal of Chinese Computer Systems 29, 1415–1419 (2008)
11. Langville, A.N., Meyer, C.D.: Deeper inside pagerank. Internet Mathematics 1, 335–380 (2004)
12. Haveliwala, T.: Efficient computation of PageRank., vol. 8090, 1998–31. Stanford University, Stanford (1999), http://dbpubs.stanford.edu
13. Kamvar, S.D., Haveliwala, T.H., Manning, C.D., Golub, G.H.: Extrapolation methods for accelerating PageRank computations. pp. 261–270 (2003)
14. Herlocker, J.L., Konstan, J.A., Terveen, L.G., Riedl, J.T.: Evaluating collaborative filtering recommender systems. ACM Transactions on Information Systems 22, 5–53 (2004)

Author Index

Printed in the United States
By Bookmasters